THE REVIEWERS

'We can get very used to the translation of the Bible which we use for reflective reading and prayer. This new translation wakes us up to new dimensions of the text and so is to be commended highly.'

GRACE AND TRUTH, SOUTH AFRICA

'All that remains is to encourage everyone to pick up this translation and think afresh about the New Testament.'

THE WAY, UK

'This is an excellent translation that well lives up to the endorsements of leading clergy and scholars. It encourages the reader to work through the New Testament and hear what it has to say. It is never dull and, with the help of the commentary, underscores the challenging and questioning nature of the New Testament.'

STUDIES, IRELAND

'This is dynamite! I anticipate this volume being open on my desk during sermon preparation for years to come.'

METHODIST RECORDER, UK

'This superb version of the New Testament may well be the most illuminating and, indeed, entertaining yet.'

THE SOUTHERN CROSS, SOUTH AFRICA

THE CLERGY

'Instantly accessible, with comments both lively and unobtrusive which bring the text home to readers of all backgrounds. This is a fine and quite distinctive addition to the ranks of Scripture translations. As a guide to the kind of study that will nourish a robust and grown-up faith, it will be hard to beat.'

ROWAN WILLIAMS, ARCHBISHOP OF CANTERBURY

'I welcome this fresh translation of the New Testament; Nicholas King has succeeded in putting into English something of the raw power that the first Christians experienced when they heard or read these documents, and I commend this new version to all Christians and to interested non-Christians also.'

CARDINAL CORMAC MURPHY-O'CONNOR, ARCHBISHOP OF WESTMINSTER

'Wonderfully refreshing, like a splash of cold water on one's face. The translation hits you between the eyes and certainly makes you sit up and take notice, waking you from the torpor of overfamiliarity with the text … amazing the new insights and understanding that come to light. A splendid piece of work.'

DESMOND TUTU, FORMER ARCHBISHOP OF CAPE TOWN

THE SCHOLARS

'Nick King's translation of the New Testament is an exciting project. His aim is to get people to read the New Testament. I was enthralled by it. I am sure that readers will find his translation and commentary highly stimulating and a book to which they will come back again and again. They are in for a real treat.'

CHRISTOPHER ROWLAND, DEAN IRELAND'S PROFESSOR OF EXEGESIS OF HOLY SCRIPTURE, QUEEN'S COLLEGE, OXFORD

'Lively touches which make this new translation gripping and attractive. I hope that this translation will become an icon for the twenty-first century.'

HENRY WANSBROUGH OSB, MASTER OF ST BENET'S HALL, OXFORD, AND GENERAL EDITOR OF THE NEW JERUSALEM BIBLE

THE NEW
TESTAMENT

Freshly translated with a
cutting-edge commentary

NICHOLAS KING

**kevin
mayhew**

Third impression

First published in Great Britain in 2004 by
Kevin Mayhew Ltd
Buxhall, Stowmarket, Suffolk IP14 3BW
Tel: +44 (0) 1449 737978 Fax: +44 (0) 1449 737834
E-mail: info@kevinmayhewltd.com

www.kevinmayhew.com

9 8 7 6 5 4 3 2 1 0

Hardback edition
ISBN 978 1 84417 324 2
Catalogue No. 1500740

Paperback edition
ISBN 978 1 84417 493 5
Catalogue No. 1500858

Cover design by Rob Mortonson
Edited by Peter Dainty and Marian Read
Typeset by Richard Weaver

Set in Adobe Garamond

Printed and bound in Great Britain

For Michael Kyne SJ (1929–1989)
and Jock Earle SJ (1925–2003)
sociis et amicis in Christo Iesu
and Pauline King, happily still with us.

My novice-master made me read the whole of the
New Testament in Greek.
My headmaster first excited me about John and Paul.
My mother always encouraged us to read the sacred texts.

Nicholas King is a Jesuit priest who teaches
New Testament at Oxford University.
He spent many years in South Africa,
where he still has a weekly column on the
Sunday Scriptures. He is fond of playing squash
and cricket. He is frequently in demand to
lecture on biblical subjects, especially St Paul.

Contents

Acknowledgements

Heartfelt thanks are owed to a variety of people who have fed, more remotely or more nearly, into this translation, most of whom are not mentioned here. Among those immediately concerned I must single out my former pupil Mrs Yolande Trainor, who read every single word, and was vigilant in spotting omissions and other eccentricities, along with Mrs Catherine Jones, mother of a present pupil. Another former pupil, Dr J. S. Whitehead, also read part of the text, and made valuable suggestions, as did my colleagues Drs Seth Turner and Will Cooper. Most important of all, however, in saving me from my own mistakes and making this translation far less unsatisfactory than it might otherwise have been, was its editor, Revd P. R. Dainty, whose suggestions were always perceptive and whose watchfulness unwavering. I am grateful also for the unfailing support I have received from Dom Henry Wansbrough OSB, Master of St Benet's Hall, and himself a proven translator of the New Testament, and from Revd Chris Rowland, Dean Ireland's Professor of the Exegesis of the Holy Scripture in the University of Oxford. And I must also thank Cardinal Cormac Murphy-O'Connor, Archbishop Rowan Williams and Desmond Tutu, not only for their inspiring leadership offered to Christians in England and South Africa, but also for their generous remarks about the translation.

Thanks are owed also to those people, family, friends, fellow Jesuits, and many others, including present and former pupils, who encouraged this project, often without realising that they were doing so.

Thanks of a very different sort should go in the direction of the cricket and squash teams of St John's College, Oxford, without whose antics this translation would undoubtedly have appeared much sooner, and my life would have been thereby notably the poorer.

Nicholas King SJ
Campion Hall, Oxford
Feast of the Conversion of St Paul 2004

Introduction

The impossibility of translation

Translation cannot be done. The Italians capture it laconically in their succinct proverb *'traditore traduttore'*, which limps into English as something like 'to translate is to betray'. When I started work on this translation, I was fiercely critical of those who had gone before; the same word was going to be translated in the same way each time, the tenses of the original would be invariably respected, and I was going to be unfailingly faithful to the text before me. Well, it cannot be done; word-for-word rendition is impossible if you are going to make sense in what is grimly termed the 'target language'. I could give several examples: let me simply mention two. First, there is a word in Greek which is a faintly irregular imperative of the verb 'to see', and in older versions tended to be translated as 'behold'. In modern translations the tendency is to omit it; but very often it functions as an attention-catching device, the author wanting us to watch carefully. So I have rather woodenly opted to translate it as 'Look!', which does not quite serve in every case. Second, tenses: Mark uses the historic present ('he says' for 'he said') a great deal, and I have in every case tried to reflect this; but Luke (and, for that matter, Matthew and John also; but Luke is a better stylist) also uses the historic present, like the Silver Age Latin historian Tacitus; but in Luke the effect is different. Or consider Greek aorists. Ordinarily they should go into English as 'he did', rather than 'he has done', which is a perfect; but try that almost anywhere in the New Testament, and you will find that you cannot catch what the original is trying to say. Or, in Revelation 21:18, I have found myself driven to translating the same word first as 'pure' then as 'clear', in order to allow the author to say what he was trying to say. Then occasionally, simply to avoid thundering boredom, you find yourself introducing a variant translation. So if nothing else, working on this translation has engendered an increase in humility, and immense admiration for those who have gone before in this field.

As well as looking like treachery, translation also causes pain. Let me give a trivial example from my own experience, if only to indicate my awareness that I may inadvertently have lit a fuse by some of my renderings. In Acts 3:6, the Douay-Rheims version, on which I was brought up, reads: 'But Peter said: Silver and gold I have none; but what I have, I give thee.' At quite a young age (certainly less than ten years old, by my calculation) I had formed a great love for the cadences of this piece of English. Then they started reading in English Catholic churches from the version of Ronald Knox, who produced: 'Then Peter said to him: Silver and gold are not mine to give; I give thee what I can', and I can still, almost half-a-century later, recall how annoyed I was at the translation, which is perfectly respectable (Knox was working from the Vulgate, not the Greek text), but lacks the rhythms of the older English version. All I can say here is that I do not intend to cause pain;

but it is inevitable that some people who read this translation will feel the pain that I experienced as a young boy.

The aim of the translation: encouraging people to read the New Testament

If my aim is not to cause pain, what am I seeking to do? The aim of the translation (and I am far from confident that I have hit the target) is to allow the reader to experience what it was like to hear or read the particular document for the first time. It will more often have been hearing than reading, since most of the Christians for whom the New Testament was originally written will have been illiterate; but I should like the reader to experience (rather than just read about) something of the raw power that lurks beneath the surface of the text of the 27 documents that make up our New Testament; so these writings should not all sound the same, and where the original is awkward and jagged, I have tried to offer a version that is similarly awkward. For the same reason I have tried to excise chapter-and-verse. These enumerations in their present form are a sixteenth-century invention, and can give the text a 'churchy' feel that I am anxious to avoid. My original idea was that people would read the documents straight off, with no interruption; but I have been persuaded a) that readers would prefer to know where they are in a text (if only so that they can check what I have written against their favourite version) and b) that I should interweave some passages of commentary after each 'unit', trying all the time to say too little rather than too much, in order to make it easier to read some of the trickier passages. I hope that at least some readers will find this helpful. Certainly my own aim will in large part have been met if you find yourself exclaiming, 'but *that's* not what it says!', and turning back to your favourite translation to see what you think it *should* say. Another aim will have been achieved if someone who would rather drop dead than read the New Testament is persuaded to open the book and to stay with it.

For this reason, what matters most to me is that readers should be persuaded to read the text. The title I first thought of, *The Interactive New Testament*, sounded a little pretentious, as though perhaps the reader were being invited to decide how a particular story should end. It points, rather, to something slightly different, a quality that the New Testament has, of 'inviting the reader aboard' in a way that may change his/her life. I would argue (although I shall not do so here) that the New Testament has a quality not often, perhaps never, found in other literature, of affecting the reader's life; it is, therefore, constitutionally 'interactive', and that is the aim of the questions and commentary. Originally, as a way of making this point, I thought of 'Just Read It' as a subtitle for this translation. The origin of this lies in a marathon race that I was misguided enough to run, at an age when I should have known better. This marathon was sponsored by a company well known for the manufacture of sporting footwear; and on almost every lamp-post, it seemed, encouraging me to the bitter end, was their advertising slogan, 'Just Do It'. If the reader will 'Just Read It', remarkable things may happen.

My approach to the translation

It is possible to know too much. In my view, I do not know nearly enough about the New Testament, although I have lived closely with the Greek text of it for upwards of 30 years now. So I do not wish to put into this translation everything that scholars say about the New Testament. Were I to do so, this project would lose the attractive lightness that Scripture has, and that God's word ought to have. For a similar reason, the translation has been done in a hurry; the idea, to shoot first and ask questions later, is that I should follow as far as may be my first instinct, in order to preserve the flow of the narrative. This had two evident disadvantages, first that a great deal of slovenliness crept in, which had to be corrected in the succeeding revisions of the text, and second that on another day I might translate a given passage in a quite different way. Nevertheless I judged these to be acceptable risks in pursuit of accessibility for the New Testament documents.

Inevitably, some of my translations will turn out to have been borrowed. Normally, I hope, this will not be plagiarism so much as the result of having a familiar version in my head. Occasionally I have produced a version of a difficult passage, and then looked at someone else's translation, and found to my delight that they had reached the identical conclusion about the meaning of the text. This may serve as a useful reminder to readers unacquainted with scholarly debate on the subject that we cannot always agree on what a particular passage actually means.

The dialogue with scholars

What of my own relationship with New Testament scholarship? Clearly I owe a huge debt to those who have given themselves to the academic study of these texts, and have found great light in what they have written, including (especially, perhaps) those scholars who are quite explicit about their lack of religious faith. Nevertheless, my agenda is not that of the scholars, and this translation is not really for them. Indeed, I should say that most (not all) of the New Testament experts with whom I have discussed this project have been somewhat discouraging about it. A part of me is slightly ashamed of not having a more scholarly agenda, but this translation is directed towards actual and potential committed readers of the texts, rather than towards academics; it is for churches and prisons, rather than libraries. My instinct suggests, what I fear many New Testament scholars will reject, that those people are most suited to read the New Testament who are prepared to 'get inside' it, who are open to faith in the Resurrection of Jesus (a belief that informs every word of the New Testament), and to an encounter with Jesus Christ. Scholars will be quite properly irritated by some of my translations, and by some of the failures to indicate in my comments how complex are some of the difficulties that the reader must face. But I hope that all the translations are at least defensible, and that the comments and notes help readers to read.

Some general observations

Where it was possible without inelegance, I have tried to use inclusive language, on the grounds that the gospel is for all. Sometimes this can misrepresent the thrust of a text, however, and many people would argue that using inclusive language is something of a cover-up. For it conceals the fact that (so far as we can tell) the New Testament was written mainly by men (though it sometimes seems possible that Mark's Gospel could have been written by a woman), and out of a view of the world where the male exercises unquestioned superiority over wives, children, slaves and camels. I am reconciled, however, to the certainty that my uneasy compromise in this matter will please nobody.

Another observation I have to make is that all punctuation is invention. The editors of the Greek texts that I have used made their guesses about punctuation; I have made mine. Once again, if you find yourself saying, 'that is not how it goes', and go feverishly back to another version, then I shall be happy.

Two slightly unsatisfactory tendencies I have noticed in myself without knowing quite how to correct them. The first is that too often I have used words that no one ever uses ('upbraid' is one example I have observed), perhaps simply because it is 'the Bible', and 'the Bible' ought to feel different from ordinary language. However I do not think that the Greek in which the New Testament is written is very different from ordinary speech, so far as the evidence goes; although it must be confessed that there are many different styles of Greek in these 27 documents.

A second tendency is that of centrally justifying longer Old Testament passages, as well as those passages that are often identified as New Testament 'hymns'. Some modern editions of the Greek New Testament follow this practice, and it has the happy function of marking out differences of style, which should evoke a correspondingly different reaction in the reader; but it is not ideal, and certainly that will not have been the practice of the original authors.

A final point: the New Testament as Word of Life

There is one more thing. The other night I attended a concert in one of the old College Chapels that abound here in Oxford. It was beautifully done, and consisted of two sixteenth-century masses, one of them a requiem mass, such as might have been sung in the chapel when it was originally built. The words were profoundly familiar to me, for they were the words that we sang in my childhood; but the difference between then and now is that when we sang the words at school, it was part of our life, in the same way as algebra and rugby practice, and we often sang the words, all of which are addressed directly to God, as a prayerful response when someone in the community had died. In that setting, the words had a life which they simply could not have, so it seemed to me, in the setting of a concert, no matter how professionally performed.

That is the kind of life that lurks beneath the text of the New Testament, which is accessible only to those who are prepared to open themselves to what these 27 documents are saying, the encounter with the God who never ceases to address us, and with Jesus whom God sent and raised from the dead. This translation has taken me something over two years; but in another sense, I find that it is a distillation of my entire life so far, and the 'post-natal depression' that comes with its despatch to the publishers is a signal that the New Testament is for me, and I hope for all readers of this translation, 'the word of life'.

What more is there to say? Just read it, and listen.

(Any words in **bold** throughout the text are my emphasis.)

According to Matthew

Introduction

It is almost certain that Matthew had access to Mark's Gospel, or something very like it, so we can often see what he was doing by reference to what he had open in front of him. As you read through Matthew, it may help to look out for four features:

1. Matthew frequently emphasises that Jesus 'fulfils' the Law, the Jewish scriptures, the history of the Jewish people.
2. Look for evidence that Matthew and his church are engaged in a debate, one which is quite bitter at times, with his Jewish neighbours. It may be helpful if at this stage I point out that Matthew is also the most Jewish of the Gospels.
3. Matthew allows us to penetrate ever more deeply into his portrait of Jesus. He often paints this portrait by way of contrast with those who appear in the same scene.
4. Sometimes it seems that Matthew's community may be one that has lost its first enthusiasm.

Matthew is sometimes said to have written the first 'catechist's handbook', to help those who are instructing others in their faith. Certainly it is a very well-organised piece of work.

This suggests that there might be something of the schoolmaster about Matthew. See what you think as you read through the Gospel.

Jesus' 'family tree'

1 ¹⁻¹⁷ The Book of the Origin of Jesus Messiah, Son of David, Son of Abraham. Abraham was the father of Isaac; Isaac was the father of Jacob; Jacob was the father of Judah and his brothers; Judah was the father of Perez and Zerah, by **Tamar**; Perez was the father of Hezron; Hezron was the father of Aram; Aram was the father of Aminadab; Aminadab was the father of Nahshon, Nahshon was the father of Salmon; Salmon was the father of Boaz, by **Rahab**; Boaz was the father of Obed, by **Ruth**; Obed was the father of Jesse; and Jesse was the father of David, the King.

David was the father of Solomon, by the **wife of Uriah**; Solomon was the father of Rehoboam; Rehoboam was the father of Abijah; Abijah was the father of Asaph; Asaph was the father of Jehoshaphat; Jehoshaphat was the father of Joram; and Joram was the father of Uzziah; Uzziah was the father of Jotham; Jotham was the father of Ahaz; Ahaz was the father of Hezekiah; Hezekiah was the father of Manasseh; Manasseh was the father of Amos; Amos was the father of Josiah; Josiah was the father of **Jeconiah and his brothers**, down to the Babylon deportation.

After the Babylon deportation, Jeconiah was the father of Shealtiel; Shealtiel was the father of Zerubbabel; Zerubbabel was the father of Abioud; Abioud was the father of Eliakim; Eliakim was the father of Azor; Azor was the father of Zadok; Zadok was the father of Achim; Achim was the father of Eliud; Eliud was the father of Eleazar; Eleazar was the father of Matthan; Matthan was the father of Jacob; and Jacob was the father of Joseph; and Joseph was the husband of Mary, of whom was born Jesus called Messiah.

Therefore all the generations from Abraham to David were fourteen generations; and from David to the Babylonian deportation fourteen generations; and from the Babylonian deportation to the Messiah fourteen generations.

This is an astonishing beginning to the Gospel. Matthew gives it a title: 'The book of the birth (or 'The Bible of the Genesis') of Jesus Messiah (or Christ)'. He then follows with a family tree, neatly divided into three groups of fourteen (actually not quite so neat, if you count carefully). Those three groups divide Jewish history into three equal portions, from the promise to Abraham to its apparent fulfilment in the reign of David, from there to the utter disaster of the Babylonian deportation, then from that lowest point of all to the moment that for Matthew is the climax of the history of God's dealings with Israel, the birth of 'Jesus called Messiah'.

But there is more to it than that, for the family tree ends with a reference to Joseph as 'the husband of Mary, of whom was born Jesus called Messiah'. Now Matthew is shortly going to make it clear to us that Joseph was not the father of Jesus, so, quite evidently, we are not invited to contemplate this gallery of rogues and saints as those whose blood courses through Jesus' veins. Matthew's point is slightly different: for him Jesus is the climax of God's dealings with Israel, in which God has always remained faithful, while the people of God have not.

In addition, the pattern 'X was the father of Y' is broken on five occasions, *marked in bold type*. Four times they are women, rather unusually inserted into the family tree: Tamar, who pretended to be a prostitute, Rahab, who actually was one, Ruth, who certainly behaved in a somewhat ramshackle way with Boaz and so became King David's great-grandmother, and finally Mrs Uriah, Solomon's mother, whose beauty in the bath aroused David to adultery and murder. The fifth break in the pattern refers to 'Jeconiah (or Jehoiakim) and his brothers', the last king in Judah, and the beginning of survival out of the disaster, which Israel saw as the fruit of disobedience. God, Matthew is delicately hinting, 'writes straight with crooked lines'.

Jesus' birth, and Joseph's first dream

18-25   Jesus Messiah – his birth was like this. When his mother Mary was engaged to Joseph, before they got together, she was found to be pregnant – by the Holy Spirit. Her man Joseph, because he was a just man, and reluctant to make an example of her, wanted to let her go secretly. When he had made this plan, look! The angel of the Lord appeared to him in a dream, saying, 'Joseph, son of David, don't be afraid to take Mary as your wife, for it is by the Holy Spirit that the child has been conceived in her. She will bear a son, and you will call his name Jesus, because he will save his people from their sins. All this has happened in order that the word spoken by the Lord through the prophet might be fulfilled:

"Look! The virgin will be pregnant and shall bear a son,
   and they shall call his name Emmanuel" (which is translated "God with us").'

Joseph awoke from sleep, and did as the angel of the Lord had ordered him. And he took his wife; and he did not have intercourse with her until she bore a son. And he called his name Jesus.

The story continues to be extraordinary. Mary is said to be pregnant, and not by Joseph, but by 'the Holy Spirit': so, remarkably, God is the father of this child. Joseph's reaction does him credit: clearly he cannot marry Mary; but he wants to do the right thing, and so decides on a discreet end to the relationship, rather than making a public fuss that might end in Mary being stoned to death.

God is however in control of the story, and sends an angel in a dream, which tells the reader that the message to Joseph is aboveboard. Joseph has his part to play, not only by providing a family to receive the child, but also by giving him a name, which in Hebrew means 'Saviour'. The conversation is reported in Greek, of course; and this may suggest that the community for which Matthew wrote was equally at ease in Greek and either Aramaic or Hebrew.

It is only in the Greek version of Isaiah (7:14) that the quotation refers to a 'virgin'; but much more important for Matthew is the first designation of Jesus as 'God with us'. We shall need to remember this phrase as the Gospel develops.

It is no surprise when Joseph faithfully and precisely obeys his instructions. That is what a 'just man' is supposed to do in Matthew's Gospel.

A central scene: the Magi and two kings

2 1-12 When Jesus had been born in Bethlehem of Judaea in the days of Herod the king, look! Magi from the east turned up in Jerusalem, saying, 'Where is the one who has been born King of the Jews? For we saw his star in the east, and we came to worship him.'

When King Herod heard [this], he was disturbed, and all Jerusalem with him, and he gathered all the chief priests and scribes of the people and asked them where the Messiah would be born. They told him, 'In Bethlehem of Judaea, for it is written so through the prophet:

> "And you, Bethlehem, land of Judah,
> you are not at all the least among the leaders of Judah,
> for from you shall come one who leads,
> who will shepherd my people Israel."'

Then Herod secretly summoned the Magi, and tried to get them to be precise about the time of the star's appearance. And he sent them off to Bethlehem, saying, 'Go and enquire precisely about the little child. When you find him, report to me, so that I too may come and worship him.'

They listened to the king, and set off; and look! The star that they had seen in the east was leading them on, until it came and stood above the place where the little child was. They saw the star and rejoiced with a great joy. They came to the house and saw the little child, with Mary his mother, and they fell down and worshipped him; and they opened their treasures and offered him gifts: gold and frankincense and myrrh. And being warned in a dream not to go back to Herod, it was by a different route that they returned to their country.

Both the family tree and this story of oriental visitors are intended to help us see who Jesus is, and what God is doing in Jesus. The heroes of this episode are clearly the Magi (astrologers, with perhaps a hint of Eastern trickery), in sharp contrast to the religious establishment, who are so shaken by the news that these Orientals bring.

In between the two lurks the title of 'king': it is in the days of King Herod that they arrive, and Matthew's readers will not have needed to be told what a nasty piece of work he was. So when they put their tactless question about the one born King of the Jews, the reader knows that there is already such a king, and it is hardly surprising that Herod and Jerusalem are 'disturbed'. It may be worth noticing that the Greek word for 'gathered' would have sounded like 'synagogued'; many scholars think that Matthew's Gospel is in polemical debate with the 'synagogue across the road'.

Another word that lurks in the text is 'worship'. We shall see as we read Matthew's Gospel that this is an appropriate response to Jesus; but we know perfectly well that what the Magi mean by worship is quite different from what Herod has in mind, just as Herod's 'secretly' summoning the Magi is more sinister than Joseph contemplating divorcing Mary 'secretly'. More sinister yet is our discovery that Herod absolutely believes the message that the Magi bring: he gets his religious experts on to the question of where the star will have been leading them, and they can produce an apt scriptural quotation (from Micah 5:2) to solve the problem. Out come their computers and the answer emerges: Bethlehem. So Herod is seen from the beginning as deliberately resisting the will of God. In this he is representative of the Jewish authorities as Matthew sees them.

We learn a bit more: the star guides the visitors on to their destination, so God is still in charge. And they give gifts, which Matthew certainly intends us to see as revealing who Jesus is: gold for a king (that word again), frankincense for a priest (rather different from the chief priests, who so effortlessly produced the Scripture quotation for Herod), and myrrh, chillingly, for a dead body. Incidentally, if you thought that there were three Magi, here is the reason: they gave three gifts. But Matthew does not tell us that it was one Magus per gift: so we have to think of at least two, with no upper limit other than their arrival not being classifiable as an invasion by a hostile power.

Finally, and reminding us that God is after all in charge, a dream removes the Magi from the stage, and their naïveté no longer threatens Jesus. As we silently applaud this, we may reflect that although Jesus has done nothing at all so far, Matthew has told us a great deal about him.

Joseph's second dream: the departure for Egypt

13-15   As the Magi were going away, look! The angel of the Lord appears in a dream to Joseph, saying, 'Up you get; take the little child and his mother, and escape to Egypt, and be there until I tell you. For Herod is about to look for the little child in order to kill him.' He got up and took the little child and his mother by night; and he went up to Egypt. And he was there until the death of Herod, that the [word] spoken by the Lord through the prophet might be fulfilled, 'out of Egypt I called my son'.

Once again Joseph shows his instant obedience to God. Matthew's readers, however, will have been rather startled by where Joseph's obedience leads him. For, of all places, it is to Egypt that the little child has to escape, fleeing not from a foreign ruler (like the Pharaoh) but from Israel's king. Not only that, but the flight takes place, like the Passover, at night, and Joseph is described as going 'up' to Egypt: Matthew's readers will have known very well indeed that Jews go 'up' to the Holy Land and to Jerusalem, never to Egypt. The story has led us into a very unexpected world, of the 'reverse Exodus'. Matthew makes his point neatly by his quotation of Hosea 11:1, which meant something rather different in its original setting.

For the third time in the Gospel, Matthew makes a Scripture quotation, introducing it with the formula 'that it might be fulfilled'. The point of this technique, which we shall see again and again in this Gospel, is to emphasise that God is in charge.

Matthew evidently reads his Scripture very carefully indeed.

Herod destroys the children

16-18 Then Herod, realising that he had been tricked by the Magi, became extremely angry; and he sent and destroyed all the boys in Bethlehem and in all its territories, of two years old and under, according to the time that he had carefully elicited from the Magi. Then the [word] spoken through Jeremiah the prophet was fulfilled:

> 'A voice was heard in Rama, wailing and much lamentation,
> Rachel weeping for her children;
> and she did not want to be comforted,
> for they are not.'

Herod's brutal response echoes the worst of the activities of the Pharaoh who had tried to destroy the children of Israel at the beginning of the Book of Exodus; and for Matthew it serves as perverse evidence that Herod acknowledges that the Magi had got it right.

This fourth 'fulfilment' citation comes from Jeremiah 31:15, and Matthew's readers will not have needed to be told that this is one of the more cheerful passages in Jeremiah, and that it carries the promise of consolation.

Two dreams bring the child safely to Israel and to Nazareth

19-23 When Herod had died, look! The angel of the Lord appears to Joseph in a dream, in Egypt, saying, 'Up you get, take the little child and his mother, and go to the land of Israel. For those who were seeking the life of the little child are dead.' He arose and took the little child and his mother and entered the land of Israel.

Hearing that Archelaus was king of Judaea instead of his father Herod, he was afraid to go there. He was warned in a dream, and so he went up to the regions of Galilee, and he came and settled in a city called Nazareth, that the word spoken through the prophets might be fulfilled, that 'he shall be called a Nazorean'.

Once more, Joseph shows his obedience to God's word, and then follows the Magi off-stage. For all this has been about Jesus, clothed in the anonymity of the 'little child', and about what God is doing in Jesus. God's action is hinted at in the 'entry into Israel', echoing that of the people of Israel under Joshua, and more explicitly framed in yet another 'fulfilment-quotation'. It is hard to be sure where this comes from, but the text may well be Judges 13:5, referring to the coming of Samson. And Samson, of course, died for the people with arms outstretched, for the people of Israel, just like Jesus.

The emergence of John the Baptist

3 1-6 In those days comes John the Baptist, proclaiming in the desert of Judaea and saying, 'Repent – for the kingdom of heaven has come near.' For he was the one spoken of through Isaiah the prophet, who said,

> 'The voice of one who shouts in the desert,
> "Make the Lord's way ready, make his paths straight."'

John himself had clothing made of camel hair, and a leather belt around his waist; and his diet was locusts and wild honey. Then there came out to him Jerusalem and all Judaea, and the whole area round the Jordan, and they were baptised by him in the River Jordan, confessing their sins.

This is a very sudden turn away from Jesus, whom we have just seen safely settled in Nazareth: we are now in quite another part of the country, with a very different main character in the narrative; and when Jesus appears, he is clearly no longer a little child. John the Baptist is an austere figure, with his rough clothing and unattractive diet, but we are evidently intended to be on his side, for he proclaims the kingdom of heaven. (That phrase, by the way, which we hear now for the first time, is Matthew's preferred form for Mark's 'kingdom of God'.) Matthew paints a powerful picture of 'Jerusalem and the whole of Judaea and the whole area round the Jordan' coming out to hear his message. We may recall that 'all Jerusalem' was disturbed along with Herod when the Magi asked their tactless question.

The Isaiah quotation is from 40:3, and it is employed in all four Gospels (which is an unusual convergence).

John's address to the Pharisees and Sadducees

7-12 When he saw many of the Pharisees and Sadducees coming to his baptism, he said to them, 'Offspring of snakes . . . who suggested to you to flee from the anger that is coming? So produce fruit that looks like repentance, and don't think of saying to yourselves, "We have Abraham as our father". For I'm telling you that God can raise up children for Abraham from these stones. Already the axe is laid to the root of the trees. So every tree that doesn't produce good fruit is cut down and thrown into the fire. I'm baptising you people with water for repentance – but the one coming behind me is stronger than me, and I'm not fit to carry his sandals. He will baptise you with the Holy Spirit and with fire. His winnowing-shovel is in his hand, and he will purify his threshing-floor and gather his grain into the barn, and he will burn the chaff with fire that cannot be extinguished.'

In this section we meet for the first time some Pharisees and Sadducees. They will be seen in a uniformly negative light in Matthew's Gospel, and it is of a piece with this that the first time they are addressed it is in the unflattering phrase 'offspring of snakes'. They are told not to rely on their ancestry; there may be a Hebrew pun underlying the saying about 'children from stones'.

We also learn something about Jesus here: he is 'stronger' than John the Baptist, who is not fit to do even a very menial task for him; Jesus' baptism is 'with the Holy Spirit and with fire', which in Matthew's view is clearly a notch above John the Baptist's 'water for repentance'. And Jesus is a slightly alarming figure, as the 'threshing' metaphor makes clear.

Jesus is publicly identified as righteous and as beloved Son of Heaven

13-17 Then Jesus comes from Galilee to the Jordan, to John, in order to be baptised by him. John tried to stop him, saying, 'I need to be baptised by you – and you are coming to me!' Jesus answered him, 'Let [it happen for] now, for it is fitting for us to fulfil all righteousness in this way.' Then he let him.

When Jesus had been baptised, he immediately came up out of the water, and look! The heavens were opened, and he saw the Spirit of God descending like a dove and coming upon him. And look! A voice from heaven saying, 'This is my beloved Son, in whom I am pleased.'

> We learn two things about Jesus here. First, the polite skirmish with John the Baptist reveals that Jesus is superior to John, but that he is also concerned to 'fulfil all righteousness'. We have already seen Joseph as a 'just' or 'righteous' man. In Matthew, this idea of righteousness has to do with fulfilling the Law, a matter of considerable importance for the evangelist.
>
> Second, Jesus is publicly affirmed as Son of God (Mark 1:11 had made it a purely *private* revelation: '*you* are my beloved Son'), and we learn that God is pleased with him, apparently for being baptised, or perhaps for all that Jesus is about to do as the story unfolds.

Jesus is tested by the devil

4 1-11 Then Jesus was led up into the desert by the Spirit, to be tested by the devil. And having fasted for forty days and forty nights he was later hungry.

And the Tester came and said to him, 'If you are the Son of God, tell these stones to turn into bread.' He answered, 'It is written: "It is not only by bread that a person shall live, but by every word that comes from the mouth of God."'

Then the devil takes him into the Holy City, and sets him on the parapet of the Temple and says to him, 'If you are the Son of God, throw yourself down; for it is written, "He gives orders to his angels about you, and on their hands they will raise you up, so that you might not strike your foot on a stone."' Jesus said to him, 'Again it is written: "You shall not test the Lord your God."'

Again the devil takes him up to a very high mountain, and shows him all the kingdoms of the world and their glory; and he said to him, 'All this I shall give you, if you fall down and worship me.' Then Jesus says to him, 'Away with you, Satan. For it is written: "The Lord your God shall you worship, and him alone shall you adore."'

Then the devil left him, and look! Angels came and served him.

> For the first time now we see Jesus in action, in a kind of single combat with the enemy. He is not quite alone, however, for we are told that the test takes place under the orders of the Holy Spirit, and at the end angels emerge from the shadows and look after him. The single combat is clearly won by Jesus, effortlessly matching quotations from Deuteronomy (8:3; 6:16; 6:13) to each of the Tester's suggestions; and notice that the devil also quotes Scripture (Psalm 91:11, 12). It is a well-crafted story; like all the best stories it

comes in three parts, and circles round the question whether or not Jesus is the Son of God. We already know that he is, of course, on the best possible evidence, so what we learn here is the kind of Son of God that he is: one who does not do selfish magic, who does not put God to the test, and who worships nothing that is not God.

That word 'worship' we have already encountered: it is what the Magi did (presumably correctly) for Jesus; on Herod's lips it was code for murder. It is a word that is frequently used in the Gospel. For the moment we need only observe that it is a gesture that is to be offered only to God.

Jesus moves from Nazara to Caphernaum-by-the-Sea to start his mission

12-17 Hearing that John had been arrested, he went up to the Galilee; and leaving Nazara he went and lived in Caphernaum-by-the-Sea, in the regions of Zebulun and Naphthali, in order that what was spoken through Isaiah the prophet might be fulfilled:

'Land of Zebulun and land of Naphthali, way of the sea,
across the Jordan, Galilee of the Gentiles.
The people that sat in darkness saw a great light,
and to those who sit in the region and shadow of death,
a light has shone upon them.'

From then on Jesus began to proclaim and to say, 'Repent, for the kingdom of heaven has drawn near.'

Now at last we see Jesus actually at work. He transfers his headquarters from Nazara (we know it as Nazareth, of course, but that is how Matthew spells it here), where Joseph had installed him, to Caphernaum, on the Sea of Galilee, and the 'slogan' for his mission is identical with that of John the Baptist. Once again, Matthew produces a fulfilment quotation (Isaiah 9:1, 2); the point of it is not so much to astonish us with the uncanny fact of prophecies being fulfilled (what is reported is not in fact all that uncanny), as to emphasise the extent to which the same God is operative in Jesus as through the prophets. This is presumably why Matthew so often speaks of a word being spoken 'through' the prophet.

Jesus calls two pairs of brothers; his missionary activity summarised

18-25 Walking by the Sea of Galilee he saw two brothers, Simon called Peter and Andrew his brother, throwing their casting-net into the sea – for they were fishermen. And he says to them, 'Come here, after me, and I'll make you fish for human beings.' They immediately abandoned their nets and followed him. And going on from there he saw two other brothers, James the son of Zebedee and John his brother in the boat with Zebedee their father preparing their nets. And he called them. They immediately abandoned the boat and their father; and they followed him.

And he would go about in all Galilee, teaching in their synagogues, and proclaiming the gospel of the kingdom, and healing every disease and every ailment in the people. And his reputation went out into the whole of Syria; and they brought to him all those who were unwell with different diseases and suffering from torments, and those who had demons, and were lunatics and paralysed; and he cured them. And many crowds followed him from the Galilee and the Decapolis and Jerusalem and Judaea and across the Jordan.

Matthew is still letting us see for the first time what Jesus does. The episode with the two sets of brothers indicates great personal magnetism, the immediacy of the call to discipleship, and even a sense of humour in Jesus (the joke about 'fishing for human beings' is surely just that). The summary, including the perhaps slightly hostile reference to '*their* synagogues', indicates that Jesus' mission involves proclamation and healing. It also involves a wide geographical spread, and a complete range of diseases.

The First 'Discourse': The Sermon on the Mount (5:1–7:29)

Having given us a preliminary glimpse of the mission of Jesus, and of the enemies of the mission, Matthew now gives us a first impression of Jesus' preaching. In all, the evangelist gives us five 'sermons' in his Gospel, which enables him to gather together Jesus' preaching material. 'This is the kind of thing he used to say', he is telling us, as he offers us a carefully constructed collection of Jesus' sayings.

The 'congratulations'

5 1-12 Seeing the crowds, he went up into the mountain; and when he sat down, his disciples came to him. And opening his mouth, he began to teach them, saying:

'Congratulations to the poor in spirit – theirs is the kingdom of heaven.
Congratulations to those who are mourning – they shall be consoled.
Congratulations to the gentle – they shall inherit the earth.
Congratulations to those who are hungry and thirsty for righteousness –
they shall be satisfied.
Congratulations to the merciful – they shall be mercied.
Congratulations to the pure in heart – they shall see God.
Congratulations to those who create peace –
they shall be called children of God.
Congratulations to those who are persecuted because of righteousness –
theirs is the kingdom of heaven.
Congratulations to you when they reproach you and persecute you and falsely talk all kinds of evil against you because of me. Rejoice, and be glad, because your reward in heaven is huge. You see, that's how they persecuted the prophets before you.'

Matthew starts the greatest of his five 'sermons' by making sure that our attention is focused. Jesus goes up the mountain, apparently because of the crowds. This reminds us of Moses, except that Moses went up a mountain to receive the Law, Jesus to give a new Law. Then we watch as he adopts the teacher's position ('he sat down'); his disciples join him, and Matthew next offers no less than three expressions to indicate that Jesus is talking: 'he opened his mouth', 'he began to teach', and 'saying'. So we know that we are privileged to hear what was intended mainly for the inner group of 'Jesus' disciples'. We are not prepared, however, for the shock that follows, this astonishing list of those who are congratulated: the destitute, the sad, the meek, those concerned for justice, the merciful, those who concentrate exclusively on God, those who refuse to go the road of violence, those who are persecuted. At first blush this sounds absurd: are Christians supposed to be wimps? But on a second reading (try it), there is a profound wisdom in what Jesus offers, quite the opposite of the congratulations that people normally offer one another. We should reflect thoughtfully on this.

Disciples give the world its flavour and its illumination

13-16 'You people are the earth's salt – but if salt loses its flavour, how can [the earth] be salted? There's no use for it, except to be thrown out and trodden down by people.

'You people are the world's light: a city can't be concealed if it's placed on top of a mountain. They don't turn on a light and then place it under a measuring-jar! They put it on a lamp-stand, and it shines for everyone in the house. Let your light shine so brightly before human beings that they see your good deeds and glorify your Father – the one in heaven.'

As Christians we can get our mission wrong in two ways. Either we can see our task as lecturing the rest of the world on their errors; or we can think that no one will listen and keep quietly to ourselves. These two striking images, of salt and light, offer a middle way. We still have to be gentle, merciful peacemakers (so the more arrogant of the two horns of the dilemma is excluded); but we have nevertheless the important function of adding 'bite' and illumination to the world (so we can't retreat behind the barricades into a false humility). That does not mean that the world is going to be impressed by us, however, so Jesus warns us to expect 'persecution'. Nor, on the other hand, is there any sign here that Jesus is condemning the 'world': that's just the way it is.

Those who think that it's not respectful to laugh in church ought to look again at the joke about the light being put under a bucket, and also learn the lesson: we have no cause to be shy about the gospel message.

What about the Torah? What about righteousness?

17-20 'Don't think that I came to undermine the Torah, or the Prophets. I haven't come to undermine [them] but to fulfil them. For – Amen I tell you – not a single letter,

23

not a single punctuation mark will pass away from the Torah until it all happens. The whole of Creation will pass away before that! Anyone who relaxes just one of these commandments (even the most insignificant), and who teaches people to do the same, will have the most insignificant status in the kingdom of heaven, whereas anyone who performs it and teaches it is the one who will have importance in the kingdom of heaven. Because, I'm telling you, unless your righteousness surpasses that of the scribes and the Pharisees, no way will you go into the kingdom of heaven.'

Jesus is different; and one of the issues for the Church in that first century was the problem of just how different he was. You can raise the problem in the form of a question: does following Jesus mean not following the demands of Scripture ('Torah' and 'Prophets')? Here the answer is a firm 'no'. However, the answer is presented in such a way as to make Jesus' hearers scratch their heads: because they have to have a more generous 'righteousness' than that of the 'scribes and Pharisees'! Now we have already met these people, for example when John the Baptist compared them to reptiles, so we may be starting to form the impression that there will be a gulf of some sort between them and Jesus. Nevertheless, our appropriate response to this remark should be a long, low whistle, because for Jesus' hearers the Pharisees would be the benchmark of 'righteousness'. So Jesus is telling us that we need to be more virtuous than the Pope, or faster than the current Olympic champion.

Six ways towards a new and better righteousness

21-48 1. 'You have heard that it was said to the ancients: "You shall not kill" [Exodus 20:13], and whoever kills will be liable to the Judgement. But *I* tell you that everyone who is angry with their brother or sister will be liable to the Judgement. Anyone who says "Raka" to his brother or sister will be liable to the Sanhedrin. Anyone who says "Fool" will be liable to the fiery Gehenna.
'So – if you are offering your gift at the altar, and at that point you remember that your brother or sister has something against you, leave the gift there at the altar and go: first get reconciled with your brother or sister, and after that come and offer your gift. Get on good terms with your opponent in litigation, right up to the moment when you are with him on the journey; otherwise your opponent may hand you over to the judge, and the judge to the usher, and you be thrown into gaol. Amen I tell you, you won't get out of there at all, until you repay the last farthing.

2. 'You have heard that it was said, "You will not commit adultery" [Exodus 20:14]. But I'm telling you that everyone who looks at a woman in order to have lustful thoughts about her has already committed adultery with her in his heart. If your right eye makes you trip up, take it out and throw it away from you! For it's more in your interest that one bit of you should be destroyed, than that your whole body be thrown into Gehenna. And if your right hand causes you to trip up, cut it off and throw it away from you. For it's more in your interest that one bit of you should be destroyed, than that your whole body go off into Gehenna.

3. 'It was said, "Anyone who divorces his wife should give her a certificate of divorce" [Deuteronomy 24:1-4]. But I'm telling you that everyone who divorces his wife (except for a matter of fornication) makes her commit adultery; and anyone who marries a divorced woman commits adultery.

4. 'Again you've heard that it was said to the ancients, "You will not swear" [roughly Leviticus 19:12]; and "you will repay your oath to the Lord" [perhaps Deuteronomy 23:22, in the Greek version]. But I am telling you not to swear at all: [don't swear] by heaven, because it's God's throne. Nor by the earth, because it is the footstool for God's feet. Nor by Jerusalem, because it's the city of the Great King. Nor by the hair of your head, because you can't turn a single hair white or black. Let your response be "Yes" (meaning "Yes") and "No" (meaning "No"). Anything more than this is from the Evil One.

5. 'You've heard it said: "an eye for an eye" and "a tooth for a tooth" [Exodus 21:24]. But I am telling you: don't resist the evil person. No – whoever slaps you on your right cheek, turn the other cheek to them also; and whoever wants to take you to court and take your tunic, let them have your garment as well. And whoever conscripts you to go one Roman mile, go two miles with them. Give to the person who asks you, and don't turn away the person who wants to borrow from you.

6. 'You have heard that it was said, "You will love your neighbour" [Leviticus 19:18] and hate your enemy. But I'm telling you: love your enemies, and pray for those who persecute you, so that you may become children of your Father in heaven, because he makes the sun rise on the evil and the good, and makes the rain fall on the just and the unjust. You see – if you love those who love you, what reward do you have? Don't the tax collectors do the same? And if you only greet your brothers or sisters, what extra are you doing? Don't the Gentiles do the same? 'You are therefore to be perfect as your Heavenly Father is perfect.'

We should be startled here not only by the authoritative tone of Jesus' teaching, but also by how strictly he interprets the Torah. He takes six sayings from the Pentateuch and notches them up by a turn or two. There could be no stronger response to those (within or without Matthew's church) who argue that Christianity involves weakening the Law's demands. On the contrary, says Jesus, his disciples have to aspire to the same degree of perfection as their Heavenly Father. This might cause us to fall thoughtfully silent.

Gehenna is the Valley of the brothers Hinnom in Jerusalem, where waste material was ordinarily burnt, so it is a metaphor, one that we shall meet again.

Matthew has added to what he found in Mark (10:2, 4) the idea of fornication as an exception to the prohibition against divorce. There are three possible meanings: it could imply that adultery is a reason for divorcing one's spouse; or it could refer, in a standard Old Testament metaphor, to idolatry; or it might refer to marriage within the forbidden degrees, i.e. incest.

Ways of being righteous: almsgiving, prayer, fasting

6 1-18 'Be careful not to do your righteousness in front of people, with a view to being seen by them. Otherwise, you don't get any reward from your Father in heaven.

- 'So – when you *give alms*, don't have a fanfare blown ahead of you, as fake-pietists do, stopping to pray in synagogues and lanes, so as to be glorified by people. Amen I tell you – they have their reward. No, when *you* give alms, your left hand should not know what your right hand is doing, so that your almsgiving may be done in secret; and [then] your Father who sees in secret will pay you back.

- 'And when you *pray*, don't be like the fake-pietists. They have a habit of praying, standing up in synagogues and on street corners, so that people can see them. No, when *you* pray, go into your private office, shut the door, and pray to your Father who is in the secret place. And your Father who sees in secret will pay you back.

  'When you pray, don't gabble like the Gentiles; for they think that they'll get a hearing because of their verbosity. Don't imitate them – for your Father in heaven knows what you need before you ask him. So pray like this:

  'Our Father in heaven, may your name be treated as holy; may your kingdom come; may your will be done, as in heaven, [so] also on earth. Give to us today our bread for the coming day. And let us off our debts, just as we have let off all our debtors. And don't bring us into temptation, but deliver us from the Evil One.

  'You see – if you let people off their offences, your Heavenly Father will let you off also. But, if you don't let people off, your Heavenly Father will not let you off your offences.

- 'And when you *fast*, don't be like the fake-pietists: [they get] sad-faced, because they disfigure their appearance so as to let people know that they are fasting. Amen I tell you, they have their reward. When you fast, anoint your head and wash your face, so as not to let people know that you are fasting, only your Father, who is in secret: and your Father who sees in secret will pay you back.'

Almsgiving, fasting and prayer have always been pillars of Jewish devotional life. Clearly Jesus is not questioning their worth, but simply drawing attention to God's quiet way of operating, and encouraging his hearers to do the same. On each of the three issues Jesus operates in a way that we can no longer represent in English, between 'you plural' and 'you singular': this explanation of how to 'be perfect as your Heavenly Father is perfect' is for the disciples as a group; but it is also directed to each of Jesus' hearers, each of Matthew's readers, as an individual.

More moral teaching – some unconnected sayings

6 ¹⁹–7 ²³ 'Don't treasure up treasures on earth, where moth and rust destroy, and where burglars break in and steal. Treasure up treasures for yourselves in heaven, where neither moth nor rust destroys, and burglars don't break in and steal. For where your treasure is, your heart will also be there.

'The eye is the body's lamp. So if your eye is clear-sighted, your whole body will be illuminated. If however your eye is evil, your whole body will be darkened. So if the light in you is darkness, what a great darkness it will be!

'No one can serve two lords: for you will either hate one and love the other, or you will put up with one and despise the other. You *cannot* serve God and Mammon.

'So I'm telling you: don't worry about your life, what you're to eat, nor about your body, what you're to wear. Isn't life more than diet, and the body more than clothing? Look at the birds in the sky: they don't sow, or reap, or gather into barns, and yet your Heavenly Father feeds them. Aren't you more important than them? Which of you can by worrying add a single cubit to your height? And why do you worry about clothing? Learn [from] the wild flowers, how they grow – they don't do hard work, nor do they do any weaving, but I'm telling you that not even Solomon in all his glory was clothed like one of these. Now – if God clothes the grass of the field like this, which is here today and thrown into the oven tomorrow, will [he not do] all the more for you, people of little faith? So don't worry and say "What are we to eat?" or "What are we to drink?" or "What are we to wear?". You see, the Gentiles pursue all these things. Your Heavenly Father knows that you need all these things. No – first seek God's kingdom and his righteousness, and all these things shall be given to you in addition. So – don't worry about tomorrow, for tomorrow will worry about itself. Today's hardship is enough for today.

'Don't judge, so as not to be judged: for you will be judged by the judgement with which you judge; and the measure that you measure out will be the measure that is measured out to you. Why do you inspect the splinter in your brother's or sister's eye, but fail to notice the plank that is in your own eye? Or how come you tell your brother or sister, "Just let me get rid of the splinter from your eye", and look! There's a plank in your own eye? Fake-pietist! First, get rid of the plank from your eye, then you'll see clearly enough to get rid of the splinter from your brother or sister's eye.

'Don't give what is holy to dogs, and don't throw down your pearls in front of pigs; otherwise they'll trample them down with their trotters and then turn on you and tear you in pieces.

'Ask, and it will be given to you; seek, and you will find; knock, and it will be opened to you. For everyone who asks receives; and the one who seeks finds; and to the one who knocks it will be opened. What human being among you, when your child asks for a loaf of bread, will give them a stone? Or if they ask for a fish, will you give them a snake? So – if you who are evil know how to give good gifts to your children, how much more will your Father in heaven give good things to those who ask him?

'So – everything that you want people to do for you, you must do just the same for them. For this is the Torah and the Prophets.

'Enter through the narrow gate; because the gate is broad and the way is spacious that leads to destruction; and many are those who enter through it. How narrow is the gate and how confined the way that leads to life! And how few are they who find it.

'Watch out for fake prophets, who come to you in sheep's clothing, but inside are rapacious wolves. Recognise them from their fruits: do people collect bunches of grapes from thorns, or figs from thistles? So any tree that is any good produces lovely fruit, while the rotten tree produces evil fruit. A good tree can't produce evil fruit, and a rotten tree can't produce lovely fruit. Any tree that doesn't produce lovely fruit is cut down and thrown into [the] fire. So by their fruits you will know them.

'Not everyone who says, "Lord, Lord" to me will enter the kingdom of heaven. No – [it will be] the one who does the will of my Father in heaven. On that day many people will tell me, "Lord, Lord, didn't we prophesy in your name? And expel demons in your name? And do many miracles in your name?" And I'll tell them straight out, "I never knew you – depart from me, you who work Lawlessness." '

This can seem like a rather random collection of sayings; and the reader may start to wonder if this is a presentation of the key values of the Gospel, or just elevated common sense. Go through it carefully, however, and you will see that what makes sense of it all, the thread running through it, is Jesus' central perception of God as a loving Father. There are several possible responses to this perception: we can go the whole hog and accept it, as Jesus does, or we can half credit it, half fail to believe it. If we do that, we are what Matthew regularly calls a 'person of little faith' (in Greek *oligopist*). At the far extreme are the 'fake-pietists' (the word means 'actors' and is transcribed into English as 'hypocrites'), who only **pretend** to regard God as their Father.

The reader may be relieved to spot some jokes in this part of the Sermon on the Mount: the absurd notion of adding to your height by worrying about it, the idea of the lilies of the field working hard to get their clothing, the splendidly comical thought of my offering to get a tiny splinter out of your eye, when my vision is obscured by a huge plank in my own, and the glorious picture of collecting bunches of grapes from thorns and figs from thistles, are all intended to raise at least a wry grin in us.

It may help the reader to know that 'Mammon' is the Aramaic word for wealth or property. Here it is represented as an alternative (and dangerously attractive) God; and we have to make our choice.

Conclusion of the Sermon, with two parables to make us stop and think

24-29 'So everyone who hears these words of mine and does them will be like an intelligent man, who built his house on rock. And the rain descended, and the rivers came, and the winds blew; and they [all] fell on that house – but it didn't fall, because it was founded on the rock. And everyone who hears these words of mine and fails to do them will be like a foolish man who built his house on sand. And the rain descended, and the rivers came, and the winds blew; and they [all] fell on that house, and it fell; and great was its fall.'

And it happened when Jesus had completed these words, the crowds were amazed at his teaching. For he was teaching them like one who had authority, and not like their scribes.

The two parables of the wise and the foolish man (here they are unmistakably male – presumably only men went in for house construction in that culture) are meant to conclude the sermon with a challenge that we may not evade, an image that Jesus' peasant hearers would have readily grasped.

The lines immediately following the Sermon will find an immediate echo in all Jesus' subsequent discourses in this Gospel (see 11:1; 13:53; 19:1; 26:1). We can see, having followed Jesus closely through the sermon, what Matthew means by speaking of Jesus 'teaching like one who had authority'. It may be interesting, however, to observe that Mark (1:27; but see 1:22) had linked Jesus' authority to his ability to expel unclean spirits. In addition, Matthew, Mark and Luke all link Jesus' authority to his power to heal and to forgive sins (Matthew 9:1-8; Mark 2:1-12; Luke 5:17-26). So it is not just a matter of teaching: Jesus 'walks his talk', as they say nowadays.

Once again Jesus is set in opposition to 'their scribes'. We can feel the battle lines being drawn. As he comes down the mountain, we observe that Jesus has after all been talking to the crowds as much as to his disciples. The reader is being asked to decide: Whose side are you on: Jesus' opponents, or the aimless crowds, or the attentive (if not terribly bright) disciples?

A leper is made clean

8 ¹⁻⁴ As he came down from the mountain, great crowds followed him. And look! A leper came up, and worshipped him, saying, 'Lord, if you want, you can make me clean.' And he stretched out his hand and touched him, saying, 'I do want – be made clean.' And immediately his leprosy was made clean. And Jesus says to him, 'See that you tell nobody. Instead, go and show yourself to the priest, and make the offering that Moses commanded, as evidence for them.'

> With this episode we begin two chapters in which Jesus demonstrates his authority with a series of healings and controversies. In this first episode we notice the characteristic effortlessness of the healing. We may also observe that the leper 'worships' Jesus – and there is no suggestion that he has made some kind of mistake. This is a further element in Matthew's portrait of Jesus.

The healing of a centurion's servant

5-13 As he entered Caphernaum, a centurion came up, asking him, 'Lord, my servant is lying ill, paralysed in the house, dreadfully tormented.' And he says to him, 'I'll come and cure him.' The centurion answered, 'Lord, I am not fit that you should come in under my roof. But just say a word, and my servant will be healed. You see I am a man under authority, and I have soldiers under me, and I say to this one, "Quick march," and he marches, and to another, "Come," and he comes, and to my slave, "Do this," and he does it.'

Jesus heard this and was astonished; and he said to the people following, 'Amen I tell you, I have not found such faith from anyone in Israel. I'm telling you that many will come from east and west, and will lie down with Abraham, Isaac and Jacob in the kingdom of heaven; but the children of the kingdom will be expelled into the outer darkness. In that place there will be weeping and gnashing of teeth.' And Jesus said to the centurion, 'Go – let it happen to you in accordance with your faith.' And his servant was healed at that hour.

Once again we read of an effortless healing; but at a deeper level we may notice once more an implicit question in Matthew about the status of Israel in the new dispensation. Matthew's Gospel is sometimes spoken of as 'the most Jewish and the most anti-Jewish of the four Gospels'.

More healings, and a fulfilment citation

14-17　And Jesus came to Peter's house and saw Peter's mother-in-law lying ill with fever; and he touched her hand, and the fever left her, and she arose [or: 'was raised'] and started to serve them. When it grew late, they brought to him many people who had demons; he would expel the demons with a word, and he cured all those who were in a bad way, so that what was spoken through Isaiah the prophet might be fulfilled, 'he has taken our sicknesses and taken away our diseases'.

Again Jesus heals anything that comes his way. We may notice, though, two points regarding his revision of Mark. First, the 'when it grew late' made sense in Mark 1:32, because it had been a Sabbath-day, and they could not bring their sick until the Sabbath was over, but Matthew has broken up Mark's pattern of 'a typical day in the life of Jesus' that we find in Mark 1:21-34. Second, Mark had written (1:34) 'he healed many . . . and expelled many demons'; Matthew has upgraded 'many' to 'all', presumably because he was uncomfortable with any limitation on Jesus' ability to cure people.

The quotation is from Isaiah 53:4, the last of the 'Songs of the Suffering Servant'.

Two would-be disciples (one of them a scribe!)

18-22　Seeing the crowd around him, Jesus gave orders to go across to the other side. One scribe approached and said to him, 'Teacher, I shall follow you wherever you go.' And Jesus says to him, 'Foxes have holes and birds of the sky have nests, but the Son of Man does not have anywhere to lay his head.'

Another of the disciples says to him, 'Lord, let me first go off and bury my father.' But Jesus says to him, 'Follow me – and let the dead bury their dead.'

The command to go to the other side leads us towards the next two episodes, but first Matthew wants us to contemplate the demands of discipleship, and he gives us two tales of would-be disciples. The first, rather surprisingly, given what we have seen of them so far, is a scribe. The second is already a disciple, but both of them are given rather discouraging responses; in the case of the second one the answer is decidedly chilling. The reader is being invited to consider what following Jesus might involve – it is not a career to be adopted lightly.

Who is this who calms the storm?

23-27　And when he went on the boat, his disciples followed him. And look! A great storm happened on the sea, so that the boat was covered by the waves – and he himself was sleeping. And they came and woke him and said, 'Lord, save – we are perishing!' And he says to them, 'Why are you cowards, people of little faith?' Then he arose and scolded the winds and the sea. And there came a great calm. And the people were astonished, saying, 'What kind of person is this, because even the winds and the sea obey him?'

> Any Gospel has to invite the reader to ask the question of who Jesus is, and this episode leaves that central question hanging in the air. We may also detect a fragment of the liturgy of Matthew's church in the phrase 'Lord, save'. The Greek for it is 'Kyrie, soson', echoing the more familiar 'Kyrie, eleison' ('Lord, have mercy').
>
> Matthew often uses the phrase (it is a single word in Greek) 'people of little faith': do you have some sympathy with the disciples here?

Two men possessed by demons

28-34   And when he went to the other side, to the land of the Gadarenes, two people possessed by evil spirits met him, coming out of the tombs, very difficult [cases], so that no one was able to go by that route. And look! They cried out, saying, 'What do we have to do with you, Son of God? Have you come here ahead of time to torment us?' Far away from them was a herd of many pigs, feeding. The demons begged him, saying, 'If you're expelling us, send us into the herd of pigs.' And he said to them, 'Go', and they went out and into the pigs. And look! The whole herd rushed down the cliff into the sea; and they died in the waters. And the herdsmen ran away; and they came to the city and reported everything, including the matter of the people possessed by demons. And look! The whole city came out to meet Jesus, and when they saw him, they begged him to go away from their territory.

> Matthew does not so much *tell* us who Jesus is, as *show* us. On the demons' lips comes the title 'Son of God', which we already know to be a correct identification. Here we are allowed to watch Jesus' effortless power over the demons, which had previously rendered that particular road impassable. We notice also the reaction of the local inhabitants, who instead of welcoming him are anxious to get rid of him.
>
> Readers may be interested to compare this version of the story with that in Mark 5:1-17, and see what details Matthew has not decided to include.

Another healing

9 1-8   And he went on board a boat and crossed over, and came to his own city. And look! They were bringing him a paralytic lying on a bed. And Jesus, seeing their faith, said to the paralytic, 'Have courage, child: your sins are forgiven.' And look! Some of the scribes said to themselves, 'This man is blaspheming.' And Jesus, seeing their thoughts, said, 'Why do you think evil things in your hearts? For which is easier, to say, "Your sins are forgiven" or to say, "Arise and walk"? But that you may know that the Son of Man has authority on earth to forgive sins' (then he says

to the paralytic) 'Up you get, lift up your bed, and go to your house.' And he got up and went off to his house! When they saw it, the crowds were afraid, and they glorified God, who gave such authority to human beings.

> Again Matthew allows us to see who Jesus is. Mark's version of the story (2:1-12) had the splendid touch of the man being lowered through the roof, because of the crowds; but for Matthew (who tends to include only the details that really seem important to him), the point of the story is Jesus' controversially claimed authority to forgive sins.

The calling of Matthew, and Jesus' undesirable friends

9-13 And passing by from there, Jesus saw a man sitting at the tax desk, called Matthew. And he says to him, 'Follow me.' And he got up and followed him.

And it happened as he was lying down to eat in his house, and look! Many tax collectors and sinners came to eat with Jesus and his disciples. And when they saw it, the Pharisees said to his disciples, 'Why is it with tax collectors and sinners that your master eats?' He heard it and said, 'It is not those who are well who have need of a doctor, but those who are in a bad way. Go and find out what "I want mercy and not sacrifice" means. For I didn't come to call the righteous – no, [I came to call] sinners.'

> The tax collector who is summoned in this way is called Levi in Mark and Luke, and it is possible that this Gospel is attributed to Matthew because his name appears at this point. More important is the continuing revelation of who Jesus is: religious people are disedified by his choice of friends; but (not for the first time in this Gospel) he is not short of a scriptural quotation to defend his policy. 'I want mercy and not sacrifice' comes from Hosea 6:6.

Controversy with the disciples of John the Baptist

14-17 Then John's disciples came to him saying, 'Why do we and the Pharisees fast, but your disciples don't fast?' And Jesus said to them, 'Surely the wedding guests can't be sad during the time that the bridegroom is with them, can they? But days will come when the bridegroom is taken from them; and then they will fast. No one puts a patch of unshrunk cloth on an old garment, for it takes the patch off the garment, and the tear gets worse. Nor do they put new wine into old flasks; otherwise the flasks break, and the wine pours out, and the flasks are destroyed. No – they put new wine into new flasks, and both are preserved.'

> Now comes another objection to Jesus: he and his disciples do not observe the fast-days observed by disciples of John the Baptist and by the Pharisees. The point of the story is that Jesus is the one they have been waiting for (at the very beginning of the Gospel we saw him as the climax of the history of Israel); and in his presence fasting is inappropriate. But he will not always be there.

Two women healed

18-26 As he was saying this to them, look! A ruler came and worshipped him, saying, 'My daughter has just died; but come and lay your hand on her and she will live.' Jesus got up and followed him; and [so did] his disciples.

And look! A woman with a flow of blood for twelve years came up behind and touched the hem of his garment. For she was saying to herself, 'If only I touch his garment, I'll be saved.' But Jesus turned and saw her and said, 'Courage, daughter; your faith has saved you.' And the woman was saved from that hour.

And Jesus came to the ruler's house, and seeing the flute players, and the crowd making a noise, he said, 'Leave the room, for the little girl hasn't died. No – she is sleeping.' And they laughed at him. But when the crowd had been thrown out, he went in and took her hand, and the little girl was raised up. And this story went out into the whole of that country.

> Mark has a much longer version of these two stories (see Mark 5:22-43). What Matthew shows us here is the absolute confidence of Jesus, and that of those who approached Jesus in their need; and their confidence is justified.

Two blind people and a dumb one are healed; a concluding summary

27-35 And as he was coming away from there, two blind people followed Jesus, shouting out and saying, 'Have mercy on us, Son of David.' As he was going into the house the blind people approached him, and Jesus said to them, 'Do you believe that I am capable of doing this?' They say to him, 'Yes, Lord.' Then he touched their eyes, saying, 'Let it happen to you, in accordance with your faith.' And their eyes were opened; and Jesus spoke sternly to them, saying, 'See that no one knows'; but they went out and made him known in the whole of that country.

As they were going out, look! They brought him a person who was dumb, possessed by a demon. And when the demon had been cast out, the dumb man spoke. And the crowds were astonished, saying, 'Nothing like this ever appeared in Israel.' But the Pharisees were commenting, 'It is by the ruler of demons that he casts out demons.'

And Jesus was going round all the cities and villages teaching in their synagogues, and proclaiming the gospel of the kingdom, and curing every disease and every ailment.

> These healings and the summary bring to an end the run of cures that Matthew has laid before us since the Sermon on the Mount. As at the end of the preceding episode, Matthew includes a remark about the story going out 'in the whole of that country', to underline the impact that Jesus was having.
>
> Once again, as with the Gadarene demoniacs, Matthew has a pair (of blind men), where Mark had only one. Once again, we may hear a fragment of the liturgy of Matthew's church, when the blind men say, 'Have mercy on us', where the Greek is again 'eleison'. And here, for the first time since the Gospel's opening verse, Jesus is called 'Son of David'. We shall see this title again in Matthew, often in a context of healing.

Finally we notice that Matthew here identifies the enemy for us. They are twofold: first the demons, who make people blind and dumb and so on, but second those who do not accept Jesus, here named as 'Pharisees', who accuse him of being a closet demon.

The Second 'Discourse': Instructions for Mission (9:36–11:1)

A careful introduction

9 ³⁶-10 ⁴ Seeing the crowds, he had compassion on them, because they were harassed and helpless, like sheep with no shepherd. Then he says to his disciples, 'The harvest is great, but the workers are few; so ask the Lord of the harvest to send out workers into his harvest.'

And calling his twelve disciples, he gave them authority over unclean spirits, to expel them, and to cure every disease and every sickness.

These are the names of the twelve apostles: first, Simon called Peter, and Andrew his brother, then James the son of Zebedee and John his brother, Philip and Bartholomew, Thomas and Matthew (the tax collector), James the son of Alphaeus, and Thaddaeus, Simon the Canaanite, and Judas the Iscariot, who also betrayed him.

As with the Sermon on the Mount, so with this second of the great speeches that Matthew threads through his Gospel; the author sets the scene with some care (and, as we shall see, also provides it with a characteristic concluding formula).

Once again, it starts with the crowds, but this time more attention is given to them, their sense of 'lost-ness' ('like sheep without a shepherd'), and Jesus' compassion for them, which he expresses in terms of a sympathetic peasant metaphor, of a harvest with not enough reapers. In response to this need he summons his 'Twelve', and commissions them with some of his own powers over demons and sickness. Then comes the list of their names, concluding with 'Judas the Iscariot, who also betrayed him', in a chilling reminder that not all the labourers in the vineyard could be relied on. The list is the same as that found in Mark, except that Matthew has placed Andrew next to his brother, and added 'the tax collector' next to the name of Matthew.

Then finally we are allowed to hear the address, which concentrates on the difficulties of the job that faces them.

The address on the difficulties of discipleship

5-42 These twelve Jesus sent out, when he had given them instructions: 'Do not go on the road of the Gentiles; and don't enter a city of the Samaritans. Go instead to the lost sheep of the house of Israel. As you go, proclaim, "The kingdom of heaven has drawn near." Cure those who are sick, raise the dead, make lepers clean, cast out demons.

'You received for free, give for free. Don't have gold or silver or bronze in your wallets; no purse for the journey, not even a spare tunic or sandals or a staff: for the labourer deserves his food. Whatever city or village you enter, find out who in it is worthy, and stay there until you leave. When you enter a house, greet it; and if the house is worthy, let your peace come upon it. Otherwise, let your peace return to you. And if anyone doesn't receive you, or listen to your words, when you come out of that house or city, shake the dust off your feet. Amen, I tell you, it will be more tolerable for the land of Sodom and Gomorrah on that day than for that city. Look! I am sending you out like sheep in the midst of wolves – so be as intelligent as snakes and as simple as doves.

'Beware of human beings – they'll hand you over to Sanhedrins, and scourge you in their synagogues; you will be taken before governors and kings for my sake, as a witness to them and to the Gentiles. But when they hand you over, don't worry about how or what to say. You see, it is not you who speak, but the Spirit of your Father speaking in you.

'Brother will hand over brother to death, and a father his child; and children will rise up against parents and kill them, and you will be hated by everybody because of my name. The one who endures to the end is the one who will be saved. When they persecute you in this city, flee to the next. For Amen I tell you, you will not complete the cities of Israel before the Son of Man comes.

'A disciple is not superior to the teacher, nor a slave to his lord. It is sufficient for the disciple that he become like his teacher, and the slave like his lord. If they call the master of the house "Beelzeboul", how much more will they do it to the members of his house! So don't be afraid of them; for nothing is hidden that will not be revealed, and nothing concealed that will not be made known. What I tell you in the darkness, speak in the light; and what you hear with your ear, proclaim on top of the houses. And don't be afraid of those who kill the body, but are unable to kill the soul. No – be more afraid of the one who can kill both soul and body in Gehenna. Are not two sparrows bought for half a cent? And not one of them falls to the ground without your Father ['s consent]. As for you, God has counted all the hairs on your head. So don't be afraid – you are worth more than any number of sparrows.

'So every one of you who declares yourself for me before human beings, I in my turn will declare myself for that person before my Father in heaven. But whoever denies me before human beings, I shall deny that person before my Father in heaven.'

'Don't think that I came to bring peace on earth: I didn't come to bring peace but a sword! I came to turn a man against his father and a daughter against her mother and a bride against her mother-in-law; and a person's enemies are the people of his household. The one who loves father or mother more than me is not worthy of me; and the one who loves son or daughter more than me is not worthy of me. And anyone who does not take up their cross and follow after me is not worthy of me. The one who finds their life will lose it; and the one who loses their life for my sake will find it.

'The one who receives you receives me; and the one who receives me receives the one who sent me. The one who receives a prophet because of being a prophet will receive a prophet's reward; and the one who receives a righteous person because of being a righteous person will receive a righteous person's reward. And anyone who gives a drink to one of these little ones, a cup of cold water, just because they are a disciple, Amen I tell you, they will not lose their reward.'

This is a formidable exhortation; perhaps one might think of the 'pep talk' given by a football manager before the most important game of the season. Certainly Jesus' hearers (and Matthew's readers) are left in no doubt of the enormity of the task that lies before them. They may, however, be charmed by some more of Jesus' 'peasant images': lost sheep, the labourer's food, and the price of two sparrows.

They may well have been puzzled (certainly *we* grope uncertainly for the meaning) by the reference to the peace that returns to its giver, and the mention of the 'one who kills body and soul in Gehenna'. Is that God or the devil? But we must not evade the challenge of the Gospel. And we should notice that the basic mission with which we are entrusted is the simple message of both John the Baptist and Jesus: 'The kingdom of heaven has drawn near.'

Conclusion

11¹ And it happened when Jesus finished giving instructions to his twelve disciples, he went away from there to teach and to proclaim in their cities.

Matthew used a very similar phrase to conclude the Sermon on the Mount; but there it introduced an appraisal of the speech. Here it acts as a springboard for Jesus' continuing missionary activity. For the moment, though, we watch, as ambassadors of a puzzled John the Baptist help us to decide whether or not Jesus is the Coming One.

A strange interlude centred on John the Baptist

2-15 John heard in prison about the deeds of the Messiah, and sent [an enquiry] by way of his disciples: 'Are you the One Who Is Coming? Or are we to expect someone else?'

Jesus answered them: 'Go and tell John what you see and hear: the blind see again, the lame walk, lepers are made clean and the deaf hear; the dead are being raised and the destitute are being gospelled. And congratulations to the one who is not scandalised by me.'

As they went off, Jesus began to talk to the crowds about John. 'Why did you go out into the desert? [Was it] to see a reed shaken by the wind? No – what *did* you go out to see? Someone wearing luxurious clothing? Look! Those with luxurious clothes are in kings' palaces. No – what *did* you go out to see? A prophet? Yes, I tell you, and something far better than a prophet. This is the one of whom it was written:

> "Behold I am sending my messenger before my face,
> who will prepare your way before you."

'Amen I tell you, there has not arisen among those born of women anyone more important than John the Baptist. But the least in the kingdom of heaven is greater than he is. But from the days of John the Baptist until now the kingdom of heaven goes its way violently [or: 'suffers violence'], and violent people ravage it. For all the Prophets and the Torah prophesied up to John the Baptist; and if you want to accept it, he is Elijah, the one who is to come. Let those who have ears listen.'

This is a mysterious passage; but like the one that follows it clearly has to do with receiving Jesus. John the Baptist is dubious about whether Jesus should be accepted as the Coming One, and his disciples are sent off with a set of quotations from Isaiah (26:19; 29:18; 35:5, 6; 42:7; 42:18; 61:1), the point of which is presumably that Jesus does all the things that Isaiah indicated would happen. John the Baptist is given an appropriate Scripture text: but is it Exodus 23:20 or Malachi 3:1? Decide for yourself.

Then Jesus turns to the matter of John the Baptist himself, and indicates first how difficult he was to accept; but nevertheless, like Jesus, he spoke God's word. Second, though, John the Baptist is put in his place – he ranks lower in importance than the lowest of Jesus' disciples. The saying about violence is hard to grasp; but at the end John's status is reaffirmed: he is Elijah, who has, as predicted, returned.

The reader may notice how Matthew has tidied up Mark. In Mark 1:2 the quotation from Exodus 23:20 about the 'messenger before my face' is muddled in with a line from Isaiah 40:3, and Matthew does not like muddle, so he left the Isaiah quotation more or less where he had found it in Mark (Matthew 3:3), making it clear that it referred to John the Baptist, and has placed the Exodus citation here, again in reference to John.

If the passage seems very obscure to you, then take courage from the closing words, which indicate that you are not alone.

John the Baptist again; still talking about 'reception'

16-19 'To what shall I compare this generation? It is like children sitting in market squares, calling out to other children,

' "We played the pipe for you – and you didn't dance!
We sang a dirge for you – and you didn't mourn!"

'You see, John came: he didn't eat or drink, and they say, "He's got a demon." The Son of Man came: he both ate and drank, and they say, "Look! A glutton and a wine-drinker, a friend of tax collectors and sinners!" And [yet] Wisdom is justified by her activities.'

Here once more Matthew brings Jesus and John the Baptist close together. Neither is well received by his contemporaries. Like children, people want to set the agenda. John the Baptist and Jesus are both refused a hearing because either they are uncomfortable to listen to or they fail to conform to the stereotype.

Jesus on those who failed to receive him

20-24 Then he started uttering reproaches to the cities in which most of his miracles had been performed, because they had failed to repent. 'Alas for you, Chorazin! Alas for you, Bethsaida! Because if the miracles that took place in you had taken place in Tyre and Sidon, they would long ago have repented in sackcloth and ashes. But I'm telling you: it will be more tolerable for Tyre and Sidon on the Day of Judgement.

Caphernaum: you don't think you'll be lifted up to heaven, do you? You will go down to hell! Because if it had been Sodom where the miracles took place that took place in you, the city would have remained until now. But I'm telling you that it will be more tolerable for the land of Sodom on Judgement Day than for you.'

It is possible that one of the problems which Matthew observed in his church was that they had lost their enthusiasm; and he may be using this passage, which is also found in Luke, as a warning to them to receive the message attentively. It is certainly a rather alarming set of sayings.

What follows is less alarming, but still has to do with the appropriate response to the message.

Privileged receivers of the message

25-30 At that time, Jesus responded, 'I give you praise, Father, Lord of heaven and earth, because you hid these things from the clever and the intelligent, and revealed them to children. Yes, Father, because so was your good pleasure before you.

'Everything was handed over to me by my Father, and no one knows the Son except the Father; nor does anyone know the Father except the Son and whoever the Son wishes to reveal him to.

'Come here to me, all you who labour and are burdened, and I shall give you rest. Take my yoke upon yourselves, and learn from me, because I am gentle, and humble in heart; and you will find rest for yourselves. For my yoke is kindly, and my burden is light.'

This lovely series of sayings is still about the mystery of who can receive the message. The chapter started with John the Baptist missing a step, and wondering if Jesus was, after all, the real thing. Then it continued with a reproach to those who should have known better, Chorazin, and Caphernaum, which Jesus used as his head-quarters. Finally, it is revealed how 'receiving the message' actually works. Revelation comes from the Father to the Son, and then to those who are open to it; and these people are not necessarily the most highly educated. They are in particular those whom life crushes, who know that Jesus' 'yoke' is 'kindly' (the word will actually have sounded like 'Christ' in Greek), the people for whom God's word is a natural 'fit'.

Breaking the Sabbath, and a plan to commit murder

12 1-14 At that time, on the Sabbath, Jesus journeyed through the grain fields. His disciples were hungry, and began to pick ears of grain and eat them. The Pharisees saw it and said to him, 'Look! Your disciples are doing what is not permitted on the Sabbath!' He said to them, 'Didn't you read what David did when he and his companions were hungry? He went into the House of God, and they started eating the Loaves of Presentation, when it was not permitted for him or his companions to eat it, but only the priests. Or didn't you read in the Torah that on the Sabbath-day the priests in the Temple profane the Sabbath, and they bear no guilt for it? I'm telling you, here is [something] greater than the Temple. If you knew what "I want mercy and not sacrifice" means, you would not have condemned those who have no guilt. For the Son of Man is Lord of the Sabbath.'

And he went away from there, and came to their synagogue. And look! A man with a withered hand, and they interrogated him, 'Is it permissible to heal on the Sabbath?' ([This was] in order to [be able to] accuse him.) He said to them, 'What person is there among you who has a single sheep, and if this sheep falls into a pit on the Sabbath-day, will not get hold of the sheep and lift it up? And how much more important is a human being than a sheep! So, yes, it is permissible to do a good deed on the Sabbath.' Then he said to the man, 'Stretch out your hand'; and he stretched it out, and it was restored, just as healthy as the other!

The Pharisees went out and made a plan against him, to kill him.

For Matthew it is very important to see Jesus as observing the Torah. So when he is accused of breaking the Sabbath Jesus is able to quote Scripture (Hosea 6:6), as easily as he had done in response to the testing by the devil in Chapter 4, to make it clear that there are good precedents for what his disciples have done: tasks are set out in Leviticus 24:8 and Numbers 28:9 for performance by the priests precisely on the Sabbath-day. So (the argument runs) the Torah itself envisages a breach of the Sabbath; and Jesus is happily able to quote the example of David, whom everyone would agree was a proper servant of God (see 1 Samuel 21:1-6).

However, we should notice two more things here. First, Jesus is different from his opponents in that he is able to heal without any difficulty at all, and in that he can claim to be 'Lord of the Sabbath'. So Jesus' opponents are nowhere near the same league.

Second, Jesus' easy triumph now seems to be leading to the death at the hands of the religious establishment that Herod had in mind for him back in Chapter 2.

This sets the scene for the controversies with his opponents that make up the rest of this chapter. We should not forget that it is now a matter of life and death. Once again, Matthew faces the reader with the question: which side are you on?

Squabbles with Jesus' religious opponents

15-50 Jesus was aware of [their plot], and went away from there. And many people followed him, and he cured them all and he gave them stern warning not to reveal him, so that the [word] spoken through Isaiah the prophet might be fulfilled:

'Look! my servant whom I chose,
my Beloved in whom my soul is pleased.
I shall place my Spirit upon him
and he will announce judgement to the nations.
He will not quarrel or brawl, nor will anyone hear his voice in the streets.
He will not break a crushed reed, nor will he extinguish a smouldering wick
until he brings judgement to a victorious issue
and the nations will hope in his name.'

Then someone with a demon was brought to him, blind and dumb. And he cured him, so that the dumb man spoke and [could] see. And all the crowds were amazed and said, 'Isn't this the Son of David?'

But the Pharisees overheard and said, 'The only way this man expels demons is by Beelzeboul, Chief of the Demons.'

Jesus knew their ideas, and said to them, 'Any kingdom that is divided against itself is laid waste, and any city or house that is divided against itself will not stand. And if Satan expels Satan, he's divided against himself, so how [can] his kingdom stand? And if I expel demons by Beelzeboul, how do your children expel them? Therefore they shall be your judges. But if it is by the Spirit of God that I expel demons, then the kingdom of God has come upon you. How do you think someone can enter the strong man's house and burgle his property unless he first ties up the strong man? And then he can really burgle the house.

'Anyone who is not with me is against me, and anyone who does not gather with me, scatters. Therefore I'm telling you, every [other] sin and irreverence will be forgiven human beings; but irreverence against the Spirit will not be forgiven. And if anyone says a word against the Son of Man, it will be forgiven them, but anyone who speaks against the Holy Spirit, it will not be forgiven them either in this present age or in the age to come. You either produce a good tree (and its fruit is good) or a rotten tree (and its fruit is rotten); you see, it's by its fruit that a tree is known. Offspring of snakes! How can you make good statements when you are evil? You see, the mouth speaks out of the fullness of the heart. A good person produces good things from the treasure chest that is good, while an evil person produces evil things from the treasure chest that is evil. I'm telling you, on the Day of Judgement, people will [have to] give an account of every careless word that they utter. For it is by your words that you will be justified, and by your words that you will be condemned.'

Then some of the scribes and Pharisees answered him, 'Teacher, we want to see a sign from you.' He replied, 'A wicked and adulterous generation looks for a sign, and it will not be given a sign except for the sign of Jonah the prophet. For as Jonah was in the belly of the sea-monster for three days and three nights, so the Son of Man will be in the heart of the earth for three days and three nights. The Ninevites will rise up at the Judgement with this generation and condemn it, because they repented at Jonah's preaching, and look! Something more than Jonah is here. The Queen of the South will rise up at the Judgement with this generation and condemn it, because she came from the ends of the earth, and look! Something more than Solomon is here.

'When the unclean spirit goes out of the person, it goes through waterless places looking for refreshment, and doesn't find it. Then it says, "I'll return to my house from which I came out"; and it goes and finds it unoccupied, swept and decorated. Then it goes and brings with it seven other spirits, more evil than itself, and they go in and live there: and that person's final state is worse than their first. So it will be for this evil generation.'

While he was still speaking to the crowds, look! His mother and his brothers were standing outside, looking to speak to him. Someone said to him, 'Look! Your mother and your brothers are standing outside looking to speak to you.' He answered the one who told him, 'Who is my mother, and who are my brothers?' And he stretched out his hand over his disciples and said, 'Look! My mother and my brothers. For anyone who does the will of my Father in heaven *is* my brother and sister and mother.'

The Jesus that Matthew presents to us is neither easy nor comfortable. The quotation with which the passage opens is from Isaiah 42:1-4, the first of the 'Songs of the Suffering Servant', which Jesus seems to have applied to himself. Matthew insists that Jesus fulfils Old Testament requirements, so that God must be working in him. His opponents take the opposite view, that it is Beelzeboul and the powers of evil who are at work. Jesus argues the absurdity of this, and then goes on the offensive. Like John the Baptist before him, he calls these opponents by the unpleasant title 'offspring of serpents' and insists on the importance of proper testing. The request of the opponents for a sign sounds like a concession on their part, but Jesus is not in the mood for concessions, and offers them 'the sign of Jonah', interpreted first as the Resurrection and then as repentance. The implication is that it is his opponents who are on the side of the demons.

Finally, Jesus' family intervenes, and our discomfort grows, until we realise that he has redefined what it means to be family: 'those who do the will of the Father'. And that could include us.

The Third 'Discourse': Images of the Kingdom (13:1-53)

Introduction to the 'parable-discourse'

13[1,2] On that day, Jesus went out of the house and sat by the sea. And great crowds gathered to him, with the result that he went on board a boat and sat down; and the whole crowd stood on the shore.

As with the Sermon on the Mount, Matthew gives quite an elaborate introduction to the sermon that is about to come, to make sure that we are paying attention. We may be startled to find that Jesus is leaving a house that we had not known he was in, but it is part of the build-up (Matthew is quite often rather casual about what you might call 'continuity'). Notice that Jesus *twice* takes up the position of a teacher, first 'by the sea' and then 'on a boat', while the crowd stands, as befits those who are disciples.

The image of the sower; the difficulties of 'images' (parables)

3-23 And he spoke many things to them in images: 'Look! The sower went out to sow. And as he sowed, some fell beside the road, and the birds came and gobbled it up. Other [seed] fell on rock, where it didn't have much soil, and immediately it sprang up, because of a lack of depth in the soil; but when the sun rose, it was scorched, and because it had no roots, it withered. Other [seed] fell on thorns, and the thorns came up and choked it. But other [seed] fell on good soil, and yielded fruit: one seed a hundred, one seed sixty, and one thirty. Let the one who has ears, hear.'

And his disciples approached and said to him, 'Why do you talk to them in images?' He answered, 'Because it is granted to you to know the mysteries of the kingdom of heaven; but it is not granted to them. For whoever has, it will be given them, and it will overflow. But whoever does not have, even what they have will be taken away from them. This is the reason that I speak to them in images, that although they see, they do not see; and although they hear they do not hear – nor do they understand. And the prophecy of Isaiah is fulfilled in their regard, which says,

> "Hearing you will hear, and no way understand
> and seeing you will see and no way perceive.
> For the heart of this people has grown fat
> and with their ears they hardly heard
> and they shut their eyes, lest they should perceive with their eyes
> and hear with their ears and understand with their heart
> and lest they turn, and I heal them."

'But as for *you*, happy are your eyes that they see, and your ears that they hear. For Amen I tell you, many prophets and righteous people desired to perceive what you see, and never did, and to hear what you hear and never did.

'So now *you* listen to the image of the sower. When anyone hears the message of the kingdom and doesn't understand it, the Evil One comes and grabs what has been sown in their heart; that person is the one sown beside the road. The one sown on the rocky bits, that's the one who hears the word and immediately accepts it with joy, but has no root in themselves, but they just last a little while, and when trouble or persecution occur because of the message, they immediately trip up. The one sown into thorns is the one who hears the message, and the world's stress and the lure of wealth suffocate the message, and it is ineffective. And the one sown on good soil, that's the one who hears the word and understands, who is effective and produces in one case a hundred, in another sixty, and in another thirty.'

Matthew has already indicated that Jesus is difficult to grasp; he has done this partly by showing the starkness of Jesus' teaching, and partly by indicating how his enemies reacted. This chapter presents 'parables'; this first section of it offers a very charming peasant image, which requires a bit of thinking about, and does not really carry its own explanation. Then the disciples underline our sense of puzzlement, by asking (slightly aggressively?) why he tells stories. Jesus' answer concedes nothing, and more or less says, 'It's meant to be difficult.' Finally, Jesus offers them an account of the sower story, which makes it into a tale about how the Word of God is received. The quotation from Isaiah 6:9-10 underlines the difficulty of understanding Jesus.

Some more images: the weeds in the wheat, the grain of mustard, and the leaven, with an explanation of the first

24-43 He offered them another image: 'The kingdom of heaven is compared to a man who sowed good seed in his field, but while people slept, his enemy came and sowed weeds in the middle of the wheat and went off. But when the grain sprouted and produced ears, the weeds also appeared at that time. The householder's slaves came and told him, "Lord, didn't you sow the right seed in your field? So how come it has weeds?" He said to them, "Some enemy has done this." The slaves said to him, "So do you want us to go and collect [the weeds]?" He said, "No, in case when you collect the weeds you uproot the wheat along with them. Let them both grow together until the harvest, and at harvest-time, I'll tell the harvesters, 'First collect the weeds and tie them up in bundles to burn them, [then] gather the wheat into my barn.'"'

He offered them another image: 'The kingdom of heaven is like a grain of mustard, which someone took and sowed in their field. It is the smallest of all the seeds; but when it grows it is bigger than the vegetables and becomes a shrub, so that the birds of the air come and roost in its branches.'

He uttered another image to them: 'The kingdom of heaven is like leaven which a woman took and hid in three measures of flour, until the whole lot was leavened.'

Jesus said all these things to the crowds in images, and he said nothing to them except with an image, so that the [word] spoken through the prophet might be fulfilled:

'I shall open my mouth in images;
I shall utter things hidden from the foundation of the world.'

Then he left the crowds and went to the house. And his disciples approached him, saying, 'Explain the image of the weeds in the field for us.' He answered, 'The one who sows the good seed is the Son of Man. The field is the world, and the good seeds are the children of the kingdom. The weeds are the children of the Evil One. The enemy who sows them is the devil; the harvest is the end of the present age, and the harvesters are angels. Hence, just as the weeds are collected and burnt in the bonfire, so it will be at the end of the age. The Son of Man will send his angels, and they will collect out of his kingdom all the things that make people stumble, and all those who work against the Torah, and they'll throw them into the fiery furnace. There will be weeping and gnashing of teeth there. Then the righteous shall shine out like the sun in the kingdom of their Father. Those who have ears, let them listen.

> Still Matthew lets us see just how difficult Jesus' teaching is, and this is emphasised by the quotation from Psalm 78:2. The story of the weeds in the wheat and its explanation together act as a frame to two rather encouraging pictures, that of the tiny seed that grows into a big shrub, and that of the yeast that has its unseen but powerful effect. In this image, God is rather daringly compared to a baker-woman. Of these images it is better not to say too much: imagination is a more appropriate tool here than microscope or scissors-and-paste.

Three images to conclude: hidden treasure, a valuable pearl, the fishing-net

44-50   'The kingdom of heaven is like a treasure hidden in the field, which a person discovers; he hides it, and in his joy goes off and sells everything he possesses and buys that field.

'Or again the kingdom of heaven is like a dealer who's looking out for good-quality pearls. When he found a single really valuable one, he went off and sold everything he possessed, and bought it.

'Or again the kingdom of heaven is like a fishing-net thrown into the sea; it brings every kind [of fish] together. When it was full, they brought it to the shore, and they sat down and collected the good quality fish into containers, and the fish that was no good they threw out. That's how it will be at the end of the age. The angels will come and will separate the evil from the middle of the righteous, and they'll throw them into the fiery furnace. There will be weeping there, and gnashing of teeth.'

> Once again, Jesus (and Matthew) offers no explanation for these three images, but lets them hang in the air, to do their work on us. Sit with the stories rather than analyse them, and notice only that they are quite challenging. Consider the possibility that Matthew's congregation had lost its first enthusiasm and needed a sharp reminder.

The conclusion of the 'image' discourse

51-53 'Have you understood all these things?' They tell him, 'Yes.' He said to them, 'Because of this, every scribe who is discipled to the kingdom of heaven is like a householder, of the kind who brings new things and old things out of his safe.'
And when Jesus had completed these stories, he moved away from there.

> Jesus puts a rather schoolmasterly question to his disciples, and they can only give a schoolboy answer: what else do you say but 'Yes'? Then Jesus produces a final image, and some people suggest that Matthew here offers his own mission-statement, as a 'scribe discipled to the kingdom of heaven'. Matthew is aware of the novelty that Jesus represents, and at the same time sees the importance of asserting Jesus' continuity with the Torah of God.

An unsatisfactory visit to home territory

54-58 And coming into his home territory, he started teaching them in their synagogue, so that they were astonished, and said, 'Where did this man get this wisdom and these miracles? Isn't this the son of the builder? Isn't his mother called Mary, and his brothers Jacob and Joseph and Simon and Judas? And aren't all his sisters here with us? So where did he get all this?' And they took offence because of him. Jesus told them, 'A prophet is honoured everywhere except in his home territory and in his household.' And because of their lack of faith, he didn't do many miracles there.

> Once again Matthew reminds us of the difficulty of understanding Jesus. Notice the distance that he creates by speaking of '*their* synagogue'; but there is another kind of distance, too, that comes from knowing Jesus too well – he is the 'local man', and therefore not to be taken seriously. See how Matthew is slowly putting a portrait together.

Herod and John the Baptist

14 1-12 At that time, Herod the tetrarch heard of Jesus' reputation, and said to his servants, 'This is John the Baptist. *He's* been raised from the dead, and that's why these miracles are working in him.'

You see, Herod had arrested him and chained him up and put him away in prison, on account of Herodias, the wife of his brother Philip. For John had been telling him, 'It's not allowed for you to have her.' And although he wanted to kill him, he was afraid of the crowd, because they regarded him as a prophet. But when Herod's birthday came, Herodias' daughter danced for him, out in the middle. And she pleased Herod; and so he swore an oath to give her whatever she should ask for. Egged on by her mother, she says, 'Give me, here on a dish, the head of John the Baptist.' And although Herod was dismayed, because of his oath, and because of those who were dining with him, he ordered it to be given her, and he sent and decapitated John in prison. And his head was brought on a dish, and given to the little girl; and she brought it to her mother. And his disciples came and took the body, and buried it, and went and told Jesus.

In this story, Matthew brings together Herod and John the Baptist, two characters who fill out his portrait of Jesus by way of contrast or counterpoint. John the Baptist has already appeared at the time of Jesus' baptism (Chapter 3), where his subordinate status was established, as it was also in Chapter 11. He will be mentioned twice more in the Gospel, once (16:14) as a possible clue to the mystery of Jesus, and once as Elijah Returned (17:13). This Herod is not the same as the King Herod who tried to kill Jesus in Chapter 2; that was the tetrarch's father. But for Matthew's purpose they are virtually the same, at least as far as behaviour is concerned. Herod's behaviour is exactly the opposite of what Jesus does. We may also compare the 'little girl' here with the last 'little girl' we saw, the one whom Jesus cured back in Chapter 9. The chillingly murderous behaviour that this little girl and her mother display puts her in quite a different category.

The feeding of more than five thousand people

13-21   When Jesus heard this, he retreated from there in a boat, to a deserted place, privately. And when the crowds heard, they followed him on foot from the cities. And he went out and saw a great crowd, and he had compassion on them; and he cured their sick. When it grew late, his disciples approached him, saying, 'This is a deserted place, and the time is already past. Let the crowds go, so that they can go into the villages and buy food for themselves.' Jesus said to them, 'They have no need to go away: *you* give them something to eat.' They said to him, 'But we have nothing here but five loaves and two fish'. He said, 'Bring them to me here.' He ordered the crowds to lie down on the grass, took the five loaves and the two fish, looked up to heaven and blessed and broke and gave the bread to his disciples, and the disciples to the crowds. And they all ate and were satisfied, and they took up what was left over, twelve full baskets of fragments. Those who ate were about five thousand men, plus women and children.

This charming story fills in further details in the portrait of Jesus. This time we see him cope effortlessly with the needs of those around him. As in the previous story, we learn who Jesus is by way of a contrast. On this occasion the contrast is with 'the disciples', who, under the guise of practical attention to detail, reveal an ungenerous spirit that is quite foreign to Jesus. He throws the ball back at them, inviting them to feed the crowd. Hastily they pass it straight back to him; and the next thing is that they actually do feed the crowd! And it seems the most natural thing in the world that they collect up such an immense quantity of leftovers. Matthew portrays Jesus by understatement and pointing, rather than with banner headlines. Note the echo of the 'Beatitudes' in Chapter 5: 'satisfied' is what was promised to those who hunger and thirst for righteousness.

Jesus the ghost; Jesus as Son of Man

22-33 And immediately he compelled the disciples to go on board the boat and to go ahead of him to the other side, while he sent the crowds away. And when he had sent the crowds away, he went up privately to the mountain to pray. When it grew late he was there alone. The boat was now a good many furlongs away from the land, buffeted by the waves, because the wind was in the wrong direction. In the fourth watch of the night, he came to them, walking on the sea! When the disciples saw him walking on the sea, they were disturbed, saying, 'It's a ghost,' and they cried out in their fear. Immediately he spoke to them and said, 'Courage, it is I. Don't be afraid.' Peter answered him, 'Lord, if it's you, order me to come to you on the water.' He said, 'Come.' And getting out of the boat, Peter walked on the water and came to Jesus! But seeing the wind, he was afraid, and as he was beginning to go under, he cried out, saying, 'Lord, save me.' Immediately Jesus stretched out his hand and says to him, 'You man of little faith – why did you hesitate?' And when they got into the boat, the wind dropped. Those in the boat worshipped him, saying, 'Truly, you are the Son of God.'

Again Matthew reveals Jesus by indirection rather than by positive statements. Jesus gives the orders, copes with the crowds, daringly goes alone up into the mountains to pray. However, it seems that he keeps an eye on the struggling disciples (is there *anything* they can be trusted to get right?), and so he comes to them in their need. Everything he does in this story is calm and unruffled, and the oddest feats are performed without his turning a hair. Contrast that with the exploits of the disciples, who go from terror ('it's a ghost!') to worship ('truly you are the Son of God'), and with Peter, who goes from foolish bravery ('order me to come to you on the water') to abject helplessness ('Lord, save me' may be another fragment from the liturgy of Matthew's church). Once again we hear the phrase 'of little faith' contrasted with 'worship', which is for Matthew the correct response to Jesus.

A summary description of Jesus' healing work

34-36 And when they had crossed over, they came to the land of Gennesaret. And the men of that place recognised him and they sent to the whole of that neighbourhood, and they brought to him all those who were unwell; and they were begging him that they might just touch the hem of his cloak, and whoever touched [it] were safely brought through [their danger].

Again Matthew stresses the effortlessness of Jesus' healings, quite unlike the dizzy dancing of an ordinary medicine man. It happens almost without anyone noticing.

Jesus uncomfortably contrasted with scribes and Pharisees, disciples, and Peter

15 **1-20** Then from Jerusalem there came Pharisees and scribes to Jesus, saying, 'Why do your disciples transgress the traditions of the elders? They don't wash their hands when they eat.'

He answered them, 'And what about you? Why do you transgress God's command because of your traditions? For God said, "Honour [your] father and [your] mother," and "Anyone who speaks ill of father or mother, let them die the death." Whereas you people say, "Anyone who tells father or mother, 'Whatever you should have had from me is a gift [to God]' shall not [have to] honour his father." And you have abrogated God's word because of your own tradition. Fake-pietists! Isaiah was correct in prophesying about you, "This people honours me with their lips, but their heart is far from me. It is in vain that they honour me, teaching teachings [that are the] commandments of human beings." '

And he summoned the crowd and said to them, 'Hear and understand. It is not what goes into the mouth that defiles the person, but what comes out of the mouth – *that* is what defiles the person.'

Then the disciples approach and tell him, 'Do you know that the Pharisees were scandalised when they heard what you said?' He replied, 'Every plant which my Heavenly Father has not planted will be uprooted. Ignore them – they are blind guides, and if a blind man guides [another] blind man, they'll both fall into a pit!'

Peter replied and said to him, 'Explain this simile to us.' He said, 'Are you people still so unintelligent? Don't you realise that everything that enters the mouth goes down into the stomach and is evacuated into the latrine? Whereas what comes out of the mouth comes from the heart, and those are the things that defile a person. You see, it is from the heart that evil thoughts come, murder, adultery, fornication, theft, perjury and blasphemy. These are the things that defile a person; eating with unwashed hands isn't what defiles a person.'

Matthew's portrait of Jesus gets sharper. The Pharisees have a point – it is good to have the ritual washing before a meal, as it stands for a reminder of what we are about, but we must not lose sight of the central thing, namely the will of God. The disciples are uncomfortable with Jesus' wholesale dismissal of the Pharisees, but he does not retreat an inch, and makes his rather dark joke about 'blind guides'; and Peter's well-meant intervention gets very short shrift. Matthew is warning us not to expect a tame and domesticated Jesus, who leaves us with our comfortable assumptions all intact. See how adroitly Matthew's Jesus marshals his quotations, from Exodus 20:12; Leviticus 20:9; and Isaiah 29:13, to answer his enemies. They are shown up as not being sufficiently serious about God.

The persistent foreigner (a woman!) defeats the disciples

21-28   When Jesus went out from there, he retreated to the district of Tyre and Sidon. And look! A Canaanite woman from that region came out, yelling, 'Have mercy on me, Lord, Son of David. My daughter is badly possessed by demons.'

But he didn't answer her a word; and his disciples approached him and started asking him, 'Get rid of her – she's yelling after us.'

But he replied, 'I was only sent to the lost sheep of the house of Israel.'

She, however, came and worshipped him and said, 'Lord, help me.'

He replied, 'It's not proper to take the children's food and throw it to dogs.'

But she said, 'Yes, Lord – but even dogs eat from the crumbs that fall from their lords' table!'

Then Jesus answered her, 'Woman – your faith is great. Let it be done to you as you wish.'

And her daughter was healed from that hour!

> This is a lovely story, and the woman, the only person in the Synoptic Gospels to make Jesus change his mind, is clearly the hero of it. The disciples are at their ungracious worst, and the reader experiences some unease with Jesus' initial silence (though we might read that as his waiting to see what will happen) and with his very sharp remark about 'dogs' ('bitches', 'lapdogs' or 'puppies' would be different possible ways of taking it, each with a different tone). Whereas she gets everything right. She addresses Jesus as 'Lord and Son of David'; she has a huge cross to carry; no one wants to know her; she makes the very simple prayer, 'Lord help me'; and, finally, she turns Jesus' discouraging (even rude) remark with considerable wit. Jesus is enormously impressed with her, and in granting her request uses a phrase that the alert reader will recognise as coming from Matthew's version of the Lord's Prayer ('May your will be done').
> Once again, the healing itself is effortless and understated.

Jesus and the crowds

29-39   And Jesus went away from there and came beside the Sea of Galilee, and he went up the mountain and sat there. And large crowds came to him; they had many lame people with them, and blind and crippled and dumb, and many others. And they put them down at his feet and he healed them, with the result that the crowd was astonished at seeing the dumb speak, the crippled [made] healthy, the lame walking, and the blind seeing. And they glorified the God of Israel.

Jesus summoned his disciples and said, 'I'm feeling sorry for the crowd; it's three days already that they've been staying with me, and having nothing to eat. And I don't want to dismiss them without eating, or they might get weary on the journey.'

And the disciples say to him, 'Where in the desert can we get enough loaves to satisfy a crowd like this?'

And Jesus says to them, 'How many loaves have you got?'

They said, 'Seven – and a few little fish.'

And he instructed the crowd to lie on the ground, then took the seven loaves and the fish, and gave thanks and broke, and gave to the disciples, and the disciples [gave it] to the crowds. And they all ate and were satisfied; and what remained of the fragments they took up: seven full baskets!

Those who ate were four thousand men, plus women and children.

He dismissed the crowds, went on board the boat, and came to the district of Magadan.

> The portrait of Jesus deepens and sharpens. Not for the first time in this Gospel he comes to 'the mountain', this time to teach rather than to pray, it seems. Included in his teaching, however, is his care for them: those in need of healing are healed, and their hunger (and, it must be said, devotion) arouses his compassion. The disciples (like other characters whom we have seen already in the Gospel) act as a kind of counterpoint to this, with their severely practical objections. The crowds do rather better, for 'they glorified the God of Israel'. And Jesus himself? He is quite unimpressed with his own miraculous powers, and simply moves on to the next place, which is Magadan (but you won't find it on any map of the Holy Land).

Jesus contrasted with a) Pharisees and Sadducees and b) disciples

16 1-12 And the Pharisees and Sadducees approached and asked him a trick question; [they wanted him] 'to show them a sign from heaven'.

He answered, 'When it's evening, you say, "Good weather, because the sky is red," and in the morning, "Storm today, because the sky is a gloomy red." You know how to discern the appearance of the sky – but you can't discern the signs of the times! An evil and adulterous generation looks for a sign, and the only sign given it will be the sign of Jonah.' And he left them and went off.

The disciples came to the other side; and they had forgotten to bring loaves of bread. Jesus said, 'See that you beware of the leaven of the Pharisees and Sadducees.' And [the disciples] discussed among themselves, '[It's] because we didn't bring loaves of bread'. Jesus was well aware [of this], and said, 'Why, people of little faith, are you discussing among yourselves "because you haven't got loaves of bread"? Have you still not grasped it? Don't you remember the five loaves for the five thousand, and how many basketfuls you took? And the seven loaves for the four thousand, and how many baskets you took? How come you don't realise that I wasn't talking to you about loaves of bread? Beware of the leaven of the Pharisees and Sadducees.'

Then they got it: he wasn't telling them to beware of the leaven [for making] bread, but the teaching of the Pharisees and Sadducees.

> The religious authorities get it wrong here by asking for a sign, when clearly they should already have seen the 'signs of the times' in what Jesus has been doing. So Jesus' dismissive comment (and abrupt departure) is sufficient comment on them. And the disciples are not much better, haven't a clue what Jesus is on about, and can only imagine that they have committed a blunder by failing to organise the picnic. Jesus is always just beyond people's grasp.

Who is Jesus? What are his disciples to be like?

13-28 When Jesus came into the area of Caesarea Philippi, he asked his disciples, 'Who do people say the Son of Man is?'

They said, 'Some [say] John the Baptist, others Elijah, and others Jeremiah or one of the prophets.'

He says to them, 'What about *you*? Who do *you* say I am?'

Simon Peter answered, 'You are the Messiah, the Son of the Living God.'

Jesus answered, 'Congratulations to you, Simon bar Jonah, because [it was] not flesh and blood that revealed [this] to you; no – it was my Father in heaven. And I'm telling you: you are Rock, and on this Rock I shall build my Church and the gates of hell shall not triumph over it. I'll give you the keys of the kingdom of heaven, so that whatever you bind on earth shall be bound in heaven, and whatever you loose on earth shall be loosed in heaven.'

Then he instructed the disciples to tell no one that he was the Messiah.

From that moment on, Jesus started to show his disciples that he had to go to Jerusalem, and suffer many things at the hands of elders and chief priests and scribes, and be killed, and on the third day be raised. And Peter collared him, and started rebuking him, saying, 'God forbid, Lord. This will certainly not happen to you!'

And he turned and said to Peter, 'Get behind me, Satan. You're a scandal to me; [now] you're not thinking God-thoughts, but human thoughts.'

Then Jesus said to his disciples, 'If anyone wants to come after me, let them deny themselves and take up their cross and follow me. For anyone who wants to save their life will lose it; and anyone who loses their life for my sake will discover it. You see, how does it help a person if they gain the whole world, and suffer the loss of their life? Or what can a person give in return for his or her own life? For the Son of Man is going to come in the glory of his Father, with his angels; and then he will repay each person in accordance with what they have done. Amen I tell you, there are some of those standing here who will not taste death before they see the Son of Man coming in his kingdom.'

This time, it is Jesus who takes the initiative; he asks for popular estimates of his significance, and then sharpens the focus, so that the disciples (and the reader) cannot avoid making a decision. In the name of all of us Simon bar Jonah gets it spectacularly right, and gets the nickname 'Rock' or 'Peter'. Then, however, without changing gear, he gets it equally wrong. For when Jesus explains that he is a Messiah who will die, Simon will have none of it. In a terrible moment, Simon turns from being congratulated to being addressed, chillingly, as 'Satan'; his nickname of 'Rock' becomes instead a 'stone for stumbling over' (scandal); and the one who had been given a revelation from God, not flesh or blood, is now 'thinking human thoughts' instead of 'God-thoughts'.

We observe the mystery of the Church, that Jesus makes his promise to the fallible and fearful, sinful and corrupt. So if the Church prevails, that has nothing to do with its personnel, and everything to do with the fidelity of God. The Church can get it spectacularly wrong, as Simon does here, and disciples must learn in every generation to follow in Jesus' way, as Jesus proceeds to explain.

One element of Matthew's portrait of Jesus that appears here for the first time is that 'the Son of Man will come in the glory of his Father, with his angels', and (quoting Psalm 62:13, where it refers to God) 'repay each person in accordance with what they have done'. Here, language is being applied to Jesus that believers have hitherto used only of God.

Jesus is identified as Son of God

17 ¹⁻¹³ And after six days, Jesus takes Peter and James and John his brother, and leads them privately up a high mountain. And he was transformed in their presence; his face shone like the sun, and his clothes became white as light. And look! Moses appeared, and Elijah; and they were chatting with him.

Peter's response was to say to Jesus, 'Lord, it's good for us to be here. If you want, I'll make three tents here: one for you, one for Moses, and one for Elijah.'

While he was still speaking, look! A bright cloud overshadowed them; and look! A voice from the cloud, saying, 'This is my Son, the Beloved, in whom I am well pleased. Listen to him.' And when the disciples heard, they fell on their faces and were very afraid. And Jesus approached and touched them and said, 'Up you get – and don't be afraid.' They lifted up their eyes; and they saw nobody, except only for Jesus himself. And as they were going down the mountain, Jesus gave them instructions, 'Don't tell anyone what you have seen until the Son of Man is risen from the dead.'

And the disciples asked him, 'So why do the scribes say that Elijah must come first?'

He answered, 'Indeed, Elijah is coming, and will restore everything. But I'm telling you: Elijah has already come, and they didn't recognise him. No – they did what they wanted with him. So also the Son of Man is about to suffer at their hands.'

Then the disciples realised that he'd been speaking to them about John the Baptist.

Not for the first time, Matthew here takes some trouble to set the scene. He has Jesus take his 'inner cabinet', Peter and the two sons of Zebedee; then they go up a mountain (which we have already seen to be a significant location for Matthew), and it is 'private'. So we are not in the realm here of instructions to the 'crowds', nor even to 'the disciples'. This is going to be special, we surmise. This indeed turns out to be the case: first Jesus is remarkably transformed (presumably giving us a glimpse of the truth about him). Second, he is presented as at least the equal of Moses (the Torah) and Elijah (the Prophets). Third, the cloud and the voice assert Jesus' Sonship in unmistakable terms, and on the best possible authority. Finally, we learn that all this will only make sense in the light of the Resurrection.

Notice also that the reaction of the disciples is fairly inept: Peter wants to build a camping site, and all of them are seen scratching their heads about Elijah and John the Baptist.

A healing that the disciples couldn't perform

14-20 And when they came to the crowd, a man approached, knelt before him, and said, 'Lord, have mercy on my son, because he has epilepsy, and suffers dreadfully; he often falls into the fire, and often into the water. And I brought him to your disciples, and they were unable to cure him.'

Jesus replied, 'Unbelieving and perverse generation – how long shall I be with you? How long shall I put up with you? Bring him to me.' And Jesus rebuked him, and the demon left him, and the boy was cured from that hour.

Then the disciples came privately to Jesus and said, 'What was the reason that we couldn't throw it out?' He said to them, 'Because of your lack-of-faith. For Amen I tell you, if you have faith like a grain of mustard, you'll say to this mountain, "Move from here to there" – and it will move. And nothing will be impossible to you.'

Once again, Jesus is set in contrast with two sets of people, the harassed father of the child, and the disciples. The father gets a good deal right: he makes an appropriate gesture; he says 'Kyrie, eleison'; he shows absolute confidence in Jesus. He is apparently rebuked (or is it the disciples?) for being part of an 'unbelieving and perverse generation', but he gets what he was after. The disciples, though, as so often in Matthew, are getting 'private' instruction (see Chapter 10, and 13:10-23, 36-53; 17:1; 20:17; 24:3), and get a great deal wrong. First, they are unable to cure the boy; then they cannot understand their failure, which Jesus attributes to their *oligopistia*, or 'having-little-faith'. Against those two backgrounds, Jesus stands out as the one who knows exactly what is going on, and who heals without breaking sweat.

Second prediction of Jesus' passion – and of his Resurrection

22, 23 As they were crowding round in Galilee, Jesus said to them, 'The Son of Man is going to be handed over into the hands of people, and they'll kill him. And on the third day he will be raised.' And they were greatly saddened.

This second passion prediction is muted in comparison with what Matthew had found in Mark (see Mark 9:30-32). Mark had placed at this point the disciples' question, 'Who is important in the kingdom of heaven?', which he clearly saw as a failure on their part. By moving that question into Chapter 18, Matthew has changed their reaction to one of sadness, which gives a rather different 'feel'.

The two-drachma piece (the Temple tax)

24-27 As they came into Caphernaum, the people who collect the two-drachma [tax] approached Peter and said, 'Doesn't your teacher pay the two-drachma [tax]?' He said, 'Yes'; and when he went into the house, before [he could say a word] Jesus was there first: 'What do you think, Simon? From whom do the world's monarchs exact tax or duty? From their sons or from others?' When he said, 'From others',

Jesus said to him, 'So the sons are free; but so that we don't scandalise them, go to the sea, cast a fish-hook, take up the first fish to rise, open its mouth, and you'll find a four-drachma coin. Take that and give it to them for me and you.'

This strange little tale is found only in Matthew. Once again it depicts Jesus by way of contrast to two sets of people. The first set is the collectors of the half-shekel tax which every adult male Jew paid for the upkeep of the Temple building. They are prepared to criticise Jesus for his lack of ethnic and religious solidarity. The second is Peter, who gives what turns out to be the wrong answer to their question, and then runs into the house without doing anything about it. Jesus, by contrast, we learn, a) knows the subject of conversations at which he has not been present, b) is not liable to the tax because he is Son of God and c) with effortless ease removes any embarrassment on Peter's part.

The Fourth 'Discourse': About the Church

18 ¹⁻³⁵ At that hour, the disciples approached Jesus saying, 'So who's the Most Important in the kingdom of heaven?' And he summoned a little child and put it in the middle of them, and said, 'Amen I tell you: unless you turn and become like children, you won't enter the kingdom of heaven. So whoever puts themselves as low as this little child, that's the one who is Most Important in the kingdom of heaven. And whoever receives one little child like this in my name, receives me. But anyone who trips up one of these little ones who believe in me, it's better for that person to have a donkey's millstone hung around his neck, and be drowned in the open sea.

'Woe to the world because of scandals! You see, it's inevitable that scandals come; but woe to the person through whom a scandal comes! If your hand or your foot cause you to stumble, cut it off, and throw it away from you. It is better for you to enter life deformed, or lame, than to be thrown into eternal fire with two hands or two feet! And if your eye trips you up, rip it out and throw it away from you. It is better for you to enter life with only one eye than to be thrown into the fiery Gehenna with two eyes!

'See to it that you don't despise one of these little ones. For I'm telling you that their angels in heaven are all the time looking upon the face of my Father in heaven.

'What do you think? If a person has a hundred sheep, and one of them goes wandering, won't the person abandon the [other] ninety-nine and go and look for the wanderer? And if it should happen that he finds it, Amen I tell you, he rejoices more over it than over the ninety-nine who never wandered at all. So it is not the will of [literally: 'before'] your Father in heaven that one of these little ones should be lost.

'If your brother or sister sins, go and correct them, just you and him or her alone. If they listen to you, you've gained your brother or sister; but if they don't listen, take one or two others with you, so that "on the oral evidence of two or three witnesses shall any charge be sustained". If the person refuses to listen to them, tell the Church; and if the person refuses to listen to the Church, let them be to you like a Gentile or a tax collector.

'Amen I tell you, whatever you bind on earth will be bound in heaven; and whatever you loose on earth will be loosed in heaven.

'Again I tell you, if two of you on earth agree about anything that they are going to ask for, it will be done for them by my Father in heaven. For where two or three are gathered in my name, I am there in the middle of them.'

Then Peter approached and said to him, 'Lord, how many times is my brother or sister to sin against me, and I forgive them? As many as seven times?'

Jesus says to him, 'I'm not saying "as many as seven times" to you, but as many as seventy times seven! So the kingdom of heaven is like a person, a king, who wanted to settle an account with his servants. As he started the process, one was brought to him, in debt for tens of thousands of talents; and because he had no way of repaying, the lord ordered him and his wife and his children and all his possessions to be sold, and the money repaid. So the servant fell down and worshipped him, saying, "Be patient with me, and I'll repay you the lot." The lord had compassion on that servant; he set him free and let him off the debt.

'That servant went out and found one of his fellow servants who owed him a hundred denarii, and he grabbed hold of him and tried to throttle him, saying "Repay anything you owe [me]." So his fellow servant fell down and begged him, "Be patient with me, and I'll repay you." But he wouldn't [hear of it]; instead, he went and threw him in prison until he should repay what he owed. So when his fellow servants saw what had happened, they were very sad, and went and revealed everything that had happened to their lord. Then his lord summoned him and said to him, "Wicked servant: I let you off all that debt, since you begged me. Should you not also have had mercy on your fellow servant, as I had mercy on you?" And in a rage, his lord handed him over to the torturers until he should pay everything that was owing. That's how my Heavenly Father will deal with you, unless each of you forgives your brother or sister from your hearts.'

This is a slightly different discourse; it has the telltale conclusion (19:1), and it comes in two halves, about little ones and about forgiveness, each starting with a disciple's question, and each ending with a parable.

The 'little ones' are clearly children here; the disciples want to know who is 'Mr Big' in Jesus' new dispensation, and have to be taught that the least important (no one counts lower than a child) is the most important, and that following Jesus means loss of status. That is something that Christians have never quite managed to work out, of course.

So the little ones have to be looked after, and not made to 'stumble' or 'trip' (the idea underlying these words is 'scandal', a stone on which you trip up or stub your toe). But there is a bit more to it than that: the eye or hand or foot that is to be thrown away looks as though it may be a member of the Church (or 'body'). The least important (and least competent, as the sheep image indicates) members of the Church are those whom the pastor really looks after. Then come instructions for dealing with a crisis in the Church: a three-step procedure, at the end of which (but only then) is the offending member to be rejected as a sinner or tax collector (rather odd, this, in the face of Jesus' known predilections). Then reassurance about prayer, resting on the central plank that 'I am in the midst of them', taking us back to Jesus as Emmanuel ('God with us') in Chapter 1, and looking ahead to the final word of the Gospel, 'I am with you until the end of time'. This presence of Jesus is the key idea that makes the Gospel possible.

Notice the characteristic citation of Deuteronomy (19:15 'on the evidence of two or three witnesses').

The mention of forgiveness prompts Peter's question and leads into the second parable, a dramatisation of the fifth beatitude, 'congratulations to the merciful, for they shall be mercied'. It is well told, with a touch of humour in the contrast between the sums owed: 'tens of thousands of talents' is simply gazillions of pounds sterling, and a 'hundred denarii' is a few weeks' wages. The comedy (and the lesson) is in the absurd behaviour of the servant who has been let off, who doesn't notice that the language his fellow servant uses is practically identical to what he had said to their master.

Jesus asked about divorce; disciples put right about children

19 ^1-15 And it happened when Jesus finished these words, he removed from Galilee and came to the Judaea region, across the Jordan, and great crowds followed him, and he healed them there.

And some Pharisees approached him with a trap for him: 'Is it permissible for a man to divorce his wife for any cause?' He answered, 'Didn't you read that the One Who Created In the Beginning, "made them male and female" and he said, "For this reason a man or woman will leave their parents and be joined together, and the two shall become one flesh?" So they are no longer two, but one flesh. So let no human being separate what God has gathered together.'

They say to him, 'So why did Moses instruct [us] to give a certificate of divorce and send her away?'

He says to them, 'Because of your hardness of heart, Moses permitted you to get rid of your wives; but it was not so at the beginning. I'm telling you: anyone who divorces his wife (other than for fornication) and marries another commits adultery.'

His disciples said to him, 'If that's the situation in the relationship of a man and a woman, there's no point in marrying!'

He said to them, 'It's not everyone who accepts this saying, only those to whom it is given. For there are eunuchs who are born like that from their mother's womb; and there are eunuchs who have been made into eunuchs by [other] people; and there are eunuchs who have made themselves so because of the kingdom of heaven. Let the one who can, accept it.'

Then children were brought to him for him to lay hands on them and pray [for them]. The disciples scolded them, but Jesus said, 'Leave the children alone, and don't prevent them from coming to me; because the kingdom of heaven is made up of people like these.' And he laid his hands on them and went away from there.

Once again, Jesus is contrasted with his opponents and with his disciples. The opponents raise with him a question that was current in contemporary Judaism, about the possibility of divorce; but their real aim is to trap him into denying the Mosaic Law. Jesus effortlessly avoids the snare by quoting the Torah (Genesis 1:27; 2:24) back at them. The disciples (not for the first time) scratch their heads in puzzlement and are given a response that may not have entirely cheered them up. And, not for the first time, they are muddled about the status of the 'little ones' in Jesus' community.

The exception allowed in respect of divorce ('other than for fornication') might mean a) if the woman has committed adultery, or b) if the marriage is within the prohibited degrees of kinship or c) (just possibly) idolatry, for which 'fornication' is a frequent Old Testament image.

The rich young man, and Jesus' teaching about wealth

16-30 And look! Someone approached him and said, 'Teacher, what good thing should I do so that I might possess eternal life?'

But he said, 'Why do you ask me about what is good? There is One who is good. But if you want to enter into life, keep the commandments.'

He says to him, 'Which ones?'

Jesus said, ' "You will not kill", "You will not commit adultery", "You will not steal", "You will not bear false witness", "Honour your father and mother", and "Love your neighbour as yourself".'

The young man says to him, 'I have kept all these things since I was young. What do I still lack?' Jesus said to him, 'If you want to be perfect, go and sell your possessions, and give to the poor, and you'll have treasure in heaven. Then come, follow me.'

When the young man heard the message, he went away saddened. Because he had many possessions.

And Jesus told his disciples, 'Amen I tell you, it's difficult for an affluent person to get into the kingdom of heaven. Again I tell you, it is easier for a camel to pass through the eye of a needle than for an affluent person to enter the kingdom of God.'

When the disciples heard [this] they were profoundly shocked, and said, 'So who can possibly be saved?'

Jesus looked at them and said, 'For human beings this is impossible, but for God – everything is possible.'

Then Peter responded, 'Look! We've abandoned everything and followed you. So what will there be for us?'

Jesus said to him, 'Amen I tell you, you people who have followed me in the New Age, when the Son of Man sits on his glorious throne, you also will be seated on twelve thrones judging the twelve tribes of Israel. And everyone who has abandoned homes or brothers or sisters or father or mother or children or estates for the sake of my name, will receive a hundred times the amount *and* will inherit eternal life. But many will be first who are last; and vice versa.'

Again a set of contrasts allows the reader to grasp the starkness of Jesus' teaching. He is set against, first, this rather bumptious young man, for whom keeping the commandments is old hat, then the disciples, who can't see the sense in Jesus' teaching about wealth, and finally Peter, who wants to know the cash values of the sacrifices that he and the others have made. Discipleship is not easy.

The image of the vineyard

20 ¹⁻¹⁶ 'For the kingdom of heaven is like a householder who went out at the crack of dawn to hire workers [and bring them] into his vineyard. He agreed with the workers on [a wage of] one denarius for the day, and sent them into his vineyard. And he went out at about 9.00 a.m. and saw other people standing in the market place with nothing to do, and said to them, "You go into my vineyard also, and I'll give whatever is the going rate (literally: 'what is just/righteous'). So they went. Then again at noon and at three in the afternoon he did the same. And at about five o'clock in the evening he went out and found others standing there, and said, "Why have you been standing [there] all day with nothing to do?" They said, "Because no one has hired us." He says to them, "You go into my vineyard also."

'When evening came, the lord of the vineyard said to his foreman, "Summon the workers and pay them their wages. Start with the last arrivals, and end up with those who came first." And those who had come at five o'clock got a denarius each! And so those [who had come] first thought they'd be getting more – but they also got a denarius each. When they got it, they made a complaint against the proprietor, "These last-comers only did an hour, and you've made them just the same as us, who carried the weight of the day and its burning sun." He answered, "My friend, I'm not doing you down; didn't you and I agree on one denarius? Take what is yours and go. I am making the choice to pay this last-comer just what I'm paying you. Don't I have the right to do what I choose with what is my own? Or are you jealous because I am being generous?" So the last will be first, and the first last.'

> This image apparently continues Jesus' response to Peter's anxiety about 'what's in it for us?' It is the wrong question: God is utterly generous (generosity is the quality that defines God), and we do not lose out because God has been equally generous to those undeserving people next door. It is all rather shocking. We may notice that the address 'my friend' is used in only two other places in Matthew's Gospel: to the wedding guest who had no wedding garment (22:12) and to Judas when he turns up with the arresting party in Gethsemani (26:50).

Third prediction of Jesus' passion – and of his Resurrection

¹⁷⁻¹⁹ And while he was going up to Jerusalem, Jesus took the Twelve aside, privately, and on the way he said to them, 'Look! We are going up to Jerusalem, and the Son of Man will be handed over to the chief priests and scribes, and they'll condemn him to death, and they'll hand him over to Gentiles to mock and flog him and crucify – and on the third day he will be raised up.'

> For the third time Jesus explicitly tells his disciples what is going to happen at the end of the journey. We call them 'Passion Predictions', but we should notice that in each case he also predicts his own Resurrection. Matthew is different from both Luke and Mark (see Mark 10:32-34; Luke 18:31-33). Luke fits the prediction into his scheme of 'the great journey', while Mark has each of these predictions immediately precede a fairly catastrophic blunder by

one or more of the disciples. However, in the episode that follows, Matthew has apparently exempted James and John, sons of Zebedee, from all blame, and placed the blame instead on their mother's shoulders.

The request of an ambitious mother

20-28   Then the mother of the sons of Zebedee approached with her sons; she worshipped him, and was asking something of him. He said to her, 'What do you want?' She says to him, 'Say that these two sons of mine may sit, one on your right and one on your left in your kingdom.'

Jesus answered, 'You people do not know what you are asking for. Can you drink the cup that I'm about to drink?'

They tell him, 'We can.'

He says to them, 'You will indeed drink my cup, but the [business of] sitting on my right and my left is not mine to give – it's for those for whom it is prepared by my Father.'

And when they heard it, the [other] ten were furious with the two brothers. Jesus summoned them and said, 'You know that the rulers of the Gentiles lord it over them, and their Big Ones tyrannise over them. It will not be like that among you. No – anyone who wants to be Big among you will be your Servant. And anyone who wants to be Number One among you will be your Slave. Just so the Son of Man did not come to be served, but to serve, and to give his life as a ransom for many.'

> Once again, Matthew paints Jesus' portrait by contrasting him with two other sets of people: there is (the mother of) the sons of Zebedee, and 'the other ones'. Both groups are looking out for the best jobs in Jesus' new community (Matthew does not long sustain the pretence that it was really Mrs Zebedee who was getting ambitious), not realising that this is a community unlike any other, because Jesus is so totally different. Jesus comes as a servant and as one condemned to death; and that is the road for the disciples to follow. Next we shall see a pair of disciples who get Jesus right.

Two blind men near Jericho

29-34   And as they moved away from Jericho, a great crowd followed him. And look! Two blind men, sitting by the road; and hearing that Jesus was passing by, they yelled out, 'Have mercy on us, Son of David!' The crowd told them off – they should shut up. But they yelled all the more, 'Have mercy on us, Lord, Son of David!' And Jesus stopped and summoned them, and said, 'What do you want me to do for you?' They tell him, 'Lord, we want our eyes opened.' Jesus had compassion on them, and touched their eyes. And immediately they saw again. And they followed him.

> This episode brings to an end the journey from Galilee to Jerusalem on which we have been following Jesus – although it is less marked in Matthew than in Luke (18:35-43), or, in his very different way,

Mark (10:46-52). Matthew has characteristically (as with the Gadarenes in Chapter 8) made Mark's single blind man into a pair; and he also allows us to hear again a phrase from the liturgy of his church (the blind men actually say 'Eleison . . . Kyrie'). But the great thing about these two is that they saw a great deal better than the Twelve. For without any jockeying for position, and very simply, 'they followed him'.

Jesus' entry into Jerusalem

21 ¹⁻²² And when they drew near to Jerusalem and come to Bethphage, to the Mountain of Olives, then Jesus sent two disciples, telling them 'Go to the village opposite you, and immediately you'll find a donkey tied up, and a foal with her. Untie her and bring her to me; and if anyone says anything, you'll tell [them], "The Lord has need of them"; and he'll send them immediately.'

This took place in order that the word spoken through the prophet might be fulfilled,

'Say to the daughter of Zion, Look! Your king is coming to you,
meek, and riding on a donkey, and on a foal, the offspring of a donkey.'

The disciples went and did as Jesus had directed them; they brought the she-donkey and the foal, and they put cloaks on them, and he sat on them. And the immense crowd laid their cloaks on the road, and others started cutting branches from the trees and laying them in the road. And the crowds that went before him, and those who followed were crying out, 'Hosanna to the Son of David, blessed is the one who comes in the Lord's name. Hosanna in the highest.'

And as he went into Jerusalem, the whole city was shaken, saying, 'Who is this?' And the crowds were saying, 'This is the prophet Jesus, the one from Nazareth in Galilee.'

And Jesus went into the Temple; and he expelled all those who performed commercial transactions in the Temple, and he overturned the tables of the moneychangers, and the chairs of those who were selling doves.

And he said to them, 'It is written, "My house shall be called a house of prayer", but you are making it "a cave for bandits".'

And blind and lame people came to him in the Temple; and he cured them. The chief priests and the scribes saw the miracles he performed, and the children shouting in the Temple, 'Hosanna to the Son of David' – and they were annoyed, and said to him, 'Do you hear what these people are saying?'

Jesus said to them, 'Yes. Have you never read that "out of the mouths of infants and those at the breast you have prepared praise for yourself"?' And he left them and went out of the city to Bethany, and camped there.

In the morning, as he returned to the city, he was hungry. And he saw a single fig tree on the way; he came to it, and found on it nothing but leaves, and he says to it, 'May fruit never ever come from you again.' And the fig tree withered straightaway! The disciples saw it and were astounded: 'How did the fig tree wither straightaway?' Jesus answered them, 'Amen I tell you, if you have faith and do not doubt, you will not only do the fig-tree thing; you'll also tell this mountain, "Be removed and thrown into the sea," and it will happen. Everything that you ask in prayer you will receive, if you have faith.'

As Jesus returns to Jerusalem, where the Magi had turned up with their naïve question, all those chapters ago, we see two familiar features of Matthew's presentation of history. The first is the emphasis on Jesus' fulfilling the Old Testament: there are several quotations here, and perhaps the most interesting is that from Zechariah 9:9 about 'a donkey and the foal of a donkey'. In the original it was intended to indicate how unthreatening the Messiah would be, and what looks like two animals is actually only one. Matthew, however, is so determined to show how Jesus fulfils Scripture that he has him perched rather uncertainly on two beasts. Matthew also has Jesus quote Isaiah 56:7 ('house of prayer') and Jeremiah 7:11 ('cave for bandits') as well as Psalm 8:2 ('out of the mouths . . . ')

Second, Jesus is once again contrasted with various groups. Disciples have to be told what to do, and they ask dim-witted questions, while the religious establishment are indignant, and the crowds get it right, shouting 'Hosanna' and other quotations from Psalm 118. And we notice that whereas Jerusalem is 'shaken' (as it was in 2:3, though the Greek verb was different there) and asks, 'Who is this?', the crowds respond (quite correctly, as far as they go), 'This is the prophet.' Contrast all this with the calm certainty with which Jesus now proceeds.

Controversies with the religious establishment, and three stories against them

21 ²³**-22** ¹⁴ And when he went into the Temple, the chief priests and elders of the people approached him as he taught, saying, 'By what authority are you doing these things? And who gave you this authority?' Jesus answered, 'Now *I* shall ask *you* a single question. And if you tell me [the answer] then in my turn *I* shall tell *you* the authority by which I am doing these things: John's baptism, where was it from? From heaven, or from human beings?' And they discussed among themselves, 'If we say "From heaven", he'll say to us, "So why didn't you believe him?" But if we say "From human beings", we're frightened of the crowd, because they all regard John as a prophet.' And their answer to Jesus was, 'We don't know.' In his turn he said to them, 'Nor am I telling you by what authority I am doing these things.'

'What do you think? A man had two children, and he approached Number One, and said, "My child, go and work in my vineyard today." But he said, "I don't want to", but later on he changed his mind [literally, 'repented'] and went. He went up to Number Two, and said the same: he said, "Aye-aye, sir" – and didn't go. Which of the two did the father's will?'

They said, 'Number One.' Jesus said to them, 'Amen I tell you, the tax collectors and prostitutes are going ahead of you into the kingdom of God. For John came to you on the road of righteousness, and you didn't believe him, but the tax collectors and prostitutes *did* believe him; but you saw him, and didn't change your minds later, so as to believe him.

'Listen to another image. There was a person, a householder, who had planted a vineyard, and put a hedge round it, and dug a winepress in it, and built a tower and leased it out to tenant-farmers, and went overseas. When the vintage-time came, he sent his slaves to the farmers, to get his fruit. And they took his slaves, and gave one of them a hiding, killed another, and stoned another. Again he sent more slaves, in greater numbers – and they did the same to them. Finally, he sent his son to them, saying, "They'll respect my son." But when the tenant-farmers saw the son, they said to themselves, "This is the one who is going to inherit! Come on, let's kill him and get his inheritance!" and they took him and threw him out of the vineyard, and killed him.

'So – when the Lord of the Vineyard comes, what will he do to those tenant-farmers?' They said to him, 'They are bad people, and he'll bring them to a bad end, and he'll lease out the vineyard to other tenants, who will return the revenues to him at the proper time.'

Jesus says to them, 'Did you never read in the scriptures:

"The stone which the builders rejected, has become the cornerstone. This came from the Lord, and is wonderful in our eyes."

'Therefore I'm telling you that the kingdom of God will be taken away from you, and given to a nation that produces its fruit.' And when the chief priests and the Pharisees heard his stories, they knew that he was speaking about them. And they were looking for a way to get him; but they were afraid of the crowd, since they regarded him as a prophet.

And Jesus answered, and spoke to them again in images: 'The kingdom of heaven is like a person, a king, who held a wedding party for his son; and he sent his slaves to summon those who'd been invited to the wedding party. And they didn't want to come! Again he sent other slaves and said, "Tell those who've been invited, 'Look! I've prepared my meal, my oxen and fatlings have been slaughtered, and everything's ready. Come to the wedding.'" But they didn't care: one went off to his farm, and another to his business. And the rest took hold of his slaves and maltreated them and killed them.

'The king was enraged, and sent his armies, and destroyed those murderers and set fire to their city.

'Then he said to his slaves, "The wedding party is ready, and those who were invited were not worthy. So go out into the exits from the city, and invite anyone you find to the wedding party." And those slaves went out into the roads, and they gathered everyone that they could find, both evil and good. And the wedding feast was full of people lying down to dine.

'But the king came in to look at the diners, and he saw there a man who was not wearing wedding clothes, and he says to him, "My friend, how did you get in here without wedding clothes?" And he was silent. Then the king said to the servants, "Tie up his feet and his hands, and throw him into the outer darkness. There shall be weeping there, and gnashing of teeth. For many are invited, but not many are selected."'

It was the religious leaders who started this, with their demand to know Jesus' authority for behaving in this way; and they were correct in doing so, for Jesus was implicitly claiming rights over the Temple. But Jesus makes no concessions, and claims to be engaged on the same task as John the Baptist. Then he tells them three parables or images, one after the other, which make the division absolutely explicit. The first indicates that his opponents commit the worst possible sin, that of refusing to do the Father's will. The second image, that of the vineyard, is in the view of many scholars the one that sealed Jesus' fate. He is unmistakably referring to Isaiah 5, where the prophet sees Israel as God's unsatisfactory vineyard, and Jesus clearly presents himself as the son who is sent last of all, then forces his hearers to think of an appropriate punishment.

The third parable perhaps does not take itself all that seriously: the final invitation is done in a slightly casual way; the punishment of the reluctant invitees (sending armies to kill them and burn their city), and then the summoning of a new and altogether less impressive guest list, asks us to suppose a long gap during which the chef's best efforts will have been getting cold. And then the king seems rather distant from the son's wedding: he only goes in to have a look, and all he does is seize on some unfortunate who is wearing the wrong clothes. Many readers find themselves thinking: 'I am not at all sure that this is the kind of God with which I wish to deal', and may perhaps like to read the story another way, starting from its ending. Try seeing the one who gets thrown out because of not wearing a wedding garment as Christ, who was thrown out to die outside the city; who pursued a very lonely furrow; and who invites us to follow the same trail. It does not, it must be confessed, solve all the problems of the story, but may serve to remind us that the story is meant to shock and surprise us into glimpsing the reality of the 'kingdom of heaven'.

The quotation about the 'stone which the builders rejected' is from Psalm 118, which is also the source of the 'Hosanna' ('save us, please') that they had shouted on Palm Sunday.

As the following stories indicate, it was not Jesus who started the trouble.

Controversies with Pharisees and Sadducees

15-46 Then the Pharisees went and made a plan to set a verbal trap for him. And they send their disciples to him, along with the Herodians, saying 'Teacher, we know that you are true, and that you truly teach God's way, and that you don't care about anybody, regardless of their status. So tell us: what do you think – is it permissible to give poll tax to Caesar or not?'

But Jesus was well aware of their malice, and said, 'Why are you trying me out, you frauds ['hypocrites']? Show me the coin of the poll tax.' They brought him a denarius, and he says to them, 'Whose picture is this? And the inscription?' They tell him, 'Caesar's.' Then he tells them, 'So pay Caesar what is Caesar's – and pay God what is God's!'

When they heard this, they were astonished, and they left him and went off.

That day some Sadducees came to him (they say there is no Resurrection) and they asked him, 'Teacher, Moses said, "If someone dies childless, his brother shall marry his widow as next-of-kin and shall raise up offspring for his brother." Now, there were seven brothers in our community. Number One married and then died, and having no offspring, he left her to his brother; and the same with Number Two and Number Three, right through all seven of them. Last of all the woman died. So in the "Resurrection", which of the seven will she be the wife of? You see, they were all married to her.'

Jesus answered them, 'You don't know the scriptures; nor do you know God's power – that's why you go astray. You see, in the Resurrection, they don't marry or get given in marriage; they're like angels in heaven. As for the Resurrection of the dead, didn't you read what God said to you, when he said "I am the God of Abraham and the God of Isaac and the God of Jacob." God is not the God of the dead, but of the living.'

And when the crowds heard, they were astounded by his teaching.

The Pharisees heard that he had silenced the Sadducees; and they got together, and one of them asked a question (trying him out): 'Teacher, what's the most important commandment in the Torah?' He told them, ' "You shall love the Lord your God with all your heart and all your soul, and all your mind." This is the most important commandment, and the Number One. Number Two is like it: "You will love your neighbour as yourself." The whole Torah (and the Prophets) depends on these two commandments.'

When the Pharisees got together, Jesus asked them, 'What is your view about the Messiah? Whose son is he?' They tell him, 'David's.' He says to them, 'So how is it that when David is inspired, he calls him "Lord", [saying]

"The Lord said to my Lord, 'Sit on my right
until I place your enemies beneath your feet' "?

'So – if David calls him "Lord", how come he's his son?'

And no one could answer him a word; nor did anyone have the nerve to ask him any more questions from that day on.

Here we have four skirmishes, all part of the bigger battle that is now a cloud on the horizon. The first is a potentially lethal trap laid by the Pharisees, with the connivance of the 'Herodians', unlikely bedfellows of the Pharisees, since they would be expected to support the Roman domination. Perhaps the point is simply their desire to make sure that Jesus is properly caught. We are to applaud his adroit response: 'give to God what belongs to God' – and what belongs to God, of course, is nothing less than absolutely everything.

The second skirmish is a slightly sillier, certainly less dangerous, trick question, trying to disprove the possibility of Resurrection, by demonstrating an absurd implication of it. They quote the Torah (Deuteronomy 25:5), and Jesus quotes the Torah (Exodus 3:6) back at them, and they have nothing more to say.

Next on the attack are the Pharisees again (for Matthew they are Jesus' most passionate opponents), this time asking his view on which of the 613 precepts of the Torah is the most important. This was a common enough question among Jewish thinkers of the time; Mark's account of the incident (Mark 12:28-34) has Jesus and a scribe in rather unusual agreement, but Matthew has none of that. Matthew has Jesus quote Deuteronomy 6:5 and Leviticus 19:18 to shut them up.

Finally Jesus goes on to the attack, asking about the ancestry of the Messiah, and quoting Psalm 110:1 to make the point that the

Messiah is more important than David. That marks the end of the attempts to trap Jesus out of his own mouth, but not the end of the campaign against his life. It is perhaps in that context that we have to understand the assault on the Pharisees that follows.

Against the Pharisees; how Christian leaders should behave

23 1-39 Then Jesus spoke to the crowds and to his disciples, saying, 'It is [indeed] on the chair of Moses that the scribes and Pharisees are seated. So whatever they tell you, do it, and hold to it; but don't be doing what they do. For they talk, but they don't perform. They bind up heavy burdens, and place them on people's shoulders; but they don't want to shift them themselves by [so much as] a finger. All that they do, they perform, in order to be seen by people. They broaden their phylacteries and lengthen their tassels, and they like [to have] the place of honour at dinner parties, and the best pews in the synagogues, and being greeted in the public squares, and being called "Rabbi" by people.

'But you people are not to be called "Rabbi", for you have just one Teacher, and you are all brothers and sisters. Don't call anyone your "Father" on earth, for you have just one Father, the Heavenly one. And you are not to be called "Guides", because you have just one Guide, the Messiah. The greatest of you will be your servant; but those who exalt themselves will be humbled, and those who humble themselves will be exalted.

'Woe to you, scribes and Pharisees, you frauds [hypocrites], because you shut the kingdom of heaven in people's faces; you don't go in, and you don't allow those who [wish to] enter to go in.

'Woe to you, scribes and Pharisees, you frauds [hypocrites], because you travel sea and land to make a single convert; and when it happens, you make him a child of Gehenna, twice as bad as yourselves.

'Woe to you, you blind guides, you say, "If anyone swears by the Temple, that's non-binding; but if anyone swears by the Temple's gold, then they are bound." Blind morons! Which is more important, the gold, or the Temple which makes the gold holy? And [you say] "If anyone swears by the altar, that's non-binding; but if anyone swears by the gift that is on the altar, then they are bound." [You're so] blind! Which is more important, the gift, or the altar which makes the gift holy? So anyone who swears by the altar swears by it, and by all that is on it. And anyone who swears by the Temple swears by it and by the One who dwells in it. And the one who swears by heaven swears by God's throne, and by the One who sits on the throne.

'Woe to you, scribes and Pharisees, you frauds [hypocrites], because you tithe mint, dill and cumin, and you have neglected legal matters of greater moment, justice and compassion and faithfulness. You should have performed these, without neglecting [your tithing]. Blind guides! You strain out a gnat and gulp down a camel!

'Woe to you, scribes and Pharisees, you frauds [hypocrites], because you purify the outside of the cup and the dish, but inside they are full of robbery and self-indulgence. Blind Pharisee! [You should] first purify the inside of the cup, so that its outside may be clean.

'Woe to you, scribes and Pharisees, you frauds [hypocrites], because you're like whitewashed tombs, which look lovely on the outside, but inside are full of the bones of the dead and every [kind of] impurity. That's how you people are: on the outside you look righteous to people, but inside you're full of hypocrisy and lawlessness.

'Woe to you, scribes and Pharisees, you frauds [hypocrites], because you build the prophets' tombs and decorate the memorials of the righteous, and you proclaim, "If we had [lived] in our ancestors' times, we'd never have shared in the prophets' blood." So you are evidence against yourselves that you are descended from those who murdered the prophets; and you people fill up the measure of your ancestors. Serpents! Offspring of snakes! How are you to escape the condemnation to Gehenna?

'For that reason, look! I am sending you prophets and wise men [and women] and scribes. You'll kill some of them and crucify them; and some of them you will flog in your synagogues, and you'll persecute them from city to city; so that all the righteous blood may come upon you that pours out on the earth, from the blood of Abel the righteous to the blood of Zachariah son of Barachiah, whom you slew between the Temple and the altar. Amen I tell you, all these things will come on this generation.

'Jerusalem, Jerusalem, who kills the prophets and stones those sent to her, how often I wanted to gather your children together, in just the way a bird gathers her young ones together under her wings – but you didn't want it! Look! Now your house is being abandoned and deserted. For I'm telling you, from now on you won't see me at all until you say, "Blessed is the one who comes in the name of the Lord."'

We feel very uncomfortable at this assault on the Pharisees, who were certainly not as unpleasant as they are painted here. Our discomfort stems from the anti-Jewish sentiments that Christians have all too often indulged, which are fed by passages like this. It may be helpful to remember three things. First, Matthew's Gospel, which seems so anti-Jewish in places, is also the most Jewish: this is a battle between two different kinds of Judaism. Second, the style is rhetorical, polemical, so we shall not do well to regard it as evidence of 'how those dreadful Pharisees behaved'. Third, the criticisms levelled here are those which could be thrown at all religious leaders who lose sight of their ideals. Matthew is writing here a warning to his own church.

The Fifth 'Discourse': The End-Time (24:1–25:46)
Optimism in the face of signs of the Return

24 1-51 Jesus went out of the Temple, and was on the move when his disciples approached, to point out the Temple buildings to him. He answered them, 'Do you not see all these things? Amen I tell you, no stone will be left on another stone here that will not be destroyed.'

He sat down on the Mountain of Olives, and his disciples came to him privately: 'Tell us, when will these things be, and what is the sign of your Return and of the end of the age?'

Jesus answered them, 'Make sure that no one fools you. For many people will come in my name; and they'll say, "I am the Messiah," and they'll fool many. You're going to hear about wars, and reports about wars. Make sure that you don't panic. For it has to happen; but the end is not yet. For one nation will rise up against another, and one kingdom against another; and there will be famines and earthquakes in places. All these things will be the start of the labour-pains. Then they'll hand you over to affliction, and they'll kill you, and you'll be hated by all the Gentiles because of my name. And then many people will be made to stumble, and they'll hand one another over, and they'll hate each other. And many fake prophets will arise and lead many astray, and because of the increase of lawlessness, many people's love will grow cold; but the one who endures to the end, that's the one who will be saved. And this gospel of the kingdom will be proclaimed in the whole world as a witness to all the nations – and then the end will come.

'So when you see the "abomination of desolation" that was spoken of through the prophet Daniel standing in the Holy Place (let the reader understand), then let those who are in Judaea flee to the mountains; the one who is on the roof must not go down to pick up things from his house; the one who is in the field mustn't turn back to pick up his cloak. Bad luck to the women who are pregnant or have children at the breast in those days!

'Pray that your flight doesn't happen in winter, or on the Sabbath. For then there will be great trouble, the like of which has not been from the beginning of the world until now – nor will ever be [again]. And if those days are not curtailed, no one would be safe. But because of [God's] chosen ones, those days *will* be curtailed.

'Then if anyone tells you, "Look, here's the Messiah," or "Here," don't believe them. For fake-Messiahs and false prophets will arise, and provide impressive signs and powers, so as to fool even the chosen ones, if possible. Look! I have told you in advance. So if they tell you, "Look! He's in the desert," don't go out, or "Look! In one of the inner rooms!", don't believe [them]. For as the lightning comes from the east and appears all the way to the west, so will it be with the Return of the Son of Man. Where the corpse is, there the vultures will gather.

'Immediately after the trouble of those days,

"The sun shall be darkened, and the moon shall not give her light,
and the stars will fall from the sky,
and the powers of the heavens shall be shaken."

'And then the sign of the Son of Man will appear in heaven, and then all the tribes of the earth shall mourn, and they'll see the Son of Man coming on the clouds of heaven in power and great glory. And he will send his angels with a great trumpet, and they will gather his chosen ones from the four winds, from one end of the heavens to the other.

'Learn [the meaning of] the illustration from the fig tree. When its branch is now tender, and it's producing leaves, you know that summer is near. Similarly, when you people see all these things, know that it is just outside the gates. Amen I tell you that this generation will not pass away before all these things happen. Heaven and earth will pass away – but my words will not pass away. But no one knows the precise chronology [literally 'that day and hour'], not even the angels of heaven, and not even the Son – but only the Father.

'You see, the Return of the Son of Man will be like Noah's time. For just as in those days before the Flood, they were eating and drinking, marrying and giving in marriage, until the day when Noah went on board the ark; and they had no idea, until the flood came and took them all: that's how it will be with the Return of the Son of Man. Then there will be two men in the field; one will be taken and one left. Two women will be grinding at the mill; one will be taken and one left.

'So keep awake; because you have no idea what day your Lord is going to come. But know this, that if the householder had known at what hour of the night the thief was coming, he would have stayed awake, and not allowed his house to be broken into. Therefore you people also must get ready, because the Son of Man is coming at an hour when you're not expecting [it].

'So who is the faithful and sensible slave, whom the lord appointed over his house-slaves, to give them their food at the right time? Congratulations to that slave whose lord will find him on the job [literally, 'doing so'] when he comes. Amen I tell you, he'll appoint him over all his possessions. But if the bad slave says to himself, "My lord is taking his time," and starts beating his fellow slaves, and has banquets with drunkards, and the slave's lord comes on a day when he doesn't expect him and at a time that he doesn't know, then he'll cut him in two, and place bits of him with the fakes. There'll be weeping and gnashing of teeth there.'

It is important to recall that this is not a prediction, a kind of cosmic weather forecast (perhaps echoing Isaiah 13:10), in which we can see the likely symptoms, and so work out at what stage we are in the disaster. This discourse (as will become clear in the paragraphs that follow) is trying to do two things. First it wants to emphasise that a fairly catastrophic set of events is about to intrude on history, apparently sooner rather than later, and that Christians will need to keep their wits about them. Second, however, the evangelist is stressing that God is in charge, and therefore believers have nothing to worry about. The Greek word for Jesus' 'Return' is *Parousia*, which means something like 'presence'.

The 'abomination of desolation' comes from Daniel 9:27.

First of three images for the end-time: the ten maidens

25 ¹⁻¹³ 'Then the kingdom of heaven shall be likened to ten maidens, who took their lamps and went out to meet the bridegroom. Five of them were foolish, and five were sensible. For when the foolish ones took their lamps, they didn't bring oil with them; but the sensible ones brought oil with them in containers, along with the lamps. The bridegroom took his time, and they all dozed off and fell asleep. In the middle of the night there was a shout, "The bridegroom! Come out to meet him." At that point all the maidens woke up and trimmed their lamps. And the foolish ones said to the sensible ones, "Give us some of your oil, because our lamps are going out," but the sensible ones said, "No; otherwise there might not be enough for us and for you. Instead, go to the people who sell [oil], and buy some for yourselves." As they went away to buy it, the bridegroom arrived, and those who were ready went in with him to the wedding feast, and the door was shut. Later on the rest of the maidens turn up, saying, "Lord, lord, open [the door] to us." But he answered, "Amen I tell you, I don't know you."

'So stay awake, because you don't know the day or the hour.'

This is a good story, though the point is perhaps not crystal clear. We are presumably meant to laugh, and learn the message, which is probably about being prepared rather than about staying awake; the story perhaps does not take itself all that seriously – there is the unexplained gap between the first announcement of the bridegroom's arrival and his actual appearance; there is the absurd picture of the 'foolish' maidens trudging off to the shops, which are presumably closed at that hour of the night; and the pragmatic attitude of the sensible virgins ('Why don't you go shopping?') is not especially attractive.

Second image: eight talents

14-30   'For as a man going overseas summoned his own slaves, and handed over his possessions to them, and he gave one five talents, one two, and to the other one he gave one talent, each one in proportion to his own abilities, and then went overseas.

'Straightaway, the one who'd got the five talents got to work on them and gained another five. In just the same way the one who'd got the two talents gained two more. But the one who'd got the single talent dug a hole in the ground, and hid his lord's money!

'A long time afterwards, the lord of those slaves comes and settles accounts with them. And the one who'd got the five talents brought the other five talents. "Lord, you handed five talents over to me; look – I've gained five more talents," he said. His lord said to him, "Well done, good and faithful slave; you were faithful over small matters. I'll put you in charge of larger matters. Enter into the joy of your lord."

'And the one [who'd got] the two talents approached and said, "You handed me two talents. Look – I've gained two more talents." His lord said to him, "Well done, good and faithful slave; you were faithful over small matters. I'll put you in charge of larger matters. Enter into the joy of your lord."

'And the one who'd got a single talent also came forward; and he said, "Lord – I knew you were a hard man, harvesting where you didn't sow, and gathering where you didn't scatter, and because I was afraid I went and hid your talent in the ground. Look! You have what is yours."

'His lord answered him, "You wicked and idle slave: you knew that I harvest where I have not sown, and that I gather where I have not scattered, so what you should have done is to deposit my money with the bankers and I would have recovered my own with interest. So take the talent from him and give it to the one who has the five talents. For everything shall be given in abundance to the one who has; and as for the one who does not have, even what he has shall be taken from him. And throw out this useless slave into the outer darkness. There will be weeping and gnashing of teeth there."'

Another stirring of discomfort here, as we feel for the unfortunate who was only given one talent, and managed to be deprived even of that. At the same time, of course, it has to be said that his response to his master was not the most diplomatic that he could have chosen. A great deal is evidently expected of disciples who live in the end-time.

The alert reader will have noticed that the phrase about 'weeping and gnashing of teeth' has become very familiar to us in Matthew. It appears also at 8:12; 13:42; 13:50; 22:13; 24:51, and only once in Luke (13:28).

Third image: when the Son of Man is enthroned as judge

31-46 'When the Son of Man appears in his glory and all his angels with him, then he will sit on the throne of his glory. And all the nations will be gathered before him; and he will separate them from each other, just as the shepherd separates sheep from goats. And he'll set the sheep on his right hand, and the goats on his left. Then the king will say to those on his right, "Come, you who have been blessed by my Father; inherit the kingdom prepared for you from the foundation of the world. For I was hungry, and you gave me to eat; I was thirsty and you gave me to drink; I was a stranger and you gave me hospitality; naked and you put clothes on me; I was sick and you visited me; I was in prison and you came to me."

'Then the righteous will answer him, "Lord, when did we see you hungry and feed you, or thirsty and give you a drink? When did we see you a stranger and give you hospitality or naked and put clothes on you? When did we see you sick or in prison and come to you?" And the king will answer them, "Amen I tell you, whatever you did to one of these brothers and sisters of mine, [even] the least of them, you did it to me."

'Then he'll say to those on his left, "Go away from me, you cursed ones, into the eternal fire prepared for the devil and his angels. For I was hungry, and you did not give me [anything] to eat; I was thirsty, and you did not give me [anything] to drink; I was a stranger and you didn't give me hospitality; I was naked and you didn't put clothes on me, sick and prison and you didn't visit me."

'Then in their turn they will answer him, "Lord, when did we see you hungry or thirsty or a stranger or naked, or sick or in prison and didn't minister to you?" Then he'll answer them, "Amen I tell you, whenever you failed to do it to one of these littlest ones, you failed to do it to me." And these ones will go away to eternal punishment, but the righteous ones will go into eternal life.'

This well-known and much-loved story, on top of the other two slightly strange images, of the ten maidens (being prepared) and the talents (being generous), now indicates the question that will be asked at the end-time: how did you treat Christ, when he appeared in the form of 'these littlest ones', who may be the poor and under-privileged, or may be the members of the Church. It is decidedly challenging, and Matthew's last word before he enters upon the climax of the Gospel, the sad tale of Jesus' Passion and death.

The Passion of Jesus (26:1–27:66)

A plot, framing a woman's mysterious action

26 1-16 And it happened when Jesus finished all these words, he said to his disciples, 'You know that after two days the Passover is happening, and the Son of Man is being betrayed, to be crucified.'

Then the chief priests and elders of the people gathered together in the courtyard of the High Priest called Caiaphas; and they laid a plot to arrest Jesus by a trick and kill him. But they were saying, 'Not during the festival – we don't want trouble with the people.'

Now Jesus was in Bethany, at the house of Simon the leper, and a woman approached him with an alabaster [jar] of highly priced myrrh, and poured it on his head, as he lay down to eat. When the disciples saw it, they were furious, and said, 'What's the point of this waste? This could have been sold at a high price, and [the money] given to the poor!'

But Jesus knew [it] and said to them, 'Why are you giving the woman trouble? For she's done a beautiful thing to me. You see, you have the poor with you all the time; but you don't have me all the time. For when she put this myrrh over my body, she did it in order to bury me. Amen I tell you, whenever this gospel is proclaimed in the whole world, there will also be talk of what this woman has done, so that she'll be remembered.'

Then one of the Twelve, the one called Judas Iscariot, went to the chief priests and said, 'What are you willing to give me? And I'll hand him over [or: betray him] to you.' They settled on thirty silver coins, and from that moment he was looking for the best opportunity to hand him over.

Matthew generally follows Mark in his account of the Passion; but he makes one or two interesting changes. When he speaks of the 'chief priests and elders' gathering, he uses the same verb as he had in 2:4, where it had been the chief priests and scribes who were gathering ('synagoguing') in order to help Herod track down the newly born 'King of the Jews'. And the myrrh, here produced by the unnamed woman, is of course one of the gifts that the Magi had brought in that same scene. The 'thirty silver coins', which are only found in Matthew, represent, according to Exodus 21:32, the price of a slave who has been gored to death. But in Zechariah 11:12, 13 it is also the unsatisfactory wages given to a prophet, which he then casts into the Treasury. For Matthew, this is a prediction of the Judas episode, and foreshadows the circumstances of Judas' death, and the reaction of the Jerusalem establishment.

Not for the first time, the evangelist contrasts Jesus' calm goodness with the murderous intentions of the religious leaders, the incomprehension of the disciples, and (in this case) the mercenary motives of Judas.

The Passover meal

17-30 On the first day of Unleavened Bread, the disciples approached Jesus and said, 'Where do you want us to prepare for you to eat the Passover?' He said, 'Go into the city, to So-and-So, and tell him, "The teacher says: My time is near; it is at your place that I am having Passover with my disciples."' And the disciples did as Jesus had directed them; and they prepared the Passover.

When it was evening, he lay down [to eat] with the Twelve. And as they were eating, he said, 'Amen I tell you, one of you will betray me [or: hand me over].' They got very sad, and each of them started saying to him, 'It's not me, is it, Lord?'

He answered, 'The one who dips his hand with me in the dish, that is the one who will betray me. The Son of Man is going [just] as it was written about him, but woe to the person through whom the Son of Man is being betrayed. It [would have been] better for that person if he had not been born.'

Judas (the one who was in the process of betraying him) said to him, 'It's not me, is it, Rabbi?' Jesus says to him, 'It is you who have said it.'

As they were eating, Jesus took bread and blessed and broke and gave [it] to the disciples and said, 'Take, eat: this is my body.' And he took a cup and gave thanks and gave [it] to them saying, 'Drink from it, all of you. For this is my blood of the covenant, which is poured out for the forgiveness of sins. I'm telling you: from now on, I shan't drink from this fruit of the vine until that day when I drink it new with you in the kingdom of my Father.'

And they sang a hymn and went out to the Mountain of Olives.

The Passover is the greatest celebration of the Jewish year, and the Passover meal should be the most joyful event within it. We notice that Jesus is very much in charge of things here, and has the venue already arranged (there would be so many people in Jerusalem at this time that it could not possibly have been organised at the last minute).

Then this joyful meal goes horribly wrong, with the prediction of betrayal; in that culture it is a terrible breach of the law of hospitality, that one might betray someone with whom one has shared a meal – and such a meal! So the remark that Jesus' betrayer is 'the one who dips his hand with me in the dish' is less a matter of identifying the traitor than an expression of horror at what is going on.

And the alert reader will notice that Judas twice addresses Jesus as 'Rabbi' (here, and when Jesus is arrested, at 26:49); and the only other time that the word is used in this Gospel is at 23:7, 8, when it is expressly forbidden for Jesus' followers. Matthew is subtly classifying Judas with Jesus' opponents.

Prediction of the disciples' failure, stoutly rebuffed by Peter

31-35   Then Jesus says to them, 'You will all be caused to stumble [or: be scandalised] because of me tonight, for it is written, "I shall strike the shepherd, and the sheep of the flock will be scattered." But after I have been raised, I shall go before you into Galilee.'

Peter answered him, '[Even] if they are all made to stumble, me, never will *I* be made to stumble.'

Jesus said to him, 'Amen I'm telling you, tonight, before the cock crows, you'll deny me three times!'

Peter says to him, 'Even if I'm required to *die* with you, no way will I deny you!' And all the disciples spoke in a similar vein.

Once again we see the contrast between Jesus and his followers, here robustly led by Peter; Jesus is quiet and accurate, Peter all noisy bluster. And Jesus is, we realise, very much alone. They have not really noticed his prediction of Resurrection and a meeting in Galilee, because they have not properly taken aboard the fact that he must die.

The prediction of the scattering of the sheep is from Zechariah 13:7.

Jesus prays in great sadness to his Father; the disciples snore

36-46 Then Jesus came with them to a place called Gethsemani, and he says to his disciples, 'Sit here, while I go there and pray.' And he took along Peter and the two sons of Zebedee, and began to be sad and to be distressed. And he says to them, 'My soul is very sad, even to the point of death. Stay here, and stay awake with me.' And he went a little bit further, and fell on his face, praying, 'My Father, if it is possible, let this cup pass [me] by; nevertheless [don't let it be] in accordance with what I want, but [with] what you want.' And he comes to the disciples and finds them sleeping, and he says to Peter, 'So you weren't even strong enough to stay awake with me for a single hour! Stay awake, and pray, that you may not enter into temptation. The spirit is eager, but the flesh is weak.' Again he went off a second time and prayed, 'Father, if it is not possible for this [cup] to pass by unless I drink it, may your will be done.' And again he came and found them sleeping, for their eyes were heavy [with sleep]. And he left them again, and went off and prayed for a third time, again saying the same prayer. Then he comes to his disciples and says, 'Go on sleeping now, and have a rest. Look! The hour has come near, and the Son of Man is being betrayed into the hands of sinners. Up you get – let's go! Look! My betrayer has come near.'

This little episode presents us with a Jesus who is doing what he has always told his disciples to do, namely entrust everything to his Father. Just as the image of the unforgiving slave in Chapter 18 was a dramatisation of the fifth beatitude ('congratulations to the merciful'), so this whole episode presents us with the meaning of the third petition of Matthew's version of the Lord's Prayer ('may your will be done'), which is quoted here.

Once again see the contrast which Matthew uses to paint Jesus' portrait, between his own alertness and grief, and the crass somnolence of his disciples.

Jesus arrested by an armed group; abandoned by his disciples

47-56 And while he was still speaking, look! Judas (one of the Twelve!) came; and with him a huge crowd, with swords and clubs, from the chief priests and elders of the people. The one who was betraying him had given them a signal: 'The one I kiss is the one; arrest him.'

And immediately he approached Jesus and said, 'Hello, Rabbi', and kissed him.

Jesus said to him, 'My friend, [do] what you are here for.' Then they approached and laid hands on Jesus and arrested him.

And look! One of those with Jesus stretched out his hand and drew his sword, and struck the High Priest's slave, cutting off his ear. Then Jesus says to him, 'Return your sword to its place; all those who take the sword will die by the sword.

Or do you think that I am unable to call on my Father, and he'll give me more than twelve legions of angels? But how then are the scriptures to be fulfilled [that say] it must happen this way?'

At that hour, Jesus said to the crowds, 'You came out to arrest me with swords and clubs – just as if I was a bandit! I used to sit teaching in the Temple every day, and you didn't arrest me. But all this happened so that the Prophets' scriptures might be fulfilled.'

Then all the disciples abandoned him and fled.

This is a sombre episode; the betrayal by a member of Jesus' intimate circle, and the arresting party, armed to the teeth, 'from the chief priests and elders' is not how it should have been.

After the detail about the excision of the High Priest's slave's ear, Matthew puts on Jesus' lips a speech that is entirely characteristic (if slightly awkward syntactically). The reference to the twelve legions of angels will remind us of the second temptation in Chapter 4, when the devil suggested that Jesus might safely throw himself down, and of the end of that scene, when the 'angels came and served him'. The point is that he can safely trust his Father. Hence the reference to the fulfilment of Scripture (we shall find the number of such references increasing once more now, as the story approaches its climax).

Jesus' gentle and somewhat wry reproach about being regarded as a 'bandit' will bring us up short a bit later, when he'll be crucified between two real bandits.

Jesus before the Sanhedrin

57-68 Those who had arrested Jesus took him to [the house of] Caiaphas the High Priest, where the scribes and chief priests had gathered. Peter followed him from a distance as far as the High Priest's courtyard; he went in and sat down with the servants, to see what the end would be.

The chief priests and the whole Sanhedrin were looking for false evidence against Jesus in order to put him to death; and they couldn't find any, even though many false witnesses came forward. Later on, two approached and said, 'This man said, "I can destroy the Temple of God and in three days rebuild it."' And the High Priest rose up and said to him, 'Do you have no answer? What is [it that] these men are testifying against you?' Jesus was silent; and the High Priest said to him, 'I adjure you, by the Living God, that you tell us if you are the Messiah, the Son of God.'

Jesus says to him, 'You have said so; but I am telling you, from now on, you will see the Son of Man seated on the right hand of power and coming on the clouds of heaven.'

Then the High Priest tore his garments, saying, 'He has blasphemed! What need do we have of any more witnesses? Look! You've heard the blasphemy now – what do you think?'

They answered, 'He deserves death.'

Then they spat on his face and struck him; and some of them slapped him, saying, 'Prophesy to us, Messiah – who was it that hit you?'

This moment has been rushing towards us from the very beginning of the Gospel; Matthew had spoken there of the religious authorities being 'gathered' or 'synagogued' to give Herod the information he needed, and the same verb is used here of them (as also, significantly, at 22:34, 41; 27:17, 62; 28:12 – and see also 24:28). Peter is contrasted with them: he is not 'gathered', but bravely alone; while they are presented as 'looking for false evidence', he is looking 'to see what the end would be'. And to heighten the contrast, Matthew deliberately makes the High Priest's question, 'I adjure you by the Living God, that you tell us if you are the Messiah, the Son of God' an echo of Peter's (quite accurate) statement at 16:16: 'You are the Messiah, the Son of the Living God.' The maltreatment with which the episode ends only confirms another contrast, between this sordid pettiness, and Jesus' quiet dignity.

Peter's triple denial

69-75 Meanwhile, Peter was sitting outside in the courtyard. And a little slave girl approached him and said, 'You were also with Jesus the Galilean.' He denied it before [them] all, saying, 'I have no idea what you are talking [about]'. He went out to the entrance, and another [slave girl] saw him, and said to the people who were there, 'This man was with Jesus the Nazarene'; and again he denied it (with an oath!), 'I don't know the man.' A little while later, the bystanders approached and said to Peter, 'You're certainly one of them, for in fact your accent shows you up.' Then he began cursing and swearing, 'I don't know the man.'

And immediately a cock crowed. And Peter remembered Jesus' words; he had said, 'before the cock crows, you will deny me three times'. And he went out and wept bitterly.

This is a dreadfully sad story, even though we could see it coming. We admire Peter's courage in being there at all, but he can't even cope with a couple of slave girls, or the evidence of that frightful Galilean accent, and he'll do anything to convince them that he's never even heard of the one whom he had, ten chapters earlier, proclaimed as 'the Messiah, the Son of the Living God', and whom he was never, ever, going to deny 'even if I'm required to *die* with you!' His tears, however, must count for something.

Judas's change of heart, and Barabbas's release, framed by the interview with Pilate. Jesus three times proclaimed innocent

27 1-26 In the early morning, all the chief priests and elders of the people took counsel against Jesus, so as to put him to death; and they tied him up and led him off and handed him over to Pilate, the governor.

Then Judas, his betrayer, seeing that he had been condemned, had a change of heart, and returned the thirty silver pieces to the chief priests and elders, saying, 'I have sinned in betraying innocent blood.' But they said, 'What is that to us? That's your problem.' And he flung the silver pieces into the Temple and departed, and went off and hanged himself. The chief priests took the silver pieces and said, 'It is not permitted to put it into the Temple treasury, since it is the price of blood.' So they took counsel, and with the money they bought the Potter's Field as a burial-ground for foreigners. That is why that field is called 'Blood Field' to the present day. Then [the word] was fulfilled that was spoken through Jeremiah the prophet, 'And they took thirty pieces of silver, the price of the one who had been priced, whom they priced from among the children of Israel. And they gave it for the Potter's Field, as the Lord had ordered me.'

Meanwhile, Jesus stood before the governor, and the governor interrogated him, 'Are you the King of the Jews?' Jesus said, 'You say so.' And while he was being accused by the chief priests and elders, he made no reply. Then Pilate says to him, 'Don't you hear how much evidence they're bringing against you?' And he didn't reply to him, not even to a single charge, which left the governor quite dumbfounded.

Now at the feast, the governor was accustomed to free a prisoner for the crowd, anyone they wanted. At that time, they had a notorious prisoner called Barabbas. So when they were gathered, Pilate said to them, 'Who do you want me to set free for you, Barabbas, or Jesus, known as Messiah?' (For he was well aware that envy had led them to hand him over.)

As he sat on his judgement-seat, his wife sent to him, saying, 'Have nothing to do with that righteous person; for I have suffered a great deal in a dream today on his account.'

The chief priests and the elders worked on the crowds to ask for Barabbas and kill Jesus. The governor said, 'Which of the two shall I release for you?' They said, 'Barabbas.' Pilate said, 'So what shall I do with Jesus called Messiah?' They all say, 'Let him be crucified.' He said, 'Why? What evil has he done?' They yelled louder than ever, 'Let him be crucified!'

When Pilate saw that he was doing no good, but that actually a riot was imminent, he took water and washed his hands in the presence of the crowd, saying, 'I am innocent of this murder. It is your problem.' And the whole people replied, 'His blood on ourselves and on our children.' Then he released Barabbas; but he whipped Jesus, and handed him over to be crucified.

Once again, Jesus, strong and silent in this scene, is contrasted with those around him: Pilate is ineffectual in his attempts to acquit 'the King of the Jews' (this title, the nearest a Roman functionary could get to 'Messiah' recalls the tactless question of those other Gentiles, who came to Jerusalem, way back in Chapter 2, looking for 'the one born King of the Jews'); Judas realises that he has got it wrong, and ends up apparently committing suicide; Barabbas, for all his criminality, goes free; and the leaders will allow nothing to deflect them from murder. Only Mrs Pilate resists the trend, although we should notice that both Judas and Pilate declare Jesus innocent.

Pilate performs a very Jewish gesture in publicly washing his hands (to understand it, look at Deuteronomy 21:6-8; and when the crowd calls for 'blood on us and on our children' (echoing the traditional formula at Leviticus 20:9-16; see also 2 Samuel 1:16), we have to remember that this is the most Jewish of Gospels, and cannot be read as justifying the anti-Jewish violence and bloodshed that has disgraced Christian history. This is a battle within Judaism on which we are eavesdropping. Unusually for Matthew, the quotation he attributes to Jeremiah is actually from Zechariah 11:12, 13 (more or less); but he may also be thinking of Jeremiah 32:6-15.

Jesus is mocked and crucified

27-44   Then the governor's soldiers took Jesus into the Praetorium; and they gathered the whole cohort round him. They undressed him and put a scarlet cloak on him; and they plaited a crown made of thorns and put it on his head, and a reed in his right hand. Then they genuflected before him and had fun with him, saying 'Hail – King of the Jews!', and they spat on him, and took the reed and beat him on his head. And when they'd had their fun with him, they took the scarlet cloak off him, and took him out to crucify him.

As they went out, they found a Cyrenean man called Simon; and they conscripted this fellow to carry his cross. And they came to a place called Golgotha, which means 'Skull Place'. They gave him a drink of wine mixed with gall. When he tasted it, he refused to drink it. They crucified him, 'dividing his garments', and 'casting lots'. And they sat down and kept watch on him there. And above his head, they put the indictment against him:

'This is Jesus, the King of the Jews.'

Then two bandits were crucified with him, one on the right and one on the left. The passers-by abused him, and shook their heads, and said, 'You are [the one] who destroys the Temple and rebuilds it in three days – save yourself, if you are Son of God, and come down from the cross!'

Similarly the chief priests had fun with the scribes and elders and said, 'He saved others – he can't save himself! He's the King of Israel; let him come down from the cross now, and we'll believe in him. He trusted in God; let [God] deliver him now, if he wants him. Because he said, "I am Son of God."'

Similarly the bandits who had been crucified with him reviled him.

The crucifixion of Jesus is framed by two pieces of mockery. First the soldiers play an elaborate game of 'King'; Jesus is dressed up in royal attire (scarlet cloak, crown, sceptre) and given a parody of royal homage, where genuflection and royal form of address turn to spitting and violence; then he is reduced to nakedness again, and an African is conscripted to play the part of a disciple and 'carry his cross'. He is crucified, with a label above his head that is presumably intended to be mocking, calling him 'King of the Jews'. Matthew notes carefully how Psalm 22 is fulfilled: 'dividing garments . . . casting lots' echoes verse 18, and 'let God deliver him' goes back to verse 8; the psalm will be explicitly quoted again when Jesus dies.

Then after Jesus has been crucified, he is mocked in turn by the spectators, by the religious establishment, and by his fellow convicts. The phrase 'if you are the Son of God' is familiar to us from the temptation, back in Chapter 4. The question it implies has faced the reader all the way through the Gospel. Jesus is Son of God, but not in that dramatic, spectacular way. As for 'King of the Jews', that is the point agreed by both the Magi and Herod.

Jesus dies

45-56 From midday, darkness came on all the earth, until three o'clock. And at about three o'clock, Jesus shouted out in a loud voice, saying, 'Eli, Eli, lema sabachthani', that is, 'My God, my God, why did you abandon me?' Some of the bystanders, when they heard it, said, 'This one's calling for Elijah!' And immediately one of them ran and took a sponge, and filled it with vinegar, put it round a reed, and gave it to him to drink. Others said, 'Leave him alone – let's see if Elijah comes to save him.' Jesus again cried out in a loud voice and gave up the spirit.

And look! The veil of the Temple was torn in two from top to bottom; and the earth quaked, and the rocks were split, and the tombs were opened, and many bodies of the saints who had fallen asleep were raised, and they came out of the tombs, after his Resurrection, and entered the Holy City and appeared to many.

The centurion and those who were watching Jesus with him saw the earthquake and the things that had happened, and they were very afraid, saying, 'Truly this man was Son of God.'

There were many women looking on from a distance; they had followed Jesus from Galilee, looking after him. Among them were Mary Magdalene, and Mary the mother of Jacob and Joseph, and the mother of the sons of Zebedee.

> The death of Jesus is starkly told, more or less following Mark. As before, Matthew subtly insists (quoting Psalms 22:1 and 69:21b) that Jesus fulfils the scriptures. His death is greeted with signs, and the party with the centurion proclaim him Son of God, answering the devil's question (4:3,6), and confirming what the reader already knows (3:17; 16:16; 17:5, not to mention the evidence of demons at 8:29, and disciples at 14:33).
>
> The women are there, though the men have fled, and the alert reader will notice the presence of the mother of the sons of Zebedee, who was last seen asking for the top jobs for her sons. Things have changed round here.

Jesus is buried (in three scenes)

57-66 When evening arrived, there came a wealthy man from Arimathea (Joseph was his name), who was himself discipled to Jesus. He came to Pilate and asked for Jesus' body. Pilate ordered it to be given to him. He took the body of Jesus and wrapped it in a clean linen cloth, and put it in his new tomb, which he had carved in the rock; and he rolled a big stone to the door of the tomb and went off.

Mary the Magdalene was there, and the other Mary, sitting in front of the grave.

The next day, which was after the Preparation Day, the chief priests and Pharisees gathered together [literally, 'synagogued'] to Pilate, and said, 'Lord, we have remembered that this impostor said, while he was still alive, "I am being raised after three days". So order the grave to be made secure until the third day; [we don't want] his disciples to come and steal him and tell the people "he's been raised from the dead", [because then] the last imposture will be worse than the first.' Pilate told them, 'You have a guard; go and secure it as you know [how].' They went off and secured the tomb, with the guard.

> Matthew tells the story in three scenes. In the first, a named and apparently prominent person provides a site that can be located

later on, a new tomb, and a clean cloth. In the second, there are two witnesses, who knew Jesus. In the third, there is an attempt to prevent the disciples from 'body-snatching' (not that they were psychologically in a position to attempt anything of the sort). Matthew's intention is to make it clear that the grave was known and clearly identified, and to exclude the possibility of error or fraud. Naturally the empty tomb does not demonstrate the truth of Christian belief in the Resurrection; but on the other hand it is hard to see how the first Christians could have proclaimed that Jesus was risen if his body could have been easily produced.

The angel tells the women 'he is risen'

28 ¹⁻⁷ Late [in the night after] the Sabbath, towards dawn on the first day of the week, Mary Magdalene and the other Mary came to see the grave. And look! There was a great earthquake; for the angel of the Lord came down from heaven and came and rolled away the stone, and sat on top of it. And his appearance was like lightning, and his clothing white as snow. Those who were keeping watch were shaken with fear of him, and they became like corpses. The angel spoke to the women, 'Don't *you* be afraid; because I know that you are looking for Jesus, the crucified one. He is not here; for he is risen, as he said. Come here; look at the place where he was lying. And quick, go and tell his disciples, "He's risen from the dead and look! He's going before you to Galilee – you will see him there." Look! I have told you.'

Matthew tells the Resurrection story in four scenes. In this first one, the women bravely come to the tomb, and discover that the angel of the Lord is there before them, the stone rolled away, and the tomb empty, because 'he is risen'. And the state-of-the-art security team? They are 'like corpses', and it was their job precisely to look after a corpse! The women are given the good news, and appointed as apostles to the apostles. The angel may remind us of the transfigured Jesus (17:2); and perhaps see also Revelation 1:14-16.

The women meet Jesus

⁸⁻¹⁰ And they went away quickly from the tomb, with fear and great joy; they were running to tell the disciples. And look! Jesus met them, saying, 'Hail' [literally, 'rejoice']; and they approached and held on to his feet and worshipped him. Then Jesus says to them, 'Don't be afraid. Go and tell my brothers [and sisters] to go to Galilee – and they'll see me there.'

Mark had the women running away into silence, telling no one (except, of course, that they must have said something to someone). In Matthew the women set out to perform their mission, and have this unexpected encounter with the one who is unmistakably he whom they had seen buried: they do the appropriate thing, like the Magi back at the beginning of the story, and 'worship', and their mission is reconfirmed, with the instruction, 'Don't be afraid.' So it's off to Galilee (where the mission is to be lived out).

What about the guard?

11-15   As they went, look! Some of the guard came to the city and reported to the chief priests everything that had happened. And they gathered together ['synagogued'] with the elders, and took counsel, and gave the soldiers plenty of silver pieces, telling them, 'Say that his disciples came by night and stole him while we were asleep. And if the report gets to the governor, we'll reassure him and see you right.' They took the silver pieces and did as they had been taught. And this story has spread about among the Jews until the present day.

> Meanwhile, the guard, so carefully posted, is doing its corpse-imitation. Matthew skilfully takes them off-stage, and in so doing confirms the fact of the empty tomb (for the story would not have been spread if the body of Jesus could be produced).

Final words of the Gospel; the mission to fearful disciples

16-20   The eleven disciples journeyed to Galilee, to the mountain which Jesus had commanded them. And when they saw him, they worshipped – but they doubted.
And Jesus approached and spoke to them, 'All authority in heaven and on earth is given to me. So go and make disciples of all the Gentiles, baptising them in the name of the Father, and of the Son and of the Holy Spirit, teaching them to keep everything that I have commanded you. And look! I am with you all the days, up to the consummation of the age.'

> This is a powerful scene with which to conclude this remarkable Gospel. Notice that the disciples are eleven now, a reminder that one of his intimates had betrayed Jesus and then committed suicide.
>
> They go to Galilee, as instructed, and to 'the mountain', a location which, though vague enough in itself, has been important throughout this Gospel.
>
> The disciples show the correct response: 'they worshipped', a gesture first performed by the Magi; but, like all disciples down the ages, they are a bit unsure: 'they doubted'.
>
> Then we are given a further clue to Jesus' identity: 'all authority in heaven and on earth' is given to him, which is a very grand claim indeed. And this leads directly into the mission to the Gentiles: 'make disciples of them', says Jesus, using the same verb that we encountered at the end of Chapter 13, when he spoke of the 'scribe discipled in the kingdom of heaven', and in Chapter 27, where Joseph of Arimathea was 'discipled to Jesus'. And they are to baptise these Gentiles in the triune name of Father, Son and Holy Spirit (another fragment of the liturgy of Matthew's church?) and pass on the teaching of the Sermon on the Mount and those other discourses that we have heard. Finally comes the promise, picking up the reference to Emmanuel in Chapter 1, and to the Church in Chapter 18, 'I *am* with you'. It is only on the supposition of that unfailing and faithful presence that Matthew can write a Gospel at all.

According to Mark

Introduction

Mark's is the shortest Gospel, and it is probably the one that was first to be written. So Mark may be said to have invented the Gospel form, which gives him a special claim on our attention. His Greek is vigorous, but not always very grammatical, and readers will find this translation jarring in places, as I have tried to preserve in English the 'feel' that it has in the original Greek.

Some things to look out for: Mark's Gospel is intended to answer two questions:

- Who is Jesus?
- What must Jesus' disciples be like?

As you read through, ask yourself how Mark approaches these questions. One thing that may help is to notice the haunting ambiguities of the Gospel, the mystery of who Jesus is, and the painful mystery of discipleship. You will notice at times that Mark leaves questions hanging in the air, such as 'Who can forgive sins, but God alone?' or 'Who is this, that even the wind and the sea obey him?' Mark does not give an answer; the reader must supply their own.

The Title

1 [1]   Beginning of the good news of Jesus Messiah Son of God.

> With this characteristically curt announcement we start our reading of the first of the Gospels to be written. 'Beginning' tells the reader where we are, of course, but may also serve as an echo of the opening words of the Bible. 'Good news' (in Greek, *euangelion*) has come, through the Anglo-Saxon 'god-spel', into English as 'gospel'. It reflects on the one hand an Old Testament background, where the word refers to the proclamation of God's great deeds, and on the other hand a background in the Roman Empire, where it can be used for something like the announcement of a birth to the royal house, or a Roman victory in far-off places. 'Messiah' comes into Greek as 'Christ', but in this Gospel, as opposed to the letters of Paul, it is a title rather than a name. 'Son of God' is not in all manuscripts, but it is likely to be what Mark wrote, and is almost certainly what he meant.

The emergence of John the Baptist

2-6   As it is written in Isaiah the Prophet:

> 'Look! I am sending my messenger before your face,
>   who will prepare your way;
>   a voice of one shouting in the desert:
>   "Prepare the way of the Lord,
>   make straight his paths."'

There arose John, baptising in the desert and proclaiming a baptism of repentance for forgiveness of sins. And there journeyed out to him the whole Judaean region, and all the Jerusalemites, and they wanted to get baptised by him in the River Jordan, confessing their sins.

And John was clothed in camel-hair; and there was a leather belt about his loins. And he was eating locusts and wild honey.

> Mark's is a mysterious Gospel, and it is mysterious from the very beginning. The quotation that he attributes to Isaiah is not in fact wholly from that source. The opening lines of it are from either Exodus 23:20 (in the Greek version) or from Malachi 3:1. Only after that does Mark revert to Isaiah (40:3, in the Greek version). Why is this so? The reader must decide – but you can exclude any idea that Mark didn't know his Old Testament.
>
> Also mysterious is the fact that Mark starts his Gospel, not with Jesus (as you might expect), but with John the Baptist. This must mean that in some sense John gives a clue to the mystery – including, apparently, that Jesus may properly be called 'Lord' in a passage that clearly referred originally to God.
>
> We notice that John's mission (and therefore presumably that of Jesus) has something to do with confronting the reality of sin ('a baptism of repentance for the forgiveness of sins . . . confessing their sins'). We also note, with perhaps a slight shudder, John's austere clothing and unattractive diet.

The message of John the Baptist

7, 8 And he started proclaiming, saying: 'The Stronger-One-Than-Me is coming after me, of whom I am not worthy to stoop down and untie the thong of his sandals. I baptised you with water, while he will baptise you by the Holy Spirit.'

> John's message turns out to be all about Jesus, pointing to Jesus' superiority: Jesus is 'stronger', incomparably superior (the task of untying sandals was a slave's job), and his baptism is 'with the Holy Spirit', a notion that Mark has yet to explain to us.

The baptism of Jesus

9-11 And it happened in those days Jesus came from Nazareth of Galilee and was baptised in the Jordan by John. And immediately coming up out of the water he saw the heavens dividing and the Spirit like a dove coming down upon him. And a voice came out of the heavens:

'You are my Son, the beloved; in you I have taken pleasure.'

> We may puzzle at this, as perhaps the early Christians did: if Jesus is so superior to John, why did he have to be baptised by him? Mark does not really give us an answer, except that a) Jesus sees the heavens dividing (which means that what happens is God's doing), and the Holy Spirit descending (as John the Baptist had indicated) and b) Jesus is publicly affirmed as God's Son. We watch with renewed interest.

Jesus in the desert

12, 13 And immediately the Spirit hurls him out into the desert. And he was in the desert forty days being tested by the Satan, and he was with the beasts. And the angels began to serve him.

> There is a breathless, urgent quality in these early chapters, partly engendered by Mark's repetition of the word 'immediately' (How many times does he use this word in the first two chapters?). What the Spirit does here is normally translated as 'sent', but the word is more powerful than this might suggest. And notice the 'historic present' ('he hurls' for 'he hurled'), which Mark favours; I have left it so in the translation, to give the 'feel' of the original.

The beginning of Jesus' mission

14, 15 Now after John had been handed over, Jesus came to Galilee proclaiming the good news of God and saying, 'The right-time has been fulfilled and the kingdom of God has drawn near. Repent and believe in the good news.'

> Note the starkness of this: the moment when the mission begins is the moment of the arrest of the 'Forerunner'. There is great urgency in Jesus' proclamation: it is *now* that a decision is required. Like

John, Jesus tells his hearers that they must repent, but he also tells them to 'believe the good news'. This is the second time the term 'good news' has been used in the Gospel.

The sudden calling of two sets of brothers

16-20   And going along by the Sea of Galilee he saw Simon and Andrew the brother of Simon casting in the sea (for they were fishermen). And Jesus said to them, 'Come here, after me, and I'll make you become fishers of human beings.' And immediately abandoning their nets they followed him.

And going a little further he saw James the son of Zebedee and John his brother – and them in the boat repairing their nets. And immediately he called them. And abandoning their father Zebedee in the boat with the hirelings they went off after him.

> Notice that this episode takes place 'by the Sea of Galilee'. You will see that whenever we hear this phrase in Mark, something important is about to happen. The call is a very striking one: first Simon, and his brother with the Greek name, simply leave everything to follow Jesus, without complaint or excuse, or even any apparent surprise, perhaps in response to the little joke about becoming 'fishers of human beings'. Then two other brothers answer the call, with the added detail that they abandon their father Zebedee and his staff.
>
> Mark's Gospel is written to answer two questions: 'Who is Jesus?', and 'What must Jesus' disciples be like?'

In the synagogue at Caphernaum

21-28   And they enter into Caphernaum. And immediately on the Sabbath going into the synagogue he began to teach. And they were amazed at his teaching. For he was teaching them as though he had authority, and not like the scribes.

And immediately there was in their synagogue a man with an unclean spirit and he shouted out, saying, 'What do we have to do with you, Jesus Nazarene? You have come to destroy us. I know who you are, the Holy One of God.' And Jesus scolded him, saying, 'Shut up and come out of him.' And the unclean spirit, convulsing and crying with a great cry, came out of him. And they were all astonished, so that they debated with each other, saying, 'What's this? New teaching with authority? He even gives instructions to the unclean spirits, and they obey him.'

And his reputation immediately went out into the whole surrounding area of the Galilee.

> Now we see Jesus, for the first time in the Gospel, doing something that is an important part of Mark's understanding of him, namely teaching. The teaching has an immediate effect: 'they were amazed'. We shall see this 'amazement' again and again in the Gospel, describing Jesus' impact on people, especially disciples. His teaching is also 'with authority', we gather. 'Authority' is another word to look out for throughout the Gospel. We also see the first mention of 'the scribes', who are going to represent (largely but not wholly – see 12:28-34) Jesus' opponents. Here already we can detect the tension.

Jesus displays effortless 'authority', telling unclean spirits where they get off, even though they try to exercise power over him by correctly identifying him as 'Jesus Nazarene – the Holy One of God'. They can do nothing against him, however.

Notice that Jesus is said to 'scold' the unclean spirit. There will be other uses of this verb in the course of the Gospel.

Simon Peter's mother-in-law

29-31   And immediately coming out of the synagogue they came into the house of Simon and of Andrew with James and John. Now the mother-in-law of Simon lay sick, fevered. And immediately they tell him about her. And approaching he raised her up, taking her hand. And the fever abandoned her. And she was serving them.

> This healing is, as always with Jesus' miracles, effortless. It shows, moreover, Jesus' complete indifference to questions of ritual purity: he touches someone who is a woman, and perhaps on the point of death. Finally, the healing brings her to a point where she can do 'service', the proud task of angels (1:13) and of Jesus himself (10:45) and of Jesus' disciples.

Healings, once the Sabbath is over

32-34   When it grew late, when the sun set, they brought to him all those who were in a bad way, including those who had demons. And the entire city was gathered at the door. And he cured many who were in a bad way with various diseases. And he hurled out many demons and he did not allow the demons to speak because they knew him.

> Here Mark gives us a little picture of what it was all like: Jesus' reputation has spread, and once the Sabbath is over people can bring their sick to him. His impact is immense: 'The entire city was gathered at the door.'
>
> Notice the command to silence (sometimes called the 'Messianic Secret'). This is the first of many times that we shall meet it. Here it is addressed to the demons, 'because they knew him'. (Later on, we shall see that, as you might expect, no one takes any notice of the command.)

Jesus at prayer; Jesus misunderstood; Jesus continues the mission

35-38   And early in the morning, when it was deep in the night, rising up he went out and went away to a deserted place. And there he began to pray. And Simon and those with him went chasing after him. And they tell him, 'Everyone is looking for you.' And he says to them, 'Let's go elsewhere, to the neighbouring market towns, so that I may proclaim there also. Because for this I came out.'

> We go further into the mystery of who Jesus is. Here we note that he is one who needs to pray. We note also that 'Simon' (already taking on a certain prominence in the group) really does not

85

understand him and clearly regards this prayer business as a waste of time. We should, however, be startled, on reading the story, to notice that Jesus neither scolds Simon for interrupting his prayer-life, nor grudgingly consents to come back with them; instead he takes us by surprise and points out new directions for his mission.

Teaching, proclamation, exorcism, the healing of a leper

39-45 And he went into their synagogues, into the whole of the Galilee, proclaiming, and hurling out demons. And a leper comes to him, begging him, falling on his knees and telling him, 'If you want, you can make me clean.' And taking pity, stretching out his hand, he touched him and tells him, 'I do want: be made clean'. And immediately the leprosy went away from him, and he was made clean. And sternly warning him he immediately drove him out. And he tells him, 'See that you say nothing to anybody. Instead, go, show yourself, and make the offering that Moses prescribed with regard to your cleansing, as a witness to them.' But he went out and he started to proclaim many things and to spread the word; so that he could no longer go into a city; instead, he was outside, in deserted places. And they started to come to him from all sides.

> This first chapter leaves us quite out of breath as it comes to its end, if we have been trying to keep up with Jesus, as we watch him travelling, teaching, 'hurling out demons'. Then there comes a major test, the encounter with the highly contagious disease of leprosy. We repress a shudder as Jesus actually touches the leper; then he states his determination to 'make him clean', and the leprosy disappears as easily as Simon's mother-in-law's fever. Once again there is the command to silence.
>
> Notice the uncertainty about the identity of 'he', 'him', 'them' in this passage. It is a difficulty in reading Mark that we often have to guess whom his pronouns are referring to.

The paralytic who came through the roof

2 1-12 And coming again into Caphernaum several days later, it was heard that he was in [the] house. And many gathered so that he could no longer go, not even to the door, and he began to speak to them The Message. And they came, carrying to him a paralytic lifted up by four [people]. And not being able to bring [him] to him, because of the crowd, they unroofed the roof [of the house] where he was, and digging out [the clay of the roof?] they let down the mattress where the paralytic lay. And seeing their faith Jesus says to the paralytic, 'Child, your sins are forgiven.' Now there were some of the scribes sitting, and arguing in their hearts, 'Why does this fellow speak in this way? He blasphemes. Who can forgive sin, except one person, namely God?' And immediately Jesus, knowing in his spirit that they were arguing in their hearts in this way, says to them, 'Why do you argue these things in your heart? What is easier, to say to the paralytic, "Your sins are forgiven you," or to say "Arise and take up your mattress and walk"? But so that you may know that

the Son of Man has authority to forgive sins on earth' – he says to the paralytic – 'To you I say, arise, take up your mattress, and go to your house.' And he arose and immediately taking up the mattress he went out before all of them.

The result was that all were beside themselves, and glorified God, saying, 'Like this we never saw.'

We are supposed to be startled by a number of things here. There is the breathless sense of the crowds surrounding Jesus, dramatically signalled by the unusual rearrangement of the roof. There is the unreferred 'he' (who can only be Jesus) in the first line. There is the reference to the 'house' (possibly that of Simon and Andrew, the only one we have previously seen). The 'house' in Mark's Gospel is often (though not here) a place where Jesus gives private instruction to his disciples.

The next thing to startle us is what Jesus says: not, as we may have been expecting, some command to the paralysis to depart, but, to the paralytic, 'Child, your sins are forgiven.' This assertion of the man's status as child may perhaps be related to Jesus' sense of God as 'Father'. This has only been hinted at so far in the Gospel, with the two references to Jesus as 'Son'. And the forgiveness of sins, presumably a diagnosis of what was *really* wrong with the man, is a great shock. And it is not only the reader who is shocked. Rather surprisingly, we learn that 'some of the scribes' (who have already been dismissed as being less impressive teachers than Jesus) were 'sitting there', and take this quite amiss. They immediately raise the question whether Jesus is claiming a function reserved to God. Jesus doesn't trouble to answer them, but offers them the expected healing as a proof that 'the Son of Man has authority (that word again) to forgive sins on earth'.

Who is this Son of Man? Clearly Jesus; but it is the first time we have met the expression, which reads like a title of some sort. We shall watch carefully for it in future. Some scholars prefer to translate it as something like 'the Human One', to preserve inclusive language; but a) it clearly refers only to Jesus, and b) it was clearly an expression that was frequently on Jesus' lips, so I have judged it worth the risk of leaving it as it stands.

Two other things: 'The Message' is capitalised because Mark has put it in a curiously emphatic place in the sentence. And, second, the result of the episode is to direct praise, not to Jesus, but first to God: 'the result was that all were beside themselves, and glorified God'.

Jesus and revenue collectors

13-17   And he went out again, beside the sea. And the whole crowd came to him, and he was teaching them. And passing by he saw Levi of Alphaeus sitting at the revenue office. And he says to him, 'Follow me.' And rising up he followed him.

And it happens that he is lying down [to dine] in his house, and many revenue collectors and sinners lay down [to dine] with Jesus and with his disciples. For they were many, and they followed him.

And the scribes of the Pharisees, seeing that he was eating with sinners and revenue collectors, started saying to his disciples, 'He's eating with revenue collectors and sinners.' Jesus overheard and says to them, 'The strong do not have need of a doctor, but those who are in a bad way. I did not come to call the just, but sinners.'

Once again, this important episode takes place 'beside the sea'; once more, Jesus attracts the crowds. There is a new departure here, however, in that Jesus is seen in company with some far-from-desirable friends, the associates of the 'revenue collector', Levi of Alphaeus. The main thing to notice, though, is how instantly Levi responds to the command: 'follow me'. This leads to a celebration with some equally undesirable characters, which raises some more disapproving questions from the 'scribes' (this time the 'scribes of the Pharisees'). Jesus then announces his rather subversive mission-statement: 'I did not come to call the just, but sinners.'

Jesus' disciples don't fast!

18-22 And the disciples of John, and the Pharisees, were fasting. And they come and say to him, 'Why do the disciples of John, and the disciples of the Pharisees fast, but your disciples do not fast?' And Jesus said to them, 'Surely the sons of the bridal chamber can't fast during the time when the bridegroom is with them? As long as they have the bridegroom with them, they cannot fast. But days will come when the bridegroom is taken away from them, and then they will fast on that day.

'No one sows a patch of new cloth on an old garment. Otherwise, the new one takes the fullness away from the old one, and the tear becomes worse.

'And no one pours new wine into old wineskins. Otherwise the wine will break the skins, and so both the wine and the skins are destroyed. So: New Wine into New Flasks.'

Clearly Jesus has been identified as a figure of religious significance; so, his opponents (now Pharisees and followers of the Baptist) ask aggressively, why don't his disciples behave more religiously? The answer that Jesus' critics are given is in terms of a wedding: he is the bridegroom in God's wedding-feast, and now is the moment for celebration, not fasting. Jesus tells his first two 'parables' to support his point, about patching old garments, and about bottling new wine. Either way, the message is the same: Jesus is Different.

Jesus' disciples don't keep Sabbath

23-28 And it happened that on the Sabbath he was journeying through the sown fields, and his disciples started to make their way plucking the ears of corn. And the Pharisees said to him, 'Look: they are doing something on the Sabbath for which there is no authority.' And he says to them, 'Did you never read what David did, when he had need, and he and those with him were hungry, how he entered the house of God, in the days of Abiathar the priest, and devoured the loaves of presentation, which no one except the priests has authority to eat, and he gave them to those who were with him?' And he said to them, 'The Sabbath came into existence for the sake of human beings, and not human beings for the sake of the Sabbath, so that the Son of Man is Lord also of the Sabbath.'

> Once again, Jesus' disciples cause trouble, this time by performing an activity that is forbidden on the Sabbath, which seems odd, given that they are followers of a clearly religious figure. Jesus defends his followers with an adroit reference to 1 Samuel 21:1-7, which reveals him as an attentive and imaginative student of Scripture. But there is a deeper point to be made here: who is the Sabbath for? And underlying all this is Jesus' implicit claim to have authority over the Sabbath. That is a high claim indeed.
>
> Notice that Jesus is not questioning Sabbath observance, so much as the Pharisees' interpretations of it.

Healing on the Sabbath (in a synagogue!) – and a plot to commit murder

3¹⁻⁶ And he came back into the synagogue; and there was there a man who had his hand dried up. And they watched him, in case he should heal him on the Sabbath, so that they could accuse him. And he says to the man who had the dried hand, 'Rise up into the middle.' And he says to them, 'Is there authority on the Sabbath to do good or to do evil? To save a life or to kill?' But they were silent. And looking around them with anger, grieving with [at] the hardness of their heart, he says to the man, 'Stretch out your hand.' And he stretched it out. And his hand was restored.

And the Pharisees, going out immediately, hatched a conspiracy with the Herodians against him, how they might destroy him.

> We go deeper into the mystery of who Jesus is: and we notice that the opposition is now overt ('they watched him'), and that by the end of the story it is turning to killing, as the unlikely combination of the 'Herodians' and the Pharisees conspires to put an end to it all. Jesus' response is purely religious, while their response is clearly wrong, from the very beginning.

A summary of Jesus' activities

7-12 And Jesus with his disciples went up to the Sea. And a great number from the Galilee followed [him]. And from Judaea, and from Jerusalem and from Idumaea and across the Jordan and around Tyre and Sidon, a great number, hearing what things he was doing, came to him. And he told his disciples that a boat should be ready for him, on account of the crowd, so that they should not press upon him. For he cured many, so that whoever had afflictions fell upon him, that they might touch him.

And the unclean spirits, whenever they saw him, fell down before him, and cried out, saying, 'You are the Son of God.' And often he scolded them, that they should not make him known.

Once again we meet the 'Sea of Galilee'; here it functions as the setting for crowds, and healings, and exorcisms, and commands to secrecy about Jesus' status as 'Son of God'.

Appointment of the Twelve

13-19 And he goes up to the mountain, and he summons whom he wanted. And they came to him. And he made twelve, that they should be with him, and that he should send them to proclaim, and to have authority to throw out the demons. And he made twelve. And he put the name on Simon of 'Rock'. And James the [son] of Zebedee and John the brother of James, and he put the name on them of Boanerges, which is 'sons of thunder'. And Andrew and Philip and Bartholomew and Matthew and Thomas and James of Alphaeus and Thaddaeus and Simon the Canaanite. And Judas Iscariot, who also betrayed him.

> The selection of his 'core group' now takes place. Presumably the fact that there are twelve of them represents Jesus' intention of founding a 'new Israel'. We notice Jesus' tendency to give nicknames: 'Rock', 'Boanerges', and perhaps 'the Canaanite' and 'Iscariot', though this is less certain. Two of the disciples (Andrew and Philip) have Greek rather than Hebrew or Aramaic names, which is striking, especially since Andrew's brother Simon has a perfectly respectable Hebrew or Aramaic name. We note the final phrase, 'who also betrayed him', and reflect, perhaps, that this is true of all of them. We may also observe the three functions of disciples: to be with him, to proclaim, and to have authority to cast out demons.

Jesus the embarrassing

20-35 And he comes to [the] house. And again the crowd comes together, so that they could not even eat bread. And 'his people' hearing [it] came out to arrest him. For they said, 'He's beside himself.' And the scribes who came down from Jerusalem said, 'He has Beelzeboul' and 'It is by the ruler of the demons that he casts out the demons'. And summoning them in parables he began to say to them, 'How can Satan cast out Satan?' And, 'If a kingdom is divided against itself, that kingdom cannot stand.' And, 'If a house is divided against itself, that house cannot stand. And so if Satan rose up against himself and is divided, he cannot stand; his end is coming. But no one can enter the house of the strong one to plunder his property unless he first binds the strong one and then plunders his house. Amen I tell you, all their sins and all their blasphemies that they blaspheme will be forgiven to human beings. But whoever blasphemes against the Holy Spirit, does not have forgiveness for ever, but is guilty of an everlasting sin.' This was because they said, 'He has an unclean spirit.'

And his mother and his brothers come; and standing outside they sent to him, calling him. And a crowd sat about him, and they tell him, 'Look: your mother and your brothers and your sisters are outside. They are looking for you.'

And answering he says to them, 'Who is my mother, and brothers?' And looking round at those who sat about him in a circle, he says, 'Look – my mother and my brothers. Whoever does the will of God, that person is my brother and sister and mother.'

Jesus now visibly embarrasses 'his people', who try to arrest him. In that culture, it was of immense importance that one should be seen to be honouring the values of the clan; and failure to do so might be evidence of insanity.

'Scribes from Jerusalem' now join 'Jesus' people', the fourth time that these characters have been mentioned. Each time it has signalled trouble. Here they make the offensive accusation that Jesus is allied to Beelzeboul, and that's how he casts out demons. Jesus exposes the shaky logic of their argument, but probably does not win any friends among them, especially when he accuses them of committing the unforgivable sin of 'blaspheming against the Holy Spirit'.

After this interlude, Jesus' family send for him, and he resists, perhaps even giving them a brush-off. We may, however, take heart from his statement that anyone who does God's will is Jesus' 'brother and sister and mother': the idea of family is redefined.

The setting for the parables; the first parable (the Sower), and an explanation of it

4 1-20 And again he began to teach by the sea; and a very great crowd gathers to him, so that he boards a ship and sits on the sea, and the whole crowd was facing the sea, on land. And he began to teach them many things in parables, and he said to them in his teachings, 'Listen – Look! The sower went out to sow, and it happened as he sowed that some fell beside the road, and the birds came and devoured it. And other [seed] fell on the rocky ground, where there was not much earth. And immediately it sprang up, because it had no depth of earth; and when the sun rose it was scorched, and because it had no root it was dried up. And other [seed] fell on thorns, and the thorns came up and suffocated it, and it did not yield fruit. And other [seed] fell on good earth, and yielded fruit, coming up and growing, and it bore as much as thirty times, and even sixty times, and a hundred.' And he said, 'Whoever has ears to hear, let them hear.'

And when he was alone, those with him, with the twelve, asked him [about] the parables. And he said to them, 'To you the mystery is given of the kingdom of God; whereas to those outside everything happens in parables, so that

> "Looking they may look and not see
> and hearing they may hear and not understand
> lest they return and it be forgiven them."'

And he says to them, 'Do you not know this parable – and how will you know all the other parables? The sower is sowing the word. But these are the ones beside the road, where the word is sown; and when they hear, immediately Satan comes, and takes the word that is sown into them. And those likewise [are] the ones who are sown on the rocky bits, who whenever they hear the word immediately accept it with joy, and do not have root in themselves, but are momentary, then when there comes trouble or persecution on account of the word, they are immediately made to stumble. And others there are who are sown into the thorns: these are the ones who hear the word, and the concerns of the world, and the deceit of wealth, and

desire for all the other things march in and suffocate the word, and it becomes
sterile. And these are the ones who are sown into good earth, who hear the word
and receive it and bear fruit, in thirties and sixties and hundreds.'

Mark has told us that Jesus is a teacher 'with authority'. Now he
actually lets us hear some of the things that Jesus teaches. Our
attention is carefully focused: once again we are by 'the Sea'; once
again there is a huge crowd, and Jesus is forced to a striking expedient,
that of sitting on a boat (Mark expresses it slightly uncomfortably,
that he 'sits on the sea'; but we know what he means).

Then comes this well-known parable; and, for the first time (of
many) in Mark, the disciples completely fail to understand, and
Jesus has (reluctantly, we feel) to explain the parable to them.

Three (or four) more parables

21-34 And he said to them, 'Surely the lamp does not come so as to be put under the
bushel or under the bed? Is it not intended to be put on the lamp-stand? For there
is nothing hidden, except so that it should be revealed; nor did it become obscured,
except that it should come into the open. If anyone has ears to hear, let them hear.'

And he said to them, 'Look at what you hear. In the measure that you measure
out it will be measured out to you, and it will be added to you. For whoever has, it
will be given to that person. And whoever does not have, even what they have will
be taken away from them.'

And he said, 'So is the kingdom of God, as a man sows seed on the earth; and he
sleeps and wakes, night and day, and the seed sprouts and lengthens, in a way that
he himself does not know. The earth yields fruit automatically, first a stalk of grain,
then an ear, then full corn in the ear. But when the fruit comes, immediately "he
sends out the sickle, because the harvest has drawn near".'

And he said, 'How shall we liken the kingdom of God, or in what parable shall
we place it? It is like a grain of mustard, which when it is sown into the earth,
being smaller than all the seeds which are on the earth. And when it is sown, it
comes up and becomes bigger than all the vegetables, and it makes big branches, so
that "under its shadow the birds of the air find shade".'

And with many such parables he spoke the word to them, just as they were able
to hear. But apart from a parable, he did not speak to them; but privately to his
own disciples he explained everything.

Mark continues to give us the flavour of Jesus' teaching, its
combination of plain commonsense and obscurity; and there is a
feeling that Jesus wanted his disciples to grasp it, but others to
remain uninitiated.

The quotation about 'he sends out the sickle' is from Joel 4:13;
that about the 'birds of the air' is from Ezekiel 17:23.

Who *is* this, then?

35-41 And he says to them on that day, as it grew late, 'Let us go through to the other
side.' And abandoning the crowd, they took him as he was in the boat. And other
boats were with him. And there comes a great storm of wind, and the waves beat

upon and into the boat; so that already the boat was beginning to be filled. And he was in the stern, sleeping on the pillow. And they arouse him and say to him, 'Teacher, don't you care that we are being destroyed?' And being thoroughly aroused, he scolded the wind, and said to the sea, 'Silence; be quiet'; and there came a great calm. And he says to them, 'Why are you such cowards? How do you not have faith?' And they feared, a great fear. And they said to each other, 'Who is this, then? Because both the wind and the sea obey him.'

> This is a remarkable story; Mark is not particularly interested in geographical details, but gets Jesus and his disciples to cross the Sea of Galilee. As often happens in these parts, a storm comes up unexpectedly, and the disciples panic, accusing Jesus of indifference to their fate. Like someone calming a boisterous dog, Jesus orders the sea to behave (and it does), then rebukes the disciples, for the first time indicating the importance of faith to them. Their response (again for the first time in this Gospel) is to 'fear a great fear'; this is a reaction that in the Old Testament signals the presence of God. Then we hear the question they ask themselves: 'Who is this, then?' It is a question that Mark does not answer. Instead, he invites the reader to respond: who *is* this, then?

The possessed man in the land of the Gerasenes

5 ¹⁻²⁰ And they came to the other side of the sea, into the land of the Gerasenes. And as he came out of the boat, immediately there met him out of the tombs a man with an unclean spirit, who had his dwelling among the tombs. And not even with chains could anyone bind him, on account of the fact that he had often been bound with fetters and chains. And the chains and the fetters had been torn apart by him, and broken. And no one was strong enough to tame him. And all night and day he was in the tombs and in the mountains, shouting out and cutting himself with stones. And seeing Jesus from afar he ran and worshipped him, and shouting in a loud voice he says, 'What have you to do with me, Jesus, Son of the Most High God? I conjure you by God, do not torture me.' For he was saying to him, 'Come out, unclean spirit, from the man.' And he asked him, 'What name [do they give] to you?' And he said to him, 'Legion is the name [they give] to me, because we are many.' And he begged him, many times over, not to send them out of the region. And there was there, near the mountain, a large herd of pigs feeding. And they begged him, saying, 'Send us into the pigs, that we may enter into them.' And he allowed them. And the unclean spirits going out went into the pigs, and the herd rushed down the slope into the sea, about two thousand, and they suffocated in the sea. And those who looked after them fled and announced into the city and into the fields. And they came to see what had happened. And they come to Jesus, and they see the possessed man sitting down, clothed and sober, the one who had had the Legion. And they were afraid. And those who saw explained to them how it happened to the possessed man, and about the pigs. And they began to beg him to go away from their frontiers. And as he was going on board the boat, the man who had been possessed begged him that he might be with him. And he did not allow him, but says to him, 'Go into your house, to your people,

and announce to them what things the Lord has done for you and had mercy on you.' And he went off and began to proclaim in the Decapolis what Jesus had done for him. And they were all amazed.

> This is yet another extraordinary story from Mark. He emphasises what a powerful opponent Jesus has here, one who dwells 'among the tombs' (something to make Mark's readers shiver); he cannot be shackled, despite numerous attempts; he shouts, and he mutilates himself. Despite all this, he runs to Jesus, worships him, and correctly identifies him as Son of God. Jesus, without turning a hair, a) discovers the demon's name, and we whistle sharply as we discover that there may have been as many as six thousand unclean spirits, b) as a special favour allows the demons to go into the nearby pigs, but their respite is illusory, since c) they drown anyway. Not surprisingly, the news of this gets about, and instead of applauding the man's healing, the locals get nervous, and get rid of Jesus. The healed man wants to stay with him; but you can't choose discipleship – it is discipleship that chooses you, and instead the man is told to go and preach at home. The effect on his compatriots is one we have encountered before, and shall see again: 'they were all amazed'.

Two stories 'sandwiched' round each other

21-43 And when Jesus had crossed in the boat back to the other side, a great crowd gathered upon him. And he was by the sea. And one of the synagogue rulers comes to him, Jairus by name, and seeing him he falls at his feet and begs him many things, saying, 'My little daughter is in extremis; do come and lay hands on her, so that she may be saved and may live.' And he went with him. And a great crowd followed him and they pressed upon him.

And a woman, who had been in haemorrhage for twelve years, and had suffered many things from many doctors, and had spent all that she had, and she was no way helped, but rather she went downhill, having heard the things about Jesus, coming in the crowd from behind touched his garment. For she was saying [to herself], 'If I were just to touch his garments, I shall be saved.' And immediately the fountain of her blood was dried up, and she knew in her body that she was healed from her scourge. And immediately, Jesus, knowing in himself that the power had gone out of him, turning round in the crowd said, 'Who touched my garments?' And his disciples said to him, 'You see the crowd pressing upon you, and you say, "Who touched me?".' And he looked about to see the woman who had done this. And the woman, afraid and trembling, knowing what had happened to her, came and fell before him, and told him the whole truth. And he said to her, 'Daughter, your faith has saved you. Go in peace, and be healed of your affliction.'

While he was still speaking, they come from the [house of the] synagogue ruler, saying, 'Your daughter died. Why still bother the teacher?' But Jesus, overhearing the message being uttered, says to the synagogue ruler, 'Do not be afraid. Only believe.' And he did not allow anyone to follow along with him except Peter and James and John the brother of James. And they came to the house of the synagogue ruler and he sees a disturbance, and people weeping, and wailing loudly. And going in he says to them, 'Why do you make a tumult and weep? The child is not dead but asleep.' And they jeered at him. And he threw them all out, and takes the father of the child, and the mother, and those with him, and he goes in where the child was. And taking the hand of the child, he says to her, 'Talitha Koum', which in translation is, 'Little girl, I say to you, arise.' And immediately the little girl arose and walked. For she was twelve years old. And immediately they were beside themselves with great ecstasy. And he strongly commanded them that no one should know this. And he said that she be given [something] to eat. And he went out from there.

Mark employs a technique that we may call 'sandwiching', wrapping one story round another, so that each story sheds light on the other. Here it is the story of Jairus's daughter that is 'sandwiched' around the story of the woman with the flow of blood. The woman's story is a charming one: she is utterly alone, for her condition alienates her from all human contact, even from her family, and therefore from any sense of self-worth, and even, we may deduce, from God. She shows initiative, however, more than any disciple so far. We are even allowed to hear what she thinks: 'If I were just to touch his garments', and what she wants: 'I shall be saved'. She is *healed* (but not yet saved), and knows it; Jesus also knows it, despite the uncomprehending jeers of his disciples, and he knows that it is a woman who has touched him. She confesses all, 'afraid and trembling', like those other women at the Gospel's end (16:8), then hears those lovely words: 'Daughter, your faith has saved you.'

The other story likewise gives us great joy. Somewhat unexpectedly, it is a synagogue ruler who asks Jesus for help (and we are even given his name). Once the story resumes, on the other side of the 'sandwich', it sounds as though it's all much too late; but Jesus is quite confident, ignoring the jeers of those who refuse to believe him, and effortlessly (as always) performs the cure, commands them to silence (this command is unlikely to be obeyed, we feel), and charmingly exhorts them to feed the child.

An unsuccessful return home

6 1-6 And he comes to his homeland. And they followed him, his disciples. And when a Sabbath arrived, he began to teach in the synagogue. And many [people] hearing were astounded, saying, 'From where [have] these things [come] to this [fellow]? And what is the wisdom that has been given to this [fellow], and such great miracles that happen through his hands? Is not this [fellow] the builder, the son of Mary and the brother of James and of Joses and of Judas and of Simon? And are not his sisters here with us?' And they were shocked by him. And Jesus said to them, 'A prophet is only dishonoured in his homeland, and among his kinsfolk, and in his household.' And he could not do any miracle there, except that he laid hands on a few sick [people] and healed them. And he was amazed on account of their unbelief.

We might expect a ticker-tape parade ('local boy makes good'); but we already know that Jesus is different. Not many people in the Gospel so far have really understood him, and his hometown continues the pattern: they are 'shocked' or 'scandalised' by him. So he can't do much in the way of miracles.

Another 'sandwich': the apostles are sent out; John the Baptist is decapitated

7-32 And he went round the villages in a circle, teaching. And he summons the twelve. And he began to send them two by two, and he gave them authority [over] unclean spirits. And he directed them not to take anything for the way, except only a staff: 'No bread, no begging-bag, no copper for the belt: just have sandals tied on. And don't put on two tunics.' And he said to them, 'Wherever you go into a house, stay there until you come out from there. And whatever place does not receive you or listen to you, marching out from there shake the dust from under your feet as a witness to them.'

And they went out and proclaimed that [people] should repent. And they threw out many demons, and they anointed many sick people with oil and cured them.

And King Herod heard; for his name had become known. And he said, 'John the baptiser has risen from the dead, and that's the reason these miracles are at work in him.' And some [people] said, 'It's Elijah', and others said, 'A prophet, like one of the prophets'. But Herod was saying, when he heard, 'That [fellow] I decapitated: John – he has risen.' For Herod himself had sent and arrested John and tied him up in gaol, on account of Herodias, Philip his brother's wife, because he had married her. For John was telling Herod, 'You have no authority to have your brother's woman.'

And Herodias had it in for him, and she wanted to kill him. And she couldn't, for Herod was afraid of John, knowing him for a just man and a saint. And he protected him, and when he was listening to him he was deeply puzzled. And he used to listen to him gladly.

And when a good chance arrived, when Herod threw a banquet on his birthday for his magnates and his kiliarchs, and the Number Ones of the Galilee, and when his daughter Herodias came in and danced, she pleased Herod and those who lay down to dine with him. The king said to the little girl, 'Ask me whatever you want, and I shall give [it] to you.' And he swore to her, 'Whatever you ask me, I shall give you, "even unto half of my kingdom".' And going out, she said to her mother, 'What shall I ask for?'

And she said, 'The head of John the baptiser.'

And immediately going in with haste to the king, she asked him, saying, 'I want you to give me, straightaway, on a dish, the head of John the Baptist.'

And the king [although] becoming very sad, because of the oaths, and because of those who lay down [to dine], did not wish to thwart her. And immediately, the king, sending a scout, ordered him to bring his head. And going off he decapitated him in the prison. And he brought his head on the dish. And he gave it to the little girl. And the little girl gave it to her mother.

And hearing it his disciples came and took up his corpse and placed it in a tomb.

And the apostles gathered to Jesus and announced to him all the things that they had done and that they had taught.

And he says to them, 'Come here, you yourselves, privately, to a deserted place and refresh yourselves for a little.' For those who were coming and going were many, and they didn't even have a chance to eat. And they went in the boat to a deserted place, privately.

> We have watched Jesus going about his mission; now it is the turn of the Twelve. Just like him, they are to have authority over unclean spirits; and they are to travel light, and (like Jesus) to expect rejection. Eventually they will return, full of all that they have done; but while they are away Mark invites us, by way of another 'sandwich', to reflect on the form which that rejection might take. The story of John the Baptist's death is a horrid one, with lively narrative and deftly drawn characters. Incidentally, the two women here are the only ones (in contrast to the blundering males) in Mark's Gospel who get things wrong. We may reflect that discipleship is not going to be easy.
>
> 'Even unto half my kingdom' is from Esther 5:3, 6, where the speaker is another unpredictable tyrant addressing a woman from his household.

A hungry crowd (five thousand of them) taught and fed

33-44 And many saw them going and recognised [them/it?], and on foot, from all the cities, they ran there together. And they got there before them.

And going out he saw a great crowd and had pity on them, because they were 'like sheep who have no shepherd', and he began to teach them many things. And when it was already very late, his disciples coming to him said, 'The place is deserted, and it's already late. Dismiss them, so that they can go to the estates and villages about and buy for themselves something to eat.' He replied and said to them, 'Give them something to eat yourselves.' And they say to him, ' [You want us to] go off and buy loaves for two hundred denarii and give them to eat?'

But he says to them, 'How many loaves have you got? Go and see.' And they found out and say, 'Five. And two fishes.' And he instructed them to make everyone lie down in picnic-groups, on the green grass. And they lay down group by group, by fifty and a hundred. And taking the five loaves and the two fish, and looking up to heaven, he blessed and broke the loaves and gave to [his] disciples for them to place before them, and the two fish he divided for all. And they all ate and were filled. And they took up fragments, twelve full baskets, and also from the fish. And those who ate were five thousand men.

> The disciples have returned from their missionary expedition, all ready for debriefing; but the crowds have their eye on Jesus, and there will be no privacy. Worse still (from the disciples' point of view) Jesus actually cares about these crowds. The disciples try to break it up, by looking at their watches and talking about food; but instead are told 'feed them yourselves'. They treat this suggestion with derision, but, in the end, feed them is precisely what they do.
>
> 'Like sheep without a shepherd' comes from Numbers 27:17 and Ezekiel 34:5. Both these texts are about how leadership should be exercised in Israel.

'Courage, IT IS I'

45-52 And immediately he compelled his disciples to embark on the boat and to go ahead to the other side, to Bethsaida, while he dismisses the crowd. And having said farewell, he went off to the mountain to pray. And when it grew late, the boat was in mid-sea; and he was alone on the land. And seeing them in distress in their rowing, for the wind was against them, around the fourth watch of the night he comes to them, walking on the sea. And he wanted to pass them by. But they, seeing him walking on the sea, thought that it was a ghost. And they cried out. For they all saw [him] and were disturbed. But he immediately spoke with them, and says to them, 'Courage, IT IS I.' And he came up to them, into the boat, and the wind abated. And they were exceedingly beside themselves in themselves. For they had not understood about the loaves. Instead, their heart was hardened.

> Who is Jesus? Who are his disciples? Jesus effortlessly feeds five thousand people, and then needs to go and pray. The disciples are sent off by boat, but meet with difficulty, and Jesus approaches them, out of compassion. They are in no way comforted; instead, they are convinced that they are being haunted. Jesus replies 'It is I', which might just mean 'It's me, Jesus'; but it also echoes what God said at the burning bush in Exodus 3:14. For the first time, we are told clearly that the disciples fail to understand; and Mark applies to them the alarming phrase, 'their hearts were hardened'.

A summary of Jesus' activities

53-56 And crossing to the land they came to Gennesaret, and they docked. And when they disembarked, immediately recognising him they ran round that whole region, and they began to carry around on mattresses those who were in a bad way, wherever they heard that he was. And wherever he would journey, into villages or into towns or into fields, they placed the sick in the market places, and they begged him, that they might touch even the hem of his garment, and whoever touched him, were being saved.

> Mark brings this chain of linked stories to an end now, by docking at Gennesaret; and, once again, Jesus is beset by the crowds, who long to be healed by him (and they are not disappointed). Notice how Mark leaves us to work out for ourselves who 'they' are in each sentence.

More disagreements on appropriate religious behaviour

7 1-23 And they came together to him, the Pharisees and some of the scribes coming from Jerusalem, and seeing some of his disciples, that with unclean (that is, unwashed) hands they eat loaves. For the Pharisees and all the Jews unless they have washed with the fist, do not eat, keeping a grip on the tradition of the elders, and [coming back] from the market place don't eat unless they have washed, and many other things which they have received to keep, washings of cups and jugs and bronzes. And the Pharisees and the scribes interrogate him, 'Why do your disciples not walk according to the tradition of the elders, but with unclean hands eat bread?'

And he said to them, 'It was well that Isaiah prophesied about you fakes [literally, 'actors'] as it is written:

"This people honours me with [their] lips,
but their heart is distant from me.
In vain do they worship me,
teaching teachings [which are] the instructions of humans."

'Abandoning the command of God, you hold firm to the tradition of human beings.'

And he said to them, 'Do you do well to nullify the command of God, so as to set up your tradition? For Moses said, "Honour your father and your mother"; and "The one who bad-mouths father or mother, let them die the death." You, on the other hand, say, "If a person says to [their] father or mother, 'Qorban,' (that is, gift) 'whatever you should have had from me.'" – you no longer let a person do anything for [their] father or mother, thus invalidating the word of your God by your tradition which you have traditioned. And you do many similar such things.'

And calling the crowd again, he was telling them, 'Listen to me all of you, and understand. There is nothing outside the person which comes into them which can make them unclean. Rather the things that come out of the person are those which make them unclean.'

And when he went into the house away from the crowd, his disciples asked him about the parable. And he says to them, 'So you too are unintelligent. Don't you understand that everything that from outside comes into the person cannot make them unclean? Because it does not come into the heart, but into their belly, and goes out into the latrine' (making all foods clean). But he went on to say, 'What comes out of the person, that is what makes the person unclean. For from within, from people's heart, come evil thoughts: fornications, thefts, murders, adulteries, greeds, wickednesses, debauchery, evil eye, blasphemy, arrogance, and foolishness. All these wicked things come out from inside, and make the person unclean.'

Once again we witness an encounter between Jesus and 'the Pharisees and some of the scribes coming from Jerusalem'. We know now that this means disagreement; and it must be said that Jesus' opponents have a point, when they observe his disciples' behaviour (though we have no idea what 'washing with the fist' might mean). When Jesus is criticised on religious grounds, he tends to quote Scripture, as he does here (Isaiah 29:13); for Jesus what counts is nothing else than doing the will of God, and he argues that his opponents tend to evade that will. He then sums up his message to the crowds, and, perhaps a little irritably, explains the matter to his not very sharp disciples.

'Qorban' is a Hebrew word, a gift consecrated to God, and therefore unavailable for charitable purposes.

A woman whose retort changed Jesus' mind

24-30 Rising up from there he went off to the boundaries of Tyre. And going into a house he wanted no one to know. And he could not pass unnoticed. Instead, immediately a woman heard about him, whose daughter had an unclean spirit, and came and fell at his feet. Now the woman was a Greek-speaker, Syro-Phoenician by race. And she asked him that he would cast the demon out of her daughter.

And he started to say to her, 'First let the children eat their fill. For it is not good to take the children's loaf and fling it to little dogs.' And she replied and says to him, 'Lord, even the little dogs eat under the table, from the children's crumbs.' And he said to her, 'Because of this remark, go; the demon has come out of your daughter.' And going into her house she found her little child hurled on the bed, and the demon gone out.

This is an extraordinary episode. Jesus retreats to non-Jewish territory, perhaps a little dispirited by inner-religious arguments, and meets a non-Jew who wants a favour, the healing of her daughter. His response is dismissive, and not apparently very polite, referring to Gentile women as 'little dogs'; but she maintains her cool, and wittily twists his words, apparently delighting Jesus so much that she gets her way. This Gospel is full of surprises.

'He has done everything well'

31-37 And again going out of the boundaries, he came through Sidon into the Sea of Galilee, up the middle of the boundaries of [the] Decapolis.

And they bring to him a deaf man with a speech impediment, and they beg him to lay his hands on him. And taking him away from the crowd in private he put his fingers into his ears, and, spitting, touched his tongue. And looking up to heaven he groaned, and says to him, 'Ephphatha', which is 'Be opened'. And his ears were opened. And the chain of his tongue was untied. And he started to talk properly. And he commanded them that they tell nobody. But as much as he tried to command them, they proclaimed [it] all the more extravagantly. And they were super-extravagantly amazed, saying, 'He has done everything well: even the deaf he makes to hear, and speechless ones to speak.'

This episode also takes place in non-Jewish territory, but on the east rather than the west side, across the Jordan. As always, the healing is effortless; as so often there is the command to silence; and we are given Jesus' word in perfectly correct Aramaic. The point of the story may be in the echo of the Old Testament (see Isaiah 35:5, 6): Jesus is everything that Scripture had led us to expect. We recall the disciples' awed question at the end of Chapter 4: 'Who is this, that even the winds and the seas obey him?'

Feeding of the four thousand, and a reflection on failures to understand (hardening of the heart)

8 1-21 In those days again, there being a great crowd, and them not having anything to eat, summoning his disciples he says to them, 'I have compassion on the crowd, because for three whole days they stick with me, and they do not have anything to eat. And if I dismiss them fasting to their home, they will dissolve on the road. And

some of them have come from a long way off.' And his disciples replied to him, 'From where will someone be able so to fill these people with loaves in the desert?' And he was asking them, 'How many loaves do you have?' And they said, 'Seven.'

And he commands the crowd to lie down on the ground. And taking the seven loaves he gave thanks and broke and gave to his disciples for them to place before [the people]. And they placed [them] before the crowd. And they had a few little fishes. And he blessed them and he said to place [them] also before. And they ate and were filled, and they took up surplus fragments, seven hampers. They were about four thousand. And he dismissed them.

And immediately he went on to the boat with his disciples, and came to the parts of Dalmanutha. And the Pharisees came out and began to contend with him, seeking from him a sign from heaven. They were testing him. And groaning in his spirit he says, 'Why does this generation seek a sign? Amen I say to you: no sign will be given to this generation [literally: 'if a sign shall be given to this generation . . .'].' And abandoning them he embarked again and went off to the other side. And they had forgotten to bring loaves. And they only had one with them in the boat. And he instructed, saying, 'Look, keep a watchful eye out against the leaven of the Pharisees and the leaven of Herod.' And they discussed with each other, because they don't have loaves. And knowing [what they were up to] he says to them, 'Why are you discussing that you don't have loaves? Do you neither understand nor comprehend? You have your heart hardened. Having eyes, do you not see, and having ears do you not hear?

'And don't you remember, when I broke the five loaves for the five thousand, how many baskets full of fragments you took up?' They said, 'Twelve.'

'When [I broke] the seven [loaves] for the four thousand, how many hampers full did you take up?' They tell him, 'Seven.'

And he says to them, 'Do you not yet understand?'

> The point of this story, which in many respects echoes that earlier story where five thousand were fed, lies apparently in the obtuseness of Jesus' disciples. The seven loaves and a few fishes are made to stretch out so that not only does everyone eat, but there are seven hampers of surplus food. The story is briefly told, but really seems to set up a contrast between Jesus and a) the Pharisees (who want a sign) and b) the disciples (who have not only forgotten to bring a picnic, but also have no real notion what is going on). Jesus speaks of their inability to see, echoing Jeremiah 5:21 and Ezekiel 12:2.
>
> The question is therefore forcefully addressed to the reader: do *you* understand?

The start of Jesus' instruction of his disciples

22-26   And they came to Bethsaida. And they bring to him a blind man and they beg him to touch him. And taking the hand of the blind man, he took him outside the village. And spitting into his eyes he laid his hands on him and asked him, 'Do you see anything?' And recovering his sight [or: 'looking up'] he said, 'I am looking at human beings, because I see them walking like trees.' Then again he laid hands on his eyes. And he saw clearly and was restored, and he beheld everything plainly. And he sent him to his home, saying, 'Don't even go into the village.'

We have established that the disciples do not understand very much. Now comes a period when they are being instructed, especially about the fact that Jesus must die. This time of instruction starts with the present story, and ends at 10:46-52. In other words, the whole instruction period is framed by two stories in which blind men have their sight restored; perhaps this symbolises what happens to Jesus' disciples in the course of the instruction.

This particular healing is unusual: Jesus leads the blind man away privately; he spits into his eyes; the miracle is initially only partially successful ('I see them walking like trees') – and then the cured man is told to go home, 'not even into the village'. All this may symbolise where the disciples are just at present.

Caesarea Philippi: a Messiah who will suffer (and has disciples who don't understand)

8 ^{27}-**9** ^{1} And Jesus went out, and his disciples, to the villages of Caesarea Philippi. And on the way he interrogated his disciples saying to them, 'Who do people say I am?' And they told him, saying, 'John the Baptist. And others Elijah, and others that [you are] one of the prophets.'

And he himself interrogated them, 'Now you: who do you yourselves say I am?' Peter replied and says to him, 'You are the Messiah.' And he scolded them, to tell nobody about him.

And he began to teach them that it was necessary for the Son of Man to suffer many things, and to be rejected by the elders and the high priests and the scribes, and to be killed, and after three days rise again. And he said the message openly. And Peter, taking him aside, began to scold him. And he turned, and, seeing his disciples, scolded Peter and says, 'Get behind me, Satan. Because you are not thinking God's thoughts but human thoughts.' And summoning the crowd with his disciples he said to them, 'If someone wants to follow after me, let them deny themselves, and take up their cross, and follow me. For whoever wants to save their life will destroy it. And whoever destroys their life, for my sake and for the sake of the gospel, will save it. For what use is it for a person to gain the entire world and suffer the loss of their life? For what would a person give in exchange for their life? For whoever is ashamed of me and of my words in this adulterous and sinful generation, the Son of Man will also be ashamed of him when he comes in his Father's glory with the holy angels.' And he was telling them, 'Amen I say to you: there are some of those who stand here who will not taste death until they see the kingdom of God coming in power.'

This central passage continues the theme of the disciples' education; the process seems to be a combination of light dawning and dark incomprehension. It starts with a survey of current views ('Who do people say I am?'), then moves to an uncomfortably direct question: 'Who do you yourselves say I am?' Peter gets it stunningly right; but then, when the implications of his answer are unfolded, stunningly wrong, for he cannot cope with a Messiah who is to be killed. And so he is, for his pains, addressed as 'Satan'. It is important for disciples to understand this business of a Messiah who has to die. Disciples have to be prepared to imitate their master, right to the end.

Continuing education: the Transfiguration

²⁻¹³ And six days later Jesus takes aside Peter and James and John and carries them up to a high mountain privately, on their own. And he was transformed before them, and his garments became radiant, very white such as a bleacher on earth could not so whiten [them]. And there appeared to them Elijah with Moses; and they were talking together with Jesus. And Peter responded and says to Jesus, 'Rabbi, it is good for us to be here. And let's make three tents, one for you, and one for Moses and one for Elijah.'

For he had no idea how to respond. For they became terrified. And there came a cloud overshadowing them; and there came a voice from the cloud, 'This is my Son, the beloved. Listen to him.'

And suddenly, looking round, they no longer saw anybody, except Jesus, on his own, with them.

And as they came down out of the mountain, he instructed them that they should narrate to nobody what they had seen, except when the Son of Man should be risen from the dead. And they hung on to the message for themselves, arguing what 'rising from the dead' was. And they interrogated him, saying, 'The scribes say that Elijah has to come first.' And he said to them, 'Elijah indeed comes first, and restores everything. And how is it written about the Son of Man that he should suffer a great deal and be treated with contempt? But I tell you that Elijah has come, and they did to him as they pleased, as it is written about him.'

> The instruction of the disciples goes on, although here it is only his 'inner cabinet', Peter, James and John, who are given their instructions. Up the mountain, two things happen: first, Jesus is 'transfigured', and whatever we make of this, it is clearly intended as a glimpse of the truth about him. Second, Jesus is seen chatting with Elijah and Moses, the Prophets and the Law, so that he is at least the equal of them. Then Peter blows it, with his willing but not very sensible suggestion of building a camping-site. Notice that 'they became terrified'. This is the sign of the presence of God; and, sure enough, there is a cloud and the voice of God, confirming what we heard at the Baptism (1:11), 'This is my Son, the beloved', with the instruction (which they will do well to observe), 'listen to him'.
>
> With these words ringing in their ears they go down the mountain. Then they (and we) are told that this can't be understood until Jesus is raised from the dead, and are invited to think about Elijah. But they don't really understand very much.

Another failure by the disciples

¹⁴⁻²⁹ And coming to the disciples they saw a great crowd about them, and scribes arguing against them. And immediately the whole crowd seeing him was amazed. And they ran up and greeted him. And he asked them, 'Why are you debating against them? And one of the crowd responded to him, 'Teacher, I brought my son to you, since he has a dumb spirit. And whenever it overtakes him, it dashes him to the ground and he foams at the mouth and gnashes his teeth and he becomes stiff. And I told your disciples that they should expel [the demon]. And they had not the strength.' He responded to them saying, 'O faithless generation! How long shall I

be with you? How long shall I put up with you? Bring him to me.' And they brought him to him. And seeing him the spirit immediately convulsed him. And falling on the ground he rolled [about], foaming at the mouth. And he asked his father, 'How long a time is it that this has happened to him?' And he said, 'From since childhood. And often it threw him into a fire and into waters, to destroy him. But, if you can, help us, having compassion on us.' And Jesus said to him, 'That "If you can" – everything is possible to the one who believes.' Immediately, the father cried out and said, 'I believe: help my unbelief!' And Jesus, seeing that a crowd was running together, scolded the unclean spirit, saying to it, 'You dumb and deaf spirit, I command you, come out of him, and never enter into him again.' And crying out and convulsing him it came out. And he became just like a corpse, so that many said, 'He's dead!' But Jesus gripped his hand and raised him up, and he stood up again [or: 'resurrected'].

And when he went into a [the?] house, his disciples asked him, 'Couldn't we cast it out?' And he said to them, 'This kind can't come out by any method but prayer.'

> Now, as they rejoin the others, comes another failure. The disciples (presumably all but the three who were up the mountain) have been unable to heal a boy who was possessed by a demon, and the crowd and the boy's father clearly want 'the organ-grinder, not his monkeys'. There is more dialogue than we are used to, as Jesus discovers the circumstances, and twice emphasises the need for faith. Then the boy is healed, although not without a struggle, and the crowds thinking he was dead. The point of the story, however, seems to be the education of the disciples, puzzled at their failure – and Jesus simply stresses the need for prayer.

Continuing education: the Messiah and his disciples

30-50 And going out from there they went through the Galilee, and he did not want anyone to know. For he was teaching his disciples and telling them, 'The Son of Man is being handed over into human hands. And they'll kill him. And having been killed, after three days he will rise up.' And they didn't know the thing. And they were afraid to ask him. And they came to Caphernaum. And being in the house, he asked them, 'What were you discussing on the road?' But they were silent. For they had been discussing against each other on the road, 'Who's greatest?' And he sat down, and addressed the twelve and says to them, 'If someone wants to be Number One, they will be last of all and servant of all.'

And he took a little child and placed it in the middle of them. And taking it in his arms, he said to them, 'Whoever receives one such child as this in my name receives me. And whoever receives me receives not me but the one who sent me.'

John said to him, 'Teacher, we saw someone in your name casting out demons, and we stopped him, because he didn't follow us.' And Jesus said, 'Don't stop him. For there's no one who can do a miracle in my name and will then quickly be able to bad-mouth me. For whoever is not against us is on our side. For whoever gives you a drink of water because you belong to Messiah, Amen I tell you, no way will that person lose their reward. And whoever makes one of these little ones stumble, who believe in me, it is good for him rather if a millstone worked by a donkey is put round his neck and he has been thrown into the sea. And if your hand causes you to stumble, cut if off: it is better for you to go deformed into life than to go with two hands into Gehenna, into the unquenched fire. And if your foot causes you to stumble, cut it off. It is better for you to enter life lame than to have two feet and be thrown into Gehenna. And if your eye causes you to stumble, throw it away: it is better for you to enter one-eyed into the kingdom of God than with two eyes to be thrown into Gehenna, where their worm does not die and the fire is not extinguished. For everyone will be salted by fire. Salt is good: but if that salt becomes saltless, with what will you season it? Have salt in yourselves. And be at peace among each other.'

A second time now Jesus predicts his own death (the first time was in the previous chapter, at Caesarea Philippi); a second time the disciples show they don't understand a word. This time, however, it's different. First, Mark emphasises that this is just for disciples ('he did not want anyone to know, for he was teaching his disciples . . . '). Second, the disciples turn out to have been discussing who was Top Apostle. So they have to be educated, but still take no notice, for no sooner has the lesson ended than John is begging for Jesus to praise him for not allowing someone to cast out demons in Jesus' name. Jesus has to tell them that the only thing that matters is to belong to the kingdom of God.

Notice how Mark has built up the final paragraph, using teachings with three 'keywords': 'stumble' (or 'scandal'), 'fire', and 'salt'. That may help you to understand what can otherwise be a rather difficult passage.

Three controversies: Pharisees and divorce; the disciples on children; the rich man and eternal life

10 ¹⁻³¹ And from there rising up he comes to the regions of Judaea and across the Jordan, and crowds came together to him, and as he was accustomed, again he started to teach them. And Pharisees approached and asked him, 'Does a man have authority to send a woman away?', testing him. But he answering said to them, 'What did Moses command you?' They said, 'Moses allowed us to "draw up a certificate of divorce and send her away".' Jesus said to them, 'It was with regard to your hard-heartedness that he wrote down this commandment for you. But from the beginning of creation, "male and female he created them. For this reason a man shall leave his father and mother and stick to his wife, and the two shall turn into one flesh". So – what God has yoked together, let human beings not separate.'

And back in the house the disciples asked him about this. And he says to them, 'Whoever sends his woman away and marries another commits adultery on her; and if she sends her husband away and marries another, she commits adultery.'

And they were offering him children, for him to touch them; but the disciples scolded them. But when Jesus saw [it] he was angry, and he said to them, 'Allow the children to come to me. Don't stop them – for of such is the kingdom of God. Amen I say to you, whoever does not receive the kingdom of God like a child, no way will that person enter it.' And taking them in his arms he blessed them, laying hands on them.

And he was going out on to the road, running up to one [person] and kneeling to him interrogated him, 'Good teacher, what shall I do in order that I may inherit eternal life?' But Jesus said to him, 'Why do you call me good? No one is good, except one, God. You know the commandments: "You shall not kill. You shall not commit adultery. You shall not steal. You shall not bear false witness. You shall not defraud. Honour your father and mother".' But he said to him, 'Teacher, all these things I have kept from my youth.' But Jesus fixed his gaze on him and loved him and said, 'One thing is missing for you. Go – whatever you have, sell it and give to the poor. And you will have treasure in heaven. And come here, follow me.'

But he was appalled at this remark and went off grieving. For he was a man who had many possessions. And looking around, Jesus says to his disciples, 'With what difficulty will those who have [material] things enter the kingdom of God.' And his disciples were astounded at his remarks. But Jesus again answering says to them, 'Children, how difficult it is to enter the kingdom of God. It is easier for a camel to go through the eye of a needle than for a rich person to enter the kingdom of God.' But they were overwhelmed beyond measure, saying to themselves, 'And who can be saved?' Fixing his gaze on them, Jesus says, 'For humans it's impossible, but not for God. You see, everything is possible for God.' Peter began to say to him, 'Look! We have abandoned everything, and have followed you.' Jesus says, 'Amen I say to you, there is no one who has abandoned home or brothers or sisters or mother or father or children or fields because of me and because of the gospel, but they will receive a hundredfold now in this time – houses and brothers and sisters and mothers and children and fields (along with persecutions) – and in the coming world, eternal life. You see, many first will be last, and last first.'

Another rather vague geographical introduction presents us with crowds and with Pharisees. The Pharisees ask an important question about when divorce is admissible. Jesus' answer is 'never'. The disciples are baffled by this, and also by his willingness to bless children; then an over-pious and over-affluent questioner interrogates him about eternal life. He goes off sad at the answer Jesus gives him. This in turn sows alarm and despondency among the disciples, and Peter. Finally Jesus gives them a clue about the mystery of discipleship: disciples 'will receive a hundredfold'.

Notice that Jesus and his interlocutors agree on the Old Testament as their starting-point: on marriage (Genesis 1:27; 2:24) and on the question of divorce (Deuteronomy 24:1-4).

More failure on the part of the disciples

32-45 Now they were on the road going up to Jerusalem, and Jesus was leading them [or: going before them], and they were astounded, and those who followed were afraid. And again taking the twelve he began to tell them the things that were about to happen to him: 'Look! We are going up to Jerusalem, and the Son of Man will be handed over to the high priests and to the scribes. And they will condemn him to death, and they will hand him over to Gentiles. And they will mock him, and they'll spit on him, and they'll whip him. And they will kill him. And after three days he will rise.'

And up to him come James and John, the sons of Zebedee, saying to him, 'Teacher, we want you to do for us whatever we ask you.' And he said to them, 'What do you want me to do for you?' And they said to him, 'Grant us that we should sit in your glory, one on your right and one on your left.' But Jesus said to them, 'You do not know what you are asking. Can you drink the cup that I drink? Or can you be baptised [in] the baptism [with] which I am to be baptised?' But they told him, 'We can.' But Jesus told them, 'The cup that I drink you will drink. And the baptism [with] which I am being baptised you shall be baptised. But to sit on the right or on the left is not mine to give; but it is [for those] for whom it has been prepared.' And hearing this, the ten began to be annoyed about James and John. And summoning them Jesus says to them, 'You know that those who think they rule the Gentiles dominate them. And their great ones exercise authority over them. Not so is it among you. Instead, whoever wants to be Number One among you will be everyone's slave. You see, the Son of Man did not come to be served, but to serve. And to give [his] life [as] a ransom for many.'

A third time Jesus explains to his disciples about his imminent death, and a third time they show that they have not understood a word. Notice how Mark sets it up: the road to Jerusalem (where we already know that he is going to die), and the fact that they were 'astounded' and 'afraid', all of this makes our mood quite sombre by the time Jesus actually starts talking about his suffering and death. Then the sons of Zebedee try and get in ahead of the rest, and have to be told, 'It's not like that'; and when the other ten start to get cross, they also have to be educated. So, linking discipleship to what Jesus is like, or to who Jesus is, we are told, with a clarity that we shall do well to heed, 'You see, the Son of Man did not come to be served, but to serve. And to give [his] life [as] a ransom for many.'

Bartimaeus: a disciple who gets it right

46-52 And they come to Jericho. And as he is going out of Jericho, and his disciples, and a fair old crowd, the son of Timaeus, Bartimaeus, a blind beggar, was sitting by the road. And hearing that it was Jesus the Nazarene, he began to cry out and say, 'Son of David, Jesus, have mercy on me.' And many people scolded him, that he should be silent. But he cried out much more, 'Son of David, have mercy on me.' And Jesus stood, and said, 'Call him.' And they call the blind man, telling him, 'Courage! Arise. He is calling you.' And he threw off his cloak, leapt up, and came to Jesus. Jesus responded to him and said, 'What do you want me to do for you?' And the blind man said to him, 'Rabbouni, that I may see again.' And Jesus said to him, 'Go. Your faith has saved you.' And immediately he saw again. And he followed him on the road.

This section of the Gospel began with one blind man being healed, and ends with another. We are invited to admire this one's persistence, despite the scolding of the people around him; we are cheered when Jesus summons him, perhaps a little alarmed as he strips off his clothes and blunders sightless through the crowd. Then he expresses clearly, and with absolute confidence, what he wants: 'that I may see again' – calling Jesus 'Rabbouni' as he does so.

Finally, this man who had been 'by the road' at the beginning of the story now 'followed him on the road'. He has become a disciple, and is cheerfully following Jesus, even though the road leads to Jerusalem and to death.

Jesus finally enters Jerusalem

11 **1-11** And when they drew nearer to Jerusalem, to Bethphage and Bethany, towards the Mountain of Olives, he sends two of his disciples and says to them, 'Go into the village that is opposite you. And immediately when you go into it you will find a colt tied up, on which no human being has ever sat. Untie it and bring it. And if someone says to you, "Why are you doing this?", say, "The Lord has need of it and he will send it back here immediately."' And they went off and found the colt tied at a door outside on the street. And they untie it. And some of those standing there started to say to them, 'What are you doing, untying the colt?' But they said to them as Jesus had said. And they let them go. And they take the colt to Jesus and they threw their cloaks on it; and he sat on it. And many people spread their cloaks on the road. And others [were] cutting leafy branches from the fields. And those who went before and those who followed cried out,

'Hosanna! Blessed the one who comes in the name of the Lord.
Blessed the coming kingdom of our father David!
Hosanna in the Highest!'

And he went into Jerusalem, into the Temple. And looking around at everything, the hour being already late, he went out to Bethany with the Twelve.

It has been a while coming, and our mood is now a bit grim, but here we are, on the outskirts of Jerusalem, the desert side, from which the Messiah was supposed to come. Jesus has it all under control, gives instructions for hijacking a donkey (one that is not used to being ridden, alarmingly enough). The procession goes ahead uneventfully, with cloaks and branches and a quotation from Psalm 118 (verses 25, 26, but read through the whole psalm, and remember that 'Hosanna' is the Hebrew for 'please save us'); and Jesus arrives in the Temple without being thrown by his beast of burden.

This has been an odd Gospel all the way through, and at this moment of apparent climax it does not cease to be so, for the Messiah comes triumphantly to Jerusalem, enters the Temple (as you would expect) and then, just as we are waiting for him to deliver independence and send the occupying Roman forces back into the sea, with an extraordinary sense of anti-climax he merely looks about the place and retires to Bethany!

The Temple and the fig tree

12-25 And on the next day, when they were coming from Bethany he was hungry. And seeing from a long way off a fig tree with leaves, he went to see if he should find anything on it. And coming to it he found nothing on it but leaves (for it was not the season for figs). And in response he said to it, 'No longer, for ever, may anyone eat fruit from you.' And his disciples heard.

And they came to Jerusalem. And going into the Temple he began to throw out those who sold and bought in the Temple. And the tables of the moneychangers and the seats of those who sold doves, he simply overturned. And he did not allow anyone to carry a vessel through the Temple. And he was teaching and telling them, 'Is it not written, "My house shall be called a house of prayer for all the Gentiles"? And you have made it a cave of brigands.' And the chief priests and the scribes heard. And they sought how they might destroy him. For they were afraid of him; for the whole crowd was overwhelmed at his teaching. And when it grew late they went outside the city.

And early in the morning as they went by, they saw the fig tree, withered from the roots. And, remembering, Peter says to him, 'Rabbi, look! The fig tree you cursed has withered!' And Jesus answering says to him, 'Have faith [in] God. Amen I tell you, whoever says to this mountain, "Be lifted up and be thrown into the sea", and does not doubt in their heart but believes that what they say is happening, it will be theirs. Therefore I tell you, everything that you pray and ask for, believe that you received it, and it will be yours.

'And whenever you stand praying, let it go if you have anything against anybody, so that your Father, the one in heaven, may let go of your transgressions for you.'

> This is an episode which has always puzzled readers. It is better, though, to see it as *two* episodes. Jesus' cursing of the fig tree often seems uncomfortably petulant, especially as 'it was not the season for figs'; but take the fig tree as a symbol of Israel, see the Temple as that which should always have borne fruit, whatever the season, if people had only been open to God, and it all starts to fall into place. What counts here is the Temple, which has become a shopping-mall ('cave of brigands') instead of 'a house of prayer' (Jesus here quotes Isaiah 56:7). For Jesus, the central relationship is his intimacy with the God whom he calls 'Father'; get that right, and Temples will be what they should be, the nation will bear fruit, and extraordinary things will start to happen; we may even learn to forgive one another.

Clashes with religious leaders about 'authority'

11²⁷-12⁴⁴ And they came again to Jerusalem. And as he was walking in the Temple the high priests and the scribes and the elders come to him, and they began to say to him, 'By what authority do you do these things? Or who gave you this authority that you should do these things?' And Jesus said to them, 'I shall ask you one thing; and you can answer me. And [then] I'll tell you by what authority I do these things. The baptism of John: was it from heaven or from human beings? Answer me.' And they argued among themselves, saying 'If we say, "From heaven", he'll say, "So why didn't you believe him?" But if we say, "From human beings . . . ".' (They were afraid of the crowd, for they all regarded John as really a prophet.) And they responded to Jesus, 'We don't know.' And Jesus says to them, 'Nor am I telling you by what authority I am doing these things.'

And he began to speak in parables, 'A man planted a vineyard; and he put a hedge round, and dug a trough, and built a tower. And he leased it to [tenant-] farmers, and went overseas. And at the season he sent a slave to the tenants, to accept some of the fruit of the vineyard from them. And they took him and flogged him and sent him away with nothing. And a second time he sent them another slave. This one they struck on the head and insulted. He sent a third slave. This one they killed, along with many others, some of whom they flogged, and others they killed. He still had one [resource?], a beloved son. He sent him last of all, saying, "They will have respect for my son." But those tenants said to themselves, "This is the heir. Come, let us kill him; and ours will be the inheritance." And they took him and killed him and flung him out of the vineyard. So what will the master of the vineyard do? He will come and destroy the tenants. And he will give the vineyard to others. Have you never even read the Scripture,

"A stone which the builders rejected,
this became the cornerstone.
This came from the Lord
and it is wonderful in our eyes"?'

And they sought to arrest him; and they feared the crowd. For they knew that it was in respect of them he told the parable. And abandoning him they went off. And they send to him some of the Pharisees and the Herodians, to catch him out verbally. And they come and say to him, 'Teacher, we know that you are for real, and you're not bothered about anybody, because you don't worry about people's status, but in truth you teach God's way. Is it authorised to pay poll tax to Caesar or not? Do we give it or not give it?' But he knew they were putting on an act, and he said, 'Why do you test me? Bring me a denarius, for me to look at.' They did so, and he says to them, 'Whose image and inscription is this?' And they said to him, 'Caesar's.' And Jesus said to them, 'What belongs to Caesar, pay to Caesar. And what belongs to God, pay it to God.' And they wondered greatly at him.

And Sadducees came to him, people who say there is no such thing as Resurrection. And they interrogated him, saying, 'Teacher, Moses wrote for us that if someone's brother dies and leaves a wife and he doesn't leave a child, then his brother should take his wife and raise up seed for his brother. There were seven brothers: and the first took a wife, and when he died he left no seed. So the second took her, and died, leaving no seed, and the third likewise. All seven left no seed. Last of all, the woman died. In the Resurrection, of which of them will she be the wife? For [all] seven had her as wife.' Jesus said to them, 'Is this not the reason that you go astray, that you do not know the scriptures or the power of God? For when they rise from the dead, they do not marry, nor are they given in marriage; instead, they are like angels in heaven. But with regard to the dead, for evidence that they are raised, did you not read in Moses' book, at the bush, how God told him, saying "I [am] the God of Abraham and the God of Isaac and the God of Jacob"? God is not God of corpses, but of the living. You are badly astray.'

And approaching, one of the scribes, hearing them argue, seeing that he had made a good answer to them, asked him, 'Which commandment is first of all?' Jesus replied, 'Number one is, "Hear, O Israel, the Lord our God is one Lord"; and "You will love the Lord your God out of your whole heart and your whole soul and your whole understanding and your whole strength." This is the second: "You will love your neighbour as yourself." Greater than these there is no other commandment.' And the scribe said to him, 'Beautifully [spoken], Teacher. Truly you said that [God] "is one and there is no other except for God". And "loving God out of one's whole heart and whole intelligence and whole strength" and "loving one's neighbour as oneself" is greater than all holocausts and sacrifices.' And Jesus, seeing that he replied thoughtfully, replied [and] said to him, 'You are not far from the kingdom of God.'

And no one dared any longer to interrogate him.

And in response Jesus was saying as he taught in the Temple, 'How do the scribes say that the Messiah is the son of David? You see, David himself said in the Holy Spirit,

> "The Lord said to my Lord:
> Sit at my right
> until I place your enemies beneath your feet."

'David himself calls [Messiah] "Lord", so how come [Messiah] is his son?' And the crowd used to listen to him with delight.

And in his teaching he was saying, 'Look away from the scribes who want to walk about in long robes, and [who want] greetings in market places, and front-row seats in synagogues, and Number One spots at banquets. These people who devour the houses of widows, and make a pretence of praying for a long time: they are the ones who will receive an overwhelming judgement.'

And sitting opposite the Treasury, he was gazing at how the crowd threw their change into the Treasury. And lots of wealthy people put in lots. Then there came a single destitute widow-woman: and she threw in two tiny [coins], a farthing.

And summoning his disciples, he told them, 'Amen I tell you: this widow, the destitute woman, threw more than all who threw [money] into the Treasury. You see, they all threw [in] from their surplus. But she, from her poverty, threw [in] everything she had, her whole life.'

The episode where Jesus threw the money-changers out of the Temple raised questions about Jesus' 'authority', an issue that has been present since the beginning of the Gospel; and now the quarrel is out in the open. It starts with an attempt to trap Jesus, which he easily turns back on his opponents, adding for good measure the parable of the vineyard, which obviously echoes Isaiah 5:1-7 ('the vineyard of the Lord of Hosts is the House of Israel'), but also clearly foreshadows Jesus' own death at his opponents' hands.

Then comes a lethal trap, set by the unlikely combination of Herodians and Pharisees whom we have seen before (3:6), about the poll tax. Jesus easily sidesteps the trap, only to be assailed by yet another group, the Sadducees, trying to demonstrate the absurdity of belief in Resurrection. Not for the first time, Jesus uses the Torah to combat their own use of it (Exodus 3:6).

Next comes what at first sight looks like yet another attack on him, concerning the difficult question of which commandment is the most important, but it turns into a most unexpected and warming meeting of minds, as Jesus and the scribe discover that they are speaking the same language.

Once again it is worth noting that Jesus draws on his easy mastery of the Old Testament, quoting Deuteronomy 6:5 (which a prayerful Jew will say three times a day) and Leviticus 19:18.

Then Jesus goes on to the attack, demonstrating (from Scripture again, see Psalm 110:1) that the Messiah is actually David's Lord – and thereby making a claim that will certainly have annoyed his opponents. From there he delivers an aggressive warning about the 'scribes', whom we have increasingly, all through the Gospel, learnt to see as the enemy. And no sooner have we heard them dismissed as those who 'devour the houses of widows' than Jesus singles out precisely a poor widow as the most generous person in that very Temple where he has just made his outrageous prophetic gesture. She, and not the buyers and sellers, nor the religious people, is attentive to God.

The coming destruction

13 ¹⁻³⁷ And as he was going out of the Temple, one of his disciples says to him, 'Teacher, look what stones, and what buildings!' And Jesus said to him, 'Do you see these great buildings? There will not be left here a stone upon a stone that will not be destroyed.'

And as he was sitting on the Mountain of Olives opposite the Temple, Peter and James and John and Andrew asked him privately, 'Tell us when these things will be, and what is the sign when all these things are about to be accomplished?' And Jesus began to say to them, 'Look out, that no one lead you astray. Many will come in my name, saying "I AM", and they will lead many astray. But when you hear of wars and rumours of wars, don't be frightened. It must happen, but the end [is] not yet. For nation shall be raised against nation and kingdom against kingdom. There shall be earthquakes in places; there will be famines. These things are the beginnings of [the] birth-pangs. But you, look at yourselves: they will betray you to Sanhedrins and Synagogues. You will be flogged, and you will be stood before procurators and kings, for my sake, as witness to them.

'And the gospel has first to be preached to all the nations. And when they take you, handing [you] over, don't get agitated beforehand [about] what you will say. Instead, whatever is given to you at that hour, say that. For it isn't you who are saying [it], but the Holy Spirit. And brother will hand over brother to death, and a father a child. And children will rebel against parents and put them to death. And you will be hated by all because of my name. But the one who endures to the end – that one will be saved.

'But when you see the abomination of desolation standing where it ought not (let the reader understand), then let those in Judaea flee into the mountains. Let the one [who is] on top of the house not come down, nor enter the house to take anything out. And the one who goes into the field, let him not turn back to take his cloak. Woe to women who are pregnant and who are suckling in those days. Pray that it doesn't happen in wintertime: for those days will be tribulation, such as has not occurred like this from the beginning of the creation which God created until now, and will not happen again. And if the Lord did not curtail the days, no flesh would be saved. But because of the chosen ones whom he chose he curtailed the days.

'And then, if anyone tells you, "Look! Here is the Messiah!" or "Look! There!" don't believe [them]. For there shall arise false Messiahs and false prophets and they shall give signs and portents, so as to lead astray, were it possible, even the chosen. But you see: I have predicted everything for you.

'But in those days after the tribulation,
    the sun will be darkened
    and the moon shall not give her light.
    And the stars shall be falling from heaven
    and the powers in the heavens shall totter.

'And then they shall see the Son of Man coming on clouds with much power and glory. And then he will send his angels, and he will gather together the chosen ones from the four winds, from the furthest point of the earth to the furthest point of heaven.

'From the fig tree learn the parable. When its branch now becomes tender and it puts forth leaves, you know that the summer [or: harvest] is near. So you, when you see these things happening, you know that he is close upon the gates. Amen I tell you, no way will this generation pass away until all these things happen. Heaven and earth shall pass away: but my words shall not pass away.

'But about that day or that hour no one knows, not even the angels in heaven, nor the Son, but only the Father. Look, stay awake. For you do not know when the time is. Like a man who went overseas, left his house and gave his slaves his authority, for each his own work, and instructed the gatekeeper to stay awake. So you stay awake. For you do not know when the Lord of the house comes, whether late in the day or in the middle of the night or at cockcrow or early in the morning. [Be careful] lest he come suddenly and find you sleeping. What I say to you I say to all: stay awake!'

This alarming and dramatic speech continues the mysterious discomfort that we have experienced throughout the Gospel. It starts with the naïve admiration of a spiritual tourist among the disciples, exclaiming over the beauty of Herod's Temple; but Jesus has twice already given his verdict on the Temple, and now he predicts its destruction. The 'inner cabinet' (plus Andrew, for once) asks him about the when and the how, but Jesus is prepared only to tell them that it will be tough, but that (also) all will be well, provided that they don't get too credulous. He quotes Isaiah 13:10 and 34:4 to give an idea of how dreadful it will all be, how unreliable all will seem to be that we have hitherto relied on. So we have to be alert for the signs, but not pretend to know too much: 'stay awake' is (literally) the watchword.

Introducing the Passion; another 'Marcan sandwich'

14 ¹⁻¹¹ Now it was the Passover and Unleavened Bread after two days. And the high priests and the scribes were trying to see how they could arrest him by stealth and kill him. For they were saying, 'Not at the festival, lest there be a popular riot.'

And while he was in Bethany at the house of Simon the leper, while he lay down to dine, there came a woman. She had an alabaster jar of myrrh, pistachio-nard, genuine and very expensive. She broke the alabaster jar and poured it over his head. And there were some people getting quietly indignant: 'To what end has this waste of myrrh taken place? For this myrrh could have been sold for more than three hundred denarii, and given to the poor.' And they snorted indignantly at her. But Jesus said, 'Leave her be. Why do you give her hassle? She has worked a good work in [regard to] me. For it is always the case that you have the poor with you; and whenever you want you can be bountiful to them. But me you do not always have. She has done what her resources allowed: she took an early opportunity to anoint my body for burial. But, Amen I tell you, wherever the gospel is preached in the whole world, even what she has done will be spoken of in remembrance of her.'

And Judas Iscariot (one of the Twelve) went off to the high priests to betray him to them. And when they heard they rejoiced; and they promised to give him money. And he started to look to see how he might betray him at an appropriate time.

Suddenly, with the imminence of the Passover (the first time that this great feast has been mentioned in the Gospel) we are rushing towards the end that we have seen coming for some time now. Mark introduces the story with one of his 'sandwiches'. He wraps the story of the high priests and scribes wanting to commit discreet homicide, and their finding a willing accomplice in Judas, round a quite different story, of the anointing at the house of Simon the leper. The woman who performs this unconventional action (presenting Jesus as Messiah) is clearly the story's heroine, her generosity contrasting with the murderous plans of the religious leaders and the treachery of Judas, and the small-mindedness of Jesus' fellow guests. Hers is not the whole story, however, for Jesus gives another verdict on what she has done; she has anointed him for his 'burial'. These two stories, mixing generosity and love with some notably less attractive emotions, are Mark's way of telling us how to read the Passion Narrative.

A Passover meal gone wrong

12-25 And on the first day of Unleavened Bread, when they were sacrificing the Passover, his disciples said to him, 'Where do you want us to go and prepare for you to eat the Passover?' And he sends two of his disciples and says to them, 'Go into the city; and a man carrying a jar of water will meet you. Follow him. And wherever he enters, tell the master of the house, "The teacher says, 'Where is my lodging, where I may eat the Passover with my disciples?'." And he will show you a big upstairs room furnished and ready. And there prepare for us.'

And the disciples went out and went to the city; and they found [things] as he had said to them. And they prepared the Passover.

And when it grows late he comes with the Twelve. And as they lay down and were eating, Jesus said, 'Amen I say to you, one of you will betray me, the one who is eating with me.' They began to grieve, and to say to him, one by one, 'Surely it's not me, is it?' And he said to them, 'One of the Twelve, the one who dips his hand into the bowl with me. Because the Son of Man goes as it is written about him. But woe to that person through whom the Son of Man is handed over. It [would be] good for him if that person had not been born.'

And as they were eating, he took bread, blessed, broke, and gave it to them, and said, 'Take, this is my body.' And he took a cup and gave thanks, and gave it to them. And they all drank of it. And he said to them, 'This is my blood of the covenant. It is poured out for many. Amen I tell you that no way any longer shall I drink of the fruit of the vine until that day when I drink it new in the kingdom of God.'

After the sandwiched story of the anointing, we attend the Passover meal. This is the greatest and most joyous meal of the Jewish year, but our expectations are going to be disappointed. We note that in the crowded city of Jerusalem the disciples have only just wondered about making arrangements. Fortunately Jesus has already set something up on his own account. That, however, is the last piece of good news for a while, because no sooner has the meal begun than Jesus predicts that one of those sharing this great occasion with him will betray him, an almost unimaginable offence against the Near Eastern code of hospitality. Nor does the mood lift very much as he takes the bread and wine and says, 'This is my body . . . this is my blood of the covenant. It is poured out for many.' Whatever else this means, it sounds like death.

Gethsemani: idle boasting, and a desperately serious prayer

26-42 And they sang a hymn and went out to the Mountain of Olives. And Jesus said to them, 'You will all be led into sin, because it is written,

> "I shall strike the shepherd
> and the sheep shall be scattered."

'But after I have been raised I shall go before you [or: lead you] into Galilee.' And Peter said to him, 'Even if all [the others] are led into sin . . . but not me.' And Jesus says to him, 'Amen I say to you: Today, this very night, before the cock crows twice, you will deny me three times.' And he started to babble with great emphasis, 'Even if it is necessary for me to die with you, no way shall I deny you.' And they all talked in the same vein.

And they come to a place whose name is Gethsemani. And he says to his disciples, 'Sit here, while I pray.' And he takes along Peter and James and John with him. And he began to be distressed and in anxiety. And he says to them, 'My soul is very sad, even to death: remain here, and keep awake.' And going a little bit forward, he fell on the earth. And he prayed that if it were possible the hour might pass away from him. And he said, 'Abba, Father, everything is possible for you. Remove this cup from me. But not "What do I want?" but "What do you want?".' And he comes and finds them sleeping, and he says to Peter, 'Simon, are you sleeping? Did you not have the strength to stay awake for a single hour? Watch and pray, that you may not come into temptation. The spirit is eager; but the flesh is sick.' And again he went off and prayed, saying the same thing. And again he came and found them sleeping. For their eyes were weighed down. And they didn't know what to say to him. And he comes the third time and says to them, 'Are you going to sleep and lounge about for the rest [of your lives]? That's it. The hour has come. Look! The Son of Man is being betrayed into the hands of sinners. Arise – let us go! Look: the one who betrays me has drawn near.'

Singing a hymn sounds cheerful enough; but there is not much else to be cheerful about, and the alert reader will in any case be reflecting that leaving the city for the Mountain of Olives sounds like a strategic withdrawal. Jesus warns them (citing the prediction of Zechariah 13:7) that they are on the point of abandoning him.

All of them, but most especially Peter, protest the impossibility of this: 'even if all the others . . . even if it's necessary for me to die with you . . .'

Then he tells the disciples to sit, and takes the 'inner cabinet', and asks them simply to keep awake while he prays to the Father. Mark permits us to eavesdrop on his prayer: 'Abba, Father' is the confident address; but the content is sad and fearful: 'Remove this cup from me.' Like all the best stories, this one comes in three parts, and each time, after his desperate prayer, Jesus finds the disciples asleep. That is all there is to it: we do not hear any response from the Father. Nevertheless it is noticeable that Jesus walks tall after this, so presumably something happened in the course of that prayer.

The loneliness of Jesus

43-52 And immediately, while he was still speaking, Judas, one of the Twelve, appears, and with him a crowd with swords and cudgels, from the high priests and scribes and elders. The one who was betraying him had given them a secret signal, saying, 'The one whom I'll kiss – that's the one. Arrest him and lead him securely away.' And when he came he immediately came to him and says, 'Rabbi', and he kissed him. And they laid hands on him and arrested him. And one of the bystanders drawing his sword struck the High Priest's slave and took off his ear lobe. And Jesus responded and told them, 'As though I were a brigand, you've come out to seize me with swords and cudgels. Every day I was with you, teaching in the Temple: and you didn't arrest me. But let the scriptures be fulfilled.'

And they abandoned him; and every one of them fled.

And a certain young man was following along with him, wearing a linen cloth over his naked body. And they arrest him. But he cast aside the linen cloth and fled naked.

At this point, Jesus is arrested (by now that comes as no surprise); the arresting party is led, as Mark emphasises, by 'one of the Twelve', and comes, armed to the teeth, representing the religious authorities. The act of betrayal is performed with a formal greeting ('Rabbi'), and a kiss, which underlines the horror of it. A pathetic attempt at resistance (cutting off a slave's ear lobe!) is clearly both irrelevant and useless. Jesus is able to manage an ironic comment on what is happening; but no one else can manage anything at all: 'they abandoned him; and every one of them fled'. The mysterious young man who runs away naked could be absolutely anybody (scholars and other readers have made some interesting guesses!) – certainly one of his functions is to emphasise Jesus' utter loneliness.

The Sanhedrin looks for (and finds) evidence against Jesus

53-65 And they led Jesus to the High Priest, and all the high priests and elders and scribes came together. And Peter followed him from a long way off, right into the High Priest's courtyard. And he was sitting in with the other servants, and warming himself towards the light.

And the high priests and the whole Sanhedrin began to look for evidence against Jesus in order to put him to death. And they couldn't find [any]. For many gave false witness against him: and their evidence didn't match up. And some got up and bore false witness, to the effect: 'We heard him say, "I shall destroy this Temple made by hand, and in three days I shall build another, not made by hands."' And not even then did their evidence match up. And the High Priest rose up in the middle and interrogated Jesus, saying, 'Do you make no response? What evidence are these people bringing against you?' But he was silent, and made no response at all.

Again the High Priest interrogated him and says to him, 'Are you the Messiah, the Son of the Blessed One?' And Jesus said, 'I AM. And "You will see the Son of Man sitting on the right side of power" and "coming with the clouds of heaven".' And the High Priest tore his garments and said, 'Why do we need any more witnesses? You heard the blasphemy. How does it seem to you?' And they all condemned him as liable to the death penalty. And some people began to spit on him and cover his head, and to strike him and say to him, 'Prophesy.' And the servants received him with blows.

> Now comes the first judicial hearing, Jesus before the High Priest and Sanhedrin. Mark is quite clear that their aim is death, but also that they want some colourable evidence. There is a promising claim about destroying the Temple and building another in three days, which they might have linked with his prophetic gesture of driving out the commercial interests from the Temple, but since Jesus is saying nothing, there is not much going for them. Finally, the High Priest asks the question that has been lurking just below the surface of the text all the way through this Gospel: 'Are you the Messiah, the Son of the Blessed One?' We, the reader, have known the answer to this question since the Gospel's very first line, but it is nevertheless a surprise when Jesus roundly declares 'I AM' (quoting as he does so our old friends Daniel 7:13 and Psalm 110:1), and so allows the charge of blasphemy to have some substance.

Peter has never heard of Jesus

66-72 And Peter was still below in the courtyard. And there comes a single little slave girl of the High Priest. And seeing Peter warming himself she had a good look at him and says, 'You were also with the Nazarene, [that] Jesus.' And he denied it, saying, 'I neither know nor understand what you are saying.' And he went out into the forecourt. And the little slave girl saw him and began again to say to the bystanders, 'This [fellow] is from that lot.' And he again denied [it]. And again after a little the bystanders started to say to Peter, 'You must certainly be [one] of them: you're a Galilean.' And he began to curse and swear, 'I don't know this fellow you're talking about.'

And immediately for the second time a cock crowed. And Peter remembered the word, how Jesus had told him, 'Before the cock crows twice, three times you will deny me.'

And he thought of it and wept.

Jesus is not, it turns out, quite alone, because Peter has 'followed from a long way off'. Now, though, Peter is going to be tested (as Jesus had warned him). Absurdly (and Mark does nothing to hide the absurdity) the instrument of testing is the not very frightening figure of just one 'little slave girl', who says, quite correctly, 'You were with the Nazarene'. Peter won't admit that, under any circumstances, even when confronted with bystanders, and with the evidence of his dreadful Galilean accent: 'I don't know the fellow you're talking about.' Then the cock crows, and Peter remembers, and dissolves into saving and healing tears.

Pilate reluctantly agrees to Jesus' death

15 [1-15] And immediately, early in the morning, they held a consultation, the high priests with the elders and scribes and the whole Sanhedrin. And they bound Jesus and led him away and handed him over to Pilate. And Pilate interrogated him, 'You are the "King of the Jews"?' But he answered and said, 'You say so.' And the high priests made many accusations against him. And Pilate interrogated him again, saying, 'You do not respond? Look how many things they accuse you of!' But Jesus no longer made any response, so that Pilate wondered.

Now at the feast he used to free for them one prisoner whom they requested. And there was the one known as Barabbas, who had been imprisoned with the revolutionaries who had committed murder in the revolt. And the crowd came up and began to ask [Pilate to do] what he used to do for them. And Pilate responded to them, saying, 'Do you want me to release the "King of the Jews" to you?' For he knew that it was out of spite that the high priests had handed him over. And the high priests incited the crowd that he should rather release Barabbas to them. And Pilate again responded; and he was saying to them, 'So what do you want me to do with the "King of the Jews"?' And they again screamed out, 'Crucify him.' And Pilate tried to say to them, 'Why? What crime has he committed?' And they screamed out all the more, 'Crucify him.'

Then Pilate, wanting to do enough [to please] the crowd, released Barabbas to them. And he handed Jesus over to be crucified, having scourged him.

> The Sanhedrin now holds a second session, after which they finally bring the local Roman governor into the matter. Pilate hardly knows what is going on, despairingly asking if Jesus is 'King of the Jews' (about the only concept he can grasp); like the High Priest before him, he gets nothing out of Jesus. Nor, when he tries to release Jesus, does he get anything out of the crowd (which Mark blames on the high priests). Everyone seems, on this account, agreed that Jesus has done nothing to deserve it; but there he is, being scourged in preparation for a horrible death.

The journey to Golgotha

[16-24] And the soldiers led him inside the courtyard, which is the praetorium. And they call together the whole cohort. And they clothe him in purple and place on him a thorny wreath which they wove. And they began to acclaim him, 'Hail, King of the

Jews.' And they started to beat his head with a reed; and they were spitting on him, and they were kneeling down and worshipping him.

And when they had mocked him, they took the purple off him, and put his own clothes on him. And they take him out to crucify him.

And they conscript a certain passer-by, Simon, a Cyrenean coming in from the countryside, the father of Alexander and Rufus, to carry his cross. And they take him to the place Golgotha, which when it is translated is 'Place of the Skull'. And they tried to give him wine flavoured with myrrh – but he didn't take it. And they crucify him. And they 'divide his garments, casting a lot over them [to see] who would get something'.

Two quite different things happen now. First, the soldiers, picking up the idea that 'this one thinks he's a king!' have a little game, dressing him up and doing a horrible parody of respect for a king. Second, though, these same soldiers conscript an African to help Jesus. Mark tells us that this Simon is 'the father of Alexander and Rufus'; now the only reason Mark mentions their names must be that his church knows them. So something must have happened to Simon of Cyrene that day, to turn his sons into disciples; and that is the first bit of good news that we have had for a long time. Someone tries to reduce Jesus' pain by giving him 'wine flavoured with myrrh', but he refuses, and Golgotha lives up to its grim name, as they squabble over who's to have his clothes.

The quotation about 'dividing his garments' is from Psalm 22:18. The early Christians had clearly meditated on this psalm, to try and find some meaning in the awful event of Jesus' crucifixion. Jesus' dying words, in the next section, may well be a quotation of its opening line. Read through the psalm, and see what other details surface in Mark's text hereabouts.

A very lonely death

25-37 Now it was the third hour, and they crucified him. And the inscription of his charge was inscribed 'The King of the Jews'. And with him they crucify two brigands, one on [the] right and one on his left. And the passers-by started to blaspheme him, nodding their heads and saying, 'Aha! The chap who destroys the Temple and builds it in three days! Save yourself [by] coming down from the cross!' Likewise the high priests were making mocking comments to each other, along with the scribes, 'He saved others; himself he cannot save. Let the "Messiah", the "King of Israel", come down from the cross, now, so that we may see and believe.'

Even those crucified along with him reviled him.

And when it came to the sixth hour, darkness came on the whole land until the ninth hour. And at the ninth hour Jesus shouted in a loud voice, 'Eloi, eloi, lema sabachthani?' which when it is translated is, 'My God, my God, for what purpose did you abandon me?' And some of the bystanders, hearing [this], started to say, 'Look – he is calling on Elijah.' And someone ran and filled a sponge with vinegar and put it round a stick and gave it to him to drink, saying, 'Wait – let's see if Elijah is coming to take him down.' But Jesus, letting out a great shout, expired.

Now Mark, with unusual exactness, tells us that Jesus was on the cross for six agonising hours. On his right and left, in a terrible parody of a ruler's enthronement, are his two 'co-rulers', whom Mark dismisses as 'brigands'. Then, instead of the normal fawning sycophancy, Jesus gets abuse from passers-by, 'Save yourself'; from high priests and scribes, 'Let the "Messiah", the "King of Israel", come down from the cross now'; and finally from his fellow convicts.

Then comes Nature's comment on what is happening: 'darkness . . . until the ninth hour', and a heart-rending cry of loneliness: 'My God, my God, for what purpose did you abandon me?' Some readers note that these are the opening words of Psalm 22, which ends with an encouraging cry of joy. That may be so, but Mark quotes the phrase in Jesus' native Aramaic, not in the Hebrew in which the Psalms were written, and I think that Mark intends us to feel the loneliness. No one understands him, anyway – they think that perhaps Elijah may drop in. As we hear this, we reflect that hope was not very far below the surface of those who watched Jesus die: perhaps after all, he might have been the real thing . . . ?

The final, remarkable verdict

38, 39 And the veil of the Temple was torn in two, from the top to the very bottom. And seeing that he expired in this way, the centurion who stood by, over against him, said, 'Truly this man was Son of God.'

Now that Jesus is safely dead, we hear the verdict on his life. First there is the tearing of the Temple veil. Clearly we are intended to read this as God's comment on Jesus' death, and on the part played in it by the Temple authorities.

The second verdict is even more remarkable. For the centurion who has watched Jesus die in this appalling, and appallingly lonely, way now gives his comment: 'Truly this man was Son of God.' Now we, the reader, have known this since the opening line of the Gospel, and even if we hadn't, we have twice heard God saying so. This verdict, on the lips of such a man, is the climax of the Gospel's remarkable treatment of who Jesus is: a mysterious and very different Messiah, but Messiah and Son of God nevertheless.

The circumstances of Jesus' burial

40-47 And there were women looking at him from afar, among whom were also Mary the Magdalene, and Mary mother of James the Little and of Joses, and Salome, the women who when he was in the Galilee used to follow him and minister to him, and many other women who came with him up to Jerusalem.

And when it had already become late, since it was Preparation Day, which is the day before the Sabbath, there came Joseph, the one from Arimathea. He was a reputable councillor; and he was also waiting for the kingdom of God. He was daring enough to go to Pilate and ask for the body of Jesus. And Pilate wondered if he was already dead [or: was surprised that he should be already dead]. And he summoned the centurion and asked if he was long dead. And when he had confirmation from the centurion, he gifted the corpse to Joseph. And he bought a linen cloth and took him down and wrapped him in the linen cloth and placed him in a tomb which was hewn out of rock. And he rolled a stone on to the door of the tomb.

And Mary the Magdalene and Mary [the mother] of Joses were watching where he lay.

> Jesus was properly dead, no question about it, and now we see him buried. First, though, we discover that he was not as alone as we had feared: it turns out that the brave women were there, who had followed him from Galilee. Then a male follower of Jesus comes out of the woodwork: Joseph of Arimathea, whom we have not heard of before, but who is clearly quite serious about his discipleship. Finally (in case we should wonder if anyone actually knew where the tomb was), we learn that two women were at the site.

Three endings to the Gospel

16 [1-20] And when the Sabbath was at last over, Mary the Magdalene, and Mary the mother of James, and Salome bought spices in order to come and anoint him. And extremely early on the first of the Sabbaths they come to the tomb. The sun had already risen. And they said to themselves, 'Who will roll away the stone for us from the door of the tomb?' And looking up [or: recovering their sight] they see that the stone has been rolled away. For it was very big. And going into the tomb they saw a young man sitting on the right wearing a white robe. And they were alarmed. But he said to the women, 'Do not be alarmed. You seek Jesus the Nazarene, the one who was crucified. He is risen; he is not here. See the place where they put him. But go, tell his disciples, and Peter, that "he is going before you [or: leading you] into the Galilee. There you will see him, as he said to you".' And going out they fled from the tomb, for quivering and astonishment had hold of them. And they said nothing to anybody. For they were afraid . . .

> Most scholars today regard this as the original ending of Mark's Gospel, and the 'long' and short endings, printed overleaf, as additions made by people who were not the original author, and who regarded this as an unsuitable ending. But it is a marvellous passage: you can feel the impatience of these women, as they grind their way through the Sabbath, before they can buy spices to do the needful for Jesus' dead body (and notice, by the way, that they evidently did not believe in the Resurrection; you can only anoint dead bodies if they stay where they are put). Mark makes, perhaps, a little joke at their expense, when he says that 'the sun had already risen'; and if the reader is inclined to berate the women for their improvidence in not thinking in advance about how to roll the stone away, then just ask where Jesus' male followers are at this moment. Then there is the young man, and the information that he already has, and the precious proclamation that he gives them: 'he is risen'. Then there is the flight of the women; but there is a clue even there: 'quivering and astonishment' is a sign of the presence of God. This is a powerful ending.

The 'long ending' [16:9-20]	The 'short ending'
But being resurrected early on the first day of the week he appeared to Mary the Magdalene, from whom he had cast out seven demons. She went and announced to those with him, who had taken to mourning and weeping. And they, hearing that he was alive and had been seen by her did not believe [or: had no faith]. And after this he appeared in a different form to two of them who were walking to the country. And they went and announced it to the rest. And they did not even believe them. Later, he appeared to the eleven themselves as they were at table and he reproached them for their faithlessness and hardness of heart, because they had not believed those who had seen him resurrected. And he said to them, 'Go into the whole world. Proclaim the gospel to all creation. The one who believes and is baptised will be saved; but the faithless [or: the one who does not believe] will be condemned. These signs will follow those who do believe: in my name, they will expel demons. They will speak in new languages. And in their hands they will lift up snakes. And if they drink anything lethal it will not harm them. They will lay hands on the sick and they will be well.' And so the Lord Jesus after speaking to them was taken up into heaven and sat at the right hand of God. Meanwhile they went out and preached everywhere, the Lord working with them and confirming their word through the signs that followed them.	They concisely proclaimed all the instructions to those [who were gathered] around Peter.

And after this, Jesus himself, from east as far as the west sent out through them the holy and imperishable proclamation of eternal salvation. Amen. |

In a fit of generosity, the manuscripts now give us not one but three endings to the Gospel. The 'long ending' and the 'short ending' probably suggest an attempt by later authors to patch up what they thought to be Mark's failure to produce a proper ending. The 'long ending' is really a series of scenes taken from other Gospels and from Acts, while the 'short ending' is just a way of bringing the story to a suitable conclusion.

It looks, therefore, as though the Gospel originally ended at 16:8, 'And they said nothing to anybody. For they were afraid . . . ' Now it may have been rats or mice that ate the original ending of the manuscript. But as we have read the Gospel together, we have seen how mysterious it is, with its subtle portrayal of what Jesus is like, and what his disciples must be like; and certainly such an ending would fit. And, of course, we know that the women must have said something to someone, or we should not be reading this extra-ordinary Gospel.

According to Luke

Introduction

Luke's Gospel is undeniably the most charming of the four; but it has an underlying toughness that we ignore at our peril.

Luke tells all the best stories. It is a fair bet, for example, that your favourite parable comes from this Gospel; and Luke is the gentlest of the evangelists, but we should notice that he is very strong indeed on the dangers of money and of material possessions.

The other thing to remember, all the time, is that this Gospel, the longest of the four, is the first part of a two-volume work that we may call Luke-Acts.

The Prologue

1 ¹⁻⁴ Seeing that a good many people have set their hand to compile a narrative of the things that have been fulfilled amongst us, just as those who from the beginning were eyewitnesses and ministers of the word have handed down to us, I also have decided, having investigated everything from the outset, to write it down for you, most excellent Theophilus, carefully and in order. My intention is that you should have a complete knowledge of the truth of the things which you have been taught.

Luke's is the only Gospel to start with a statement of what he is about (unless you count the rather brief heading which Mark offers); and it may be helpful for our reading of the Gospel if we start by looking at what he says. First, it is addressed to 'most excellent Theophilus', who might be a real person, of high social standing, perhaps one of the Equites, who formed the second rank of Roman society. Or, given that the name Theophilus means 'Lover of God' or 'Beloved by God', it might be addressed to any interested Christian.

Second, Luke's language shows that he is aiming at some kind of historical accuracy: he even suggests that his predecessors (Mark?) have not succeeded in this aim. And we notice his insistence on careful investigation, and his stated intention of writing 'carefully and in order', and his stress on the importance of 'eyewitnesses'.

Third, however, Luke is not just trying to write history. The alert reader will have noticed one or two words that belong rather in the area of religious education: 'hand down', 'fulfilled', 'ministers', 'truth' (or 'infallibility') of the things which you have been taught (or 'catechised'). So there is a religious aim here also.

Finally, notice that Jesus is not mentioned here, nor anywhere in Chapter 1 until we reach the encounter between the angel Gabriel and Mary; so presumably this work is intended for circulation only among Christians, who already know what it is about.

The Annunciation of John the Baptist (5-25)

Setting the scene

⁵⁻⁷ There was in the days of Herod, King of Judaea, a certain priest, Zachariah by name, of the division of Abijah; and his wife was of the daughters of Aaron, and her name was Elisabeth. They were both upright before God, walking blameless in all the commandments and precepts of the Lord. And they had no child, because Elisabeth was barren, and they were both advanced in their days.

Luke is the most artistic of all the Gospels, and probably more of Luke's stories have been painted than those in any other Gospel. We see his artistry here, deft touches that set the scene; and we need to stand back and admire the entire composition. He starts with the story of John the Baptist, who is in turn going to point to the more important reality of Jesus. Neither figure has been mentioned so far, and yet the reader is following without difficulty. Such is Luke's skill.

Now look at the details. First of all, the air we are breathing here is that of the Old Testament. Even Luke's language makes that point (though it is hard to put it into English without sounding contrived). We notice this charming couple, both of priestly ancestry (she is 'of the daughters of Aaron'); so John the Baptist's parentage is similar to that of the prophet Jeremiah. They are observant Jews, 'walking blameless in all the commandments and precepts of the Lord'. And they have no child – so readers familiar with the Hebrew Bible know that, according to the rules of the game, a child is on its way. Even the names signal that something important is going ahead. Zachariah means 'the Lord has remembered', Abijah, 'My Father is the Lord', and Elisabeth, 'My God has sworn an oath'.

Finally, look at the first name we meet: 'in the days of Herod, King of Judaea'. Here we see another instance of Luke's artistry. For there is a clear echo here of the Books of Kings, where events are frequently dated by the reigns of one or other of the Kings of Judah or Israel (see, for example, 1 Kings 15:1, 9); and so the reader is immediately transported into the world of the Old Testament. The name of Herod, however, strikes a jarring note; any member of that family is liable to mean trouble, and this particular one was 'Herod the Great', the most remarkable fact about whom is that he succeeded in dying in his bed (albeit very unpleasantly, according to the Jewish historian Josephus). The readers of Luke's Gospel will have been well aware that it was his son who would appear in Luke's account of Jesus' last days (Luke 23:7ff.).

First appearance of the angel Gabriel

8-25   It came to pass, as [Zachariah] was doing his priestly duty, in the appointed order of his division, before God; according to the custom of the priesthood it fell to his lot to enter the Temple of the Lord and burn incense. And the whole crowd of the populace was praying outside at the hour of the incense offering. And the angel of the Lord appeared to him, standing on the right of the altar of incense. And Zachariah was disturbed when he saw it; and fear fell upon him. And the angel said to him, 'Do not be afraid, Zachariah, because your supplication has been heard, and your wife Elisabeth will bear a son for you, and you will call his name John. And there shall be joy and exultation and many will rejoice at his birth, for he shall be great before the Lord. "And he shall not drink wine and strong drink" and he shall be filled with the Holy Spirit right from his mother's womb. And he shall turn many of the children of Israel to the Lord their God. And he shall go before him in the spirit and power of Elijah, to turn the hearts of fathers to their children and the disobedient [so as to walk] in the understanding of justice, to prepare for the Lord a people that has been made ready.'

And Zachariah said to the angel, 'How shall I know this? For I am old, and my wife is advanced in her years.'

And the angel replied and said to him, 'I am Gabriel, who stands before God. And I was sent to speak to you, and to give you these good tidings. And look! you will be silent and unable to speak until the day when these things came to pass, because you did not believe these words of mine, which *will* be fulfilled at their right time.'

And the populace [was] waiting for Zachariah, and they were astonished that he took so long in the Temple. When he came out, he could not speak to them, and they realised that he had seen a vision in the Temple. And he kept nodding to them, and he remained dumb. And it came to pass that when the days of his service were fulfilled, he went back to his home.

After these days, Elisabeth his wife conceived, and she hid herself for six months, saying, 'Thus the Lord has done for me in the days when he looked with favour on me, to take away my shame in the eyes of human beings.'

Luke the artist is very much in evidence here. The biblical tone of his Greek continues, and I have tried to hint at it in the translation. The scene is painted with great skill: the Temple setting is depicted in a couple of effortless strokes of the brush. And then there is 'the populace'. Luke has them there from the beginning, 'praying outside'. This has two effects: first, they act as the background of the dialogue between Zachariah and the angel. Second, Luke is going to employ them later in the scene, to emphasise the startling nature of what has occurred.

Another name appears (still no Jesus!), that of John ('God has acted graciously'). We learn of him first, looking back, that 'he shall not drink wine and strong drink', which is a direct quotation of Leviticus 10:9 and Numbers 6:3; and we recall 1 Samuel 1:11, where Hannah, another childless wife, is praying for a boy. Her prayer will be granted, and she will produce the prophet Samuel (be careful what you pray for!). Second, looking forward, 'he shall be filled with the Holy Spirit'. The two-volume work Luke-Acts is the story of what happens when people allow themselves to be 'filled with the Holy Spirit'. Others to whom it will happen are: Elisabeth, Mary, Jesus, Peter, Stephen, and, of course, Paul.

Zachariah's question may strike us as a perfectly reasonable one, and not all that different from what Mary says a few verses later ('How will this be?'); but Zachariah is punished for his question, and Mary is not. Why this unequal distribution of sanctions? First, Mary's question accepts what is going to happen, and simply indicates a perfectly sensible difficulty. Second, it is artistically necessary for Luke to make Zachariah a bit (but not too much) inferior to Mary – because her child, who has still not been mentioned, is going to be much more important than his.

Lastly, the perceptive populace realises that Zachariah has seen a vision. Later on we shall meet 24:23 where the same word is used to refer, disparagingly, to the evidence of the women who found Jesus' tomb empty. And they, of course, were right to believe what the angels had told them . . .

Second appearance of Gabriel

26-38 In the sixth month the angel Gabriel was sent to a city of Galilee whose name is Nazareth, to a virgin engaged to a man whose name was Joseph, of the house of David; and the name of the virgin was Mary.

And going in to her he said, 'Rejoice, you who have received favour: the Lord is with you.'

She was deeply disturbed at the remark, and wondered what kind of thing this greeting might be.

And the angel said to her, 'Do not be afraid, Mary. For you have found favour with God. And look! you will conceive in the womb, and bear a son. And you shall call his name Jesus. This one will be great, and will be called Son of the Most High. And the Lord will give him the throne of his ancestor David. And he shall rule over the house of David for ever and of his reign there shall be no end.'

And Mary said to the angel, 'How will this be, since I do not know a man?'

And the angel answered and said to her, '[The] Holy Spirit will come upon you, and the power of the Most High will overshadow you. Therefore that which is conceived is holy and will be called Son of God. And look, Elisabeth, your kinswoman, she too has conceived a son in her old age, and this is the sixth month for her who was called "Barren"; because there is no such thing as an impossibility to God.'

Mary said, 'Look, the Lord's slave-woman. Let it happen to me in accordance with your word.' And the angel went from her.

This lovely picture, which a thousand artists have tried to paint, needs to be seen together with its companion-piece, the announcement to Zachariah. Like him, Mary is told 'do not be afraid'; like him, she notes the difficulty of it. The difference is that this is not depicted as an answer to Mary's prayer (how could it be?), and that Mary is more straightforwardly ready to go along with the divine invitation. We may also notice (as something that we shall see in Luke's Gospel) that Mary, the girl of no status from an utterly insignificant village, turns out to be the person in whom Luke is most interested in the opening two chapters.

Or rather, not quite; for one character is not mentioned, and yet underlies every line of the text, namely God. Consider what Luke is saying when he says at the beginning of this section, 'the angel Gabriel was sent': by whom? By, clearly, God, who is in sole charge of all the events that Luke narrates. That is something for us to remember in our reading of the whole of the rest of the Gospel.

Two mothers are brought together

39-56 Mary arose in those days and journeyed in a hurry to the hill-country, to a city of Judah, and she entered the house of Zachariah and greeted Elisabeth. And it happened when Elisabeth heard Mary's greeting, the unborn child leapt in her womb, and Elisabeth was filled with the Holy Spirit, and she cried out in a loud voice and said, 'Blessed are you among women, and blessed is the fruit of your womb. And how does this happen to me, that the Mother of my Lord should come to me? For look! As the sound of your greeting came to my ears, the unborn child leapt with exultation in my womb. And happy is she who believed that there would be a fulfilment of the things spoken to her from the Lord.'

And Mary said,

'My soul extols the Lord
and my spirit has exulted in God my Saviour
because he has looked [favourably] on the humble state of his slave girl.
For look! From now on, all generations will congratulate me
because the Powerful One has done great things for me,
and holy is his name.
And his mercy is for generation after generation on those who fear him.
He has done a mighty deed with his arm.
He has scattered those who are haughty in the thoughts of their heart.
He has deposed rulers from their thrones
and raised up the humble.
The hungry he has filled with good things
and the wealthy he has sent away empty.
He has helped his servant Israel, remembering his mercy.
As he spoke to our ancestors,
to Abraham and his descendants for ever.'

Mary remained with her about three months, and she returned to her home.

In this episode, with consummate artistry, Luke brings two stories, those of John the Baptist and Jesus, effortlessly together. Notice two themes that are becoming familiar: those of 'journeying', and being 'filled with the Holy Spirit'. Luke also delicately indicates that although John the Baptist comes first, he is actually inferior to Mary's child.

Another theme that is of importance to Luke's Gospel underlies the Magnificat. Possibly because his church was from the more well-to-do section of society (you must decide as you read the Gospel whether or not you agree with this possibility), Luke emphasises more than the other Gospels God's preference for those at the bottom of society's priorities: Mary is a 'slave girl' and 'humble', and God exalts the 'hungry'. The 'great things' that God is praised for having done to Mary are etymologically connected with the word that we have translated 'extols'; sometimes it is rendered 'magnifies'.

First birth and its attendant circumstances

57-80 Meanwhile, for Elisabeth her time was fulfilled to bring forth her child – and she bore a son. And her neighbours and relatives heard that the Lord had multiplied his mercy in regard to her; and they rejoiced with her. And it happened on the eighth day that they came to circumcise the child; and they were trying to call him by the name of his father Zachariah. And his mother responded and said, 'No – on the contrary; he shall be called John.'

And they said to her, 'There's no one from [among] your kinsfolk who's called by this name.' And they started nodding to his father, [to know] what he wanted him to be called. And he asked for a little writing-tablet and wrote, 'John is his name'.

And they were all amazed. And his mouth was opened immediately, and he spoke, blessing God. And there came fear upon all their neighbours; and in the whole hill-country of Judaea all these events were discussed; and all those who heard [them] placed [them] in their hearts, saying 'so what is this child going to be?' For indeed the hand of the Lord was with him.

And Zachariah his father was filled with the Holy Spirit, and prophesied, saying,

'Blessed is the Lord, the God of Israel,
for he has looked at his people, and brought about their release
and raised up a horn of salvation for us
in the house of David his servant,
as he spoke through the mouth of the holy ones of old, his prophets,
salvation from our enemies, and from the hands of all those who hate us,
to work mercy with our ancestors
and to remember his holy covenant,
an oath which he swore to Abraham our ancestor
to grant to us, once we had been fearlessly delivered from enemy hands,
to worship him in holiness and righteousness
before him all our days.
And you, little child, you shall be called a prophet of the Most High;
for you shall go before the Lord, to prepare his ways,
to give knowledge of salvation to his people, through forgiveness of their sins
through the compassionate heart of our God,
by which he will visit us, the risen sun from on high,
to appear to those who sit in darkness and in the shadow of death,
to straighten our feet into the way of peace.'

And the little child grew and was strengthened in the spirit; and he was in the desert until the day of his revelation to Israel.

John the Baptist's birth is splendidly told: Elisabeth's independence of spirit, as she insists that the boy is not to be called Zachariah, and the comic touch of the relatives frantically 'nodding' to Zachariah, pardonably forgetting that his problem is not deafness, but an inability to speak. He recovers the power of speech when he supports his wife's assertion that the boy is to be called 'God has acted graciously'.

Zachariah is, like his wife and Mary before him, 'filled with the Holy Spirit', and utters another song like Mary's, which the Church still sings to itself in the morning, just as it sings Mary's song in the evening.

Notice, finally, how artistically Luke places John the Baptist in the desert, from where he will be reintroduced at the beginning of Chapter 3.

Second birth and its attendant circumstances

2 1-7   It came to pass in those days that a decree went out from Caesar Augustus that the whole world [or: 'empire'] should be registered. This, the first registration, took place when Quirinius was governor of Syria. And everyone journeyed to be registered,

each to their own city. Joseph also went up from Galilee, from the city of Nazareth, to Judaea, to the city of David which is called Bethlehem, because he was of the house and family of David, to be registered along with Mary, his betrothed – who was pregnant. It came to pass while they were there that the days were fulfilled for her to give birth and she brought forth her son, the first-born; and she wrapped him round with swathing-bands, and laid him down in a feeding-trough, because there was no room for them in the lodging house.

This all-too-familiar passage is in certain respects a shocking one. It is far from the birth that we should expect of one who 'will be called great, and Son of the Most High', who will 'sit on the throne of his ancestor David', and 'will reign over the house of Jacob for ever, and of his reign there shall be no end'. The references to Caesar Augustus, the most powerful man in the world, and to Quirinius, his local representative, flatter only to deceive. These two potentates know nothing of Jesus, and their actions have the unforeseen consequence (unforeseen by them at any rate) that Jesus is born in Bethlehem. Not only that, but he is born in less than ideal circumstances: there is no room in the town's single lodging house, so the child is born like one of the poor and put in a 'feeding-trough'.

As a matter of fact, Luke has got his dates a bit muddled, since Quirinius was governor of Syria about ten years after Jesus was born, and we know nothing of the 'registration' of which Luke speaks. That, however, is not important. What matters to Luke is the contrast between the 'great ones' of the earth and the child that has been born.

Lastly, notice the shock of the reference to Mary's pregnancy. It is true that we already know the circumstances; nevertheless, the way Luke expresses it brings us up short, and I have tried to reflect this in the translation.

Luke's Greek retains its biblical flavour here, and I have made some attempts to represent the sound in English.

Third appearance of the angel

8-20 And there were shepherds in the same region, who were living in the fields, and keeping careful watch by night over their flock. And the angel of the Lord stood near them; and the glory of the Lord shone about them; and they feared with a great fear.

And the angel said to them, 'Do not be afraid. For look – I bring you good news, great joy which will be for all the people, that there has been born for you today a Saviour, who is Christ the Lord in the city of David; and this is the sign for you: you will find the baby wrapped in swathing-bands and lying in a feeding-trough.'

And suddenly there was with the angel a crowd of the heavenly army praising God and saying,

'Glory in the highest to God
and on earth peace among human beings who are pleasing to God.'

And it came to pass, when the angels went from them into heaven, the shepherds started saying to each other, 'Let us go to Bethlehem, and see this thing that has happened, which the Lord has made known to us.'

And they went in a hurry, and they searched for Mary and Joseph, and the baby, which lay in the feeding-trough. When they saw [them], they revealed about the word that had been spoken to them about this little child. And all those who heard were astonished about the things spoken to them by the shepherds.

But Mary kept all these words, pondering them in her heart.

And the shepherds went back, glorifying and praising God for all that they had heard and seen, as it had been spoken to them.

This third angelic appearance confirms all that has gone before, including the superiority of Jesus over John the Baptist. There is also at least one shock, however; for the recipients of the vision are not, like Zachariah, Temple priests going about their business, nor, like Mary, quietly ready to do God's bidding; they are, frankly, cowboys, people living on the margins of society, and making up their rules as they go along, perhaps the very people that Luke's well-to-do Christians would have had least in common with. They live out of doors, and are not even respectable enough to sleep at nights.

Nevertheless, it is to these 'cowboys' that the Lord's revelation comes; and, remarkably, they do not hesitate to believe, especially after the 'heavenly army' has sung a chorus for them. This is of a piece with the (repeated) shock that the 'Saviour, Christ the Lord' is currently lying in a feeding-trough. Another repetition or echo is that, like Mary earlier, the shepherds respond 'in a hurry'.

Lastly, notice how Luke enables us to reflect on the episode by offering three separate reactions to it: 'those who heard' are astonished by it; Mary is quietly reflective about it; the shepherds go home glorifying God for it. There is a kind of completeness about this.

Jesus' circumcision and presentation

21-40 And when the eight days were fulfilled for him to be circumcised, his name was called Jesus, which [he] had been called by the angel before he had been conceived in the womb.

And when the days of their purification were fulfilled according to the Law of Moses, they took him up to Jerusalem, to offer him to the Lord, as it is written in the Law of the Lord that 'every male that opens his mother's womb shall be called holy to the Lord', and to give sacrifice according to what is written in the Law of the Lord, 'a pair of turtle-doves, or two young doves'.

And look! There was a man in Jerusalem, whose name was Simeon, and this man was righteous and pious, and waiting for Israel's comfort; and the Holy Spirit was on him. And it had been revealed to him by the Holy Spirit [that he would not] see death before he saw the Christ of the Lord. And he came in the Spirit into the Temple; and as the parents brought in the child Jesus, for them to act in accordance with the Law about him, he himself took him into his arms and blessed God and said,

'Now you are letting your slave go, Master,
according to your word in peace;
because my eyes have seen your salvation
which you have prepared before the face of all the peoples,
a light for the revelation of the Gentiles
and the glory of your people Israel.'

And the child's father and mother were in a state of astonishment at the things being said about him; and Simeon blessed them, and said to Mary his mother: 'Look! This one is destined for the fall and rising of many in Israel, and as a sign of contradiction (and your own soul will be pierced by a sword) so that the thoughts of many hearts may be revealed.'

And there was Hanna, a prophetess, a daughter of Phanuel, of the tribe of Asher; she was advanced, with many days, having lived with her husband for seven years from her virginity, she was now a widow of as many as eighty-four years; she did not leave the Temple, worshipping with fasting and prayer, day and night. And at that hour, she stood and praised God and spoke of him to all those who were waiting for the redemption of Israel.

And when they had completed everything in accordance with the Law of the Lord, they returned to Galilee, to their own city of Nazareth.

And the child grew and gained strength, filled with wisdom, and God's favour was on him.

In this combination of episodes, Luke shows his skill at creating atmosphere. Five times it is emphasised that Jesus' parents observe the Law, and Simeon and Hanna, another couple straight from the pages of the Old Testament, reinforce this picture. However, the reader will know that by the end of the two-volume work of Luke-Acts, the group of Jesus' followers will have clearly separated from their Jewish matrix; and for Luke it is the Holy Spirit that directs that separation, so the Spirit is mentioned no less than three times in this passage. Likewise Simeon's song, which has been for a millennium and a half part of the Church's night prayer, refers implicitly to the separation, with its reference to 'revelation of Gentiles', along with 'glory of Israel'. Simeon sides with the lowly, classing himself as a slave, just as Mary does.

Above all, though, it is a central theme of Luke-Acts that God is in charge; and this is indicated quite emphatically in the account of Jesus' circumcision, which is performed in accordance with God's Law, but also (and more specifically) in accordance with the instruction of the angel Gabriel to Mary. As before, we are invited to contemplate the meaning of the child, through the lens of his parents' 'astonishment', Simeon's song of farewell, and Hanna's praise of God.

One last point to notice is the theme, once more, of journeying. Count carefully in these first two chapters, and you will find that the scene shifts no less than nine times, between Judaea and Galilee. The rest of the Gospel can be seen as a steady journey towards Jerusalem; then Acts is a journey outwards, concluding in Rome, but with occasional returns to Jerusalem, until the Gospel definitively turns its back on that city.

Passover in Jerusalem

41-52 And his parents used to journey each year to Jerusalem for the Passover festival. And when he was twelve years old, when they went up according to the custom of the feast, and when they had completed the days, as they returned, the boy Jesus stayed behind in Jerusalem; and his parents did not know. Thinking that he was in the caravan, they went a day's journey, and then started to hunt for him everywhere among their relatives and acquaintances; and when they couldn't find him, they returned to Jerusalem in their hunt for him; and so it was that after three days they found him sitting in the Temple in the middle of the teachers, and [he was] listening to them and asking them questions; and all those who heard him were astonished at his intellect and at his responses. And when they saw him they were overwhelmed; and his mother said to him, 'Child, why did you do this to us? Look – your father and I have been looking for you in agony.'

And he said to them, 'Why were you looking for me? Didn't you know that I had to be on my Father's business [or: 'in my Father's house']?' And they did not understand the word that he had spoken to them.

And he went down with them to Nazareth, and put himself under their authority. And his mother kept all these events [or: 'words'] in her heart.

And Jesus advanced in wisdom and stature and favour before God and human beings.

> Luke ends his account of Jesus' early years with a characteristically dramatic vignette. Once again the parents are presented as observant Jews, going up to Jerusalem on pilgrimage; but a note of suspense is injected into the story when they discover that they have actually lost this child that has been so carefully entrusted to them.
>
> The drama is not just for its own sake, however, but for what it hints about Jesus' future. The Jesus of Luke's Gospel is not about to be easily pinned down; and the child who reacts harshly to 'your father and I' by deliberately redefining his parentage ('my Father'), is the one who is going to 'cause division' (Luke 12:49-53; and see also 8:19-21).
>
> Yet again the evangelist encourages us to reflect on Jesus through the lens of Mary, who 'kept all these things in her heart'; and household order is restored, with Jesus submitting to parental authority and then growing up in the normal way.

John the Baptist begins his mission

3 [1, 2] In the fifteenth year of the Imperium of Tiberius Caesar, when Pontius Pilate was governor of Judaea, and Herod was tetrarch of Galilee, and Philip his brother was tetrarch of Iturea and the district of Trachonitis, and Lysanias was tetrarch of Abilene, under the High Priesthood of Annas and Caiaphas, the word of God came to John, the son of Zachariah, in the desert.

> This very elaborate introduction to John the Baptist's mission contains the only date in the whole of the New Testament (AD 28–29). It is quite a good example of Luke's 'sleight of hand', whereby he feints in one direction, when his intention is to go somewhere else altogether. He lists, in descending order of priority, the most important people as far as the history and geography of the region are concerned: Tiberius, the unpleasant emperor of Rome (successor to Augustus, who was mentioned in the last chapter), his local

representative Pontius Pilate (the literary if not political successor to Quirinius); then Herod, son of the King Herod of Chapter 1, and his brothers, who share, under moderately strict Roman conditions, their father's empire; then come the local religious figures, Annas and Caiaphas. Finally, while we ponder this list, as unwholesome a collection of brigands as you could wish to meet on a dark night, Luke brings us to the person he is really interested in, our old friend 'John, son of Zachariah'. And he is in the desert, where Luke had conveniently placed him, a chapter ago.

John's mission

3-9 And he came to the whole country around the Jordan, proclaiming a baptism of repentance for the forgiveness of sins, as it is written in the scroll of words of Isaiah the prophet:

> 'A voice of one shouting in the desert:
> "Prepare the way of the Lord,
> make straight his paths."
> Every valley shall be filled in,
> and every mountain and hill made low,
> and the crooked places shall turn straight
> and the rough places turn into smooth roads.
> And all flesh shall see the saving power of God.'

So he would tell the crowds who journeyed out to be baptised by him, 'Offspring of vipers, who taught you to flee from the anger that is coming? So produce fruits worthy of repentance; and don't start saying to yourselves, "We have Abraham as our father". Because I tell you that God can raise up children for Abraham from these stones. Already the axe is laid to the root of the trees. So every tree that does not give fruit is cut down and cast into the fire.'

John the Baptist here introduces a theme that will be very important in the Gospel of Luke, that of 'repentance for the forgiveness of sins', though here the phrase is taken over directly from Mark 1:4, and the 'fruits worthy of repentance' is almost identically found in Matthew 3:8. The quotation is from Isaiah 40:3-5.

You might have expected the crowds to drift away, seeing John the Baptist's rather aggressive speech to them; but it doesn't seem to have put them off.

John and the crowds

10-18 And the crowds asked him, saying, 'What are we to do, then?'

In answer he said to them, 'Let the one who has two tunics share with the one who has none; and let the one who has food to eat do the same.'

Tax collectors also came and said to him, 'Teacher, what are we to do?'

He said to them, 'Exact nothing beyond what is commanded you.'

There were also some who were serving in the army; they asked him, 'What about us? What are *we* to do?'

And he said to them, 'No extortion; no false accusations; be satisfied with your wages.'

The populace was agog; everyone was arguing about John [wondering] whether perhaps he might be the Messiah. So John responded to them all, 'I'm baptising you in water – but the one who is stronger than me is on his way, and I am not fit to untie the thong of his sandals. He will baptise you with the Holy Spirit and with fire. His winnowing-shovel is in his hand to clean the threshing-floor thoroughly – and the chaff he will burn with a fire that cannot be extinguished.'

With many other consoling remarks he spread the good news among the people.

> Luke is a very gentle evangelist; but that should not blind us to the starkness of his message. John the Baptist's message will have struck Luke's Christians as chillingly severe, especially if, as I suspect, they were relatively comfortably off: sharing tunics and food comes less easily to the rich. Tax collectors and soldiers will have wondered how they could possibly make a living under this dispensation; and am I alone in hearing a touch of irony in Luke's concluding remark about 'consoling' and 'good news'?
>
> The alert reader will have noticed yet another reference here to the 'Holy Spirit', but in connection with Jesus' mission, now, not John's.

John the Baptist and Herod

19, 20   Now Herod the tetrarch, having been rebuked [by John] in respect of Herodias his brother's wife, and in respect of all the evil things that Herod had done, added this also to everything else, and locked John up in prison.

> The starkness continues; if this is John the Baptist's fate, what is going to happen to Jesus? This is, we observe, now the third reference in the Gospel to this unpleasant family.

The baptism of Jesus

21, 22   It happened when the whole populace had been baptised, and as Jesus had been baptised and was praying, heaven was opened and the Holy Spirit came down in bodily form, like a dove, upon him, and a voice came from heaven, 'You are my Son, the Beloved – in you I am well pleased.'

> Luke's is very much the Gospel of prayer; at several keypoints, as we shall see, Luke shows us Jesus at prayer, and this is the first such occasion.
>
> All the way through the Gospel, we need to be asking, 'Who is Jesus for Luke?' The first two chapters gave us a number of implicit and explicit clues. Here, Luke makes the contrast between Jesus and John the Baptist; he does not explicitly mention, we notice, that Jesus was baptised by John, but hurries on to assert that Jesus is Son of God. This assertion is now supported in a rather different way in the genealogy.

135

Jesus' genealogy

23-38 And Jesus himself was, when he started, about thirty years old. He was the son, so it was supposed, of Joseph, son of Heli, son of Matthat, son of Levi, son of Melchi, son of Jannai, son of Joseph, son of Mattathias, son of Amos, son of Nahum, son of Esli, son of Naggai, son of Maath, son of Mattathias, son of Semein, son of Josech, son of Joda, son of Ioanan, son of Rhesa, son of Zerubbabel, son of Shealtiel, son of Neri, son of Melchi, son of Addi, son of Kosam, son of Elmadam, son of Er, son of Joshua, son of Eliezer, son of Jorim, son of Matthat, son of Levi, son of Symeon, son of Judah, son of Joseph, son of Jonam, son of Eliakim, son of Melea, son of Menna, son of Mattatha, son of Nathan, son of David, son of Jesse, son of Obed, son of Boaz, son of Sala, son of Nahshon, son of Aminadab, son of Admin, son of Arni, son of Hezron, son of Perez, son of Judah, son of Jacob, son of Isaac, son of Abraham, son of Terah, son of Nahor, son of Serug, son of Ragai, son of Peleg, son of Eber, son of Shela, son of Cainan, son of Arphaxad, son of Shem, son of Noah, son of Lamech, son of Methusaleh, son of Enoch, son of Jared, son of Mahaleel, son of Kainan, son of Enos, son of Seth, son of Adam, son of God.

> Luke puts in a genealogy at this point, after Jesus' baptism and as he starts his ministry. Matthew, by contrast, *begins* with Jesus' genealogy. For Matthew, Jesus' family tree sums up the whole of Israel's history. Luke, on the other hand, traces the story back to 'Adam, son of God', so embracing the whole human race; by the end of this two-volume work, the Gospel will have reached all humanity. Beyond this observation, there is no great need to worry too much about the genealogy. Gallant attempts have been made to reconcile this one with what we find in Matthew; generally they have not carried conviction. The alert reader will notice here several repetitions, which may suggest that Luke was short of information on the matter.

The temptation of Jesus in the desert

4 1-13 Jesus, full of the Holy Spirit, returned from the Jordan, and was led by the Spirit in the desert, being tempted by the devil for forty days. And he ate nothing in those days; and when they were completed, he was hungry.

The devil said to him, 'If you *are* the Son of God, tell this stone to become a loaf of bread.'

And Jesus answered him; 'It is written, "Human beings shall not live by bread alone."'

And leading him up, he showed him all the kingdoms of the world in an instant of time, and the devil said to him, 'I shall give you all this authority, and the glory of them, because it has been handed over to me, and I give it to whomsoever I want. So, as for you, if you bow down before me, it will all be yours.'

And Jesus answered and said to him, 'It is written, "The Lord your God shall you worship – and him alone shall you adore."'

He led him up to Jerusalem, and set him on the summit of the Temple, and said to him, 'If you *are* the Son of God, throw yourself down from here. For it is written, "He will command his angels about you, to protect you" and "On their hands they will bear you up, lest you strike your foot on a stone." '

And Jesus in reply said to him, 'It is said, "You shall not tempt the Lord your God."'

And having completed the whole temptation, the devil withdrew from him until a suitable occasion.

This episode starts, possibly for our comfort, with a double reference to the Holy Spirit (Mark at this point has a rather violent-sounding reference to the Spirit 'expelling' Jesus into the desert; Luke, characteristically, is more gentle). Luke and Matthew have a threefold pattern of temptation from the devil, trying to persuade Jesus to gratify some immediate need, and also, more importantly, to take his eyes off the mission that he has been given by God. Each time Jesus effortlessly repels the temptation by quoting Deuteronomy. The three temptations are in a slightly different order in Matthew and Luke. Some scholars think that Luke deliberately made the 'Temple' temptation the climax: Luke's Gospel begins and ends in the Temple, and the Temple is clearly of importance to him.

The final line ('until a suitable occasion') sounds like a threat, whose implication only becomes clear as we approach the end of the Gospel story.

The ministry begins in Nazareth

14-30   And Jesus returned to Galilee in the power of the Spirit. And a report about him went out through the whole district; and he was teaching in their synagogues, being glorified by everybody.

And he came to Nazareth, where he had been brought up, and, as was his custom, he went in on the Sabbath-day to the synagogue, and rose up to read. And there was given to him the scroll of the prophet Isaiah, and unrolling the scroll he found the place where it was written,

'The Spirit of the Lord is upon me,
therefore he has anointed me
to give good news to the destitute.
He has sent me
to proclaim freedom to prisoners
and recovery-of-sight to the blind,
to set the oppressed free,
to proclaim an acceptable year of the Lord.'

And rolling up the scroll he gave it back to the assistant and sat down. And all eyes in the synagogue were gazing at him. He began to speak to them, 'Today this Scripture is fulfilled as you listen.'

And they all bore witness to him, and they wondered at the graceful words that came out of his mouth; and they started saying, 'Isn't this Joseph's son?'

And he said to them, 'Certainly you'll tell me this proverb, "Doctor, heal yourself. Do also here in your home territory the things that we have heard of occurring in Caphernaum." Amen I tell you, no prophet is acceptable in his home territory. In truth I tell you, there were many widows in Israel in Elijah's day, when heaven was shut for three years and six months, when a great famine hit the whole earth; and Elijah was sent to none of them, but to Sarepta of Sidon, to a widow-woman [there]. And there were many lepers in Israel in the time of Elisha the prophet; and none of them was cleansed but Naaman the Syrian.'

And they were all filled with rage in the synagogue as they heard this; and they arose and started throwing him out of the city; and they led him to the brow of the hill on which their city was built, so as to throw him down. But he passed through the middle of them and travelled on.

Luke has placed this Nazareth episode (which takes place at a later stage in both Matthew and Mark) right at the beginning of Jesus' ministry, apparently because he wants various themes to surface from the very start. I may mention the following:

- the 'ripple' effect conveyed by the phrase 'a report went out through the whole district' – an oral extension of the journeying motif that we have already encountered;

- the reader will have to get used to the idea of the 'Lucan summary': the opening lines of this passage, which do not refer to any particular episode, but create atmosphere, give an impression of what it was like. This is something that we shall see again. Luke uses it very effectively in Acts;

- the text of Jesus' sermon. Luke is the Gospel of the poor and oppressed, as the author signals once more by the text that Jesus is given to read (Isaiah 61:1, 2a). This message is hammered home by Jesus' sermon, the shortest on record. He claims, 'today this Scripture is fulfilled';

- and the word 'today', one of great importance in Luke: it is used in the annunciation to the shepherds, in the Zacchaeus story, and will be used in the story of the thief who recognised Jesus on the Cross. Each of these stories is important in the unfolding of the Gospel narrative;

- finally, another important theme of this Gospel is the spread of the gospel to the Gentiles, symbolised here by the widow of Sarepta, and by Naaman the Syrian.

The first day of the apostolate

31-44 And he went down to Caphernaum, a city of Galilee, and he used to teach them on the Sabbath-day; and they would be amazed at his teaching, because his speech was marked with authority.

And in the synagogue there was a man who had the spirit of an unclean demon; and it cried out in a loud voice, 'Leave us alone – what have we got to do with you, Jesus the Nazarene? Have you come to destroy us? I know who you are – the Holy One of God!'

And Jesus rebuked it, 'Be silent, and come out of him.'

And the demon threw him into the middle and came out of him, causing him no harm! And astonishment came upon them all, and they spoke to each other saying, 'What is this word? Because he commands the unclean spirits with authority and with power – and they come out!' And the rumour about him started to go out to every place in the area round about.

He arose out of the synagogue and went into the house of Simon. Simon's mother-in-law was in the grip of a great fever, and they asked him about her. And he stood over her and rebuked the fever; and it left her. Straightaway she arose and ministered to them.

When the sun set, all those who had people sick with different kinds of diseases brought them to him. He laid his hands on every single one of them, and healed them. Demons came out from many people, shouting and saying, 'You are the Son of God.' He rebuked them, and did not allow them to speak – because they knew that he was the Messiah.

When day came, he went out and journeyed to a desert place; and the crowds went looking for him, and they came up to him and restrained him from journeying away from them. He told them, 'It is necessary for me to proclaim the good news of the kingdom of God in the other cities also, because this is my mission.'

And he was preaching in the synagogues of Judaea.

We can see here signs of Luke's careful planning of his material, to give a sense of what Jesus' mission was like, and what it was about, from the very beginning. This passage begins and ends with a 'Lucan summary', setting the mood, but with the important difference that whereas the first summary is set in Galilee, the second is in Judaea, thereby stressing the 'journeying' theme.

Second, the demons correctly identify Jesus as 'Holy One of God' and 'Son of God' – but this has to be kept quiet.

Third, we see once more the 'ripple effect' in the 'rumour' that went out about him.

Fourth, feminists sometimes get irritated when Simon Peter's mother-in-law is cured, only to start waiting on the males; but notice that, like Mary (1:39) and Jesus (4:16) before her, she 'arose'. We are meant to applaud and imitate her.

Fifth, Luke once more underlines respect for Jewish traditions – it is only when the sun sets, and therefore the Sabbath ends, that the sick are brought to Jesus.

Finally, one of the oddest features of Luke as the Gospel of prayer is that when Jesus goes out to the desert place (where in Mark and Matthew he prays), prayer is not mentioned. And in this Gospel it is the crowds, and not Simon Peter, who come and try to stop his 'journeying'.

The calling of Simon

5 ¹⁻¹¹ It happened when the crowd was pressing upon him and listening to the word of God, and he was standing by the Lake Gennesaret; and he saw two boats standing by the lake. The fishermen had come ashore and were washing the nets. He went on board one of the boats, which was Simon's, and asked him to put out a little bit from the land. He then sat down and taught the crowds from the boat.

When he stopped speaking, he said to Simon, 'Put out into the deep, and let down your nets to catch something.'

In response, Simon said, 'Master, the whole night we have been labouring and caught nothing – but at your word I shall let down the nets.' They did this – and they enclosed an enormous number of fish – and their nets were starting to break; and they signalled, nodding to their colleagues in the other boat to come and assist them. They came, and they filled both boats, to a point where they were sinking!

When Simon Peter saw this, he fell at Jesus' knees and said, 'Go away from me, because I am a sinful human being, Lord.' For astonishment had seized him, and all those with him, at the catch of fish which they had taken, and similarly James and John the sons of Zebedee, who were colleagues of Simon.

And Jesus said to Simon, 'Do not be afraid. From now on, you will be catching human beings.' And drawing up their boats on to the shore, they abandoned everything and followed him.

This is an extraordinary story, different from and similar to the version told by Mark (1:16-20). The reader must decide whether there are two different stories here, or whether Luke has adapted Mark's story for his own purposes. Certainly some scholars have found echoes here of Mark 4:1, 2 and John 21:1-19.

However you answer this question, you will notice some familiar touches that are typical of Luke. In the first place, Jesus breaks into Simon's life, without a by-your-leave, as Gabriel did into the lives of Zachariah and Mary.

Second, like Mary to Gabriel, Simon (no doubt a very sceptical professional fisherman), expressly acquiesces in Jesus' 'word'.

Third, he becomes 'Peter' as well as Simon, as soon as he gives his consent.

Fourth, he discovers in the light of the miracle of the fish that he is a 'sinful human being', and he learns to call Jesus 'Lord'. He is mistaken, however, in thinking that this means that Jesus must go away from him. Sinners have to repent, not send the Lord away.

Finally, and this is something we shall see frequently in Luke, discipleship is a matter of 'abandoning everything'. This may count as evidence in favour of the view that Luke is writing for a well-to-do church, a group that needed to be reminded that their possessions could be an obstacle to the work of the Holy Spirit in them.

A leper asks to be healed

12-16 And it happened, when he was in one of the cities, and look! A man full of leprosy, seeing Jesus, fell on his face and implored him, 'Lord, if you want, you can cleanse me.' And stretching out his hand he touched him, saying, 'I want – be cleansed.' And immediately the leprosy went away from him.

And he commanded him, 'Tell nobody. Instead, go and show yourself to the priest and offer [the offering] as prescribed by Moses for your cleansing, as evidence to them.' The report about him spread even further; and great crowds started gathering to hear and to be cured of their sicknesses; but he was [ever] withdrawing in[to] desert places and praying.

This passage feels a bit like one of those 'Lucan summaries', a story that serves to set the mood, a typical incident in the life of Jesus. Certainly it ends with what is unmistakably such a summary.

Once again there are some typical Lucan touches. The theme of the 'Gospel of prayer' is twice touched upon, first in the prayer of the leper (he 'implored him'), and then at the end, when we learn of Jesus' regular habit of prayer.

Like his own parents, and like Zachariah and Elisabeth, Jesus is presented to us as very observant of the Jewish Law ('as prescribed by Moses', he orders the cured leper).

And we see once more our familiar 'ripple effect': 'the report about him spread even further . . .' which is a variation on the 'journeying theme'.

The cure of a paralysed man – and the first signs of official opposition

17-26 And it happened on one of the days that he was teaching, and Pharisees and teachers of the Law were sitting; they had come from every village of Galilee and Judaea and Jerusalem. And the power of the Lord was that he should heal. And look! Men carrying someone on a bed, who was paralysed. And they were looking for a way to bring him in and to put him before him. When they did not find any way of bringing him in, because of the crowd, they went up to the roof, and let him down through the tiles, with [his] little bed, in the middle, in front of Jesus. And seeing their faith, he said, 'Man, your sins are forgiven you.' And the scribes and the Pharisees began to argue, saying, 'Who is this who is talking blasphemies? Who can forgive sins, except only God?'

Jesus, knowing their arguments, said to them in response, 'Why are you arguing in your hearts? What is easier – to say, "Your sins are forgiven you" or to say "Arise and walk"? But in order that you people may know that the Son of Man has authority on earth to forgive sins' – he said to the paralytic – 'I tell you, arise, take up your little bed, and go to your house.'

And straightaway he arose before them, taking up that on which he had been lying, and went off to his house, glorifying God. And amazement seized all of them, and they glorified God, and were filled with fear, saying, 'We have seen glorious things today.'

Luke found this story in Mark's Gospel, though he has added one or two touches of his own. The first thing we notice is a heavy overload of Pharisees and teachers of the Law; at first blush it seems as though there is no room for anyone else, especially since they come from every single village in the land. We shall probably be correct in detecting here our 'journeying' theme in the reference to Galilee, Judaea and Jerusalem.

If you look carefully at Mark's version, you will notice that where Mark speaks of 'unroofing the roof', Luke speaks of going through the tiles. It may well be that they have in view two different styles of building: Mark the rougher Palestinian construction, and Luke thinking of the roofs of Greek-style villas. This could be another indication that he has a more affluent audience in view.

The references at the end to 'glorifying God' are very Lucan: we have already seen shepherds (2:20) and crowds (4:15) doing the same; and there will be other examples.

The call of Levi: the first 'disastrous dinner party'

27-32 And after this he went out, and he saw a tax collector named Levi sitting at the tax-collecting place, and he said to him, 'Follow me.' And abandoning everything he rose up and followed him. And Levi gave a great reception in his house, and there was a great crowd of tax collectors and others who were with him, lying down to eat. And the Pharisees and their scribes complained to his disciples, 'Why do you people eat and drink with tax collectors and sinners?'

Jesus in reply said to them, 'The healthy have no need of a doctor – no, it's those who are ill. I did not come to call the just, but sinners, to repentance.'

> Levi's call, like that of Peter and his colleagues, clearly involves 'abandoning everything'; and like Mary and Jesus before him, we learn that he 'arose' or 'rose up'. At the end of the episode we notice the characteristic Lucan theme of repentance for sin. We learn, too, that for Luke the 'Pharisees and their scribes' stand for those who do not see the possibility (or the need?) of repentance.
>
> This is the first of a series of what I call 'disastrous dinner parties' in Luke's Gospel. Not all of them are really dinner parties, and not all of them are utterly disastrous; but it is one of the ways he has of organising his material, and perhaps such a setting would have sent a message to his affluent Christian community.

Is Jesus a serious religious figure? No – he's something new

33-39 They said to him, 'John's disciples fast frequently, and make intercessions, just like those of the Pharisees, but yours [just] eat and drink.'

Jesus said to them, 'Surely you can't compel the wedding guests [or: 'bridegroom's attendants'] to fast while the bridegroom is with them? But days will come, and when the bridegroom is taken from them, then they will fast in those days.'

He also spoke a parable to them: 'No one tears a patch from a new garment and patches it on to an old one. Otherwise the new one will tear, and the patch from the new one won't match with the old one. Likewise no one puts new wine into old flasks. Otherwise the new wine will burst the flasks; then it will spill out, and the flasks will be destroyed. No – new wine must be put into new flasks. No one who has drunk old wine wants new wine, for they say, "The old is good."'

> Luke has slightly tidied up Mark's version here, to make it a bit clearer how the parables about new cloth and new wine fit the controversy with the Pharisees. There is a slight puzzle at the end: the reader feels that the new wine stands for Jesus, but it is the old wine that is 'good'. Perhaps Luke's well-to-do audience were accustomed to vintage wine. Or perhaps it is the attitude of the Pharisees that Jesus is trying to describe here: people who prefer the 'old wine' of the Law to the 'new wine' of the gospel. Or perhaps he's just keeping us on our toes.

Can you pluck grain and heal on the Sabbath? Two examples

6 1-11 It happened on a Sabbath-day that he was going through the grain fields; and his disciples started plucking and eating the ears of grain, rubbing them in their hands.

Some of the Pharisees said, 'Why are you doing what is not allowed on the Sabbath?'

And Jesus responded to them, 'Haven't you even read what David did when he and those with him were hungry? How he went into the house of God, and took the Loaves of Presentation and ate them and gave them to those with him? But no one is allowed to eat those loaves, except the priests alone.' And he said to them, 'The Son of Man is Lord of the Sabbath.'

On another Sabbath-day, it happened that he went into the synagogue and taught. And a man was there, and his right hand was paralysed [or: 'withered']. And they were watching him, the scribes and the Pharisees, to see if he cured on the Sabbath, in order that they might find something to accuse him of. He however knew their thoughts, and said to the man with the paralysed hand, 'Up you get, and stand out into the middle.' And he arose and stood.

Jesus said to them, 'I ask you: is it allowed on the Sabbath-day to do good, or to do evil? To save life or to destroy it?' And he looked round at all of them and told the man, 'Stretch out your hand.' He did so – and his hand was restored! They were mad with rage, and they discussed with each other what they might do to Jesus.

> This passage with its two controversies confirms our impression of the way things are going: there's trouble ahead, symbolised by the readiness of Jesus' opponents to criticise, and by the fact that 'they were watching him'. Evidently he is already regarded as a menace; and being right is not going to make it any easier for him. But Luke's version of the story is less stark than Mark's account (Mark 2:23–3:6).

Jesus prays and then chooses the Twelve

12-16 It happened in these days that he went out on to the mountain to pray. And he was spending the whole night in prayer to God. And when day dawned, he called his disciples, and chose twelve from among them, whom he named 'apostles': Simon, whom he named 'Rock', and Andrew his brother, and James and John, and Philip and Bartholomew, and Matthew and Thomas, and James of Alphaeus, and Simon, nicknamed 'Zealot', and Judas of James; and Judas Iscariot, who became a traitor.

> Luke typically inserts the reference to prayer. Some readers may feel that after a night spent in meditation, the Lord might have selected a more satisfactory team than this particular group of cowards and traitors. But there is consolation for us here: we do not have to be out of the top drawer in order to be close to Jesus.

The 'Sermon on the Plain' (17–49)

Introduction

17-19 And he came down with them, and stood on a level place, he and a crowd of his disciples, and a great throng of the populace from all of Judaea and Jerusalem and the sea-coast of Tyre and Sidon, who came to listen to him, and to be healed from their diseases; and those who were troubled by unclean spirits were getting cured, and the whole crowd tried to find ways of touching him, because power was coming from him, and was healing everybody.

> Luke places this 'sermon' on a 'plain' or a 'level place'. Matthew's equivalent, which in some ways is like Luke's and contains almost all of Luke's material, is placed on a 'mountain', and is altogether a much more organised affair. Luke introduces the sermon with these various healings, as a kind of 'Lucan summary'.

Congratulations and woes

20-26 And he raised his eyes up to his disciples and said,

'Congratulations to the poor – for yours is the kingdom of heaven.
Congratulations to those who are hungry now – for you will be sated.
Congratulations to you who weep now – because you will laugh.
Congratulations when people hate you, and when they ostracise you and heap insults on you, and spurn your name as evil, for the sake of the Son of Man.
Rejoice in that day, and leap about.
For look! Your reward is great in heaven;
for in just the same way their ancestors used to treat the prophets.
BUT woe to you who are rich – for you have your comfort in full.
Woe to you who are filled now – for you will be hungry.
Woe to you who laugh now – for you will mourn and weep.
Woe to you whenever all people speak well of you.
For in just the same way their ancestors used to treat the false prophets.'

> Again the reader must decide whether Luke is speaking to an audience that is largely affluent. Certainly he does not, as Matthew does, speak of the 'poor in spirit'; and although he has fewer 'congratulations' than Matthew in the Sermon on the Mount, he sharpens the effect by throwing in four 'woes' to match the 'congratulations'. These two sections, the woes and the congratulations, are nicely balanced; some scholars see here the original version of the beatitudes.

On being children of the Father

27-49 'But I am speaking to you who are listening:

Love your enemies.
Do good to those who hate you.
Bless those who persecute you.
Pray for those who threaten you.
To the one who strikes you on the cheek, turn the other also.
And from the one who takes away your cloak, do not refuse your tunic.
To everyone who begs from you, give.
And to those who take what is yours, do not demand it back.

'And as you want people to do to you, do likewise to them. If you only love those who love you, what credit is that to you? For even sinners love those who love them. And if you do good to those who do good to you, what credit is that to you? Even sinners do that same thing. And if you lend money to people from whom you expect to get it back, what credit is that to you? Even sinners lend money to sinners in order to get the same amount back. No – love your enemies, and do good and lend without any expectation of return, and your reward will be great, and you will be children of the Most High, for he is kind even to the ungrateful and the wicked.

'Learn to be compassionate, just as your Father is compassionate. And don't judge, and you won't be judged. Don't condemn, and you won't be condemned. Let people off, and you will be let off. Give, and it will be given to you; they will give a generous measure, pressed down, shaken up and overflowing into your lap. For in the measure that you measure out, it will be measured to you in return.'

He also told them a parable: 'Can a blind person guide a[nother] blind person? Will they not both fall into a pit? The pupil does not have a higher status than the teacher; if they are fully trained, they will be just like their teacher.

'Why do you look at the [tiny] speck that is in your fellow's eye, but do not perceive the [huge] beam that is in your own eye? How can you say to your brother or sister, "Brother/sister: let me get rid of the speck that is in your eye", and all the while you yourself do not see the beam that is in your eye? Hypocrite [literally, 'actor'], first get the beam out of your eye, and then you will see the speck that is in the eye of your brother or sister.

'You see, there is no such thing as a good tree that produces rotten fruit. Nor is there such a thing as a rotten tree that produces good fruit. For each tree is recognised by its own fruit. They don't, you see, gather figs off thorn bushes; nor do they pick a bunch of grapes off brambles. A good person produces good things from the good treasure chest of their heart; the wicked person produces wickedness from what is wicked. You see, their mouth speaks out of the fullness of the heart.

'Why do you call me "Lord, Lord", and not do what I say? Everyone who comes to me and hears my words and does them – I'll show you what they are like. They are like a person building a house, who dug deep, and laid a foundation on the rock; and when the flood came, the river burst against that house, and it could not shake [the house], because it was well built.

'However the one who hears and does not perform is like a person who built a house on soil, with no foundation; the river burst on it, and immediately it fell in, and the collapse of that house was enormous.'

Read one way, this can sound like very stark teaching indeed. Try seeing it, however, as springing from Jesus' central insight that we are all children of the one Father, and it all falls into place: all of us are equal, no one is better than anyone else, and the affluent (to whom alone, surely, the instructions about lending are directed) should be delighted to be generously at the service of other human beings.

Notice the difference, in the parable of the house which comes at the end of the discourse, between house-building techniques in Luke and in Matthew. The houses at the end of Matthew's Sermon on the Mount (Matthew 7:24-27) are built either on rock or on sand; whereas the Lucan houses, perhaps in Greek cities rather than the Palestinian countryside, either have or do not have proper foundations.

A centurion's slave is healed

7¹⁻¹⁰ When he had completed all his words in the ears of the populace, he went into Caphernaum.

Now a certain centurion had a slave who was in a bad way and on the point of death. The slave was valuable to him; and hearing about Jesus, he sent elders of the Jews to him, asking him to come and save his slave. They came to Jesus, and begged him earnestly, saying, 'He deserves that you should grant him this. For he loves our people, and has himself built a synagogue for us.'

Jesus journeyed with them. When he was now not far off from the house, the centurion sent friends, saying, 'Lord, do not trouble yourself, for I am not good enough for you to enter under my roof. Therefore I didn't even think that I deserved to come to you. Just say the word, and let my servant be healed. For I am also a man placed under authority, with soldiers under me. And I say to this one, "Quick march," and he marches, and to another, "Come here," and he comes, and to my slave, "Do this," and he does it.'

When Jesus heard this, he was astonished at him; and he turned to the crowd that followed him and said, 'I tell you – not even in Israel have I found so much faith.' And those who had been sent returned and found the slave in good health.

> This remarkable story is also in Matthew 8:5-13 and John 4:46-54, though it is far more detailed here, and the centurion is very sympathetically treated by Luke. He is perhaps a symbol for Luke of Gentile openness to the Gospel. Luke alone offers the detail about the centurion building the synagogue, and his friendly relationship with the Jews of Caphernaum; and Luke omits Matthew's severe judgement on Israel.

The widow's son at Nain

¹¹⁻¹⁷ The next thing that happened was that he journeyed to a city called Nain, and his disciples and a large crowd were journeying with him. When he drew near to the gate of the city, look! There was being carried out one who had died, the only son of his mother – and she was a widow. And there was a good crowd of the city with her. And when he saw her, the Lord had pity on her and said to her, 'Do not weep.' He approached and touched the coffin; the bearers halted, and he said, 'Young man, I say to you, arise.'

And the young man sat up and began to talk. And he gave him to his mother. Fear seized all of them, and they glorified God, saying, 'A great prophet has been raised up among us, and God has visited his people.' And this report went out about him in the whole of Judaea, and the whole area round about.

> This is a charming story, characteristic of Luke, not least in the fact that it concerns a widow; widows, like lepers, are among Luke's favourite class of people, for they are marginalised in such a society. We notice, with no real surprise, that Jesus is unafraid to contract ritual impurity by touching the corpse. Once again we hear the people glorify God, and they even quote the Benedictus (1:68): 'God has visited his people.' Once again we have an instance of the 'ripple effect': ('this report went out about him . . . ').

When Luke says 'the Lord had pity', it is the first time that as narrator he has explicitly named Jesus with the awesome title of 'the Lord'. This title is used in the Greek translation of the Old Testament for the sacred and unpronounceable name of God, and in the language of the Roman Empire it was being increasingly used for the Emperor, often in connection with his divination. So Christian use of it for Jesus is subversive in two directions at once.

Comparing Jesus (once more) with John the Baptist

18-35 And his disciples repeated to John about all these things. And John summoned two of his disciples and sent them to the Lord, saying, 'Are you the Coming One, or are we to expect another?' And when they reached him, the men said, 'John the Baptist sent us to you. He said, "Are you the Coming One, or are we to expect another?".'

At that moment he cured many from diseases and afflictions and evil spirits, and gave many blind people the free gift of sight. He replied to them, 'On your way, and tell John what you saw and heard: "The blind see again; the lame walk; lepers are cleansed and the deaf hear; the dead are raised; the poor have the good news preached to them." And happy is anyone who is not affronted by me.'

As John's messengers went off, he began to talk to the crowds about John: 'What did you go out into the desert to see? A reed shaken by the wind? No? What *did* you go out to see? A man dressed in gorgeous clothes? Look – people who wear splendid clothing and live in luxury are in palaces. No? What *did* you go out to see? A prophet? Yes, I tell you, and far better than a prophet. This is the one of whom it is written, "Look – I am sending my messenger before my face, who will prepare your way before you." I tell you: no one is greater among the sons of women than John – but the most insignificant in the kingdom of God is greater than he.'

And the whole populace who heard, and the tax collectors, justified God by being baptised with John's baptism. But the Pharisees and lawyers set aside God's will, refusing to be baptised by him.

'So to what shall I compare the people of this generation, what are they like? They are like children who sit in the market place and call out to each other and say,

"We piped for you – and you didn't dance.
We mourned – and you didn't weep."

'For John the Baptist came, not eating bread, nor drinking wine, and you say, "He's got a demon!" The Son of Man came, eating and drinking, and you say, "Look! A glutton and a wine drinker! A friend of tax collectors and sinners!" And Wisdom is justified by *all* her children.'

This is a slightly enigmatic passage. Clearly Luke wants us to accept that Jesus is John the Baptist's superior; we have already seen as much in the opening chapters of the Gospel. In this passage, moreover, John is uncertain enough to have to send a deputation, to check whether Jesus really is the expected one. Jesus shows no doubts whatever. John is said to be inferior to 'the most insignificant in the kingdom of God'; and Jesus reminds us of his 'mission statement' at Nazareth in Chapter 4: 'the poor have the gospel (good news) preached to them', and John is criticised for being 'affronted' by Jesus.

At the same time, John is praised for being an austere and serious religious figure, and Jesus indicates that John's mission was foretold in Scripture. John's baptism gives glory to God. The accusation that Jesus' opponents are like children, at the end of the passage, implicitly affirms the mission of both Jesus and John: the one more austere, the other less so, 'and Wisdom is justified by *all* her children', both John and Jesus, and anyone else who listens to God.

The ones who are on the outside are those who see no need to listen to God, here classed as 'Pharisees and lawyers'. We have already seen the former as opponents of Jesus; the latter appear here for the first time. We shall see them a few times more in Luke's Gospel, nearly always behaving badly, or at least in opposition to Jesus. It is one of the former who behaves badly in the story that immediately follows.

The second 'disastrous dinner party'

36-50 One of the Pharisees invited him to eat with him; and he went into the house of the Pharisee and lay down.

And look! A woman who was a sinner in the city, and who had found out that he was lying down in the house of the Pharisee, bringing an alabaster jar of myrrh, and standing behind, weeping beside his feet, began to wet his feet with her tears, and with the hair of her head began wiping [them] and kissing his feet and anointing them with myrrh.

When the Pharisee who had invited him saw [this], he said to himself, 'If this fellow were a prophet, he would know who this woman is who is touching him, and what sort of person – she's a sinner!'

Jesus responded to him, 'Simon, I have something to tell you.'

He said, 'Speak, teacher.'

'A moneylender had two people in debt to him. One owed fifty denarii, and the other five hundred. Because they had no way of repaying, he let them both off. Which of them, then, will love him more?'

Simon replied, 'I suppose the one whom he let off the most.'

He said to him, 'Right verdict.' And he turned to the woman and said to Simon, 'Do you see this woman? I came into your house – you didn't give me water for my feet. She by contrast wet my feet with her tears and wiped them with her hair. You gave me no kiss – she by contrast, ever since I entered, has not stopped kissing my feet. You did not anoint my head with oil – she, by contrast, anointed my feet with myrrh. Therefore, I tell you, they are forgiven, her many sins, because she loved much. A person who is forgiven [only] a little loves [only] a little.'

He said to her, 'Your sins are forgiven.' And those who were lying down with him began saying to themselves, 'Who is this, who can forgive sins?'

He said to the woman, 'Your faith has saved you – on your way in peace.'

This is the second of several 'disastrous dinner parties' in Luke's Gospel. Jesus cannot have been altogether an easy guest to have for a meal, and we may imagine the host or hostess rolling their eyes in despair at the flickering tensions that Jesus engendered; Luke's affluent readers may also have felt the unease. This story is in some ways very similar to that which the other three evangelists place at the beginning of the Passion story (Matthew 26:6-13; Mark 14:3-9; John 12:1-8), but not all scholars agree that it is the same story.

Certainly the point of the story is different. As we have seen several times already in this Gospel, and will see again, Jesus shocks his contemporaries by having some thoroughly disreputable friends, sinners who repent (we have already seen that repentance and forgiveness is a major theme of this Gospel). The woman is a good example, and she is singled out for praise, in contrast to Jesus' rather negligent (but religiously observant) host. The Pharisee (why on earth did he invite Jesus?) is watching Jesus like a hawk, and notices that Jesus allows this impure woman to touch him. The reader, however, has already seen Jesus voluntarily touch a coffin, a few verses earlier, so we already know that he is indifferent to ritual taboos.

Luke's Jesus is not afraid to shock, and not afraid, either, to attack his host. The beautiful and gentle ending to the story should not blind us to the fact that he is an uncomfortable guest at a party.

Jesus' men and women companions

8 1-3 And the next thing was that he made his way through town and village proclaiming, and preaching the good news of the kingdom of God; and the Twelve [were] with him, and certain women, who had been cured from evil spirits and sickness, Mary called Magdalene, from whom seven demons had come out, and Joanna the wife of Chuza, Herod's steward, and Susanna, and many other women, who ministered to them from their resources.

> This is something of a 'Lucan summary', describing Jesus' itinerant group, and the 'support group' of women, apparently from the upper end of the social scale, whose relative wealth made the ministry possible. This may count as further evidence that Luke is writing for fairly affluent Christians.

Parables told and explained

4-18 A large crowd accompanied him, consisting of those who journeyed to him, town by town; and he spoke in a parable:

'The sower went out to sow his seed. And as he sowed, some fell by the way and was trampled underfoot, and the birds of the air gobbled it up. And another fell on the rock, and it grew up and withered, because it had no moisture. And another fell in the middle of thorns, and the thorns grew up with it and choked it. And another fell on good soil, and when it grew up it produced fruit, a hundredfold.' When he said this, he called out, 'Let those who have ears listen.'

His disciples asked him what this parable might mean.

He said, 'To you it is given to know the mysteries of the kingdom of God, but to the rest – in parables, that "seeing they may not see and hearing they may not understand". This is the parable: the seed is the word of God. Those who are "by the way" are those who hear, [but] then the devil comes and takes the word from their hearts; otherwise they might believe and be saved. Those who are "on the rock" are the ones who, when they hear the word, receive it with joy, and they have no root – they believe for a time, and in the time of temptation they withdraw. That which falls into the thorns, they are the ones who hear, and as they journey they are suffocated by the cares and affluence and pleasures of life; and they do not bring it to maturity. The seed in the "good soil" are those who hear with a noble and right heart; they hold on to the word and bear fruit patiently.

'No one who lights a lamp hides it in a pot or puts it under a bed. No – they put it on a lamp-stand, so that all who come [or: 'journey'] in may see the light. For there is nothing hidden which will not become visible; and there is nothing secret which will not become known, and come into the open.

'So watch out how you listen. For whoever has, it will be given to them, and whoever does not have, even what they think they have will be taken from them.'

> Luke makes less of the parable section than either Mark or Matthew (though, as we shall see, he has plenty of very memorable parables of his own). As befits his gentler temperament, Luke is more lenient than Mark in his verdict on the uncomprehending disciples, and on those who do not grasp Jesus' message (see Mark 4:11-13).
>
> The interpretation of the 'seed that fell among thorns' sounds a warning against the dangers of affluence, rather different from Mark's version (4:19); this may be further evidence for the view that Luke's church was a wealthy one.

Jesus' mother and brothers

19-21 His mother and his brothers came to him, and they could not meet up with him, because of the crowd. It was reported to him, 'Your mother and your brothers are standing outside wanting to see you.' He replied to them, 'A mother to me, and brothers to me, are those who hear God's word and perform it.'

> In comparison with the rather stark version of this at Mark 3:31-35, this is quite gentle, as befits the gentlest of the evangelists.

Jesus calms a storm on the Lake

22-25 It happened on one of the days that he went on board a boat, along with his disciples; and he said to them, 'Let us go to the other side of the Lake'; and they put out to sea. As they were sailing, he fell asleep. And a fierce gust of wind came down on to the Lake; and they were being swamped, and were in danger. They came and woke him up, saying 'Master, master, we're dying!' He woke up and rebuked the gale and the roughness of the waves. And they stopped; and there was a great calm. He said to them, 'Where's your faith?' They were awestruck, and they said to each other in astonishment, 'So who *is* this? Because he even gives order[s] to the winds and the water – and they obey him!'

Luke more or less reproduces here what he found in Mark (4:35-41). He has tidied it up, softened its rough edges, and omitted unnecessary material. One example of Lucan 'softening' is the way he has the disciples repeat their title for Jesus: 'Master, master'. And we shall see a similar repetition later, at 10:41: 'Martha, Martha'.

A demoniac in the land of the Gerasenes

26-39 And they sailed away to the land of the Gerasenes, which is opposite Galilee. As he disembarked on to land, a man from the city met him, who had demons; and for a good long time he had not worn a cloak, and would not stay in a house, but among tombs. Seeing Jesus, he cried out and fell down before him, and said in a loud voice, 'What do you want with me, Jesus, Son of God Most High? I implore you, don't torment me.' For he was directing the unclean spirit to come out of the man. For on many occasions it had seized him; and so he was bound in chains and kept secure with fetters; and he would break the shackles, and be driven by the demon into the desert places.

Jesus asked him, 'What is your name?' He said, 'Legion', because many demons had entered into him. And they begged him not to direct them to go off into the Abyss. Now there was there a sizable herd of pigs, grazing on the mountain. And they begged him to allow them to enter them; and he allowed them. The demons went out of the person, and entered the pigs; and the herd rushed down the cliff into the lake and was drowned.

When the herdsmen saw what had happened, they ran away and reported it in the city and in the countryside. They came out to see the phenomenon; and they approached Jesus and found the person from whom the demons had come out, sitting, wearing clothes, and in his right mind, at Jesus' feet. And they were awestruck.

Those who had seen [it] reported to them how the one who had been possessed by demons had been saved. And the whole throng of the area of the Gerasenes asked him to leave them, because they were seized with great awe. He went on board ship and returned. The man from whom the demons had come out begged to be with him; but he let him go, saying, 'Back to your house, and recount what great things God has done for you.'

And he went off through the whole city proclaiming what great things Jesus had done for him.

This is a powerful and dramatic story, revealing a good deal about how Luke sees Jesus. The demoniac moves from living naked among graves (an exceedingly bad sign) to sitting quietly at Jesus' feet (a very good sign). Not only is he 'saved', which is altogether a more powerful thing than being healed; but Jesus was up against immense odds: the demons were numerous, powerful enough to break chains, and sufficient in numbers to send a herd of pigs to a watery grave in Galilee (and thereby cease to be a threat). Jesus' mastery of them is effortless, and as we ask Luke who Jesus is we may notice that the man, who has been told to recount what great things *God* has done for him, ends up by proclaiming the great things that *Jesus* has done for him. There is no hint here that Luke thinks that the man has disobeyed Jesus, or got him wrong.

Jairus's only daughter, and a woman with a haemorrhage

40-56 As Jesus returned, the crowd welcomed him. For they were all waiting for him. And look! A man came, whose name was Jairus; and he was ruler of the synagogue, and falling at Jesus' feet he begged him to come into his house, because his only daughter was about twelve – and she was dying.

As he went, the crowds were crushing him. And a woman who had had a flow of blood for twelve years, who had spent all her livelihood on doctors, couldn't be cured by anybody, approached from behind and touched the hem of his garment. And straightaway the flow of her blood stopped!

And Jesus said, 'Who is the one who touched me?' They all denied it, and Peter said, 'Master, the crowds are pressing hard on you and jostling you . . .'

But Jesus said, 'Someone touched me, because I felt power going out of me.' The woman realised that she had not got away with it. Trembling, she came and fell before him, and, before all the populace, recounted the reason why she had touched him, and how she had been healed straightaway.

He said to her, 'Daughter, your faith has saved you – go in peace.'

While he was still speaking, someone comes from the president of the synagogue's house saying, 'Your daughter is dead. Don't bother the teacher any more.'

Jesus heard [this] and answered him, 'Don't be afraid – just believe, and she will be saved.' When he came into the house, he allowed no one to come with him except Peter and John and James, and the father and mother of the child. They were all weeping and mourning for her; but he said, 'Don't weep; she hasn't died, but is asleep.'

And they laughed at him – they knew that she was dead.

And he took her hand and spoke to her, saying, 'Girl, arise.' And her spirit returned, and she arose straightaway; and he gave instructions that something [should] be given her to eat. And her parents were amazed; but he directed them to tell no one what had happened.

> Luke found this story ready-made in Mark's Gospel, two tales, one wrapped round the other. He has made some changes, but mainly in the direction of tidying up Mark's roughnesses and smoothing his angularities. Mark portrays Peter's response as harsh and sarcastic, for example, where Luke has made it gentler. They remain two very charming stories, and demonstrate Jesus' ease with women and his indifference to ritual impurity (a woman with a haemorrhage and a woman who might be a corpse were serious snares for those who worried about such things).

The Twelve are sent out (and there is an interlude)

9 1-10 Summoning the Twelve, he gave them power and authority over all demons, and to cure diseases, and he sent them to proclaim the kingdom of God and to heal the sick; and he said to them, 'Do not take anything for the way, neither a staff nor a bag, nor bread nor silver – and not even to have two tunics. And whatever house you enter, remain there and come out from there. And whoever fails to give you hospitality, when you come out from that city, shake the dust off your feet as a sign against them.'

They went out and went through one village after another, preaching the gospel, and healing everywhere.

INTERLUDE

Herod the tetrarch heard the things that were happening; and he was quite perplexed, because it was being said by some people that John the Baptist had been raised from the dead, by some that Elijah had appeared, and by others again that one of the prophets of the ancients had arisen. But Herod said, 'John? I beheaded him; but who is this about whom I hear such things?'

And he was wanting to see him.

And when they returned, the apostles explained to him what great things they had done. And he took them and retreated in privacy to a city called Bethsaida.

> Luke is more or less following Mark here, though he emphasises the healing of the sick slightly more. One change that he has apparently made concerns the 'interlude'. While the apostles were out on the mission, Mark inserted the story of the death of John, partly, no doubt, to fill the gap, but also partly to remind the reader of what discipleship might involve. Luke has done something slightly different. He has placed the imprisonment of John the Baptist, and its reason (accusations about Herodias) back in Chapter 3, where it brings John's ministry to an end. Then in our present passage, he adds that 'he was wanting to see him', which will be picked up at the time of Jesus' Passion, when Luke alone reports a meeting between Jesus and this same Herod (Luke 23:6-12, especially verse 8).
>
> The apostles report having done 'great things'.

The feeding of the five thousand men

11-17 But the crowds found out and followed him. And he welcomed them and started speaking to them about the kingdom of God; and those who had need of healing he cured. The day began to wane, and the Twelve approached and said to him, 'Let the crowd go, so that they may journey to the villages and farms round about, and rest and find provisions, because here we're in a desert place.'

He said to them, 'Give them something to eat yourselves.'

But they said, 'We have no more than five loaves and two fish. Unless we are to go ['journey'] and buy foodstuffs for the whole of this crowd?' (For they were about five thousand men.)

He said to his disciples, 'Make them lie down to eat in groups of about fifty.' And they did so, and made them all lie down.

And taking the five loaves and the two fish, he looked up to heaven and blessed them and broke them and gave them to the disciples to set before the crowd. And they all ate and were satisfied, and their surplus was taken up, twelve baskets of fragments.

This is a powerful story; Luke tells it more or less as Mark has told it, except that Luke and John have only one story of feeding the multitudes, where Mark and Matthew have two. Luke characteristically adds the action of Jesus' 'hospitality' ('he welcomed them') and the healing of diseases. We are taken back to the story of God's feeding the People of Israel in the desert (see, for example, Exodus 16:13-18).

The idea of 'hospitality' is very important in Luke's Gospel.

Peter's identification of Jesus, and the teaching it provokes

18-27 And it happened when he was praying on his own, his disciples were with him, and he asked them, 'Who do the crowds say I am?' They answered and said, 'John the Baptist; and others Elijah; and others that one of the prophets of old has arisen.'

He said to them, 'But you people, who do *you* say I am?'

Peter replied and said, 'The Messiah of God.' He scolded them, and instructed them to say this to nobody, saying, 'The Son of Man must suffer many things and be rejected by the elders and high priests and scribes and be killed – and on the third day be raised up.'

He said to everyone, 'If anyone wants to come after me, let them deny themselves, and take up their cross every day and follow me. For whoever wants to preserve their life will lose it, and whoever loses their life for my sake, that person will preserve it. For how is a person helped, if they gain the whole world and lose or forfeit their very self? For whoever is ashamed of me and of my words, the Son of Man will be ashamed of that person, when he comes in his splendour, and in the splendour of his Father and of the holy angels. I tell you truly, there are some of those standing here who will not taste death until they see the kingdom of God.'

Luke, we have said, is the Gospel of prayer, and it is characteristic that he presents Jesus as praying at this important moment of Peter's accurate recognition of him. Much less is made by Luke than by Mark and Matthew of Peter's subsequent failure to grasp what *kind* of Messiah he is.

You may puzzle about how Jesus can be both 'on his own' and with his disciples. Perhaps we should not ask Luke this question. Another puzzle concerns Jesus' statement that 'there are some of those standing here who will not taste death until they see the kingdom of God'. Jesus and the early Church certainly seem to have expected the Second Coming fairly soon after the Resurrection. We have learnt not to expect it to be coming so soon.

Notice that the range of answers to the question who Jesus is coincides, almost exactly, with the suggestions earlier in the chapter. Luke is perhaps here tidying up what he found in Mark; but he is also making this recognition moment far less central than it was in Mark's Gospel; he even removes the reference to Caesarea Philippi. At the same time, the reference to the 'splendour of the Son of Man', in the context of the Father and the angels, indicates that Luke has a very 'high' view of who Jesus is; he is God, or the nearest thing to God. And, in the same vein, notice the references to 'splendour' in the story that now follows.

The glory of Jesus with Moses and Elijah

28-36 It happened about eight days after these words [or: 'events'] that taking Peter and John and James he went up onto the mountain to pray. And it happened as he prayed that the appearance of his face was different; and his clothing was white, gleaming like lightning. And look! Two men were speaking with him, who were Moses and Elijah. They appeared in splendour, and were speaking of his departure [or: 'exodus'] which he was to accomplish in Jerusalem.

Now Peter and those with him were overcome with sleep; and when they were fully awake, they saw his splendour, and the two men standing with him. And when they were separated from him, Peter said to Jesus, 'Master, it is right for us to be here – and let's make three tents, one for you and one for Moses and one for Elijah (having no idea what he was saying)'. As he was saying this, there was a cloud, and it overshadowed them. They were afraid when they entered the cloud; and a voice came from the cloud, saying, 'This is my Son, the Chosen One – listen to him.' And when the voice had come, Jesus alone was there. And they were silent; and in those days they reported to nobody any of the things which they had seen.

> Luke makes some small changes (and we may notice that he has omitted much of Mark's Chapters 6 to 8). Once again, he has Jesus at prayer; the transfiguration itself is in a slightly lower key (unlike Mark, he does not even use the word). Luke alone has Moses and Elijah speaking of Jesus' 'exodus' or 'departure'. This could also refer to his death, of course, and it looks ahead, as this Gospel has always done, to Jerusalem. The 'overshadowing' is also in Mark, but it reminds Luke's reader of what happened to Mary when Jesus was conceived (1:35). Luke alone has the disciples weighed down by sleep. Finally, Luke has softened Mark's abrupt command to silence at the end of the story.

The spirit the disciples couldn't expel

37-43a It happened on the next day, as they went down from the mountain, that a great crowd met them. And look! A man shouted from the crowd, 'Teacher, I implore you to look kindly on my son, because he is my only one, and look! A spirit takes him, and he suddenly cries out, and it convulses him and he foams; and it hardly leaves him, and it wears him out. And I asked your disciples to expel it – and they couldn't!'

Jesus responded, 'O faithless and perverted generation – how long shall I be with you and put up with you? Bring your son here.'

As he was still approaching, the demon threw him down and convulsed him. Jesus rebuked the unclean spirit, and healed the boy, and restored him to his father. They were all struck by the greatness of God.

> This is a much briefer version than Mark's account of the incident (Mark 9:14-29), and Luke is gentler with the disciples. There are at least three characteristic Lucan touches: 'the next day' (see 7:11); 'look kindly' (1:48), and 'the greatness of God' (see, for example 1:46, 49, 58; 9:43, each of which uses the same Greek root). There is less detail in Luke's version, but he has introduced a typical reference to 'healing'.

The suffering of the Son of Man; the unresponsive disciples

43b-50 While everyone wondered at everything that he was doing, he said to his disciples, 'Put these words into your ears: you see, the Son of Man is about to be handed over into the power of human beings.'

But they had no idea of this matter, and it was concealed from them, so that they should [not] understand it – and they were afraid to ask him about this matter.

An argument arose among them – 'Who was likely to be the Most Important?' Jesus knew about the argument of their heart; and he took hold of a little boy, and stood him next to him, and said to them, 'Whoever welcomes this little boy in my name welcomes me. And whoever welcomes me welcomes the one who sent me. For the least significant among you, that is Mr Big.'

John responded, 'Master, we saw someone casting out demons in your name – and we tried to prevent him, because he is not a disciple with us.'

Jesus said, 'Don't prevent him – for whoever is not against you is on your side.'

> The three elements that make up this section are all in Mark 9:30-41, but Luke is gentler, less harshly mysterious than Mark, and includes less detail.

The Journey to Jerusalem (9:51–19:40)

The journey begins

51-62 It happened when the days of his taking-up were fulfilled, he also set his face to journey to Jerusalem. And he sent messengers before his face. And as they journeyed, they went into a village of the Samaritans, to prepare for him. And they did not offer him hospitality, because his face was journeying to Jerusalem. When they saw it, disciples James and John said, 'Lord, do you want us to tell fire to come down from heaven and annihilate them?'

But he turned and rebuked them – and they journeyed to another village.

And as they journeyed on the way, someone said to him, 'I'll follow you wherever you go.'

And Jesus said to him, 'Foxes have lairs, and birds of the sky have places to live, but the Son of Man has nowhere to recline his head.'

He said to another, 'Follow me.' But he said, 'Lord, let me first go and bury my father.'

But he said to him, 'Let the corpses bury their own corpses – as for you, off you go and proclaim the kingdom of God far and wide.'

And another said, 'I'll follow you, Lord – but first allow me to say farewell to those at my house.'

Jesus said to him, 'No one who puts his hand to the plough and looks back is suitable for the kingdom of God.'

> At this point, Luke turns his Gospel very firmly in the direction of Jerusalem. The use of the word 'fulfilled' takes us back to 1:1, where we have the same idea, if not precisely the same Greek word. He uses the word 'taking-up' here. The verb is the one used in Acts for Jesus' Ascension; but in the light of the recent conversation that we

have overheard between Moses, Elijah and Jesus, we also know that it refers to Jesus' Death and Resurrection.

Luke uses his 'journeying' word five times in these few lines, to underline that something is starting here, which only ends with his arrival in Jerusalem at the end of Chapter 19. There are other aspects to the journey:

- it includes Samaria (important in the journey, and also in the reverse journey that is Acts, at least at its beginning; we should note that Samaritans generally get a good press in Luke – see 10:33; 17:16. They were highly unpopular with the inhabitants of Judah, for they were thought to be of mixed race and doubtful orthodoxy);
- the quotation about 'messengers before his face' is used by Mark (1:2) and Matthew (11:10) for John the Baptist;
- note the three (rather discouraging) remarks to would-be disciples. Luke has collected them here as a preface to the journey, just as he made the episode in the synagogue at Nazareth a preface to Jesus' ministry as a whole. The third episode is not paralleled in Matthew, but echoes the call of Elisha in 1 Kings 19:20;
- the fiery desires of James and John may explain why (according to Mark) they were nicknamed 'Sons of Thunder'. It may be significant that they echo Elijah (2 Kings 1:10, 12);
- notice that Jesus 'turns' to these would-be terrorists. In Luke this word denotes careful attention. See 7:9, 44; 10:29; 14:25, and especially perhaps 22:61 (Peter) and 23:28 (the women of Jerusalem).

The mission of the seventy-two, and their joyful return

10 ¹⁻²⁴ After this, the Lord appointed another seventy-two, and sent them in pairs before his face to every town and place where he was intending to go. He said to them, 'The harvest is great, but the labourers are few; therefore implore the Lord of the harvest to send out labourers into his harvest.

'Go. Look! I am sending you as lambs in the midst of wolves. Do not carry a money bag or a knapsack, or sandals, and greet no one on the way. Whatever house you enter, first say, "Peace upon this house!" and if there is a peace-person [literally: 'son of peace'] there, your peace will rest upon that person. Otherwise it will return to you. Stay in that house, eating and drinking their food and drink; for the labourer is worthy of his hire. Do not transfer from house to house. And whatever city you enter, and they give you hospitality, eat what is put before you, and cure the sick who are in the city, and tell them, "The kingdom of God has drawn near upon you." Whatever city you enter, and they fail to give you hospitality, go out into its streets and say, "Because of you [or: 'for you'] we shall even wipe off the dust that clings to us from your city. But be aware that the kingdom of God has drawn near." I am telling you: it will be more bearable for Sodom on that day than for that city.

'Woe to you, Chorazin; woe to you, Bethsaida. Because if the miracles that took place in you had happened in Tyre and Sidon, they would long since have sat down and repented. But for Tyre and Sidon it will be more bearable at the Judgement than it will be for you.

'And you Caphernaum – do you want to be exalted up to heaven? You will go down to Hades!

'The one who listens to you people, listens to me; the one who rejects you rejects me; and the one who rejects me rejects the one who sent me.'

The seventy-two returned joyfully; they said, 'Lord – even the demons do what we tell them [literally: 'are subordinated to us'] in your name!'

He told them, 'I saw Satan falling from heaven like lightning. Look! I have given you authority to tread on snakes and scorpions, and on all the Enemy's power – and no way will anything hurt you. But don't rejoice because the spirits do what you tell them; instead, rejoice that your names are written in heaven.'

At that moment, he rejoiced in the Holy Spirit and said, 'I give thanks to you, Father, Lord of heaven and earth, because you have hidden these things from clever and intelligent people, and revealed them to infants. Yes, Father, because that was the way you wanted it to be. Everything is handed over to me by my Father; and no one knows who the Son is except the Father, nor who the Father is except the Son, and whoever the Son wishes to reveal it to.'

And turning privately to the disciples he said, 'Happy are the eyes who see what you see. For I tell you that many prophets and kings wanted to see what you see, and didn't see it, and to hear what you hear and didn't hear it.'

> These instructions before the seventy-two go out, and the comments on their return, are really a version of the 'ripple effect', and so part of the journeying theme. Matthew (9:37, 38; 10:7-15) has a good deal of the material, but only Luke makes it a preliminary to Jesus' mission. Luke has some slightly daunting touches, such as the instruction to 'greet nobody on the way'. Luke alone has the tail-wagging return of the emissaries, to which he joins Jesus' thanksgiving to the Father, which is also in Matthew, but not part of this episode. The same is true of the congratulations to the disciples. Luke has made a coherent unit out of it, perhaps an indication of the importance he gives to the 'ripple effect'.

The lawyer's question, and a *good* Samaritan!

25-37 And look! A certain lawyer stood up, putting him to the test, and said, 'Teacher, what shall I do to inherit eternal life?'

He said, 'In the Torah what is written? How do you read [it]?'

He answered, '"You will love the Lord your God with all your heart and with all your soul and with all your strength and with all your understanding, and your neighbour as yourself."'

He said to him, 'You have given the correct answer. Do this, and you will live.'

But he wanted to put himself in the right, and said to Jesus, 'And who *is* my neighbour?'

Jesus took up the thread and said, 'A man was going down from Jerusalem to Jericho, and he fell into the hands of muggers. They took his clothes off, rained blows on him, and went off leaving him half dead. By coincidence, a priest was going down on that road, and, seeing him, passed by on the opposite side. A Levite also went down by that spot, and when he saw him, similarly passed by on the opposite side. Then a travelling Samaritan came upon him, and when he saw [him] he had compassion! He approached and bound up his wounds, pouring olive oil and wine on them; and he put him on his own animal, and took him to an inn, and looked after him. And the next day he took out two denarii and gave them to the innkeeper, and said, "Look after him, and whatever extra you spend, I'll repay you when I return."

'Which of these three, in your view, acted as neighbour to the one who had fallen into the muggers' hands?'

He said, 'The one who did the mercy on him.'

Jesus said to him, 'Journey on, and [make sure] you do the same.'

This is the first of many lovely Lucan parables. A version of this episode is in both Mark (12:28-31) and Matthew (22:35-40), each with their own differences. Lawyers on the whole do not do well in Luke's Gospel, whereas Samaritans generally get a good press from him.

The alert reader will notice that the story is set in the context of some rather dangerous journeying, and that at the end the lawyer is told to 'journey'.

The road on which the story is set will doubtless have been familiar to Jesus' hearers, as will the perils of it, for it runs through the desert, with hills on either side, ideal for setting an ambush.

The best stories are told in threes ('an Englishman, an Irishman and a Scotsman', for example), and the third member contains the key. We may imagine Jesus' audience chuckling at the behaviour of the clergy, expecting No. 3 to be 'an ordinary layman' perhaps, and then getting a dreadful shock when he turned out to be a hated Samaritan.

The third 'disastrous dinner party': Martha and Mary

38-42 As they journeyed, *he* went into a village. Now a woman called Martha gave him hospitality; and she had a sister called Mary, who, when she had sat down by the Lord's feet, kept listening to what he said. Now Martha was distracted with much service, and she came up and said, 'Lord – don't you care that my sister has abandoned me to serve all alone? So tell her to come and help me.'

The Lord said to her in reply, 'Martha, Martha: you're over-anxious and disturbed about many things; there is need only of one thing. You see, Mary has chosen the better portion, and it won't be taken away from her.'

This is another lovely story; the companions of the journey suddenly disappear, and we find Jesus alone with two women, which must have seemed odd for a religious teacher. The women, however, are presented as people in their own right: Martha is the hostess (no man in sight), and Mary a disciple. Martha is not given the help that she asks for, but the gentle repetition of her name softens any lurking rebuke, though we may observe that, just as the lawyer in the previous story could not sully his lips with the word 'Samaritan', so here Martha cannot bring herself to mention her sister's name.

159

Mary is like that other woman (7:38), sitting at Jesus' feet; Martha's plight is neatly expressed in the notion of 'much service' and 'serving all alone': 'service' is a value in Luke's Gospel, but when it is experienced as heavy, and as lonely, then it has turned into something else, and Martha finds herself giving orders to her eminent guest, which puts her mildly in the wrong, although Luke does not tell us how the remainder of the dinner party goes.

Teaching about prayer

11 **1-13** And it happened when he was in a certain place praying. When he ceased, one of his disciples said to him, 'Lord, teach us to pray, as John also taught his disciples.'
He said to them, 'When you pray, say:

> Father – may your name be sanctified.
> May your kingdom come.
> Each day, give us our bread for the coming day.
> And forgive us our sins,
> for we ourselves also forgive everyone who is in debt to us.
> And do not put us to the test.'

And he said to them, 'Suppose one of you has a friend come to him in the middle of the night and say to him, "My friend, lend me three loaves, because my friend has appeared at my house after a journey, and I have nothing to put before him" – would any of you reply from inside, "Don't bother me: the door is already locked, and my children and I are in bed. I can't get up and give you [anything]"? I tell you – even if he won't get up and give him something because he's a friend, his friend's persistence will make him arise and give him all he needs.

'And *I* am telling *you*: ask, and it will be given you; seek, and you will find; knock [at the door], and it will be opened to you. For everyone who asks receives; the one who seeks, finds; and to the one who knocks [on the door] it is opened.

'Suppose that one of you is a father, and his son asks for a fish – is he going to give him a snake instead of a fish? Or suppose he asks for an egg – is he going to give him a scorpion?

'So – if you people (who are wicked) are competent to give appropriate gifts to your children, will not your Heavenly Father all the more give the Holy Spirit to those who ask him?'

Luke, as we have already said, is the Gospel of prayer; this passage is the first place where the evangelist has put together any explicit teaching on prayer. The beginning and the end are in Matthew's Sermon on the Mount (6:9-13 and 7:7-11), while the middle section, the quietly humorous tale of the friend who arrives at midnight, is only in Luke. The first section is Luke's version of the Lord's Prayer, different in many respects from Matthew's (which Christians know better), but still recognisably the same. Luke's version is shorter, and many scholars think it may be more original.

What is the teaching about prayer? First, the disciples regard it as a bit puzzling, but something that they ought to do, and that Jesus ought to teach them to do, if only to keep up with the spiritual Jones's ('the disciples of John the Baptist'). Second the parable of the friend at midnight with gentle humour (imagining God as someone who would rather stay in bed!) teaches what prayer is like: it is a relationship between friends, who will cheerfully give other friends what they need. There are three 'friends' in the parable, the one in bed, the one who wants bread, and the one who has been on a journey, and the repetition of the word may seem a bit clumsy, until we realise what Luke is doing: the key to prayer is friendship. God is not, therefore, a drinks dispenser, which discharges the appropriate substance when the appropriate coin is inserted and the right button pressed. That is the explanation of the otherwise very difficult passage, 'ask and it will be given you . . . '; and when Luke uses the 'divine passives', such as 'it will be given', he is reminding us that we are speaking of God. We can be confident of God's unfailing generosity; but it is not for us to lay down the rules. And we are positively encouraged to be persistent, to the point of shamelessness. Third, though, we should notice that Jesus uses quite powerful, active verbs for talking about prayer: 'ask', 'seek', and 'find' suggest that we are supposed to take an initiative in prayer, and present our needs: Luke's version of the Lord's Prayer is all requests, although of course we may always have to recognise that God may know better than we do what we need.

Is Jesus working *with* the demons or *against* them?

14-26 And he was expelling a demon; and it was dumb. It turned out that when the demon left, the dumb man spoke – and the crowds were astonished. Some of them, however, said, 'It is by Beelzeboul, the ruler of the demons, that he casts out demons,' while others put him to the test by asking him for a sign from heaven. But he knew their thoughts, and told them, 'Every kingdom that is divided against itself is laid waste, and house falls on house. Now – if Satan is divided against himself, how is his kingdom going to stand, since you say that it is by Beelzeboul that I am expelling demons? You see, if it is by Beelzeboul that I am expelling demons, by whom do your people expel them? So it is they who will be your judges. If, on the other hand, it is by the finger of God that I expel demons – then the kingdom of God has come upon you!

'When the strong man, fully armed, is guarding his own palace, then his possessions are at peace. However whenever someone who is stronger than he is comes and defeats him, he takes away the full armour that he had relied on; and he shares out his booty.

'The one who is not with me is against me; and the one who does not gather with me scatters.

'When the unclean spirit leaves the person, he goes through waterless places, looking for rest, and not finding it. Then it says, "I'll go back to the home I came from." And it comes and finds it swept and decorated. Then it goes on a journey and finds seven other [demons] wickeder than it is – and they go in and dwell there. And that person's final state is worse than their first.'

Like Jesus' contemporaries, Luke's readers have to decide who Jesus is: clearly he meets with demons as a worthy opponent. So is he on their side or on God's side? Jesus here makes one or two sensible observations to help answer the question – and we cannot evade the conclusion, that 'the kingdom of God has come upon you', nor the challenge: are we for him or against him? And we are warned to take the demons seriously.

A woman's intervention is capped

27, 28 It happened as he was saying this that a woman from the crowd raised her voice and said to him, 'Happy the womb that bore you, and the breasts which you sucked.' But he said, 'On the contrary – happy are those who hear the word of God and keep it.'

Luke is the Gospel of women; but that does not mean that women always get it right. Here, a woman's attempt to congratulate Jesus' mother turns into a congratulation of all disciples 'who hear the word of God and keep it'. We remember Mary, of course, in the previous chapter, who did just that, not to mention that other Mary, Jesus' mother, who 'kept all these words, pondering them in her heart' and 'kept all these events in her heart'.

Teaching: repentance and visibility

29-36 When the crowds had gathered even more, he began to say, 'This generation is a wicked generation: it looks for a sign, and it won't be given a sign, except for Jonah's sign; for just as Jonah was a sign for the people of Nineveh, that's how the Son of Man will be for this generation. The Queen of the South will rise up at the Judgement with the men of this generation, and condemn them – because she came from the ends of the earth to hear the wisdom of Solomon; and look! There's [something] more than Solomon here. The men of Nineveh will rise up with this generation at the Judgement and condemn it – because they repented at Jonah's proclamation. And look! There's [something] more than Jonah here.

'No one lights a lamp and puts it in a cellar, but on the lamp-stand, so that those who journey into [the house] may see the light.

'The light of the body is your eye. When your eye is healthy [or: 'simple', 'clear'], then the whole of your body is illuminated. But if it is bad, then your body is darkened. Watch out: [you don't want] the light that is in you to become darkness. So if your whole body is illuminated, not having even a little bit [of it] darkened, it will be entirely illuminated, as when the lamp illuminates you with its beam.'

These bits of teaching are found also in Matthew, though in different places (Matthew 12:38-42; 5:15; 6:34), so perhaps it is Luke who has brought them together, except that they do not obviously belong together. We may notice, though, that the 'sign of Jonah' in Matthew 12:40 had to do with the Resurrection, whereas in Luke, the 'Gospel of repentance', it is about repentance. The alert reader will have noticed that Luke has already used a different version of the saying about 'lighting a lamp' back in 8:16. We may also observe that it is men, and not women, who are going to be judged, and that the Queen of Sheba, not only a woman, but also a foreigner, will be doing the judgement. Luke is the Gospel of the marginalised.

The fourth 'disastrous dinner party'

37-54 As he was speaking, a Pharisee invited him to have breakfast with him at his house. He went in and lay down. When the Pharisee saw [it], he was surprised that he didn't have a ritual washing first, before breakfast. The Lord said to him, 'Now you Pharisees, you clean the outside of cup and dish; but your inside is full of robbery and wickedness. Fools! Did not the One who made the outside also make the inside? So – give alms on what is within, and see, everything will be clean for you.

'No – woe to you Pharisees: you pay tithes of mint and rue, and every kind of vegetable, and you overlook God's judgement and love; *that's* what you should have performed, without overlooking the other things.

'Woe to you, Pharisees: you love the chief seats in the synagogues and being greeted in the market place.

'Woe to you: you are like graves which are not seen, and people walk on top without knowing.'

One of the lawyers answered, 'Teacher, when you say this, it's us also whom you are insulting.' And he said, 'And to you lawyers also, woe! Because you put hard-to-bear burdens on to people; but you yourselves do not touch the burdens with [even] a single finger!

'Woe to you, because you build the prophets' tombs. Your ancestors killed them: you are witnesses, and you approve of your ancestors' deeds, because they killed them and you build [their tombs]. For this reason, the Wisdom of God said, "I shall send them prophets and apostles, and some of them they will kill and persecute," in order that vengeance may be exacted for the blood of all the prophets which has been shed since the foundation of the world, from Abel's blood to the blood of Zechariah, who was killed between altar and Temple. And, I tell you, it will be exacted from this generation.

'Woe to you lawyers, because you took away the key of knowledge: you yourselves didn't enter, and you managed to thwart those who were trying to enter.'

And when he went out of there, the scribes and the Pharisees started to be very resentful and to watch closely what he said on a wider range of topics, and to plot to catch him out in something he might say.

> This fourth 'disastrous dinner party' ends with the battlelines clearly drawn. Jesus has deliberately annoyed Pharisees, lawyers and scribes, admittedly after his host had thought disapproving thoughts about his lack of ritual observance (the word translated as 'surprised', with more than a hint of disapproval, elsewhere in Luke means, positively, 'marvel'), and now they are out to get him. Some of what Jesus says to the lawyers is very obscure, especially the utterance by the 'Wisdom of God' and the talk about 'building' – but there is nothing obscure about our sense that conflict is brewing.

Teaching the disciples

12 ¹⁻¹² In the middle of this, as vast numbers of the crowd had gathered, [so many] that they were trampling each other, he began to speak to his disciples: 'First and foremost, steer clear of the leaven (which is hypocrisy) of the Pharisees.

'Nothing is hidden which will not be revealed; and nothing concealed which will not be made known. Therefore whatever you say in the darkness will be heard in the light, and whatever you speak confidentially [literally: 'into the ear'] in the innermost rooms will be proclaimed on the rooftops.

'I am telling you, who are my friends: don't be fearful of those who kill the body, and after that have nothing further [that they can] do; I'll show you whom to fear: be afraid of the one who, after he has killed you, has authority to throw you into Gehenna. Yes, I tell you: be afraid of that one.

'Are not five sparrows sold for two assaria? And not one of these is forgotten by [literally, 'before'] God. No – the hairs of your head are all numbered. Don't be afraid; you are worth more than many sparrows.

'I tell you, everyone who speaks up for me before human beings, the Son of Man will speak up for that person before God's angels. And the person who denies me before human beings will be denied before the angels of God.

'And whoever says a word against the Son of Man, it will be forgiven him; whereas the one who blasphemes against the Holy Spirit will not be forgiven.

'When they bring you in before synagogues and authorities and magistrates, don't get anxious about how to make your defence or what to say. For the Holy Spirit at that moment will give you what you must say.'

The connections between the various parts of this speech are not easy to see, unless the link is the idea of unfailing faithfulness even when persecution comes. Jesus' disciples must expect the same treatment as he received. This passage starts with a reference back to the Pharisees of the previous episode ('beware of their leaven'), continues with some general warnings: don't presume confidentiality; don't fear the wrong people; be confident of your worth before God; don't be ashamed of the Son of Man; (above all) don't blaspheme the Holy Spirit, who will tell you what to say when you are arraigned.

Assarion: one-sixteenth of a denarius. Just think of the smallest coin that you can imagine. The word Gehenna means (or nearly means) 'Valley of the Brothers Hinnom', a valley in Jerusalem where waste was burnt and corpses buried, so a symbol of decay and pollution.

Teaching about riches

¹³⁻²¹ Someone spoke to him from the crowd, 'Teacher, tell my brother to divide the inheritance with me.'

But he said to him, 'Man! Who appointed me a referee or arbitrator over you people?'

He said to them, 'Look out and guard yourselves from all greed; because a person's life does not consist in having enough-and-to-spare in the way of possessions.'

He told them a parable: 'A certain wealthy person had an estate that had done well. And he debated with himself: "What then am I to do? I have nowhere to put my produce." He said, "This is what I shall do: I'll pull down all my storehouses and build bigger ones; and I'll bring all my grain and all my goods together in them. And I'll tell my soul, 'Soul – you have many good things stored up for many years. Take it easy – eat and drink and have a good time.'" But God said to him, "Fool! This very night your life [or: 'soul'] is being asked back from you. The stuff that you prepared – whose will it be?" That's how it is with people who save up for themselves and are not wealthy in regard to God.'

This passage is only in Luke, the request and Jesus' response. It is characteristic of Luke's rather negative attitude to wealth, which may have sent a shiver down the spine of his affluent church (assuming that is what they were). The parable is a bit starker than Luke generally goes in for, and the characterisation rather more two-dimensional (though see also the story of Lazarus and the rich man – Luke 16:19-31), but that may simply reflect the urgency he gives to the principle of detachment from possessions in the Christian life.

Jesus' response 'Man' may sound like modern American slang, but a) it is a literal translation and b) it probably catches the tone of the original. The phrase translated as 'is being asked back' literally means 'they are asking back'. Like 'these things will be added to you' in the next section (12:31), this is Luke's discreet way of indicating that God is at work.

No material worries: God will look after you

22-34 He said to his disciples, 'For this reason, I'm telling you: Don't worry about your life [or: 'soul'], what you are to eat, nor about your body, what you're to wear. For life is more than food, and the body is more than clothing. Think of the ravens: they don't sow or reap; they have no cellars or storehouses, and God feeds them! How much more important are you than [mere] birds? Which of you, by worrying, can add an hour to the length of your life? So if you can't even do the tiniest thing, why are you worrying about the rest? Look at how lilies grow: they don't work [for a living]; nor do they weave [cloth]. But I'm telling you, not even Solomon in all his glory was dressed like one of them! Now – if God dresses up hay like this, which is in the field today, and tomorrow thrown into an oven, won't [he do] all the more for you, people of little faith? So don't you start looking for something to eat or something to drink; and don't be anxious. You see this is what the nations of the world are looking for; but your Father knows that you need these things. Just look for his kingdom, and God will supply you with these things in addition. Don't be afraid, little flock – because your Father in heaven has been pleased to give you the kingdom.

'Sell your possessions and give alms. Manufacture moneybags for yourselves that never grow old, inexhaustible treasure in heaven, where no burglar approaches, and no moths gobble [it] up. For where your treasure is, that is where your heart will be.'

This passage fits well enough with the previous passage and Luke's emphasis on the danger of possessions, although it is a text that Luke largely shares with Matthew, with the order slightly altered.

The starkness of discipleship: on being ready for the end-time

35-59 'Be dressed for action; have your lamps burning. You [are to be] like people expecting their Lord when he returns from the wedding, so that when he comes and knocks they immediately open up for him. Happy are those slaves whom the Lord finds still awake when he comes. Amen I tell you: he will put on his clothes, make them lie down to eat, and come and wait on them. Congratulations to them if he comes even in the second watch or even in the third watch and finds them like this. But be sure of this: if the householder knew what time the burglar was coming, he wouldn't allow his house to be broken into. And so you must be ready, because the Son of Man is coming at a time when you don't think he will.'

Peter said to him, 'Lord, are you telling this parable to us or to everybody?'

And the Lord said to him, 'So who is the reliable and sensible steward, whom the Lord will appoint over his servants, to give out the food-allowance at the proper time? Congratulations to that slave whom the Lord when he comes finds doing this. Truly I tell you that he will appoint him in charge of all his possessions. If however that slave says in his heart, "My Lord is taking his time in coming," and begins beating the male and female slaves, and [starts] eating and drinking and getting drunk, that slave's Lord will come on a day when he does not expect, and at a time [that] he does not know – and he'll cut him in two and set his portion with the unbelievers.

'That slave who knows what his Lord wants, and hasn't prepared or acted in accordance with his will, shall be beaten many times. On the other hand, the one who did not know, but has done what deserves chastisement, shall be beaten fewer times. Everyone to whom God has given much, God will demand much from them. The one to whom God has entrusted much, God will demand much more from them.

'I have come to set fire to the earth, and what do I want, if it is already kindled? [or: 'how I wish it were already blazing']. I have a baptism to be baptised with – and how great is my distress until it is accomplished. Do you think that I came to give peace on earth? No, I tell you: I came to bring division. For from now on, there will be five in a single house, divided three against two and two against three; father will be divided against son, and son against father, mother against daughter and daughter against mother, mother-in-law against daughter-in-law, and daughter-in-law against mother-in-law.'

And he said to the crowds, 'When you see a cloud arising in the west, immediately you say, "A rainstorm is on its way" – and so it turns out. And when [you notice] the south wind blowing, you say, "It'll be a scorcher" – and it happens. Hypocrites [or: 'actors']! You know how to interpret the appearance of earth and sky, but you have no idea how to interpret this moment?

'Why don't you assess what is right on your own account? When you are going to the magistrate with your opponent, while you are travelling, take the trouble to settle with him, in case he drags you to the judge, and the judge hands you over to the constable, and the constable flings you into prison. I'm telling you, no way will you come out of there, till you have paid the last penny.'

> There is some uncomfortable teaching here; some fragments of it appear in Matthew, but Luke has made much more of a discourse of it. In one way it seems to continue the previous discourse; but the sudden shift to 'readiness for the end' and the change of tone seem to justify making a new section of it.

There are one or two shocks:

- the idea of the Lord (or Master) putting on his waiter's outfit and feeding his own slaves is decidedly unexpected. Perhaps Luke is trying to startle his affluent readers;
- the word Lord/Master shifts between Jesus and the slave-owner in an interesting and startling way, although when Jesus' hearers are warned that they'll be placed with 'unbelievers' if they are asleep when he comes, it is clear that we are not precisely speaking of real servants, but of disciples;
- Jesus asks if we think that he has come to bring 'peace on earth'. The answer is 'Yes', because that is what the angels indicated to the shepherds in 2:14;
- even Luke's grammar becomes rather jarring here, but it can't be done in English.

On repentance – the parable of the fig tree

13 **1-9** At that time some people were there, telling him about the Galileans whose blood Pilate had mixed with their sacrifices. In reply he said to them, 'Do you think that these Galileans were worse than all other Galileans, that they suffered this? No, I tell you: unless you all repent, you will die in a similar way. Or what about the eighteen people on whom the tower at Siloam fell and killed them – do you think that they were worse sinners [or: 'debtors'] than everyone else who lives in Jerusalem? No, I tell you: unless you all repent, you will die in just the same way.'

He told this parable: 'A person had a fig tree planted in his vineyard, and he came looking for fruit on it, and found none. He told the vinedresser, "Look – it's three years I've been coming to look for fruit on this fig tree and not finding it. So cut it down – why [should] it occupy [the ground] to no purpose?" But he replied, "Lord – let it go for this year too; give me a chance to dig it round and put manure on it, and [see] if it yields fruit in future . . . otherwise you can cut it down."'

Luke is the Gospel of repentance, and we have here a story and a parable that both emphasise the urgency of repentance. Jesus is told of some of his fellow Galileans who have been butchered by Pilate (just as he will in the end be butchered by Pilate), and he attacks the implied comment that they deserved it more than anyone else. Then he mentions some Jerusalemites who were killed in an accident, and applies a similar interpretation to them: *everyone* needs to repent, and soon. Then he tells a fig-tree parable, which is possibly Luke's version of the difficult story in Mark 11; it also, however, echoes the angry parody of a love song in Isaiah 5, about Israel as the Lord's unfruitful vineyard. Sinners, like fig trees, are given another chance – but not indefinitely.

Luke is also, of course, the journeying Gospel, and the reader will notice that once again the two terminus points, Galilee and Jerusalem, are mentioned; currently Jesus is on his journey from the first to the second (although we might be pardoned for thinking here that he has already arrived).

The cure of a woman, crippled for eighteen years

10-17 He was teaching in one of the synagogues on the Sabbath. And look! A woman who had had a diseased spirit for eighteen years, and was bent over and unable to straighten up at all. When he saw her, Jesus addressed her and said, 'Woman – be freed from your disease'; and he laid his hands on her, and immediately she straightened up – and she glorified God. The ruler of the synagogue was annoyed that Jesus had healed on the Sabbath; and he told the crowd, 'There are six days when [we] have to work: so come and be cured on those days, and not on the Sabbath-day.'

The Lord answered him, 'Hypocrites: doesn't each of you on the Sabbath untie your ox or your ass from the trough and take them to drink? But this woman is a daughter of Abraham, whom – look! – Satan had bound for eighteen years: wasn't it necessary for her to be freed from this captivity on the Sabbath-day?'

When he said this, his opponents were all embarrassed; and the whole crowd rejoiced at all the glorious things that were being done by him.

> This story displays two possible reactions to Jesus: the cured woman glorifies God, which, as we have already seen, is an appropriate reaction as far as Luke is concerned. The reaction of the synagogue-ruler is inappropriate: his target is Jesus, but it is the crowds whom he addresses, telling them that work is forbidden on the Sabbath, even though it is not *they* who have been working. Jesus' response is stern, and aimed more widely than at just the ruler, since it is addressed to 'hypocrites' in the plural. Once again the battlelines are drawn, and at the end of the story we see two possible reactions to Jesus: either embarrassment or rejoicing at glorious things.

Two parables (one male, one female) and a 'Lucan summary'

18-22 And so he said, 'What is the kingdom of God like, and to what shall I compare it? It is like a grain of mustard, which a man took and threw into his garden; and it grew and turned into a tree, and "the birds of heaven lived in its branches".'

And again he said, 'What shall I compare the kingdom of God to? It is like a leaven which a woman took and hid in three measures of flour until it was all leavened.'

And he was journeying through cities and villages, teaching, and making a journey to Jerusalem.

> Luke often balances his references to men and to women, indicating that the gospel is for all humanity; so here we have a male gardener and a baker woman standing as icons of God. The 'and so' with which the first parable opens may suggest that it is linked with the preceding rejection in the synagogue: the man's gesture of 'throwing' the grain of mustard into the garden feels more like rejection, less like serious gardening. Either way, the point of the story lies in the restless power of God, which is also present in the 'journey' motif of the 'Lucan summary' which ties the two parables together.
>
> The quotation about the 'birds of heaven' comes from Psalm 103:12.

The difficulty of getting into the kingdom of God

23-30   Someone said to him, 'Lord, is it [just a] few who are being saved?' He said to them, 'Keep struggling to go in through the narrow gate, because, I tell you, many will try to get in, and won't manage it, once the master of the house has got up and locked the door. And you'll begin to stand outside and knock on the door saying, "Lord, open up for us"; and he'll answer you, "I don't know where you people come from." Then you'll start saying, "We ate and drank in your presence, and you taught in our streets." And he'll tell you, "I don't know where you come from: Depart from me, all you doers of evil."

'Then there will be weeping and gnashing of teeth, when you see Abraham, Isaac and Jacob and all the prophets in the kingdom of God, and you people thrown outside. They'll come from east and west, and from north and south. And see – the ones who are going to be first are [now] last; and the ones who are going to be last are [now] first.'

The whole of Chapter 13 has sin and rejection as its deepest theme. Here our attention is more explicitly on who gets into the kingdom. For the first time this 'universal gospel' speaks of the inclusion of the Gentiles, and the concomitant exclusion of some of those who think they have an automatic right of entry. This is not necessarily addressed only to Jesus' Jewish hearers; Luke may also have the over-comfortable members of his church in view. Notice how an individual's question at the beginning provokes an address to a wider audience: 'he said to *them*'. This is not the first time that we have seen this technique in Luke's Gospel.

'Depart from me, all you doers of evil' comes from Psalm 6:8.

Pharisees, Herod, Jerusalem

31-35   At that moment, some Pharisees came up and said to him, 'Get out, and journey away from here, because Herod is wanting to kill you.' And he said to them, 'Go ['journey', of course] and tell that fox: "See, I am expelling demons and performing healings today and tomorrow, and on the third day I am being consummated." But today and tomorrow and the next day I *must* journey, because it is not possible for a prophet to die outside Jerusalem.

'Jerusalem, Jerusalem, she who kills the prophets, and stones those who are sent to her, how often did I want to gather your children, like a bird gathers her young under her wings, and you didn't want it. Look – your house is abandoned. I tell you, you won't see me until you say, "Blessed is the one who comes in the Lord's name."'

The 'journeying' theme is to the fore here, and it is made clearer than at any point in the Gospel so far that the journey must end in death: see the references here to 'consummated' (like the 'exodus' at the Transfiguration, it must be Jesus' Death and Resurrection), to dying in Jerusalem, and to killing the prophets. Once again there is the theme of rejection, symbolised by Herod, clearly, and by Jerusalem, and perhaps also by the Pharisees, who are on the face of it trying to help Jesus, but a) their advice would mean interrupting his journey,

b) Jesus assumes that they are in regular contact with Herod, and c) all references to them thus far in the Gospel have led us to expect the worst. Notice the characteristic 'I *must* journey': the word 'must' is only three letters in Greek, but it punches well above its weight in Luke-Acts.

Jesus' reference to them saying 'Blessed is the one who comes . . .' refers, of course, to his arrival in Jerusalem. See how Luke always gently reminds us of where the journey is headed.

The fifth 'disastrous dinner party'

14 1-24 And it happened as he was going into the house of one of the rulers of the Pharisees on a Sabbath to eat bread: and they were watching him carefully.

And look! A man suffering from dropsy was before him; and in response Jesus said to the lawyers and Pharisees, 'Is it permitted to heal on the Sabbath or not?' They were silent. And he took him and healed him and let him go; and he said to them, 'If one of you has a son or an ox fall into a well, won't he immediately pull him out on the Sabbath-day?' And they couldn't manage any answer in response to this.

He told his fellow guests a parable, as he noticed how they chose the top places, saying to them, 'When someone invites you to a wedding, don't lie down in the top place, in case someone more honoured than you may have been invited by him; and when he arrives, the one who invited both you and him will tell you, "Give way to this man," and then you'll be embarrassed, and will start to occupy the bottom place! No – when you're invited, go ['journey', once more] and lie down in the bottom place, so that when the person who invited you comes he can tell you, "Friend, come up higher." Then you'll have glory in the presence of all those who are lying down with you. Because everyone who exalts themselves will be humbled, and those who humble themselves will be exalted.'

And he said to the one who had invited him, 'When you hold a breakfast or supper party, don't go inviting your friends or your brothers and sisters or your kinsfolk or your affluent neighbours; you don't want them to invite you in return, so that it becomes "tit-for-tat". No – when you have a party, invite poor people, crippled people, lame and blind. And you'll be blessed, because they have no way of giving you "tit-for-tat": your reward will come at the Resurrection of the dead.'

One of his fellow guests, when he heard this, said, 'Blessed is the one who eats bread in the kingdom of God.'

He said to him, 'A certain person was having a big party; and he invited many people. And he sent his slave at the time for the party, to tell the people who had been invited: "Come along, because it's ready now." And with one voice they all started to make excuses. The first one told him, "I've bought a farm, and I really *have* to go out and see it. Please, count me excused." And another one said, "I've purchased five pair of oxen, and I am going ['journeying'] to try them out. Please, count me excused." And another one said, "I have married a wife; and for that reason I can't come."

'The slave arrived and recounted all this to his lord. Then the householder was furious, and told his slave, "Quick – go out into the streets and alleys of the city; and bring here the poor and crippled and blind and lame."

'The slave said, "Lord, what you commanded has been done – and there is still room." And the lord said to the slave, "Go out to the roads and hedges, and *force* them to come in, that my house may be filled. For I'm telling you people that none of those men who were invited will taste my meal." '

This 'dinner party' is, of course, a complete disaster. As a matter of fact, the 'dinner' is just a loose setting that Luke provides for some very stark teaching on Jesus' part; as Luke tells it, we have to admit, Jesus undoubtedly started it, and he directs his fire absolutely everywhere: at the lawyers and Pharisees (who mean trouble, we know; but they haven't actually said anything at this point), at his fellow guests, at his host, and even at someone who makes a pious remark about eating in the kingdom of God.

The 'parable' about choosing the bottom place sounds remarkably pragmatic (better to be summoned upwards than booted downwards) – or perhaps Luke is sniping at wealthy Christians? Certainly there is humour in the story, and we should read it with something of a smile.

The host is told he's invited the wrong people. He should instead have invited the ritually impure (see Leviticus 21:18-20 for something like this list), as indeed the householder eventually does in the parable of the banquet, even though at least one of the invited guests had a scripturally warranted excuse (see Deuteronomy 24:5; 20:6).

One attractive feature of this passage is that the man with dropsy forms a 'Lucan pair' with the woman in the previous chapter.

Be serious about discipleship: exhortation to the journeying crowd

25-35 Many crowds were journeying with him, and he turned and said to them, 'If someone comes to me and fails to hate their father and their mother and their wife and their children and their brothers and their sisters – yes, and even their own life – they cannot be my disciple. Whoever does not carry their own cross and come after me, can't be my disciple.

'For which of you who wants to build a tower, doesn't first sit down and calculate the expense, to see if they have sufficient to complete it? [This is] so as not to have all the spectators/onlookers start to make fun of him, if he lays the foundation and doesn't have the resources to finish it off: "This fellow began to build, and didn't have the resources to finish it off."

'Or what monarch, journeying to engage in war with another monarch, will not first sit down and consider if he is able, with ten thousand [troops], to encounter the one who is coming at him with twenty thousand [troops]. And if he can't, then while the other monarch is still a long way off, he sends an embassy and asks for negotiations for peace.

'In just the same way, any of you who does not say farewell to all their possessions *cannot* be my disciple.

'To sum up: salt is good; but if the salt loses its sharpness, how will it be seasoned? It's no good for the soil or for the dunghill – it's thrown out.

'Let them hear who have ears to hear.'

These are uncomfortable words. Luke's (and Jesus') view of discipleship is decidedly stark. Once again we notice 'journeying' and Jesus' attentive 'turning'. We cannot help being struck by the strong language of 'hating' the various members of one's family. We have all done that occasionally, of course; but what is meant here is the quite radical detachment that the two sets of brothers showed in Chapter 5, verse 11, and which is expressed in this passage as 'say farewell to all your possessions'.

The two parables, of the tower builder and the militant monarch, likewise express the importance of knowing what you are about, in terms of the experience of Jesus' hearers, who may have reflected that only in the previous chapter they had heard of a tower that was not especially well built, and fell down!

Jesus' Terrible Friends: An Introduction, and Three Stories (15:1-32)

Introduction

15 [1,2] And they were getting close to him, all the tax collectors and sinners; [they wanted] to listen to him. And the Pharisees and the scribes grumbled, 'This fellow gives hospitality to sinners – and eats with them!'

Christians have consistently given 'scribes and Pharisees' a bad press; but it is important to remember what they were about. The Pharisees were a 'lay' organisation, who wanted to create an Israel to which the Messiah might come. To that end, they applied the Levitical laws of purity (intended for the priestly caste) to themselves; in particular, they aspired to a pure 'table fellowship' – so that the Messiah might join them at their meals. Imagine their shock and horror when they saw Jesus, who was in some respects very close to them, associating with such absolutely disreputable people. But Jesus' 'terrible friends' were part of his message, that the kingdom of God is open to absolutely everybody. Including, of course, scribes and Pharisees, if they are open to God's love. That is the context of the three lovely stories that make up this chapter.

A man rejoices at getting his sheep back

3-7 And he told them this parable: 'Suppose one of you has a hundred sheep, and loses one of them – won't he leave the [other] ninety-nine in the desert, and go journeying after the lost one till he finds it? And when he finds it, in his delight he puts it on his shoulders; and when he gets home, he summons his friends and neighbours, saying to them: "[Come and] rejoice with me, because I have found my lost sheep." I'm telling you, that's how much joy there'll be in heaven over a single sinner who repents, as opposed to ninety-nine righteous ones who see no need for repentance.'

This is an enormously challenging story. Remember the context in which it is told, of complaints that Jesus' friends were not religiously respectable (like the shepherds back in Chapter 2). Jesus' answer is that this is the way that God behaves. No shepherd with half an eye on the bottom line would do anything as unwise as what is suggested here, nor would he carry the miscreant home: sheep have twice as many legs as human beings, and are not designed to be carried. The point is that God behaves in that irrational way, because God loves all human beings, including, of course, the 'tax collectors and sinners' who flocked so enthusiastically to Jesus.

A woman celebrates with her girlfriends when she recovers her housekeeping money

8-10   'Or think of a woman who has ten drachmas: if she loses one drachma, won't she light a lamp and sweep the house, and hunt carefully until she finds it? And when she finds it, she summons her women friends and neighbours, saying, "[Come and] rejoice with me, because I have found the drachma that I had lost." I'm telling you, that's how much joy there'll be among the angels of God, over one sinner who repents.'

The previous story, of the sheep that was lost, appears also in Matthew's Gospel (18:12-14), where it is a tale about looking after members of the Christian body who go astray. Luke has turned it into a story of God's joy over sinners who repent, and has then hammered the point home by adding a story where God is presented as a woman who loses some of her precious (and pitifully small) housekeeping allowance and likewise throws a party. Luke repeats several of the same phrases ('summons friends and neighbours', 'rejoice with me', 'I'm telling you, that's how much joy there'll be') to emphasise that it is the same God we are talking about. So this is not only yet another story about repentance and forgiveness in Luke, but also yet another 'Lucan pairing'.

A scapegrace son is welcomed home – with a party!

11-32   He said, 'A certain person had two sons. And the younger of them said to his father, "Father, give me the portion of the property that falls to me." And he divided his life between them. Not many days later, the younger [son] gathered everything together and went abroad to a distant country; and there he squandered his property by living extravagantly.

'When he had spent the lot, a serious famine occurred throughout the country; and for the first time he was without resources, and so he went ['journeyed'] and joined one of the citizens of that country; and he sent him into the fields, to feed pigs; and he longed to stuff himself from the carob pods on which the pigs were feeding – and no one gave him permission. He came to himself and said, "How many of my father's employees have more than enough bread – and here am I, dying of hunger! I'll get up and journey to my father; and I'll tell him, 'Father – I've sinned against God and sinned before you; I'm no longer fit to be called a son of yours. Make me like one of your employees.' "

'But while he was still a long way away, his father saw him, and had compassion on him; and he ran and fell on his neck and kissed him. The son said to him, "Father – I've sinned against God and sinned before you; I'm no longer fit to be called a son of yours . . ."'

'The father said to his slaves, "Quick – bring out the Number One robe, and put it on him; and give a ring on his hand, and sandals on his feet; and bring the fattened calf, and kill it, and let's have a banquet and celebrate, because this son of mine was a corpse – and he has come alive again; he was lost, and has been found." And they began to celebrate.

'Now the elder son was in the field; and as he came nearer the house, he heard music and dancing. And he summoned one of the servants and asked what this was all about. He said, "Your brother has arrived, and your father has killed the fattened calf, because he got him back safe and sound."

'He was furious, and refused to go in. His father came out and started pleading with him. But he replied to his father, "Look! For so many years I've been slaving for you, and never disobeyed your commandment, and you never even gave me a goat to have a party with my friends. But when this son of yours comes, who ate up your life with prostitutes, you killed the fattened calf for him!"

'But he said to him, "Child, you're always with me, and everything that's mine is yours. We *had* to celebrate and rejoice, because this brother of yours was a corpse – and he is alive; and lost, and has been found." '

When Rembrandt painted this most famous of all Lucan parables, he portrayed the father with his arms round the son: the left hand is that of a man, and the right hand that of a woman. The artist had spotted that the parent in this parable is both father and mother.

It is an extraordinary story. The younger son is brutally rude and arrogant to his father, who is astonishingly docile. There is nothing at all to be said for the young man, *except* that he decides to go home. Even the employment he finds, in a not wholly satisfactory attempt to stave off hunger, is horrifying to Jewish ears: looking after pigs. Set that against the behaviour of the father, who was actually on the look-out, then ran to his son and kissed him and with every possible external attention restored to him his lost status as 'a son of mine' – and then, as in the two previous stories, the party begins.

The story should have ended there, but that would mean leaving unanswered the complaints that started the chapter. They are now personified in the steaming, sulking, loitering-outside figure of the elder brother. There are some hints that he may stand for the Jewish authorities who were opposed to Jesus' indiscriminate hospitality. This ill-tempered elder son has apparently also forgotten that his father had given him half of his 'life'. He speaks of not disobeying 'the commandment'; and father and son play the same game as Moses and God in Exodus 32:7, 11 at the time of the Golden Calf, where God and Moses each speak to the other of '*your* people'. In just the same way the elder brother speaks of 'this son of yours' (like the lawyer at 10:37 and Martha at 10:40, he can't bear to give him a name), and God replies with 'this brother of yours'. The Golden Calf story is also alluded to in the mention of 'music and dancing' that had so annoyed the elder brother (see Exodus 32:19).

With supreme artistry, Luke does not say whether or not the elder brother went in to the party. That is for you, the reader, to decide.

The steward whom the Lord praised

16 ¹⁻⁹ He also said to his disciples, 'There was a certain wealthy man who had a steward. Now this steward had been charged with squandering his possessions, and he called him and said to him, "What's this I hear about you? Give an account of your stewardship, because you can no longer be a steward."

'The steward said to himself, "What am I to do, seeing that my Lord is taking away my stewardship from me? I don't have the strength to dig, and I'm [too] embarrassed to beg . . . *I* know what I'll do, so that when I'm removed from the stewardship they'll give me hospitality in their houses." And he summoned each of his Lord's debtors; and he said to the first one, "How much do you owe my Lord?" And he said, "A thousand gallons of olive oil." He said to him, "Take your documents, sit down, and quickly write five hundred." Then to the next one he said, "What about you? How much do you owe?" He said, "Ten thousand gallons of wheat." He says to him, "Take your documents, and write eight thousand." And the Lord praised the steward for his unrighteousness [or: 'praised the unjust steward'], because he had acted prudently. Because the children of this world are more prudent than the children of light with regard to their own generation. And I'm telling you, make yourselves friends of the Mammon of Iniquity [or: 'unjust wealth'], so that when it runs out you may be given hospitality in the eternal tents.'

Like its predecessor, this is a deeply subversive story, challenging us to look at the world with fresh eyes. The man who was wealthy enough to have a steward (like some of Luke's intended audience, perhaps) is certainly not the hero of the story. If there must be a hero, then the only candidate is the steward, who is charged (perhaps falsely) with squandering his master's possessions, and who is dismissed without being permitted to offer his version of events, and who shows such a ready wit in organising allies for himself.

There are two other points to give salt to our reading of the story. First, the word that I have translated and capitalised as 'Lord' could mean no more than the 'master' of the steward; but it is possible to read the story as meaning that 'Jesus praised the unjust steward', which would be subversive indeed (it is bad enough if it is the steward's master).

Second, the conclusion of the story, 'make yourselves friends of the Mammon of Iniquity, so that when it (what?) runs out you may be given hospitality in the eternal tents', leaves the reader in a moral fog: is it a joke? a piece of practical advice? irony?

Now try fitting all that to the teaching that follows.

Loosely connected sayings, some of them concerning money

¹⁰⁻¹⁸ 'The one who is reliable on the tiniest matter, is also reliable on a big issue; the one who is dishonest on the tiniest matter is also dishonest on a big issue. So – if you are not reliable in regard to dishonest wealth [or: 'unjust mammon'] – who's going

to entrust you with the real thing? And if you are not reliable on other people's affairs, who's going to give you what is your own?

'No servant can be a slave to two lords; for either he'll hate the one and love the other, or he'll be devoted to the one and look down his nose at the other. You can't serve God and Money.'

The Pharisees (being lovers of money) heard all of this, and they scoffed at him. And he said to them, 'You're the ones who justify yourselves before human beings – but God knows your hearts; because what human beings regard as top priority is an abomination to God.'

'The Law and the Prophets went up to John; but from then on, the good news of the kingdom is being proclaimed, and everyone forces their way into it [or: 'suffers violence']. But it is easier for heaven and earth to pass away than for a single serif [on a single letter] of the Law to fail.

'Every man who divorces his wife and marries another one commits adultery; and the man who marries a woman who is divorced from her husband also commits adultery.'

It is not easy to know what to say about these, hard to link them adequately. The first two sound as though they might be continuing the story of the steward: in both of them Jesus speaks of money/ Mammon, but not in quite the ironic way that the story had led us to expect. The injunction to be reliable about other people's affairs is precisely what the steward disobeyed; and as for not being able to serve two masters, that seems to be precisely what the steward adroitly did! Luke's church must have listened uncomfortably to all this; but it is hard to see how it all fits.

The next paragraph charges the Pharisees (not at all justly) with being 'lovers of money'; and it is certainly as subversive as the rest of the teaching. Then comes the mysterious saying about the kingdom of God and violence: is it a good thing that people force their way in, or a bad thing that it suffers violence? Finally comes a characteristically strong statement from Jesus on divorce, in which the rights of the woman are firmly upheld.

All of which leads into yet another of Luke's subversive stories.

The wealthy man who went to hell

19-31 'A certain man was wealthy; he wore purple and linen, and he had sumptuous feasts every day.

'But a poor man called Lazarus was flung down at his gateway, covered with sores. And he wanted to fill himself on what fell from the rich man's table. Instead, the dogs came and licked his sores!

'It turned out that the poor man died, and was carried by the angels into the bosom of Abraham. The rich man died and was buried. And, in hell, he lifted up his eyes, since he was in torment; he sees Abraham a long way off, and Lazarus in his bosom. And he called him and said, "Father Abraham, have mercy on me, and send Lazarus to dip the tip of his finger in water and cool off my tongue, because I'm in pain in this flame." But Abraham said, "Child – remember that you received good things during your life; and similarly Lazarus got bad things. Now he's being comforted here, and you're in pain. And, as if all that were not enough, between us and you there's a huge chasm established, so that people who want to cross over from here to you can't, nor do they make the crossing from there to us." But he said, "So I'm asking you, Father, to send him to my father's house (you see, I've got five brothers), to warn them not to come into this torture chamber." Abraham says, "They have Moses and the prophets – let them listen to *them*." He said, "No, Father Abraham: if someone journeys to them from the dead, they'll repent." He said to him, "If they don't listen to Moses and the prophets, they won't be convinced even if someone were to rise from the dead." '

This is another thoroughly subversive story. As soon as we read of the (unnamed) rich man's clothing and parties, we know there'll be trouble. Lazarus (whose name means 'God has helped'), by contrast, *is* given a name, and his sufferings are described in unpleasant detail. Then comes a sudden reversal. Lazarus can't afford a funeral, so is instead transported straight to 'Abraham's bosom'. The rich man, on the other hand is buried properly, and Luke assumes as a matter of course that he goes to hell. He has not learnt his lesson, however, and some delightfully lively dialogue shows that he is still imperiously inclined (giving indirect orders to Lazarus), while Abraham carefully explains the facts of life. Abraham calls him 'child', as the Father did the Elder Brother in Chapter 15; this is perhaps picked up in the two senses of 'father' ('Father Abraham' and 'my father's house'), reminding us of a similar ambiguity about the word at 2:48-49. But the verdict is irresistible, and we tremble as we read.

Instructions to disciples

17 ¹⁻¹⁰ He said to his disciples, 'It is impossible that scandals should not come. But woe to the one through whom they come. It is better for that person to have a millstone round their neck and be hurled into the sea, than that they scandalise one of these little ones. Mind yourselves!

'If your fellow Christian commits a sin, rebuke them; and if they repent, forgive them. And if they commit a sin against you seven times a day, and seven times come back to you saying "I repent", you will forgive them.'

And the apostles said to the Lord, 'Increase our faith.' The Lord said, 'If you have faith like a mustard seed, you would say to this mulberry tree, "Be uprooted and plant yourself in the sea," and it would obey you.

'Suppose one of you has a slave ploughing or looking after the sheep, are you going to tell him, when he comes in from the field, "Come along right away, and lie down [for a meal]"? No – won't you tell him, "Make something for me to eat; put your livery on and wait on me while I eat and drink – and you can eat after that!"? Do you *thank* the slave because he did what was ordered? It's just the same with you people: when you've done everything that you were ordered, [just] say, "We are unprofitable slaves – we have done [only] what we ought to have done." '

These instructions, except for the last paragraph about the treatment of slaves which may have been directed at Luke's affluent audience, are found in Chapter 18 of Matthew, although not in quite the same order (this may be because of Matthew's tidy mind). And Luke characteristically adds an emphasis on 'repentance and forgiveness'. The 'uprooting of the fig tree' is in Mark (9:24), where it is in fact a mountain that is uprooted; perhaps Luke has combined this with the 'cursing of the fig tree' (Mark 11:12-14), which he does not include.

A 'Lucan summary' and a grateful Samaritan

11-19 And it happened as [he was] journeying to Jerusalem, that he himself was proceeding through the middle of [or: through the borders of] Samaria and Galilee.

And as he was entering a village, ten leper men met him; they stood far away, and raised their voices to him, 'Jesus, master, take pity on us.' He saw them and said to them, 'Go ['journey'], and show yourselves to the priests.' And it turned out that as they were on their way, they were made clean!

Now one of them, when he saw that he had been cured, came back, glorifying God in a loud voice; and he fell on his face at his feet. And he was a Samaritan! Jesus responded, 'Weren't [all] ten made clean? The [other] nine – where [have they gone]? Were none to be found returning to give glory to God, except this foreigner?' And he said to him, 'Up you get – continue your journey. Your faith has saved you.'

> The 'Lucan summary' characteristically reminds us of the journey, and its (slightly confusing?) landmarks of Samaria and Galilee. The next story also continues the 'journeying' theme: the lepers are told to 'journey' (as is the grateful one). And there are other points at which we can detect the hand of Luke: the Samaritan ex-leper glorifies God, like the shepherds in Chapter 2. And the fact that he is a non-Jew, and, worse, a Samaritan, emphasises Luke's sense of the gospel moving out from its Jewish base to include 'everyone'.

What about the end-time?

20-37 When he was asked by the Pharisees, 'When is the kingdom of God coming?', he replied to them, 'The kingdom of God doesn't come with close observation. And they won't say "Look – here [it is]," or "There [it is]." For look! The kingdom of God is right inside you!'

And he said to his disciples, 'Days will come when you will long to see one of the days of the Son of Man – and you won't see it. And they'll tell you, "Look – there [it is], look – here [it is]." Don't go off in pursuit. For as lightning when it flashes lights from one end of the horizon to the other, so will the Son of Man be in his day. First, however, it is necessary for him to suffer much, and to be rejected by this generation. And as it happened in Noah's days, so it will be in the days of the Son of Man. They were eating, they were drinking, they were marrying and they were getting married – right up to the day when Noah went on board his Ark. Then the deluge came, and destroyed every one of them. Just like it happened in Lot's days: they were eating, they were drinking, they were buying, they were selling, they were planting, they were building. But on the day when Lot went out of Sodom, [the Lord] rained fire and sulphur from heaven, and destroyed every one of them.

So it will be on the day when the Son of Man is revealed. On that day, if someone is on the rooftop, and their belongings are in the house, they should not go down to fetch them. Similarly, someone who is in the field shouldn't come back. Remember Lot's wife. You see, everyone who looks to preserve their life will lose it, while everyone who [is prepared to] lose their life will revive it. I'm telling you: on that night, there'll be two people in one bed: one will be taken, and the other left. And there will be two women grinding in the same place; one will be taken, and the other left.'

They replied, 'Where, Lord?' He said to them, 'Where the body is, there the vultures will gather too.'

The material gathered together here is found elsewhere, mainly in Matthew 24, but also in Mark 13; in those Gospels, however, it comes nearer to the end. The one exception is the introductory verses, the exchange between Jesus and Pharisees. We have learnt in our reading that for Luke Pharisees mean trouble.

The disciples' question, 'Where, Lord?', is undeniably puzzling – but the answer is not particularly enlightening. Perhaps we should realise that we are dealing with the unknown.

Two Lucan parables on prayer

18 ¹⁻¹⁴ He told them a parable about the need to pray all the time, and not give up. He said, 'A particular magistrate in a particular city had no respect for God, and no regard for human beings. Now there was a widow in that city; and she kept coming to him and saying, "Give me justice against my opponent." And for a time he refused. Later, though, he said to himself, "Perhaps I don't respect God, and have no regard for human beings – but because this widow is pestering me, I'll give her justice. Otherwise she'll end up by coming and giving me a black eye!" Do you think that God won't bring about justice [or: 'vindication'] for his elect who shout to him day and night, even though he is slow in dealing with them? I'm telling you – he'll quickly bring about justice for them. Nevertheless, when the Son of Man comes, will he find faith on earth?'

He also told this parable to some people who trusted in their own righteousness, and were contemptuous of everyone else:

'Two people went up into the Temple to pray. One was a Pharisee, and the other was a tax collector. The Pharisee stood and prayed to himself as follows: "God, I give you thanks that I'm not like the rest of humanity: thieves, dishonest [or: unrighteous/unjust], adulterers – or like this fellow, the tax collector. I fast twice a week; I give away a tenth of everything I possess."

'The tax collector, on the other hand, stood a long way off; he didn't even dare lift up his eyes to heaven. Instead, he beat his breast, and said, "God, be merciful to me, the Sinner." I'm telling you, he's the one who went to his house counted-as-righteous, not the other one. Because everyone who lifts themselves up will be put down; but those who put themselves down will be lifted up.'

These two parables are only found in Luke's Gospel. Both of them (rather unusually) are given headings, so that the reader knows what they are about. Both of them have to do with prayer, and both of them make use of a whole series of words connected with righteousness and justice: the word for opponent could nearly be translated 'the one who is against the righteous'. They are both good stories, memorably told and with a touch of humour (the widow's threat of a black eye, the Pharisee's tedious catalogue of his virtues); we can feel Luke's artistry at work here. The words for 'justice' and for 'opponent' both have the same root here.

Jesus and babies

15-17 They tried to bring babies to him also, for him to touch them. The disciples saw, and rebuked them. Jesus, however, called the babies to him and said, 'Let the little children come to me, and don't get in their way. You see, the kingdom of God consists of people like this. Amen I tell you, whoever doesn't accept the kingdom of God like a little child, no way will they get into it.'

> This charming story is also in Mark 10:13-16 and Matthew 19:13-15, except that Luke has omitted the detail that Jesus 'took them in his arms, laid his hands on them and blessed them'.

An affluent ruler asks about inheriting eternal life

18-30 And a certain ruler asked him, 'Good teacher, what am I to do to inherit eternal life?'

Jesus said to him, 'Why do you say that I am good? No one is good except One – namely God. You know the commandments: "Thou shalt not commit adultery; thou shalt not kill; thou shalt not steal; thou shalt not bear false witness; honour thy father and mother."' But he said, 'I've kept all of these since my youth.' When Jesus heard [this], he said to him, 'You still lack one thing: whatever you have, sell it, and distribute [the money] to the poor, and you'll have treasure in heaven. And, here, follow me.' When he heard this, he became very sad. You see, he was extremely affluent.

When Jesus saw him getting so very sad, he said, 'How difficult it is for those who have possessions to journey into the kingdom of God! For it is easier for a camel to go in through the eye of a needle than for someone who is affluent to go into the kingdom of God.'

Those who heard [this] said, 'In that case, who can be saved?' He said, 'Things that are impossible for human beings are possible for God.'

Peter said, 'Look! We've abandoned our own and followed you.' He told them, 'Amen I tell you – there's no one who has left house or wife or brothers or parents or children, for the sake of the kingdom of God who doesn't receive many times over in this [present] age, and in the age that is coming, life eternal.'

> This episode is also in Mark and Matthew; Luke has tidied up what he found in Mark, and perhaps also emphasised the detachment that disciples require, and the dangers of affluence (writing, perhaps, for a wealthy congregation); but otherwise he leaves it much as he found it, except that he turns Jesus' interrogator into a 'ruler'. We also notice that the question put to him by the ruler is identical to that on the lips of the lawyer who was rewarded with the disconcerting parable of the Good Samaritan.

Jesus warns the Twelve about what will happen at the end of the journey

31-34 He took the Twelve with him and said to them, 'Look – we're going up to Jerusalem; and everything written through the prophets will be accomplished for the Son of Man: he'll be handed over to the Gentiles, and be ridiculed, and insulted, and spat upon. And they'll flog him and then kill him – and on the third day he'll rise again.' And they didn't understand any of this – and the matter [or: 'word'] was hidden from them; and they couldn't grasp what was being said.

> This is the third Passion prediction (see 9:22; 9:44), though Luke makes much less of them than Mark does (see Mark 10:32-34). The attentive reader will note two changes that are characteristic of Luke. First, the prediction is narrowed to just 'the Twelve', and, second, there is his typical emphasis on fulfilling prophecy. It is Luke's way of saying that God is in charge. Luke also omits the disciples' blunder.

A blind man near Jericho gets his sight back

35-43 It happened as he drew near to Jericho a blind person was sitting begging beside the way. He heard a crowd journeying through, and asked what it was. They told him, 'Jesus the Nazarene is passing by.' And he shouted, 'Jesus, Son of David, have pity on me!' And the people in front told him sharply to be silent. But he cried out all the more, 'Son of David, have pity on me!' Jesus stopped, and ordered him to be brought to him; when he approached, he asked him, 'What do you want me to do?' He said, 'Lord, that I may see again.' And Jesus said to him, 'See again. Your faith has saved you.' And straightaway he saw again, and followed him, glorifying God. And when they saw it, the whole populace gave praise to God.

> This story is also in Mark 10:46-52 and Matthew 20:29-34; but Luke has made some characteristic changes. Mark sets the story at the moment when Jesus departs from Jericho, which is a bit puzzling. Luke locates it as part of the ongoing journey up to Jerusalem. He emphasises that the crowd was 'journeying'; he eliminates Mark's rather alarming disrobing on the part of the blind man, and emphasises the verb 'see again'. He changes the form of address from Rabbouni to Kyrie, and (how many times have we heard this phrase?) has the beggar 'glorifying God', and the 'populace' giving praise to God.
>
> Also characteristic of Luke is the fact that the blind man's persistence gets him what he wants; and of course we remember that 'sight for the blind' was part of Jesus' 'mission-statement' at Nazareth, back in 4:18.

Zacchaeus of Jericho

19 1-10 And he entered and passed through Jericho. And look! A man called Zacchaeus; and he was a head tax collector; and he was affluent. And he was trying to see Jesus ('which one is he?'); and he couldn't, because of the crowd, because he was small in stature. And he ran on ahead, and went up a sycamore tree to see him, because he

was going to pass by it. And when he got to the spot, Jesus looked up and said to him 'Zacchaeus! Quick – down you come: because today I must stay in your house.' And he came down in a hurry, and joyfully gave him hospitality. And they all saw it, and complained, 'He's gone in to stay with a man who is a sinner.' Zacchaeus stood there, and said to the Lord, 'Look, Lord; I'm giving half of my possessions to the poor; and if I have defrauded anyone of anything, I'm giving it back fourfold!' Jesus said to him, 'Today salvation has come to this house, because this man is also a child of Abraham; you see, the Son of Man came to look for the lost, and to save them.'

This story is only in Luke. As in the previous episode, Luke simplifies the introduction in a way that emphasises the journeying theme. The man's name will give us a clue: it is an abbreviation of Zachariah, 'the Lord has remembered', so despite the fact that he has so much going against him as an 'affluent tax collector', we feel optimistic about the outcome of the story. There is the memorable detail about Zacchaeus' lack of height, and the unforgettable moment when everyone is looking at him up in the tree, waiting for Jesus' condemnation, which never comes (though we may imagine an eternal pause after Jesus first addresses him). Twice in the passage Luke uses his characteristic 'today'; Zacchaeus hurries, as Mary had done in Chapter 1, and his 'joy' reminds us that Luke is the Gospel of joy. We notice also, as always in Luke, the radical demands of hospitality, indicated by Zacchaeus' more than generous compensation for what he has done wrong. It is 'repentance in action'.

The parable of the absentee landlord

11-27 As they listened to this, he told another parable, because he was near Jerusalem, and they thought that the kingdom of God was about to appear straightaway. So he said, 'A certain nobleman journeyed to a distant country, to accept his kingdom and return. He summoned his ten slaves, and gave them ten minae, and told them, "Do some trading while I'm away." Now his citizens hated him, and sent an embassy after him to say, "We don't want this man to rule over us." And it turned out, when he returned, having accepted his kingdom, he gave orders for these slaves to be called, the ones to whom he had given the money, to find out what they had earned in their trading. The first one came and said, "Lord – your mina has yielded ten minae." And he said to him, "Well done, good slave: because you turned out to be faithful on a tiny matter, assume authority over ten cities." And the second one came and said, "Here's your mina, Lord: it's made five minae." He told this one also, "You, too, be in charge of five cities." And the other one came and said, "Lord – here's your mina. I kept it hidden in a handkerchief, because I was afraid of you; you're a severe man – you take up what you didn't put down, and you harvest what you didn't sow." He said, "Out of your own mouth I condemn you, wicked slave. You knew that I'm a severe man, taking up what I didn't put down and harvesting what I didn't sow – so why didn't you give my money to a bank, so that on my arrival I could have claimed it with interest?" And he said to the bystanders, "Take the mina from him, and give it to the one who has ten minae." And they said to him, "Lord – he [already] has ten minae." "I tell you, it will be given to everyone who has, and from the one who has not, even what they have will be taken from them. But these enemies of mine who didn't want me to be king over them, bring them here and slaughter them in front of me." '

> This is really a very audacious story. Luke tells us in the introduction that it's meant to correct misapprehensions about the kingdom of God, given that the journey has now almost reached Jerusalem. But the king, who is presumably meant to represent God, turns out to be a thoroughly unpleasant fellow, with more than a passing resemblance to Herod. His subjects loathe him; he rewards initiative, but (on his own admission) he is very severe in his dealings with slaves, and is something of a greedy capitalist; and, finally, his response to any kind of opposition takes the form of public murder.

The journey ends with the entry into Jerusalem

28-40 And with these words, he continued to journey onwards to Jerusalem. And it happened, when he drew near to Bethphage and Bethany, near the mountain called 'Of Olive Trees', he sent two of the disciples, saying, 'Go into the village opposite; when you journey into it you'll find a colt tied, on whom no human being has ever sat. Untie it and bring it. And if anyone asks you why you are untying it, you'll say this, "The Lord has need of it." ' The ones who had been sent went off and found [things] as he had told them. As they were untying the colt, its masters [or: 'lords' – *kyrioi*] said to them, 'Why are you untying the colt?' They said, 'The Lord has need of it,' and they brought it to Jesus, and they threw their garments over the colt and sat Jesus on it. As he journeyed, they spread their garments underneath him on the road. As he was now drawing near to the slope of the Mountain of Olives, the whole crowd of disciples began to rejoice and praise God at the top of their voices, for all the miracles they had seen: 'Blessed is the Coming One, the King in the Lord's name, in heaven peace and glory in the highest places.'

And some of the Pharisees in the crowd said to him, 'Teacher, speak severely to your disciples.'

And he answered them, 'I'm telling you – if they are silent, the stones will cry out.'

> After a characteristic Lucan summary, with the familiar reference to a journey, Luke retains more or less what he found in Mark, but makes some typical changes. We notice the interplay between different senses of Kyrios/Lord (the owners of the donkey and the Lord), which may remind us of a similar ambiguity about 'Father' in 2:48, 49. Jesus' ride on the donkey is described in terms of a journey. We also notice how the crowd 'began to rejoice and praise God', and how their welcoming song quotes Psalm 118.

Jesus, Jerusalem and the Temple

41-48 And as he drew near, when he saw the city, he wept over it, saying, 'If [only] you also had known on this day the things that lead to peace; but now it's hidden from your eyes. Because the day will come on you, and your enemies will throw up an earthworks alongside you, and they'll encircle you and hem you in from all sides, and they'll dash you to the ground, and your children within you because you didn't know the time of your visitation.'

And he went into the Temple; and he started to expel the sellers, telling them, 'It is written: "And my house shall be a house of prayer" – but you've made it a den of thieves.'

And he was teaching every day in the Temple. The chief priests and the scribes were looking for a way to destroy him – and so were the Most Important People; and they could find nothing to do with him – because the whole populace hung upon his words.

> The 'things that lead to peace' echoes 14:32 (the king going out to war), and appears in only these two places in the entire New Testament. The equivalent verb for the idea of 'visitation' is also in Luke 1:68, 78; 7:16. The quotation about 'my house shall be a house of prayer' is from Isaiah 56:7, and the 'den of thieves' is from Jeremiah 7:11. Luke has rather oddly (despite his interest in the Gentile mission) missed out the reference to the Gentiles in the first of these quotations, although Mark has it. Perhaps Luke thought that his readers would make the connection.
>
> The Temple story is introduced by another 'Lucan summary': 'he was teaching every day in the Temple'. The 'Most Important People' (literally 'first') might perhaps be a dig at Luke's affluent church.

The battlelines are drawn: an awkward question and a dangerous parable

20¹⁻¹⁹ And it happened on one of the days, while he was teaching the people in the Temple, and giving the good news, the Chief Priest and the scribes came up to him, along with the elders; and they spoke, saying to him, 'Tell us, by what authority do you do these things? Or who is it that gives you this authority?'

He replied to them, 'Now I'll ask you something. So tell me – was John's baptism from heaven, or from human beings?'

They debated among themselves, 'If we say "from heaven", he'll say, "Why did you not believe him?"; but if we say "from human beings", the whole populace will stone us to death, for they are convinced that John is a prophet.' So they replied that they didn't know where it was from. And Jesus said to them, 'And I'm not telling you by what authority I do these things.'

He started to address this parable to the populace: 'A man planted a vineyard, and he leased it out to cultivators, and went abroad for a considerable time. And at the appropriate moment, he sent the cultivators a slave, for them to give him some of the fruit of the vineyard; but the cultivators beat him and sent him away empty-handed. And he did it again and sent them a second slave, but they beat him too, and when they had dishonoured him they sent him away empty-handed. And he did it again and sent them a third slave. And this one too they wounded and flung him out. The lord of the vineyard said, "What shall I do? I'll send my beloved son. Perhaps they'll respect him." But when the cultivators saw him, they discussed [it] with one another, "This is the heir – let's kill him, so that the inheritance may be ours." And they flung him out of the vineyard and killed him.

'So what do you think the lord of the vineyard will do to them? He'll come and destroy the cultivators and give the vineyard to others.'

When they heard it, they said, 'God forbid!' He looked at them and said, 'So what is this Scripture: "The stone which the builders rejected, this is the one that has turned into the cornerstone." Everyone who falls over that stone will be dashed to pieces; but the person on whom it falls, it will crush him.'

And the scribes and the chief priests sought to lay hands on him at that moment; and yet they were afraid of the people, because they knew that it was at them that he had spoken this parable.

> The tone of the Gospel is now unmistakably menacing. Luke has left this more or less as he found it in Mark (12:1-12), though the alert reader may notice how he tidies things up, so that the parable (in which Jesus pulls no punches, as he adapts Isaiah 5 to the present situation) is told to the 'populace', a favourite Lucan word. Luke also makes it clear that it is Jesus to whom the parable refers, by speaking of the 'beloved son'.

Three attempts to trap Jesus, and Jesus' adroit responses

20-47   They watched him carefully; and they sent spies, who pretended to be on the right side, to seize on something he said, so as to hand him over to the magisterial authority of the procurator. And they asked him, 'Teacher, we know that you speak and teach correctly, regardless of who you are talking to, but that you truly teach God's way: is it allowed for us to pay tribute to Caesar or not?'

He however detected their cunning, and said to them, 'Show me the denarius – whose image and likeness does it have?' They said, 'Caesar's'; and he said to them, 'So pay back Caesar's property to Caesar – and God's property to God.'

And they were unable to seize on anything he said, in the presence of the populace; and they were stunned by his response and fell silent.

Some of the Sadducees came up; these people deny that there is a Resurrection; and they interrogated him: 'Teacher, Moses wrote down for us that "if someone's brother dies, and [the brother] was married and childless, his brother should take his wife, and raise up seed for his brother". So – there were seven brothers. Number One took a wife, and died childless; and Number Two and then Number Three took her, and all seven of them took her, and they died, without leaving children. At last the woman died. So – in the "Resurrection", whose wife does she become? (You see, all seven had had her as wife!)'

And Jesus said to them, 'The sons of this world marry and are given in marriage – but those who are judged worthy of that [other] world, and worthy to reach the Resurrection, don't marry or get married; and neither will they die, because being children of the Resurrection they are on a par with the angels, and they're children of God. But Moses pointed out at the bush that corpses are raised, when he says, "The Lord is the God of Abraham and the God of Isaac and the God of Jacob." But he's not the God of corpses – no, he's the God of the living, for they're all alive to him.'

Some of the scribes replied, 'Teacher, well said.' For they didn't dare interrogate him any longer.

He said to them, 'How do they say that the Messiah is David's son? For David himself says in the Book of Psalms,

> "The Lord said to my Lord,
> 'Sit at my right
> until I make your enemies
> a footstool for your feet.'"

'So David calls him "Lord": how, then, is he his son?'

In the hearing of the entire populace, he told his disciples: 'Beware of the scribes who want to go about in long robes; they love being saluted in the public squares, and front seats in the synagogues, and top places at banquets. And they make a pretence of long prayers. These people will get a much more severe condemnation.'

Luke has left this more or less as he found it in Mark, except that he has shifted the question about the 'Great Commandment' back to Chapter 10, and placed it on a lawyer's lips; at this point he has simply left a couple of traces of it, the scribes' 'well said', and the reluctance to press his interrogations any further. He has, too, a much briefer version of Matthew's assault (23:1-36) on the scribes and Pharisees (although you might point out that Luke has already said his piece about the Pharisees in 11:39-44).

But we can feel the doom pressing in on Jesus, now that his journey is over and he has arrived in Jerusalem.

A destitute widow

21 1-4 He looked up and saw the people putting their gifts in the Treasury. They were affluent; but he also saw a needy widow putting two tiny coins in there, and he commented, 'Truly, I'm telling you, this poor widow put in more than all the others. You see, all of these contributed to the gifts from out of their surplus, while she contributed to the gifts from out of what she *didn't* have. She put in all the life she had.'

Beyond a little bit of tidying, Luke has not changed very much of what he found in Mark 12:41-44; but as we read we need to recall that widows get an especially good press from Luke, and that Luke compares the widow to the Father of 15:12, who 'divided his life'. Luke's affluent congregation will no doubt have pondered these things.

An innocent remark about the Temple leads to a prediction of the end

5-36 And when some people remarked about the Temple, that it was adorned with lovely stones and votive-offerings, he said, 'All these things which you are looking at – the days will come when no stone will be left on another stone that will not be pulled down.' They asked him, 'Teacher, so when will this happen? And what's the sign when these things are about to take place?' He said, 'Watch out that you don't get misled. For many people will come in my name, saying, "I AM!" and "The Time Has Come." Don't go journeying after them; but when you hear of wars and revolution, don't get panic-stricken. For these things have to happen first – but the end is not immediately.'

Then he said to them, 'Nation will rise up against nation, and kingdom against kingdom; and [there will be] great earthquakes; and in places there will be famines and epidemics, and terrors and great signs from heaven. But before all this, they'll lay hands on you, and hunt you down, handing you over to synagogue and prison; [you will be] brought before kings and governors for the sake of my name. It will give you the opportunity to bear witness. So make it your policy not to practise your speech for the defence beforehand. For I shall give you eloquence and wisdom which none of your opponents will be able to resist or refute. What is more, you will be handed over by parents and siblings, cousins and friends – and they'll kill some of you, and you'll be loathed by everyone because of my name. Nevertheless, not a hair of your head will be destroyed: through your unflinching endurance you will take possession of your lives.

'But when you see Jerusalem encircled by armies, be sure that her devastation is close. Then let those who are in Judaea flee to the mountains, and let those who are inside Jerusalem get out; and those who are in the rural areas must not go into the city, because these are the days of her punishment, for all that is written to be fulfilled. Woe to those who are pregnant or who have children at the breast in those days, for there will be great distress on the land, and wrath on his people, and they'll fall at the edge of the sword, and they'll be taken captive to all the Gentiles. And Jerusalem shall be under the jackboot of the Gentiles, until the Times of the Gentiles are completed.

'And there shall be signs in the sun and the moon and the stars; and on earth there shall be anguish of nations, and perplexity from the roaring and raging of the sea. Human beings will stop breathing, in fear and anticipation of the things that are coming on the world – for the powers of heaven shall be shaken.

'And then they shall see the Son of Man coming on the cloud with power and great glory. When these things start to happen, look up, and lift your heads – because your redemption is approaching.'

And he told them a parable, 'Look at the fig tree (and indeed all trees): as soon as they bud, from the evidence of your eyes you know that the summer is now at hand. And so you also, when you see these things happening, be aware that the kingdom of God is at hand. Amen I tell you, no way will this generation pass away before everything happens. Heaven and earth will pass away, but my words will not pass away.

'Be careful not to get your senses dulled by being hung over, or drunk, or by everyday preoccupations. Otherwise that Day will come suddenly upon you, like a trap; for it will come on all the inhabitants of the earth [or: 'to all those who dwell on the face of all the earth']. Stay awake, all the time, asking to have the ability to escape all these things, and to stand before the Son of Man.'

> Luke has taken over this long passage more or less as Mark left it, but making some characteristic changes of his own; 'famines and epidemics' for example, which sound the same in Greek, and 'terrors and great signs in heaven', which add to the general sense of foreboding. Luke adds 'prisons' to 'synagogues' as places where Christians might expect to be taken. Some scholars take the reference to 'Jerusalem encircled by enemies' as evidence that Luke wrote this on the basis of reports of the siege of Jerusalem that ended in AD 70, and likewise the predictions of trouble for Israel, and for 'this people' and for 'Jerusalem'. Some of the material Luke has already used in Chapter 17 (23, 24, 37), where it is about the delay in the coming of the Son of Man.

The reader may reflect, on hearing what Christians may expect in the shape of betrayal and death and hatred, that there has not been a century in the Church's existence, when this has not been the case.

A 'Lucan summary' concluding Jesus' work in Jerusalem

37, 38   In the daytime, he would teach in the Temple; but at night he went out and camped on the Mountain called 'Of Olives'. And the whole populace would get up early in the morning [and come] to him in the Temple to listen to him.

> We are now on the point of moving into the sombre and chilling story of Jesus' Passion, and Luke brings to an end Jesus' ministry in Jerusalem (to which the Gospel had been aiming since Chapter 9, and in a sense from its very beginning) with one of his 'summaries'. He reminds us here of two themes of great importance to him. First, there is the Temple, where the Gospel started, and where it will end and Acts begins. Acts will not end there, however, but in Rome, having turned its back on Jerusalem. So it is that Luke deliberately surprises us with the information that Jesus has no permanent HQ in Jerusalem, but only a temporary base on the Mountain of Olives, from which direction the Messiah was popularly expected to come.
>
> The second theme is that of the 'populace' (a favourite term of Luke) who have never been far from the surface of the narrative, open enough to the Gospel, if not fanatical about it, but often listening to Jesus.

Luke's Account of Jesus' Suffering and Death (22:1–23:56)

Introductory Lucan summary

22 ^{1, 2} The feast of Unleavened Bread, called Passover, was drawing near; and the chief priests and the scribes were looking for a way to destroy him; for they were afraid of the populace.

> This is very nearly exactly what Mark had written, with one or two small changes; in context, however, it functions as a 'Lucan summary', creating atmosphere, and signalling (as so often in Luke) the importance of the populace.

Judas' betrayal

3-6   Satan had entered Judas, the one called 'Iscariot', who was of the number of the Twelve; and he went off and talked with the chief priests and captains, how to betray [or: 'hand over'] him. And they rejoiced, and made an agreement to give him money. He gave his consent, and started looking for a good moment to hand him over [or: 'betray'], without a crowd to [bother] them.

Although Luke is largely following Mark, we shall notice at several points in the Passion Narrative that Luke and John seem to graze in the same paddock. One example is here, where he says that 'Satan had entered Judas', something we find also at John 13:2, 27.

Preparing the Passover meal

7-13 The day of Unleavened Bread came, the day on which the Passover lamb had to be sacrificed; and he sent Peter and John, saying, 'Go [or: literally, 'journey'] and prepare the Passover for us, so that we may eat.' They said to him, 'Where do you want us to prepare [it]?' He said, 'Look! As you go into the city, a man will meet you who is carrying a water-pot. Follow him into the house into which he goes ['journeys', of course]. And you will tell the master of the house, "The teacher says to you, 'Where is the chamber where I am to eat the Passover with my disciples?'." And he will show you a large upstairs room, spread with couches. Prepare [the meal] there.'

They went off, and found it as he had said, and prepared the Passover.

Luke has made some small changes from what he found in Mark (14:12-17). In the latter, it had been the disciples who took the initiative; here it is Jesus, who singles out Peter and John. Luke also inserts his beloved 'journeying' word.

This is my body . . .

14-20 And when the moment came, he lay down [to eat], and his apostles with him. And he said to them, 'I have eagerly desired to eat this Passover with you before I suffer. For I am telling you that I shan't eat it at all until it is fulfilled in the kingdom of God.' And he took a cup and gave thanks [or: 'did Eucharist'] and said, 'Take this, and divide it among yourselves. For I'm telling you, from now onwards, I shan't drink from the produce of the vine, until the kingdom of God comes.' And taking bread, he gave thanks, broke and gave it to them saying, 'This is my body which is being given for you. Do this for my remembrance.' And the cup likewise after they had eaten, saying, 'This cup, the new covenant in my blood, is what is poured out for you.'

Luke calls Jesus' companions the 'apostles', where Mark had 'the Twelve'. He has also changed the order slightly: the mood is made perhaps slightly less sombre by the fact that he puts the prediction of his betrayal after the distribution of bread and cup. Luke also introduces a blessing of a cup before the bread, perhaps to underline that it is a Passover ritual.

Prediction of the betrayal, a squabble, and warnings

21-30 'But look! The hand of the one who is betraying me is with me at the table. Because the Son of Man is going on his journey in accordance with what has been appointed. But alas for that person through whom he is being betrayed.' And they started arguing among themselves who it would be that was about to do this.

And there was a quarrel, about which of them seemed to be Top [Apostle]. He said to them, 'The kings of the Gentiles act as lords over them, and those who are authorities over them are known as benefactors. With you it [must] not [be] so. No – let the top one among you become like the youngest, and the leader like one who serves. Tell me – who is top: the one who lies down, or the one who serves? Isn't it the one who lies down? Well, *I'm* in the middle of you as the one who serves.

'You people are the ones who have stuck it out with me in my trials. And I am assigning [a kingdom] to you, just as my Father has assigned a kingdom to me, that you may eat and drink at my table in my kingdom, and you may sit on thrones, judging the twelve tribes of Israel.'

> Luke departs here from Mark: he inserts two characteristic phrases, 'journey', and 'in accordance with what has been appointed', to underline his conviction that Jesus (and his disciples) are 'on their way', and that God is in charge. He has also placed here something like the squabbling that arose in Mark 10:41-45 when James and John made their bid for power; but Luke has turned it round neatly in the direction of the washing of the disciples' feet that John reports at this point (John 13:4, 5, 12-17). Luke also places here the material about judging the twelve tribes of Israel, which Matthew places earlier (Matthew 19:28).

Prediction of Simon's lapse of faith

31-34 'Simon, Simon, see, Satan sought to sift you like wheat; but I prayed for you that your faith should not fail. And then you in your turn, come back to yourself and support your brothers [and sisters].'

He said to him, 'Lord – with you I'm even ready to journey to prison and to death!'

He said, 'I'm telling you, Peter, the cock won't crow tomorrow before you've denied, three times, that you know me!'

> The series of s-sounds with which this section begins does not come out very well in English, but it reflects what appears to be deliberate alliteration in Luke's Greek.
>
> The material does not appear quite like this in Mark (14:27-31). Characteristic of Luke is the double repetition of Simon's name (cf. 'Master, master' at 8:24, and 'Martha, Martha at 10:41); and it is interesting that Luke also has Jesus address him here by the nickname 'Rock'.

Armed to the teeth?

35-38 And he said to them, 'When I sent you off without purse or bag or sandals, did you lack anything?'

They said, 'Nothing.'

He said to them, 'Right – but now let anyone who has a purse take it, and the same with a bag; and anyone who doesn't have a sword should sell his cloak and buy one. For I'm telling you that this Scripture passage must be fulfilled in me:

"And he was reckoned with the lawless"; you see, what is written about me is nearing accomplishment.'

They said, 'Lord, look – here are two swords.'

He said, 'It's enough.'

This baffling passage is only in Luke. It picks up the instructions about travelling light that we saw in 10:4, but seems to argue that things are now so bad that previous instructions are now to be disregarded, and they must invest in an arsenal. On the other hand, when they admit to having a small selection of weapons (only two!), Jesus tells them that it's sufficient. What do you think he meant?

Notice the characteristic Lucan notion that a 'Scripture passage must be fulfilled'. This particular one comes from Isaiah 53:12, the fourth and last of the 'Songs of the Suffering Servant'.

'What is written about me is nearing accomplishment': this is one possible meaning of a phrase that has always stumped scholars.

Jesus prays to the Father

39-46 And he went out and journeyed, in accordance with his custom, to the Mountain of Olives; and the disciples followed him. When he got to the place, he said to them, 'Pray not to enter into temptation.' And he withdrew from them, about a stone's throw; and he fell on his knees and prayed, 'Father, if you wish, take this cup from me. But not my will – let yours be done.' And he arose from [his] prayer, and came to the disciples; and he found them asleep because of their grief, and he said to them, 'Why are you asleep? Arise and pray not to enter into temptation.'

Luke changes what he found in Mark (14:32-38); the story is no longer a triptych (three separate episodes of prayer); he adds 'in accordance with his custom', as he had when speaking of Zachariah's turn to sacrifice (1:9), and Jesus' first visit to Jerusalem for Passover (2:42). He also calls it (as so often before, and look at the first chapter of Acts) 'the Mountain of Olives' rather than Gethsemani. Quite unlike Mark's version, Jesus twice tells his disciples to 'pray' (Luke's is the Gospel of prayer, we remember). And Jesus is less evidently miserable here than he was in Mark's account. Charitably Luke ascribes the disciples' somnolence to 'grief', just as in 24:41 he will ascribe their lack of belief in the Resurrection to 'joy'.

Between 'let yours be done' and 'And he arose from [his] prayer', some early manuscripts have 'there appeared to him an angel from heaven, strengthening him. And being in an agony, he started to pray more intently. And his sweat became like drops of blood, falling on to the ground.' It was probably not what Luke originally wrote, however.

The arresting party

47-51 While he was still speaking, look! A crowd, and the one called Judas (one of the Twelve!) approached them. And he drew near to Jesus, to kiss him. Jesus, however, said to him, 'Judas – is it with a kiss that you are betraying the Son of Man?'

When his companions saw what was about to happen, they said, 'Lord, are we to hit [someone] with a sword?' And one of them hit the Chief Priest's slave and cut off his ear (the right-hand one). Jesus responded, 'Let them be; that's enough!' And he touched the ear and healed it!

Again Luke offers a rather briefer account than what we find in Mark. It is only Luke, however, who comments on the inappropriateness of a kiss as an accompaniment of the betrayal. Then comes some violent (if wholly ineffective) resistance. Whoever it was (and unlike John, Luke is not telling) might argue, I suppose, that Jesus had only a few minutes earlier been speaking of the importance of being well armed. But then Jesus negates the gesture by healing the fairly trivial (though doubtless tiresome to the slave in question) wound that had been inflicted.

Jesus' reproof to the religious authorities

52, 53 Jesus said to the chief priests and captains of the Temple who had come upon him, 'You've come out with swords and clubs, as though [arresting] a bandit! But every day, when I was with you in the Temple, you never stretched out your hands against me. No – this is your hour, and the domain of darkness.'

This is an odd passage, for the most part only in Luke. It shows a Jesus who is very much in command, and with some gentle irony, or even humour ('I'm not really dangerous'). He refers back to 19:47 ('teaching daily in the Temple'), which was only in Luke; and Luke is the only one to make the enigmatic remark about 'your hour, and the domain of darkness', which takes us back to the end of the temptation narrative (Luke 4:13).

Peter doesn't know Jesus

54-62 When they had arrested him, they took him and led him to the house of the Chief Priest. But Peter followed from a long way off. When they had kindled a fire in the middle of the courtyard, and they had sat down together, Peter sat in the midst of them.

A little slave girl saw him sitting facing the light. She looked closely at him and said, 'This one was with him, too.' But he disagreed and said, 'I don't know him, woman.'

And after a short time, someone else saw him and said, 'You're one of them, too!' But Peter said, 'Man, I'm not!' And an hour or so later, someone else insisted, 'For sure he was with him – he's a Galilean!'

Peter said, 'Man – I've no idea what you're talking about.'

And immediately, while he was still speaking, a cock crowed.

And the Lord turned and looked at Peter. And Peter recalled the Lord's comment, that he'd told him, 'Before the cock crows today, you'll deny me three times.' And he went out and wept bitterly.

This saddest of all stories is in all the Gospels, but Luke tells it in his own way. He places it slightly earlier than it was in Mark, and produces a most telling touch when he has Jesus (who appears from nowhere) turn and look at Peter, which is sufficient to remind him of what he has just done and said.

The mocking of Jesus

63-65 And the men who held him mocked him and beat him, and they covered him up and interrogated him, 'Prophesy, who's the one who struck you?' And they addressed him with many other impertinent remarks.

Luke places this episode slightly later than Mark does, and makes it lead into the interrogation by the religious authorities. In some ways this is closer to Matthew's version, although Luke is the only one to speak of 'impertinent remarks' (literally, 'blaspheming').

In the Sanhedrin

22 66–23 1 And when day broke, the presbyterium of the populace gathered, chief priests and scribes; and they led him into their synagogue, saying, 'If you are the Messiah, tell us.' He said to them, 'If I tell you, you won't believe; but if I interrogate [you], you won't answer. But from now on, the Son of Man will be seated at the right hand of the power of God.'

They all said, 'So – you are the Son of God, then?' He said to them, 'It is you people who say that I am.' They said, 'What need do we still have of evidence? For we have heard from his mouth.' And the whole crowd of them got up and led him to Pilate.

Luke has shortened Mark's account, omitting the allegation about 'destroy this Temple and in three days I shall rebuild it', and going straight on to the difficult question: is Jesus, or is he not, the Messiah? It is no longer, according to Luke, the Chief Priest who finds Jesus guilty, but all of them. And it is hard, on this account, to know what Jesus is guilty *of* !

Jesus is accused before Pilate

2-5 They began to accuse him, saying 'We found this man subverting our nation and preventing them from paying tax to Caesar, and saying that he is a King-Messiah.'

Pilate interrogated him, 'Are you the King of the Jews?'

He answered, 'You say so.'

Pilate said to the chief priests and the crowds, 'I find no crime in him'; but they insisted, 'This man is stirring up the populace, teaching in all of Judaea, and starting from Galilee right up to this point.'

Luke gives a slightly different introduction to the scene between Jesus and Pilate. He makes the accusations against Jesus demonstrably false: the reader knows perfectly well that Jesus was not 'subverting' the nation or 'preventing them from paying tax to Caesar' or 'stirring up the populace'. But they are all the kind of thing that the affluent in society might unthinkingly say. He also adds his familiar 'journeying' theme, with the reference to Judaea and Galilee.

Jesus is sent to Herod

6-12   Pilate pricked up his ears, and asked if the fellow was a Galilean. When he found out that he was from Herod's jurisdiction, he sent him up to Herod, since he was also in Jerusalem at that time.

When Herod saw Jesus, he greatly rejoiced. For [he'd been] wanting to see him for a long time, because he'd been hearing about him, and he was hoping to see a miracle being done by him. He interrogated him at some length – but he didn't respond to him in any way. The chief priests and the scribes were standing there, vigorously accusing him. Herod, along with his troops, regarded him with contempt, and played a game with him, dressing him up in gorgeous clothing, and sending him back to Pilate. Herod and Pilate became friends with each other on that day; for they had previously been at enmity.

This passage is only in Luke, and once again we meet Herod, in whom Luke has more than a passing interest. Like John the Baptist and Jesus at the beginning, so now Herod and Pilate are brought together at the end. Herod's superficial interest in 'Jesus the miracle-worker' marks him out as someone who can't cope with who Jesus is for Luke, so it is not surprising that he plays his silly game and cements a trivial alliance.

We may contrast Herod, who 'was hoping' to see one of Jesus' party-tricks, with Cleopas and his companion in the following chapter, who 'had been hoping' that Jesus was to redeem Israel.

Pilate is reluctantly forced to condemn Jesus

13-25   Pilate called the chief priests and the rulers, and the populace, and said to them, 'You brought me this person on the grounds that he is causing rebellion among the people, and look here – speaking for myself in your presence, I have examined this person, and I've found in him no evidence that he is guilty of the accusations that you are bringing against him. And nor did Herod (because he sent him up to us); and look – nothing worthy of death has been done by him. So I am going to have him flogged and release him.'

But they all cried out together, 'Take this one away; release Barabbas to us!' (This one had been flung into gaol because of a riot that had taken place in the city, and for murder.) Pilate addressed them again; he wanted to release Jesus. But they went on shouting, 'Crucify him, crucify [him].' He addressed them a third time, 'Why? What evil has this man done? I have found no capital crime in him. So I'm going to flog him and release him.' But they insisted, with loud shouts, demanding that he be crucified – and their shouts prevailed, and Pilate decided that their request should be granted. He released the one they had been demanding, the one who had been flung into gaol because of rioting and murder – and Jesus he handed over to their will!

Luke departs from Mark here, and runs a bit closer to John's account of the scene before Pilate. He shares with John the strong sense that Pilate tried very hard to release Jesus. Luke manages to convey this with the awkward sentence 'nothing worthy of death has been done by him'. Luke is also closer to John than he is to Mark in the reference to 'crying out' and to the demand for Barabbas rather than Jesus. On the other hand, it is Luke alone who makes it clear that Jesus' flogging, with monstrous injustice, is for being innocent-but-accused.

Jesus' companions on the way to death

26-32   And as they led him away, they took hold of Simon, a Cyrenean, who was coming from the field, and put the cross on him to carry it behind Jesus.

A great crowd of the populace was following him, and also [a crowd] of women, who were mourning him and weeping for him. Jesus turned to the women and said, 'Daughters of Jerusalem, don't be weeping over me. No – weep for yourselves and for your children. Because, look! Days are coming when they will be saying, "Congratulations to the women who are barren, and the wombs that have not given birth, and the breasts that have not suckled." Then they will start saying to the mountains, "Fall on us," and to the hills, "Cover us." Because if they do these things when the wood is green – what might happen when it's dry?'

And two other criminals were led out with him to be executed.

Luke has grouped together three groups of companions for Jesus as he goes out to his execution. The first and the third are already in Mark, although Luke's account of Simon of Cyrene is less stark than Mark 15:21. The second group, however, the 'women of Jerusalem', who have the courage to show their affection for Jesus, is only in Luke, and is part of the evidence that makes people want to call Luke the 'Gospel of women'. Jesus' sensitive response to their mourning, and the characteristic Lucan note that he '*turned* to the women', give the incident great emotional weight. The line about asking the mountains and the hills to bury them is already in Hosea 10:8, in the context of the destruction of the Northern Kingdom. Here it is clearly the destruction of Jerusalem that is in view.

Jesus' companions at Skull Place

33-43   And when they came to the place that was known as 'Skull', there they crucified him, and the criminals, one on the right, and one on the left. Jesus said, 'Father forgive them, for they do not know what they are doing.' When they divided his garments, they threw lots.

And the crowd stood, watching. And the rulers sneered at him, saying, 'He saved others; let him save himself, if this is the "Messiah of God", the "Chosen One".' And the soldiers who came up also made a game of him, offering him sour wine, and saying, 'If you *are* the King of the Judaeans, save yourself!' There was also a placard on him, 'This is the King of the Judaeans.'

One of the crucified criminals started blaspheming him, saying, 'Aren't you the Messiah? Save yourself – and us as well!' The other scolded him in response and said, 'Have you no reverence even for God? Because you're under the same sentence; but we deserve it, because we are getting the going rate for what we did. But this man hasn't done anything wrong.' And he said, 'Jesus – remember me when you come into your kingdom.' And he said to him, 'Amen I tell you, *today* you will be with me in Paradise.'

Luke presents three possible reactions to Jesus: the 'populace' watch; the rulers (familiar Lucan term), soldiers, and one of his fellow criminals, turn the word 'save' on Jesus, to show that he's a fake; finally the other criminal gets him triumphantly and dramatically right, and turns into one of Jesus' 'terrible friends'. This perceptive murderer asserts that Jesus is indeed a King (or Messiah) and all but says that he is God. In addition the reader knows that whatever the rulers may think, Jesus is indeed 'Messiah of God' (9:20) and 'Chosen One' (9:35). The episode ends, with arresting solemnity, with 'Amen I tell you' and a striking Lucan 'today', and a most unexpected conclusion.

The circumstances of Jesus' death

44-49   And it was now about the sixth hour, and a darkness came on all the earth until the ninth hour, because there was an eclipse of the sun. The veil of the Temple was torn in the middle, and Jesus cried in a loud voice, 'Father, into your hands I commit my spirit.' As he said this, he expired. When the centurion saw what had happened, he started to glorify God, saying, 'This person really was innocent.' And all the crowds who had come together for this spectacle, and had watched what took place, went back beating their breasts. All the men who were known to him stood a long way off, and also the women who had followed him from Galilee, watching these [events].

Luke is still clearly following Mark's account, but he makes one or two changes, where we can see his hand at work. He adds the detail about the eclipse of the sun, perhaps giving a scientific explanation for his educated readers. He omits Mark's terrible cry of abandonment ('My God, my God – why have you forsaken me?', Mark 15:34), and the sponge filled with vinegar (though the soldiers have given Jesus something like that earlier on). Jesus' last words are reported as a much more gentle quotation from Psalm 31:6. And the centurion, in a characteristic phrase, 'started to glorify God', and instead of the verdict 'Son of God', which in some ways is the climax of Mark's Gospel (Mark 15:39), we read, 'This person really was innocent'; and Luke adds the dramatic detail that the watching crowds (verse 48 picking up verse 35) 'went back beating their breasts'. Finally, where Mark had the disciples all run away, Luke is rather emphatic that 'all the men known to him' were, after all, still there, though he agrees with Mark that the faithful women were witnesses. And he does have the men standing 'a long way off'.

How Jesus was buried

50-56 And look! A man called Joseph, who was a member of the Sanhedrin, and a good and just man (he had not voted for their decision and action), from Arimathea, a city of the Jews, who was waiting for the kingdom of God, this man approached Pilate and asked for the body of Jesus. And when he had taken it down, he wrapped it in a linen cloth, and placed him in a tomb hewn out of the rock, where no one had yet lain. And it was the Day of Preparation, and Sabbath was about to begin (literally, 'dawning').

And the women who had followed with him from Galilee, saw the tomb, and [saw] how his body was placed. They went back and prepared spices and perfumes, and for the Sabbath-day they rested in accordance with the commandment.

Once again, Luke is following Mark, but with some shades of meaning of his own. He specifically exempts Joseph of Arimathea from any blame in Jesus' death. He follows Mark in saying that Joseph was 'waiting for the kingdom of God'. But in Luke that phrase has a special meaning. Basically it means to 'receive'; but in 2:25 Luke uses it of Simeon 'waiting for the comfort of Israel'; at 2:28 Simeon 'received' or 'took' Jesus into his arms; at 12:36 it refers to people 'expecting' their Lord when he comes back from the wedding. And in 15:2, it refers to Jesus' unfortunate propensity to lavish hospitality on undesirables. If in the previous passage Luke seems to have downgraded the women by emphasising that they weren't alone, he now makes handsome amends, by repeating that they had 'followed' (or 'been disciples') 'from Galilee'. He also points to their faithfulness and love, in preparing spices for anointing Jesus' body, to their status as witnesses (they saw 'how his body was placed') and their fidelity as Jews ('for the Sabbath-day they rested in accordance with the commandment'); for this very Lucan idea about the 'commandment', see also 1:6; 15:29; 18:20.

No body, but two men in white clothes

24 1-12 But on the first day of the week, in the deep dawn, they came to the tomb, bringing the spices they had bought. And they found the stone rolled away from the tomb; and when they went in, they did not find the body of the Lord Jesus. And as they were puzzling about this, look! Two men stood by them in dazzling clothes. They became fearful, and bowed their faces to the ground; [the two men] said to the women, 'Why are you looking for the Living One among the corpses? He is not here – no, he has been raised! Remember how he told you, while he was still in Galilee, that "the Son of Man must be delivered into the hands of sinners and be crucified and on the third day rise again".' And they recalled his words.

And when they returned from the tomb, they announced all these things to the Eleven, and to all the rest. They were the Magdalene Mary, and Joanna, and Mary of Jacob, and the rest of the women with them. They said these things to the apostles. And these words appeared to them like nonsense; and they didn't believe them. And Peter arose and ran to the tomb and stooped down and saw the cloths, and went off home, marvelling at what had happened.

Luke, for the last time, uses what Mark (16:1-8) had written, but makes several changes. There is no conversation about rolling the stone away; they simply find it so, and no dead body. Then they encounter 'two men', clearly angels, in an encounter that echoes the Transfiguration (9:28-36). The two men rebuke them for looking in the wrong place, and remind them that Jesus had actually predicted his Resurrection. There is here no mission to Galilee, no instructions to Peter and the disciples. And Luke has avoided Mark's astonishing ending, 'They said nothing to anyone – for they were afraid'.

In addition, Luke reports a visit by Peter to the tomb, with a characteristic Lucan phrase, 'marvelling at what had happened', but also using some words that will appear in John's version of the scene: 'ran', 'bent down and saw the cloths', 'he went off home (or: to himself)'.

The journey from Jerusalem to Emmaus and (rather rapidly) back to Jerusalem (a liturgy?)

13-35 And look! Two of them on that day were journeying to a village called Emmaus that was sixty stades (seven or eight miles) distant from Jerusalem. And they were talking to each other about all these things that had happened. And as they talked, Jesus himself actually drew near and was journeying with them. Their eyes were prevented from recognising him. He said to them, 'What words are these which you are exchanging with each other as you walk?' And they stopped dead, looking sullen.

One of them, called Cleopas, answered him, 'Are you the only one visiting Jerusalem, and you don't know the things that have taken place in Jerusalem during these days?'

And he said to them, 'What sort of things?' They told him, 'Things about Jesus the Nazarene, who appeared as a man, a prophet, powerful in word and deed before God and before the entire populace? How they handed him over, our chief priests and rulers, to a death sentence, and they crucified him? We had been hoping that he was going to be the one to ransom [or: 'liberate'] Israel. On top of all this, it is the third day since all this happened. And now, some women from our lot have astonished us; they got to the tomb at dawn, and didn't find his body, and they came saying that they'd seen a vision of angels, who said he was alive. And some of those with us went off to the tomb; and they found it just as the women had said – but they did not see him.'

And he said to them, 'What *fools* you are! [So] lacking in imagination, [not] to believe all that the prophets had said! Wasn't it *essential* for the Messiah to suffer this and [so] enter into his glory?' And he started with Moses and with all the prophets, and explained the stuff about himself in all the scriptures.

And they drew near to the village to which they were journeying – and he pretended to be journeying further. But they pressed him, saying, 'Stay with us, because it is towards evening, and the day has already declined.' And he went in to stay with them. And it turned out, as he lay down [to eat] with them, he took the loaf, and blessed [it] and broke [it] and handed [it] over to them – and their eyes were opened wide, and they recognised him! And he vanished from them.

And they said to each other, 'Wasn't our heart burning within as he was talking to us on the journey? As he was opening up the scriptures to us?'

And they got up at that moment and returned to Jerusalem, and found the Eleven gathered, and their companions, who were [all] saying, 'The Lord really is risen, and he's appeared to Simon.' And they in their turn related the things that had happened on the way, and how he'd been recognised by them in the breaking of the bread.

This episode is only reported in Luke, and it may be helpful to make two points about it. First, it is a journey, perhaps a microcosm of the whole journey that is Luke-Acts, and indeed (for Luke) the entire Christian life. It starts, like the Gospel, in Jerusalem, and, like the Gospel, it ends there – but much has gone on. The journey started slow and plodding; its pace quickened up when Jesus 'journeyed with them'; it seemed to have come to a pleasant halt as the day declined – but it culminated in a rapid sprint back to Jerusalem. And that, it turns out, is only the beginning of a quite new journey.

Second, it is a Eucharistic service. Standardly, the Christian Eucharist begins with 'where the worshippers are', what in some traditions is called the 'Penitential Rite'. That is represented by the sullen disciples speaking to each other and (rather reluctantly) to Jesus of their disillusionment. Next comes the 'service of the word', Jesus taking them through the Scripture readings, and tying it together in a homily (though most preachers these days avoid addressing their congregations as 'fools', whatever their private opinions). Then, in the form of a request to Jesus to stay on, come the 'prayers of intercession'. This is then taken up in the service of communion (taking, blessing, and distributing bread) in which Christians have, ever since that Easter Sunday evening, momentarily recognised their Lord. Finally there is the dismissal, where the congregation is told to 'go in peace'. That is precisely what happens to Cleopas and his companion. As all Christians should be, they are animated by the liturgy they have attended, and go hastily on the journey for which the liturgy has equipped them. And the liturgy and the journey both take them back (at least from time to time), to the Church, 'the Eleven and those with them'.

The real Jesus – not a ghost – appears

36-43 As they were saying these things, he himself stood in the middle of them, and he says to them, 'Peace [be] with you.' They were panic-stricken and terrified – they thought they were seeing a spirit! And he said to them, 'Why are you so disturbed, and for what reason do doubts arise in your mind? See my hands and my feet: it is me, in person. Feel me, and see that a spirit does not have flesh and bones, as you see that I have.' Saying this, he showed them his hands and feet. As they still didn't believe (it was too good to be true), and were [just] marvelling, he said to them, 'Do you have anything edible here?' They gave him a piece of grilled fish, and he took it, in front of them, and ate it!

This passage finds echoes in John's Gospel (see John 20:19-23 and 21:5,10). The point of it is twofold: first, that Jesus is different. He can suddenly appear in their midst; and they are clearly not sure that it is he. Second, he is real: he can be felt; he still bears (presumably) the marks of crucifixion; and he can eat. Resurrection, Luke is telling us, is not just a feeling that Jesus is 'still very much with us' – it is much more precise and purposeful than that.

The summary of the teaching of Luke's Gospel

44-49 He said to them, 'This was the meaning of my words, which I spoke to you while I was still with you, that everything written about me, in the Law of Moses, and in the Prophets, and in the Psalms, must inevitably be fulfilled. Then he opened their minds to understand the scriptures and he told them, 'So it is written that the Messiah suffered and rose from the dead on the third day; and repentance for the forgiveness of sins be preached in his name to all the Gentiles, beginning from Jerusalem. You are witnesses of these things. And, look, I am sending you the Father's promise upon you. You [are to] settle down in the city until you are clothed with power from on high.'

Here Luke weaves together a good many themes from the Gospel which is now ending, themes that will also be part of the narrative of Acts that is about to begin. We may mention the following:

- Jesus' words are explained in terms of a continuity with the message of the three sections (Law, Prophets, Psalms) of the Hebrew Bible, what we call the Old Testament;
- the idea of 'opening the mind' reminds us that not everyone in the Gospel has been able to see Jesus in this way; and we shall see that in Acts likewise there are those who fail to see Jesus as the fulfilment of the Hebrew scriptures;
- the heart of the matter is that the Messiah suffered and rose. At the end of Acts, Paul is about to suffer;
- the message, of both Jesus and the infant Church of Acts, is 'repentance for the forgiveness of sins';
- the message is both a journey and an invitation to a journey 'starting from Jerusalem'. It never loses touch with its roots, but proceeds to 'the ends of the earth' (Acts 1:8);
- the message, which was first delivered in the Temple, is now to go out to 'all the Gentiles (or nations)', which is what we shall see happening in Acts;
- the journey continues by means of 'witnesses': primarily witnesses to the Resurrection. In the first place, it will be 'the Twelve and those with them'; later the task is handed over to Stephen, Philip, Paul and any single reader of the Gospel and Acts who responds with an open mind;
- the journey is not under their control: for the moment, they must 'settle down in the city' and wait;
- the journey is under the control of 'the promise of my Father . . . power from on high', what elsewhere in Luke-Acts is called 'the Holy Spirit', whose journey this is.

Jesus leaves them; they survive

50-53   He led them out towards Bethany, and he raised his hands and blessed them. And it happened as he blessed them that he parted from them, and was being taken up to heaven. They worshipped him and returned to Jerusalem with great joy; and they were all the time in the Temple, blessing God.

> This is a powerful ending. Three times the word 'bless' is used, echoing the four times it was used in the Infancy Narratives (1:42; 1:64; 2:28; 2:34). The last act of the Gospel is the same as its first, in the Temple, blessing God. Now, however, it is no longer an old man with no descendants, but a young group, on the point of expanding rapidly. They have also learnt the correct approach to Jesus, for Luke tells us that they 'worshipped' him, and the alert reader will recall 4:7, 8, when it was established from Scripture that 'you shall worship the Lord your God'. Luke is understated in his assertion of who Jesus is; but follow him carefully and you will see that he has a very lofty view of him indeed.

According to John

Introduction

As soon as you open John's Gospel you are aware that you are breathing a different air from that which you encountered in Matthew, Mark and Luke. It has often been described as 'a magic pool, in which an elephant may swim and an infant paddle'. My sense of it is that it is a journey into the mystery of who Jesus is, inviting us ever deeper, as the story unfolds. One aspect of Jesus' identity that the reader might find helpful is to think of him as a being who performs on two stages: the heavenly stage ('up there'), which he leaves for a while to walk on the earthly stage ('down here'), from which he returns, but taking with him all those who belong 'up there'.

The reader will do well to remember that this is a very rich Gospel, whose meaning emerges slowly, over a lifetime of reading.

The Prologue

1 ¹⁻¹⁸
In the beginning was the Word,
and the Word was with God,
and the Word was God.
This [Word] was in the beginning with God.
Everything came to be through [the Word],
and apart from [the Word] nothing at all came to be.
What came to be in [the Word] was Life,
and the Life was the Light of human beings.
And the Light shines in Darkness,
and the Darkness did not master [the Light].

There arose a man sent from God, his name [was] John. This [John] came for witness, that he might bear witness about the Light, so that all might believe through him. That [John] was not the Light; his function was to bear witness about the Light.

The Genuine Light, which enlightens every human being, was coming into the World.

He was in the world,
and the world came to be through [the Light];
and the world did not know [the Light].
[The Light] came to his own,
and his own did not accept him.
But as many as accepted him,
he gave them power to become children of God.
[They were the ones] who believed in his name,
who were not born of blood,
nor of the will of flesh,
nor of the will of a man,
but of God.

And the Word became flesh and pitched his tent among us. And we saw his glory, [the] glory as of the only-begotten of the Father, full of grace and truth.

John bears witness about him and cried out, saying, 'This was the one I spoke of, "The one coming after me came-to-be before me, because he was earlier than I."'

For we have all received of his fullness, and grace after grace. For the Law was given through Moses, grace and truth through Jesus Christ. No one has ever seen God. The only-begotten Son, the one who rests in the bosom of the Father, he has made [God] known.

This is an astonishing and powerful opening to the Gospel. My suggestion is that you read it out loud to yourself, and simply let it speak to you. You might notice how John introduces this 'Word' of God without any explanation at all; we are supposed to understand it right away. Only at the very end of the Prologue are we told that it is Jesus who is God's 'Word'.

A second point to notice is the way our author weaves this high poetry about the 'Word' with the more prosaic story about John the Baptist. This is the first instance of what will become a theme throughout the Gospel, that it is a drama played out on two stages. The

'Word' belongs on the stage 'up there', with God, but leaves his natural home for a while to play his stuff on the stage 'down here', in search of those who would listen to him, 'those who were . . . born . . . of God'.

Third, notice the audacious statement that 'the Word became flesh, and pitched his tent among us'. This 'Word' has been presented in unimaginably lofty terms, as Light, and as Life, and as God; and now, with a bump, it 'became flesh', took on the ambiguities and frailty of human nature. And not only that, but it made its uncertain, mobile dwelling with human beings. There is much here to make us reflect.

Next, a word on the paragraph that begins 'For we have all received of his fullness . . .' Here (and often elsewhere in the Gospel) it is not clear whether this is the continuation of someone's speech, or the evangelist's own comment. Here I have opted for the latter, and have punctuated accordingly. But the original manuscript would have carried no indication that might help.

Lastly, is the 'Jesus Christ' mentioned in these final sentences the same as 'the Word'? Perhaps, and even presumably, but notice that the evangelist does not say so.

John gives his evidence

19-28 And this is the witness of John, when the Judaeans from Jerusalem sent priests and Levites to ask him, 'Who are *you*?' And he confessed, and he did not deny, and he confessed, '*I* am not the Messiah.' And they asked him, 'What then? Are you Elijah?' And he said, 'I am not.'

'Are you the Prophet?' And he replied, 'No.' So they said to him, 'Who are you, so that we may give a response to those who sent us? What do you say about yourself?' He said, 'I [am] a voice of one crying in the desert, "Make straight the way of the Lord" (as Isaiah the Prophet said).' And they had been sent from the Pharisees. And they asked him, and said to him, 'So why are *you* baptising, if you are not the Messiah, and not Elijah and not the Prophet?' John responded to them, saying, 'I baptise with water. In the middle of you stands [someone] whom you do not know, the One Coming Behind Me. And I am not worthy to untie the thong of his sandal.'

These things happened in Bethany across the Jordan, where John was baptising.

> The Gospel gradually unfolds the mystery of who Jesus is. Here, in this second section, the evangelist allows us to glimpse it negatively, through the 'evidence' or 'witness' of John the Baptist. The Greek word, which I have generally translated as 'witness', represents a very important idea in the fourth Gospel: it links together the two 'stages' on which the drama is played out.
>
> Clearly the talk here is all about Jesus; the evangelist makes use of some curiously emphatic word-positioning here. We cannot manage the same in English, so I have tried to express it with the use of bold type. The evangelist often attracts our attention by the use of odd, or awkward language also: 'he confessed and did not deny, and confessed' is as awkward in Greek as it is in English. John the Baptist's

interrogators run through a list of possible options as to who he might be: Messiah (or Christ), Elijah, the Prophet, and he denies them all; instead he defines his function in relation to Jesus, first by the quotation from Isaiah 40:3 (which all the Synoptic Gospels also use), about 'the voice of one crying in the wilderness', and second by the statement about the 'One Coming Behind Me'.

The passage ends with one of John's indicators about where it all happened. The reader will observe that we quite often find these, and it is not always clear what purpose they serve.

You may also notice the reference to the 'Judaeans' at the start of the passage. This is by way of alternative to translating the word as 'Jews' (the same word is used for both in Greek), and may serve to mitigate the anti-Semitism that, too often, this Gospel has been used to justify.

Two days, on which John the Baptist recognises Jesus, and gives him his first two disciples

29-43 On the next day he sees Jesus coming to him and says, 'See! The Lamb of God, the one who takes away the sin of the world. This is the one about whom I said, "Behind me comes a man who came-to-be before me, because he was earlier than I." And I did not know him; but in order for him to be revealed to Israel – that was the reason why I came baptising with water.' And John bore witness, saying, 'I beheld the Spirit coming down like a dove out of heaven. And it remained on him. And I did not know him – but the one who sent me to baptise with water said to me, "The one on whom you see the Spirit coming down on to him and remaining, this is the one who baptises with the Holy Spirit." And I have seen, and I have borne witness, that this is the Son of God.'

On the next day again, John stood, and two of his disciples, and looking at Jesus walking he said, 'See! The Lamb of God.' And his two disciples heard him speaking. And they followed Jesus. And Jesus turned, and seeing them following says to them, 'What do you seek?' But they said, 'Rabbi' (which carries the meaning, when translated, of 'Teacher'), 'where do you stay?' He says to them, 'Come and you will see.' So they came and saw where he was staying. And they stayed with him that day. It was about the tenth hour.

It was Andrew, the brother of Simon Peter, who was one of the two who heard [this] from John and followed [Jesus]. He finds first his own brother Simon and says to him, 'We have found the Messiah (which is, translated, Christ).' He led him to Jesus. Jesus fixed his gaze on him and said, 'You are Simon, the son of John. You shall be called Kephas (which is translated 'Rock').'

Now John the Baptist sees Jesus for the first time, and gives him a title ('Lamb of God'), that appears nowhere else in the New Testament, except the Book of Revelation (where the Greek word is different). We cannot be precisely sure of its force, but evidently it worked as a title, since it found a place in the Christian Eucharistic liturgy. The 'Lamb' probably evokes the 'Passover Lamb', and probably also the scapegoat is suggested by the idea that this Lamb 'takes away the sins of the world'. There are other possibilities, but these seem the most likely. We should also pay attention to the second use of the term, because John repeats the phrase to two of his disciples; and whatever they understand by it, the upshot is that John loses them to Jesus.

We may also observe that in this passage, unlike the Synoptic Gospels, Jesus is not actually said to have been baptised by John, but simply identified with the one on whom the Spirit rests.

We should be astonished to observe that it is only now, for the very first time in the Gospel, that the one called 'Word' actually speaks. And notice his first two utterances: 'What do you seek?' (that word, 'seek', is very important in the Gospel of John), and 'Come and you will see.' Those two sayings should leap from the page at us, and accompany our reading of the Gospel.

This episode has the further consequence of introducing into the story 'Simon', the brother of Andrew (the evangelist shows no surprise at this man's Greek name), and the application to him of the nickname 'Rock'. We shall watch this character with some interest from this point onwards.

Philip and Nathanael meet Jesus

44-51 On the next day, he wanted to go to the Galilee, and finds Philip. And Jesus says to him, 'Follow me.' Now Philip was from Bethsaida, from the city of Andrew and Peter. Philip finds Nathanael and says to him, 'The one Moses wrote about in the Torah, and [the one] the prophets [wrote about] – we've found him, Jesus, the son of Joseph, from Nazareth.' And Nathanael says to him, 'From Nazareth can any good thing come?'

Philip says to him, 'Come and see.' Jesus saw Nathanael coming and says of him, 'See! Truly an Israelite in whom there is no guile.' Nathanael says to him, 'Where do you know me from?' Jesus replied and says to him, 'Before Philip called you, when you were under the fig tree, I saw you.' Nathanael replied to him, 'Rabbi, you are the Son of God, you are King of Israel.' Jesus replied and said to him, 'Because I told you that I saw you under the fig tree do you believe? Greater things than this you shall see.' And he says to him, 'Amen, Amen, I tell you: You shall see heaven opened, and the angels of God going up and going down upon the Son of Man.'

This is an enigmatic episode. We are not told why Jesus wants to go 'to the Galilee', and there is not much indication of where we are at present. And, apparently because of these travel plans, he invites Philip (another Greek name, we may notice; but he comes from a pagan city) to discipleship. Then Philip, going way beyond any evidence that we have seen, summons Nathanael, and indicates to him that Jesus is 'the one Moses wrote about in the Torah'. Like Thomas later on (20:24-29), Nathanael expresses incredulity, but then (again on no evidence that we can see), simply when he is told 'I saw you under the fig tree', acclaims Jesus as 'Rabbi, Son of God, King of Israel'. Then something more is added: 'You shall see the heavens opened, and the angels of God going up and going down upon the Son of Man'. No question, of course, but that this Son of Man is Jesus; and see how, once again, the evangelist links together the two 'stages' on which the drama is played out.

The wedding at Cana

2 1-12 And on the third day, a wedding took place at Cana of the Galilee. And the mother of Jesus was there. Jesus was also invited, and his disciples, to the wedding, and when the wine ran out, the mother of Jesus says to him, 'They don't have [any] wine.' Jesus says to her, 'What is that to me and you, woman? My hour has not yet come.' His mother says to the servants, 'Whatever he tells you, do [it].' Now there were six stone water-jars standing in that place, in accordance with the purification rites of the Judaeans, going up to two or three measures. Jesus says to them, 'Fill up the water-jars with water.' And they filled them, right to the top. And he says to them, 'Now draw and take to the master of the feast', and they took it. And when the master of the feast tasted the water, which had become wine, he didn't know where it was from, although the servants who had drawn the water knew, the master of the feast calls the bridegroom and says to him, 'People generally set out the good wine first, and [then] when people are drunk, the inferior. *You* have kept the good wine till now.'

This first of the signs Jesus did in Cana of Galilee and revealed his glory, and his disciples believed in him. After this he went down to Caphernaum, and his mother and brothers and his disciples, and they remained there for a few days.

This is an extraordinary story, and we are invited by it to go deeper into the mystery of Jesus. It starts 'on the third day', and a Christian reader inevitably reads this as a reference to the Resurrection. Notice the order in which people are named: 'the mother of Jesus' (not actually named here, of course, nor at 19:25, the other occasion on which she is mentioned; both episodes are important in the unfolding of Jesus' story).

Next we notice the conversation between Jesus and his mother. Her observation (it is no more than that) about the lack of wine receives what sounds like a sharp rebuff, except that she does not read it so: 'Whatever he tells you, do it,' she says, confidently, to the servants. Next, and with no apparent effort at all, we discover that we have an enormous quantity (something like 180 gallons!) of the very best wine, to the astonishment of the headwaiter, and no doubt that of the bridegroom also.

The point of the story comes at the end; there is no interest in the miracle as such, only in its function as a 'sign', to reveal his 'glory'. We shall listen out for these two words; they are important in identifying Jesus. We notice that 'his disciples believed in him'; but the same is not said of his mother, presumably because she was already a believer.

Jesus in the Temple

13-25 And the Passover of the Judaeans was near, and Jesus went up to Jerusalem. And he found in the Temple those selling cows and sheep and doves, and the money changers in their seats. And he made a whip out of ropes and started to throw everyone out of the Temple, including the sheep and cows, and he began to pour out the coins of the money changers, and to overturn the tables. And to those who were selling doves he said, 'Get these things out of here. Don't make my Father's house a market place.' His disciples recalled that it is written, 'Zeal for your house devours me.'

So the Judaeans responded and said to him, 'What sign do you show us, that you do these things?' Jesus replied and said to them, 'Undo this Temple, and in three days I will raise it up.' So the Judaeans said to him, 'Forty-six years this Temple was [being] built – and you'll raise it up in three days?' But he was speaking about the temple of his body. So when he was raised from the dead, his disciples recalled that he had been saying this. And they believed the Scripture and the word that Jesus said.

And when he was in Jerusalem at the Passover, at the feast, many came to faith in his name, seeing his signs that he was doing. Jesus, however, did not entrust himself to them, because he knew everybody, and he had no need for anyone to bear witness to him about humans – for he knew what was in human beings.

Suddenly Jesus is in Jerusalem, and we are on the point of celebrating Passover (which happens three times in the Gospel of John, but only once in the Synoptics). Then he makes his powerful prophetic gesture, whipping people out of the Temple. The natural response on the part of 'the Judaeans' is to ask for his authority for doing something like this. The reader knows the answer already: he is Son of God (and the Temple is 'my Father's house'), but Jesus' opponents can only see what a large claim he is making.

The disciples receive two insights here: first, they can apply Psalm 69:9 to what has happened. Second, after the Resurrection, they can look back to this episode and understand. This theme of Resurrection was hinted at in Cana; now it is played loud and clear.

Notice the phrase indicating that 'they believed the Scripture and the word that Jesus said'. He is already extraordinarily authoritative.

There is also an ominous warning: 'many came to faith in his name . . . Jesus did not, however, entrust himself to them'. The same verb is used for 'coming to faith' and for 'entrust'; the theme of faith, and of the refusal of faith, are going to be important in the rest of the Gospel.

Nicodemus by night

3 1-21 There was a man from the Pharisees, Nicodemus his name, a ruler of the Judaeans. This [Nicodemus] came to him by night and said to him, 'Rabbi, we know that you have come as a teacher from God. For no one can do these signs that you do unless God is with him.' Jesus replied and said to him, 'Amen, Amen, I tell you; unless a person is born from above, he cannot see the kingdom of heaven.' Nicodemus says to him, 'How can a human being be born when they are old? Surely they can't enter their mother's womb a second time and be born?' Jesus replied, 'Amen, Amen, I tell you, unless [they are] born of water and Spirit, they cannot enter the kingdom of God. What is born of flesh is flesh, and what is born of the Spirit is spirit. Don't be astonished that I said to you, "You must be born again from above." The Spirit blows where it wants, and you hear its sound. But you don't know where it comes from or where it's going. That's the way everyone is

who is born of the Spirit.' Nicodemus replied and said to him, 'How can these things be?' Jesus replied and said to him, '*You* are the Teacher of Israel, and you do not know these things? Amen, Amen, I tell you: we speak what we know and we bear witness to what we have seen, and you [people] do not accept our witness. If I speak to you of earthly things and you don't believe, how will you believe if I speak to you of heavenly things?'

And no one has gone up to heaven, except the one who came down from heaven, the Son of Man. And as Moses lifted up the serpent in the desert, so the Son of Man must be lifted up, so that everyone who believes may have eternal life. For God so loved the world that he gave the only-begotten Son, so that everyone who believes in him may not be destroyed, but may have eternal life. For God did not send his Son into the world in order that he should judge the World, but in order that the world should be saved through him. The one who believes in him is not judged. But the one who does not believe is already judged, because he has not believed in the name of the Only-Begotten Son of God. This is judgement, that the Light entered the World, and human beings loved Darkness more than Light – for their deeds were wicked. For everyone who does evil things hates the Light and does not come to the Light, so that his deeds may not be exposed. Those who do Truth come to the Light, so that their deeds may be revealed, because [their deeds] are done in God.

This is the first clear example in the Gospel of John of what is sometimes called 'Johannine irony'. This occurs when Jesus is talking to someone who completely fails to understand him, while the reader understands perfectly well. This reveals the 'two stages' on which the Gospel operates. If you belong 'up there', you understand Jesus; if you belong 'down here', you do not. The evangelist perhaps labours the point by having Nicodemus come 'by night'. The stage 'down here' is threatened by darkness, unacquainted with light. So Nicodemus has no idea what is meant by being born 'again' or 'from above' (the Greek word could mean either).

We should not, however, get too impressed with our own ability to understand Jesus. At the end of Chapter 1, and the beginning of Chapter 2, we are uncomprehending eavesdroppers on the conversations between Jesus and Nathanael and Jesus and his mother, so there the irony is on us.

Notice the opening phrase, 'a man from the Pharisees': the word for 'man' is the same word that I translated 'humans' and 'human beings' in the previous sentence. Nicodemus is therefore an example of those to whom Jesus does not entrust himself.

You will see from the punctuation that I have taken the final paragraph as evangelist's commentary, rather than the continuation of Jesus' words to Nicodemus. Certainly, many of the ideas in this paragraph are very important in the Gospel: 'going up', and 'coming down'; 'lifting up' (understood, we shall learn later, as crucifixion), 'Son of Man', 'eternal life', especially when associated with 'belief' or 'faith' (the same word in Greek), 'world', 'sending' (especially God sending the Son), 'judgement', 'Light', 'Darkness', 'Truth', 'deeds', 'reveal'.

John the Baptist once more

22-36 After this, Jesus came, and his disciples, into the Judaean territory; and there he was spending [time] with them, and baptising. And John was also baptising, at Aenon near Saleim, because there were many waters there, and they were appearing and being baptised, for John had not yet been flung into prison. So there arose a controversy on the part of the disciples of John with a Jew about purification. And they came to John and said to him, 'Rabbi, the one who was with you across the Jordan, to whom you have borne witness, look! He's baptising – and they're all coming to him.' John replied and said, 'A person cannot accept a single thing, unless it be given them from heaven. You bear witness to me that I said, "I am not the Messiah but that I am sent before him." The one who has the bride is the bridegroom: but the friend of the bridegroom, who stops and hears him, rejoices with joy because of the bridegroom's voice. So this joy of mine is fulfilled. He must increase and I must decrease.'

The one who comes from above is above everything. The one who is from the earth is from the earth and speaks from the earth. The one who comes from heaven, what he has seen and heard, that he testifies, and no one accepts his testimony [or: 'evidence', 'witness']. The one who accepts his testimony certifies that God is True. For the one whom God has sent speaks God's words – for he gives the Spirit with unstinting generosity. The Father loves the Son, and has given everything in his hand. The one who believes in the Son has eternal life. But the one who disobeys the Son will not see life – but the wrath of God remains on him.

Throughout the New Testament, the figure of John the Baptist is important for helping Christians to see who Jesus is. So once more the Gospel reverts to John, to help the reader go deeper into the mystery by way of the contrast between Jesus and John. The episode starts with a disagreement of some kind, and the Baptist's disciples complaining about Jesus. This produces his final verdict on Jesus: he is the 'Messiah', the 'Bridegroom', and 'he must increase and I must decrease'.

Then comes what I have taken as a paragraph of commentary by the evangelist, reverting to our 'two stages', above and below, heavenly and earthly. Once again we have the theme of testimony (or 'evidence' or 'witness'), of 'Truth', of 'love' and the connection between 'belief' and 'life'.

An encounter by a well; deeper into the mystery

4 1-42 So when Jesus knew that the Pharisees had heard that Jesus was making and baptising more disciples than John (and yet it was not Jesus himself who was baptising, but his disciples), he abandoned Judaea and went back to the Galilee, and he had to pass through Samaria. So he comes to a city of Samaria called Sychar, near the place which Jacob had given to Joseph his son. Jacob's well was there. So Jesus, worn out from the journey, sat, just like that, on the well. It was about the sixth hour (12 noon). There comes a woman from Samaria to draw water. Jesus says to her, 'Give me a drink.' For his disciples had gone into the city,

to buy food. So the Samaritan woman says to him, 'How come you who are a Judaean ask for a drink from me, a Samaritan woman?' (For Judaean males do not have intercourse with Samaritan females.) Jesus replied and said to her, 'If you knew the gift of God, and who it is that says to you 'Give me to drink', you would ask him, and he would give you Living Water.' She says to him, 'Lord, you have no bucket and the well is deep. From where do you have [this] Living Water? Are you [can you be?] greater than our ancestor Jacob, who gave us the well, and he used to drink of it, and his sons and his animals?' Jesus replied and said to her, 'Everyone who drinks of this water here will be thirsty again. But whoever drinks of the water which *I* shall give them will never thirst and it will become in them a fountain of water which bubbles up to eternal life.' The woman says to him, 'Lord, give me this water that I may not be thirsty, and not come here to draw [water].'

He says to her, 'Go, call your man and come here.' The woman answered and said to him, 'I don't have a man.' Jesus said, 'Well said: "I don't have a man." For you've had five men; and now the one you have isn't your man. You spoke [the] truth there.' The woman says to him, 'Lord, I see that *you* are a prophet. Our ancestors worshipped on this mountain; and you people say that it is in Jerusalem, the 'place' where worship must happen.' Jesus says to her, 'Have faith in me, woman; because the hour is coming when you people will worship the Father, not on this mountain, and not in Jerusalem. You people worship that which you do not know. We worship what we do know, because salvation is from the Jews. But the hour is coming, and is [here] now, when genuine worshippers will worship the Father in spirit and truth. For the Father seeks people like this who worship him. God is Spirit, and those who worship God must worship in Spirit and in Truth.' She says to him, 'I know that Messiah is coming, the one called Christ. When that one comes, he will announce everything to us.' Jesus says to her, 'I AM, the one who is speaking to you.'

And at this, his disciples came; and they were startled that he was actually talking to a woman. But no one said, 'What are you looking for?', or 'Why are you speaking with her?'

So the woman abandoned her bucket and went off into the city and says to the people, 'Come here and see a person who has told me all the things I have done. Do you think he's the Messiah?' They went out of the city and they came to him.

In the meantime his disciples were asking him, saying, 'Rabbi, eat.' But he said to them, 'I have food to eat which you do not know.' So the disciples said to each other, 'Do you think someone has brought him something to eat?' Jesus says to them, 'My food is that I should do the will of the one who sent me, and complete his work. Don't you people say, "Another four months and the harvest is coming"? Look, I tell you, lift up your eyes and see the fields – they are white for the harvest. Already the Reaper is taking his wages and gathering fruit for eternal life, so that the sower may rejoice together with the reaper. For in this the saying is true, that "The Sower is one person, and the Reaper another". I sent you to reap where you did not labour. Others have laboured, and you have entered into [the fruits of] their labour.'

From that city, many of the Samaritans came to faith in him because of the report [or: 'word'] of the woman, who testified, 'He told me all the things that I had done.' So when the Samaritans came to him, they asked him to stay with them. And he stayed there for two days. And many more came to faith because of his word. And to the woman they said, 'It's no longer because of your talk that we believe. For we ourselves have heard, and we know that this one is truly the Saviour of the World.'

The Gospel aims to take us deeper into the mystery of who Jesus is. Here is a story where we can see it happening. It starts with an awkward and baffling introduction, which may remind us of the introduction to the Nathanael story, at 1:43.

It continues awkward: 'boy meets girl', so to say, by the well; and in the Old Testament such a situation always leads to a betrothal. And then there is the mysterious sentence about Judaean males and Samaritan women (I have to admit that this is not the only way of translating it; but a Greek reader or hearer would not have missed this possibility).

Slowly, however, the mist clears. The woman comes to the well at midday, a time which, as any African will tell you, is wrong for that kind of heavy work. She is told, perhaps slightly abruptly, to 'give me a drink', which Jesus never gets. (We may think of Jesus' thirst on the cross (19:28) and the remark in Matthew 25:42 'I was thirsty, and you gave me no drink'. Perhaps it is accurate to think of Jesus as thirsting for our kindness and compassion, but failing to get it.) There is 'Johannine irony' when Jesus refers to 'Living Water' and the woman understands this in terms of buckets. We notice, however, that she is exceptionally quick on the uptake: she calls him 'Lord' (the first person in the Gospel to do so); she identifies him as perhaps greater than Jacob; she picks up his talk of 'eternal life'.

Then she is able to follow Jesus through his abrupt change of subject to the question of the men in her life, and identifies him as a prophet. This enables her to pose a question about appropriate worship, which takes the discussion on to an even higher level. Finally, she is almost there, implicitly raising the question of whether Jesus is indeed Messiah. To this, now that she is ready to understand, Jesus responds with 'EGO EIMI' ('I AM'); this is not simply saying 'you've got it', but is also making a claim about divinity. Just at this very important moment, the disciples intrude (there is no other word for it), and purse their lips at the company he is keeping.

Next, very significantly, the woman abandons her bucket, symbol of her former life (she has previously noticed that Jesus has no bucket), and takes up the new task of being a missionary.

The disciples, in sharp contrast to the woman, do not understand anything of what is going on, and have to have the 'harvest' explained to them. Meanwhile, of course, the woman (and a foreigner at that) is actually reaping the harvest. It may be of interest to the reader to know that the word for 'labour', something they show no signs of doing, is closely connected with the word translated 'worn out', referring to Jesus at the beginning of the story.

Finally, the story ends with another title for Jesus. We have seen him identified in this episode as 'Lord', 'Greater-than-Jacob', 'Prophet', 'Messiah' and 'Ego Eimi'. Now he is described as 'Saviour of the World'.

Another awkward introduction; and a 'second' sign

43-54 After the two days, he went out from there into the Galilee. For Jesus himself had borne witness that a prophet has no honour in his own country. Therefore when he came to the Galilee, the Galileans received him, having seen everything that he had done in Jerusalem at the feast; you see, they themselves had gone to the feast.

So he went back into Cana in the Galilee, where he had made the water [into] wine. And there was a certain princeling whose son was sick in Caphernaum. This one, hearing that Jesus had come out of Judaea into the Galilee, went off to him and asked him to come down and heal his son; for he was about to die. So Jesus said to him, 'Unless you see signs and portents, you will not believe.' The princeling says to him, 'Lord, come down before my little child dies.' Jesus says to him, 'Go – your son lives.' The man believed the word which Jesus spoke to him, and went. As he was already coming down, his slaves met him, saying his child was alive. So he found out the time from them at which he had begun to improve. So they told him, 'Yesterday at the seventh hour the fever left him.' So the father knew that it was at that hour at which Jesus had said to him, 'Your son lives.' And he came to faith, as did his entire household. Jesus did this again as his second sign, coming out of Judaea into the Galilee.

John narrates another sign, 'the second', according to the evangelist (even though Nicodemus thought there had been lots – 3:2; see also 2:23). Yet again the introduction is awkward. He is going to the Galilee, apparently *because* of his belief that he will not be honoured there. Contrary to what we are expecting, however, the Galileans accept him, because they had been in the Galilee at the time of the feast (when Jesus had made his gesture in the Temple). After that, the healing of the 'princeling's son is effortlessly accomplished, and at precisely the time when Jesus said that he was alive. The effect is 'faith' on the princeling's part, and that of his entire household. Finally, the evangelist emphasises that this took place in the Galilee, not Judaea.

The cure of 'Old Grumpy', and Jesus' defence of his actions

5 1-47 After this, there was a feast of the Jews, and Jesus went up to Jerusalem. There is in Jerusalem, at the Sheep [Gate] a pool which is called in Hebrew Beth Zatha, which has five porticoes. In these [porticoes] there lay a number of ailing people, blind, lame, paralysed. And there was a certain man who had been thirty-eight years in his ailment. Seeing him lying [there], and knowing that he was already [there] a long time, he says to him, 'Do you want to be healthy?' The ailing one said to him, 'Lord, I don't have anyone, when the water is disturbed, to throw me into the pool. And while I am on the way, someone else goes down ahead of me.' Jesus says to him, 'Arise, take up your mattress, and walk.' And straightaway the man became healthy, and he took up his mattress and walked. Now it was a Sabbath on that day. So the Judaeans said to the cured man, 'It is Sabbath: and it is not permitted for you to lift up your mattress.' He answered them, 'The one who made me healthy, that one told me, "Lift up your mattress and walk."' They asked him, 'Who is the man who said to you, "Lift up and walk"?' But the healed man did not know who it was, for Jesus had withdrawn, there being a crowd in the place. After this, Jesus finds him in the Temple and said to him, 'Look! You have become

healthy. Don't sin any more, so that nothing worse may happen to you.' The man went off and told the Judaeans that Jesus was the one who had made him healthy.

And because of this the Judaeans went after Jesus, because he used to do these things on the Sabbath. He responded to them, 'My Father is working up to now, and [now] I [also] am at work.' So because of this the Judaeans sought even more to kill him; because not only did he undo the Sabbath – but he also spoke of God as his own Father, making himself equal to God. So Jesus replied and said to them, 'Amen, Amen, I say to you: the Son can do nothing unless he sees the Father doing something. For whatever That One does, the Son likewise does these things. For the Father loves the Son, and shows him all the things which he does; and he will show him greater things, so that you may wonder. For as the Father raises the dead and gives them life, so the Son gives life to those whom he wishes. For neither does the Father judge anyone, but he has given all judgement to the Son, so that all may honour the Son as they honour the Father. The one who does not honour the Son does not honour the Father who sent him.

'Amen, Amen, I tell you, the one who hears my word and believes in the one who sent me has eternal life, and does not come to judgement, but has transferred out of death into life.

'Amen, Amen, I tell you, the hour is coming and now is when the dead will hear the voice of the Son of God, and those who hear [it] will live. For as the Father has life in himself, so he has given life to the Son, to have in himself. And he gave him authority to do judgement, because he is Son of Man.

'Do not wonder at this, because the hour is coming in which all those in the tombs will hear his voice; and they will come out, those who did good to a Resurrection of Life, and those who did evil to a Resurrection of Judgement.

'I cannot do anything of myself. As I hear I judge, and my judgement is just, because I do not seek my will, but the will of the One who sent me. If I bear witness about myself, my witness is not true. There is Another who bears witness about me, and I know that his witness is true, which he witnesses about me. You people sent to John, and he witnessed to the truth. I do not take witness from [any] human being – but I say these things so that you people may be saved. He was the lamp, burning and shining; but you people wanted to rejoice for an hour in his light. But I have a witness greater than [that] of John. For the works which the Father gave me for me to complete them, the very works that I do, bear witness about me that the Father sent me. And the Father who sent me, he has borne witness about me. You have never heard his voice, nor have you seen his shape. And you do not have his word abiding in you, because the One whom he sent, this is the One whom you people do not believe. You people investigate the scriptures, because you think that you have eternal life in them – and those are the [scriptures] that witness about me. And you people do not wish to come to me in order that you might have life.

'I do not accept glory from human beings: but I know you people – you do not have the love of God in yourselves. I came in the name of my Father, and you did not believe me. If another [person] came in his own name, him you will receive. How is it that you people can believe, taking glory from each other, and you do not seek the glory [that comes] from the only God? Do not think that I shall accuse you people to the Father. It is Moses who is your accuser, Moses in whom you hoped. For if you believed Moses, you would believe me. For he wrote about me. But if you do not believe his writings, how will you believe my words?'

I call this man 'Old Grumpy'. Some readers leap to his defence, and call this a harsh judgement, but consider: he whines, when Jesus asks him if he wants to be healthy, about his lack of servants; he reports his benefactor to the 'Judaeans'; he fails to recognise what has happened to him, or to show the slightest gratitude, ducking the Sabbath controversy; and, finally, he sneaks on Jesus to the authorities. He is not a sympathetic character.

This episode provokes a murderous campaign against Jesus, partly because he exercises a claim over the Sabbath, and partly because he refers to God as 'Father'. The alert reader may also observe that he claims that God may also have been at work on the first ever Sabbath (see 1:17, and read Genesis 2:2 – carefully).

In response, Jesus gives the first of the major discourses that run through this Gospel, not merely in self-defence, but explaining the relationship of the Son to the Father, and the Son's 'subordination' to the Father. Once again we meet the ideas of 'sending' and of 'life'. Here there is an explicit link made to Resurrection. Once again there is talk of 'witness' and of 'truth' and of 'glory'. Finally we note the audacious claim that Moses is, after all, on Jesus' side.

Jesus feeds the five thousand

6 ¹⁻¹⁵   After this, Jesus went off across the Sea of Galilee, of Tiberias. And there followed him a great crowd, because they were observing the signs that he was doing with regard to the ailing. And Jesus went up into the mountain and there he sat down with his disciples. And the Passover was near, the feast of the Jews. And so, lifting up his eyes, Jesus, and seeing that a great crowd was coming before him, says to Philip, 'From where are we to buy loaves so that these ones may eat?' He said this testing him; for he himself knew what he was about to do. Philip replied to him, 'Two hundred denarii's worth of loaves are not sufficient for them, for each of them to take a tiny bit.' One of his disciples says to him (Andrew, the brother of Simon Peter), 'There is a little boy here who has five barley loaves and two dried fish – but what are these in the face of so many people?' Jesus said, 'Make the people take their places.' There was much grass in the area. So the men took their place, in number about five thousand. So Jesus took the loaves, and having given thanks, distributed to the guests, and likewise of the dried fish – as much as they wanted. And when they had eaten their fill, he says to his disciples, 'Gather the fragments that are surplus, so that nothing be lost.' So they gathered, and they filled twelve baskets of fragments from the five barley loaves that were surplus to [the needs of] those who had eaten. So the people, seeing [the] sign he had done, said, 'This is indeed the prophet who is coming into the world.' So Jesus, knowing that they were about to come and take him away to make him king, withdrew again into the mountain, just himself alone.

This story is also in the Synoptic Gospels, and, as in the Synoptic versions, it is followed by the episode where Jesus walks on the water. In John, however, the two episodes together form a platform for the long discourse about the Bread of Life. Once again, John offers a slightly mysterious geographical indicator by way of introduction; once again he gives the impression that a whole series of 'signs' has been taking place, possibly because he expects his readers to know the traditional Synoptic narrative. We notice the test for Philip, who, like Andrew mentioned a few lines later, has a Greek name. Philip's incredulity at Jesus' suggestion shows that he has failed the test (as does Andrew); but the evangelist emphasises that Jesus, by contrast, 'knew what he was about to do'. This knowledge of Jesus is a regular theme in the Gospel; and it is offered also to the Gospel's readers (more 'Johannine irony'). Less knowledgeable, however, is the crowd who, on seeing the 'sign', correctly identify Jesus as 'the prophet who is coming into the world', and then, incorrectly, seek to make him king. As we shall see at the end of his life, he is indeed king, but not in the sense which they understand. So at the end of our episode, Jesus is symbolically left on the mountain, 'just himself alone'. No one else really understands him.

'I AM – do not be afraid'

16-21 And when it grew late his disciples came down to the sea. And going on board a boat they went across the sea to Caphernaum. And darkness had already fallen, and Jesus had not yet come to them. And the sea was becoming aroused, with a strong wind blowing. And so when they had rowed about three or four miles, they see Jesus walking on the sea and coming near the boat. And they were afraid; but he says to them, 'I AM – do not be afraid.' So they wanted to take him into the boat – and immediately the boat was on the land for which they were making!

> For the first time, the disciples do something on their own in the Gospel, and they encounter darkness and fear; to be fair to them, the fear is provoked by Jesus 'walking on the water and coming near the boat'. Their fear provokes a response from Jesus; he uses the same words, 'I AM' that we find in the equivalent passage, Mark 6:49; but it means so much more here – in John's Gospel, 'I AM' has become a divine title.
>
> Then, quite remarkably, as though to underscore the significance of the title, the boat suddenly arrives where they were going; this deepens our sense that extraordinary things are afoot.

The words about the 'Bread of Life'

22-59 On the next day, the crowd that had stood on the other side of the sea saw that there was no other boat (except for one), and that Jesus had not gone into the boat with his disciples, but his disciples had gone off on their own. Other boats came from Tiberias, near the place where they had eaten the bread, when the Lord gave thanks. So when the crowd saw that Jesus was not there, nor his disciples, they embarked on the boats, and came to Caphernaum seeking Jesus. And finding him across the sea, they said to him, 'Rabbi, when did you come to be here?' Jesus replied and said, 'Amen, Amen, I say to you, you seek me, not because you saw signs, but because you ate of the loaves and were filled. Don't work for the food that decays; but [work for] the food that remains for eternal life, which the Son of Man will give you. For the Father, God, has sealed this One. So they said to him,

'What are we to do that we may work the works of God?' Jesus replied and said to them, 'This is the work of God, that you should believe in the one whom [God] has sent.' So they said to him, 'So – what sign are you doing, that we may see and believe you? What work are you doing? Our fathers used to eat manna in the desert, as it is written, "bread from heaven he gave them to eat".' So Jesus said to them, 'Amen, Amen, I tell you, it was not Moses who gave you the "bread from heaven". Instead, it is my Father who gives you the "bread from heaven" – the true bread. For God's bread is the one who comes down from heaven and gives life to the world.' So they said to him, 'Lord, always give us this bread.'

Jesus said to them, 'I AM the Bread of Life. The one who comes to me, will never be hungry, and the one who believes in me, will never be thirsty. But I spoke to you because you also saw me, and you do not believe. Everything that the Father gives me will come to me, and the one who comes to me, I will never expel them outside. Because I have come down from heaven, not to do my will but [to do] the will of the One who sent me. Now this is the will of the One who sent me, that I shall not lose anything that he has given me; instead, I shall raise them up on the last day. For this is the will of my Father, that everyone who sees the Son and believes in him has eternal life – and I shall raise him or her up on the last day.'

So the Judaeans grumbled about him, that he said, 'I AM the bread that came down from heaven.' And they were saying, 'Isn't this Jesus the son of Joseph? Don't we know his father and mother? How come he's now saying "I have come down from heaven"?' Jesus replied and said to them, 'Don't grumble to one another. No one can come to me unless the Father who sent me drags them. And I shall raise them up on the last day. It is written in the prophets, "And they shall all be taught by God." Everyone who hears and learns from the Father comes to me. Not that anyone has seen the Father, except for the One who is from God – he has seen the Father.

'Amen, Amen, I tell you, the one who believes has eternal life. I AM the Bread of Life. Your ancestors ate the manna in the desert – and they died. This is the bread that comes down from heaven, that someone might eat of it and live. I AM the living bread that comes down from heaven. If someone eats from this bread they will live for ever. And the bread which I shall give is my flesh, on behalf of the life of the whole world.'

So the Judaeans fought with each other, saying, 'How can this fellow give us his flesh to eat?' So Jesus said to them, 'Amen, Amen, I say to you, unless you eat the flesh of the Son of Man and drink his blood you do not have life in yourselves. The one who munches my flesh and drinks my blood has eternal life. And I shall raise them up on the last day. For my flesh is true food and my blood is true drink. The one who munches my flesh and drinks my blood remains in me, and I in them. Just as the Living Father sent me, I also live because of the Father. And the one who munches me, that person will also live because of me. This is the bread that came down from heaven, not as the ancestors ate and died. The one who munches this bread will live for ever.'

These things he said in a synagogue, teaching at Caphernaum.

Once again John gives us a mysterious introduction. The long speech that is now recounted is prefaced by a baffled question, 'Rabbi, when did you come to be here?', as a flotilla of vessels is 'seeking' (that important word again) Jesus. The episode starts with dialogue, as the crowd wrestle with the mystery, and are charged with failing to see 'signs'. Once more there is reference to 'eternal life', and to belief in the one whom God has sent; once more there is the contrast with Moses, though the reader already knows that Jesus is superior to Moses. Finally, we plunge deeper than ever into the mystery, with the electrifying statement, 'I AM the Bread of Life'. This raises the question: how can Jesus have 'come down from heaven' (the upper stage) if he is also Joseph's son, and they know his parents (the lower stage)?

Then the metaphor about bread is treated in a different way: the bread has not only come down from heaven; it must also be eaten, by those who would live for ever. Jesus' language becomes almost crude, as he lays down the challenge. From the very earliest days, Christians have read this as referring to the Eucharist that has been celebrated every Sunday since that first Easter day.

'Bread from heaven he gave them to eat' could come from Exodus 16:4, Nehemiah 9:15, Psalm 78:24 or Psalm 105:40. 'And they shall all be taught by God' refers to Isaiah 54:13, and perhaps Jeremiah 31:33, 34, on the 'New Covenant'.

The words about 'Bread of Life' repel Jesus' hearers

60-71 Therefore many of his disciples who heard [this] said, 'This is a harsh message [or: 'Word']. Who can hear him?' But Jesus, knowing in himself that his disciples were grumbling about this, said to them, 'Does this scandalise you? And so [what] if you see the Son of Man going up where he was before? The Spirit is the one that makes alive – the flesh is of no use at all. The words that I have spoken are spirit and life. But there are some of you who do not have faith.' (For Jesus knew from the beginning who they were who did not have faith, and who was the one who would betray him.) And he said, 'Because of this I told you that nobody can come to me unless it be granted them from the Father.' As a result of this many of his disciples went off backwards, and no longer walked with him. So Jesus said to the Twelve, 'Surely you don't want to go, too?' Simon Peter replied to him, 'Lord, to whom shall we go? You have the words of eternal life. And we have come to believe and to know that you are the Holy One of God.' Jesus answered them, 'Did I not choose you, the Twelve? And of you, one is a devil.' He was referring to Judas, son of Simon Iscariot. For he was about to betray him – one of the Twelve!

Both in the Gospel of John and in the Synoptic Gospels, Jesus always brings division. Some accept him; he horrifies others. The 'Word' (or: 'message') is too harsh, they feel. But in John's Gospel, Jesus does not retreat an inch and insists on the reality that the Son of Man belongs elsewhere ('going up where he was before' – the upper stage). This leads to an exodus of disciples, and Jesus is apparently left only with the Twelve. In their name, and in ours, Simon Peter indicates that there isn't much choice, and leads us deeper into the mystery with his affirmation (and we notice his use of the words 'believe' and 'know') that Jesus is the 'Holy One of God'. We applaud the recognition and the loyalty, even as we are chilled by the revelation that 'of you, one is a devil'.

Jesus seen through the eyes of his brothers and of the 'Judaeans'

7 ¹⁻⁵² And after this Jesus was walking about in the Galilee, for he did not wish to walk about in Judaea, because the Judaeans were seeking to kill him. And the feast of the Judaeans was near, Tabernacles. So his brothers said to him, 'Move on from here and go into Judaea, so that your disciples also may see the works that you do. For no one does anything in secret, and himself seeks to be publicly known. If you are doing these things, show yourself to the world.' For neither did his brothers believe in him. And so Jesus says to them, 'My time is not yet here; but as for you people, your time is always ready. The world cannot hate you – but it hates me, because I bear witness about [the World] that its works are wicked. You all go up to the feast. I am not going up to this feast, because my time is not yet fulfilled.'

When he said this, he himself was for remaining in the Galilee. However, when his brothers went up to the feast, then he also went up, not openly, but in secret. So the Judaeans were seeking for him, and they were saying, 'Where is he?' And there was a good deal of grumbling talk about him in the crowds. Some were saying, 'He's good,' while others were saying, 'No – on the contrary, he's leading the crowd astray.' But no one spoke out publicly, because of fear of the Judaeans.

When the feast was already halfway through, Jesus went up into the Temple and began to teach. So the Judaeans were astonished, saying, 'How does this man know letters, when he has never learnt?'

So Jesus answered them and said, 'My teaching is not mine. No – it is [the teaching] of the One who sent me. If someone wants to do his will, they will know about the teaching, whether it is from God or whether I speak from myself. The person who speaks for him or herself seeks their own glory. The one who seeks the glory of the one who sent them, that one is true [or: 'genuine'], and unrighteousness is not in that person. Did not Moses give you people the Torah? And none of you does the Torah. Why do you seek to kill me?'

The crowd answered, 'You have a demon! Who's "seeking to kill" you?'

Jesus answered and said to them, 'I did a single deed, and you're all astonished. This was the reason that Moses gave you the circumcision – not that it is from Moses, but from the ancestors – and you circumcise a man on the Sabbath. If a man receives circumcision on the Sabbath, so that the Torah of Moses may not be broken, are you getting cross with me because I made a whole person healthy on the Sabbath? Don't judge by sight; instead, judge [with] a righteous judgement.'

So some of the Jerusalemites said, 'Isn't this the one they are seeking to kill? And look – he's talking openly and they say nothing to him! Surely the rulers haven't realised that this is the Messiah? No – we know where this one comes from. But when the Messiah comes, no one knows where he's from.'

So Jesus cried out in the Temple as he was teaching, and said, 'You both know me and know where I'm from. And I didn't come from myself; no – the one who sent me is genuine [or: 'true'], the One whom you people don't know. I know him, because I am from him and he sent me.'

So they sought to arrest him, and no one laid a hand on him, because his hour had not yet come. Of the crowd, some believed in him, and they said, 'The Messiah, when he comes, surely won't do more signs than what this one has done, will he?' The Pharisees heard the crowd uttering these dark remarks about him. And the chief priests and the Pharisees sent servants to arrest him. So Jesus said, 'Just a little time still I am with you; and [then] I go to the One who sent me. You will seek me, and you will not find me. And where I am, you are unable to go.'

And so the Judaeans said to themselves, 'Where is this one going that we shan't find him? Surely he's not about to go to the Diaspora of the Greeks and teach the Greeks, is he? What is this word that he spoke, "You will seek me and you will not find" and "Where I am you are unable to come"?'

And on the great last day of the feast, Jesus stood up and cried out, saying, 'If anyone is thirsting, let them come to me and drink. The one who believes in me, as the Scripture said, "Streams from his belly shall flow, of running water."' Now he said this about the Spirit which those who believed in him were about to receive. For the Spirit was not yet, because Jesus was not yet glorified.

And so from the crowd, people who heard these words started to say, 'This man is truly the Prophet.' Others were saying, 'This man is the Messiah.' Others said, 'No – surely Messiah doesn't come from the Galilee? Doesn't the Scripture say that [it's] from the seed of David, and from Bethlehem, the village where David was, that the Messiah comes?' And so a division happened in the crowd on his account. But some of them wanted to arrest him, but no one laid hands upon him. And so the servants came to the high priests and Pharisees, and they said to them, 'Why didn't you bring him?' The servants replied, 'Never did a human being speak so.' And so the Pharisees answered them, 'Are you also led astray? Has any of the rulers come to faith in him? Or any of the Pharisees? But this crowd, which doesn't know the Law, they're all accursed.' Nicodemus says to them, the one who had come to them before, being one of them, 'Surely our Law doesn't judge the man without first hearing from him and finding out what he's doing?' They replied and said, 'You're not from the Galilee too, are you? Investigate and see that from the Galilee a prophet is not raised up.'

Once again, this episode begins with a rather baffling introduction; Jesus is apparently skulking in the Galilee, because of people in Judaea looking to kill him; but his brothers (who, according to the evangelist, did not believe him) want him to get more public exposure in Judaea. His decision, however, is apparently to remain in the Galilee; but then, secretly, he goes up after all, and starts to teach in the Temple. This teaching then raises the question of where exactly he gets it all from, and he answers by indicating his Father as the source of his teaching. Once again there is talk of glory, and more talk (denied by Jesus' opponents) of a plot against his life. The reader, of course, already knows that there is indeed such a plot.

Jerusalemites are divided about whether Jesus is the one, and they make the important comment that 'when the Messiah comes, no one knows where he's from'; and we see that this is indeed the case, at any rate for those who belong on the 'lower stage'. Jesus' response is to go back to the proclamation that he has been 'sent'.

There is an attempt to arrest Jesus, who responds enigmatically, 'You will seek me and you will not find me.' This provokes a nice example of 'Johannine irony', when his audience asks if he's going off to teach the Greeks. The crowd is divided: is Jesus prophet, or Messiah, or none of the above? Even the High Priest's servants, and the Pharisees (at least in the form of Nicodemus), are divided. The official verdict, however, is finally that prophets do not come from the Galilee (another 'Johannine irony').

'Streams shall flow from his belly'. It is not clear what text is being cited here, but the metaphor of God quenching the thirst of human beings is often found in the Bible. See, for example, Isaiah 55:1.

A beautiful story, not written by John

7 ^{53}-8 ^{11} And they each went off to their own house. Jesus went to the Mount of Olives.

And early in the morning he came again to the Temple, and the whole people came to him. And sitting down, he began to teach them. But the scribes and the Pharisees lead [in] a woman who had been detected in adultery. And standing her in the middle, they say to him, 'Teacher, this woman was detected in the act [of] committing adultery. Now in the Law Moses commanded us to stone women like this. So – what do you say?' (They were saying this as a test for him, in order to have something to accuse him of.) But Jesus bent down, and with his finger drew figures on the ground. But as they persisted [in] asking him, he straightened himself and said, 'Let the Sinless One of you be the first to throw a stone at her.'

And again he bent down and wrote on the ground.

But they heard; and they went out, one by one, beginning from the elders. And he was left alone, and the woman who was in the middle. And Jesus straightened up and said to her, 'Woman, where are they? Did no one condemn you?' And she said, 'No one, Lord.' And Jesus said, 'Neither do I condemn you. Go – and from now on, sin no longer.'

This lovely story is not in all the manuscripts of John's Gospel; some manuscripts put it in various places in Luke's Gospel. It does not sound like John, and certainly interrupts the flow of the narrative here. For all that, we should be grateful to whoever thought this story too good to exclude. The story sounds like Jesus, has his unmistakable accents; it starts, like so many of the stories in all the Gospels, with an attempt to trap him, and culminates in the beautiful dialogue in which the woman is no longer treated as bait, but as a human being, invited to speak for herself, and regarded by Jesus as a responsible adult. We may also notice that it 'takes two to tango'. There is no sign here of her presumed partner in adultery. It was not just women who were supposed to be punished for this offence.

Discourse and disagreement: the Light of the World?

12-59 So Jesus spoke to them again saying, 'I AM the Light of the World. The one who follows me will not walk in the darkness, but will have the light of life.' So the Pharisees said to him, 'You are witnessing about yourself. Your witness is not true.' Jesus replied and said to them, 'Even if I do bear witness about myself, my witness is true, because I know where I come from and where I am going. You people do not know where I am coming from, nor where I am going. You people judge according to the flesh – but I judge nobody. And if I do judge, my judgement is true. Because I am not alone: it is I and the Father who sent me. And in your Law it is written that the witness of two is true: there is I, who bear witness about myself, and there is the Father who sent me, who bears witness about me.' And so they said to him, 'Where is your Father?' Jesus replied, 'Neither me nor my Father do you know. If you did know me, you would also know my Father.'

These words he spoke in the Treasury, while teaching in the Temple. And no one arrested him, because his hour had not yet come. And so he said to them again, 'I am going, and you will seek for me. And in your sins you will die. Where I am going you cannot come.' So the Judaeans said, 'Surely he's not going to kill himself? Because he's saying "Where I am going, you can't come."' And he said to them, '*You* are from the things below, while *I* am from the things above. *You* are from this world, *I* am not from this world. And so I said to you that you will die in your sins. For if you do not believe that I AM, you will die in your sins.'

And so they said to him, 'Who are *You*?' Jesus said to them, 'I said to you at the beginning what I am also saying to you [at present]. I have many things to say and judge about you. But the one who sent me is true; and the things that I heard from him, these are the things that I speak [to] the world.' They did not know that he was speaking of the Father to them. And so Jesus said, 'When you lift up the Son of Man, then you will know that I AM, and of myself I do nothing. Instead, as the Father taught me, these [are the] things I speak. And the One who sent me is with me. He has not left me alone, because I do the things that are pleasing to him, all the time.'

As he was saying these things, many people came to faith in him. And so Jesus spoke to the Judaeans who had come to faith in him, 'If you remain in my word, truly you are my disciples, and you will know the truth, and the truth will free you.' They replied to him, 'We are seed of Abraham, and were never enslaved to anyone, ever. How is it that you say, "You will become free"?' Jesus replied to them, 'Amen, Amen, I tell you, everyone who does sin is a slave of sin. But the slave does not remain permanently in the house, while the Son remains for ever. And so if the Son sets you free, you will really be free. I know that you are seed of Abraham. But you are seeking to kill me, because my word does not make headway among you. What I have seen at my Father's side, I speak. And so, you people, do what you hear from the Father.' They replied and said to him, 'Our father is Abraham.' Jesus says to them, 'If you are children of Abraham, do the works of Abraham. But now you are seeking to kill me – and I am [the] person who spoke to you the truth that I heard from God. Abraham did not do this – but you people do the deeds of your father.' They said to him, '*We* weren't born of fornication. We have one father, namely God.' Jesus said to them, 'If God were your Father, you would love me, for I came out from God – and I have arrived. For I did not come on my own account, but *He* sent me. Why do you not know my language? Because you are unable to hear my message. You people are from [your] father, the devil, and you want to do your father's desires. That one was a murderer from the beginning, and did not take his stand [on] the Truth, because Truth is not in him. When he speaks falsehood, he speaks out of his own, because he is a liar – and the father of falsehood. Because I speak the Truth, you do not believe me. Who of you convicts me of sin? If I speak Truth, why do you not believe me? The one who is from God hears God's words. Because of this you do not hear [them], that you are not from God.' The Judaeans replied and said to him, 'Do we not rightly say that you are a Samaritan, and have a demon?' Jesus replied, '*I* have no demon; but I honour my Father, while *you* dishonour me. But *I* do not seek my glory: there is one who seeks and who judges. Amen, Amen, I tell you: if someone keeps my word, they will not see death for ever.'

So the Judaeans said to him, 'Now we know that you have a demon. Abraham died, and so did the prophets, and *you* say, "If someone keeps my word, they will not taste death for ever." Can you possibly be greater than our father Abraham, who died? And the prophets also died – who are you making yourself [out to be]?' Jesus replied, 'If I glorify myself, my glory is nothing. It is my Father who glorifies me, of whom you say, "He is our God." And *you* don't know him, but *I* know him. And if I were to say that I do not know him, I shall be a liar, just like you. But I know him, and I keep his word. Abraham, your 'father', was overjoyed that he might see my day. And he saw it, and he was glad.' And so the Judaeans said to him, 'You are not fifty yet – and you've seen Abraham!' Jesus said to them, 'Amen, Amen, I tell you: before Abraham was, I AM.' And so they picked up stones to throw at him. But Jesus hid, and went out of the Temple.

After the previous charming interlude, the story resumes its interrupted flow, with another EGO EIMI/I AM statement by Jesus. This time he is starting a theme that will take us to the very end of the next chapter, the 'Light of the World' (something that the reader has known about Jesus ever since the Prologue).

Jesus' opponents raise the important question: 'is his witness true?' Jesus' answer refers back to our 'upper stage', the place to which he will return, and from which he was sent. This leads to a long discussion about his 'Father' who 'sent' him. There is another nice Johannine irony as they ponder (rather implausibly) whether he is contemplating suicide when he says, 'Where I am going you cannot come.' This in turn introduces another EGO EIMI/I AM, and a question about who is father to whom. Various ancestors are suggested for Jesus' interlocutors: Abraham, God, and the devil. The temperature rises, and Jesus is accused of being born of the wrong race, of being possessed, and, perhaps, of being the product of fornication. Jesus repeats the familiar theme of 'glory', and concludes the discussion with the powerful phrase: 'before Abraham was, I AM', which his audience takes to be blasphemy. And they are right, of course, in that there is a claim here which is certainly blasphemous if it is false.

The Light of the World – and several kinds of blindness

9 1-41 And passing by, he saw a man blind from birth. And they asked him, his disciples, saying, 'Rabbi, who sinned? Was it this man or his parents, that he should be born blind?' Jesus replied, 'It wasn't that this man sinned, or his parents. It was so that the works of God might be revealed in him. We have to work the works of the One who sent me while it is day. Night is coming, when no one can work. When I am in the world, I am [the] Light of the World.' Saying this, he spat on the ground, and made mud out of the spittle, and anointed the mud on his eyes, and said, 'Go wash in the pool Siloam (which means 'Sent'). So he went, and washed. And he came back seeing! So his neighbours and those who used to see him before, because he was a beggar, said, 'Isn't this the one who sits and begs?' Some said, 'This is he.' Others said, 'No – but it's like him.' He said, 'I am.' So they said to him, 'So how were your eyes opened?' He answered them, 'The man known as Jesus made mud and anointed my eyes and told me, "Go to Siloam and wash." So I went and washed and saw again.' They said to him, 'Where is he?' He says, 'I don't know.' They take him to the Pharisees, the one who was once blind.

Now it was a Sabbath on the day when Jesus had made the mud and opened his eyes. So once more the Pharisees also asked him how he saw again. He said to them, 'He put mud on my eyes. And I washed. And I see.' So some of the Pharisees said, 'This fellow is not from God, because he does not keep Sabbath.' But others said, 'How can a fellow who is a sinner do signs of this sort?' And there was division among them. So they say to the blind man again, 'What do *you* say about him, because it was *your* eyes that he opened?' He said, 'He is a prophet.'

So the Judaeans did not believe [it] of him that he had been blind and saw again, until [the time] when they called the parents of the one-who-saw-again. And they interrogated them, saying, 'Is this your son, whom you say was born blind? So how come he sees now [or: 'who opened his eyes']? So his parents replied and said, 'We know that this is our son, and that he was born blind. But how he now sees we do not know. Ask *him* – he is of age. He will speak for himself.' His parents said this because they were afraid of the Judaeans. For the Judaeans had already agreed that if anyone should acknowledge him as Messiah, they would be [put] out of the synagogue. For this reason his parents said, 'He is of age – ask *him*.'

So for a second time they called the man who had been blind, and said to him, 'Give glory to God. *We* know that this fellow is a sinner.' So he replied, 'Whether or not he is a sinner, I do not know. One thing I do know [is that] [having been] blind I now see.' So they said to him, 'What did he do to you? How did he open your eyes?' He replied to them, 'I told you already. And you didn't listen. Why do you want to hear [it] again? Surely *you* people don't want to become his disciples also?' And they reviled him and said, '*You're* a disciple of *him*, but *we* are disciples of Moses. We know that God spoke to Moses: but as for this fellow, we don't know where this one is coming from.' The man replied and said to them, 'Now there's a remarkable thing: *you* don't know where he's coming from – and [yet] he opened my eyes! We know that sinners God doesn't listen to: but if someone is God-fearing and does [God's] will, then God does listen to that person. From all time it is unheard of that anyone opened the eyes of someone who was born blind. If this fellow were not from God, he could do nothing.' They replied and said to him, 'You were utterly born in sin, and do *you* teach us?' And they threw him out.

Jesus heard that they had thrown him out, and finding him he said, 'Do you believe in the Son of Man?' He replied and said, 'And who is it, Lord, that I may believe in him?' Jesus said to him, 'Not only have you seen him; but the one speaking to you – that's him.' And he said, 'Lord, I believe.' And he worshipped him. And Jesus commented, 'For judgement *I* came into this world, so that those who do not see might see, and those who see might become blind.' From the Pharisees those who were with him heard this, and they said, 'Surely we're not blind, are we?' Jesus said, 'If you *were* blind, you would have no sin. But as it is, you claim, "We see." Your sin remains.'

This story continues the theme of the 'Light of the World' from the previous chapter. It starts with the man born blind, and an idiot question from Jesus' disciples, and then moves through several different kinds of blindness. First, obviously, is the blindness of the blind man; but follow the story through, and see how he grows in confidence and vision, and deals spiritedly with Jesus' opponents, finally coming to full faith ('sight') in Jesus as the Son of Man. The second blindness is that of the disciples: 'Rabbi, who sinned?', they ask, brightly, and with ignorant piety. Then there is the blindness of the neighbours, uncertain whether this is or is not the blind man. Fourth there is the blindness of Jesus' opponents, here classed as 'Pharisees', who decree that Jesus cannot possibly be from God, affirm that '*We* know that this fellow is a sinner', and, (significantly), 'we don't know where this one is coming from', and finally ask, 'Surely we're not blind, are we?'. Fifth, there is the blindness of the man's parents, fearfully reluctant to get involved. All this contrasts splendidly with the wit and independence of mind of the one who at the beginning of the story was undeniably blind, and by the end is seeing more than anyone around him except Jesus.

Jesus the 'ideal shepherd'

10 ¹⁻²¹ 'Amen, Amen, I tell you, the one who does not enter through the entrance into the sheepfold, but comes up at some other place, that one is a thief, and a brigand. But the one who comes through the entrance is shepherd of the sheep. This is the one to whom the doorkeeper opens. And the sheep hear his voice; and he calls his own sheep by name and leads them out. When he drives out all his own [sheep], he goes before them; and the sheep follow him, because they know his voice. They will not follow a stranger – they will flee from him, because they do not know the voice of strangers.'

This parable Jesus told them – but they did not know what he was telling them. And so Jesus said again, 'Amen, Amen, I tell you that I AM the sheep's entrance. All who came before me were thieves and brigands. But the sheep did not hear them. I AM the entrance: through me if anyone enters, they will be saved; and they will come in and go out and find pasture. The thief only comes in order to steal and slaughter and destroy: I came in order that they might have life, and have it abundantly.

'I AM the ideal shepherd. The ideal shepherd lays down his life on behalf of the sheep. The hireling, and the pretend-shepherd, who does not own the sheep, sees the wolf coming and abandons the sheep and flees, and the wolf plunders and scatters them. [That is] because he is a hireling, and doesn't care about the sheep.

'I AM the ideal shepherd. And I know my [sheep], and mine know me, as the Father knows me and I know the Father, and I lay down my life on behalf of the sheep. And I have other sheep that are not from this fold; and I must lead them. And they will hear my voice; and they will become a single flock of sheep, [with] a single shepherd. Because of this the Father loves me, that I lay down my life, that I may take it up again. No one takes it from me, but I lay it down on my own initiative. I have authority to lay it down; and I have authority to take it up again. This [is the] command I received from my Father.'

A division again arose among the Judaeans on account of these words. Many of them said, 'He has a demon – and he's crazy. Why are you people listening to him?' Others said, 'These are not the words of one possessed by a demon. Can a demon open [the] eyes of [the] blind?'

This seems to follow directly on from the drama around the Light of the World. But a different idea is in play here, that of the 'shepherd', and especially Jesus as the 'model' or 'ideal' or 'good' shepherd, who is distinguished from fake shepherds by his relation to the flock, in two ways: first he knows them, and they know and recognise him, and second he 'lays down his life' for them.

Once again, though, Jesus' talk leads to division: some regard Jesus as possessed, while others say he can't be, and hark back to the previous episode, appealing to the fact that he opened the eyes of the blind.

'If you are the Messiah, tell us openly'

22-42   Then there took place the Hanukkah in Jerusalem; it was winter and Jesus was walking in the Temple, in Solomon's Porch. And so the Judaeans encircled him and said to him, 'How long do you keep us in suspense? If you are the Messiah, tell us openly.'

Jesus answered them, 'I told you; and you do not believe. The works that I do in the name of my Father, they are what bears witness to me. But you people do not believe, because you are not of my sheep. My sheep listen to my voice; and I know them, and they follow me, and I give them life for ever, and they will not be destroyed for ever; and no one will plunder them from my hand. My Father – what he has given me is greater than everything, and no one can plunder from the Father's hand. I and the Father are one.'

The Judaeans again took up stones, in order to stone him. Jesus answered them, 'Many good works I showed you from the Father. On account of what kind of work of them do you stone me?' The Judaeans answered him, 'For a good work we do not stone you – but [we do stone you] for blasphemy, because you, a human being, make yourself God.' Jesus replied to them, 'Is it not written in your Torah, "I said: 'You are gods' "? If he said [that] they were gods to whom the word of God came, and [if] the Scripture cannot be undone, [then] the one whom the Father sanctified and sent into the world, do you people say, "You are blaspheming", because I said, "I am God's Son"? If I do not do the works of my Father, don't believe me. But if I am doing [them], believe the works, that you may know and understand that in me [is] the Father, and I [am] in the Father.'

And so they sought again to lay hold of him. And he went out of their grasp. And he went off again across the Jordan to the place where John was baptising at first; and he remained there. And many came to him and said, 'John did no sign, but everything that John said about this man was true.' And many believed in him there.

The reader may feel that it is utterly obvious that Jesus is the Messiah, but that is because we are privileged readers of the 'Johannine irony'. We can see clearly what his irritated interlocutors cannot, 'because you are not of my sheep'. Jesus tells them, 'The Father and I are one', taking us deeper into the mystery, but provoking his opponents to stone him for blasphemy. Slowly people are coming to believe in him, but many are also opposed to him.

We notice that this episode takes place at the Feast of Hanukkah, and previous stories have been linked to Passover (6:4) and the feast of Sukkoth (6:22). John the evangelist is clearly saying something about who Jesus is. The quotation, 'I said: "You are gods" ' comes from Psalm 82:6.

Once again we hear that impressive sound of the EGO EIMI/I AM.

Two women do theology, and Lazarus is raised from the dead

11 ¹⁻⁴⁴ And someone was ailing, Lazarus from Bethany, from the village of Mary and Martha, her sister. It was Mary who anointed the Lord with ointment and wiped his feet with her hair – her brother was ailing. And so the sisters sent to him, saying, 'Lord, look! The one whom you love is ailing.' When Jesus heard, he said, 'This ailment is not to death, but for the glory of God, so that the Son of God might be glorified by means of it.' Now Jesus loved Martha and her sister. And Lazarus. So when he heard that he was ailing, then he stayed in the place where he was for two days. Then, after this, he says to the disciples, 'Let us go to Judaea again.' The disciples say to him, 'Rabbi, [just] now the Judaeans were seeking to stone you – and you're going there again!' Jesus replied, 'Are there not twelve hours in the day? If someone walks in the day, they do not stumble, because they see the light of this world. But if someone walks in the night they stumble, because the light is not in them.' He said this, and after this he tells them, 'Lazarus our friend has gone to his slumbers; but I am going to wake him up.' So the disciples said to him, 'Lord – if he is slumbering, he will be saved.' But Jesus had spoken of his death: *they* thought that he was speaking of the slumber of *sleep!* So then Jesus said to them openly, 'Lazarus is dead – and for your sakes I rejoice, that you may believe, *because* I was not there. But let's go to him.' And so Thomas, the one called 'Twin', said to his fellow disciples, 'Let us go too, in order to die with him.'

So when Jesus came he found that he was already four days in the tomb. Now Bethany was near Jerusalem, about two miles away. And many of the Judaeans had gone to Martha and Mary in order to console them about their brother. So when Martha heard that Jesus was coming, she [went to meet] him, and Mary sat at home. So Martha said to Jesus, 'Lord, if you had been here, my brother would not have died; but even now I know that whatever you ask of God, God will give you.' Jesus said to her, 'Your brother will rise.' Martha says to him, 'I know that he will rise at the Resurrection on the last day.' Jesus said to her, 'I AM the Resurrection and the Life. The one who believes in me, even if they die, will live. And everyone who lives and believes in me, they will not die for ever. Do you believe this?' She says to him, 'Yes, Lord. I have come to believe that you are the Messiah, the Son of God, the one coming into the world.'

And saying this, she went off and called Mary her sister, secretly, saying, 'The teacher is present, and is calling you.' She, when she heard this, arose quickly and went to him. Jesus had not yet come to the village, but was in the place where Martha had met him. And so the Judaeans who were with her in the house and consoling her, seeing that Mary had swiftly arisen and gone out, followed her, thinking that she was going to the tomb, in order to weep there. So Mary, when she came [to the place] where Jesus was, when she saw him, she fell at his feet, saying to him, 'Lord, if you had been here, my brother would not have died.' So Jesus, when he saw her weeping, and the Judaeans who accompanied her [also] weeping, was deeply moved in spirit, and disturbed himself. And he said, 'Where have you placed him?' They say to him, 'Lord, come and see.' Jesus wept. And so the Judaeans said, 'See how he loved him.' But some of them said, 'Could not the one who opened the eyes of the blind man have brought it about that this one should not die?'

So Jesus, again deeply moved in himself, comes to the tomb. It was a cave, and a stone lay upon it. Jesus says, 'Lift up the stone.' The sister of the dead man, Martha, says to him, 'Lord, he smells already – for he's four days [gone].' Jesus says to her, 'Didn't I tell you that if you believe, you will see the glory of God?' So they lifted up the stone. And Jesus lifted his eyes upwards and said, 'Father, I thank you that you have heard me. I knew that you hear me all the time. But I said [this] because of the crowd standing about, that they may believe that you sent me.' And saying this, he cried out in a loud voice, 'Lazarus, here, outside!' The dead man came out, bound as to his feet and hands with grave-clothes. And his face was bound round with a sweat-cloth. Jesus says to them, 'Untie him and allow him to go.'

This story is sometimes called 'the raising of Lazarus'; but it is far more noteworthy for the manner in which Martha, and in a different way Mary, go deeper into the mystery of who Jesus is, and take us with them. As often in this Gospel, the story has a mysterious beginning, with the reference to the episode when 'Mary anointed the Lord with ointment and wiped his feet with her hair'. John has not yet told this story!

There is no doubt that Jesus is a mystery: for one thing, when he is summoned to Lazarus's sickbed, he delays for two days; and it seems that he is doing it as part of the disciples' training. They clearly think that he is quite crazy, but humour him by going along with him anyway ('to die with him', as Thomas gloomily mutters).

When they arrive, Lazarus has been dead for four days (so the two-day pause made no difference); then Martha shows a remarkable depth of theological awareness, proclaiming her faith in the Resurrection, and being invited to accept Jesus' next EGO EIMI/ I AM: 'I AM the Resurrection and the Life.' She responds with a resounding declaration of faith: 'I have come to believe that you are the Messiah, the Son of God.'

The scene now switches to Mary. Like Martha, only perhaps more strongly, Mary reproaches Jesus for his absence at the critical moment; but her tears cause Jesus also to shed tears, which in turn leads to complaints from the observers about his failure to save his friend. Then Jesus orders the stone to be 'lifted up', not pausing to listen to Martha's severely practical objection about the stench, but praying instead to the Father (with yet another reference to his being 'sent'), and the miracle is effortlessly completed.

Reactions to the raising of Lazarus: Judaeans, chief priests, Pharisees

45-57 So many of the Judaeans, who had come to Mary, and had seen what [Jesus?] had done, came to faith in him. But some of them went off to the Pharisees, and told them the things that Jesus had done. So the chief priests and the Pharisees gathered a Sanhedrin, and they said, 'What are we doing, because this man is doing many signs? If we leave him like this, they will all come to faith in him. And then the Romans will come and take our Temple and our nation.' But one of them, Caiaphas, who was High Priest that year, said to them, 'You know nothing, nor do you reckon that it is to your benefit, that one man should die on behalf of the people, and not the whole nation be destroyed.' He did not say this of himself, but being High Priest that year he prophesied that Jesus was about to die on behalf of the nation. And not just on behalf of the nation, but so that he might gather the scattered children of God into one. So from that day, they plotted to kill him.

So Jesus no longer walked about openly among the Judaeans, but went off from there to a place near the desert, to a city called Ephraim. And there he stayed with his disciples. And the Passover of the Judaeans was near, and many went up to Jerusalem from the district before the Passover in order to purify themselves. And so they sought Jesus and spoke with each other, standing in the Temple, saying, 'What does it seem to you? That he will come to the Feast?' And the chief priests and the Pharisees gave orders that if anyone should find out where he was, they should report [it], so that they might seize him.

> Once again, Jesus causes division. Some of the witnesses 'came to faith in him' while others go and sneak to the Sanhedrin, who then discuss the matter. Most of them foresee disaster, but Caiaphas explains to them, in an involuntary prophecy, as the evangelist notes, that 'one man should die on behalf of the people'. Murder is therefore now plainly on the agenda. Jesus opts for discreet tactics, but the reader sees no way of avoiding the crisis. And for the third time in the Gospel (see 2:13; 6:4) the Passover is near. The evangelist reports the general reaction: 'they *sought* Jesus' (that word again), while the chief priests and Pharisees give orders for his arrest. The scene is set for the final trial of strength.

A thanksgiving meal at Bethany: reactions to Jesus

12 1-11 So Jesus, six days before the Passover, came to Bethany, where Lazarus was, whom Jesus had raised from the dead, and so they had a dinner there, and Martha was serving, and Lazarus was one of those who lay down [to eat] with him. So Mary, taking a pound of oil of pistachio nard, very expensive, anointed Jesus' feet and with her hair wiped his feet. The house was filled with the smell of the myrrh. And Judas Iscariot, one of his disciples, who was about to betray him, says, 'Why was this myrrh not sold for three hundred denarii and given to the poor?' He said this, not because he cared about the poor, but because he was a thief, and having the money box he used to steal what was put into it. So Jesus said, 'Leave her alone, that she may guard it for the day of my burial. For the poor you always have with you – but me you do not always have.'

So a great crowd of the Judaeans knew that he was there, and they came, not just on Jesus' account, but also in order to have a look at Lazarus, whom he had raised from the dead. But the chief priests plotted to kill Lazarus also, because on his account many of the Judaeans were coming; and they believed in Jesus.

> This meal, which is placed at the same point in the narratives of both Mark and Matthew, in this Gospel has the air of a 'thank-you' to Jesus for Lazarus' restoration to life; and Mary's gesture of anointing, intimate as it is, feels like an act of gratitude. As we have seen so often in this Gospel, however, there is division, and John makes Judas Iscariot the spokesman for the opposition (with an uncharitable sideswipe at his kleptomaniac tendencies). And there is more: a group of gawking tourists, to look at Jesus and at Lazarus. So the decision is taken to kill Lazarus also (Jesus' fate is, of course, already sealed).

Jesus enters Jerusalem: murmurings from the Pharisees

12-19 On the next day, the great crowd which came to the feast, hearing that Jesus was coming into Jerusalem, took the palm branches and came out to meet him, and they were crying out,

'Hosanna – blessed is the One coming in the name of the Lord,
Blessed is the King of Israel!'

And Jesus, finding a little donkey, sat on it, as it is written,

'Do not fear, Daughter of Zion,
behold, your king is coming,
seated on the foal of a donkey.'

These things the disciples did not understand at first, but when Jesus was glorified, then they remembered that these things were written about him, and that these things were done to him. And so they bore witness – the crowd which was with him when he called Lazarus from the tomb and raised him from the dead. Because of this the crowd came to meet him, because they heard that he had done this sign. And so the Pharisees said to themselves, 'You see – you're getting nowhere. Look – the world has gone after him.'

> This is unmistakably a triumphant entry, and very similar to what we find in the Synoptic Gospels. Like them, John emphasises how Jesus fulfils the scriptures; the crowds quote Psalm 118:25, 26, and Jesus follows the suggestion of Zechariah 9:9: 'Your king is coming, seated on the foal of a donkey.'
>
> Once again the disciples fail to understand, but realise later what had been going on (something similar is reported in connection with the cleansing of the Temple, at 2:22). The crowds testify to Jesus (here the evangelist places the word which I have translated 'bore witness' very emphatically at the beginning of the sentence). And the Pharisees complain, menacingly, 'the world has gone after him'.

The Greek intervention: now is the crisis

20-50 There were some Greeks [among] those who went up to worship at the feast. And so these went to Philip, the one from Bethsaida in the Galilee, and they asked him, saying, 'Sir, we want to see Jesus.'

Philip comes and tells Andrew. Andrew and Philip come and tell Jesus. But Jesus answered them, saying, 'The hour has come for the Son of Man to be glorified. Amen, Amen, I tell you, unless the grain of wheat falling into the ground dies, it remains itself alone; but if it dies, it bears much fruit. Those who love their life lose it, and those who hate their life in this world will keep it for eternal life. If anyone serves me, let them follow me – and where I am, there also will my servant be. If anyone serves me, the Father will honour them. Now is my soul disturbed – and what am I to say? "Father, save me from this hour"? But it was for this that I came to this hour. Father, glorify your name.'

And so a voice came from heaven, 'I both glorified it, and shall glorify it again.' And so the crowd that stood [by] and heard [this] said that there was thunder. Others said, 'An angel has spoken to him.' Jesus answered and said, 'It was not on my account that this voice came, but on yours. Now is the judgement of this world; now the ruler of this world shall be cast outside. And I, if I am lifted up from the earth, shall draw all to myself.' This he said, indicating what sort of a death he was about to die. And so the crowd answered him, 'We heard from the Law that the Messiah stays for ever. And how come *you* say that the Son of Man must be lifted up? Who is this "Son of Man"?' So Jesus said to them, 'A little while still the Light is among you. Walk while you have the Light, lest the Darkness master you – and the one who walks in the Darkness does not know where he is going. While you have the Light, believe in the Light, that you may become children of the Light.'

Jesus said these things, and went off and hid from them. Although he had done so many signs before them, they did not believe in him, that the word of Isaiah the Prophet might be fulfilled, which he spoke,

'Lord, who believed our hearing?
And the arm of the Lord, to whom was it revealed?'

This was the reason they could not believe, what Isaiah again said,

'He has blinded their eyes
and hardened their heart,
lest they should see with their eyes
and understand with their heart, and turn.
And I shall heal them.'

Isaiah said these things, because he saw his glory, and he spoke about him. Nevertheless, however, many even of the rulers believed in him; but because of the Pharisees they did not admit it, for fear they would be [put] out of the synagogue. For they loved the glory of humans over and above the glory of God.

Jesus cried out and said, 'The one who believes in me does not believe in me, but in the One who sent me. And the one who sees me sees the One who sent me. I have come as Light into the World, so that no one who believes in me should remain in the Darkness. And if anyone hears my words, and does not keep them, *I* do not judge them (for I did not come in order to judge the World, but in order to save the World). The one who rejects me and does not accept my words has One who judges him. The word which I spoke, that is what will judge him on the last day. Because I did not speak from myself – but the Father who sent me, He Himself gave me a commandment, what I should say, and what I should speak. And I know that his commandment is eternal life. And so – what I say, just as the Father has spoken to me, that is how I say.'

Now, obscurely, the crisis comes, in the shape of 'some Greeks', presumably Jews of Greek-speaking background, as opposed to Aramaic or Hebrew speakers. They approach the two apostles who have Greek names, and Jesus recognises that 'the hour has come for the Son of Man to be glorified'. We hear the parable of the seed falling into the ground, and we know that death is walking the streets. We also learn that Jesus' disciples must go his way (and that the Father is still in control). 'Now', says Jesus (and this is the nearest that the Gospel of John ever gets to the 'Agony in the Garden' that we find in the Synoptics) 'is the crisis' (or: judgement); and the crisis takes the form of the Son of Man being 'lifted up'. Once again, we hear of the interplay (battle, rather) between Light and

Darkness. Significantly the evangelist quotes from Isaiah 53:1 (about God's 'Suffering Servant') and Isaiah 6:10 (the people's reluctance to listen to God).

Jesus' final speech underscores the sense of looming crisis, with its contrast of Light and Darkness, faith and unbelief, the mission of the Father, and the offer of eternal life.

Chapters 13–17: The Last Supper, and Jesus' Last Discourse

This long section, deliberately placed by the evangelist before Jesus' death, serves to answer what you might call the 'sad question', on our lips, quite as much as on the lips of those disciples round the table with him: 'How can we survive without the presence of the Lord?' The speech offers various answers: the disciples must serve each other, stay in the light, listen to the 'Paraclete', remain 'in Jesus', keep his commands, remain in contact with the Father, preserve unity.

Jesus washes the feet of the disciples

13 ¹⁻²⁰ Before the feast of the Passover, Jesus, knowing that his hour had come for him to go from this world to the Father, having loved his own who were in the world, loved them to perfection; and when supper took place, the devil having already thrust it into the heart of Judas [son] of Simon Iscariot that he should betray him, knowing that the Father had given everything into his hands, and that he had come out from God and was going to God, he arises from the meal and takes off his garments, and taking a linen cloth he tied it round his waist. Then he pours water into the washbasin, and began to wash the feet of his disciples, and to wipe them with the towel which he had tied around. And so he comes to Simon Peter. He says to him, 'Lord, are *you* washing *my* feet?' Jesus replied and said to him, 'What I am doing you do not know now – but you will know after this.' Peter says to him, 'You will not wash my feet – ever.'

Jesus replied to him, 'If I don't wash you, you have no part of me.' Simon Peter says to him, 'Lord, [then] not just my feet but also my hands and head.' Jesus says to him, 'The one who has been cleansed only needs to have his feet washed but is completely pure. And you people are pure; but not all of you.' For he knew who was betraying him; for this reason he said, 'You are not all pure.'

And so when he had washed their feet and taken his clothes and lain down again, he said to them, 'Do you know what I have done for you? You people call me the "Teacher" and the "Lord"; and you are right to say so, for I am. So – if I washed your feet (I, who am "Lord" and "Teacher"), you also ought to wash each other's feet. For I gave you a model, so that just as *I* did for *you, you* also should do. Amen, Amen, I tell you: there is no slave greater than his lord, nor an apostle greater than the one who is sent. If you people know these things, you are happy if you do them. I do not speak of you all: I know whom I have chosen; but let the Scripture be fulfilled,

"The one who munches my bread
tried to kick me."

'From now on, I tell you before the event, that you may believe when it happens that I AM. Amen, Amen, I tell you, the one who receives anyone whom I shall send receives me, and the one who receives me receives the One who sent me.'

> This is an extraordinary episode, placed precisely where in the Synoptic Gospels we find the institution of the Eucharist. I assume that John and his readers knew of this tradition, and that therefore Jesus is offering here a new understanding of the Eucharist, namely that you are not celebrating it properly unless you bring to it, or take from it, a commitment to service, even menial service. See how many familiar Johannine terms we find here: 'knowing', 'love', 'hour', 'world', 'Father', all appear in the opening lines of the story. Simon's resistance increases the drama of the story, and enables the lesson to go home. Some scholars read the difficult line about 'the one who has been cleansed only needs to have his feet washed' as a reference to both baptism (having been cleansed) and the continuing need for confession and absolution (having one's feet washed to get rid of the stains that one picks up on the journey through life).
>
> Jesus concludes with the moral of the story; disciples must behave in precisely this way to each other. This adds poignancy to the prediction that immediately follows, which has already been hinted at here in the quotation from Psalm 41:9.

Judas goes out into the night

21-30 Saying this, Jesus was disturbed in spirit, and bore witness and said, 'Amen, Amen, I tell you that one of you will betray me.' The disciples started looking at each other, scratching their heads as to whom he might be talking about. One of the disciples was lying on Jesus' breast, the one whom Jesus loved. And so Simon Peter nods to him, to find out who it might be that he's talking about. And so he, lying just like that on Jesus' chest, says to him, 'Lord, who is it?' Jesus replies, 'It is that one for whom I dip the bit of bread and give it to him.' So, having dipped the piece of bread, he gives it to Judas [son] of Simon Iscariot. And after the piece of bread then Satan entered into him. And so Jesus says to him, 'What you are doing, do rather quickly.' Now none of those lying there knew the purpose of his saying this to him. For some thought, since Judas had the money box, that he was telling him, 'Buy some things that we need for the feast', or that he should give something to the poor. So taking the piece of bread *he* went out immediately.

It was night.

> Unlike the Synoptic Gospels, John's Gospel does not present the Last Supper as a Passover meal. But he still has the chilling prediction of Judas' betrayal, with a coded message between Simon Peter and the 'disciple whom Jesus loved'; and an indicator from Jesus (showing who the betrayer was) that no one seems to have noticed. All our attention is concentrated on that dramatic final sentence, 'and it was night', symbolising the last, and unsuccessful, effort of the forces of darkness.

Glorification of the Son of Man; Peter's betrayal predicted

31-38 And so when he had gone out, Jesus said, 'Now the Son of Man is glorified, and God is glorified in him. And God will glorify him in him, and will glorify him immediately. Children, I am with you for a little [while] still. You will seek me, and as I said to the Judaeans, "Where I am going, you cannot come," I tell you also now. A new commandment I give you, that you love each other; as I loved you, that you also love each other. By this everyone will know that you are my disciples, if you have love among each other.' Simon Peter says to him, 'Lord, where are you going?' Jesus answered him, 'Where I am going you cannot follow me now – but you will follow me afterwards.' Peter says to him, 'Lord, why can't I follow *now*? I'll lay down my life for you!' Jesus replies, 'Lay down your life for me, will you? Amen, Amen, I tell you – the cock will not crow until you've denied me three times!'

Judas' departure into the night is signalled by Jesus as the 'glorification' of the Son of Man. This glorification is also interpreted in terms of Jesus' absence, which they are to survive by loving each other. Simon Peter, gallant as ever (with perhaps a hint of petulant adolescence), takes no notice of this, but offers to lay down his life for Jesus. Jesus puts all this heady enthusiasm into its context by indicating that Simon is in fact going to deny him, and very soon.

All of which is the context for Jesus' final words.

Jesus' last discourse, first part – peace and the Paraclete

14 1-31 'Do not let your hearts be troubled. Believe in God, and believe in me. There are many dwelling places in my Father's house. Otherwise would I have told you that I am going to make ready a place for you? And if I go and prepare a place for you, I shall come again and take you to myself, so that where I am you also may be. And where I am going you know the way.' Thomas says to him, 'Lord, we don't know where you are going – how can we know the way?' Jesus says to him, 'I AM the Way, the Truth and the Life. No one comes to the Father other than through me. If you people know me, you will know my Father also. And from now on, you know him and you have seen him.' Philip says to him, 'Lord, show us the Father, and it's enough for us.' Jesus says to him, 'For so much time am I with you, and you don't know me, Philip? The one who has seen me has seen the Father: how [can] you say, "Show us the Father"? Do you not have faith that I am in the Father and the Father is in me? The words that I speak I do not speak on my own account – the Father who stays in me does his own works. Believe me that I am in the Father and the Father is in me. Otherwise, believe on account of the works themselves. Amen, Amen, I tell you, the one who believes in me, the works that I do, that person will also do. And they will do greater works than these, because I am going to the Father. And whatever you ask in my name, I shall do it, in order that the Father may be glorified in the Son. If you ask anything in my name, I shall do it.

'If you love me, you will keep my commandments; and I shall ask the Father, and he will send another Paraclete to be with you for ever, the Spirit of Truth, which the world cannot accept, because the world does not notice the Spirit, nor does it know the Spirit. You know the Spirit, because the Spirit remains by you and is among you. I shall not abandon you as orphans – I am coming to you. Still a little while, and the world no longer sees me, but you see me. Because I am alive, you also shall be alive. On that day you will know that I am in my Father, and you in me and I in you. The one who has my commands and keeps them, that is the one who loves me. And the one who loves me will be loved by my Father, and I shall love that person and shall show myself to them. Judas (not the Iscariot) says to him, 'Lord, what happened, that you are about to show yourself to *us* and not to the world?' Jesus replied and said to him, 'If someone loves me, they will keep my word, and my Father will love them, and we shall come to them, and we shall make a dwelling place with them. The one who does not love me does not keep my words. And the word that you hear is not mine – it belongs to the One who sent me, the Father.

'These things I have spoken to you while remaining with you. But the Paraclete, the Holy Spirit whom the Father will send in my name, that one will teach you everything, and will remind you of everything that I have said to you. Peace I leave to you, the peace that is mine I give you: it is not as the world gives that I give. Do not let your heart be disturbed, nor let it be timid. You heard that I told you, "I am going," and "I am coming [back?] to you." If you loved me, you would rejoice that I am going to the Father, because the Father is greater than I. And now I have told you before it happens, that when it happens you may have faith. I shall no longer be saying much in your presence – for the Ruler of the world is coming. He has nothing on me; but so that the world may know that I love the Father, and as the Father instructed me, so I am acting.

'Arise, let us go from here . . .'

This is a lovely collection of sayings, which we find only in John's Gospel. This part of the speech starts with the calming words, 'Do not let your hearts be troubled', further interpreted as 'believe in God, and believe in me'. This part of the discourse is structured on three not very bright questions from Thomas, Philip and Judas, and on two references to the 'Paraclete'. Each of these takes us deeper into the mystery: Thomas's question yields another powerful 'I AM' saying: 'I AM the Way, the Truth and the Life'; Philip's question provokes Jesus to restate the identity (or something near it) that he has with his Father. Judas's question gives him the opportunity to restate the centrality of love in his new dispensation: disciples must love each other and so be loved by the Father.

The 'Paraclete' is one of John's happiest contributions to Christian theology. The word means something like a 'lawyer for the defence', someone I 'call to my side', though it has often been understood also as 'Comforter', which is not wholly inaccurate, although grammatically implausible. Here the Paraclete functions first as a token that the disciples are not, after all, abandoned by Jesus, but alive and beloved. Second, the Paraclete's job is to 'teach you everything'.

This chapter ends with the words 'Arise, let us go', which has made many scholars suppose that Chapters 15–16 are an editorial intrusion; but we have seen several times already that the linking of episodes in this Gospel can be mysterious, so perhaps this is only part of the evangelist's style.

Jesus' last discourse, second part – do you belong to Jesus or to the world? The choice is yours

15 ¹**-16** ³³ 'I AM the True Vine, and my Father is the Farmer. Every branch in me that does not bear fruit, he takes it off, and every branch that does bear fruit, he cleans it off, in order that it may bear more fruit. You are clean because of the word that I have spoken to you. Remain in me and I [shall remain] in you. As the branch cannot bear fruit of itself, unless it remains on the vine, so neither can you unless you remain in me. I AM the Vine, you are the branches. The one who remains in me, and I in them, that one bears much fruit – because apart from me you can do nothing. If a person does not remain in me, like the branch they were cast out and were withered up. And they gather them up and throw them in the fire – and they are burnt. If you remain in me, and my words remain in you, ask for whatever you want, and it will happen to you. In this was my Father glorified, that you bear much fruit and become my disciples. As the Father loved me, I also loved you: remain in my love. If you keep my commands, remain in my love, as I have kept my Father's commands and I remain in his love.

'These things I have spoken to you, in order that my joy may be in you and your joy may be fulfilled. This is my command, that you love each other as I loved you. No one has greater love than this, that someone should lay down their life for their friends. You are my friends, if you do the things that I command you. I no longer speak of you as slaves – for the slave has no idea what his Lord is doing. Instead, I have spoken of you as friends, because everything that I have heard from my Father I made known to you. You did not choose me – instead I chose you; and I have appointed you, that you should go and bear fruit, and that your fruit should abide, so that whatever you ask the Father in my name [the Father] may give you. These things I command you, that you love each other.

'If the world hates you, you know that it has hated me before [it has hated] you. If you were from the world, the world would love 'its own'. But because you are not from the world, but I chose you out of the world, that is the reason the world hates you. Keep in mind the remark I made to you: "A slave is not greater than his Lord." If they went after me, they will go after you also. If they kept my word, they will keep yours also. But they will do all these things to you because of my name, because they do not know the One-who-sent-me. If I had not come and spoken to them, they would not have sin. As it is, they have no excuse with regard to their sin. The one who hates me hates my Father also. If I had not done the works in their midst which no one else has done, they would have no sin. As it is, they have seen and hated, not only me, but also my Father, in order that the word may be fulfilled which is written in the Law, "They hated me for nothing."

'When the Paraclete comes, whom I shall send you from the Father, the Spirit of Truth which comes out from the Father, that one will bear witness about me. And you too will bear witness, because from the beginning you are with me.

'I have said these things to you, that you should not be made to stumble. Out of the synagogues they will put you. But an hour is coming when everyone who kills you will think they are offering worship to God. And they will do this because they do not know the Father or me. But I have spoken these things to you so that when their hour comes you may bear them in mind – because I told you.

'I did not tell you these things from the beginning, because I was with you. Now I am going to the One-who-sent-me, and none of you asks me, "Where are you going?" But because I have spoken these things to you, grief has filled your heart.

But I tell you the truth: it is to your advantage that I am going. For unless I go, the Paraclete will not come to you. But if I go, I shall send [the Paraclete] to you. And when he comes he will correct the world about sin, and about justice, and about judgement:

- about sin, because they do not have faith in me;
- about justice, because I am going to the Father, and you no longer see me;
- about judgement, because the Ruler of this world has been judged.

'I have still much to say to you – but you are incapable of bearing it now. But when that one comes, the Spirit of Truth, he will guide you in all Truth. For he will not speak on his own account. Instead, he will speak whatever he hears – and he will proclaim to you what is to come. That one will glorify me, because he will take from what is mine and will proclaim it to you. Everything that the Father has is mine. That is why I said that he takes from what is mine and will proclaim it to you.

'A little [while], and you no longer see me; and again a little [while] and you will see me.' And so [some] of his disciples said to each other, 'What is this that he is saying to us, "A little [while] and you do not see me, and again a little [while] and you will see me" and "I am going to the Father"?' And so they said, 'What is this "little"? We have no idea what he is talking about.' Jesus knew that they wanted to ask him, and said to them, 'Is it about this that you are seeking [from] each other, because I said, "A little [while] and you do not see me, and again a little while and you will see me"? Amen, Amen, I tell you that you will weep and lament but the world will rejoice. You will grieve, but your grief will turn into joy. The woman, when she gives birth, has grief because her hour has come. But when she bears the child, she no longer remembers the agony, because of the joy that a human being is born into the world. Just so you people for the moment have pain: but again I shall see you, and your heart will rejoice – and no one shall take your joy away from you. And on that day you will not ask me anything. Amen, Amen, I tell you, whatever you ask the Father in my name, he will give you. Hitherto, you did not ask anything in my name. Ask and you will receive, that your joy may be fulfilled.

'These things I have spoken to you in metaphors. The hour is coming when I shall no longer speak to you in metaphors, but I shall be quite open in proclaiming to you about the Father. And in that day you will ask in my name – and I do not tell you that I shall ask the Father about you. For the Father himself loves you, because you have loved me, and you have believed that I came forth from God. I came forth from the Father, and I came into the world. Again I am abandoning the world, and am on the way to the Father.' His disciples say, 'See – now you are being quite open in what you say, and you are not really telling a riddle. Now we know that you know everything and you have no need for anyone to ask you. Because of this we believe that you have come forth from God.' Jesus replied to them, 'Now do you believe? Look – an hour is coming, and has come, for each of you to be dispersed to your own and leave me alone. And [yet] I am not alone, because the Father is with me. These things I have spoken to you, that you may have peace in me. In the world you have agony – but, courage: I have conquered the world.'

This passage starts off with the powerful image of Jesus as the Vine; the image has a double point to it. First, the believer is invited to belong to Jesus; but, second, the pruning associated with this belonging is an uncomfortable activity, although we may reflect that it is more comfortable than being 'thrown into the fire and burnt'.

Once again, love and joy are to the fore, but we note with unease the link that Jesus makes between loving and laying down our lives for our friends. Once again, the world is presented as a force opposed to Jesus; but (once again) the Paraclete is promised, who will help disciples to remain in contact with the Father, and, in bearing witness to Jesus, enable disciples also to bear witness.

Once again, the disciples ask dim questions, and admit 'we have no idea what he is talking about'. Then, just towards the end, they finally brighten up and announce 'now . . . we believe that you have come forth from God'. In response, Jesus warns them that they are all about to run away; and this part of the discourse ends with peace, in contrast to the 'agony' that the world offers, and, in a final flourish, 'courage: I have conquered the world'.

'They hated me for nothing' is a quotation from Psalm 35:19.

Jesus' last discourse, third part – 'Glorify your Son'

17 1-26 Jesus said this, and lifting up his eyes to heaven said, 'Father, the hour has come. Glorify your Son, that your Son may glorify you. Just as you gave him authority [over] all flesh, so that everything that you have given him, he may give to them: eternal life. This is eternal life, that they should know you as the only True God, and the one whom you sent, Jesus Messiah. I glorified you on earth, completing the work that you gave me to do. And now *you* glorify *me*, Father, at your side, with the glory that before the world existed I had at your side.

'I revealed your name to the people whom you gave me from the world. They were yours; and it was to me that you gave them, and they have kept your word. Now they know that everything that you gave me [comes] from you; because the words that you gave me, I have given to them, and they accepted [them] and knew truly that I came from you – and they believed that you sent me. I ask with regard to them; I do not ask about the world, but about those whom you gave me, because they are yours. And everything that is mine is yours, and what's yours [is] mine – and I am glorified in them.

'And I am no longer in the world – and they are in the world, and I am coming to you. Holy Father, keep them in your name which you have given to me, that they may be one just as we [are one]. When I was with them, I kept them in your name which you have given to me, and guarded them. And not one of them is destroyed except the son of destruction, that the Scripture might be fulfilled.

'But now I am coming to you, and I say these things in the world, that they may have my joy fulfilled in them. I have given them your word, and the world hates them, because they are not from the world, just as I am not from the world. I do not ask that you should take them from the world, but that you should keep them out of [the clutches of] the Evil One. Of the world they are not, just as *I* am not of the world. Consecrate them in Truth. Your word is Truth. Just as you sent me into the world, I also send them into the world. And on their behalf *I* consecrate myself, that *they* also may be consecrated in Truth.

'I do not ask just on behalf of these, but also on behalf of those who through their word come to faith in me, that they may all be one, just as you, Father, are in me and I in you, that they may also be in us, in order that the world may believe that you sent me. And for my part, the glory which you have given to me I have given to them, in order that they may be one as we are one, I in them and you in me, that they may be perfected into one, that the world may know that you sent me, and you loved them as you loved me. Father, what you have given me, I want that where I am they also may be with me, that they also may see my glory which you have given me, because you loved me before the foundation of the world. O Just Father, the world did not know you, and I know you and these know that you sent me. And I made your name known to them, and I shall continue to make it known, that the love with which you loved me may be in them, and I also in them.'

> At this point, it is really no longer a 'discourse', as Jesus turns, almost priest-like, to address the Father, and offers a prayer, which has a number of elements to it. There is the familiar element of glory, the mutual glorification of Father and Son. Then there is the prayer for the people the Father gave him from the world: 'keep them in your name'. Next there is the warning that the world will hate them. Then comes the prayer for those whom this little group will reach: 'may they all be one, just as we are one, I in them, and you in me'. Finally the whole discourse ends, just as it had begun (see 13:1), with several mentions of the word 'love'.

Chapters 18 and 19: The Passion and Death of Jesus

> John's story, in its account of the last hours of Jesus' life, presents a picture of him that is different from that which we find in the Synoptics. Watch and see how very much Jesus is in control, at every stage.

The arrest of Jesus

18 ¹⁻¹² Saying these things, Jesus went out with his disciples across the Wadi Kedron, where there was a garden, which he entered, as did his disciples. And Judas who was betraying him also knew the place, because Jesus had often gathered there with his disciples. So Judas, taking the cohort, [and] servants both from the high priests and from the Pharisees, comes there with lamps and torches and weapons. So Jesus, knowing everything that was coming upon him, came out and says to them, 'Whom are you looking for?' They answered him, 'Jesus the Nazarene.' He says to them, 'I AM.' Now Judas, who was betraying him, stood with them. And so when he said to them 'I AM', they went backwards and fell to the ground. Again therefore he interrogated them, 'Whom are you looking for?' And they said, 'Jesus the Nazarene.' Jesus answered, 'I said that I AM. So if it is me you are looking for, let these go.' [This was] in order that the word might be fulfilled which he had spoken, 'Those whom you gave me, I have not lost [any] of them.'

And so Simon Peter, having a sword, drew it, and struck the slave of the High Priest, and cut off his ear lobe, the right-hand one. The name of the slave was Malchus. And so Jesus said to Peter, 'Put the sword in its scabbard; the cup which my Father has given me, shall I not drink it?' And so the cohort and the tribunus militum, and the servants of the Judaeans, arrested Jesus and tied him up.

The garden in which this episode takes place reminds us of the garden at the very beginning of the Bible (see Genesis 2:8), and therefore, perhaps, of the opening lines of the Gospel. It also looks forward to the rather different garden of 19:41, and perhaps also to the 'gardener' of 20:15.

Consider Jesus' opponents, armed to the teeth, and grimly hanging on to their torches, which simply reveal their fear of the one whom we know to be the 'Light of the World'. Jesus, by contrast, is in sole charge here; he 'knows' what is happening; it is he who conducts the interview with the arresting party; and when he identifies himself (EGO EIMI/I AM), the phrase is so powerful that it knocks them to the ground. He then gives orders that they are not to arrest anyone else. Notice also that his words (about 'those whom you gave me') have now become Scripture, to be fulfilled.

From the other angle, contrast Jesus' majestic assurance with Simon Peter's absurd act of resistance (what on earth is the use of cutting off a 'right ear lobe'?), and with the might of the Roman army that is required to take Jesus to Annas and Caiaphas. Both of these show something of the powerful mystery that is Jesus.

Jesus and Simon Peter at the High Priest's house

13-27 And they took him to Annas first, for he was the father-in-law of Caiaphas, who was high priest that year. It was Caiaphas who had advised the Judaeans that it was expedient for one person to die on behalf of the people.

Now Simon Peter followed Jesus, along with another disciple. That disciple was known to the High Priest, and he went in with Jesus to the palace of the High Priest. But Peter stood outside, beside the door. And so the other disciple went out, the one who was an acquaintance of the High Priest, and spoke to the lady gate-watcher and introduced Peter. And so the slave girl who was the gate-watcher says to Peter, 'Aren't you among the disciples of that fellow?' He says, 'I am not.'

The slaves and the servants stood, having made a charcoal fire, because it was cold, and were warming themselves. And Peter also was with them, standing and warming himself.

And so the High Priest interrogated Jesus about his disciples and his teachings. Jesus answered him, 'I have spoken openly to the world. I always taught in synagogue[s] and in the Temple, where all Judaeans come together; and I said nothing in secret. Why do you interrogate me? Interrogate those who heard what I said to them. Look – these people know what I said.' As he was saying this, one [particular] bystander from [among] the servants gave Jesus a slap, saying, 'Is this the way you respond to the High Priest?' Jesus answered him, 'If I spoke evilly, testify about the evil. But if [I spoke] well, why do you beat me?' And so Annas sent him, bound, to Caiaphas the High Priest.

And Simon Peter was standing and warming himself. And so they said to him, surely you are also one of his disciples?' He denied and said, 'I am not.' One of the slaves of the High Priest, being a cousin of the one whose ear lobe Peter had cut off, says, 'Didn't I see you in the garden with him?' So again Peter denied. And immediately a cock crew.

The centre of this episode is the interrogation of Jesus, or rather Jesus' entirely authoritative statement, highlighted by the trivial violence of the slap from a sycophantic servant, and by Jesus' cool dismissal of it.

Framing this picture of assurance is a most unassured performance from Simon Peter, who is brave enough to follow, right into the lion's den, but not brave enough to admit to a slave girl that he was a disciple of Jesus. Twice more, as he warms himself (his cold was that of incipient treachery), he denies the plain truth, even to a witness who had cause to remember him in the garden. John concludes the story, 'and immediately a cock crew'. There is no need to say anything more.

A drama of judgement, played out on two stages

18²⁸**-19**¹⁶ᵃ And so they led Jesus from the house of Caiaphas to the praetorium. It was early in the morning. And they themselves did not enter into the praetorium, so that they should not be defiled but [be able to] eat the Passover. And so Pilate came outside to them, and says, 'What accusation do you bring against this man?' They replied and said to him, 'If this fellow were not an evildoer, we would not have handed him over to you.' And so Pilate said to them, '*You* people take him – and according to *your* law judge him.' And so the Judaeans said to him, 'It is not permissible for us to kill anybody.' [This was in order] that Jesus' word might be fulfilled, signalling by what kind of a death he was about to die. And so Pilate went back into the praetorium, and he called Jesus and said to him, 'Are you the King of the Judaeans?'

Jesus replied, 'On your own account do you say this, or did others tell you about me?' Pilate answered, 'Do you think that *I* am a Judaean? Your nation, and the high priests, handed you over to me. What have you done?' Jesus replied, 'My kingdom is not of this world. If my kingdom were of this world, my servants would have struggled so that I should not be handed over to the Judaeans. As it is, my kingdom is not from here.' And so Pilate said to him, 'Then you are a king, are you not?' Jesus replied, 'You say that I am a king. *I* was born for this, and for this I came into the world, that I might bear witness to the Truth. Everyone who is of the Truth listens to my voice.' Pilate says to him, 'What is Truth?'

And saying this he went out again to the Judaeans, and says to them, 'I find no grounds [against] him. But you have a custom, that I should release one person to you at the Passover. So – do you want me to release the King of the Judaeans to you?' And so they cried out again saying, 'Not this one, but Barabbas.' Barabbas was a bandit.

And so then Pilate took Jesus and scourged him. And the soldiers, weaving a wreath out of thorns, placed it on his head, and a purple cloak they put round him, and they came to him and started to say, 'Hail, King of the Judaeans.' And they rained blows on him. And again Pilate comes out and says to them, 'Look – I am leading him out to you, that you may know that I find no grounds [against] him.' And so Jesus came out, wearing the wreath of thorns and the purple cloak. And he says to them, 'Behold – the man.' And so when the chief priests and the servants saw him, they cried out, saying, 'Crucify, crucify.' Pilate says to them, '*You* take him and crucify [him]. For *I* find no grounds against him.' And so the Judaeans replied, '*We* have a Law. And according to the Law, he ought to die – because he appointed himself Son of God.' And so when Pilate heard this statement he was more afraid. And he went into the praetorium again, and says to Jesus, 'Where are you from?'

But Jesus gave him no reply. And so Pilate says to him, 'Do you not talk to me? Don't you know that I have power to release you, *and* I have power to crucify you?' Jesus replied to him, 'You would have no power against me, unless it were given you from above. For this reason, the one who handed me over has [the] greater sin.' From that [moment] Pilate was seeking to free him, but the Judaeans cried out saying, 'If you free this fellow, you are not a friend of Caesar; everyone who appoints himself King is opposed to Caesar.' And so Pilate, taking these words aboard, led Jesus outside, and he sat on [the] judgement-bench in a place called 'Lithostrotos' ['Pavement'], [or], in Aramaic, 'Gabbatha'. It was the Preparation Day of the Feast; the hour was about midday.

And he says to the Judaeans, 'Look – your King.' And so *they* cried out, 'Take [him] away! Take [him] away! Crucify him!' Pilate says to them, 'Your King, shall I crucify?' The high priests replied, 'We have no king but Caesar.' And so he handed him over to them that he should be crucified.

The evangelist has carefully constructed this episode. It starts with the unhealthy contrast (of which he does not make very much) between what Jesus' opponents were engaged upon, and their desire not to be polluted before the Passover.

More impressively, look at his 'stage directions'; look for words such as 'enter', 'outside', 'back into the praetorium', 'went out again', 'comes out', 'went into the praetorium again', and you will see that the story alternates between two stages, not this time 'upper' and 'lower', but 'inner' and 'outer'. The outside is all noise and baying for blood and attempts at manipulation; inside is a serene authority, radiating from Jesus. Between these two stages scurries Pilate, like a frightened rabbit. At the heart of it all is a debate about kingship: who is King, Tiberius Caesar (and therefore also Pilate, his local representative), or Jesus? Pilate's verdict, delivered three times, is that Jesus is indeed a king; but the question remains: who is sitting in judgement on whom? The soldiers join in and play a game of 'King' with Jesus, but only throw his quiet dignity into sharp relief. Pilate, unmistakably alarmed now, asks Jesus the all-important question: 'Where are you from?' He gets no answer, but Jesus' next response to his words absolutely strips him of any authority at all. Then, in a terrible abrogation of what Israel stood for, the religious leaders solemnly declare, 'We have no king but Caesar.' There should be a shocked silence after these words.

The crucifixion and death of Jesus

16b-30 And so they accepted Jesus. And carrying his cross for himself, he went out to the [place] known as Skull Place, which in Aramaic is known as Golgotha, where they crucified him, and with him two others, on this side and on that, and Jesus in the middle. And Pilate wrote an inscription and put it on the cross; and it was written:

'Jesus the Nazarene, the King of the Judaeans.' And so this inscription was read by many of the Judaeans, because the place was near the city where Jesus was crucified, and it was written in Aramaic, Latin, Greek. And so the high priests of the Judaeans said to Pilate, 'Do not write, "the King of the Judaeans", but that "The man said, 'I am the King of the Judaeans'." ' Pilate replied, 'What I have written, I have written.'

And so the soldiers, when they had crucified Jesus, took his garments and made four parts, a part to each soldier, and his tunic. But the tunic was seamless, [being] woven from the top throughout. And so they said to each other, 'Let us not divide it; instead, let us cast lots [for] it [to see] whose it will be.' [This was] that the Scripture might be fulfilled which says:

> 'They divided my garments [among] themselves,
>   and over my garments they cast lot[s].'

And so the soldiers did that.

There stood by the cross of Jesus his mother, and his mother's sister, Mary of Clopas and Mary the Magdalene. And so Jesus, seeing his mother, and the disciple standing by whom he loved, says to [his] mother, 'Woman, look – your son.' Then he says to the disciple, 'Look – your mother.' And from that hour the disciple took her to his own.

After this, Jesus, knowing that already everything was brought to perfection, in order that the Scripture might be perfected, says, 'I thirst.' A vessel lay there, full of wine vinegar. And so, wrapping a sponge full of the vinegar on a piece of hyssop they offered it to his mouth. And when he had taken the vinegar, Jesus said, 'It is perfected.' And inclining his head, he handed over the Spirit.

> Now comes the last act (or is it?); and although Jesus must inevitably die at the end of it, just notice how very much in charge he is. There is here no sign of Simon of Cyrene; instead Jesus is 'carrying his own cross for himself'; and there is the affirmation, solemnly written out by the local representative of the most powerful man in the world, and in all the relevant languages, that Jesus is indeed the 'King'.
>
> We do not in John, as we do in the Synoptic Gospels, feel that Jesus is alone and abandoned on the cross. Instead, the cross is more like a royal throne, from which he forms a royal dynasty, of his mother and the disciple that he loved.
>
> Finally, 'knowing that already everything was brought to perfection', he makes sure that the final Scripture text is fulfilled, and announces his thirst, perhaps making us think of Psalm 22:15, just as 'they divided my garments among themselves . . .' comes from Psalm 22:18, accepts some vinegar, and graciously allows Death to do his part: 'it is accomplished (or: perfected).' Even the description of his death, which could equally well have been translated 'he gave up his life', is probably to be read as a royal distribution of the Spirit.

Jesus' royal burial

31-42   And so the Judaeans, since it was Preparation [Day], so that the bodies should not remain on the cross on the Sabbath, for that was a special Sabbath-day, asked Pilate that the legs might be broken, and the bodies taken away. And so the soldiers

244

came, and of the first one they broke the legs, and [then] of the other who had been crucified with him. But coming to Jesus, when they saw him already dead, they did not break his legs. Instead, one of the soldiers, with a spear pierced his side. And there came out straightaway blood and water. And the one who saw it has testified, and true is his testimony, and he knows that he speaks true things, in order that you may believe. For these things happened that the scriptures might be fulfilled:

'Not a bone of him shall be broken.'

And again another Scripture says:

'They shall look on [him] whom they have pierced.'

After this, the request was put to Pilate by Joseph from Arimathea, who was a disciple of Jesus, although hidden, because of fear of the Judaeans, that he might take away Jesus' body. And Pilate gave permission. And so he came and took his body. And Nicodemus came, who came to him by night in the first place, with a mixture of myrrh and aloes, about a hundred pounds. And so they took the body of Jesus and wrapped it in linen cloths with the spices, as is the custom for Judaeans to bury [corpses]. And there was in the place where he was crucified a garden, and in the garden a new tomb, in which no one had yet been laid. And so there, because of the Preparation Day of the Judaeans, because the tomb was nearby, they laid Jesus.

> Jesus' opponents once more show themselves concerned about ritual purity; even in death, however, Jesus stands for something far more exalted. His legs remain unbroken; his corpse royally discharges blood and water; he fulfils Scripture. Finally he is given a burial fit for a king, with enormous quantities of aloes and myrrh, and a new tomb in a garden; and the story ends, gently and respectfully, with 'Jesus' as the very last word: 'they laid Jesus'.
>
> 'Not a bone of him shall be broken' comes from Psalm 34:20 (and see also Exodus 12:46, Numbers 9:12, which link the words to the Passover. Remember that John sees Jesus as the Passover lamb). 'They shall look on him whom they pierced' is from Zechariah 12:10.
>
> What does it mean to call Jesus a king?

The empty tomb; the encounter with Mary Magdalene

20 [1-18] On the first day of the week Mary the Magdalene comes early, while it is still dark, to the tomb, and sees the stone taken away from the tomb. And so she runs, and comes to Simon Peter and to the other disciple whom Jesus loved, and says to them, 'They took the Lord out of the tomb, and we do not know where they have put him.' And so Peter and the other disciple went out; and they came to the tomb. The two of them were running side by side; and the other disciple ran more quickly than Peter, and went ahead, and got to the tomb first. And stooping down he sees the linen cloths lying – but he did not go in. And so Simon Peter also comes, in second place, and went into the tomb. And he sees the linen cloths lying [there] and the sweat-cloth, which was on his head, not lying with the linen cloths, but rolled up on its own, in one place. And so then the other disciple also went in, the one who had come first to the tomb; and he saw and he believed. For they did not yet understand the scriptures, that it was inevitable that he [should be] raised from the dead. And so the disciples went back [home].

But Mary stood outside by the tomb, weeping. And so, as she wept, she stooped down [to look] into the tomb; and she sees two angels in white [garments] sitting [there], one at the head and one at the feet, where Jesus' body had lain. And they say to her, 'Woman, why are you weeping?' She says to them, 'They took my Lord away, and I don't know where they have put him.' Saying this, she turned around backwards and sees Jesus standing there – and she did not know that it was Jesus. Jesus says to her, 'Woman, why are you weeping? Whom are you looking for?' She, thinking that it was the gardener, says to him, 'Sir [or: 'Lord'], if you have taken him, tell me where you have put him, and I shall move him.' Jesus says to her, 'Mary.' She turns round and says to him in Aramaic, 'Rabbouni' (which means 'Teacher'). Jesus says to her, 'Don't touch me – for I have not yet gone up to the Father. But go to my brethren, and tell them, "I am going up to my Father and your Father, and my God and your God."' Mary the Magdalene comes announcing to the disciples, 'I have seen the Lord', and [that] he had said these things to her.

There is an air of uncertainty about this story: the stone is rolled away, and there is no body. Everyone suddenly starts running, a sign of the general confusion; linen cloths are lying all over the place (which shows that it wasn't grave-robbers). Finally, the beloved disciple, who has courteously waited outside for his elder to arrive, puffing and panting, goes in 'and he saw and he believed'. What did he believe? The inevitability, it would seem, of Jesus' Resurrection.

Mary, however, has not yet tumbled to it, and remains weeping. Then she goes deeper into the mystery, because there are two angels who ask her, not unkindly, 'Woman, why are you weeping?'

Her answer concerns the loss of her much-loved Lord; and now that same Lord appears, although unrecognised, mistaken for the local garden attendant. Her illusion is rapidly dispelled, however, when she is addressed by name, and she replies in her native Aramaic. Then we are reminded of the 'two stages': Jesus no longer belongs on the 'lower stage'; his place is on the 'upper stage', with his Father. Then Mary does what disciples must do, and proclaims the Resurrection. The story comes full circle, as she announces: 'I have seen the Lord.' At this point, we remember Jesus' opening words: 'What do you seek . . . Come and you will see' (1:38, 39). We also recall the testimony of the Baptist ('I have seen and I have borne witness, that this is the Son of God', 1:34; 'See! The Lamb of God', 1:36), and the response to Mary's tears ('Whom are you looking for?'), a few lines ago.

The mystery explored to the full

19-29   And so when it was late on that day, the first day of the week, and the doors were closed where the disciples were, for fear of the Judaeans, Jesus came and stood in the midst, and says to them, 'Peace be with you.' And saying this, he showed his hands and his side. And so the disciples rejoiced, seeing the Lord. And so Jesus said to them again, 'Peace to you. As the Father sent me, I also send you.' And saying this, he breathed on them and says to them, 'Receive [the] Holy Spirit. If you let go the sins of any, they are let go for them – if you hold them bound, they are held bound.'

Now Thomas, one of the Twelve, known as 'Twin', was not with them when Jesus came. And so the other disciples said to him, 'We have seen the Lord.' But he said to them, 'Unless I see in his hands the mark of the nails, and thrust my finger into the mark of the nails, and thrust my hand into his side, I shall never believe.'

And after eight days, again the disciples were inside, and Thomas with them. Jesus comes, the doors being closed, and stood in the middle and said, 'Peace to you.' Then he says to Thomas, 'Bring your finger here and see my hands, and bring your hand here and thrust it into my side, and don't be an unbeliever, but [be] a believer.' Thomas replied and said to him, 'My Lord and my God.' Jesus says to him, 'Because you have seen me, you have come to faith. Happy are those who did not see *and* believed.'

> This passage unfolds in two scenes. In the first, it is established a) that the disciples are frightened, and certainly do not believe in the Resurrection; b) that Jesus is risen; and c) that the disciples have a mission, described in terms of the Holy Spirit and of letting go of sins. The second scene goes much deeper into the mystery, thanks to Thomas's incredulity, and, frankly, thanks to his rather crude demand for verification. It is a repeat of the first scene, a week later; but after the opening greeting it takes a very unexpected turn. Thomas is granted his rather unpleasant wish (though we are not told whether or not he takes advantage of the offer), but instead, like Nathanael before him (see 1:46-52), he leaps beyond the evidence, and makes the affirmation to which the Gospel has been leading, all this time: 'My Lord and my God.' Then, just as we applaud his insight, we find ourselves purring in self-satisfaction as we hear the next stage in the story: 'Happy are those who did not see *and* believed'. That clearly refers to us who read this Gospel.

Final words to the reader

30, 31 And so there were many other signs that Jesus did in the presence of his disciples, which are not written down on this scroll. But these things are written, so that you may have faith that Jesus is the Messiah, the Son of God, and that through your faith you may have life in his name.

> Now the evangelist turns and speaks directly to us. He admits that he has not told the whole story, only that bit of it that brings us, the readers or hearers, to 'have faith that Jesus is the Messiah, the Son of God'. And why should he do this? So that through our faith we 'may have life in his name'.

Final appearance (mainly to Peter)

21 1-25 After this, Jesus revealed himself again to the disciples on the Sea of Tiberias. He revealed [himself] in this way:

They were together, Simon Peter, and Thomas called Twin, and Nathanael, the one from Cana in the Galilee, and the [sons] of Zebedee, and two others of his disciples. Simon Peter says to them, 'I am going to fish.' They say to him, 'We're also coming with you.' They went out, and they boarded the boat, and on that night they caught nothing. When it was already morning, Jesus stood on the shore – but the disciples did not know that it was Jesus. And so Jesus says to them, 'Children, don't you have any fish?' They answered him, 'No.' He said to them, 'Cast the net out on to the starboard side of the boat and you will find [something].' And so they did, and they no longer had the strength to pull it, because of the number of fish. And so that disciple whom Jesus loved says to Peter, 'It is the Lord.' So Simon Peter, hearing that it was the Lord, put on his outer garment (for he was naked) and threw himself into the sea. Meanwhile the other disciples came by boat, for they were not far from the land, but about a hundred yards [away], dragging the net of fish. And so when they went on shore they see a charcoal-fire set up, and fish and bread on top. Jesus says to them, 'Bring [some] of the fish which you have just caught.' And so Simon Peter went up and dragged the net to the land, full of big fish, one hundred and fifty-three; and although there were so many, the net was not split. Jesus says to them, 'Come here and eat your breakfast.' None of the disciples dared to ask him, 'Who are you?', knowing that it was the Lord. Jesus comes and takes the bread and gives it to them, and the fish likewise. And this [was the] third [time] Jesus appeared to the disciples, having risen from the dead.

So when they had had breakfast, Jesus says to Simon Peter, 'Simon [son] of John, do you love me more than these?' He says to him, 'Yes, Lord, you know that I love you.' He says to him, 'Feed my lambs.' He says to him again a second time, 'Simon [son] of John, do you love me?' He says to him, 'Yes, Lord, you know that I love you.' He says to him, 'Pasture my sheep.' He says to him a third time, 'Simon [son] of John, do you love me?' Peter was grieved that he said to him a third time, 'Do you love me?', and he says to him, 'Lord, *you* know everything, you know that I love you.' Jesus says to him, 'Feed my sheep. Amen, Amen, I tell you, when you were younger, you girded yourself, and you walked where you wanted. But when you grow old, you will stretch out your hands, and someone else will gird you, and will take you where you don't want [to go].'

He said this, indicating by what kind of a death he was going to glorify God. And having said this, he says to him, 'Follow me.'

Peter turns and sees the disciple whom Jesus loved following, who at the supper had laid down on his breast and said, 'Lord, who is the one who is betraying you?' So seeing him, Peter says to Jesus, 'Lord, what about this one?' Jesus says to him, 'If I want him to remain till I come, what is that to you? *You* follow me.' And so the rumour went out to the brethren that that disciple was not going to die; but Jesus didn't tell him that he was not going to die, but 'If I want him to remain till I come, what is that to you?'

This is the disciple who bears witness about these things, and who wrote these things; and we know that his witness is true. There are many other things that Jesus did, which if each of them was written individually, I don't think the world would contain the written scrolls.

Some scholars, by no means all, regard the last two verses of Chapter 20 as the original ending, so that Chapter 21 is an appendix, perhaps written after the death of the evangelist. That is possible, but we have seen sufficient mysterious introductions and connections in the course of reading this Gospel to know that we cannot always be sure of too-confident conclusions of this sort.

The episode is about Peter, who has spoken up, impressively if not always accurately, at several places in the Gospel, since that moment in Chapter 1 when his brother Andrew brought him to Jesus. Since then, however, we have heard him deny that he was a disciple, and have seen him make a fruitless visit to the empty tomb. So there is unfinished business here. The episode starts with him exercising leadership in the group (just as he had when he went first into the tomb), telling a select number of them that he was returning to his profession (in which, as it turned out, he was mistaken). Somehow the reader is not surprised when they catch nothing (Jesus is not with them). As soon as Jesus appears, however, they have more fish than they can cope with (153, according to the evangelist – and you should see the flights of fancy to which readers and scholars have been led by this figure down the centuries!). Then there is a charming picture of the Lord cooking the food for breakfast (and we notice that the beloved disciple recognises who it is, while the rest are not quite so sure); but as the meal progresses, we (and Peter) are uneasily aware of the unfinished business, and nervously hear Jesus turn to ask the question, 'Do you love me?' The question is asked three times, and we should have to be very insensitive not to see in this the most delicate possible reference to Peter's triple denial. In that moment, he is given his task, precisely as sinner: 'Feed my lambs [or: sheep].'

Then he is given a warning, or a prediction of his death. Only after that does Jesus say 'Follow me' – and Peter, impetuous to the last, fails to respond directly to this invitation, but gets distracted, and starts worrying about the 'beloved disciple', and demands to know what will happen to **him**. He is given no answer, but simply told, once more, 'Follow me.' Finally there is a comment on this beloved disciple: 'This is the disciple . . . who wrote these things.' Is it the author of the Gospel? Perhaps, but it doesn't quite say so. The Gospel is all about the Word, who was with God, not about his disciples; and so it ends with yet another disclaimer. The Gospel, we learn, does not contain **everything** that Jesus did. It couldn't possibly.

And so this astonishing composition tails away into silence. Only it doesn't, because in the silence there lies hidden an invitation to you, the reader.

Acts of the Apostles

Introduction

The racy tale that you are about to read is the second part of our two-volume narrative and it is likewise addressed to 'Theophilus'. If the Gospel was the Gospel of Jesus, you might say that Acts is the 'Gospel of the Holy Spirit'. Two ways in which you will notice the power of the Spirit: first, Acts is a journey, always 'on the move', until it reaches Rome; and even then it is restless – the last word (two words in English, only one in Greek) of the two volumes is 'without hindrance'. Second, in his account of the Pentecost incident, Luke represents this Holy Spirit as 'fire' and 'mighty wind'. Watch how this power is made evident throughout this extraordinary story.

Prologue

1 ¹⁻⁵ Theophilus: the first account I drew up about all the [things] which Jesus began to do and teach, from the day when he gave orders to the apostles whom he had chosen, through the Holy Spirit; and then he was taken up. He had showed himself alive to them, after his passion, by many convincing proofs, appearing to them through [a period of] forty days, and speaking the things that concern the kingdom of God. While he was staying with them, he directed them not to depart from Jerusalem, but to await 'the promise of the Father, which you have heard me [talking about]. For John baptised with water, while you will be baptised with the Holy Spirit, not many days from now.'

Luke here rapidly and skilfully summarises 'the story so far'. The two-volume work that we call 'Luke-Acts' (and an untranslatable particle in the Greek here makes it clearer than we can in English that we are now beginning Volume II) is addressed to the 'Most Excellent Theophilus'. This form of address is appropriate for one of the Equites, the second (but still decidedly exalted) rank of Roman society. The name 'Theophilus' might be that of a real person, perhaps Luke's well-to-do patron. Or, since it means 'Beloved by God' or 'Lover of God', it might be addressed to any Christian reader.

One aspect of Acts that we shall frequently notice is the way it echoes Volume I, the 'Gospel of Luke'. The first example of such an echo comes here, with the reference to 'forty days'. Just as Jesus prepared for his mission with forty days in the desert, he now prepares the Church for its mission with forty days of appearances. We note, too, the first mention of the Holy Spirit, whose chronicle Acts is, and the phrase 'the promise of the Father', referring to the Holy Spirit.

Notice that Resurrection is part of the 'given' of Acts, as it is of the New Testament as a whole.

The Ascension: final instructions, attentive prayer

⁶⁻¹⁴ So they came together, and asked him, 'Lord, is it at this time that you are re-establishing the kingdom for Israel?' He said to them, 'It is not your right to know times and seasons which the Father has fixed by his own authority. Instead, you will receive power when the Holy Spirit comes on you, and you will be my witnesses, in Jerusalem, and in all Judaea and Samaria, and until the end of the earth.'

As he said these things, while they looked, he was lifted up, and a cloud took him up, out of their sight. As they were gazing intently into heaven, while he journeyed, look! Two men were in their presence, in white clothes; and these men said, 'Men of Galilee, why do you stand looking into heaven? This Jesus, who was taken up from you into heaven, so he will come in [just the same] way you see him journeying into heaven.'

Then they returned to Jerusalem from the Mount called 'The Olive Grove', which is near Jerusalem, a Sabbath-day's journey. When they entered [the city] they went up to the upper room where they were staying: Peter and John and Jacob and Andrew, Philip and Thomas, Bartholomew and Matthew, Jacob of Alphaeus and Simon the Zealot and Judas of Jacob. All these were engaged unanimously in prayer, along with the women, and Mary the mother of Jesus, and his brothers.

The disciples do not really understand at present; this incomprehension continues a theme from the Gospel, of course. That will change when 'the Holy Spirit comes on you'; in a sense, Acts is the working out of this promise. Acts also shows how the apostles became Jesus' 'witnesses in Jerusalem and in all Judaea and Samaria' (reversing the order of the Gospel, where Jesus journeyed from Galilee through Samaria to Judaea and finally to Jerusalem) and 'as far as the end of the earth', which will be first Athens (Chapter 17) and finally Rome (28:30, 31).

Two favourite words of Luke that come in this text are translated here, 'gazing intently' and 'journeyed'. 'Went' is the more common translation of the latter, but does not reflect the weight that Luke puts upon it in the 'journeying Gospel'. 'A Sabbath-day's journey': orthodox Jews may not travel more than a thousand yards outside the city limits on the Sabbath-day. As in the opening of his Gospel, Luke is careful to show that the heroes of his story are observant Jews.

The list of apostles is the same as in Luke 6:14-16, but in a different order, and, of course, without Judas Iscariot. Some scholars feel that Luke puts the women 'in their place' by mentioning them last.

Note the word translated 'unanimously'; we shall see this again as a description of the infant Church.

Selecting a replacement for Judas

15-26   In those days, Peter stood up in the middle of the brethren and said (and the crowd of names together was about a hundred and twenty), 'Men and brothers, it was necessary for the Scripture to be fulfilled which the Holy Spirit foretold through the mouth of David, regarding Judas, who became a guide to those who arrested Jesus, because he was numbered with us, and he had been allotted this ministry. So this fellow obtained a piece of land out of the wages of iniquity, and falling head-long he burst open in the middle, and all his guts poured out. This became known to all who dwell in Jerusalem, so that that piece of land was called in their own language 'Haceldama', that is 'Field of Blood'. For it is written in the Book of Psalms:

"Let his residence become a desert, and let the one who dwells in it not be"; and
"Let another take over his office-as-overseer."

'Therefore it is necessary that one of the men who came together with us all the time when the Lord Jesus came in and went out among us, beginning from the baptism of John until the day when he was taken up from us, should become with us a witness of his Resurrection.'

They set up two, Joseph called Barsabbas, who was nicknamed 'Justus', and Matthias. They prayed and said, 'You, Lord, knower of the hearts of all, show which one out of the two you have chosen, to take the place of this service and this apostolate from which Judas transgressed, to journey to his own place.' They gave them lots; and the lot fell on Matthias, and he was voted in with the eleven apostles.

Peter exercises here a leadership which he does not always have in Acts, initiating God's choice of a successor to Judas. We notice that once he has performed his task of making Eleven into Twelve, Matthias is never heard of again.

Twice in this passage Luke uses, what in Greek is a three-letter word, translated 'it is/was necessary'; and notice also the word 'fore-told'. Both these words subtly convey the message that God is in charge; the Holy Spirit is irresistibly running the show.

The two quotations applied to Judas and the problems of his successor are from Psalm 69:25 and 109:8 respectively.

We also notice that the function of an apostle is to be a 'witness of his Resurrection'.

Fire and wind at Pentecost

2 [1-4] At the fulfilment of the day of Pentecost they were all together in the same place. Suddenly there came from heaven a sound, as of a violent wind rushing, and it filled the whole house where they were sitting, and divided tongues, as if of fire, appeared to them, and sat on each single one of them, and they were all filled with the Holy Spirit, and they began to speak in different languages, as the Spirit granted them to utter.

> Now we 'see' the Spirit in action, with sound and sights (mighty wind, tongues of fire); we are meant to recall Jesus' baptism at Luke 3:22, with its own sound and sight (the Holy Spirit in bodily form, and the voice from heaven). The word 'fulfilment' is related to that which the evangelist uses at Luke 1:1; the work of God is being done. The fire and mighty wind are symbols of what we shall see in the rest of Acts, as the story of the Holy Spirit unfolds. The 'violent wind' blows throughout Acts, driving the story on, powerfully changing people's lives, driving Saul and Peter and the rest of them on the journey to the 'ends of the earth'; you can see it in the way intense opposition is overcome, in the signs and wonders and healings that accompany the gospel. 'Tongues of fire' stand as a symbol for the speeches that constitute one third of Acts of the Apostles. See how on that first Pentecost the gospel was preached to 'all the world' (5-13), how Stephen and Peter and Paul cannot be prevented from speaking of Jesus to everyone they meet. Acts is the dramatic illustration of how the fire of the gospel spread round the Mediterranean world, of how the wind blew from Jerusalem to Rome, and then onwards down the centuries and across the world to wherever you are reading these words today.

The gospel is preached to the entire world

[5-13] There were Jews living in Jerusalem, devout men from all the nations under heaven. When this sound happened, the crowd came together and were confused, because each one of them heard them speaking in their own language. They were astounded and amazed, saying, 'Look! All these people who are speaking, aren't they Galileans? How do we each hear in our own language in which we were born?

Parthians and Medes and Elamites and those who dwell in Mesopotamia, and Judaea and Cappadocia, Pontus and Asia, Phrygia and Pamphylia, Egypt and the parts of Libya round Cyrene, and Roman visitors, both Jews and proselytes, Cretans and Arabs, we hear them speaking in our [own] languages the great things of God.'

They were all amazed, and greatly perplexed, one saying to another, 'What's all this about?' But others said, mockingly, 'They are full of sweet [wine].'

> Notice how the good news is already reaching 'to the end of the earth', and look at a map for all the places mentioned, to see how it makes a great circle round the Ancient Near East. The 'great things of God': the root is a favourite of Luke – see Luke 1:46, 58; 9:43; Acts 5:13; 10:46; 19:17.
>
> The theme of initial rejection or mockery (in this case the allegation that the speakers are drunk) will reappear frequently in Acts. It is part of the energy of the Spirit that it arouses opposition as well as driving the story and the gospel forcibly onwards.

Peter's Pentecost speech

14-36 But Peter stood up with the eleven and raised his voice, and addressed them, 'Men of Judaea, and all you who are living in Jerusalem, let this be known to you, and give ear to my words. For these people are not drunk, as you suppose, for it is the third hour of the day. No – this is what was spoken through the prophet Joel:

"And it shall be in those days, says the Lord,
I pour out some of my spirit on all flesh;
and your sons and your daughters shall prophesy,
and your young men shall see visions,
and your elders shall dream in dreams.

"And on my servants, male and female, in those days
I pour out some of my spirit and they shall prophesy,
and I shall give portents in heaven above
and signs on the earth below,
blood and fire and smoky vapour.
The sun will be changed into darkness,
and the moon into blood
before the Day of the Lord comes, great and glorious.
And it shall be that all who call upon the name of the Lord shall be saved."

'Men of Israel, hear these words: Jesus the Nazarene, a man marked out from God to you by miracles and portents and signs, which God did through him in the midst of you, just as you yourselves know, this same man, by the predetermined plan and foreknowledge of God [when he had been] delivered up through the hand[s] of the lawless, you nailed and destroyed him. God raised him up, undoing the birth pangs of death, because it was not possible that he should be held fast by it. For David says, with regard to him:

"I saw the Lord before me throughout,
because he is at my right, so that I be not shaken.
Therefore my heart rejoiced
and my tongue exulted
and still my flesh shall dwell in hope.

> Because you will not abandon my soul to Hades,
> nor will you permit your Holy One to see destruction.
> You made me know the ways of life.
> You fill me full of joy with your face."

'Men, and brothers, it is allowable [for us] to speak to you with confidence about the patriarch David. He died and was buried, and his tomb is in our midst to the present day. Now, since he was a prophet, and since he knew that God, with an oath, "had sworn to him that the fruit of his loins would sit on his throne" [Psalm 132:11; 2 Samuel 7:12, 13] he spoke prophetically about the Resurrection of the Messiah, "He was not abandoned into Hades, nor did his flesh see destruction" [Psalm 16:10]. This is Jesus, whom God raised up; and we are all Jesus' witnesses. And so he has been exalted to God's right hand; he received the promise of the Holy Spirit from the Father, he poured out the Spirit; that is what you people are seeing and hearing. For David did not go up to heaven, but it is David who says [in Psalm 110:1]:

> "The Lord said to my Lord: Sit on my right
> until I make your enemies a footstool for your feet."

'So let the entire house of Israel know infallibly that God appointed him Lord and Messiah, this Jesus, whom you people crucified.'

The first of several speeches in Acts: like many ancient historians, Luke uses these speeches to interpret to the reader what he thinks is going on. At the same time, however, he writes in a way appropriate to the speaker.

The long quotations from Joel 2:28-33 and Psalm 16:8-11, and the reference to 'God's foreknowledge' emphasise that the Holy Spirit is directing operations. The rather complicated argument about David is meant to demonstrate that the scriptures really refer to Jesus.

As Luke does throughout Acts, Peter here emphasises Jesus' death, to which God's response is Resurrection, making Jesus 'Lord and Messiah'.

The powerful effects of the speech

37-41 When they heard [him], they were pierced to the heart; and they said to Peter and the rest of the apostles, 'What shall we do, brothers?' And Peter said to them, 'Repent, and let each of you be baptised in the name of Jesus Messiah, for the forgiveness of your sins, and you will receive the gift of the Holy Spirit. For the promise is to you, and to your children, and to all those a long way off, whomsoever the Lord our God shall summon.'

In many more words he testified, and he invited them, saying, 'Be saved from this crooked generation.' So those who accepted what he said were baptised; and there were added on that day about three thousand souls.

The preaching of the word has an immediate effect; and, as in the gospel, it comes in terms of 'repentance and forgiveness of sins'.

As in the early part of Luke's Gospel, one is given the impression of immense and immediate success: three thousand added in a single day.

Life in the early Church – 1

2 ⁴²-3 ¹ᵃ They were holding fast to the apostles' teaching, to the breaking of the bread and to communion, and to the breaking of the bread and the prayers. There came awe on every soul; and many portents and signs came about through the apostles. And all the believers were in the same place, and they held everything in common; and they sold their possessions and their belongings, and divided them [among] everybody according as anybody had need. Every day they persisted unanimously in the Temple, breaking bread at home. They received their share of food joyfully and in simplicity of heart, praising God, and having favour with the whole people. And the Lord was every day adding the number of saved to the same place.

> This paragraph is the first of several examples in Acts of the 'Lucan summary', a device that we have seen the evangelist employ quite often in the Gospel, but which he uses more especially in Acts. Its function is to create atmosphere rather than report events. It is also Luke's way of telling the reader, 'this is what it should be like today'.
>
> Notice the phrase 'in the same place (1:44)', and, later, 'to the same place' (3:1a). This is the fourth time in Acts that we have encountered this rather obscure expression (see also 1:15 and 2:1), which presumably is intended to emphasise the unity of the infant Church. See also the word translated as 'communion'. The Greek for it is 'Koinonia'; it is an idea of immense importance in early (and not just early) Christianity, with a wide range of meanings, including unity, partnership, close relationship, sharing, and participation.

A beggar receives more than he had asked for

1b-10 Now Peter and John used to go up to the Temple at the hour of prayer, the ninth hour. And a certain man, who was crippled from his mother's womb, used to be carried, and they would place him every day by the gate of the Temple; [this was the gate] known as the Beautiful Gate. [The purpose was] for him to beg alms from the people going into the Temple. When he saw Peter and John on the point of going into the Temple, he asked to receive alms. Looking intently at him, Peter, with John, said, 'Look at us.' And he fixed his attention on them, expecting to receive something from them. But Peter said, 'Silver and gold are not at my disposal; but what I have, that I give you. In the name of Jesus Messiah the Nazarene, rise up and walk.' And taking hold of him by the right hand, he raised him up. Straight-away, his feet were strengthened, and his ankles; and he leapt up, and stood, and walked, and went into the Temple with them, walking and leaping, and praising God. And the whole people saw him walking and praising God. And they recognised him because he was the one who used to sit [begging] for alms at the Beautiful Gate of the Temple, and they were filled with astonishment and terror at what had happened to him.

> Now the apostles are clearly carrying on the work of Jesus. In this scene, John is somewhat redundant, and his presence is always just a little awkward; it is Peter who is the centre of attention.
>
> 'Praising God': this is the effect of the Spirit on ordinary people. See Luke 2:20; 18:43; 19:37; Acts 2:47.

The 'whole people' is also an important theological idea for Luke. For example, they were waiting in astonishment outside the sanctuary while Zachariah talked with the angel Gabriel (1:21), and Simeon describes Jesus as 'the glory of your people Israel (2:32), and Jesus' accusers allege (23:5) that 'he stirs up the people by teaching them'.

Peter's second speech

11-26 As he held on to Peter and John, the whole crowd ran up to them, at the colonnade named after Solomon, utterly astonished. When Peter saw the people, he responded to them, 'Men of Israel, why are you amazed at this, or why do you look intently at us, as though it were through [our] own power and godliness that we had made him walk? The God of Abraham and the God of Isaac and the God of Jacob, the God of our ancestors, glorified his servant Jesus, whom you people handed over and denied to Pilate's face, when [Pilate] had passed a verdict of acquittal. But you lot denied the Holy One and the Just One, and demanded for yourselves the gift of a murderer. And the Prince of Life you murdered; God [then] raised him from the dead. Of this we are all witnesses. And by faith in his name, this man whom you see and know, his name has strengthened him, and the faith that is through him gave him this wholeness before all of you. However, as it is, brothers, I know that [it was] through ignorance [that] you acted; and the same for your rulers. But this was how God brought to fulfilment the things he had fore-announced through the mouths of all the prophets, the Messiah's suffering. So – repent, and turn, to have your sins erased, so that times of refreshment may come from the Lord and he may send you Jesus Messiah who was fore-appointed for you, whom heaven must receive until all the times of restoration which God spoke through the mouths of his prophets, holy from all time. Moses, for example, says, "The Lord your God will resurrect a prophet for you, from among your brethren, like me. You will listen to him according to all the things that he speaks to you. And it shall be that every person who does not listen to that prophet shall be rooted out from the people."

'And all the prophets from Samuel and his successors who spoke also announced these days. It is you people who are the children of the prophets, and of the covenant that God covenanted with your ancestors, saying to Abraham, "And by your seed all the families of the earth shall be blessed." For [to] you in the first place God resurrected his Servant and sent him, blessing you [through] each one of you turning away from your wickednesses.'

Peter's second speech; he is visibly growing in confidence, and we find ourselves asking if this can possibly be the same man as in the Gospel (see Luke 22:54-60). This is how the Spirit works. At the same time we notice the awkwardness of speech that Luke has given him, which I have tried to represent in the translation.

The burden of his speech is about how the Spirit works: the same God, operating in the same way, in the stories from the Hebrew Bible, in the life of Jesus, and in the life of the Church. See the cumbersome translation of words compounded with 'fore', which make exactly the same point. Another typical Lucan idea is that of 'repentance'. Repentance means 'changing your ways', turning your life round through 180 degrees, like the Prodigal Son in Luke 15:11-32 or

Zacchaeus in Luke 19:1-10, or the thief to whom Jesus said, 'Today you will be with me in Paradise' (Luke 23:39-43).

Once again Peter insists on his hearers' responsibility for the death of Jesus, and on the apostles' role as witnesses to the Resurrection.

Opposition and success

4 ¹⁻⁴ As they were talking to the people, the priests and the captain of the Temple and the Sadducees approached him, greatly annoyed because they were teaching the people and proclaiming in the person of Jesus the Resurrection from the dead; and they laid hands on them, and placed them in custody until the next day. For it was already evening.

Many of those who heard the speech came to faith, and the number of men turned out [to be] about five thousand.

Now we see what Luke regards as a typical reaction on the part of the authorities: irritation and imprisonment, and another Lucan summary, to point the contrast.

Peter's third speech – the power of the Holy Spirit

5-31 It happened on the next day that the rulers were gathered together: the elders and the scribes in Jerusalem, and Annas the High Priest, and Caiaphas and John and Alexander, and whoever were of high priestly stock. And setting them in the middle, they enquired, 'By what power, or in what name, did you do this?'

Then Peter, filled with the Holy Spirit said to them, 'Rulers of the people and elders, if we today are under investigation because of a kindness done to a sick man, [and] by what means this man was saved, let it be known to all of you, and to the entire people of Israel, that [it was] in the name of Jesus Messiah the Nazarene whom you lot crucified, whom God raised from the dead, that is how this man stands before you, cured. This is the stone, the one despised by you, the builders, that became the cornerstone. And there is no other name wherein salvation lies; for there is no other name under heaven which is given among human beings in whom we must be saved.'

Seeing the confidence of Peter and John, and grasping that these people were illiterate and untrained, they marvelled; and they recognised them as having been with Jesus – and seeing the man standing with them, the one who had been healed, they had no answer to give. They ordered them to leave the Sanhedrin and conferred with each other, saying, 'What shall we do to these people? For what has happened through their agency is a sign well-known and evident to all those who dwell in Jerusalem; and we can't deny it. Instead, to prevent further distribution to the people, let's threaten them not to speak in this name any longer to anybody.'

They summoned them and instructed them absolutely not to utter nor to teach in the name of Jesus. In response, Peter and John said to them, 'Consider whether it is right before God to listen to you rather than to God. For as for us, we cannot *not* speak the things that we have seen and heard.'

They added further threats and released them; they had found no grounds for punishing them. This was because of the people, for they were all glorifying God after what had happened. For more than forty years old was the man on whom this sign of healing had happened.

When they had been released, they went to their own, and reported all the things that the chief priests and elders had said. When they heard [it], unanimously they lifted up their voice to God and said, 'Master, you who made the heaven and the earth and the sea, and all that is in them, the one who said by the Holy Spirit through the mouth of our father David your servant:

> "Why were the Gentiles arrogant,
> and peoples think vain thoughts?
> The kings of the earth have appeared,
> and the rulers gathered for a [common] purpose
> against the Lord and against his Messiah."

'For in truth, they gathered in this city against your holy Child, Jesus whom you anointed: Herod and Pontius Pilate, with the Gentiles and the peoples of Israel, to bring about whatever your hand and your counsel had predestined [should] happen. And now, Lord, look upon their threats, and grant to your slaves to speak your word with all confidence, when you stretch out your hand for healing and signs and portents to happen through the name of your holy Servant Jesus.'

As they made their intercession, the place was shaken in which they were gathered, and they were all filled with the Holy Spirit, and they began to speak the word of God with confidence.

Like Jesus, the apostles now get brought before the authorities. Like Elisabeth (Luke 1:41) and Jesus (Luke 4:14, 15, 18), Peter is filled with the Holy Spirit (compare Acts 2:4; 4:31), and will not retract by an inch. He quotes Psalm 118, just as Jesus had done at Luke 20:17.

Notice, too, the insistence on the 'name' of Jesus, which we shall meet frequently throughout Acts.

The astonishing confidence of these apostles, and their lack of education, and the fact that they had known Jesus, taken together count as evidence for their central claim, that Jesus was indeed raised from the dead.

The authorities' response is to attempt to silence them. The attempt is foredoomed, and the disciples' prayer dramatically confirmed by an earthquake, the equivalent of the 'fire and wind' of Pentecost.

Life in the early Church – 2

32-37 There was a single heart and soul in the group of believers. And not one of them would say that any of his possession was his own, but everything they had was in common.

With great power the apostles would give witness of the Resurrection of the Lord Jesus; and great grace was on all of them. For there was no one among them who was impoverished. For as many as were owners of lands or houses, they would sell [them] and bring the proceeds of what they had sold and they would lay [it] at the feet of the apostles; and distribution was made to each one according as anyone had need. Joseph who was surnamed Barnabas by the apostles, which when translated is 'Son of Comfort', a Levite, Cypriot by race, since he had a field, sold it, brought the money, and placed it at the feet of the apostles.

Another Lucan summary – a charming picture of the 'communism' of the early Church; though Luke knows perfectly well that it wasn't just as simple as this. See the dark story that follows.

Ananias and Sapphira: you can't cheat the Holy Spirit

5 ¹⁻¹¹ A certain man, Ananias by name, along with Sapphira his wife, sold a property, and misappropriated some of the purchase price, with the connivance of his wife, and bringing along a certain portion [of it] he laid it at the feet of his apostles. Peter said, 'Ananias, why has Satan filled your heart, that you should cheat the Holy Spirit and misappropriate part of the price of your land? [Was it not the case that] while it remained with you it remained, and that when it had been sold it was within your authority? Why did you put this business in your heart? It is not human beings whom you have cheated, but God.'

When Ananias heard these words, he fell down and breathed his last; and there came awe on all those who heard of it. The younger men wrapped him up and carried him out and buried him.

There was a delay of about three hours; and his wife came in, not knowing what had happened. Peter said to her, 'Tell me, was it for such-and-such a sum that you sold the field?' And she said, 'Yes, that was it.' Peter said to her, 'Why did you have a conspiracy to test the Spirit of the Lord? Look – the feet of those who buried your husband are at the door, and they will carry you out.' Straightaway she fell at his feet and breathed her last. The young men came in and found her dead, and carried her out and buried her by her husband. Great awe came upon the whole Church and on all who heard these things.

> It is hard to imagine that we are meant to take this particularly seriously. There are several touches of dark humour here that suggest that we would do best to read it as a playful depiction of the major theme of Acts, that you cannot impede the work of the Holy Spirit. The alternative would be to regard the story as a chilling warning against dishonesty. We have to say that this is a very difficult passage.

Life in the early Church – 3

12-16 Through the hands of the apostles, there were many signs and portents among the populace; and they were all together of one mind in Solomon's colonnade. None of the remainder [of the populace] dared to associate with them; but the people praised them. More than ever [the number of] those who believed in the Lord was increasing; [there were] crowds of men and of women. So they carried out the sick into the streets, and placed them on beds and mattresses, so that as Peter went [by], even [just] his shadow might overshadow one of them. And the group of cities in the vicinity of Jerusalem assembled, bringing sick people and those tormented by unclean spirits, who were all cured.

> Yet another Lucan summary. The new element here is that of healing. The apostles continue the work of Jesus in the Gospel. (See, for example, Luke 3:33, 38; 5:12-26, etc.). It is important not to get

too dispirited or too condemnatory about the present state of the Church. Rather we should recognise the unfailing action of the Holy Spirit, even today.

The irresistible work of the Spirit

17-42   The High Priest and all those who were with him rose up, the ones who are the sect of the Sadducees; they were filled with fanaticism, and they laid hands on the apostles and placed them in the Public Prison. But the angel of the Lord by night opened the gates of the gaol, and led them out, saying, 'Go, stand up and in the Temple speak to the people all the words of this life.'

They obeyed, and went into the Temple just before dawn, and began to teach.

[Meanwhile] the High Priest and his people arrived, and they summoned the Sanhedrin, and the whole Council of Elders of the sons of Israel, and sent to the guardhouse to have [them] brought. The minions arrived, but failed to find them there; they went back and reported, 'We found the prison securely locked, and the sentries in position at the gates; but when we opened up we found no one inside.' When they heard these words, the Captain of the Temple and the high priests were puzzled about them – what could this mean? Then someone arrived and reported to them, 'Look – the men whom you put in prison are standing in the Temple, teaching the people.' Then the captain went off with his minions and brought them along; but without violence – because they were afraid of the people. [They didn't want] to be stoned.

They brought them and put them in the Sanhedrin. And the High Priest interrogated them, 'Didn't we give you strict orders not to teach in this name? And look! You have filled Jerusalem with your teaching, and you want to bring this man's blood on *us*!' Peter responded (and the apostles) and said, 'We must obey God rather than human beings. The God of our ancestors raised Jesus, whom you had murdered by nailing him to the cross. This Jesus God elevated to his right hand as Prince and Saviour, to provide repentance for Israel, and forgiveness of sins. And we are witnesses of these things; and [so is] the Holy Spirit which God gave to those who obey him.'

When they heard, they were infuriated, and wanted to destroy them. But someone rose up in the Sanhedrin, a Pharisee called Gamaliel, a teacher of the Law, who was held in high regard by the whole people. He ordered [them] to put the men outside for a short time.

Then he said to them, 'Men of Israel, take care what you propose to do to these men. For before these present days, Theudas appeared, claiming to be somebody, and a number of men, something like four hundred, favoured him. He was assassinated; and all those under his command were dispersed. Then there arose Judas the Galilean, in the days of the census, and he got the people to follow him in rebellion. He too was destroyed, and all those under his command were scattered. And as for the present matter, I warn you, keep away from these people, and let them go. Because if this plan or this work is of human origin, it will be destroyed, but if its origin is divine, you will be unable to destroy them. Be careful that you do not turn out as God-fighters.'

They went along with his advice, and summoned the apostles. They flogged them, instructed them not to speak in the name of Jesus, and set them free. So they went their way rejoicing from the presence of the Sanhedrin, because they had been considered worthy to be dishonoured for the sake of the name, and all day long, in the Temple and at home, they never stopped teaching and gospelling the Messiah Jesus.

> The authorities' resistance is as unsuccessful as that of Pharaoh in the original Passover. The 'angel by night' is meant to make us recall Exodus 12:42, and the irrational opposition of the authorities is meant to deprive us of all sympathy for them.
>
> The apostles cannot be prevented from their task of being 'witnesses', whatever the authorities do. Gamaliel has seen the problem clearly.

Racial tensions in the early Church

6[1-6] In these days, as the disciples multiplied, there arose a complaint, Hellenists against Hebrews, because their widows were being neglected in the daily distribution. The Twelve summoned the group of disciples and said, 'It is not desirable for us to abandon the word of God to wait at tables. Instead, brothers [and sisters], select seven men of attested merit from among you, full of the Spirit and of wisdom, whom we shall appoint; as for us, we shall devote ourselves to prayer and the ministry of the word.'

This speech was pleasing to the whole group, and they chose: Stephen, a man full of faith and the Holy Spirit, and Philip and Prochorus and Nicanor and Timon and Parmenas and Nicolaus, a proselyte of Antioch, whom they set before the apostles. They prayed over them, and laid hands on them.

> Now there arises a spot of racial tension, Greek-speakers against speakers of Aramaic. Luke gives 'the Twelve' a central role; it is they, for example, who find a solution, in terms of the 'Seven' (another significant number). The Seven, like Peter, Elisabeth and Jesus, are to be 'full of the Spirit', and are to be appointed by the 'Twelve' on the recommendation of their fellow Greek-speakers. The seven who are chosen all have impeccably Greek names; but it is striking that the only two who are ever mentioned again, Stephen and Philip, turn out to be preachers, rather than officials at the soup-kitchen.

Life in the early Church – 4

[7] The word of God increased, the number of disciples in Jerusalem multiplied very greatly; and a great crowd of priests came under obedience to the faith.

> Another Lucan summary (note the strange, but to Luke important, title for the Church: 'the word of God') introduces the crisis over Stephen, one of the 'Seven'. He is accused, as Paul will be later, of blaspheming Moses and God; like Jesus (in Mark 14:56, 57, but not in Luke's Gospel) he is accused by false witnesses.

Stephen's success and death; another 'tongue of fire'

6⁸-**7**⁵³ Now Stephen, full of grace and power, was performing portents and great signs among the populace. And some people rose up from the synagogue that was called 'Libertines' – Cyreneans and Alexandrians and of those from Cilicia and Asia, arguing with Stephen. They did not have the resources to resist the wisdom and the Spirit with which he spoke. Then they secretly instigated men, who said, 'We heard him saying blasphemous things against Moses and God.' They aroused the people and the elders and the scribes, and they approached and dragged him off and took him to the Sanhedrin. Then they set up false witnesses, who said, 'This man is endlessly speaking words against this Holy Place and against the Torah. For we heard him saying that this Jesus the Nazarene will destroy this place and will change the customs that Moses handed down to us.'

They all looked intently at him, all those who were sitting in the Sanhedrin; and they saw his face, just like the face of an angel.

The High Priest said, 'Is this so?' But he said, 'Men, brothers and fathers, listen. The God of glory appeared to our ancestor Abraham when he was in Mesopotamia, before he lived in Haran, and said to him, "Come out from your country and from your kinsfolk, and come to the country that I shall show you." Then coming out of the land of the Chaldees, he went to make his home in Haran. And from there, after the death of his father, he changed his home to this country, in which you now have your home. And he did not give them an inheritance in it, nor even a foot of ground; and he promised 'to give him it for a possession, and to his descendants after him', though he had no child. This is how God spoke: "Your descendants shall be homeless in a country that belongs to others. And they shall enslave them and mistreat them for four hundred years. And the nation that enslaves them I shall judge," said God, "and after this they shall come out and worship me in this place." And he gave Abraham a covenant of circumcision; and so he fathered Isaac, and circumcised him on the eighth day: and Isaac [did the same for] Jacob, and Jacob [for] the Twelve Patriarchs.

'The patriarchs were jealous of Joseph; and they sold him into Egypt. And God was with him, and rescued him from all his tribulations, and gave him grace and wisdom before Pharaoh, King of Egypt, and he appointed him ruler over Egypt and over his entire house. And there came a famine over all of Egypt and Canaan, and great tribulation; and our ancestors could not find fodder, but Jacob heard that there was food in Egypt, and sent our ancestors on reconnaissance. And on the second [mission] Joseph was made known again to his brothers; and Joseph's family became known to Pharaoh. And Joseph sent and summoned Jacob his father, and all his kinsfolk, about seventy-five souls; and Jacob went down to Egypt, and he and our ancestors died. And they were brought back to Shechem, and placed in the tomb that Abraham had bought, for the price of silver, from the children of Emmor at Shechem. As the time of the promise drew near which God had made to Abraham, the people grew and multiplied in Egypt, until "there arose another king over Egypt, who did not know Joseph". This [new king] did some sharp practice on our race, and mistreated our ancestors, to have their infants exposed so that they [should] not be kept alive.

'At that point, Moses was born, and he was divinely beautiful. He was nurtured for three months in his father's house; but when he was put out, the daughter of Pharaoh rescued him, and brought him up as a son for herself. And Moses was educated in all the culture of the Egyptians, and he was powerful in his words and deeds. But when his forty-year period was done, [the idea] arose in his heart to see his brothers, the sons of Israel. And seeing someone being maltreated, he came to their aid, and wrought vengeance for the one who was being oppressed, [by] striking the Egyptian. He thought that his brethren understood that God was giving them salvation through his hand; but they did not understand. On the next day, he turned up as they were fighting, and tried to reconcile them [to bring them] to peace, saying, "Men, you are brothers! Why are you maltreating each other?" But the one who was maltreating his neighbour repudiated him, saying, "Who appointed you ruler and judge over us? Do you want to murder me, the way you murdered the Egyptian yesterday?"

'Moses fled at this remark, and ended up homeless in the land of Midian, where he produced two sons. And when forty years were fulfilled, there appeared to him in the desert of Mount Sinai an angel, in [the] flaming fire of a thorn bush. Moses marvelled at the vision when he saw it; when he approached to look at it, the Lord's voice came, "I am the God of your ancestors, the God of Abraham and Isaac and Jacob."

'And Moses was all atremble and did not dare to look. And the Lord said to him, "Untie the sandal [from] your feet; for the place on which you stand is holy ground. Seeing I have seen the maltreatment of my people in Egypt, and I have heard their groan; and I have come down to rescue them. And now, come, I am sending you to Egypt."

'This Moses, whom they denied, saying, "Who appointed you as ruler and judge?" – this Moses God sent as Ruler and Redeemer, [by] the hand of [the] angel who appeared to him in the bush. This [was the one who] led them out, performing portents and signs in the land of Egypt, and in the Red Sea, and in the desert for forty years. This is the Moses who said to the sons of Israel, "God will raise up a prophet for you from among your brothers, [a prophet] like me." This [Moses] is the one who was in the Assembly in the desert, with the angel who spoke with him on Mount Sinai (and with our ancestors), [Moses] who accepted to give us living words. [This was the Moses] to whom our ancestors were reluctant to become subject; instead, they rejected him, and in their hearts turned [back] to Egypt, telling Aaron, "Make gods for us who go before us. For this Moses, who led us out of the country of Egypt, we do not know what has happened to him."

'And they made a calf in those days, and brought up sacrifice to the idol; and they rejoiced at the work of their hands. And God turned, and handed them over to worship Heaven's Army, as it is written in the scroll of the prophets:

> "Did you not offer me sacrificial offerings,
>> for forty years in the desert, House of Israel?
> And you took along the tent of Moloch
> and the constellation of your god Rompha,
>> the statues which you had made to worship them;
> and I shall move your home beyond Babylon."

'The tent of witness was for our ancestors in the desert, and the One who spoke to Moses had commanded, to make it according to the model which he had seen. [That was] what our ancestors in their turn brought in, with Joshua, when they restrained the Gentiles, whom God expelled before the face of our ancestors . . . right down to the days of David, who found grace before God, and asked to find a dwelling for the house of Jacob. But Solomon built a house for it nevertheless; the

Most High does not make his home in [buildings] made by hand. As the prophet says:

"The heaven is my throne
and the earth is the footstool of my feet.
What kind of a home will you build for me, says the Lord,
or what is the place of my rest?
Is it not [that] my hand made all these things?"

'You stiff-necked people, and uncircumcised of heart and ears, you people always resist the Holy Spirit, as your ancestors so also you. Which of the prophets did your ancestors not persecute? And they killed those who foretold the coming of the Just One, whose betrayers and murderers you people became, you who received the Torah by the directions of angels, and failed to keep it.'

Stephen's defence consists in a rereading of the nation's history, in terms largely of the way God's word has invited Abraham, Joseph and Moses to go on unexpected and uncomfortable journeys. It also recalls to the listeners the occasional infidelities of the people. The way Stephen tells the story leaves a huge gap from the entry into the Promised Land to the reigns of David and Solomon, where the story abruptly ends. This speech has far more 'biblical echoes' than anything Peter has said so far, and it makes two points, as far as Acts is concerned. First, the word of God is for ever on the move; second, there is a history of resistance to that word. These two furnish the premises of a conclusion that is only partly spelt out: the Temple is not definitively God's dwelling place. The reader should keep an eye on this conclusion as the story of Acts develops.

The quotation about 'sacrificial offerings' is from Amos 5:25-27; 'the heaven is my throne . . .' is Isaiah 66:1, 2.

There is no mealy-mouthed diplomacy in Stephen's speech.

Stephen dies; Saul tries to destroy the Church

7 ⁵⁴–8 ³   When they heard this, they were infuriated in their hearts, and they gnashed their teeth at him. But being full of the Holy Spirit, looking intently at heaven, he beheld the glory of God, and Jesus standing at the right hand of God and he said, 'Look – I see the heavens opening, and the Son of Man standing on the right hand of God.' But they shouted with a loud cry and stopped their ears, and rushed as one man against him, and they threw him out of the city and stoned him.

And the witnesses stored their garments at the feet of a young man called Saul. They stoned Stephen, who was making invocation and saying, 'Jesus, Lord, do not hold this sin against them.' Saying this, he fell asleep.

And Saul agreed with his murder.

On that day a great persecution took place against the Church in Jerusalem; and they were all scattered up and down the country of Judaea and of Samaria. And some pious men buried Stephen and made loud lamentation over him.

Meanwhile Saul was trying to destroy the Church, going up and down the houses. He dragged [away] both men and women and handed them over to imprisonment.

This episode, linking the scattering of the early Church to the death of Stephen, and the death of Stephen to the death of Jesus, at the same time evokes the programme outlined in 1:8: 'You will be my witnesses in Jerusalem and in the whole of Judaea and Samaria.' Almost the central message of Acts is that you cannot prevent the work of the Holy Spirit. We notice, however, that the apostles are not 'scattered': they remain in Jerusalem, to give the infant Church the stability that it needs. At the same time the Saul theme is played, quietly, reminding us once again that the Holy Spirit is not to be frustrated.

Life in the early Church – 5

4-8 So those who were scattered went about gospelling the word. Philip [for example] went down to a city of Samaria and preached the Messiah to them. The crowds unanimously paid attention to what Philip said when they heard and saw the things that he did. For many of those who had unclean spirits came out shouting in a loud voice, and many who were lame and paralysed were cured. And there was much joy in that city.

> This is almost a 'Lucan summary', creating atmosphere, but using Philip (who we thought was waiting at table!) as a kind of example of the early preaching and its effects. Note that Luke is quite vague about where it happened. One oddity here is that the reader feels that it ought to be the unclean spirits, rather than their owners, who 'came out shouting in a loud voice'; but that is not what the Greek says. Some scholars feel that this and other similar looseness of expression suggest that Acts of the Apostles was not finally revised.
>
> 'Joy' for Luke is a mark of the presence of the Holy Spirit.

Simon the magician is impressed by the power of the Holy Spirit

9-13 A man called Simon, who had practised magic [or: who was a foremost practitioner of magic], was already in the city. He amazed the race of Samaritans, alleging that he was someone special; and they all paid attention to him, from the least to the greatest, saying, 'This man is the power of God which is called Great.'

They paid attention to him because he had amazed them for quite a time with [his] magic tricks. But when they came to believe Philip, who was gospelling them about the kingdom of God and the name of Jesus Messiah, they started to get baptised, both men and women. Simon also came to believe, got baptised, and attached himself to Philip, because he saw signs and great miracles happening – he was amazed.

> The reader notices that the word 'amazed' is now used for the third time. Like 'joy' it is evidently an important idea for Luke, indicating the presence of the Holy Spirit. We also observe the artistry with which Luke has set up the dénouement of the Simon story, which now continues.

Simon the magician surrenders to the Holy Spirit

14-25 Now when the apostles in Jerusalem heard that Samaria had received the word of God, they sent Peter and John to them. These [two] came down and prayed for them that they might receive the Holy Spirit. For [the Spirit] had not yet fallen on any of them; but they were only baptised in the name of the Lord Jesus. Then they laid hands on them, and they received the Holy Spirit.

Simon saw that it was through the laying on of hands by the apostles that the Spirit was given, and he offered them money, saying, 'Give me also this power, so that anyone I lay hands on may receive the Holy Spirit.' Peter said to him, 'May your cash and you go to hell, because you thought you could secure the gift of God with money. You have no part or share in this matter, for your heart is not straight before God. So repent from this vice of yours, and ask the Lord to see if the intention of your heart will be forgiven you. For I see that you are in bitter gall, and the chains of unrighteousness.' Simon answered, '[Please will] you turn to the Lord in prayer for me, so that nothing may come upon me of the things that you have seen.'

So they bore witness and spoke the word of the Lord. Then they returned to Jerusalem, and they gospelled many villages of the Samaritans.

> So this part of the story ends; notice how the gospel is unflinchingly preached, despite internal and external problems, partly thanks to the central group of apostles (of whom, evidently, Peter is not the leader, since 'the apostles' send him and John into Samaria). Now Philip's story continues, the gospel spreading ever wider. This time it is to Africa that it goes – but see also how this wave of evangelisation has its roots in the racial problems that originally caused the appointment of the deacons, nearly three chapters ago.

The gospel reaches Africa

26-40 The angel of the Lord spoke to Philip, saying, 'Rise up and go southwards, on to the road that goes down from Jerusalem to Gaza.' (This is desert.) He arose and went. And look! An Ethiopian man, a eunuch, a man of influence with Candace, Queen of the Ethiopians (he was in charge of her entire treasury), who had come with the intention of worshipping in Jerusalem, was now returning. He was seated in his chariot and reading the prophet Isaiah. The Spirit told Philip, 'Approach and hang on to the chariot.' Philip ran up, and heard him reciting Isaiah the prophet and said, 'Do you know what you are reading?' He said, 'But how can I, unless someone guide me?' He invited Philip to get up and sit with him. The portion of Scripture he was reading was this:

'Like a sheep to the slaughter he was led.
And like a lamb that is dumb before the one who shears him,
so he does not open his mouth.
In his humiliation his verdict was denied him.
Who will describe his generation?
Because his life is taken from the earth.'

The eunuch responded and said to Philip, 'This is my question to you: about whom does the prophet say this? About himself or about some other?' Philip opened his mouth, and starting from this Scripture, he gave him the gospel of Jesus. As they journeyed on the way, they came to some water, and the eunuch said, 'Look! Water! What stops me from being baptised?'

And he gave orders for the chariot to stop, and they both went down into the water, Philip and the eunuch, and he baptised him. And when they came up out of the water, the Spirit of the Lord snatched up Philip, and the eunuch did not see him any more, for he was going on his way, rejoicing. Meanwhile Philip was found at Azotus, and he went through and gospelled all the cities until he reached Caesarea.

> Another extraordinary story, giving us a flavour of what is really going on in Acts. Four times the word for 'journeying' is used in the Greek (8:26, 27, 36, 39), including the striking phrase 'as they journeyed on the way' (though it was impossible so to translate them all into English). It is a little glimpse of how the gospel spreads all over the world (Azotus, Caesarea, even Africa). It continues the theme of the Holy Spirit triumphing over all obstacles, in particular the storyline that started with the racial tensions between Greek- and Hebrew-speakers. That theme will now open out into the Christian life and ministry of one whom at present we know only as Saul. He will come to dominate the second half of Acts.
>
> Finally, it is worth noting that we never hear anything more of the eunuch, and not much of Philip; they have served the narrator's purpose.
>
> The quotation from Isaiah 53 is a familiar one in the New Testament – but this is one of the rare cases where it is explicitly linked to Jesus.

Saul encounters Jesus

9 1-19a Meanwhile, Saul was still breathing murderous threats against the Lord's disciples. He approached the High Priest and asked him for letters to Damascus, for the synagogues, so that if he should find any who were of The Way (both men and women) he might handcuff them and take them to Jerusalem.

Now as he journeyed, he happened to be drawing near to Damascus. Suddenly a bright light from heaven shone about him. Falling on to the ground, he heard a voice saying to him, 'Saoul, Saoul, why are you persecuting me?' He said, 'Who are you, Lord?' He [said], 'I am Jesus, whom you are persecuting. [Some manuscripts here add: 'It is hard for you to kick against the goad.' And in fear and trembling he said, 'Lord, what do you want me to do?' But the Lord said to him, ' . . .] But up you get, and go into the city, and it will be told you what you must do.' The men who were journeying with him stood speechless. They had heard the voice, but saw nobody. Saul arose from the ground; and when he opened his eyes he could see nothing. Taking him by the hand they led him into Damascus; and he was three days without seeing – and he neither ate nor drank.

Now there was a disciple in Damascus named Ananias, and the Lord said to him in a vision, 'Ananias.' He [said], 'Here I am, Lord.' The Lord [said] to him, 'Arise and go to the street called Straight, and look in Judas's house for a man of Tarsus called Saul. Look! He is at prayer, and he has seen in a vision a man called Ananias coming in and laying hands on him, so that he may see.' Ananias replied, 'Lord – I have heard from many people about this man, how much evil he has done to the saints in Jerusalem. And here he has a commission from the high priests to handcuff everyone who calls on your name.' The Lord said to him, 'Go, because this one is a chosen vessel to carry my name before Gentiles and kings and children of Israel. For I shall show him how much he must suffer for the sake of my name.' Ananias went off and entered the house and laid hands on him and said, 'Brother Saoul, the Lord has sent me, Jesus, who appeared to you on the way by which you came, so that you may see again and be filled with the Holy Spirit.' And immediately there fell from his eyes [something] like fish-scales, and he saw again. He arose and was baptised; he took food and regained his strength.

This is an excellent story, related with elegant economy by Luke, who regards it as so important that he tells it twice more, putting it as a first person narrative on Paul's lips, first to Jews (in Chapter 22), and then to distinguished Gentiles (Chapter 26). Notice the theme of journeying, the importance of visions, and yet Luke's restraint in reporting them. The reversal, from arresting officer to 'Brother Saul', that Paul experiences is characteristic of Luke; the identity of Jesus and the Church is something that becomes very important in Paul's later writings. The 'name' is a very important idea in Acts; we have seen it quite often already. Some people have argued for the authenticity of this episode from the fact that Saul's name is preserved in its Semitic form ('Saoul'). Above all, notice how Jesus dominates the scene, and how right Paul is to address him as 'Lord.'

This is the first explicit mention in Acts of Paul's mission to the Gentiles, and we should note it with care. We note also that it is Ananias to whom the message is entrusted. We may also admire Ananias's courage in approaching the rather alarming person of Saul.

Saul begins his mission: rejection on all sides

19b-30 He was with the disciples in Damascus for some days, and immediately he began to preach Jesus in the synagogues, saying, 'This man is [the] Son of God.' All those who heard him were amazed, and started saying, 'Isn't this the one who at Jerusalem ravaged those who call upon this name, and came here on purpose to handcuff them and take them to the high priests?' Saul, however, was all the more empowered, and confused the Jews who lived in Damascus, demonstrating that 'He [Jesus] is the Messiah'.

When a fair number of days were fulfilled, the Jews plotted to murder him. Saul knew their plot. They watched the gates day and night, in order to murder him. The disciples, however, took him by night; they let him down through the wall, winching him down in a hamper.

When he got to Jerusalem he attempted to join the disciples – and they were all afraid of him. They didn't believe that he was a disciple. Barnabas, however, took hold of him, led him to the apostles, and explained to them how he had seen the Lord on the way, and that he had spoken to him, and how he had spoken boldly in Jesus' name in Damascus. And he was with them, going in and out of Jerusalem, and speaking boldly in the Lord's name. And he was also arguing with the Greek-speakers – but they attempted to murder him. The brethren however knew about it, and led him down to Caesarea – and they sent him off to Tarsus.

So Luke gets Saul off-stage for the moment; but it is a significant moment, continuing the remarkable story of the character who will dominate most of the rest of the book. This second part of the story of his encounter with Jesus contains a number of themes that are important in Acts: preaching that Jesus is Messiah, the power given to evangelists, preaching first to synagogues, the threat of violence, and the solidarity of the Church.

Paul encounters suspicion from his fellow Christians and attempted murder on the part of his fellow Jews.

Life in the early Church – 6

31 And so the Church, through the whole of Judaea and Galilee and Samaria, was at peace. It was building up, and journeying in the fear of the Lord; and it was filled with the comfort of the Holy Spirit.

This is another 'Lucan summary'; see how the author creates a mood, and also reminds us of the command given in 1:8 about being 'my witnesses in Jerusalem and in all Judaea and Samaria'. As before, the mood he creates is slightly at odds with reality: we have just seen hints of internal and external problems in the Church. Above all, though, Luke insists on the activity of the Holy Spirit.

The 'summary' also provides a cushion, separating Paul's narrative from a story where the reader's attention is more on Peter.

Peter heals Aeneas and Tabitha

32-43 It happened that as Peter went through everywhere he also went down to the saints who dwell at Lydda. There he found a man called Aeneas, who for eight years had been lying on a stretcher; he was paralysed. And Peter said, 'Aeneas, Jesus Messiah heals you. Arise and make your own bed.' Immediately he arose. All those who lived in Lydda and Sharon knew about it; and they turned to the Lord.

In Joppa there was a lady-disciple named Tabitha. Translated, the name means 'Gazelle'. She was full of good works and of acts of charity that she performed. It happened in those days that she fell sick and died. They washed her [corpse] and put her in an upstairs room. Since Lydda was near Joppa, the disciples, hearing that Peter was there, sent two men to him, asking, 'Don't delay to come across to us.'

Peter arose and went with them. When he arrived they took him up to the upstairs room; and all the widows came to him, weeping and showing [him] tunics and garments that 'Gazelle' had made when she was with them. Peter flung everybody out, and fell on his knees and prayed; and he turned to the body and said, 'Tabitha, arise.' She opened her eyes, and seeing Peter, sat up. He gave her [his] hand and raised her up. Calling the saints and the widows he gave her [to them] alive. It became known through the whole of Joppa; and many believed in the Lord. It happened that for a good few days he stayed in Joppa, with Simon the Tanner.

These two 'healing stories', the first of them done explicitly in Jesus' name, the second echoing the story of Jairus's daughter in Luke 8 and Mark 5, serve to focus the reader on Peter as precisely continuing the mission of Jesus. That is what Acts is about. Now comes a very important moment, which we might call 'the conversion of Peter'.

The conversion of Peter to the Gentile mission

10 [1-48] There was a man in Caesarea, Cornelius by name, a centurion of the 'Italian' cohort. He, along with his entire household, was pious and a God-fearer, doing many acts of charity to the people, and praying constantly to God. At about the ninth hour he saw clearly in a vision a messenger of God coming to him and addressing him, 'Cornelius.'

He looked intently at him, and, becoming fearful, said, 'What is it, Lord?' He said to him, 'Your prayers and your acts of charity have ascended as a memorial offering before God. Now – send some men to Joppa, and summon one Simon, who has the surname Rock. He is staying as a guest with a certain Simon the Tanner, who has a house alongside the sea.'

When the messenger who had spoken to him had departed, [Cornelius] summoned two of the house slaves, and a devout soldier from among those who were attached to him; he explained everything to them, and sent them off to Joppa. On the next day, as they were en route, and approaching the city, Peter went up to the roof to pray, at about the sixth hour. He was hungry, and he wanted to eat. And as they were preparing [the meal] a trance came over him, and he sees heavens opening, and a container coming down, like a large linen cloth with four corners being let down on the earth. In this container there were all the animals and creepy-crawlies of the earth, and the birds of the sky. A voice came to him, 'Arise, Peter, kill and eat.' But Peter said, 'No way, Lord; I have *never* eaten anything profane or unclean.' [The] voice [spoke] to him again, a second time, 'What God has made clean, you are not to call profane.' This happened three times; and the container was immediately taken up to heaven. As Peter was scratching his head [about] what the vision might [mean], look! The men who had been sent by Cornelius [were] enquiring for Simon's house, and stood at the gate, and they called and enquired, 'Is Simon with the surname "Rock" here?' and as Peter reflected about the vision, the Spirit said, 'Look! Three men who are looking for you. Up you get now, go down, and travel with them. Have no doubt that it is I who have sent them.' Peter went down to the men and said, 'Look! I am the one whom you seek. What is the reason for your being here?' They said, 'Centurion Cornelius, a good man and a God-fearer, who is of good reputation among the whole nation of the Jews, was directed by a holy messenger to send for you [to come] to his house, and [for him] to hear words from you.' So he invited them in and entertained them.

The next day he arose and went out with them; and some of the Joppa Christians went with him. The next day he entered Caesarea. Cornelius was expecting them; he had invited his kinsfolk and his close friends. When Peter arrived Cornelius met him; he fell at his feet and worshipped him. Peter, however, raised him up, saying, 'Up you get – I am also a human being [just like you].' And chatting with him he went in, and found that many people had come together. He said to them, 'You people know that it is unlawful for a Jewish man to associate with or approach someone of another nation. Yet God has taught even me not to call anyone profane or unclean. So when I was sent for, I came without refusing. Therefore may I ask you on what grounds you sent for me?' And Cornelius said,

'Four days ago to this hour I was praying the prayers of the ninth hour in my house. And look! A man stood before me in resplendent clothing and says, "Cornelius – your prayer has been heard, and your acts of charity remembered before God. So send to Joppa, and summon Simon who is surnamed Peter. He is a guest of Simon Tanner, by the sea." So immediately I sent for you; and you have done a lovely thing in coming. So now all of us are present, before God, to hear everything that the Lord has enjoined on you.'

Peter opened his mouth and said, 'In truth I recognise that God is not one to show partiality – in every nation, those who reverence God and do justice are acceptable to God. The message which he sent to the children of Israel, gospelling peace through Jesus Messiah (he is the Lord of all) – you people know the thing that happened throughout the whole of Judaea, beginning from Galilee, after the baptism which John proclaimed, Jesus of Nazareth, how God anointed him with the Holy Spirit and power, who went about doing good, and healing all those who were tyrannised by the devil, because God was with him. We are witnesses of everything that he did, both in the area of the Judaeans, and in Jerusalem [itself]. He is the one whom they murdered, by nailing to a tree. He is the one whom God raised on the third day, and granted to him [the gift] of becoming visible, not to all the people, but to the witnesses whom God had appointed beforehand, that is us. We are the ones who ate and drank with him after he was raised from the dead. And he instructed us to proclaim to the people, and to give testimony that this is the one appointed by God as judge of [the] living and [the] dead. He is the one to whom all the prophets bear witness, for everyone who believes in him to receive forgiveness of sins through his name.'

While Peter was still uttering these words, the Holy Spirit fell upon all those who heard the word. And those of the Circumcision Party who were believers, who had come with Peter, were astounded that even on the Gentiles the gift of the Holy Spirit could fall. For they heard them speaking in tongues and extolling God's greatness. Then Peter responded, 'Surely no one can refuse water for these people to be baptised? They have received the Holy Spirit just as we did.' And he gave orders for them to be baptised in the name of Jesus Messiah.

Then they asked him to remain for some days.

As once before, Luke seems to be emphasising the awkwardness of Peter as a speaker. The first sentence of the major speech is hardly a sentence at all, and it is impossible to find one's way through it. The last sentence of the same speech has a very awkward order. We should again consider the possibility that Luke is trying to catch Peter's awkward diction (or a style of speaking appropriate to the character). Other Lucan touches include the 'fore' idea hidden in 'appointed be*fore*hand' and 'speaking in tongues and extolling God's greatness', which remind us of Pentecost and Mary's Magnificat.

This episode is one of immense importance in the Church's history. The question of whether or not non-Jews could be admitted was a fearsomely difficult one, and might have destroyed the Church at its very beginning. We could perhaps call this 'Peter's conversion'; and like Saul's 'conversion' Luke regards it as of sufficient importance to tell it again, in Chapter 11. The issue is still painfully alive in Chapter 15 (the 'Council of Jerusalem'). Since the beginning of his

Gospel, Luke has been preparing us for the admission of the Gentiles – see Luke 2:32; 24:47; Acts 1:8; 9:15, and it seems entirely natural to us. We should never forget, however, that this was a very neuralgic issue.

The Holy Spirit here enables Peter to face and overcome his own prejudices, and to take a brave step that was going to land him and the Church in hot water.

Peter is challenged by the Church; his defence

11 ¹⁻¹⁸ The apostles and the brethren who were throughout Judaea heard that the Gentiles had received the word of God. And when Peter went up to Jerusalem, the people of the Circumcision took issue with him, saying, 'You went into [the houses of] men with foreskins – and you ate with them!' Peter started up and explained it to them point by point.

'I was in the city of Joppa, and in a trance I saw a vision, a container coming down, like a big sheet with four corners being let down from heaven – and it came up to me. As I gazed intently at it, I contemplated it and saw the four-footed animals of the earth, and the wild beasts and the creepy-crawlies and the birds of heaven. I also heard a voice saying to me, "Arise, Peter, kill and eat." And I said, "No way, Lord, because profane or unclean [food] has never entered my mouth." The voice replied a second time from heaven, "What God has made clean you are not to call profane!" This happened as many as three times, and everything was pulled up to heaven again. And look! Straightaway three men approached the house where we were. They had been sent to me from Caesarea. The Spirit told me to go with them without argument. These six fellow Christians came with me, and we entered the man's house. He [then] reported to us how he had seen the messenger standing in his house and saying, "Send to Joppa and summon Simon who has the surname Peter, who will speak words to you by which you and your entire household will be saved." As I began to speak, the Holy Spirit fell on them, just as [it had] on us at [the] beginning; and I remembered the Lord's word, how he had said, "John baptised with water, but you people will be baptised by the Holy Spirit." So if God has given them the identical gift that he gave to us who believe in the Lord Jesus Messiah, who was I to thwart God?'

When they heard this they were silent, and they glorified God, saying, 'Indeed God has given the Gentiles the repentance that leads to life.'

This is such an important moment that Luke reports it twice, in third and first persons; or three times, if you include what Peter says in Cornelius's house, more if you include his speech in Chapter 15 to the 'Council of Jerusalem'. The opening lines, detailing the complaint of the 'Circumcision Party', sound like the beating of a menacing drum. However, what happened at Cornelius's house and its aftermath is a classic instance of the work of the Holy Spirit in Acts, effortlessly surmounting all obstacles, especially the major problem of the admission of non-Jews into the Church. When Luke tells us that Peter reported the circumstances 'point by point' that is high praise – for that was how the evangelist described his own aim at the beginning of the two-volume work.

It may console us in our era, when Christianity is still divided, to notice that the intervention of the Holy Spirit does not automatically solve all problems. Notice how the gospel is restricted to 'Jews only', at least initially, in the episode that follows.

Continuing aftershocks from the death of Stephen; the gospel is preached to the Gentiles

19-26 So those who had been scattered as a result of the oppression that happened in connection with Stephen came through as far as Phoenicia and Cyprus and Antioch, speaking the word to nobody other than Jews. Some of them were men of Cyprus and Cyrene, who came to Antioch, gospelling the Lord Jesus to the Greek-speakers. The Lord's hand was with them, and great was the number that believed and turned to the Lord. The report about them came to the ears of the Church in Jerusalem, and they sent Barnabas to go through as far as Antioch. He came, and saw God's grace; he rejoiced and encouraged them all to remain true to the Lord with devotion of heart, because he was a good man, and full of the Holy Spirit and of faith. And a fair crowd was added to the Lord. He came out to Tarsus to look for Saul; and when he found him he took him to Antioch. For a whole year they gathered with the Church and taught [them]. Calling disciples 'Christians' [or 'Messianists'] first happened in Antioch.

> In charting the move away from Judaism, Luke plays on us his favourite 'three-card trick', distracting our gaze to 'Phoenicia', 'Cyprus' and even 'Cyrene' in Africa, when all the time his interest is only in Antioch. We have seen this device of his before, and will meet it again. Now the gospel moves gently away from 'Jews only' to 'Greek-speakers' and includes all those who could call Jesus 'Messiah'. Luke has effortlessly linked the stories of Peter and Saul by means of Barnabas, who is an accredited witness because he is 'full of the Holy Spirit', like Elisabeth, Jesus, Peter, and Stephen before him.

The 'collection' for Christians in Jerusalem

27-30 In those days, prophets came down from Jerusalem to Antioch. One of them, called Agabus, arose and foretold through the Spirit that there would be a great famine over the whole inhabited world. This happened under Claudius. Each of the disciples, according to their prosperity, determined to send to their fellow Christians who lived in Jerusalem. They did this and sent [it] to the elders, through the agency of Barnabas and Saul.

> The three-card trick again, perhaps: Barnabas comes first, but it is Saul in whom Luke will soon start to show primary interest. Jerusalem is still very important in Luke's understanding of the Church, as this episode indicates: prophets come from there, and in return 'food parcels' are sent back. For Luke this has the happy effect of bringing Barnabas and Saul together, and of getting Saul to Jerusalem. With his reference to an event that took place in Claudius's reign, Luke also reminds 'Theophilus' that this Christian story takes place in the real Roman Empire.

Peter imprisoned and released

12 ¹⁻¹⁹ At just that moment King Herod laid hands on some people from the Church to maltreat them. He had James, John's brother, put to death with a sword. Seeing that the Jews approved of [this step], he proceeded to have Peter arrested (it was the days of Unleavened Bread). He took him into custody, and handed him over to four detachments of soldiers to guard him. [Herod's] intention was to bring him before the people, after the Passover. So Peter was under guard in the gaol; and prayer for him was eagerly going up to God from the Church.

When Herod was just on the point of bringing him forward, on that very night, Peter was sleeping between two soldiers, immobilised with two sets of handcuffs; and there were guards before the door keeping an eye on his cell. And look! The Lord's messenger approached; and a light shone in the building. Striking Peter's side, he aroused him, saying, 'Quick! Up you get.' And the handcuffs fell off his hands, and the messenger said to him, 'Get dressed and put on your sandals.' And he did so. And he says to him, 'Put on your cloak and follow me.' And he went out and followed; and he had no idea that what the messenger was doing was the real thing – he thought he was seeing a vision! But they went through the first guard, and through the second, and they came to the iron gate that gave on to the city, which opened for them of its own accord. They emerged and went one street further on; and immediately the messenger left him. Peter came to himself and said, 'Now I know for sure that the Lord has sent his messenger, and has rescued me from the power of Herod, and from all that the people of the Jews expected.'

When he realised [this] he went to the house of Mary, John's mother (he was the one who was surnamed 'Mark'), where there were a good number gathered together in prayer. When he knocked on the door of the gatehouse a little slave girl approached to answer. Her name was Rhoda; and when she recognised Peter's voice, in her joy she didn't open the door, but ran and announced that Peter was standing at the gate! They said to her, 'You're crazy!' But she insisted that it was so, and they said, 'It's his angel.'

Meanwhile Peter carried on knocking. They opened and saw [that it was] him, and were astounded. He motioned to them with his hand to be silent, and reported how the Lord had led him out of prison, and said, 'Report this to James and the brethren.' And he went out and travelled to another place.

When day broke, there was considerable consternation among the soldiers: what had happened to Peter? Herod [initiated a] search for him, and, failing to find him, interrogated the guards, and ordered them to be led away. And he went down from Judaea to Caesarea and spent time there.

> This is a remarkable story: a breathless adventure at its beginning, with some high comedy over the slave girl relieving the tension halfway through (and the reader will remember the last time that Luke had Peter and a slave girl together, at Luke 22:56), and, finally, a calm ending. 'Herod' is Herod Agrippa, grandson of Herod the Great, and he died in AD 44. By the end of the story, Herod, who had been 'on a roll' at the beginning, with one vote-catching execution behind him, and another in prospect, has been easily defeated; and while Peter is moving freely about the place, Herod has to make an undignified departure to Caesarea. Luke is quietly showing us how the Holy Spirit works. See also how skilfully Luke has linked the

start of this episode with the preceding story, which brought together the Christians of Antioch and Jerusalem. Notice, too, some echoes of the death of Jesus, with the reference to Passover, always a tricky time in Jerusalem; and presumably this is now one year after Jesus died, so the memory will have been fresh and expectations high. Another echo is of the light that shone round those shepherds in Luke's second chapter. The evangelist keeps all kinds of threads together.

The death of Herod

20-23 He was very angry with the people of Tyre and Sidon. They came to him as a body; they had persuaded Blastus, who was Gentleman of the Royal Bedchamber, and sued for peace, because their country supported itself [by importing grain] from the King's country. On the appointed day, Herod, arranged in [his] royal finery, and sitting on the rostrum, addressed them publicly. The people cried out, 'The voice of God, not a human being.' Straightaway, the angel of the Lord struck him, because he had not given glory to God, and he expired, eaten by worms.

This story may owe something to Ezekiel's abuse of the 'Prince of Tyre' for his presumption (Ezekiel 28:2, 6, 9). But in its rough outline it is found also in the Jewish historian Josephus, and it completes the story of Herod's downfall; the reader will think of what was predicted in the Magnificat. From being in control, Herod is now history. The story is exceptionally well told. Contrast it now with the 'Lucan summary' that follows, and note the way in which Luke picks up the story of Barnabas and Saul, and prepares us for their ministry, which is shortly to start.

The Church of all nations and many cultures

12²⁴-13³ The word of God increased and multiplied. Barnabas and Saul returned to Jerusalem, having fulfilled their service; they took John, who was surnamed Mark, along with them.

There were in Antioch, in the Church there, prophets and teachers: Barnabas and Simeon (called Niger), and Lucius the Cyrenean, Menahem who was foster-brother of Tetrarch Herod, and Saul. As they worshipped the Lord, and fasted, the Holy Spirit said, 'Set apart for me Barnabas and Saul for the work to which I have summoned them.' Then they fasted and prayed and laid hands on them, and sent them on their way.

As occasionally happens in Luke-Acts, there appears to be some confusion: we had supposed John-Mark to be in Jerusalem with his mother, and Barnabas and Saul to have already returned to Jerusalem. But Luke is more interested in setting up the missionary team than in getting the times and places exactly right.

Very gently the passage hints at the catholic nature of the Church in Antioch. No less than five cultures or languages are represented, it seems: Aramaic (Barnabas, Saul), Hebrew (Simeon, Menahem),

Latin (Niger), Greek (Lucius), and (somewhat vaguely) African (Cyrenean). With the statement that Menahem was foster-brother to the Tetrarch Herod, our mind goes back to the previous episode; and our admiration for the work of the Holy Spirit increases.

The Holy Spirit tends to make the Church all-embracing, rather than exclusive.

The gospel is more powerful than magic

4-12 Having been sent out by the Holy Spirit, they went down to Seleucia, and from there they went to Cyprus. And, being at Salamis, they proclaimed the Word of God in the synagogues of the Jews; and they had John as their assistant. They went through the whole island as far as Paphos; and they found a man who was a magician, a Jewish pseudo-prophet of the name of Bar-Jesus. He was with the proconsul Sergius Paulus, a man of some intelligence. This man sent for Barnabas and Saul, and demanded to hear the word of God. Elymas (for so his name is understood) the magician resisted them, seeking to divert the proconsul from the faith. But Saul (who is also Paul), filled with the Holy Spirit, gazed intently at him and said, '[You are] full of all cunning and all villainy, son of the devil, enemy of all righteousness, will you not stop [attempting to] divert the Lord's straight ways? And now look! The hand of the Lord is upon you, and you will be blind; you shall not see the sun until an appropriate time.'

Straightaway there fell on him mist and darkness, and he needed guides to get about. Then the proconsul, having seen what had happened, came to faith, overwhelmed by the Lord's teaching.

Saul (now starting to be given the name by which we know him best) is seen here for the first time as a full-blown apostle. From now on he outstrips Barnabas; and the episode before Sergius Paulus reminds the reader of Moses' feats of magic against the Egyptian necromancers in the presence of Pharaoh. The account of Sergius's conversion also fits with Luke's general notion of commending Christianity to a Roman audience. We may observe that Elymas's fate is precisely the opposite of what happened to Saul when he first heard the voice of Jesus.

Another theme to notice here is that of the 'journey', an idea very important to Luke. We must not think in terms of a 'travelogue' so much as of a theological idea, of these apostles being Jesus' witnesses 'to the ends of the earth'. So he goes from Antioch down to Seleucia, its port, then across to Cyprus, and the length and breadth of the island: we should, however, be marvelling less at Paul's travelling, and more at the power of the Spirit which it demonstrates.

The gospel is the power of the Holy Spirit, not fakery and trickery.

Paul's first speech – in the synagogue at Pisidian Antioch

13-41 Having put out from Paphos, Paul and his group arrived at Perga in Pamphylia; but John deserted them and returned to Jerusalem. Meanwhile they went through from Perga and arrived at Pisidian Antioch. They entered the synagogue on the

Sabbath-day, and sat down. After the reading of the Torah and the Prophets, those in charge of the synagogue sent to them saying, 'Brothers, if you have some word of comfort for the people, speak.' Paul arose, and, motioning with his hand, said, 'Men of Israel, and you who are God-fearers, listen! The God of this people Israel chose our ancestors and made the people great during the stay in the land of Egypt, and with uplifted arm led them out of that [land]. And for about forty years he put up with their moods in the desert. He destroyed seven nations in the land of Canaan, and gave their land as [Israel's] inheritance, for about four hundred and fifty years. And after that he provided judges, down to Samuel the prophet. After that they asked for a king, and God gave them Saoul son of Kish, a man of the tribe of Benjamin, for forty years. And after he had removed him [from the throne] he raised up David as their king; and he authenticated David, saying, "I have found David the son of Jesse, a man after my heart, who will carry out all my wishes."

'It was from David's seed, in accordance with [his] promise, that [God] brought Jesus as a saviour for Israel, with John the Baptist acting as his harbinger, prior to his entry, preaching a baptism of repentance for the whole people of Israel. When John had finished his course, he said, "Who do you suppose I am? I am not [The One]; he is coming after me, the one whom I am not worthy to untie the sandals of his feet."

'Brethren, children of the race of Abraham, and the God-fearers among you, it is to us that this message of salvation has been sent out. For those who live in Jerusalem, and their rulers, failed to know him; and they fulfilled the prophets' words that are read every Sabbath-day when they condemned him. And they found no capital crime, so they asked Pilate that he should be done away with. And when they had accomplished everything that had been written about him, they took him down from the cross and put him in a tomb. But God raised him from the dead; and he appeared for several days to those who had come up with him from Galilee to Jerusalem: these are the people who are now his witnesses to the people. And *we* are gospelling *you* the good news of the promise made to the ancestors. God fulfilled it for their children, when he raised Jesus up, as it says in the Second Psalm, "You are my Son – I have fathered you today." And that he raised him from the dead [in such a way that] he would never again return to corruption, he declared, "I shall give you David's holy promises." Therefore in another place he says, "You will not allow your Holy One to see corruption." For David in his own generation served God's purpose; then he slept, and was added to his ancestors, and saw corruption. But the One whom God raised did not see corruption.

'So, let it be known to you, brethren, that it is because of this that forgiveness of sins is being proclaimed to you – and from all the things from which you could not be justified by the Law of Moses, in him "everyone who believes is justified". So – watch out that it doesn't happen to you, what was spoken in the prophets:

> "See, you scoffers; wonder and disappear.
> For I am working a work in your days,
>   a work that you will never believe,
>   even if someone tells it to you in detail."'

Paul is from now on clearly the leader of the mission, and this is his first speech in Acts. It is a careful argument from Scripture, appropriate to a synagogue audience (though we may notice that its account of the history of Israel is quite as truncated as that offered by Stephen in Chapter 7). In some ways it does not sound much like Paul, as we know him from his letters, except for the Old Testament basis of the argument, and, towards the end, the link of 'faith' and 'justification'.

The line 'I have found David the son of Jesse . . .' is from 1 Samuel 13:14; 'I shall give you David's holy promises' is Isaiah 55:3; 'you will not allow your Holy One to see corruption' is Psalm 16:10; and 'See, you scoffers . . .' is Habakkuk 1:5. I have put 'everyone who believes is justified' in quotation marks because it sounds like Paul quoting himself.

It is worth checking the travels of Paul on a map; notice, for example, that there are two Antiochs, and that this speech has been delivered in Antioch in Pisidia, not Syrian Antioch.

Resistance to the Holy Spirit

42-52 As they went out, they invited them for the next Sabbath, for a discussion of these words. When the synagogue had broken up, many of the Jews and of the proselytes who worshipped there followed Paul and Barnabas; they spoke to them, and convinced them to continue in God's grace.

On the next Sabbath, almost all the city was gathered to hear the word of the Lord. When the Jews saw the crowds they were filled with fanaticism, and tried to contradict the things that Paul was saying – they defamed him. Paul and Barnabas, however, spoke fearlessly, and said, 'It was obligatory that the word of God should be spoken to you people first; since you have rejected it, and since you do not judge yourselves worthy of eternal life, look! We are turning to the Gentiles; for so the Lord has commanded us:

"I have set you [as] a light [for the] Gentiles,
    so that you may mean salvation to the end of the earth."'

When the Gentiles heard this, they rejoiced, and they glorified the word of the Lord; and those who were set in the way of eternal life came to faith. The word of the Lord spread through the whole area; but the Jews incited female worshippers of high repute and the first men of the city, and they aroused persecution [against] Paul and Barnabas, and they expelled them from their district. They simply shook the dust off their feet against them, and came to Iconium. And the disciples were filled with joy and the Holy Spirit.

This is the first example of a pattern that we shall encounter frequently in Paul's ministry in Acts: the gospel is preached first to the synagogue. Often it meets with success at first; then, however, it is rejected, and the missionaries turn to the Gentiles, who are thirsty for it. Disciples expect persecution, and even rejoice in it. 'Joy' and 'the Holy Spirit' belong very close together, in Luke's view.

The reference to 'a light [for the] Gentiles, etc.' is from Isaiah 49:6. Alert readers will remember the phrase on Simeon's lips at the very beginning of Luke's Gospel (Luke 2:32).

The preaching causes divisions in Iconium

14 ¹⁻⁷ It happened in Iconium as before: they went into the synagogue of the Jews, and spoke in such a way that a crowd of both Jews and Greeks came to faith. But the Jews who were unbelievers instigated and poisoned the minds of the Gentiles against the brethren. So they spent a fair time speaking boldly, with the Lord bearing witness to the message of his grace, and allowing signs and portents to occur through their agency. The city crowd was divided: some were on the Jews' side, while others were with the apostles. Then the Gentiles and Jews made an attempt, with [the complicity of] their leaders, to maltreat them and stone them; when they became aware of it, they fled to the cities of Lycaonia – Lystra and Derbe, and the area round about; and they were gospelling there.

> This episode brings another of Luke's themes to the fore: persecution always has the opposite effect to that which the persecutors intend. This has continued to be true in the history of the Church. So Augustine could say, 'The martyrs were bound, imprisoned, scourged, racked, burnt, rent, butchered – and they multiplied', and Tertullian, 'We multiply whenever we are blown down by you; the blood of Christians is seed.' Because the Spirit is in charge of events, the stoning of Stephen brought about a wider preaching of the gospel. The same is now happening in the life of Paul.

Paul and Barnabas (almost) deified

⁸⁻¹⁸ At Lystra, there was a man who had no power in his feet; he had been lame since [he left] his mother's womb, and had never walked. This man heard Paul speaking. [Paul] looked at him intently, saw that he had [enough] faith to be saved, and said in a loud voice, 'Rise up, and stand straight on your feet.' And he leapt up and walked.

And when the crowds saw what Paul had done, they lifted up their voices in the Lycaonian language, saying, 'Gods have come down to us in the form of human beings.' And they started calling Barnabas 'Zeus' and Paul 'Hermes', since he was the chief speaker. And the priest of the Zeus that was before the city brought bulls and garlands to the gates, along with the crowds. And he wanted to offer sacrifice. But when the apostles Barnabas and Paul heard, they tore their garments and rushed out into the crowd shouting and saying, 'Men – why are you doing this? We are also human beings, with feelings just like yours; and we are gospelling you to turn away from these useless gods to the Living God, "who made heaven and earth, and everything in them". [This God], in bygone generations, allowed all the Gentiles to travel by their own ways – and yet he did not leave himself without witness, conferring benefits, giving you rains from heaven, and seasons of fruitfulness, filling your hearts with food and cheerfulness.'

And with this speech he only just managed to stop the crowds from sacrificing to them.

> We notice that Paul has not yet fully displaced Barnabas; for it is Barnabas who is named first. But it is Paul who does the speaking. Here we have his third speech in Acts. The first was to serious-minded Jews; the second indicated the move from Jews to non-Jews; this one, finally, is to over-excited Gentiles.

An attempt at murder helps to spread the gospel

19-28   Some Jews came from Antioch and Iconium and they persuaded the crowds, and stoned Paul, and dragged him out of the city, thinking he was dead. The disciples surrounded him, and he got up and went into the city. The next day he went out with Barnabas to Derbe. They gospelled that city, and made a good few disciples, then returned to Lystra, Iconium and Antioch, where they strengthened the souls of the disciples, encouraging them to remain in the faith, 'because we have to enter the kingdom of God through many tribulations'. They installed elders for them in each Church; they prayed and fasted and offered them to the Lord in whom they had come to believe.

Then they crossed Pisidia and came to Pamphylia; they spoke the word in Perga and came down to Attalia. From there they sailed to Antioch, where they had been commended to the grace of God for the work that they had fulfilled. When they arrived and summoned the whole Church, they reported what great things God had done with them, and that he had opened a door of faith to the Gentiles. They spent no small period of time with the disciples.

> See once again Luke's narrative skill. Paul has a remarkable (but effortless) escape from death, which in no way deters him. He even goes *back* into the city, and only moves on the next day. This now allows the two of them to revisit churches they have previously founded, building up the necessary ecclesial infrastructures. Then more journeying (though Luke does not indicate much of what they did in the various places) until they come back to square one, with the important exception that the Gentile mission is now well and truly under way.

What about circumcision?

15 1-21 And some people coming down from Judaea started teaching the brethren, 'Unless you were circumcised [according] to the custom of Moses, you can't be saved.' Paul and Barnabas had a good deal of disagreement and argument with them; and it was arranged that Paul and Barnabas, and certain others of them, should go up to Jerusalem [to talk] to the apostles and elders about this issue.

So the Church sent them on their way, and they went through Phoenicia and Samaria. [As they went] they gave a detailed report of the conversion of the Gentiles; and they caused great joy to all their fellow Christians. When they reached Jerusalem, the Church, apostles and elders welcomed them. They related what great things God had done with them; but some of the Pharisee party who had joined the faith stood up and said, 'You must circumcise them and instruct them to keep the Law of Moses.'

The apostles and elders gathered to see about this affair. After a good deal of argument, Peter stood up and told them, 'Brethren – you [all] know that from early days God made his choice among you, that through my mouth the Gentiles should hear the word of the gospel and come to faith. And God, the knower of hearts, bore witness to them, giving them the Holy Spirit, just as [he had] to us. And God made no distinction in faith between us and them when he purified their hearts. So now why are you testing God, by putting a yoke on the disciples' neck, which neither our ancestors nor we had the strength to bear? On the contrary, through the grace of the Lord Jesus we believe that we are saved in just the same way as them.'

The whole group was silent as they listened to Barnabas and Paul recounting what signs and portents God had done through them among the Gentiles. After they had finished speaking, James responded, 'Brothers, listen to me. Simeon has explained how God first deigned to acquire from among the Gentiles a people for his name. And the prophets' words are in tune with him, as it is written, "After this I shall turn, and I shall rebuild David's tent which had fallen, and I shall rebuild the parts of it that had been torn down; and I shall put it to rights, so that the rest of humanity may seek the Lord, and all the nations on whom my name has been invoked, says the Lord, who does these things that have been known from all time."

'So my verdict is: not to cause trouble for those of the Gentiles who have turned to God, but to write to them to keep away from pollution by idols, and from fornication, and from meat that has been strangled, and from blood. For from the earliest generations Moses has those who proclaim him in every city, in the synagogues each Sabbath-day.'

This is a very important moment in Acts. The issue, bluntly stated by the intruders from Judaea, is whether you have to be circumcised in order to be a Christian. The meeting at Jerusalem is meant to find a way out: there were strong views on both sides. For Luke, narrating what has happened is a way of listening to God: Acts itself is a narrative listening, and so is Peter's story; but it is also the case with Paul and Barnabas (we notice that Paul normally gets mentioned first in this episode). Unusually their speech is not reported: 'They related what great things God had done with them . . . recounting what signs and portents God had done through them among the Gentiles'. Now it all rather turns on which way James will jump; he is, after all, the brother of the Lord, and might be thought to represent the more 'conservative' viewpoint (i.e. in favour of compulsory circumcision), and so it is uncertain how he will react. As it turns out, his speech is not all that coherent; but clearly he is doing his best to find a compromise, using a text from Amos (9:11, 12) for the purpose, while not surrendering so much of his heritage that the Pharisee Christians would feel uncomfortable. It may be relevant to note that Luke has him use 'Simeon', the Semitic form of Peter's original name. Some scholars feel that Luke may have smoothed things over a bit here. The puzzling opening remark from Peter's speech, that 'you know that . . . God made his choice among you . . . that through my mouth the Gentiles should have the word of the gospel and come to faith' seems not to fit with what we have seen already. Nor does it fit with Galatians 2:7, where it is agreed that Paul is to go to the Gentiles and Peter to the Jews. Moreover Luke does not offer any evidence from those opposed to the Gentile mission, nor Paul's (no doubt spirited) defence of the mission to the Gentiles. Perhaps in abbreviating his account Luke has followed his practice of emphasising the unity rather than the divisions of the Church.

Once again, it is theologically important, and relevant to the matter in hand, that Paul and Barnabas journey ('to the end of the earth') 'through Phoenicia and Samaria'. This both provides them with useful support from the wider Church and enables them to draw on a useful range of pastoral and missionary experience. Perhaps there is something here for the Church of our own day to learn.

The Church authenticates the mission of Paul and Barnabas

22-35   Then the apostles and the elders, along with the entire Church, decided to choose men from their number and send them to Antioch with Paul and Barnabas: Judas called Barsabbas, and Silas. These were prominent among the brethren; and they wrote this letter for them to carry:

> The Apostles and the Elder Brethren, Greetings to the Gentile Brethren in the territories of Antioch, Syria and Cilicia. Since we have heard that some people from here have disturbed you with what they said, unsettling your souls with things that we had not commanded, we have reached a unanimous agreement to choose men and send them to you along with our beloved Barnabas and Paul, people who have handed over their lives for the name of Our Lord Jesus Christ. So we have sent Judas and Silas (and the others) to announce this verbally. For we and the Holy Spirit have decided to put no greater burden on you than these (which are necessary): to abstain from things offered to idols, and blood, things strangled, and sexual vice. If you keep yourselves from these, you will do well. Farewell.

So they were sent off, and they came to Antioch; and gathering the group, they handed over the letter. They read it, and rejoiced at the encouragement. Judas and Silas, being prophets themselves, comforted the Christians and strengthened them with much talking; and having spent some time, they took their leave of the brethren [and went back] to those who had sent them. Paul and Barnabas spent time in Antioch, teaching and gospelling, with many others also, the word of the Lord.

> The last phrase, 'the word of the Lord', is of immense importance in Acts. The reader notices that the letter and the theological argument were not enough by themselves. What counts is the personal contact, which means a willingness to travel. It is possible to see here a lesson for the Church of our day. We should also observe Luke's emphasis on Church infrastructures: the 'apostles and elders' have to validate the policy decisions taken by missionaries 'in the field'. Otherwise we are not Church.

The quarrel between Paul and Barnabas

36-41   After some days, Paul said to Barnabas, 'Let us return and visit the Christians in each city where we proclaimed the word of the Lord, to see how they are getting on.' Barnabas, however, wanted to take with them John called Mark; and Paul insisted that they should not take him along, since he had abandoned them in

Pamphylia, and had not gone to work with them. A sharp disagreement arose, and they separated from each other. Barnabas took Mark and sailed to Cyprus, while Paul chose Silas, and set out, having been commended to the Lord's grace by his fellow Christians. He went through Syria and Cilicia, strengthening the Churches.

> Paul is now quite clearly calling the tune. Not for the last time in his missionary work, he has a row, on a matter of principle, with a fellow missionary. Luke's Paul (and the Paul who reveals himself in his letters) is gratifyingly human. We may find ourselves longing to know what really caused John Mark to disappear.

Paul's sensitivity to cross-cultural issues

16¹⁻⁵ He reached Derbe and Lystra. And look! There was a disciple there named Timothy, the son of a Jewish woman who was a believer, but a Greek father; Timothy was vouched for by the Christians in Lystra and Iconium. Paul wanted him to accompany him; he took him and circumcised him, because of the Jews in those parts – for they all knew that he had a Gentile father. As they journeyed through the cities, they handed down to them the decisions for them to observe, that the apostles and elders in Jerusalem had decided upon.

So the Churches were strengthened in the faith, and every day they increased in number.

> This 'Lucan summary' concludes an important section, in which Luke neatly brings together some issues of great importance to his understanding of the story. These include the 'journeying' theme, obviously; the appointment of Timothy as successor to Barnabas; the need for the awkward and painful circumcision, which dramatically highlights the sensitivity of the Jewish-Gentile issue; the need to enforce the compromise that has been arrived at in Jerusalem; the central position of the Jerusalem Church. Finally, the summary tells us that despite the uncomfortable issues involved, the Spirit's work is proceeding from strength to strength.

How the Spirit guides the mission

6-9 They came through Phrygia and the Galatian region, having been prevented by the Holy Spirit from speaking the word in Asia. They came down towards Mysia and tried to journey to Bithynia – and the Spirit of Jesus did not permit them. They bypassed Mysia and came down to Troas. And a nocturnal vision appeared to Paul, a Macedonian man standing, beseeching him and saying, 'Come over into Macedonia and help us.'

> Two important ideas lurk in this passage: first, as so often in Acts, note the liberal sprinkling of place names. It is quite a good idea to trace them on a map, and, perhaps with the help of commentaries, look at the difficulty about what is meant by 'Galatia'. But it is important not to worry too much about it; what most interests Luke here is the 'journey' that the gospel is following, rather than

precise geographical detail. Second, see how three times the trajectory of the mission is adjusted in response to divine intervention: the 'Holy Spirit', the 'Spirit of Jesus' and 'a Macedonian man', all serve to direct the gospel as it makes its huge (psychologically if not geographically) leap into Europe.

Paul's first European mission: Philippi

10-13   When he had seen the vision, we immediately tried to go out to Macedonia; we inferred that God had called us to gospel them. We put out from Troas and ran a straight course for Samothrace, and the next day to Neapolis, and thence to Philippi, which is a leading city of the district of Macedonia, a [Roman] colony.

On the Sabbath-day we went outside the city, along a river, where we thought there was a prayer-place. We sat down and spoke with the women who came together.

> This passage is the first of the four 'we' passages that we find in Acts, and it continues a few lines further, down to the beginning of the strange story of the slave girl. The four stories are at: 16:10-17, 20:5-15; 21:1-18, and 27:1–28:16. The reader might care to reflect on why Luke switches so abruptly to writing in the first person plural. There are various possible explanations: a) that this was how you narrated sea voyages in the ancient world, to make them more direct and hence more exciting; b) that this is simply the way that Luke liked to tell the story; c) that Luke was at this stage making use of some kind of written source, such as someone's travel diary; d) that Luke is here signalling to the reader that he was at this point in the story a companion of Paul. The last seems the most obvious, but you can make up your own mind about what he is doing here. Scholars are far from agreed on the subject.
>
> Since it was a 'Sabbath-day', we assume that it was *Jewish* women who were meeting by the river (although it turns out that Lydia was not Jewish but interested in Judaism). Once again we see Paul's familiar pattern of going first to the Jews.

Lydia demands to be allowed to offer hospitality

14, 15   A particular woman was listening. Her name was Lydia, and she was a dealer in purple cloth from the city of Thyatira, and a God-fearer. The Lord opened her heart to pay attention to the things that Paul was saying. When she and her household had been baptised, she begged [us], saying, 'If you have decided that I am a believer in the Lord, come into my house and stay there'; and she prevailed on us.

> Once again we see the familiar pattern: Paul preaches first to the Jews, as the reference to 'Sabbath' indicates; although it is interesting that here in Philippi he seems to have targeted primarily Jewish women – and Lydia is not even Jewish. As in the Cornelius story, so here we have not just an individual but an entire household coming

to faith. This is something we shall see again soon, with the story of the gaoler/prison commissioner of Philippi. It may make us reflect on how evangelisation should be done.

Trouble in Philippi, and the effortless resolution of it

16-40   As we journeyed to the prayer-place, it happened that a slave girl encountered us. She had a spirit of divination, and she provided her owners with a tidy income by her prophesying. She dogged Paul's footsteps, and ours, and cried out, saying, 'These people are servants of the Most High God. They are proclaiming the Way of Salvation to you.'

She did this over several days. Paul was at the end of his tether; he turned round and told the spirit, 'I command you, in the name of Jesus Messiah, to come out of her.' And it went out of her at that [very] moment. When her owners realised that their chance of income had gone away, they seized hold of Paul and Silas, and dragged them to the agora, before the authorities. And taking them to the praetors, they said, 'These people (who are Jews) are turning our city upside down; and they are proclaiming customs that it is not permissible for us (who are Roman [citizens]) to admit or to practise.'

The crowd joined in the attack on them; and the praetors tore off their clothes and ordered them to be caned. They laid a large number of strokes on them, and threw them into prison, and ordered the prison commissioner to keep a very careful eye on them. When he received this order, he flung them into the innermost prison, and he fastened their feet to the stocks. Round about the middle of the night, Paul and Silas were praying and singing hymns to God, and the [other] prisoners were listening to them. Suddenly, there was a huge earthquake, [which] shook the foundations of the prison. Immediately all the gates were opened and everyone's chains were unfastened. The prison commissioner woke up, saw the doors of the prison open, and drew his sword. He was just on the point of killing himself (because he thought that the prisoners had escaped). Paul, however, cried out in a loud voice, saying, 'Don't do yourself any harm – for we're all here.' He asked for light, and rushed in. Trembling, he fell at the feet of Paul and Silas; he led them out and said, 'My Lords: what must I do in order that I may be saved?' They said, 'Believe in the Lord Jesus, and both you and your household will be saved.' And they spoke the word of the Lord to him, along with all those in his house. Even at that time of night he took them in, washed [away] the results of their beating, and he and all his people were baptised right away. He took them to his house, set food before [them], and with his whole household rejoiced, because he had found faith in God.

When day came, the praetors sent the lictors, saying, 'Release those people.' The prison commissioner reported these words to Paul: 'The praetors have sent for you to be released. So out you go, and go off in peace.' Paul however said, 'They have publicly flogged us without a proper trial – although we are Roman citizens; they have flung us into gaol, and now they want to get rid of us without any fuss! No way – they can come and get us out themselves!'

The lictors reported these statements to the praetors, who were alarmed to hear that they were Roman [citizens]. They came and begged them; they took them out and asked them to leave the city. When they left the prison, they went to Lydia; they saw the Christians [in her house], comforted them, and left [the city].

Here is another story that gives us Luke's understanding of how the Holy Spirit works. First there is a victory, in that Paul effortlessly exorcises the servant girl who has correctly identified them. Next comes an apparent setback: opposition from those who are financially threatened leads to flogging and imprisonment. From then on, however, it is all success: Paul and Silas entertain their fellow prisoners by singing hymns; they are miraculously released; Paul orders the gaoler not to commit suicide, and receives him and his household into the Church; Paul lays down the law to the local authorities, who are embarrassed, and reduced to begging the evangelists to get out of town! Finally Paul does condescend to leave; but it is in his own good time, not theirs, and only after reassuring the infant Church in Lydia's house. We may also notice the change in meaning of 'Lord': the gaoler uses it to address Paul and Silas, but they use it only for Jesus. In a sense this is a little vignette of the entire battle that is Acts of the Apostles: who is Lord round here?

Persecution brings the gospel to Athens

17 1-15 Travelling through Amphipolis and Apollonia, they came to Thessalonica, where there was a synagogue of the Jews. In accordance with [his] custom, Paul went into them, and for three Sabbaths he held discussions with them on the basis of the scriptures, explaining [them] and demonstrating that it was inevitable for the Messiah to suffer and rise from the dead, and that 'This is the Messiah, Jesus, whom I am proclaiming to you.'

Some of them were persuaded, and they threw in their lot with Paul and Silas; there was a good number of Greek [God-]fearers, and not a few of the leading women. The Jews got jealous; and taking along some degenerates who hung about the market place, they called in Rentamob, and set the city in an uproar. They attacked Jason's house, and wanted to bring them before the assembly; but they didn't find them, so they dragged Jason and some of the Christians to the politarchs, shouting: 'These are the ones who are upsetting the [entire] world – and here they are, and Jason has given them hospitality! And all these people are acting against Caesar's decrees, saying that there's an alternative king in [this] Jesus.'

They succeeded in unsettling the crowd and the politarchs; when they heard this they took bail from Jason and the others, and let them go.

The Christians sent Paul and Silas out [of the city] to Beroea, then and there, by night. When they got there, they visited the synagogue of the Jews. These were more open-minded than those in Thessalonica, and they received the word with all eagerness; every day they would examine the scriptures [to see] if it was so. Many of them therefore came to faith; and there were a good number of prominent Gentile women, and men.

However, when the Jews from Thessalonica found out that Paul had preached the word of God in Beroea as well, they came [along], and there also they upset and disturbed the populace. Then and there the Christians sent Paul off, to travel to the coast; and Silas and Timothy waited there. Those who were conducting Paul escorted him to Athens; and they departed, with an order to Silas and Timothy to get to him as soon as possible.

Jason has appeared rather from a clear sky, and it seems that Luke supposes that we know who he is. Once again we see the familiar pattern of Acts: preaching leads to persecution, which brings about the spread of the gospel, to Athens and then Corinth, where Paul had one of his most successful ministries. We have come a long way from Jerusalem and Judaea, and are now at 'the end of the earth', at least in the sense that Athens was the commercial centre of the ancient world.

Paul in Athens

17 ^{16}-**18** ^{1} While Paul was waiting for them in Athens, he was exasperated to see that the city was full of idols. So he held discussions in the syngogue with the Jews and God-fearers, and every day in the agora, with anyone who happened to come along. Some of the Epicurean and Stoic philosophers fell in with him, and some said, 'What is this rag-picker on about?' Others said, 'He seems to be a proponent of outlandish deities' (because he was giving the gospel message of Jesus and the Resurrection).

They took him and led him to the Areopagus, saying, 'Can we know what this new teaching is to which you are giving utterance? For you are imparting certain outlandish matters into our hearing. So – we want to know what is the meaning of it.' (All Athenians, and the foreigners passing through there, had no time for anything but talking or hearing about the latest [fad]).

Paul stood in the middle of the Areopagus and said, 'Men of Athens, you seem to me exceptionally devout. For as I was coming through [this city], and examining the objects of your worship, I also found an altar on which was inscribed "To the Unknown God". Therefore what you worship without knowing is what I am proclaiming to you. The God who made the universe and everything in it, being the Lord of heaven and earth, does not dwell in temples that human hands have made, and is not served by human assistance, as though he had need of anything. For it is he who gives life and breath and everything to all. Out of one [person] he made the whole human race to dwell over the entire face of the earth, having set the appointed times and fixed boundaries of their habitation, [for them] to seek God, [to see] if they might grope their way to finding him. For he is not far off from each one [of us]. For in him we live, and move, and are; and as some of your poets say, "We are of his family." So, being of God's family, we should not think that the deity is like gold or silver or stone, or something fashioned by human technology or thought. So God, overlooking the times of ignorance, now commands people everywhere to repent, for he has appointed a day on which he is going to judge the world in righteousness, by means of a man whom he appointed, and he has given an assurance to all by raising him from the dead.'

When they heard 'resurrection from the dead', some of them sneered; but others said, 'We'll hear you again on this matter.'

So Paul went out of their midst; but some men joined him, including Dionysus the Areopagite, and a woman called Damaris, and others along with them. After this he left Athens, and came to Corinth.

Once more we see the pattern, that Paul first attends the synagogue, and normally (though apparently not in Athens) gets rejected and turns to the Gentiles. Here, though, the pattern is modified; for

Luke reports a speech that would seem well crafted for his intellectual Athenian audience, and yet it is only minimally successful. We notice, however, that Luke uses Athens as the springboard for Paul's very fruitful ministry in Corinth.

The mysterious Jason in Thessalonica is one of Luke's 'loose ends'. Another feature of Luke here is, I suspect (it is hard to be sure, but I have so translated it) the slightly pompous invitation to the Areopagus, and Paul's rather stilted speech when he gets there.

Paul arrives in Corinth: the familiar patterns repeated

2-8 [In Corinth] he found a Jew called Aquila, who was a native of Pontus. He had recently come from Italy with his wife Priscilla, because Claudius had decreed that all Jews should depart from Rome. [Paul] came to them because they were fellow professionals (their trade was tent-making); and with them he lived and worked.

Every Sabbath he would hold discussions in the synagogue, trying to convert both Jews and Greeks. When Silas and Timothy came down from Macedonia, he was wholly absorbed in preaching, testifying to the Jews that Jesus was the Messiah; but they resisted and abused [him]. So he shook out his clothes and told them, 'Your blood be on your heads. I am clear of responsibility – from now on, I shall travel to the Gentiles.'

He went away from there and entered the house of a God-fearer called Titus Justus, whose house was adjacent to the synagogue. Crispus, the head of the synagogue, came to faith in the Lord, with his entire household, and many of the Corinthians heard, and believed, and were baptised.

Corinth was not a promising place for Paul's mission; it was a rich and thriving and multiracial society, a byword in its day for sexual activity of various kinds. Yet it was here that Paul stayed for a year and a half. Once again, we notice, he goes first to the synagogue, and not without success, since his 'fellow professionals', Priscilla and Aquila, are fairly prominent in his letters. Nevertheless, this time Paul has apparently come to the conclusion that he is never going to get anywhere, although, as we shall see, he continues to go to the Jews first. Here Luke makes his point by having Paul echo Ezekiel 33:3-5, which Matthew picks up in his Gospel, at 27:25, that terrible moment when Jesus' own people reject him before Pilate.

What happened in Corinth

9-17 The Lord told Paul in a vision at night, 'Don't be afraid: speak up, and don't be silent, because I am with you, and no one will attack you to do you harm – because I have many in this city who are my people.' He settled [there] for a year and six months, teaching God's word among them.

When Gallio was proconsul of Achaia, the Jews combined against Paul, and took him to court, saying, 'He incites people to worship God in a way that is contrary to our Law.' When Paul was about to open his mouth, Gallio said to the Jews, 'If it were some evil crime or villainy, then, [my] Jewish [friends], I should reasonably put up with your complaint. If, however, the argument is about a discourse, and vocabulary, and law that is all your own, then *you* [are the ones who] must see to it. I have no desire to sit in judgement on these matters.' And he threw them out of court. They all took Sosthenes, the head of the synagogue, and beat him up in front of the tribunal. None of this was of any concern to Gallio.

> This Gallio was brother to Seneca, the Roman philosopher who was Nero's tutor; inevitably some later Christians dreamed up a correspondence between Paul and Seneca. An inscription at Delphi dates Gallio's time in Corinth to AD 51 or 52. When Gallio supposed Christianity to be just another Jewish sect, that would have been to their advantage, since Judaism, though considered rather odd because of insisting on only one God, had the status of a 'permitted religion', and was therefore exempt from taking part in imperial worship.

Paul moves on; return to the Holy Land

18-22 Paul remained many more days; he said goodbye to the Christians and sailed off to Syria, with Priscilla and Aquila in tow, having cut his hair at Cenchreae (for he had a vow). They arrived at Ephesus, and he left them there; meanwhile he went into the synagogue and held discussions with the Jews. However, when they asked him to stay a bit longer, he did not give his consent, but bade them farewell and said, 'I shall come back to you, if God wills.' He set sail from Ephesus and reached Caesarea. He went up [to Jerusalem] and greeted the Church [there]; and then he went down to Antioch.

> Why has Paul suddenly left Timothy and Silas, Priscilla and Aquila? The reader may notice the apostle's tendency to split with his fellow workers; he was not altogether an easy man. Cenchreae, where he shaved his head, was the eastern port of Corinth. We observe that at Ephesus Paul has continued his practice of going to the synagogue first.

Back to Asia Minor

23 Having spent some time, he went to one place after another in the Galatian and Phrygian regions, and strengthened all the disciples.

> This is another 'Lucan summary', getting Paul off stage, perhaps to prepare for Apollos's visit to Corinth, the background to the controversy that emerges in Paul's first letter to the Corinthians.

Apollos in Corinth

18 24-19 1a   A Jew by the name of Apollos, of Alexandrian origin, an educated man, arrived at Ephesus; he was very good on the scriptures. He had been taught the Way of the Lord, and was brimming with enthusiasm; he was speaking and teaching all about Jesus, [quite] accurately – but he only knew about the baptism

of John. Apollos began to express himself freely in the synagogue. Priscilla and Aquila heard him; they got hold of him and explained the Way more accurately to him. Because he wanted to cross over to Achaia, the Christians wrote a letter, encouraging the disciples to welcome him. He arrived, and by [God's] grace helped the faithful greatly. For he vigorously refuted the Jews in public, showing through the scriptures that Jesus was the Messiah.

Now while Apollos was in Corinth, Paul went through the inland parts, and came to Ephesus.

> Apollos is in Ephesus while Paul is in the Holy Land and Paul comes to Ephesus while Apollos is in Corinth; 1 Corinthians tells us about the divisions based on their two factions in Corinth. Was Ephesus too small for the two of them? Luke gently but firmly points out that Apollos's background and teaching may have been a bit deficient – only John's baptism, and perhaps not much on the Holy Spirit.
>
> Later on in Corinth there was (at least) an Apollos-party and a Paul-party, with quite serious divisions between them.

The coming of the Holy Spirit

1b-7 He found some disciples and said to them, 'Did you receive the Holy Spirit when you came to faith?' They said to him, 'We hadn't even heard if the Holy Spirit exists!' And he said, 'What were you baptised into?' They said, 'Into John's baptism.'

Paul said, 'John baptised [with] a baptism of repentance, telling the people to believe in the One coming after him – that is Jesus.'

When they heard this, they were baptised [in] the name of the Lord Jesus. When Paul laid his hands on them, the Holy Spirit came on them, they spoke in tongues, and they prophesied. The men were about twelve in number.

> This is not the first time that Acts has spoken of the 'coming of the Holy Spirit', but other than at Pentecost, we have not really grasped what it was. At Pentecost it was tongues of fire, the sound of a mighty wind, and speaking in languages that everyone could understand. Clearly for the early Church the coming of the Holy Spirit was something tangible. Here it is represented as a matter of 'speaking in tongues' and 'prophesying', which may not take us much further. Evidently, though, it was something about which there could be no doubt and we need to bear this in mind as we continue our journey through this 'Gospel of the Holy Spirit'.
>
> The coming of the Holy Spirit was obviously something that no one could doubt.

Paul's exploits in Ephesus

8-20 Going into the synagogue, he spoke freely for three months, holding discussions, and trying to convince [them] about the kingdom of God. But as some people were obstinate, and disbelieved, and reviled the Way before the people, he withdrew from them, and took the disciples on their own, and held discussions with them every day in Tyrannus's lecture hall. This lasted for two years; the result was that all those who lived in Asia, both Jews and Greeks, heard the word of the Lord. Through Paul's agency, God worked miracles that were quite out of the ordinary. For example, the sick had facecloths or handkerchiefs that had touched him taken to them, and their diseases left them, and evil spirits departed.

Some of the wandering Jewish exorcists attempted to name the name of the Lord Jesus, saying, 'I adjure you, by Jesus whom Paul proclaims.' There were seven sons of Sceva, a Jewish Archpriest, who were doing this. The evil spirit answered and said to them, 'Jesus I recognise and Paul I know – but who are you people?' And the man in whom the evil spirit was, leapt on them, and overmastered them all, so that they fled, naked and wounded, from that house. All the Jews and Gentiles who lived in Ephesus came to know of this; awe fell on all of them, and the event magnified the name of the Lord Jesus. Many of those who had come to faith came, acknowledging and declaring their acts. Several of those who had practised magic brought their scrolls, and burnt them before everybody; and they added up the price of them – it came to more than fifty thousand silver pieces! So by the Lord's might the word increased and grew.

This adroit combination of 'Lucan summary' and the story of the sons of Sceva creates an impressive atmosphere, of the gospel effortlessly overcoming every possible obstacle and reaching out to all humanity ('all those who lived in Asia . . . all the Jews and Gentiles who lived in Ephesus'). The facecloths and handkerchiefs that had touched Paul remind us of the effects of Peter's shadow (5:15). Notice, once again, the emphasis on the 'name of the Lord Jesus'. Notice, too, how 'Lord' has become a divine title for Jesus: contrast Luke 1:46, where it clearly referred to God. Now it is apparently 'God or Jesus' or 'God in Jesus'. Paul is still, we observe, going to the Jews first.

Towards Jerusalem and Rome

21, 22 When these things were fulfilled, Paul resolved to pass through Macedonia and Achaia, and so journey to Jerusalem. He said, 'After I have been there, it is necessary for me to see Rome as well.' He sent two of his assistants, Timothy and Erastus, to Macedonia; meanwhile Paul himself stayed on for a time in Asia.

Is Paul splitting up yet again with his apostolic assistants? Luke does not say so, but we cannot help asking. Once again we notice the theme of travelling, and the fact that the gospel never stops anywhere, but presses on to Jerusalem and to Rome, where Acts will end, having arrived, presumably, at 'the end of the earth'.

Trouble averted in Ephesus

23-41 At about that time there was a fairly considerable disturbance with regard to the Way. For someone called Demetrius, a silversmith, who made silver shrines of Artemis, and provided the craftsmen with a good deal of business, called them all together, along with others who worked in related trades, and said, 'Men, you know that our livelihood depends on this trade. You [can] see and hear that this fellow Paul has been misleading vast numbers of people with his arguments, not just here, but almost everywhere in Asia. He says that [statues] made by human hands aren't gods! The risk is that not only will our profession come into disrepute, but also the temple of the great goddess Artemis will be reckoned as nothing, and it will be stripped of its majesty, which Asia, and [indeed] the whole world, worships.'

They heard him, and were filled with anger, and shouted out, 'Great is Artemis of the Ephesians'; and the city was filled with confusion. Unanimously, they rushed to the theatre, and dragged off the Macedonians Gaius and Aristarchus, Paul's travelling companions. Paul wanted to go into the crowd, but the disciples wouldn't allow him. Some of the Asiarchs, who were friendly towards him, sent to him and begged him not to venture into the theatre. People were shouting different things, for the assembly was in uproar, and most people had no idea why they had come together. Some of the crowd gave instruction to Alexander, as the Jews pushed him to the front. Alexander gave a signal that he wanted to make [his] defence to the people. When they realised that he was Jewish, a single slogan arose from the whole lot of them; for about two hours, they shouted, 'Great is Artemis of the Ephesians.'

The Secretary quietened the crowd and said, 'Ephesians, is there anyone who does not know that the city of Ephesus is the guardian of the Temple of the Great Artemis and of the image that fell from heaven? Since this is undeniable, you must show restraint, and do nothing reckless. For you brought these men, who are neither temple-robbers nor blasphemers of our God. So if Demetrius and his fellow professionals have a case against someone, the courts are in session, and there are proconsuls – let them accuse each other. If, however, there is anything further you wish to know, it will be settled at the statutory assembly. In fact we run the risk of being charged with sedition for [what has gone on] today, since there is no charge to which we shall be able to respond regarding this commotion. And having said these things, he dismissed the assembly.

> Why has Luke given a relatively large section to this account of civil disorder at Ephesus? Perhaps to indicate to 'Theophilus', the archetypal Roman reader, that the disturbances that surrounded this new 'Way' are not just inner-Jewish problems; they also have implications for pagan religion. Demetrius's claim that Paul preaches against idols 'almost everywhere in Asia' suggests that the apostle was quite impartial about whom he annoyed: Jews with his claims about Jesus as Messiah, and pagans with his strict monotheism. And we have already heard Paul arguing this case in Athens. We also notice, not for the first time, that Luke presents Roman officials as inclined to protect Christians. At the same time, however, Luke wants to make it clear that the troubles are not the Christians' fault. It serves to stand as an example for many such problems that must have occurred in cities throughout the Mediterranean as Christianity made its way westwards.

Paul's travel plans changed by attempted murder

20 ¹⁻⁶ After the trouble had died down, Paul sent for the disciples and comforted them. [Then] he took leave of them and left to travel to Macedonia. As he went through those parts, he comforted them with much talking, and reached Greece, where he spent three months. As he was about to sail to Syria, there was a plot against him on the part of the Jews, and he decided to go back through Macedonia. He was accompanied by Sopater, son of Pyrrhus, a Beroean; of the Thessalonians there were Aristarchus and Secundus, Gaius from Derbe, and Timothy; the Asians were Tychicus and Trophimus. These people went ahead of us and waited for us at Troas. We left by boat from Philippi after the days of Unleavened Bread, and reached them at Troas within five days. We spent a week there.

> This is the beginning of the second 'we' passage. The reader notices that, once again, the context is that of travel, including a sea voyage, and that there is the flurry of names (not all of them known to us) that we have come to expect in Acts. The Church of Acts is catholic in that it signals a broad mixture of cultures within its ample bosom.

Eutychus and the dangers of long sermons. Farewell to the elders of Ephesus

7-38   On the first day of the week, when we had gathered to break bread, Paul gave them an address, since he was due to leave the next day; and he prolonged his discourse till midnight; there were many lamps in the upper room where we had gathered. A young man called Eutychus was sitting at the window, and sank into a deep sleep as Paul talked longer and longer. Finally overcome by his somnolence, he fell down from the third storey, and was taken up dead. Paul went down and threw himself upon him. He embraced him and said, 'Don't be distressed – there is life in him.' He went up and broke bread and ate, having chatted for a long time, until daylight. They took the boy alive, and were comforted in no small measure.

Meanwhile we went on ahead to the boat and sailed to Assos. The plan was that we should take him on board there. For he had arranged it so – he was going to travel on foot. When he met us at Assos we took him on board and came to Mitylene. From there we sailed the next day and reached [a spot] off Chios. The following day we approached Samos, and the day after we came to Miletus. Paul had decided to sail past Ephesus, so as not to waste time in Asia. For he was hurrying to be in Jerusalem for the day of Pentecost, if possible.

From Miletus he sent to Ephesus and summoned the elders of the Church. When they arrived, he said to them, 'You know how from the first day that I came to Asia, I spent the whole time with you, serving the Lord with all humility and tears, and the trials that happened to me with the Jews' plots. You know how I did not keep silent about anything that is profitable, and proclaimed to you and taught you both in public and at home, testifying to Jews as well as Greeks [about] turning to God in repentance, and [about] faith in our Lord Jesus. Now look – I am bound in the Spirit to travel to Jerusalem, not knowing what will happen to me there, except that in each city the Holy Spirit testifies to me, telling me that imprisonment and anguish lie in wait for me. As for myself, I regard my life as in no sense precious to me, so long as I can complete the race, and the ministry that I have received from the Lord Jesus, to spread the witness of the gospel of God's grace. Now look – I know that none of you, among whom I have gone about proclaiming the kingdom, will ever see my face again. So I call you to witness, this very day, that I am innocent of the blood of all. For I never held back from announcing God's entire plan to you. Look after yourselves; look after the whole flock in which the Holy Spirit made you overseers to shepherd God's Church, which he got through the blood of his own [Son]. I know that after my departure ruthless wolves will come in to you. They will not spare the flock; and men will arise from among you who will utter travesties [of the truth], so as to draw away the disciples after them. So, stay awake. Remember that for three years, day and night, I never stopped admonishing each one with tears. Now I am offering you to God, and to the message of God's grace. God is able to build up, and to give the inheritance to all who have been sanctified. I never desired anyone's silver, or gold, or clothing. You [of all people] know that it was my own hands that took care of my needs, and of my companions. In every way I have shown you that [you] must strive to help the weak, and remember the words of the Lord Jesus. He himself said, "Happiness consists in giving rather than receiving." '

Saying this, he fell to his knees, and prayed with all of them. There was much weeping on the part of all, and they fell on Paul's neck and embraced him. They were especially saddened by his remark that they were destined to see his face no more. And they escorted him to the boat.

> There is much in this episode that is characteristic of Paul: talking freely about himself as an example; his insistence on the centrality of the gospel ministry; his obsession with Jesus; his intense conviction about what is right. At the same time there is much that Luke regards as typical of the work of the Holy Spirit in general. Like Peter (9:36-41) and Jesus (Luke 7:11-17; 8:40-56), Paul brings someone back to life, for example. And there is the role of the Holy Spirit in appointing 'overseers' or 'bishops' to the Churches. There is the expectation that disciples will be persecuted and seduced from the faith. There is also the sadness that comes with the realisation that Paul is making his final farewell. He is on his way to Jerusalem, where there is likely to be trouble; although, as we know, Jerusalem is not his final destination. He is quite right, however, in saying that he will not see the elders of Ephesus again.

From Miletus to the Holy Land

21 1-14 When we set sail and drew away from them, we steered a straight course to Cos, and the next day to Rhodes, and from there to Patara. [There] we found a boat that was crossing over to Phoenicia; we went aboard and sailed away. We sighted Cyprus, and leaving it to port, we sailed for Syria, and came down to Tyre, since that was where the vessel was unloading its freight.

We searched for the disciples and stayed here a week. They told Paul through the Spirit not to embark for Jerusalem; but when our time was up, we left on our journey. All of them, including the women and children, escorted us out of the city; and we fell on our knees at the shore, and prayed and parted from them; then we went on board the boat, while they returned home.

Meanwhile we continued our voyage from Tyre, and reached Ptolemais. [There] we greeted the brethren, and spent a day with them. The next day we departed and came to Caesarea. We entered the house of the Gospeller Philip. He was one of the 'Seven', and we stayed with him. He had four virgin daughters who spoke the word of God. We remained for [a few] more days; [then] someone came down from

Judaea, a prophet called Agabus. He came to us, took Paul's girdle, bound his own hands and feet, and said, 'Thus says the Holy Spirit: "The man whose girdle this is, the Jews shall bind after this fashion in Jerusalem, and they shall give him over into the hands of Gentiles."'

When we heard this, both we and the locals begged him not to go up to Jerusalem. Then Paul responded, 'What are you doing, weeping and breaking my heart? For I am prepared not just to be arrested, but even to die on behalf of the Lord Jesus.' Since he could not be persuaded, we all held our peace and said, 'The Lord's will be done.'

> This important passage combines two Lucan themes. First, there is the familiar travel story (it is the third 'we' passage), with plenty of place names, and an itinerary that we can check against the map. Second, however, and this is a part of the 'Gospel of the Holy Spirit', there is a note of impending doom. At Tyre Paul is warned (and should he have obeyed the Holy Spirit?) not to go up to Jerusalem; then there is another tearful farewell. Then at Caesarea there is yet another prophetic warning, and Paul's companions endeavour to dissuade him. But, like Jesus in Luke's Gospel, he has to go on with the journey, at all costs (see Luke 9:31, 51; 13:31-33), and no tears will dissuade him. His final remark sounds like Paul's authentic voice (see, for example Philippians 1:21-26; 3:7-11). Agabus we have already met, making another correct prediction at 11:28.

Arrival in Jerusalem: a tense encounter with James

15-26 After this, we made our preparations and were on our way up to Jerusalem. Some of the disciples from Caesarea came with us. They brought one Mnason, a Cypriot, a disciple of long standing, with whom we had been lodging. When we reached Jerusalem, the brethren welcomed us gladly.

On the following day, Paul went in with us to James; and all the elders were there. He greeted them, and explained in detail everything that God had done among the Gentiles through his ministry. When they heard [it], they glorified God, and said to Paul, 'Do you see, brother, how very many there are who have come to faith among the Jews? And they are all ardent observers of the Torah. They have been given information about you, that you were teaching rebellion against Moses, telling all the Jews in the Diaspora not to circumcise their children, and not to follow our way of life. So what about it? They will certainly hear that you have arrived. Therefore do what we tell you. We have four men who have taken a vow. Take them along with you; get yourself purified, and pay for them to have their heads shaved. Then they'll all know that there is nothing in the stories they've heard about you, and that in fact you are still keeping the Torah. With regard to the Gentiles who have come to faith, we have written, giving our verdict that they should avoid meat sacrificed to idols, and [meat that still has the] blood, and [meat that was] strangled, and sexual misbehaviour.'

Then Paul took the men, on the very next day; he had himself purified with them, and he went into the Temple, giving notice that the days of purification were completed, until the sacrifice had been offered by each one of them.

We might have been expecting fireworks at this meeting; it was clearly a tense and formal affair. Not only is Paul encountering James the brother of the Lord, but it is the 'liberal' Gentile mission meeting the 'conservative' Jewish Christian tradition. In addition, both sides have their supporters present at the meeting; and we already know how prickly Paul can be. The threatened explosion does not materialise, however, and Paul acquiesces like a lamb to their demands. He is made aware that his own supporters are outnumbered; he will in any event have known how tense things were in Jerusalem at festival-time – and this was just such an issue as to light the fuse. We have already seen how aware he is of the delicacy of the issues involved, as when he circumcised Timothy (16:3), the vow he took at Cenchreae (18:18), and his insistence, already mentioned, on keeping the Jewish feasts (20:6, 16; 27:9). At the same time, we must remember that Paul's insistence on the mission to the Gentiles, and on tempering for them the Law's demands, did create enormous tensions among those first Christians, especially, it seems, in Jerusalem. On his side, of course, Paul will be glad to have known that they implicitly acquit him of the charge of 'preaching rebellion against Moses'. He never did that – see Romans 9-11, for example.

Trouble in the Temple

27-30   When the seven days were almost up, the Jews from Asia spotted him in the Temple, and stirred up the crowd; and they laid hands on him and said, 'Help! Israelites! This is the fellow who's teaching everyone everywhere against Israel and the Torah and this Temple. And now he's brought Gentiles into the shrine and has defiled this holy place!' The reason was that they had already seen Trophimus from Ephesus in the city with him; and they thought that Paul had brought him to the Holy Place. The whole city was aroused; the people rushed together, and they got hold of Paul and dragged him out of the Temple. And immediately the gates were closed.

This is an important moment. The reader knows that the trouble-makers had misread the situation, or exploited it for their own purposes. Paul was not such a fool as to have defiled the Temple – nor would he have thought of doing so. Now, for the last time, Luke leaves the Temple where he had set the opening and closing scenes of his Gospel (and many scenes in between), and the opening scene (and many subsequent scenes) of Acts. This is the end; the gospel, however, continues its charted course 'to the end of the earth'.

Paul rescued by Roman soldiers

31-36   As they attempted to kill him, a report went up to the tribune of the cohort that the whole of Jerusalem was in an uproar. He immediately took some soldiers and centurions, and came down on them at the double. They saw the tribune and the soldiers, and stopped raining blows on Paul. Then the tribune approached, arrested him, and gave orders that he was to be bound in double chains. He asked who he was and what he had done. Different [people] in the crowd said different things; and because of the noise, he couldn't get at the facts. So he had him brought to the barracks. But when Paul got to the steps, the soldiers, because of the force of the crowd, were actually carrying him. For the mob was behind him, shouting, 'Away with him!'

> For Luke, violence and unjustifiable arrest is to be expected for those who preach the gospel of the Spirit. He may also have been glad to point out to his Roman readers that it was imperial troops who had saved Paul from being lynched.

Second account of Paul's conversion; the help of a friendly tribune

21 ^{37}-22 ^{29} As they were just about to enter the barracks, Paul said to the tribune 'Is it permissible to say something to you?' He said, 'Do you know Greek? Aren't you the Egyptian who started a rebellion some time ago, and led the four thousand assassins out into the desert?' Paul said, 'I am a Jew; but I'm also an inhabitant of Tarsus in Cilicia – citizen of a city of some significance. I ask you, let me speak to the people.' He let him, and Paul stood on the steps, and motioned with his hand to the people. A great silence descended, and he spoke to them in Aramaic:

'Brethren and fathers, listen now to my defence before you.' When they realised that he was talking to them in Aramaic, their silence became more intense. He said, 'I am a Jewish man, born in Tarsus in Cilicia, but brought up here in Jerusalem, educated at the feet of Gamaliel, in accordance with the strictness of the Torah of our forefathers. I was just as fanatical for God as you people are today. I persecuted this "Way" to death; I arrested and handed over both men and women, as the High Priest and the entire Presbyterium can bear me witness. I had letters from them, and travelled to our brethren in Damascus, so as to bring the people who were there also in chains to be punished. However, as I was travelling, and getting near to Damascus, round about noon, suddenly a great blaze of light shone round me, and I fell to the ground, and heard a voice saying to me, "Saoul, Saoul, why are you persecuting me?" I answered, "Who are you, Lord?" He said to me, "I am Jesus the Nazarene, whom *you* are persecuting." Those who were with me saw the light; but they did not hear the voice of the one who was speaking to me. I said, "What shall I do, Lord?" The Lord said to me, "Arise, go to Damascus, and there you will be told about all the things that you have been ordered to do." Since I could not see, because of the radiance of that blaze of light, those who were with me led me by the hand into Damascus. Ananias, a devout man, and an observer of the Torah, who is vouched for by all the Jews who live there, came to me, stood over me, and said, "Saoul, brother, receive your sight back." And at that moment my sight came back [and I saw] him. He said, "The God of our forefathers has predestined you to know his will, and to see the Just One, and to hear a voice from his mouth, that you are to be a witness, to all people, of the things that you have seen and heard. And now, why do you delay? Up – get yourself baptised, and wash away your sins, calling on his name."

'When I returned to Jerusalem and was praying in the Temple, I fell into a trance, and I saw him saying to me, "Hurry – leave Jerusalem quickly, because they will not listen to your testimony about me." And I said, "Lord, they know that in all the synagogues I was committing to prison and flogging those who believe you, and that when the blood of Stephen (your witness) was poured out I myself was at hand, and approving, and looking after the clothes of those who killed him." And he said to me, "Go – because I am sending you a long way, out to the Gentiles." '

As they yelled and cast their garments and threw dust in the air, the tribune ordered him to be taken into the barracks, telling [them] to examine him with whips, to find out on what grounds they were screaming out against him. However, as they stretched him out for the flogging, Paul said to the centurion who was standing there, 'Is it permissible for you to flog a Roman [citizen] who has not been condemned?' When the centurion got the message, he went up to the tribune and reported to him, 'What are you going to do? This man is a Roman [citizen].'

The tribune came to Paul and said, 'Tell me, are you a Roman [citizen]?'

He said, 'Yes.' The tribune replied, 'I acquired this citizenship for a considerable sum of money.' Paul said, 'I was born [a citizen].' So those who had been about to examine him stood back; and the tribune was alarmed that he had had him bound.

This is the second time that we have heard the story of Paul's encounter with Jesus. This time, however, it is given a highly dramatic setting. Paul is allowed to tell the story himself, as an angry crowd presses round him. The interaction is on two levels. At one level, he is speaking Aramaic to fellow Jews and explaining why he has taken the road that he has followed. Like the Paul we know from his letters (see, for example, Philippians 3:4-6), he is not afraid to list his qualifications. We may notice that in this version he emphasises Ananias's orthodoxy rather more than the narrator had in Chapter 9, when the event was first reported, and that Paul is made to talk of returning to Jerusalem and praying in the Temple.

At another level, Paul's interaction is with the Roman authorities, with whom Luke's readers will have been more in sympathy than with what they would have regarded as a fanatical mob. So he talks Greek to the tribune, and makes the centurion jump with the revelation that he is a Roman citizen. Now begins the final thread in the narrative, the one that will lead him to Rome, the 'end of the earth'.

Paul before the Sanhedrin

22 ³⁰-23 ⁵ The next day, wanting to get at the facts of the Jewish accusation against him, he released [Paul], and ordered the high priests and the entire Sanhedrin into his presence. He brought Paul down and stood him [before] them.

Paul looked intently at the Sanhedrin and said, 'Brothers, I have conducted my life with a clear conscience before God, down to this very day.'

The High Priest Ananias ordered the bystanders to strike him on the mouth. Then Paul said to him, 'God is going to strike you, you whitened wall: do you sit in judgement in accordance with the Torah, and [then], contrary to the Torah, order me to be hit?' The bystanders said, 'Do you revile God's High Priest?' Paul said, 'Brothers, I had no idea that it was a High Priest. You see, it is written, "You shall not speak badly of a leader of your people."'

This is a very odd incident; Paul can hardly have been in ignorance of Ananias's identity. Perhaps the point is simply that high priests should not behave in that way; but the Exodus citation does not sit well with that interpretation. Perhaps Paul is the leader who is being 'spoken of badly'.

The Lord is in charge: to Rome!

6-11 Now Paul was aware that one part consisted of Sadducees, and the other part consisted of Pharisees, and so he cried out in the Sanhedrin, 'Brethren, I am a Pharisee and a son of Pharisees; and I am on trial about the hope for the resurrection of the dead.' When he said this, there arose a difference of opinion between the Pharisees and the Sadducees, and the meeting was divided. For Sadducees say that there is no resurrection, no angels, and no spirits, while Pharisees acknowledge the whole lot. There was a great clamour, and some of the scribes who were on the Pharisee side rose up and argued, 'We find no evil in this man; perhaps a spirit or an angel has spoken to him?' As the temperature of the discussion increased, the tribune was fearful that Paul might be torn in pieces by them, and ordered the troops to go down and seize him, and carry him out of their midst and into the barracks. The next night, the Lord stood over him and said, 'Have courage; as you bore witness to me in Jerusalem, so you must also do in Rome.'

Whatever happens, God is in charge, and the 'end of the earth' comes nearer, even though at present the witnessing is only in Jerusalem.

What Paul says of himself in this speech is not unlike his boast in Philippians 3:5, 'a Hebrew of Hebrew stock, a Pharisee as far as the Torah is concerned'.

The plot against Paul

12-35 When day came, the Jews called together a secret meeting. They bound themselves under a curse, that they would fast from food and drink until they had killed Paul. More than forty of them had entered into this conspiracy. They went to the High Priest and the elders and said, 'We have put ourselves under an oath to taste nothing until we have killed Paul. So now you people, along with the Sanhedrin, [must] make it clear to the tribune that he is to bring Paul down to you, because you are going to decide his case more precisely. Before he gets anywhere near, we'll be ready to do away with him.'

The son of Paul's sister heard about the ambush, and came and got into the barracks and reported to Paul. Paul summoned one of the centurions and said, 'Take this young man to the tribune, for he has something to report to him.' So he took him, and led him to the tribune and says, 'The prisoner Paul summoned me, and asked me to bring this young man to you, because he has something to say to you.' The tribune took him by the hand, and going aside with him in private, asked, 'What is it that you have to report to me?' He told him, 'The Jews have agreed to ask you to take Paul down to the Sanhedrin tomorrow, because it is going to decide his case more precisely. But don't do what they say – more than forty of them are going to ambush him. They have bound themselves by an oath not to eat or drink until they have done away with him – and now they're waiting for a promise from you.'

So the tribune let the young man go, and said, 'Don't tell anyone that you've revealed this to me.' He summoned two of the centurions and said, 'Prepare two hundred soldiers, to travel to Caesarea, and seventy cavalry and two hundred lightly armed troops, any time after the third watch of the night.' [He told them] to produce animals to give Paul a mount and bring him safely to Felix the procurator. He wrote a letter, and this was its content:

Claudius Lysias to the Most Excellent Procurator Felix, Greetings.

I came upon this man when the Jews had arrested him, and he was on the point of being killed by them. I rescued him when I discovered that he was a Roman citizen. I wanted to know what they were accusing him of, and so I took him down to their sanhedrin. I discovered that he was indicted on some questions of their Torah; but there was no charge [against him] that deserved death or imprisonment. Then I got information that there was going to be a plot against him, and I immediately sent him to you. And I have also ordered his accusers to put their case against him in your presence.

So the soldiers took Paul, in accordance with their orders, and brought him by night to Antipatris. The next day they let the cavalry go on with him, while they returned to barracks. The cavalry entered Caesarea, gave the letter to the procurator, and handed over Paul as well. He read the letter, and asked what province he was from. When he discovered that Paul was from Cilicia, he said, 'I shall give you a hearing when your accusers arrive.' He ordered him to be kept in Herod's praetorium.

There is a touch of James Bond about the story now, narrow escapes, and the battlelines clearly drawn: Paul's (mortal) enemies are his Jewish opponents, and it is Romans, aided by informers from his kinsfolk, who come to his rescue, in, it must be said, absurdly large quantities. The escort provided would look extravagant if they were protecting the Emperor! We notice (not for the first time) that Paul is very much in charge, giving orders to a passing centurion about what do to with his nephew. It is, no doubt, a tribute to Roman military discipline that these orders are faithfully carried out.

The story of the projected 'ambush' is told three times, like the stories of Paul's and Peter's conversions, so Luke obviously regards it as being of some importance.

Interestingly, the tribune's letter to Felix has the right 'feel' about it; and if it was not the actual letter, it was certainly the kind of thing that such an officer might have written to his political boss.

There is an echo here of Luke's version of Jesus' passion when the procurator finds out what province of the empire Paul comes from, and in consequence decides to postpone his hearing; Pilate did something of the same at Luke 23:6-12.

The case against Paul – who is stuck in prison for two years!

24 [1-27] Five days later, the High Priest Ananias came down with some elders, and a barrister [called] Tertullus. They informed the procurator of [the charges] against Paul. Paul was summoned, and Tertullus began the speech for the prosecution:

'Most Excellent Felix, thanks to you we have experienced great peace; many improvements have come about for this nation, thanks to your foresight, as everywhere in every way we acknowledge with great gratitude. However, not to delay you any further, I beg you to listen briefly to us, with your [customary] graciousness. The fact is, we find this man to be a pest; he causes dissension among all the Jews throughout the world, and is a ringleader of the sect of the Nazarenes. He tried to desecrate the Temple, and we arrested him. You can interrogate him yourself about all these things and ascertain the grounds of our accusations.'

The Jews also joined in the accusation, and alleged that it was so.

When the procurator gave him the nod to speak, Paul responded, 'I know that for many years you have been judge for this nation; and so I cheerfully make my defence. You can ascertain that it is no more than twelve days since I came up to Jerusalem, with the intention of worshipping [there]. And they did not find me in the Temple disputing with anyone, or collecting a crowd; nor [was there anything of that sort] in the synagogues or anywhere in the city. And they cannot prove any of the accusations that they now level against me. However, I [will] admit this [much] to you: it is in accordance with this Way, which they call a "sect", that I worship our ancestral God. I believe everything that is written according to the Torah and in the prophets. My hope is in God, and these people themselves entertain the same hope, that there will be a resurrection of the just and the unjust alike. Therefore I do my best to have a clear conscience towards God and towards human beings in every respect. After several years I arrived, to provide alms and offerings to my nation. In the middle of this they found me in the Temple, after I had been purified. There was no crowd, and no uproar; but there were some Jews from Asia, and [it is they] who should appear before you and make accusations, if they had anything against me. Or let these people themselves say what crime they discovered when I was up before the Sanhedrin. Or was it this single expression that I uttered when I stood among them, that "I am on trial before you today on the issue of the resurrection of the dead"?'

Felix adjourned them, being well informed on the subject of the Way. He said, 'When Tribune Lysias comes down, I shall decide your case.' He instructed the centurion that [Paul] was to be kept in custody, and that he was to have some freedom; the centurion was not to prevent his own people from looking after him.

Some days later, Felix arrived with his wife Drusilla, who was Jewish. Felix sent for Paul, and listened to him on the subject of faith in Messiah Jesus. As he talked about righteousness and self-control and the judgement to come, Felix became alarmed, and responded, 'For the time being, go. If I get a chance, I shall send for you.' At the same time he hoped that Paul would give him money. For that reason he sent for him quite frequently, and chatted with him. When two years were up, Felix got Porcius Festus as his successor; and wanting to do the Jews a favour, Felix left Paul in custody.

> We are perhaps to make a contrast here, between the odious (and entirely probable) sycophancy of the barrister Tertullus, and Paul's honesty and integrity. Once again, Luke puts the blame on Paul's Jewish opponents, though Felix ('a mere freedman', they might have muttered, dismissively, since Felix was a former slave, who had been set free by the Emperor Claudius) does not escape unscathed; he wants money, and for political reasons is happy to leave Paul in prison for two years, though he knows that he does not deserve it.

The appearance before Porcius Festus, and before Herod Agrippa and Bernice

25 ¹⁻²⁷ Three days after Festus had taken up his governorship, he went up to Jerusalem from Caesarea, and the high priests and leading Jews brought up the case against Paul, and begged him, asking for a favour (against Paul), to send for him to Jerusalem. They were going to set an ambush and kill him on the way. So Festus replied that Paul was in custody in Caesarea, while he himself was on the point of departing shortly. He said, 'So the influential people among you should come down with [me]; and if there is anything wrong about the fellow, let them accuse him.'

He spent no more than eight or ten days among them, and went back to Caesarea. The next day he was in session at the tribunal, and ordered Paul to be brought. When he arrived, the Jews who had come down from Jerusalem stood around him. They brought several serious charges [against him], which they were unable to substantiate, while Paul in his own defence said, 'I have not sinned against the Law of the Jews, nor against the Temple, nor against Caesar, in any respect.'

However, Festus, wishing to curry favour with the Jews, replied to Paul, 'Do you want to go up to Jerusalem, to be judged in my court on these matters?' Paul said, 'I am standing at Caesar's tribunal, and that is where I must be tried. I have done no wrong to the Jews, as you yourself know perfectly well. So if I am in the wrong, and have done something worthy of capital punishment, I am not trying to talk my way out of a death sentence. If, however, there is nothing in what they accuse me of, no one can throw me to them as a gift. I appeal to Caesar.'

Then Festus, having talked with his Council, replied, 'You have appealed to Caesar; to Caesar you shall go.'

Some days went by, and King Agrippa and Bernice arrived in Caesarea. When they had spent a number of days there, Festus brought up Paul's case. He said, 'There is a man who was left behind as a prisoner by Felix. When I arrived in Jerusalem, the high priests and the elders of the Jews told me about him, asking for a verdict against him. I told them that it is not [the] Roman custom to give a man over, with no questions asked, until the accused has been faced with his accusers and has had an opportunity for a defence against the indictment. So they came here; I made no delay, but immediately went into session, and had the man brought. They stood round him, but brought no charge of the crimes that I had been imagining, just certain questions about their own religion, and about one Jesus, a dead man, whom Paul alleged was alive. I was at a loss over the investigation of these things, and said [that] if he wanted he was to go to Jerusalem and there be tried on these matters. But when Paul appealed to be kept in custody, for Augustus's decision, I ordered him to be imprisoned until I should send him to Caesar.'

Agrippa said to Festus, 'I should like to hear the fellow.' 'Tomorrow,' he said, 'you shall hear him.'

So the next day, Agrippa and Bernice came in full state, and entered the auditorium, along with tribunes and with the most prominent men of the city. At Festus's command, Paul was brought [in]. Festus said, 'King Agrippa, and all you men who are here with us, you see this man. The whole crowd of the Jews appealed to me, both in Jerusalem and here, shouting that he ought not to live any longer. I realised that he had done nothing that was worthy of death; but when he appealed to Augustus, I decided to send him. I have nothing definite to write to the sovereign about him, so I produce him before you all, and especially you, King Agrippa, so that after a hearing, I may have something to put on paper. For it seems absurd to me to send a prisoner and not communicate the charges against him.'

The reader notices the similarities with Luke's account of Jesus' passion: a baying crowd of Jewish leaders is looking to kill someone who does not deserve it, and we have a weak and self-serving Roman official (we already know that Festus's speech to Agrippa is self-exculpating mendacity). And all the time, as throughout this book, the Holy Spirit is at work. Rome is now the destination (so there can be no question of a return to Jerusalem), the 'end of the earth' foreshadowed in the very first chapter of the work. It is no accident, therefore, that when Festus says, 'to Caesar you shall go', he uses Luke's favourite 'journeying' word.

This Agrippa is Herod Agrippa II, son of the one whom we earlier heard about, when he died in that unfortunate way (12:20-23), and therefore great-grandson of Herod the Great.

Paul's defence before Herod Agrippa: third account of his meeting with Jesus

26 ¹⁻³² Agrippa said to Paul, 'You have permission to speak about yourself.' Then Paul stretched out his hand and made his defence.

'With regard to all the matters of which I am accused by the Jews, King Agrippa, I think myself lucky that I am going to make my defence before you today, especially since you are an expert in all the customs and issues among Jews. So I implore you to listen patiently.

'All the Jews know [about] my way of life that I have followed since my youth, from the very beginning, amongst my people and in Jerusalem; for they know me from time past from the beginning, if they are willing to give evidence; because I lived according to the strictest school of our religion, as a Pharisee. And now I stand trial on the hope of the promise that came to our ancestors from God, the hope which our twelve tribes hope to attain to, as they persevere in their worship day and night: this is the hope for which I am accused, Your Majesty. Why do you people regard it as incredible that God raises the dead?

'Now I myself thought it incumbent on me to do lots of things in opposition to the name of Jesus the Nazarene. That is what I did in Jerusalem; and I locked many of the saints in prison; I had authority from the high priests – and I cast my vote against them when they were killed. In all the synagogues I punished them frequently – I tried to force them to speak against God; my fury knew no bounds, and I persecuted them even in cities outside this land [of Israel].

'In the middle of all this, I was journeying to Damascus, with authority and full power from the high priests. And about noon, Your Majesty, I saw a light from heaven shining, round me and those who journeyed with me, brighter than the sun. All of us fell to the ground, and I heard a voice speaking to me in Aramaic: "Saoul, Saoul, why are you persecuting me? It is hard for you to kick against the goad." I said, "Who are you, Lord?" And the Lord said, "I am Jesus, whom you are persecuting. Now – up you get, and stand on your feet. This is why I have appeared to you, to appoint you a servant and witness of what you have seen, and how I shall appear to you. I have rescued you from the people of Israel, and from the

Gentiles, to whom I send you to open their eyes, to turn them from darkness to light, and from the power of Satan to God, so that they may receive forgiveness of sins, and a place among those who are made holy by faith in me."

'This being the case, King Agrippa, I did not disobey this heavenly vision, but, first to those in Damascus, then in Jerusalem, and the whole region of Judaea I preached that they should repent and turn to God, by doing deeds appropriate for repentance. Because of this, some Jews arrested me in the temple and tried to murder me. So I have had help from God, down to the present day, and stand giving witness to small and great; I say nothing other than what the prophets and Moses said was destined to happen, that the Messiah was liable to suffer, that as the first to rise from the dead he would proclaim light, both to Israel and to the Gentiles.'

When he had made this speech for the defence, Festus said in a loud voice, 'You're mad, Paul: [too] much education is turning you to madness.' Paul said, 'I'm not mad, Most Excellent Festus; no – I am uttering words of sober truth. The king, before whom I speak fearlessly, knows about these things – for I cannot persuade myself that any of this has escaped his attention. For this was not done in a corner. King Agrippa, do you believe the prophets? I know that you do.' Agrippa said to Paul, 'Soon you [will] persuade me to become a Christian!' Paul said, 'Would to God that sooner or later, not only you, but also all those who hear me today will become as I am, apart from these chains.'

The king arose, as did the procurator and Bernice, and all those who sat with them. As they withdrew, they started speaking to each other, saying, 'This man is doing nothing that deserves death or imprisonment.' Agrippa said to Festus, 'This fellow could have been freed if he had not appealed to Caesar.'

This is a highly dramatic, and quite personal, confrontation. It contains the third account of Paul's encounter with Jesus. It also establishes for the reader Paul's complete innocence of the charges, while at the same time setting him irrevocably on the final journey to Rome. There is a personal 'electricity' between Paul and King Agrippa, which takes us rather by surprise, both at the beginning, where he refers to Agrippa's knowledge of Judaism, and at the end, where Agrippa does not join in Festus's abuse of Paul, but seems almost on the verge of succumbing to his eloquence. There is a real passion in Paul's final remarks, which sounds very much like the Paul whom we know from his letters.

The excitements of the journey to Rome; landfall at Malta

27 1-44 When it was decided that we should sail to Italy, they handed over Paul and some other prisoners to a centurion called Julius, of the Augustan cohort. We boarded a boat that belonged to Adramyttium, whose sailing-plan included various places down the coast of Asia, and set off. Aristarchus was with us, a Macedonian from Thessalonica. The next day we called at Sidon. Julius dealt kindly with Paul, and allowed him to go to his friends and get some attention from them. From there we put out to sea and sailed under the lee of Cyprus because the winds were contrary; we sailed across the open sea along Cilicia and Pamphylia, and came down to Myra in Lycia. There the centurion found an Alexandrian vessel that was sailing to Italy,

and he put us on board. For some days we sailed slowly, and barely made it to Cnidos. Since the wind was against us, we sailed under the lee of Crete, off Salmone. We barely coasted past it, and came to a place called 'Lovely Harbours'; the city of Lasaea was nearby.

A considerable time had elapsed, and sailing was already dangerous, because the Day of Atonement had come and gone. Paul therefore gave them some advice: 'Men – I see that the journey is going to involve damage, and much loss, not just of the cargo and the vessel, but also of our own lives.' The centurion, however, followed the advice of the steersman and the captain, rather than what Paul said. Since the harbour was not suitable for wintering in, the majority decided to sail from there, to see if they could get to Phoenix for the winter. Phoenix is a harbour in Crete that faces the south-west and north-west winds.

When a moderate south wind began to blow, they thought they had secured their objective. So they sailed along closer to Crete. Quite soon, though, the hurricane called Euraquilo tore down on Crete. It seized the boat, which could not sail into the teeth of the gale; so we gave in, and were carried before it. We ran under the lee of an island called C[l]auda, and were only just able to get the ship's dinghy under control. They used cables and undergirded the ship. Now they were afraid of running aground on the Syrtis, so they lowered the floating anchor, and simply drifted. The next day, because we were being violently battered by storms, they jettisoned [the cargo]. The day after that, they threw the tackle overboard with their own hands. For several more days we saw neither sun nor stars, and a violent storm raged. From now on, all hope of being rescued was gradually abandoned. No one was eating very much at the time, and Paul stood up among them and said, 'You should have followed my advice not to sail from Crete, and spared [yourselves] this damage and loss. Now I recommend you to keep up your courage. For none of your lives will be lost; all you will lose is the boat. This very night, you see, a messenger of the God to whom I belong, the God I worship, stood by me. The messenger said, "Do not be afraid, Paul. It is *inevitable* that you will stand before Caesar; and behold! God has granted you as a gift [the lives of] all those who are sailing with you."

'So be of good spirits, men. For I trust God: it will be just as it was uttered to me. We shall certainly run aground on some small island.'

When the fourteenth night arrived, and we were still drifting around in the Adriatic, about the middle of the night, the sailors suspected that land was close by. They took soundings, and found twenty fathoms; after they had sailed a short distance further they took soundings again, and found fifteen fathoms. Fearful that we would run aground on some rocky areas, they let down four anchors from the stern, and prayed for daybreak to come. Then the sailors tried to escape from the boat; they let the ship's dinghy down into the sea, pretending that they were going to lay out anchors from the prow. So Paul told the centurion and the soldiers, 'If these people don't stay on board, you can't be saved.' So the soldiers cut the dinghy's ropes, and let it drift away.

Until just before daybreak, Paul kept encouraging all of them to take food, saying, 'Today is the fourteenth day that you have been waiting, and still you are hungry and taking nothing. So I am encouraging you to take food. This is required for your preservation – for none of you will lose a hair of your heads.'

Saying this, he took bread and gave thanks to God before all of them, broke it, and began to eat. They all cheered up, and took some food. (In all we were 276 souls on the boat.) When they had eaten their fill, they lightened the ship by throwing the wheat-grain into the sea.

When day broke, they did not recognise the land, but they noticed a bay with a good beach, and they planned to run the vessel on to [this] beach, if they could. They slipped the anchors all round, and let them fall into the sea. At the same time they loosened the couplings that held the rudders, hoisted the foresail to the wind, and steered for the beach. They struck a reef, and ran the ship aground. The prow was stuck fast and remained immovable, while the force of the waves was breaking up the stern.

The soldiers decided to kill the prisoners; otherwise someone might swim off and escape. However, the centurion wanted to save Paul, and stopped them from doing what they intended. He ordered those who could swim to lead the way and jump overboard, then get to land; the rest were to go, some on planks, and some on bits and pieces of wreckage from the ship. So it was that everyone got safely to land.

This part of the fourth 'we' passage is a breathless adventure story. For Luke's purposes, three themes come usefully together here: there is the excitement, which he maintains with considerable skill, the first person narrative giving us the feeling that we are actually there. Second, there is the character of Paul. Notice his steadfast courage, and his certainty about what is going to happen ('the journey is going to involve damage . . . You should have followed my advice . . . If [the sailors] don't stay on board, you can't be saved'). Like Jesus, in Luke 5:1-11, Paul's supernatural knowledge defeats the expertise of professionals. He is only a prisoner; but it is he who is giving the orders round here (and it sounds, we note, just like the Paul whom we know from his letters!). Third, as the boat drifts helplessly in this Mediterranean storm, the reader, while wondering how they are going to get out of it, is nevertheless confident that they will do so. The reason is that again and again we have been told that Paul will get to Rome, the 'end of the earth'. Notice Paul's divinely inspired confidence that it is '**inevitable**' that he will stand before Caesar. For Luke, the Holy Spirit is in charge, and the Spirit cannot be thwarted by anything, whether accident or human malice. It is a bit like the storms in Homer: we always know that Odysseus will get home to Ithaca.

Excitement in Malta: Paul and a snake

28 [1-10] When we had got safely through, we found out that the island was called Malta. The natives (they were not Greek-speakers) showed unusual kindness. They lit a fire, and welcomed all of us, because of the rain that had come on, and because of the cold.

As Paul was gathering a heap of brushwood and putting it on the fire, a viper, driven out by the heat, came out and fastened on his hand. When the natives saw the snake hanging from his hand, they said to each other, 'This man is definitely a murderer; he was rescued from the sea, but justice has not permitted him to survive.' Paul shook the snake off into the fire, and suffered no harm. They waited for him to swell up, or suddenly fall down dead; but they looked and waited for a long time, and nothing untoward happened, so they changed their minds and said he was a god.

In the neighbourhood of that place, there was a property belonging to the chief official of the island, a man named Publius. He welcomed us, and for three days entertained us very kindly as his guests. Now Publius's father was sick, suffering from fever and dysentery. Paul went to him, prayed, and laid his hands on him and healed him. When this happened, everyone else on the island who had diseases approached [him] and were cured. They showed us great honour, and when we were going away they gave us all that we needed.

> As the story moves to its end, the adventures are still not over. We see Paul through the eyes of the Maltese, first as a murderer, then as a god; and we know that neither is the case. Luke allows a touch of comedy here, perhaps even a patrician sneer, to enter into his portrayal of them. As always, it is the figure of Paul that catches the eye. Vipers have no terror for him; the sick are cured, just as effortlessly as Jesus used to cure them (see Luke 4:38, 39 for a parallel to Publius's father). And there is absolutely no sign at all that he is a prisoner.

Finally the story reaches Rome

11-14 After three months, we set sail in a boat that had wintered on the island. It was Alexandrian, and had Castor and Pollux as its figurehead. We put in at Syracuse, and stayed [there] for three days. We cast off from there and reached Rhegium. A day later, the south wind came up, and on the second day we came to Puteoli. There we found some fellow Christians; they begged us to stay for a week. And so we came to Rome.

> So the journey is over; but for Luke the journey is never over, because the Holy Spirit is running it. The narrative has still a way to go; but at least the seasickness and the attendant storms are behind us, and we are among Christians for the first time since Paul left James's house, back in Chapter 21.

Paul's discussions with the Jewish community in Rome

15-28 The brethren from Rome had heard all about us, and they came out to meet us, as far as Forum Appii and Tres Tabernae. Paul saw them, and gave thanks to God, and took courage.

When we entered Rome, Paul was permitted to live on his own, with the soldier who was guarding him.

After three days, he called together the most prominent among the Jewish community. When they gathered, he said to them, 'Brethren, although I for my part have done nothing against the people [of Israel], or against our ancestral customs, I was handed over [by those in Jerusalem] as a prisoner, and put in the hands of the Romans. They examined me, and wanted to set me free, because there was no capital offence in me. But because the Jews opposed this, I was compelled to appeal to Caesar, not that I had any accusation to make against my nation. For this reason, I requested you to [come and] see me and talk to me, because it is for the sake of the hope of Israel that I am wearing this chain.' They said to him, 'We have not received any letters about you from Judaea; nor has any of the brethren come and reported or spoken anything evil about you. We desire to hear from you what you think. For what we know about this sect [of yours] is that it is contradicted everywhere.' They agreed a date with him, and came to him in his lodgings, in large numbers. He expounded to them and bore witness to the kingdom of God. He tried to persuade them about Jesus from the Torah of Moses, and from the prophets. Some believed his words; but others refused to trust him. They were at variance with each other, and they broke up. Paul uttered a single remark: 'The Holy Spirit spoke accurately to *your* ancestors, saying:

> "Go to this people and say:
> Hearing you will hear and not understand.
> Seeing you will see, and not look.
> For the heart of this people has grown gross.
> With their ears they hear with difficulty,
> and they have shut their eyes,
> lest they should see with their eyes
> and understand with their hearts,
> and turn back and I should heal them."

'So let it be known to you that it is to the *Gentiles* that this saving power of God has been sent. *They* will listen.'

This is an important moment. The reader has completed the journey to the 'end of the earth', and Paul follows the familiar pattern, of speaking first to his fellow Jews. In this case they do not precisely reject the message, but are divided about it, and are given the quotation from Isaiah 6:9, 10 to meditate upon, which Matthew has already used in his Gospel (Matthew 13:14) in a similar way. In this setting it seems a bit harsh, but from Luke's point of view the gospel has now arrived at its destiny, and that means, as Paul indicates in his final flourish, that it, the 'saving power', demands to be heard instantly. It is worth pointing out that the word that I have translated as 'saving power' appears elsewhere in the whole of Luke-Acts only at Luke 2:30 (where Simeon uses it in reference to Jesus) and 3:6 (where Isaiah is quoted, to explain the significance of John the Baptist). It is this opening of the 'saving power' to the wider world that engages Luke's attention, not the rejection of Judaism.

The point for Luke is, as always, nothing else than the work of the Holy Spirit. That is why the Isaiah quotation is referred specifically to the Spirit; that is why Paul needs the courage that he gains from the brethren who came out from Rome to meet him. The Spirit is free, and, although we hear of a soldier guarding him, so is Paul; he is free, for example, to summon the Jewish leaders, and address them with authority. We notice, too, how Paul has grown in independence and fearlessness in the course of the narrative. That is what the Holy Spirit does for a disciple.

Journey's end

30, 31 He remained for two whole years at his own expense, and received all those who journeyed to him. He proclaimed the kingdom of God to them, and taught everything about the Lord Jesus Christ, in all freedom, and without hindrance.

> This is a remarkable ending to the two-volume work. It ends, at 'the end of the earth', and an apostle (not one of the original Twelve) is witnessing to Jesus; Luke's final two phrases insist that nothing is preventing – nothing can prevent – the preaching. There is not a hint here of Paul's eventual martyrdom, which Christian tradition remembers, and of which presumably Luke's readers were well aware. The gospel's journey has ended, and instead, would-be disciples now journey to Paul. Luke does not encourage us to contemplate the fact, but Paul has at this stage been a prisoner for something over four years. Nevertheless, he has 'made it'.
>
> The gospel's journey, one of 'fire and mighty wind', never ends. The Western world is for the moment apparently indifferent to the promptings of the Spirit, but there are many places in the world where the wind and fire receive an enthusiastic welcome.

The Letter to the Romans

Introduction

Romans is Paul's longest and most influential letter. It is also very hard going, and the translator faces a formidably difficult task. A single phrase in Romans 5:12, for example, may have as many as eleven different meanings, and the jury is still out on which of them best suits the context. Since, however, the aim of this translation is to persuade the reader 'back to the text', the measure of its success will be whether you are inclined to stop and ask: what is Paul saying to me, here and today? And behind what Paul may be saying (for he would have been very surprised to learn that we should still be reading his letters so many centuries later) is a further question: what is God saying? Or: what does all this have to do with the meaning of my life?

Some of the commentary sections are longer than I should wish. This is partly because of the difficulty of this epistle; you can ignore them if they do not help your reading.

Since the Old Testament is so important to the argument, I have given Paul's quotations from it in footnotes. Consult them if you think it will shed light on the argument.

At times, I have to say, I have despaired of making Romans intelligible to a modern reader who has not much acquaintance with the Christian tradition; but if you persevere, you will find this letter, though frustrating in places, enormously worth reading. What he has to say is worth saying, and needs to be heard today. It is our task to find language for it that makes some sense to those around us.

313

Introduction

1 [1-7] Paul, a slave of Jesus Christ, called as an apostle set apart for the gospel of God, which [God] promised earlier through his prophets in the holy scriptures, about [God's] Son who came from the seed of David according to the flesh, who was marked out as Son of God, in power according to the Holy Spirit, as a consequence of the Resurrection [from the] dead, Jesus Christ our Lord, through whom we have received grace and a mission for faithful obedience among all the Gentiles for the sake of his name. Among those Gentiles you too are called [to belong to] Jesus Christ – to all those who are in Rome, beloved of God, called [to be] saints, grace to you and peace from God our Father and the Lord Jesus Christ.

This opening to Paul's most difficult and most majestic epistle (and it feels more like an epistle than a letter, more a formal treatise than a scribbled note) is astonishingly dense. In Greek it is a single sentence. In certain moods, I imagine Paul roaring out his dictation of the letter, back in Corinth, with poor Tertius, his secretary for the occasion, struggling to keep up. In other moods, Romans reads like a very carefully planned document. As the letter continues we shall be looking for clues as to why he wrote it. For the moment, just get the feel of it.

The secret of the whole letter, and of the whole of Paul's Christian life, is in the opening four words (in Greek; they have to be six in English). There are, however, one or two other words and phrases that we need to keep an eye on:

- 'called . . . set apart': the mission is something thrust upon Paul, not something he has chosen for himself;

- 'an apostle': this is an enormously important title for Paul. If ever you want to annoy him, just tell him that he is not a real apostle, because he persecuted the Church, and because he did not know Jesus in the days of his ministry;

- 'the gospel of God': this is a very important phrase in Paul in general, and in Romans in particular. As you read through the document, try to build up your own understanding of the content of this gospel;

- 'promised earlier through his prophets in the holy scriptures': central to Paul's theology (and it runs through the whole New Testament) is the certainty that the same God is at work in the Hebrew scriptures, in the life of Jesus, and in the Church's mission;

- 'God's Son': Paul traces this a) through descent from David, and b) through what happened at the Resurrection. It is an important idea for Paul – try, as you read, to see what it means for him;

- 'according to the flesh . . . according to the Holy Spirit [or: spirit of holiness]': this is the first mention of a contrast that will be important for the argument of Romans;

- 'in power': another important idea for Paul. In his view, the message about Jesus makes a difference that you can feel;

- 'Resurrection from/of the dead': for Paul, there is no gospel without Resurrection;

- 'Jesus Christ our Lord': do not even try to count the number of times you will encounter this phrase in Paul. It is important to him, as naming the one he loves. Unlike the evangelists, Paul uses 'Christ' as a name, not a title. Calling him Lord means three things: First, Paul refers everything to Jesus and offers him unshakable allegiance. Second, he is using here 'Lord' language of Jesus, which until his life changed so dramatically he would have used only of God. Third, the word 'Lord' is a title that Roman emperors were now allowing to be used of themselves. A clash was inevitable;

- 'grace and [apostolic] mission': we let these words go by almost without noticing; but they are of immense importance for Paul. 'Grace' means God's unconditional love for us, which is absolutely at the heart of his argument, and of Paul's dramatic change of life. 'Apostolic mission' is a consequence of what happened to him – his astonished discovery that God wanted him to tell non-Jews about this 'unconditional love' that God had shown in Jesus;

- 'faithful obedience': this densely packed phrase includes 'obedience which consists in faith', 'obedience into faith', and 'obedience which springs from faith'. Don't try so much to understand as to experience it;

- 'Among those Gentiles you too are called': the unconditional love is even on offer to non-Jews! And Paul delicately reminds the Roman Church that some of them (perhaps most of them) are in fact non-Jews;

- 'beloved of God, called to be saints': this is not something that the Romans have achieved for themselves;

- 'grace to you and peace from God our Father and the Lord Jesus Christ': a phrase of profound theological weight. It starts off looking like a regular formality of Greek correspondence – but there is nothing merely formal about God's unconditional love, nor about the 'peace' which only comes with God's gift of justice. As you read the letter, and the rest of Paul, you need to make up your mind about how Paul sees the relationship between 'God our Father' and 'the Lord Jesus Christ'. Here it seems that he holds them very nearly equal.

Chapters 1–4: First Main Section – The Human Plight and God's Response

Thanksgiving (or diplomatic tiptoeing?)

8-15 First of all, I thank my God through Jesus Christ with regard to all of you; because your faith is proclaimed in the whole world. For God is my witness (God whom I worship in my spirit and in the gospel of his Son) that unceasingly I make mention of you all the time in my prayers, begging that somehow, some time, at last I shall succeed in coming to you, by God's will. For I long to see you, in order that I might impart some spiritual gift to you, for you to be strengthened; [by] this means to receive some comfort with you, through our shared faith, yours and mine. I do not want you to be unaware, my fellow Christians, that I frequently intended to come to you – and up to this point I have been prevented – so that I might bear some fruit among you as among the rest of the Gentiles. I am under an obligation to Greeks and non-Greeks, to wise people and to fools – hence my eagerness to preach the gospel to you in Rome as well.

The thanksgiving is almost always a part of a letter from Paul, but look closely at the text here, and you will see that it is slightly perfunctory. What Paul is chiefly aiming to do, it seems, is to win them over. The Jerusalem Church and the Roman Church had links, so they will have heard about the fluttering in the dovecotes that had been caused by Paul's rather strong language in Galatians (despite its position in the New Testament, Romans was written after Galatians, and partly in an attempt to undo the damage). Paul did not found the Roman Church, but he wants to go there (as we learn also from Acts); and he wants to underline this desire of his. Why does he want to go there? He can hardly say that it is 'in order to preach the gospel to you', since they are already believers in Jesus; but he does hint at some such intention: 'to impart some spiritual gift to you, for you to be strengthened', before retreating from this position and making it more of a mutual preaching of the gospel. In the end, though, he is clear that evangelisation in Rome is his aim: 'that I might bear some fruit among you . . . to preach the gospel to you in Rome as well'. We shall not go far wrong if we think of him as treading on eggshells here.

A summary of Paul's gospel?

16, 17   For I am not ashamed of the gospel. It is the power of God for the salvation of everyone who believes, whether Jew (in the first place) or Gentile. For God's Righteousness is revealed from faith to faith, as it is written, 'the just [person] shall live by faith'.

For many readers, these few lines summarise the whole epistle, and Paul's particular 'slant' on the gospel of Jesus Christ. The emphasis, all the time, is on what God has done, and it is 'power', something that they can see and feel. It is also unrestricted, no longer addressed exclusively to God's chosen race. It has to do with 'God's Righteousness' (and you must try to work out the meaning of this phrase as the letter unfolds. I capitalise it, to underline its importance in his thinking); it has to do with 'faith', perhaps 'beginning and ending in faith', and it is underpinned by the Habakkuk quotation that we shall hear again, 'the just person shall live by faith'.[1]

---

1. Habakkuk 2:4

The human plight

18-32 The wrath of God is revealed from heaven on all human impiety and unrighteousness, of those who hold back the truth by unrighteousness, because what may be known of God is revealed among them. For God revealed [it] to them. God's invisible attributes from the [very] creation of the world are understood, and perceived, by means of the things that God has made: I mean his personal power and divinity. The result is that they are without excuse; because they knew God, and yet failed to glorify God as such, or give thanks [to him]. Instead they were infatuated by their own thoughts, and their undiscerning heart was darkened. They told [everyone] that they were wise, but lapsed into folly. They swapped the glory of God Imperishable for a statue of a human being, or of birds, or quadrupeds, or creepy-crawlies!

For that reason, God handed them over to the desires of their hearts, to impurity, so that they dishonoured their own bodies with them. They swapped God's truth for falsehood; they gave worship and service to creatures, not to the Creator – Blessed be God for ever. Amen.

For that reason, God handed them over to degrading passions. For example, their womenfolk exchanged natural for unnatural sexual intercourse. Similarly the men abandoned natural sexual intercourse with women, and burnt with desire for each other: men committing disgusting deeds with other men, and receiving the inevitable penalty of their aberration.

Just as they did not think it creditable to recognise God, God handed them over to a discreditable state of mind, [so as to do] things that are not fitting, filled with all kinds of unrighteousness, wickedness, greed, evil; filled with spite, murder, strife, treachery, malignity; whisperers, slanderers, God-haters, insolent overweening braggarts, inventors of evil, disobedient to their parents, unintelligent, undutiful, unloving, unmerciful. Such people, though they know perfectly well what God commands, and that people who do such things deserve to die, nevertheless don't just do them – they actually applaud those who act in this way!

> We mop our brow upon reading this, and mutter 'Steady on, Paul; there are ladies present!', for he uses decidedly strong language; indeed, so powerful are his emotions that the syntax rather falls apart, as I have tried to convey in the translation. We need to keep our nerve, however, for he has a trick or two up his sleeve. In the first place, he is not so much describing what actually happens, as imagining The Worst. Second, he is leading us into a trap. So if you find yourself nodding your head in approval of his denunciation of contemporary morality, be careful, because he is going to turn on you ('anyone who judges') in the very next section. You might be encouraged in this restraint by noticing, third, that the list of vices is a fairly uneven one. It includes various kinds of homosexuality, but also lists idolatry of several sorts, as well as 'unintelligence . . . wickedness . . . greed . . . quarrelling . . . whispering . . . disobedience to parents'. Almost anything will do here to indicate the plight of human beings without God. We should read it as a picture of the loveless morass that we can drift into if we forget what we are made for.
>
> And that, fourth, is the point. For Paul it is self-evident (in a way that it may not be to us) that homosexuality (and all the rest of the

list) is something in which people get trapped through their own folly or failure, not an authentic expression of human love and goodness.

Finally, as always with Paul, especially in Romans, we have to see what he is really about. Paul is talking about God, and God's mercy on the mess that we have made. We have a long way to go in this letter, of course, but unless we see that central to its teaching is God's free gift, we shall simply have a lovely time condemning others, without recognising our own desperate need of God.

A terrible shock

2 ¹⁻¹¹ So you have no excuse, my friend, whoever you are who judges. For on that precise point on which you judge your neighbour, you condemn your own self – for you who do the judging do the very same things yourself! We know that God's judgement is in truth on those who do such things. Is this what you think, my friend who judges those who do such things, and yet do them yourself, that you will escape from God's judgement? Or do you despise the riches of God's generosity, and clemency, and forbearance? Don't you realise that God's kindness is [meant to] lead you to repentance? But because of your hardness and unrelenting heart, you are storing up a treasure-chest of wrath for yourself on the Day of the Wrath of God and the Day of the Revelation of God's Righteous Judgement, when 'he will repay each person in accordance with their deeds'. Some, because of their perseverance in good work [will receive] glory and honour and immortality – those who are seeking eternal life. Others, who are characterised by self-seeking, and who are disobedient to the truth and [instead] obey unrighteousness, will [receive] wrath and rage. Distress and anguish [will come] on the soul of every person who works evil – Jews first, and then Gentiles. Glory and honour and peace to everyone who works good – Jews first and then Gentiles. For there is no snobbery in God.

The reader here gets a salutary shock. When Paul says, 'So you have no excuse', we think that he is still getting after those Gentiles. Suddenly, though, and out of a clear sky, it is his Jewish readers who are on the receiving end, the very ones who had been saying 'I hope those Gentiles are listening to this.' As always, the key is the generosity of God, and it may help to remember that the two words that I have translated as 'generosity' and 'kindness' will have sounded in the Greek of Paul's day a bit like 'the Christ of God'. When Paul speaks of the Day of the Revelation of God's Righteous Judgement, it is important for us not to glance nervously at the calendar, in case it is falling due; instead we must focus on the mystery of who for Paul is 'righteous', and how.

A dense passage

12-16 For all those who have sinned outside the law will die outside the law. And those who have sinned under the law will be judged by the law. You see, it is not those who hear the law who are righteous before God; it is those who do the law who will be Regarded-as-Righteous.

For when Gentiles, although they do not get the law with their mother's milk, actually manage to do what the law prescribes, these people are their own law, even though they don't know the law. They demonstrate that the working of the law is written on their hearts; their conscience bears them witness, and among them their thoughts accuse them or even excuse them, on the day when God judges the things that human beings keep hidden, according to my gospel, through Christ Jesus.

> This is a very tightly packed reflection on law and Being Righteous. It is not easy to translate the set of words associated with 'righteousness' or 'justification' in Paul, especially in Romans and Galatians; and his use of the word that I have translated as 'law' is not an easy one to put confidently and consistently into English. Perhaps at this stage the best thing is not to worry too much about the precise meaning but just get the 'feel', as you read the rest of the epistle, of the complex realities to which Paul refers. When he is obscure, it is sometimes better not to wrestle with him, but to move on.
>
> Notice that towards the end of this passage a part of the intention of this letter surfaces, a defence of 'my gospel through Christ Jesus'. News of the ill-tempered confrontation in Galatia will have reached Rome, and Paul wants the Roman Christians to accept his own slant on the gospel of Jesus.
>
> A question to reflect on throughout Romans: What is wrong with the law, according to Paul?

A difficult passage

17-24 If, however, you call yourself a Jew and rely on the law and boast in God; and if you know the will of [God], and discern what is best, because of having been instructed by the law you are convinced that you are a guide for the blind, and a light to those in darkness, and a tutor for those who can't think, a teacher for those who can't speak; [and if you think that you have] the embodiment of knowledge and truth in the law – do you then who teach your neighbour not teach yourself? Do you proclaim 'No Stealing' and yet steal? Do you tell [people] 'No Adultery' and commit adultery yourself? Do you abhor idols and [yet] rob temples? You who boast in the law, by your transgression of the law you dishonour God. For, as it is written, 'Because of you the name of God is blasphemed among the Gentiles'.

> This is not easy; clearly Paul now has in his sights those Jews whom he imagined as criticising the Gentiles' disgraceful behaviour; but are we to suppose that he thought that all his fellow Jews were thieves, adulterers and temple robbers? All we can confidently say is that he wants them to hear, 'don't think you're safe'.

Real Judaism

25-29 For circumcision is useful, if you do [what] the law [commands]. If on the other hand you are a transgressor of the law, then your circumcision has become uncircumcision. So if uncircumcision keeps the law's commands, will not his uncircumcision be reckoned as circumcision? And [then] the [one who is] uncircumcised and who does the law will judge you who, for all your education and your circumcision, are a transgressor of the law. For it is not the one who is outwardly a Jew, nor the one who is outwardly circumcised, i.e. in the flesh, but the one who is a Jew in secret, and is circumcised in the heart, in spirit rather than in the letter, that is the one whose praise is not from human beings but from God.

This is another difficult passage; the point towards which he is working, however, does begin to emerge, that there is to be a new, and far less secure, definition of what it means to be a member of God's people. This is clearly something that Paul's Jewish readers are expected to find rather shocking.

An imaginary dialogue

3 1-20 'In that case [you may want to ask], what advantage [does] the Jew have? How does circumcision help?'

[My Answer:] A great deal, in every way. For, Number One, they were entrusted with the oracles of God. You see, what if some have gone back on their trust, does their failure in trust undo God's trustworthiness? No way – let God be true, though every human were a liar, as it is written,

'So that you may be recognised as righteous by your words,
and you will be victorious when you are judged.'[2]

'Now if our unrighteousness serves to show God's righteousness, what shall we say? Can God who lets loose his anger be (humanly speaking) un-righteous?'

No way. For how will God judge the world?

'But if God's truth has redounded to his glory because of my falsity, why am I still being judged as a sinner?'

Surely it is not the case, as the slander against us goes, that (so some people allege) we do evil things so that good may come? These people deserve their condemnation.

'What then? Are we [Jews] superior?'

Not at all; for I have already charged that both Jews and all Gentiles are under sin, as it is written,

'There is no one righteous, not even one;
none who understands,
none who seeks God.
They have all turned aside, together they have become depraved.
There is none who does what is right,
not even one.'[3]
'An open grave is their throat;
with their tongues they have deceived.'[4]
'The poison of cobras is under their lips.'[5]
'Their mouth is full of cursing and bitterness.'[6]
'Their feet are swift to shed blood;
destruction and misery are in their way.'[7]
'And the way of peace they do not know
there is no fear of God before their eyes.'[8]

---

2. Isaiah 51:4
3. Psalm 14:1; Psalm 53:1-3
4. Psalm 5:9
5. Psalm 140:3
6. Psalm 10:7
7. Isaiah 59:7, 8
8. Psalm 36:1

We know that whatever the law says, it speaks to those under the law, so that it might stop every mouth, and the whole world become liable to God's righteous judgement.

Therefore no human being shall be reckoned-as-righteous in his sight, for through the law [comes merely] consciousness of sin.

> A difficult passage, and not really a dialogue at all, though it looks as though Paul is imagining possible objections to 'my gospel'. I have laid it out as a dialogue, however, so that you may see how it might have gone.
>
> The two key ideas here are, first, the primary reality, which is God's righteousness, and, second, the human response, 'faith', or, as I have translated it in the second paragraph, 'trust'. When Paul says of his opponents that they 'deserve their condemnation', and when he says of God that he 'will judge the world', the words used link with the idea of righteousness or justification. Paul also reiterates his important conviction that Jew and Gentile are on an equal footing in the face of God's judgement. He starts, moreover, at this point to hint at what is wrong (or insufficient) about the law. It is still only a hint, though, so we shall do well to withhold judgement until the end.

The heart of the matter: equality of all before God

21-26 As it is, God's righteousness has been revealed independently of law, although the law and the prophets testified to it; and God's righteousness, moreover, through Jesus Christ's faith [reaches out] to all who have faith. There is no distinction; for all have sinned and lack God's glory, reckoned-as-righteous at no cost, by his own free gift through the ransom [or: 'redemption'] that took place in Christ Jesus. God offered Christ Jesus as a means of expiation, through faith, by his own blood, as a demonstration of his righteousness through the leaving unpunished of the sins that were committed in former times, by God's forbearance, to demonstrate his righteousness at the present time, so that he should be both righteous and righteous-maker, the one who is from Jesus' faith.

> This is another densely packed passage, of which there are several interpretations. Rather than insist on one interpretation over against another (though I confess that translation is always already an interpretation) let me ask you to reflect on the following questions:
>
> 1. What is the contrast between 'law' and 'righteousness of God'?
> 2. What is the meaning of 'faith of Jesus Christ'? Is it 'faith in Jesus' or 'the faith that Jesus showed'?
> 3. What does it mean to refer to Jesus as a 'means' (or 'place') of expiation?
> 4. Who is 'both righteous and righteous-maker'?
>
> The following ideas are clearly of importance here; work out for yourself how they come together:

- God is just, and wants human beings to be so also.
- The scriptures tell us this.
- There are no 'front seats' in the theatre; all human beings have equal rights.
- Human sin is a reality that has to be dealt with. One metaphor for dealing with it is drawn from the slave-market. 'Ransoming' slaves ends up, via Latin, as 'redeeming' in English. Another metaphor is connected with the law courts, and means something like 'being acquitted', though it is more complicated than that. This is the idea that comes into English as 'justified' or 'made righteous'.

Triumphant conclusion

²⁷⁻³¹ So – what room is there for boasting? It is eliminated. On what kind of law? On the law of 'works'? No – on the law of 'faith'. For we calculate that a person is reckoned-as-righteous by faith, independently of works of the law.

Or [are you saying that] God is only [a God] for Jews? Surely God is God of the Gentiles also? Of course he is. For [it is] one [and the same] God who will reckon-as-righteous [both] the circumcised (as a result of faith) and the uncircumcised (through faith).

So – are we abrogating the law through faith? No way – on the contrary, we *confirm* the law.

It is evident from the tone here that Paul regards this as the successful culmination of his argument, but he leaves us trailing in his jet-stream, not without turbulence. Some key-ideas surface again here: law (which I have rather woodenly translated as such throughout, although occasionally 'principle' might be better here); faith; works; righteousness/justification. There is a final baffling rhetorical question about whether faith means the abrogation of law (which is what you might have supposed, up to this point), and which Paul now indignantly denies: 'we confirm the law'.

Perhaps the main thing to say, or rather to repeat, is that underlying all this is a question about God. And the heart of the matter is that there is not one God for Jews and another for Gentiles, but the same God for both.

A neat illustration

^{4 1-12} What then shall we say that Abraham found, our ancestor according to the flesh? If it was by [his] works that Abraham was reckoned-as-righteous, then he has grounds for boasting – but not before God. What does the Scripture say? 'Abraham had faith in God, and it was reckoned to him as righteousness' – but if someone is working, his wages are not reckoned as a 'freebie', but as something he is owed. Whereas if someone is not working, but has faith in the One who 'reckons-the-godless-as-righteous', then his faith is reckoned to him as righteousness.

In just the same way, David also speaks a blessing over the person to whom God has reckoned righteousness independent of works:

'Blessed are those whose lawlessness is forgiven
and whose sins are covered.
Happy the one whose sins God does not reckon up.'[9]

Now – is this blessing [called down] on the circumcised or the uncircumcised? For we say 'his faith was reckoned to Abraham as righteousness'. So how was it reckoned? When he was circumcised or when he was uncircumcised? Not when he was circumcised, but when he was uncircumcised. And he took the sign of circumcision as a seal of the righteousness-by-faith which [he received while he was still] uncircumcised – so that he is the ancestor of all those who believe through uncircumcision, so that righteousness-is-reckoned to them also; and he is the ancestor of all those who have faith through uncircumcision, so that it is reckoned-to-them-as-righteousness, and the ancestor of circumcision for those who don't just depend on circumcision, but who also follow in the footsteps of the faith that our ancestor Abraham had when he was still uncircumcised.

This is still not particularly easy, but the general lines of the argument are perhaps becoming clearer to the reader. Paul adopts a rather neat way of arguing. He takes the example of Abraham, whom all Jews revere as their ancestor; and he argues that Abraham is also the ancestor of uncircumcised Gentiles! Why? Remember that Paul is arguing that Gentiles who become Christians do not need to fulfil requirements of the Jewish law, such as circumcision, but they have been given righteousness-by-faith, which Paul contrasts with 'righteousness-from-observing-the-law'. But Abraham, he shrewdly points out, had righteousness attributed to him because of his faith as early as Chapter 15 of Genesis, whereas he is not circumcised until Chapter 17.

So Abraham had not done anything, only responded to God's love; certainly he had not observed the Torah at this stage – and yet he was made 'father of many nations', which in Greek is the same as 'father of many Gentiles', as many as the stars of the heaven or the sands of the seashore.

Still finding it difficult? Don't worry – read on.

Paul's explanation

13-17 For it was not through law that the promise came to Abraham or to his seed, [the promise of] inheriting the world; that promise came through 'righteousness-by-faith'. You see, if the law-dependent people inherit, then faith is emptied of content, and the promise is abrogated. Because the law brings about wrath; whereas where there is no law, there is no transgression.

Hence the 'from faith' bit, so that it would be according to God's-unconditional-gift, so that the promise would be sure for 'all his seed', not just for the Abraham who was law-dependent, but for the Abraham who depended on faith, who is the ancestor of us all, as it is written, 'I have made you the ancestor of many nations

---

9. Psalm 32:1, 2

[or Gentiles]',[10] in the sight of the God in whom he trusted, [the God] who makes the dead alive, and calls that which is non-existent into existence.

> Still puzzled? It may help to notice how Paul's attention is exclusively on God. One difficulty that you may still feel is how 'the law brings about wrath': as you read through the rest of this chapter you can ask whether he manages to answer this question, which is obviously important for the working of his argument. Paul does not perhaps trouble too much about the steps of the argument, since he has already long since arrived at the conclusion, which is that God has given us as a free gift the not-guilty verdict that the law failed to achieve. To receive the free gift, humans have only to respond (like Abraham) in faith. Then even the deadness of Abraham and the deadness of Jesus is no longer an obstacle to the power of God's love.

The conclusion

18-25 So [Abraham], hoping against hope, made-an-act-of-faith that he [could] become the father of many nations [or Gentiles], according to what had been said, 'So [i.e. according to the number of the stars] shall your seed [or descendants] be.'[11] And Abraham did not weaken in faith when he considered the deadness of his own body (for he was about a hundred years old) and the deadness of Sarah's womb. In the face of God's promise, he was not in doubt through lack-of-faith; instead, he was empowered through faith, and gave glory to God, and was fully convinced that what [God] had promised, God was capable also of putting into action. Therefore 'it was reckoned to him as righteousness.'[12] Now this 'it was reckoned' was not written just for him, but also for us, to whom it is going to be 'reckoned', us who believe in the One who raised Jesus Our Lord from the dead, Jesus who was handed over on account of our sins, and was raised up on account of our righteous-making.

> So this difficult argument comes gently into harbour, and the reader may be glad to know that the hardest part of Romans is behind us. The key to not being driven mad by the argument is to recall that Paul always has his eye on the destination, what God has ready for those who believe, and is a bit casual in his description of the voyage itself, perhaps because it seemed so obvious to him. Paul is obsessed by God and by Christ, and by what God has done in Christ, and wants nothing else to get in the way (such as circumcision, law, 'works'). God has given believers a free gift that in no way depends on anything we can do for God, and demands only the loving response that Paul calls 'faith' or 'trust' or 'commitment'.

10. Genesis 17:5
11. Genesis 15:5
12. Genesis 15:6

Chapters 5–8: Second Main Section – Reasons for Hope

Paul has now got the difficult bit out of the way (though not all of what follows is going to be plain sailing). We may not have understood every step of his journey so far, but clearly the heart of the matter is that what God does for us or offers to us is not dependent on what we deserve or achieve, but on God's 'free gift', for which Paul has used metaphors from the slave market ('ransomed/redeemed') and from the law court ('acquitted/ reckoned-as-righteous'). Our response is to be that commitment and trust which Paul calls 'faith'. The importance of this is that non-Jews, to whom Paul feels especially called, don't have to observe all the details of Torah, if they are to respond to what God has done in Christ. For such people, Abraham acts (rather surprisingly) as a kind of icon, because he showed his faith before his circumcision took place. Now read on.

God's unbelievable generosity in Christ

5 ¹⁻¹¹ So we have been reckoned-as-righteous as a result of [our] faith. We have peace with God through Jesus Christ, through whom we have gained access by faith to this free gift in which we stand, and boast in [the] hope of the glory of God.

Not only that; but let us also boast of our afflictions, knowing that affliction brings about steadfastness, and steadfastness brings about character, and character brings about hope. And hope does not disappoint, because the love of God is poured out in our hearts through the Holy Spirit that is given us.

You see, Christ, when we were still weak, nevertheless died at the right time on behalf of the impious!

Now you *might* just about die for a righteous person [literally, 'for with difficulty someone will die on behalf of a just man'].

Perhaps a person might have the guts to die in a good cause.

But God demonstrates his own love for us, in that while we were still sinners, Christ died on our behalf!

How much more, then, now that we have been reckoned-as-righteous by his blood, shall we be saved through him from the wrath? For if when we were [his] enemies we were reconciled to God through the death of his Son, how much more, now that we have been reconciled, shall we be saved by his life?

Not only that, but we actually boast in God through our Lord Jesus Christ through whom we have now received reconciliation.

In the three chapters that follow, Paul abandons the polemical tone and the slightly impenetrable argumentation that we have grappled with hitherto. Now he is trying to offer the grounds for hope. The reasoning is that a) we have peace with God; b) this peace comes for free; c) difficulties of various kinds do not count against this peace; d) God's gift in Christ is given to the undeserving; e) the icing on the cake is Jesus' resurrection: not just his generous death, but also the conquest of death.

Adam and Christ contrasted: the catastrophe reversed (and then some!)

12-21 Because of this, just as through one human being sin entered the world, and through sin death [entered the world], and so death came to all human beings seeing that all sinned.

For before law, sin was in the world; sin [could] not be charged to our account while law did not yet exist. Nevertheless, death was sovereign from Adam to Moses, even over those who had not sinned, in the likeness of the transgression of Adam, who is the 'type' of the One who is to come.

BUT the free gift doesn't simply balance out the original transgression.

The thing is, many people died because of that one man's transgression, and all the more God's grace, and the free gift by the grace of that one man Jesus Christ, [simply] overflowed to the many.

And the gift was not just a consequence of one man having sinned. For the judgement, arising out of that one man, issues in a verdict of 'guilty', and the free gift that arose out of many transgressions issued in a verdict of 'not guilty'.

Now – if because of the one man's transgression death reigned through that one man, how much more will those who have received the abundance of grace and the free gift of righteousness, rule, through the one man Jesus Christ!

So then, it goes like this: just as the result of that one man's transgression issued in a verdict of 'guilty' on all human beings, so one man's righteousness issued in a verdict of 'not guilty' [or: 'acquittal', 'righteousness'] and of life.

[To put it another way]: just as that single man's disobedience resulted in many peoples being made sinners, so, because of that other man's obedience, those many people are made righteous [or: 'not guilty'].

And then law sneaked in, to increase the transgression. But where sin increased, grace was present in even greater abundance, so that:

just as sin ruled by means of death
so grace should rule through righteousness
and lead to everlasting life, through Jesus Christ Our Lord.

> Once again Paul brings the difficult argument to a smooth end with that gentle and entirely characteristic conclusion, 'through Jesus Christ Our Lord'. But as we look back we can see the shape of the argument. First he makes a contrast between the powers: sin-guilt-death against obedience-righteousness-life where righteousness is the 'not guilty' verdict, and life is the idea, all-important to Paul, of resurrection.
>
> Second, the phrases 'all the more' and 'how much the more', which appear three times in the first part of Chapter 5, remind us that it is not a simple contrast between Adam and Christ; God's response to our plight is one of overwhelming generosity that reverses the catastrophe, and then a whole lot more. At times in this section, the thought may cross the reader's mind that Paul is so excited that he can hardly dictate coherently.

A possible objection answered

6 1-11 'What shall we say then? Are we to persist in sin, so that grace may be on the increase?'

No way! Given that we have died to sin, how shall we continue to live in it? Or don't you realise that we who were baptised into Christ Jesus were baptised into his death? So through [our] baptism we were buried with him into death, so that just as Christ was raised from the dead by the Father's glory, so we also should walk in newness of life.

You see, if we have 'grown together' in the likeness of his death, then we shall also 'grow together' in the likeness of his resurrection. So we know that our 'old humanity' has been crucified along with [Jesus], so that the sinful body is destroyed, with the result that we are no longer in slavery to sin. For the one who has died has been justified from sin.

If we have died with Christ, we have faith that we shall also live with him. We know that because Christ was raised from the dead he does not die any more: death no longer exercises its Lordship over him. You see, [the death] which he died, he died to sin – once and for all – whereas [the life] which he lives, he lives for God. So you [must all] reckon yourselves as dead to sin, but alive to God – in Christ Jesus.

Paul starts this portion off with another of his rhetorical questions, perhaps an objection from an imaginary opponent. The answer he gives enables him to do three things:

1. He makes the contrast between our plight and what God in Christ has done for us (from death to life);

2. he links the Romans' experience of their own baptism to this contrast (from death to life);

3. he asserts the absolute centrality, for Jesus, and then for all Christians, of the Resurrection (from death to life).

The whole story, for Paul, is one of movement from one power (sin-death) into another power (life-resurrection). So he is expressing in another way the contrast made in the previous chapter between what Adam did and what Jesus did.

Let God rule, not sin and death

12-14 Therefore:

- don't let sin rule in your mortal body, so that you obey sin's passions;
- don't give over your limbs as weapons of unrighteousness for sin;
- but do give yourself over to God, like people who are alive after death.

And do give your limbs over as weapons of righteousness for God. Sin does not Lord it over you; for you are not under the law, but under God's free gift.

Just at the end there, Paul raises once again the problem of the relationship of law and sin. Try, as you read, to ask the question, 'What, for Paul, is wrong with the law?' It may be helpful to notice the almost feudal idea of one's limbs as weapons offered in the service of a higher authority.

Notice also the wide range of ideas collected under the verb that I have translated as 'Lord it over': this includes the following:

- language hitherto reserved in Jewish culture for God;
- language that was now increasingly being used for the Roman Emperor, which was therefore an alternative power;
- language applied to Jesus, in an increasingly exalted way.

Another specious argument answered: the battle of the powers

15-23 'What then: are we to sin [seeing] that we are not under the law, but under grace?'

No way – don't you know that if you present yourselves as slaves, with a view to obedience, you are slaves to that which you obey, whether that is sin that leads to death, or obedience that leads to life. Thanks [or: 'grace'] be to God, because you were slaves of sin; but you obeyed wholeheartedly in accordance with the pattern to which you have been committed: you have been set free from sin and 'enslaved' to righteousness.

I am speaking in human terms, because of the weakness of your [frail] humanity. So, just as you presented your limbs as slaves to impurity and lawlessness to achieve iniquity, so now present your limbs as slaves to righteousness to achieve holiness. For when you were slaves to sin, you were free with regard to righteousness. And so what fruit did you have then? [Things] of which you are now thoroughly ashamed – for these things end up in death.

As it is, you have been freed from sin, and 'enslaved' to God; you have your fruit [which leads] to holiness – and that ends up in eternal life. For the wages of sin is death; whereas God's free gift is eternal life in Christ Jesus Our Lord.

> Once again, Paul poses an objection from an imaginary opponent, raising the spectre that sin might be a good thing; once again, he comes safely into harbour, concluding his argument 'in Christ Jesus Our Lord'. (Sometimes it seems that Paul cannot write a sentence without mentioning Jesus!) The basic answer, however, has to do with the clear sense of a battle between two opposing powers: death and life. One difficulty here is that Paul does occasionally use the same word in more than one meaning. For example, the word translated here as 'thanks' is his normal word for 'grace', a key idea in Romans; and in the same sentence I have had to translate one word both as 'lawlessness' and as 'iniquity'. Likewise I have put 'enslaved' in speech marks, because for Paul the believer's relationship to God is in principle quite different from that which people have to 'impurity and lawlessness'.

The problem of the law – an illustration

7 1-6 Or are you unaware, my brothers and sisters (for I speak to those who know the law), that the law lords it over the human being for as long as he or she is alive?

Let me give you an example: the married woman is bound by law to her husband while he is alive. If he dies, however, she is then released from the law [that binds her to] her husband. While her husband is alive, therefore, she is called an 'adulteress' if she belongs to another man; if, however, her husband dies, she is free of his law, so that she isn't an adulteress if she belongs to another man.

In just the same way, my brothers and sisters, you too have died to the law through the body of Christ, so that you belong to Another, the One who was raised from the dead, in order that we might bear fruit for God. For when we were in the 'flesh', the sinful passions which come through the law are at work in our limbs – so that they bear fruit for death. As it is, we are released from the law; we have died to that by which we were subjugated, so that we live a new sort of 'slavery', that of the Spirit, not the old sort, that of the letter.

> Paul is here seeking to explain his 'gospel of freedom' by an illustration from marital law: just as the wife is no longer bound to her husband when he dies, so the individual is freed by death from the law. You can see what Paul is getting at – but the death in the case of the believer is of course that of Jesus Christ, which slightly unbalances the illustration.
>
> Paul uses here and elsewhere the contrast between 'flesh' and 'spirit'. One helpful way of looking at this may be to think of 'flesh' as humanity when closed to God, and 'spirit' as humanity when it is open to God. This latter use is connected to, but also distinct from, Paul's use of the term 'Holy Spirit'.

Two more Jewish objections answered

7.13   'What shall we say, then? Does this mean that law is sin?'

No way – nevertheless, I only know sin through law. For I should not have known desire if the law had not said, 'Thou shalt not desire.'[13] Sin took its opportunity from the commandment and called forth all kinds of desire in me. For without law, sin is dead. I was once alive, independent of law; then when the commandment came sin sprang to life, but I died, and it turned out in my case that the commandment that was supposed to lead to life was the very one that led to death. For sin took its opportunity; through the commandment sin cheated me, and through it sin killed me.

[My conclusion is] that the law is holy, and the commandment is holy, and righteous, and good.

'Does that mean that the good for me became death [for me]?'

No way – what happened was that sin [became death to me]. In order that sin might appear, [as sin], sin brought about death [to me] through what was good for me, in order that sin might become exceedingly sinful through the commandment.

> Paul is still wrestling with this desperately difficult question of the relationship of sin and law. In certain moods, the idea that law brings about sin can seem mysterious to us; in other moods, we know the contrary effect that the words 'thou shalt not' can have on us.
>
> We must never lose sight of Paul's main contention: there is a battle between death and life, and only God's free gift in Jesus Christ can put us on the side of life. One answer that is sometimes given to the question 'What is wrong with the law for Paul?' is that 'It's not Jesus Christ'.

---

13. Exodus 20:17; Deuteronomy 5:21

The plight of sinners

14-23 You see – we know that the law is spiritual, whereas I am flesh, sold in bondage to sin, and I [hardly] know what I am doing. What I want to do is not what I [succeed in] doing; what I loathe is what I [end up] doing! Now, when I do what I do not want to do, I agree with the law, that it is good. And so in this case it is no longer I that am at work, but [the power of] sin that dwells in me.

I know, you see, that no good dwells in me (that is, in my flesh [my humanity as not open to God]). For I find it easy to will what is good; but actually to do it – not at all! For I don't [manage to] do the good that I want to do; instead it is evil, which I don't want to do, that I end up performing.

But if I'm doing what I don't want to do, it is no longer I who am at work, but the sin that dwells in me.

So this is the principle that I have discovered: when I want to do what is morally good, it is easy for me to do evil. For in my inner self, I joyfully resonate with God's law; but there is another law that I see in my limbs, which is at war with my mind's law, and keeps me imprisoned by the law of sin which is in my limbs.

> Paul is still struggling with the question of how sin and law are related; and perhaps we can only follow his argument occasionally. This passage includes what feels at times like Paul's own personal experience; many Christians have been encouraged by the thought that Paul too struggled to do what he knew to be right. Some scholars argue, however, that Paul's use of 'I' is here intended to capture the experience of those who live the old life, not his present experience of living in the new life of Christ.
>
> As always, that is the unfailing direction of his argument, and now this portion of the text comes to a stirring conclusion: the answer is Jesus Christ.

Jesus is the answer

24, 25 What wretched human beings we are! Who will deliver us from this body of death? Thanks to God through Jesus Christ our Lord. To sum up: with my mind I am a slave of God's law; but in my unregenerate humanity, I am a slave of the law of sin.

> Once again the reader asks: Is Paul talking about himself (and clearly Paul was not perfect) or about the plight of human beings without Christ? Turn the argument the other way round, though, and perhaps it does not matter: the solution for every problem that faces us, whether Paul or me or you, is Christ. So Paul, struggling through his argument, shouts (though not as loudly as he will soon be shouting) 'Thanks [or: 'grace'] to God!'

What has God done for us in Christ?

8 1-8 In conclusion, then, there is no condemnation for those who are in Christ Jesus: the law of the Spirit (i.e. life in Christ) has freed you from the law of sin and death.

What the law was incapable of, because of its weakness, through the flesh, God achieved. God sent his own Son, in the likeness of sinful flesh; and to atone for

Sin, God condemned Sin in the flesh, so that the decree of the law might be fulfilled in us who behave, not according to the flesh [humanity closed to God], but according to the Spirit [humanity open to God].

For those who live according to the flesh are flesh-minded; those who live according to the Spirit are Spirit-minded. For flesh-thought is death, whereas Spirit-thought is life and peace.

Because flesh-thought is hostility towards God, it doesn't obey the law of God – it can't. Those who are in the flesh are incapable of pleasing God.

> We stumble along after Paul; this is not really our thought-world. Nevertheless, we can keep our eyes on the main point: the battle-lines are drawn between spirit and flesh, life and death. God in Christ has given us the opportunity of doing what we could not do for ourselves, ending up on the right side in the conflict.

What the Spirit does

9-11 You, however, are not in the flesh, but in the Spirit, if indeed the Spirit of God dwells among you. If, however, someone does not have the Spirit of Christ, that person does not belong to [Christ]. If Christ is in you, then, while the body may be dead because of sin, the Spirit is life because of righteousness. If the Spirit of the One who raised Jesus from the dead dwells among you, the One who raised Christ from the dead will also give life to your mortal bodies through his Spirit that dwells among you.

> Once again, we are aware of two worlds: the world of death and the world of the Spirit; but here Paul's emphasis is on what the Spirit can do. We notice again, as so often in Paul, the central position that he gives to the Resurrection.
> At this point the reader may also want to start asking 'Who is the Spirit?'

What the Spirit gives

12-17 So, brothers and sisters, we are under obligation – but not to the flesh, to live according to the flesh. For if you live according to the flesh, you're going to die, whereas if in the Spirit you put to death the doings of the body, you will live. You see, whoever are led by the Spirit of God, these are the ones who are children of God; for you did not receive the spirit of slavery, [to fall] back into fear – you received the spirit of adoption-as-sons, which causes us to cry out, 'Abba, Father'. The Spirit testifies in support of our spirit, that we really are children of God. Now if we are children, then we are also heirs, heirs of God, and co-heirs with Christ, if we have joined in his passion in order to join also in his glory.

> From speaking of two realms, Paul moves almost imperceptibly into talking of only one realm. He starts this part by speaking of 'flesh' and 'death', but soon moves into that other realm, of the Spirit, and what the Spirit gives: the move out of slavery, and fear, and death into freedom, or what I had to translate 'adoption-as-sons' (even

though it applies equally to woman believers). The situation from which Paul draws this underlying image is that of the Roman and Greek household, in which the eldest son was normally the heir; and although there would be slaves in the same household, there would ordinarily be no question of their inheriting. But adoption was a very common device, so that the father of the house should not die childless, and those who might be adopted could include either slaves of one's own house or children of another family. 'Adoption' is now the third image that Paul has used in Romans for what God has done for us in Christ, after 'acquitting' and 'ransoming'. It links closely with Jesus' frequent presentation of God-as-Father, which reaches its striking climax in Mark's account of Gethsemani, with the cry, to which Paul here alludes, of 'Abba, Father'. This cry for Christians signifies a new life and undeserved status.

Looking ahead to God's gift

18-30   For I reckon that the sufferings of the present epoch are not worth balancing against the glory that is about to be revealed to us. You see, the eager expectation of the creation is awaiting the revelation of the children of God. For the creation became subject to frustration, not by its own volition, but because of the One who had subjected it in hope. Creation itself will also be set free *from* the slavery of decay *for* the freedom of the glory of God's children.

We know, don't we, that the whole of creation groans and suffers labour pains together right up to the present moment. Not only that, but those who have the Spirit's first fruits, that is we ourselves, groan inside ourselves, waiting for our adoption-as-sons, waiting for the redemption of our bodies.

We were saved in hope: now a hope [whose object] can be seen isn't hope [at all], for who 'hopes' for something they can actually see? But if we are hoping for what we [can't] see, then we are waiting patiently.

In just the same way, the Spirit comes to the aid of our weakness. We have no idea what to pray for in the proper way; instead the Spirit itself pleads on our behalf, with wordless groans. The one who searches hearts knows what is the thought of the Spirit, because according to God's will the Spirit prays for the saints.

We know that for those who love God, everything cooperates to bring about good; those are the ones who are also called according to [God's] purpose: those whom he knew in advance, he also decided upon in advance as being like his son, so that he is the first-born among many brothers and sisters. Those whom he decided upon in advance [are] the ones he also called; and those whom he called, are the ones whom he reckoned-as-righteous; and those whom he reckoned-as-righteous are the ones whom he also glorified.

> Paul, in this long section that has run from the beginning of Chapter 5, has been trying to give us grounds for hope. The invitation here is to look into a future that we can't quite see, and therefore have to hope for. Paul's tactic is to encourage us to hope by lifting our gaze from the present upwards into God's plan. The present finds us 'groaning' and 'frustrated'; but thanks to the Spirit we can look ahead to God's incomprehensible dispensation. This is

good news for those whom God has chosen; they are the ones whom Paul is trying to encourage here. His attention is at this point not at all on people who have not responded to God; so there is no room here for the dreadful doctrine of 'double predestination' ('I'm in and you're out') that has caused so much trouble in my country of South Africa. This passage is for our encouragement, not for anyone else's discouragement.

A glorious conclusion

31-34   So what shall we say to this? If God is on our side, who is against us? God [you remember] did not spare his own son, but handed him over on behalf of all of us – how can he help but give us everything as a free gift, along with him [the greatest of God's gifts]? Who shall bring charges against God's chosen ones? God is the One who reckons-as-righteous – who is the condemner? Christ Jesus is the one who died, and – more than that – was raised!

He is the one who is at God's right hand.

He is the one who intercedes for us.

We may not have followed the argument all the way, but we cannot help being buoyed up by the lyrical certainty of Paul's optimism as (once again) we come gently into harbour after the rough seas of some decidedly tricky argument.

A 'purple passage'

35-39   Who shall separate us from Christ's love?

Affliction? Anguish? Persecution? Famine? Nakedness? Danger? Execution? As it is written:

'For your sake we are done to death all day [long].
We are Reckoned as sheep for the slaughter.'[14]

No – in these matters we are winning a most glorious victory through the one who loved us. I am persuaded, you see, that neither death nor life, nor angelic nor demonic rulers, nor present nor future events, nor powers, nor height nor depth, nor any other created thing, will be able to separate us from the love of God, which is in Christ Jesus our Lord.

This is one of those 'purple passages' that enable the critical reader to forgive Paul all his prickliness and the numbing obscurity of some of his arguments. We may not understand quite how the arguments work, nor what precisely are the threats that Paul refers to, which might 'separate us from Christ's love', but there is no mistaking his confidence at the end, with that final phrase, so characteristic of Paul, so very much at the heart of this great lover: 'the love of God, which is in Christ Jesus our Lord'.

---

14. Psalm 44:22

333

Chapters 9–11: Third Main Section – What About Paul's Fellow Jews?

The story so far: Paul has worked out a heavily scriptural argument to defend 'his gospel', that what God has done for us is God's free gift, and therefore does not depend on anything we can do, including having ourselves circumcised. In the second section, he showed why non-Jews who are committed to faith in Christ have grounds for hope. That, however, leaves unanswered the question of God's Chosen Race. This was an existential question for Paul, who never ceased to regard himself as a Jew, and for many of his Roman readers, several of whom will have been Jewish.

How do Jews fit into God's plan?

9[1-5] It is the truth that I am speaking in Christ. I am not lying; my conscience bears me witness in the Holy Spirit – I have a great grief, and a constant pain in my heart. For my prayer was to be accursed and [separated] from Christ for the sake of my brothers and sisters, my fellow Jews according to the flesh.

They are Israelites. Theirs is the adoption-as-children, and the glory, and the covenants, and the law-giving, and the cult, and the promises. Theirs are the ancestors. From them came the Messiah, according to the flesh, the one who is God over all, blessed for ever. Amen. [Or, with a different punctuation of the Greek: 'May God who is over all be blessed for ever. Amen.']

You may make a number of objections to Paul; one thing, however, that you cannot say of him is that he is a liar. You can hear the sincerity in his voice as he contemplates the possibility of being cut off from his beloved Christ in order to have his fellow Jews take up their rightful place in God's dispensation. Christians, with our embarrassing and wholly unjustified tradition of anti-Semitism, need to listen carefully to Paul as he lists all the assets that his fellow Jews have: the privilege of being Israel, of being 'sons-and-daughters-of-God', of being the spectators (at Sinai, presumably) of the glory of God, of having received the covenants (at least those to Abraham and to Moses), having had the privilege of being told how to worship (in the tent and in the Temple), who gave the world the Twelve Patriarchs and, best of all for Paul, who produced Jesus Christ.

Notice the very different, far less negative, sense of 'flesh' here when Paul speaks of his fellow Jews as his 'kinsfolk according to the flesh' and of Christ as having come from the Jews 'according to the flesh'.

The final sentence of this portion might, if you punctuate it in one way, be a rare explicit reference on Paul's part to Christ as God. Punctuate it another way, and it becomes an 'arrow prayer' of praise to God for the excellence of the divine dispensation.

Just are the ways of God

6-13 Of course, it is not the case that God's word has failed. For not all those descendants of Israel are [real] Israel. Nor is it the case that all who are physically descended from Abraham are in fact his children. No – 'from Isaac physical descendants shall be called [forth] for you'.[15]

What this means is not that the children of the flesh really are children of God, but that the children of the promise are reckoned-as-descendants. For this is how the promise is expressed: 'At this time I shall come, and Sarah shall have a child.'[16]

Not only that: Rebecca conceived [children] by one man, Isaac our ancestor. When they were not yet born, and had not done anything good or evil, so that God's purpose of election might be assured, not by works but by the one who issues the invitation, she was told 'the older one will be a slave to the younger one',[17] as it is written, 'I loved Jacob and hated Esau.'[18]

One thing Paul has to do here is to demonstrate to his Jewish readers (and his reference to 'Isaac our ancestor' makes it clear that it is they whom he has in mind here) that God has not gone back on his promise. One of the ways of managing this is to argue that it was all foreshadowed in Scripture, which, for Paul, is God's dictated word; and so he is able to use texts that point a) to Abraham as the father of many 'Gentiles' and b) to the unexpectedness of God's election, as when of Isaac's two children the older is placed after the younger. Underneath all that, of course, is God's sovereign freedom to do exactly as he pleases. Like a 400lb-gorilla.

Once again you can see how later readers of Paul built on what he writes here, about the 'children of the flesh' over against the 'children of the promise', the dreadful doctrine of 'double predestination'. Once again, though, it is necessary to remind ourselves that Paul's interest is in the positive, 'what God has done in Christ', not the negative, 'those who are beyond God's love'. For Paul, no one is beyond God's love.

Two more imaginary objections answered: God is not unjust, but merciful

14-23 'What shall we say then? Surely there is no unrighteousness in God?'

No way – he tells Moses: 'I shall have mercy on the one on whom I shall have mercy, and I shall pity the one whom I shall pity.'[19] It is not therefore a matter of [human] will or of [human] exertion [literally: 'running'], but of God's mercy. For Scripture tells Pharaoh, 'For this very reason I have raised you up, so that I may reveal my power in you, and so that my name may be proclaimed in all the earth.'[20] Therefore, to whomsoever God wishes God shows mercy, and whomsoever God wishes, he hardens.

---

15. Genesis 21:12
16. Genesis 18:10
17. Genesis 25:23
18. Malachi 1:2, 3
19. Exodus 33:19
20. Exodus 9:16

So you'll now say to me, 'Then why does God blame [people like Pharaoh]? Who can resist God's will?'

My dear fellow, on the contrary; who are *you* to answer back to God? Will what is moulded say to its moulder, 'Why did you make me like this?' Does not the potter have authority over the clay, to create out of one and the same batch one vessel for honourable use and another vessel for less creditable purposes?

And suppose God wanted to show his wrath and to reveal his power, and so with great patience put up with vessels of wrath, ripe for destruction? And [suppose that it was] in order to reveal the riches of his glory, on vessels of mercy which he had prepared beforehand for glory?

All the way through this epistle, Paul has been wrestling (as we must all wrestle) with the mystery of the freedom of God, which can seem dark and harsh at times, but which for Paul is a gracious mercy, one that wants the best for human beings. 'It isn't fair,' the cry regularly goes up from the Society for the Protection of Oppressed Pharaohs – and all we can do is speak of God's gracious freedom! As we worry, however, about the clay that is turned into chamber pots instead of wine goblets (is Paul making a slightly heavy joke here, when he speaks of 'vessels for honourable use . . . vessels for less creditable purposes'?), we need to remember that his attention is far more on the undeserving clay that ends up in the place of honour at a banquet than on its sibling thrust unceremoniously under the bed at night.

God concentrates mainly on those whom he has called

24-29 These are the ones whom he called, not only from [among the] Jews, but also from [among the] Gentiles; as he says in Hosea:

'I shall call not-my-people, my-people,
and unloved, beloved.'[21]

'And it shall be in the place where it was said to them
"you are not-my-people",
there they shall be called "children-of-the-living-God".'[22]

And Isaiah cries out over Israel:

'If the number of the children of Israel were like the sand of the sea,
the Remnant shall be saved.
For the Lord will act on earth by accomplishing his word, and doing it quickly.'[23]

And as Isaiah predicted:

'Unless the Lord of Sabaoth had left behind offspring for us
we should have become like Sodom
and we should have resembled Gomorrah.'[24]

21. Hosea 2:23
22. Hosea 1:10
23. Isaiah 10:21, 22
24. Isaiah 1:9

Again and again we have to allow Paul to force our attention, not on our own plight, nor on that of those (like oppressed Pharaohs) whom we worry about, but on what God's gracious mercy is about. So here Paul is bringing the argument home by way of a string of Old Testament quotations that point to the unexpected mercy of God's action.

Conclusion

30-33 'What then shall we say?' The Gentiles who did not go seeking for righteousness have attained it – but it was the righteousness that came from faith. Whereas Israel, who did go seeking for the law of righteousness, did not even get there. Why? Because they [weren't looking] for the righteousness that comes from faith, but for the righteousness that comes from works. And they stumbled over the stone of stumbling, as it is written:

> 'Look – I am placing in Sion
> a stone for stumbling and a rock for tripping
> and the one who believes in it will not be ashamed.'[25]

In conclusion Paul leaves his imaginary opponent with nothing to say. We cannot deserve what God is offering for free, and any attempt to merit it leads to our stubbing our toes (or, to transcribe the Greek rather than translate it, 'being scandalised').

The Law and the Lord

10 1-13 Brothers and sisters, the desire of my heart, and my prayer for them [the Israelites] to God [is] for [their] salvation. For I [can] bear witness that they do [indeed] have zeal for God – but it is not directed by knowledge. For they fail to recognise God's righteousness, and seek [instead] their own righteousness, and have not submitted to the righteousness of God.

You see, Christ is the law's end-and-aim, for reckoning-as-righteous for all who have faith. Moses writes about the righteousness that comes from the law, that 'the one who does them will live by them'.[26] Righteousness that comes by faith, however, says,

> 'Do not say in your heart
> "Who will go up to heaven?"
> (That is, bringing Christ down)
> or: "Who will go down into the abyss?"[27]
> (That is, bringing Christ up from the dead).'

Instead, what does it say?

> 'The word is near by your mouth and your heart.'[28]
> That 'word', of course, is the 'word' of faith that we proclaim.

---

25. Isaiah 28:16
26. Leviticus 18:5
27. Deuteronomy 30:12, 13
28. Deuteronomy 30:14

> Because if you confess the Lordship of Jesus with your mouth;
> and if you believe with your heart that God has raised him from the dead,
> you will be saved.

The point is that it is with the heart that people believe – and that leads to righteousness.

And it is with the mouth that people confess – and that leads to salvation. For Scripture says, 'No one who believes in [him] will be put to shame.'[29]

You see, there is no distinction between Jew and Greek. For they all have the same Lord, who is generous with his wealth to all who call upon him: 'For all who call on the name of the Lord will be saved.'[30]

Paul in this section is still wrestling with the question of his beloved fellow Jews. Once again he is considering what is wrong with the Law; once again, the answer is that it is not Jesus. Paul surfaces an important idea here, that of the Lordship of Jesus. Remember that calling Jesus 'Lord' (Kyrios, in Greek) sets him explicitly up against whoever is the Roman Emperor for the time being, and sets him explicitly in relation to God. Read this passage carefully, and see just how close is the relationship that Paul envisages.

We should also note Paul's clever use of Deuteronomy 30:11-14. In its original context, as Paul and his readers will have known perfectly well, it was about how easy it is to obey the Torah. In Paul's hands, it comes to mean almost the opposite. What matters is not Torah, but Jesus Christ. This underlines the radical novelty of Paul's teaching.

The position of the Jews

14-21 So how shall they call on the one in whom they have not come to faith? But how shall they come to faith in one of whom they have not heard? And how shall they hear without a proclaimer? And how shall anyone proclaim unless they are sent? (As it is written, 'How beautiful are the feet of those who preach the gospel of good things!')[31]

Ah – but not everyone has obeyed the gospel! For Isaiah says, 'Lord, who believed our report?'[32] So: faith comes from hearing, and hearing is through the word of Christ.

But – I may say – did they not know? Indeed they did: 'Their sound has gone forth to all the earth, their words to the end of the world.'[33]

But – I may say – did Israel [really] not know? In the first place, Moses says,

> 'I shall provoke you to jealousy over what is not a nation,
> over a nation that is foolish I shall provoke you to anger.'[34]

---

29. Isaiah 28:16
30. Joel 2:32
31. Isaiah 52:7
32. Isaiah 53:1
33. Psalm 18:5
34. Deuteronomy 32:21

Secondly, Isaiah even has the nerve to say,

> 'I was discovered by those who were not looking for me,
> I became visible to those who were not enquiring after me.'[35]

And to Isaiah he says,

> 'The whole day I held out my hands,
> to a disobedient and obstinate people.'[36]

Paul is still defending God against the charge of lacking integrity for having turned to the Gentiles; and he considers various possible defences ('They never had a chance'), only to dismiss them ('Oh yes, they did'), with a series of scriptural quotations that are probably intended to lay bare the structure of the plight of the Jews:

- their problem was not that they had not heard the gospel;
- their problem was that they had heard and rejected it;
- they should have known; they had been warned;
- instead, they were 'disobedient' and 'obstinate'.

But, as we shall see, that is not quite the end of the story.

Has God rejected his people?

11 [1-10] My question is then: surely God [cannot have] rejected his people? No way! You see – I am an Israelite, descended from Abraham, of the tribe of Benjamin. God has not rejected his people, whom he foreknew.

Or do you not know what Scripture says about Elijah, how he prays to God against Israel? 'Lord, they have killed your prophets, they have destroyed your altars, and I alone am left – and they are seeking my life.'[37] And how does the oracle respond to him? 'I have left for myself seven thousand men, who have not bent the knee to Baal.'[38]

So therefore, even in the present time, there is a remnant, selected by grace. Now if it is by grace, it is no longer dependent on works, since [in that case] grace [would] no longer be grace.

What is the conclusion, then? What Israel was striving for, it did not attain, but those who were chosen did attain it, and the rest were 'hardened'. As it is written,

> 'God gave them a spirit of stupor,
> eyes not to see, and ears not to hear
> until the present day.'[39]

And David says,

> 'Let their table become a snare to them, and a trap
> and a stumbling block and a retribution to them.
> Let their eyes become darkened so as not to see.
> Cause their backs to bend for ever.'[40]

---

35. Isaiah 65:1
36. Isaiah 65:2
37. 1 Kings 19:10, 14
38. 1 Kings 19:18
39. Deuteronomy 29:4; Isaiah 29:10
40. Psalm 69:22, 23

We need to watch Paul carefully here; he is heavily involved emotionally, between his love for Christ on the one hand, and his love for his people on the other. The argument has three stages:

1. I am a loyal Israelite (this is an important 'plank'; Paul wants to eliminate any possible counter-objection that he might be 'against Jews').

2. He points to a pattern, found for example in the career of Elijah, a man with whom Paul may have sympathised as sharing his loneliness. It is the people who have rejected God and God's missionaries, not the other way round.

3. God always graciously raises up a 'chosen remnant' in Israel, in contrast to those who are (for reasons we do not really understand) 'hardened', perhaps by God himself (like Pharaoh).

Conclusion (of a sort)

11, 12   So then, my question is: Surely they didn't stumble so as to fall, did they?

No way – [what happened was that] because of their fall, salvation came to the Gentiles, in order to make them jealous.

> If their transgression enriched the world
> and if their defeat enriched the Gentiles,
> how much the more [will] their fullness . . . ?

Here the argument seems to reach a term. It may not make much sense to us, unless we recall that all the time, just below the surface of the text, is Paul's conviction of God's unfailing grace (and, of course, his puzzlement that his fellow Jews cannot see what to him is as plain as a pikestaff). The argument goes that Israel got it wrong, so the offer went to the Gentiles, not, however, in order to reject Israel, but so that in the end Israel, and everyone else, would return to God.

Gentiles – wipe that sneer off your face!
An illustration from horticulture

13-24   [Now] I'm speaking to you Gentiles. Insofar as I am 'missioned to the Gentiles' I glorify my ministry, to see if I might stimulate my fellow Jews ['flesh'] to jealousy, and save some of them.

You see, if their rejection [meant] the world's reconciliation, what will their acceptance [mean]? It can only [mean] life out of death.

If the first-fruits are holy, so is the whole lump. If the root is holy, so are the branches. And if some of the branches were broken off, and you, who are a wild olive, were grafted on and you became a partner with the root in the olive's richness, don't go boasting over against the branches – if you do that, [remember] it isn't you that support the root, but the root that supports you.

You may say, 'Branches were cut off, so that I might be grafted on.' OK – they were broken off because of a failure in faith.

And you are in place because of faith. Don't start thinking high-and-mighty thoughts: be in awe! Because if God didn't spare the branches that belong by right to the tree, he won't spare you, either.

So keep an eye on God's generosity – but also God's severity. God is severe on those who fail, but generous to you, *provided* that you persevere in his generosity, since you also will be cut off.

As for the Jews, provided they do not continue in their failure in faith, they will be grafted on; for God is well able to graft them on. You see, if you, who were from the wild olive [which is of a different species], have been grafted on to the domestic olive, how much more will those who are of the same species be [able to be] grafted on to an olive of the same species?

> Paul now comes at last to the question that he has been circling since that agonised opening to Chapter 9. It seems that he almost drifts into the illustration of the branches of the 'wild olive' grafted on to the root of the 'domestic olive', and we may fear that Paul's grip on the techniques of olive-farming is a bit sketchy; nevertheless, the point is clear enough:
>
> • it is all about the undeserved generosity of God,
>
> • to which we (whether Jew or Gentile) must respond in faith;
>
> • it is underpinned (as so often before in this letter) with a 'how much the more' argument.

Conclusion: God's mercy

25-32 You see, brothers and sisters, I want you to understand this secret, so that you should not regard yourselves as clever, because Israel underwent a partial hardening until the full number of Gentiles should come in – and that is how all Israel will be saved, as it is written,

> 'From Sion the Deliverer shall come forth;
> he shall turn away godlessness from Jacob
> and my covenant shall be theirs.'[41]
> 'When I take away their sins.'[42]

As far as the spread of the gospel is concerned, they are enemies [of God], on your account.

However, as far as election is concerned, they are beloved, on account of the ancestors.

You see, God's gracious gifts, and God's calling, are not to be revoked. Just as you, once upon a time, had no faith in God, but now have received mercy because of their failure in faith, so [your Jewish brothers and sisters] failed in faith, and you received mercy, only so that they also should now receive mercy.

For God has imprisoned everyone in failure-in-faith, in order to have mercy on everyone.

---

41. Isaiah 59:20, 21
42. Isaiah 27:9

We shall not really grasp what Paul is saying, all the way through the letter to the Romans, unless we focus all the time on the inner logic of his argument, which is, quite simply, that God gives his gift out of love for us, not out of admiration for our achievements. It follows that any complacent smirking on our part is a huge misunderstanding, not to say perversion, of God's offer of salvation. We are all on the same footing.

Conclusion: triumphant hymn to God's mercy

33-36
O the depth of God's wealth and wisdom and knowledge!
You can't search out his judgements!
You cannot track down his ways!
For 'Whoever knew the mind of the Lord?
or who was his counsellor?'[43]
'Or who ever gave [God] anything on account,
so that they would be repaid?'[44]
For from him
and through him
and to him
is all.
To God be glory for ever. Amen!

The third main section of the epistle now ends with another of Paul's 'purple passages'. Readers should allow themselves to be 'swept up' by the flood of joy here, because it is really this outpouring of love, rather than the impenetrable argumentation, that animates Paul's profoundest insights about what God has done for us in Christ.

Chapters 12–16: Final Section – 'Bits and Pieces'

The argumentation is all behind us now, and Paul spends the remaining five chapters dealing with what, from some angles, looks like a series of practical instructions such as he frequently offers in other epistles – how to live out the gospel. Is he (very diplomatically) referring to difficulties in the Roman Church (or churches)? The reader must decide. Notice the great big 'So' with which this new section starts, linking the whole story together. In Romans 1-4 he outlined the plight from which God in Christ has delivered humanity; in 5-8 he outlined our grounds for hope; in 9-11 he considered God's hidden plan with particular reference to the painful question 'What about my fellow Jews, then?' Now, finally, he draws out the practical implications for Christian living, probably with special reference to difficulties in the Roman Church that he and his readers knew about, but which we can only dimly reconstruct.

43. Isaiah 40:13
44. Job 41:11

General exhortation

12 ¹⁻³ *So* I invite you, brothers and sisters, by the mercies of God, to offer your bodies as a living, holy sacrifice that is pleasing to God, your rational worship. And don't conform to this world – instead let yourselves be transformed by renewing your minds, so as to test what is God's will, that which is good and pleasing and perfect.

For, through the grace that was given me, I tell everyone among you not to think high-and-mighty thoughts, over and above what it is appropriate to think. No – I'm telling you that your thinking should lead to sober thoughts, each of you as God has apportioned [your] measure of faith.

> For once, Paul's directness of speech seems to have left him; apart from a reference to 'worship', where he uses Old Testament language, it is hard to be sure what he has in mind here. Perhaps we should hear the sound of tiptoeing on eggshells. It might be that he is building on that splendid passage on which Chapter 11 ended, appealing to his readers to respond to the God whose love and mercy he celebrated there. But their response must be in terms of the new life that Christ offers, not the old life, the sacrifice of dying animals.
>
> Alternatively, if, as some scholars think, Paul only inserted Chapters 9-11 at a later stage, after writing the rest of the letter, then these words go back to the equally splendid passage at the end of Chapter 8.

The image of the Body (borrowed from 1 Corinthians)

⁴⁻⁸ For just as in a single body we have several limbs (or members), but not all the limbs (members) have the same function, so we are one body in Christ, although we are many; and we are individually limbs (or members) of each other. We have different gifts according to the grace that has been given us:

> If it is prophecy, let it be proportionate to the faith;
> or if it is service, let it be done in service.
> If one is a teacher, let them do it in teaching.
> If someone is a comforter, let it be done in comforting.
> If someone is a contributor, let it be done with single-minded generosity.
> If someone gives aid, let them be in earnest.
> If someone shows mercy, they should do it cheerfully.

> In 1 Corinthians, which was written before Romans, Paul made excellent use, humorous and penetrating, of the image of the 'body', trying to bring healing to a divided Church. Here he seems to make less use of the possibilities of the image, perhaps because the Roman Church is less divided than its Corinthian counterpart or (if what follows later is taken to hint at divisions in Rome) because he is being diplomatic. Notice, though, that, as in 1 Corinthians, he uses the image very adroitly, slipping between 'individual bodies' (12:1) and the Body of Christ, which is made up of those individuals with their bodies.

On Christian living

9-21　Your love should not have any 'acting' about it. You should hate evil, clinging to the good, devoted to each other in Christian love, giving each other the lead in mutual respect. Don't be idle [when you should be] serious. Stay 'on the boil' spiritually, serve the Lord. Rejoice in hope; bear up in trouble, be persistent in prayer. Take your share in the needs of the saints; make a thing of hospitality. Bless your persecutors. Bless them, not curse them! Rejoice with those who rejoice, weep with those who weep.

Think along the same lines as each other. Don't think high-and-mighty thoughts – accommodate yourselves to what is lowly. Don't become thinkers in your own esteem. Don't pay back evil for evil. Have a regard for what is honourable in everybody's eyes.

If it is possible on your side, be at peace with everybody. Don't get your revenge, beloved, but leave room for God's wrath, for it is written, 'Mine is the vengeance – it is I who shall repay',[45] says the Lord. On the contrary, 'if your enemy is hungry, feed them. If they are thirsty, give them a drink. For if you do this you will pile coals of fire on their head.'[46] Do not be overcome by evil; instead, overcome evil by good.

> In places here one has simply to guess at the grammar, and sometimes also at the meaning; but the gist is clear. Paul paints an agreeable and attractive picture of Christianity at work. Is he implying that the Roman Church was not doing some of the things he mentions here as desirable for Christians; or is it simply a list of generally desirable qualities?

Respect for the powers that be

13 1-7　Let everyone submit to the supreme authorities. For there is no authority except [that which comes] from God; and those which exist, are appointed by God.

It follows that everyone who resists authority is opposed to the ordinance of God; and those who are opposed will receive judgement for themselves. For rulers are not a terror for [those of] good behaviour but for [the] bad. Do you want not to be afraid of authority? Do what is good, and you will have praise from [them]. For the authority is God's servant for you, to bring about the good. If on the other hand you do what is evil, then be afraid. Not for nothing does authority wear a sword – for authority is God's servant, an avenger [who brings God's] wrath on the one who does evil.

It is necessary therefore to submit, not only because of the wrath of God, but also for the sake of conscience. For this reason also [you should] pay taxes; for they are God's ministers who are engaged on this very task. Repay your debts to everybody, tax to the taxman, and excise duty to the excise-man, reverence to those to whom reverence is due, honour to those to whom honour is due.

> Readers are taken quite by surprise when they come to this passage, which seems to come out of a clear sky, quite unexpectedly. Worse

---

45. Deuteronomy 32:35
46. Proverbs 25:21, 22

than that, it was shamefully used by the apartheid régime in South Africa to lecture Church leaders on the importance of obeying the law.

What is going on here? Does it mean that Christians can never resist an unjust government? Clearly Christians down the centuries have not reached that conclusion. It may be useful to make the following points to help the reader think through this passage:

1. This is Christianity's first attempt to work out the relationship of the group of Christians to the secular law. It may be doubted whether Paul would have expressed himself in quite these terms after he encountered the persecution of Nero, a few years later.

2. Paul will have seen for himself the advantages that the Roman empire gave to the would-be apostle, not least the possibility of speedy and safe travel, and the relatively secure despatch of letters.

3. It is quite possible that Paul knew that there was an issue about paying taxes among the Roman Christians. If the very negative attitude to Roman political authority that we find in the Book of Revelation was one of the strands of opinion in Rome, or if some of the members of that church knew some version of the story of Jesus' response to the question about the census tax (Mark 12:13-17 and parallels) that may have led to a clash with Christians or Jews whose instincts were to preserve the status quo, then Paul may here be attempting to solve a problem at long range.

4. There may also be a hidden warning to rulers, such as you often find in the Old Testament (see, for example, 1 Samuel 8:10-18), that they are obliged to exercise their authority appropriately.

Fulfilling the law

8-10   Actually, the only debt you should have is to love each other. For anyone who loves [their neighbour] has fulfilled the law. You see, all that stuff about 'You shall not commit adultery, you shall not kill, you shall not steal, you shall not desire',[47] and any of the other commandments, are summed up in this saying: 'You shall love your neighbour as yourself.'[48] Love does not do any evil to the neighbour – therefore love is the fulfilment of the law.

It is almost impossible to imagine that Paul does not have in mind the story of Jesus' strikingly sympathetic dialogue with the scribe, reported at Mark 12:28-34, significantly, perhaps, in the same chapter to which we pointed with regard to the previous passage, about submission to authority.

---

47. Exodus 20:13, 14
48. Leviticus 19:18

On staying awake

11-14 And especially since you know what time it is, because it is now time for you to be aroused from sleep; for our salvation is nearer now than when we came to faith. The night is far gone, and the Day has drawn near. Therefore lay aside the works of darkness, and let us put on the weapons that belong to the light. Let us behave decently, as though in broad daylight, not in carousing and drunkenness, not in sexual excesses, not in quarrelling and jealousy.

Instead, put on the Lord Jesus, and it should not be for the flesh that you are taking forethought, to satisfy its appetites.

> Two features of Paul's thought come together here. First, his sense that the Day (presumably of Jesus' Second Coming) is not far off. Second, Paul holds that Christians should maintain very high standards of behaviour.
>
> Is Paul making general observations about appropriate Christian behaviour (as perhaps he did in Chapter 12)? Or is he hinting at things that may be amiss in the Roman Church? The reader must decide.

When Christians disagree

14 1-23 When someone is weak in faith, accept them, but not for the purpose of getting into quarrels about ideological positions. One person thinks that he can eat anything; the weak person eats [only] vegetables. The person who [is willing to] eat anything shouldn't disparage the person who doesn't – for God has accepted him. [Likewise] the person who does not eat should not condemn the one who does. Who are you [to] judge a fellow slave? He will stand or fall before his own Lord; in fact he will stand, because the Lord is capable of causing him to stand. One person regards one day as more important than another; another person treats all days as the same – each of them is fully convinced in his own mind. The person who takes account of days does so for the Lord. The one who eats, eats for the Lord – because he gives thanks to God. And the one who does not eat – it is for the Lord that he abstains from eating; and he gives thanks to the Lord.

You see, none of us lives just for ourselves, and none of us dies just for ourselves. If we live, it is for the Lord that we live. If we die, it is for the Lord that we die. So: whether we live or whether we die, we belong to the Lord. This was the purpose for which Christ died and lived, that he might be Lord over both the dead and the living.

But you [over there], who are you to judge your fellow Christian?

And you, why do you disparage your fellow Christian? For we shall all stand before God's tribunal, because it is written,

'I live, says the Lord, for to me every knee shall bow
and every tongue confess to God.'[49]

Therefore each of us shall give an account of ourselves to God.

So – let us not go in for any more judging of each other. Instead, make this your [aim in] judging: not to put an obstacle or a scandal before your fellow Christian.

---

49. Isaiah 45:23

I am certain, I am convinced in the Lord Jesus that nothing is profane of itself; the exception is that when someone regards it as profane, then it is profane for that person.

For if your fellow Christian is grieved because of dietary considerations, you are no longer behaving in a loving manner. *Don't* let your diet destroy the one for whom Christ died. Therefore don't allow what you regard as good to be reviled. Because God's kingdom is not food and drink; God's kingdom is righteousness and peace and joy in the Holy Spirit. For the person who serves Christ in this respect is pleasing to God and esteemed among human beings.

To sum up: let us make our goal whatever tends to each other's peace and upbuilding. Don't tear down God's work, just for the sake of food. Everything is pure, but food is evil when a person eats it in such a way as to cause scandal.

It is good neither to eat meat nor to drink wine, or anything else over which your fellow Christian takes offence. As for you, keep to yourself the faith that you have before God. Congratulations to the person who does not reproach himself or herself on a matter which they approve. The person who is in two minds whether to eat will stand condemned, because [what he does] does not spring from faith; and everything that does not spring from faith is sin.

We may (once more) hear the sound of Paul tiptoeing through a minefield. Not all the details of what he is saying are clear to us; but we must assume that they would have been to his readers. Paul distinguishes a weak person from a strong; the latter ignores dietary rules, and may in so doing shock a weak fellow Christian; it also seems that there may have been disagreement over certain 'days', perhaps Sabbath and Jewish feasts. The answer, as always for Paul, goes back to 'the Lord' and what Paul sees as the inevitable consequence of knowing the Lord: absolute respect for fellow Christians. The teaching here echoes his earlier teaching, in Chapter 13, and in 1 Corinthians 12, about the Body of Christ.

It always comes back to Christ

15 [1-13] We who are capable have a duty to put up with the weaknesses of those who are less capable and not to please ourselves. Let each of us please our neighbour with the aim of doing good, and building [people] up. You see, Christ did not please himself; instead, as it is written, 'the reproaches of those who reproach you fell on me.'[50] For what was written earlier was written in order to teach us, so that we might have hope through the endurance and comfort of the writings.

May the God who is endurance and comfort grant you the gift to think the same thoughts with each other according to Christ Jesus, in order that with one mouth and with one mind you may glorify the God and Father of Our Lord Jesus Christ.

Therefore accept each other, just as Christ accepted you, to the glory of God. For my position is that Christ became a servant of the circumcision on behalf of God's truth, in order to confirm the promises given to the ancestors, and in order that the Gentiles should [through the (divine) mercy] glorify God, as it is written,

'Because of this I shall acknowledge you among the Gentiles,
and I shall sing praise to your name.'[51]

---

50. Psalm 69:9
51. 2 Samuel 22:50; Psalm 18:49

And again he says,

> 'Rejoice, Gentiles, with his people.'[52]

And again,

> 'All Gentiles, praise the Lord,
> and let all the people praise him.'[53]

And again Isaiah says,

> 'There shall be a root of Jesse
> and the one who shall arise to rule the Gentiles;
> in him the Gentiles shall hope.'[54]

May the God of hope fill you with all joy and peace by your faith, so that you may abound in hope, by the power of the Holy Spirit.

Notice, not for the first time, how for Paul it always comes back to Christ; what he has done, we must also do, and then Christian communities will look as they should. The reference to 'thinking the same thoughts' is also found in Philippians 2, as he introduces the great hymn to Christ, and we may remember that it was in Philippi that Evodia and Syntyche were squabbling, seriously enough for the news to have reached Paul in prison. Notice, too, the coherence of Paul's thought; when he sums up his message, 'accept each other, just as Christ accepted you to the glory of God', we are right back in the main argument of the epistle.

Paul talks to the Jewish Community in Rome

14-16   My brothers and sisters, I too, for my part am certain about you, that you are full of goodness, replete with all knowledge, well able to give each other admonitions. I have written to you a little bit boldly, just as a reminder to you, because of the grace given to me by God, for me to be a minister of Christ Jesus to the Gentiles, to serve the gospel as a priest. This is in order that the Gentiles' offering should be acceptable, consecrated in the Holy Spirit.

This is not the only time in Romans that Paul uses this liturgical language: see 12:1. Is he trying to snare the attention of his Jewish readers, and win them to his side?

Paul's ministry

17-21   Therefore I have matter for boasting in Christ Jesus, in my work for God. For I shall not have the nerve to speak of anything that Christ did not accomplish through me, [to bring] the Gentiles into obedience, in word and deed, by powerful signs and portents, by the power of God's Spirit.

---

52. Deuteronomy 32:43
53. Psalm 117:1
54. Isaiah 11:10

The result is that I have completed [the task of] preaching the gospel from Jerusalem, in a circle as far as Illyricum. I made it my ambition to preach the gospel where Christ had not been named, so that I should not build on anyone's foundation, but, as it is written,

> 'They shall see to whom it has not been announced about him,
> and those who have not heard will understand.'[55]

See how it always comes back to Christ. Remember the opening words of the epistle: 'Paul, a slave of Jesus Christ'. That is the ground and root of all that he is trying to do in this letter, the basis of his mission to the Gentiles, the insistence on what Christ, God, the Spirit have done. That is why he has gone from Jerusalem to what used to be called Yugoslavia, and why he is proposing to travel still further.

Why Paul wants to come to Rome

22-33 For this reason I have often been prevented from coming to you. Now, however, since I no longer have opportunity in these regions, and since I have for many years cherished a desire to come to you, so as to journey to Spain; for I am hoping to see you as I pass through, and to be helped on my way by you, as long as I can have some enjoyment of your company first.

My plan at present is to go to Jerusalem, to give [material] support to the saints. For Macedonia and Achaia have decided to offer some solidarity with the poor among the saints who are in Jerusalem. They have decided – and indeed they owed them something. For given that those Gentiles have shared in [Jerusalem's] spiritual gifts, they owe it to them to minister to them with material gifts. So when I have accomplished this, and have 'signed, sealed and delivered' this sum into their hands, I shall return by way of you into Spain. I am certain that when I come to you it will be in the fullness of Christ's blessing.

I implore you, brothers and sisters, through our Lord Jesus Christ, and through the love of the Spirit, to be my allies in the battle, supporting me with your prayers on my behalf to God, that I may be delivered from disobedient unbelievers in Judaea, and that my assistance to Jerusalem may turn out to be acceptable to the saints, so that I may come to you with joy, and, if God wills, have some rest and recreation with you.

The God of peace be with you all. Amen.

Paul has already indicated (1:10-15) why he wants to visit the Roman Church. The reasons there were:

1. to share a spiritual gift with them and strengthen them;
2. to get some mutual comfort from each other's faith;
3. to bear fruit in Rome, as he had among other Gentiles;
4. to preach his gospel in Rome.

---

55. Isaiah 52:15

He gives two further reasons here. First, he has done all he can, from Rome to what we used to call Yugoslavia, and he wants to go to Spain, passing through Rome on the way. Second, and we may hazard a guess that this was uppermost in his mind, he wants their prayers and moral support when he takes the collection from 'Macedonia and Achaia' (Philippi and Corinth, perhaps his two favourite churches) to the impoverished Christians in Jerusalem. It is even possible that his collection might be rejected; the intemperate language of Paul's letter to the Galatians (which was, we recall, written before Romans) will have cost him dear in Jerusalem, and it was possible that they might refuse to accept the collection 'from such a tainted source'. There were strong connections between the Jerusalem Christians and those in Rome, and Paul may have wanted the Roman Church to assist him, not only with their prayers, but also with a friendly 'e-mail' to the effect that 'Paul's all right'. Hence the uncharacteristically diplomatic tone of the Letter to the Romans.

The ending sounds almost like a brief farewell; and some have argued that the letter originally ended here; but Paul normally concludes with several personal greetings, which is what Chapter 16 now gives us.

The commendation of Phoebe

16[1,2] I recommend Phoebe to you, a fellow Christian of ours, and deacon of the Church of Cenchreae. I ask you to welcome her in the Lord, in a manner appropriate to the saints, and to help in any matter in which she may need your [help]. For she has been of great assistance to many, including myself.

The translators tend to call Phoebe a 'deaconess', but that is not what the Greek says. Now it must be admitted that a 'deacon' has presumably not yet taken on quite the hierarchical sense that it would attain just a little bit later, but Phoebe, unmistakably a woman, is equally unmistakably a figure of some importance for Paul. If Chapter 16 belongs here, it looks as though she may have been the person entrusted with bearing this weightiest of Pauline letters to its intended recipients. Not only that, but she has evidently helped Paul and many other Corinthians. And she is an official of some kind in the church at Cenchreae. Cenchreae was the easternmost port of Corinth, therefore certainly a wealthy suburb in its own right; and Phoebe may well have been influential among the Christians of Corinth also. Paul was not necessarily the 'male chauvinist pig' that his detractors sometimes depict.

An endless (and pointless?) list of greetings

3-16   Greet Prisca and Aquila, my fellow workers in Christ Jesus. They put their necks on the line for me, and I am grateful to them; and not just me, but all the Gentile churches also. And do greet the church at their house.

Greet Epainetus my beloved, the first convert [literally 'first-fruits', another usage of Old Testament cultic language] to Christ in Asia.

Greet Maria, who has laboured hard among you.

Greet Andronicus and Junia, my kinsfolk and fellow prisoners; they are conspicuous apostles, and were Christians before I was.

Greetings to Ampliatus, my beloved in the Lord.

Greetings to Urbanus, my fellow worker in Christ, and Stachys my beloved.

Greetings to Apelles, a respected Christian. Greet those in the house of Aristoboulos.

Greetings to Herodion, my fellow Jew.

Greetings to those in the house of Narcissus who are in the Lord.

Greetings to Tryphaena and Tryphosa, who worked hard in the Lord.

Greetings to beloved Persis – she worked hard in the Lord.

Greetings to Rufus, that outstanding Christian; greetings to his mother (whom I regard as my own mother).

Greetings to Asynkritos, Phlegon, Hermes, Patrobas, Hermas, and all the brothers and sisters with them.

Greetings to Philologus and Julia, Nereus and his sister, and Olympus, and all the saints who are with them.

Greet each other with a holy kiss.

All the churches of Christ send you greetings.

This section is never read in church; and you can see why. The reader may be puzzled why Paul should in this case single out so many people for mention. The reason, I suggest, is quite a simple one: Paul is on something of a diplomatic mission here, and one of his aims at this point is to remind the Christian churches in Rome that they have a good many people known to them who can vouch for him. They might live in Rome, or they might be frequent visitors to the capital. Nor is this at all improbable: Rome was that sort of place, for one thing, 'all roads lead to Rome', and a good many of the empire's inhabitants drifted through, rather to the annoyance of some old-fashioned Romans. For another thing, Paul himself was an inveterate traveller, and all Christians who travelled will have sought out the group of fellow believers in whatever city they reached. So there will have been a good many meetings and conversations, in various parts of the Mediterranean world, on which Paul can build his appeal here.

There are two things for us to notice here. First, the number of women (Prisca, Maria, Junia, Tryphaena, Tryphosa, Persis, Julia, Rufus's mother, Nereus's sister, and any others included in the general list). Second, notice the range of cultures and social classes. Among those with Latin names we have: Prisca, Aquila, Maria (if she is not Miriam, in which case her name would be Hebrew or Aramaic), Junia, Ampliatus, Urbanus, Rufus and Julia. Greek names include several that may well belong to freedmen or slaves: Epainetus, Andronicus, the household of Narcissus, Tryphaena and Tryphosa, Persis, Asynkritos, Phlegon, Hermes, Patrobas, Hermas, Philologus, Nereus, Olympas. And there are names that suggest a Semitic background: Miriam (if she is not Maria), Apelles, the household of Aristoboulos, and Herodion. In addition, we should remember the Jewish practice of having a Hebrew name as well as a name in the local vernacular, so some of the Latin and Greek names may also be given to people of Jewish origin. This is certainly the case for Prisca and Aquila, for example.

Paul may be making a point here about the inclusiveness of God's love. That is what the whole letter has been about, of course.

A final plea for unity

¹⁷⁻²⁰ I implore you, brothers and sisters, to watch out for those who cause divisions and offence, contrary to the teaching that you have learnt. Avoid them. For people like this are not slaves of Jesus Christ. Instead they are slaves of their own bellies, and because of their plausible speech and pious language, they [can] deceive the hearts of the unsuspecting.

You see, everyone has heard about your obedience, and so I rejoice over you; but I want you to be wise with regard to the good, but innocent with regard to what is evil.

The God of peace will swiftly crush Satan under your feet.

The grace of Our Lord Jesus be with you.

For Paul, unity was one of the indispensable marks of the Christian churches; and rebuilding unity is in part what this letter has been about. Whatever makes for division, according to Paul, cannot be from the Spirit of God. If we are, like Paul, and, unlike 'those who cause divisions and offence', genuinely 'slaves of Jesus Christ', then our tendency will be to foster unity rather than division. We can guess from Chapter 14 that there have been divisions in Rome, though Paul does not precisely say so, and Paul is determined to help them out of their strife.

Greetings from Christians in Corinth

²¹⁻²³ Greetings to you from Timothy my co-worker, and from Lucius and Jason, and Sosipater, my fellow Jews.

Greetings to you from *me*, Tertius, who am writing this letter in the Lord!

Greetings to you from Gaius, my host, and host of the whole Church here.

Greetings from Erastus, the city treasurer, and Quartus, who is also a Christian.

Once again, Paul insists on passing on greetings; for him this was an important thing to do. Timothy, half-Jewish and a team-mate of Paul's; Lucius, Jason and Sosipater could be Jewish, by the sound of their Greek names. Tertius (Paul's unfortunate secretary), Quartus (Tertius's brother?), and Gaius (who has a house big enough to contain a huge group of Christians at once), all have Latin names. Erastus has a Greek name, and is evidently an important city official. Incidentally, he could be the 'aedile' (or 'treasurer') named in an inscription on a pavement that was recently discovered in old Corinth.

A mysterious conclusion

25-27   To the One who can strengthen you, according to my gospel and according to the preaching of Jesus Christ, according to the revelation of the mystery that was wrapped in silence for eternal ages, but has at last been made known in the prophetic writings, in accordance with the decree of the eternal God, and has been made known to all the Gentiles for the obedience of faith, to the only wise God, through Jesus Christ, to whom be the glory for ever. Amen.

These closing verses, which are unmistakably from Paul's hand, and clearly fit the main argument of the epistle, are found in various places in the manuscripts: after Chapter 14, or after Chapter 15, or both at the end of Chapter 14 and in their present position. For our purpose that does not really matter, though it may raise questions about whether Chapter 16 was originally a part of the letter.

Notice how Paul begins and ends (as always) with God and Jesus Christ; how he speaks of 'my gospel', which Paul has been defending; how he links his message to the 'prophetic writings', while admitting the divine silence on the matter; notice his phrase 'obedience of faith'; and, finally, the fact that the message is made known to 'all the Gentiles'.

The First Letter to the Corinthians

Introduction

If you move from Romans directly to 1 Corinthians, you cannot help but be struck by the difference of tone, far less measured and far more intimate than the previous letter. When Paul wrote to the Romans, he was addressing a community that he had not founded, and who had reason to be suspicious of him. With the Corinthians he had a more intimate relationship, so that the reader will find that he mixes affection and anger to a degree that can seem remarkable until we remember that this is how things happen in families.

The opening address

1 ¹⁻³ Paul, called [to be] an apostle of Jesus Christ through the will of God; and Sosthenes [our] fellow Christian, to the Church of God which is in Corinth; to those who have been made holy in Christ Jesus, [who have been] called [to be] saints, along with all those who call upon the name of Our Lord Jesus Christ in every place, both their Lord and ours: grace to you and peace, from God our Father and the Lord Jesus Christ.

> In the ancient world, as in the modern world, the opening lines of a letter could very often be a mere formality; but Paul makes the conventions of letter writing work for him. We notice the following points:
>
> - He is 'called to be an apostle . . . through the will of God'. This is not a job which he has chosen for himself, but one for which he believes he has a divine vocation.
> - Paul is not alone, but operating in solidarity with other 'fellow Christians', such as Sosthenes.
> - Notice his obsession with Jesus, who is mentioned four times in these three verses. It sometimes seems that Paul can hardly write a sentence without mentioning his beloved.
> - One of the difficulties of Corinth was that the Christians there had something of an obsession with their own spiritual achievements. See how delicately he reminds them 'who have been made holy . . . who have been called to be saints', that like him they are the beneficiaries of God's generous action.
> - Obsession with our own achievements can blind us to the claims of others. Hence Paul's reference, again rather delicate, to 'all those who call upon the name (i.e. not just in Corinth) and to 'both their Lord and ours' (i.e. Jesus is not their private property).
> - Note, finally, the end of the address: 'grace and peace' are wished on them, 'from God our Father and the Lord Jesus Christ'. Keep in mind, but do not yet answer this question: what is the relative status for Paul of God and the Lord Jesus Christ?
>
> It may help you in your reading of the letter to know that (as Paul indicates at 7:1) the Corinthians have written him a (possibly rather self-satisfied) letter, with lots of questions to Paul; we may imagine them wondering, all the way through the first six chapters, when he is going to get round to answering it.

The thanksgiving

⁴⁻⁹ I give thanks to my God all the time about you, because of the grace that has been given to you in Christ Jesus. Because you have been enriched in him in every respect, in every kind of speech, and in every kind of knowledge, just as the testimony of Christ has been confirmed in you. The result is that you are lacking in none [of God's] free gifts, and you are waiting for the revelation of Our Lord Jesus Christ. He will confirm you to the end as blameless in the day of Our Lord Jesus Christ. God is faithful, through whom you were called into the solidarity of his son Jesus Christ Our Lord.

It was conventional in Paul's world to add a thanksgiving to the gods after the opening of a letter; but Paul really makes it work for him – it is no mere formality. Once again, he emphasises that what has happened to the Corinthians is not their achievement. He speaks of 'the grace that has been given to you in Christ Jesus . . . you have been enriched . . . the testimony has been confirmed in you . . . God's free gifts' (or 'charisms'). He even tells them that 'you are waiting for the revelation of Our Lord Jesus Christ', when perhaps they thought they had already received it, and that any 'blamelessness' of theirs was their own doing.

We should also notice Paul's use of the word that I have translated as 'solidarity'. This is a very important part of his understanding of Christianity. The Greek word is *koinonia*, and it means things like 'partnership, union, community, communion, teamwork'. So it is a very rich word – and it points to something that the Corinthians desperately lacked.

Notice, once again, Paul's obsession with Jesus Christ, and ask, once more, what status he gives him. See in particular how the Old Testament idea of the 'Day of the Lord' has become 'the Day of Our Lord Jesus Christ', and ponder what Paul is saying here.

Confronting division

10-17 I beg you, my fellow Christians, through the name of Our Lord Jesus Christ, that you all say the same thing; and [I beg you] not to have divisions among you, but that you should be made complete in the same mind and the same way of thinking. For it has been revealed to me about you, my fellow Christians, by Chloe's people, that there are squabbles among you; what I mean is that each of you is saying 'I'm for Paul,' or 'I'm for Apollos,' or 'I'm for Kephas.' Well *I'm* for Christ!

Is Christ divided? Was it Paul that was crucified for you? Was it in Paul's name that you were baptised? I give thanks to God that I baptised none of you (except Crispus and Gaius), so that no one can say you were baptised in *my* name. (And I also baptised the household of Stephanas; but I don't know that I baptised anyone else.)

You see, Christ did not send me to baptise but to preach the good news – not with clever speeches. Otherwise, the Cross of Christ might be emptied [of meaning].

Paul wastes no time in approaching the point. The Christians in Corinth were divided. They were not 'saying the same thing' (compare Philippians 2:2 for a similar appeal, based likewise on Christ and on the gospel). Paul is clearly furious about the divisions, which the Corinthians have presumably not mentioned in their letter to him.

How many parties were there at Corinth? At least three, and perhaps four, each attached to a particular personality. In the translation I have taken it as three (and there is a weight of scholarship on what each of these might have stood for), and the fourth as Paul's grim comment on their divisions: 'as for me, *I* belong to Christ'; but it has to be said that not all scholars would agree.

Then Paul attacks those who were marching up and down with placards reading 'Viva Paul, viva!' (and presumably he would apply the same analysis to the other parties, but diplomatically avoids the trap). Christ is (as always) the central figure for Paul; Christ (not Paul) was crucified for them, and it was in Christ's name that they were baptised (not Paul's, or Apollos's or Kephas's). This is perhaps why Paul gets into that confusion about whom precisely he had baptised, a confusion that I have tried to convey by the use of parentheses. I imagine him dictating in a room in Stephanas's house in Ephesus, perhaps in Stephanas's presence; he says, 'I baptised none of you', at which Stephanas hisses, 'You baptised Crispus and Gaius'; Paul then makes the necessary correction and proceeds, only to be stopped by another hiss: 'You baptised *our* household!' But you may like to think of other explanations of the text as it stands. He returns, however, to Christ, as always, and to the importance of the Cross, a theme with which he will stay for a while.

The rhetoric of the Cross

18-25 For the rhetoric of the Cross is stupidity to those who are on their way to destruction, whereas to us who are on our way to salvation it is the power of God. For it is written,

> 'I shall destroy the wisdom of the wise
> and the intelligence of the intelligent I shall bring to nothing.'

Where is the clever man? Where is the literate person? Where is the debater of this age? Has not God rendered stupid the world's 'cleverness'? For since – by God's wisdom – the world did not know God through its wisdom, God was pleased to save believers through the stupidity of [our] proclamation. Furthermore, since Jews demand miraculous signs and Greeks go looking for wisdom, we for our part proclaim Christ – Christ crucified! For Jews this is an affront; for Gentiles it is stupidity. However, to those who are called, whether they are Jews or Gentiles, it is Christ, God's power and God's wisdom. Because God's stupidity is wiser than human beings and God's weakness is stronger than human beings.

This is a passage of breathtaking audacity on Paul's part. The word that I have translated 'rhetoric' is 'word', and can also mean 'speech', and even 'reason' or 'rationality'. For Paul, the 'spin doctors' of Corinth had nothing to do with God's message, which is so different from their quest for applause that Paul expresses it in a series of daring paradoxes, between 'cleverness' (or 'wisdom') and 'stupidity', and between 'strength' and 'weakness'. The ultimate paradox, of course, is that of the Cross – the miserable death of a condemned and rebellious slave – which Paul sees as God's key move in the saving of the world. This insight enables Paul even to talk of 'God's stupidity' and 'God's weakness'!

The quotation is from Isaiah 29:19.

When God called the Corinthians

1 26–2 5 Think about how you were called, brothers and sisters. Not many of you were 'clever', as people understand it; not many were influential or nobly born. It was the stupid things of the world whom God chose, to shame the 'clever'; it was the weak things of the world whom God chose, to shame the 'strong'; and it was the 'low-born' and the 'despised' of the world whom God chose, the 'non-existent', in order to cancel out the 'existent', so that no human being might boast before God.

But it is [thanks to] him that you exist in Christ Jesus, who became our 'cleverness from God' and 'righteousness' and 'sanctification' and 'redemption', so that as it is written,

'Let the one who boasts, boast in the Lord.'

And so it was that when I came to you, my fellow Christians, I came not with any superior rhetoric or cleverness when I proclaimed God's mystery to you. For I determined that all I would 'know' among you was Jesus Christ – and [Jesus Christ] crucified, at that! And as for myself, it was in weakness and fear and great trembling that I came to you. And my speaking was not a matter of seductive and clever rhetoric; I simply demonstrated the power of the Spirit. My aim was that your faith should not depend on human cleverness, so much as on God's power.

We must imagine a stunned and perhaps indignant silence as these words were read out in whichever house the Corinthian Christians were gathered that Sunday. If they were rather fancying themselves as a cut above the rest they will not have been terribly pleased to hear themselves described as 'stupid things', 'weak things', 'low-born and despised' and 'non-existent'. But we shall get Paul wrong if we think of him here as simply trying to put them in their place. There is, undeniably, a touch of that, but Paul's main aim is to lead the focus of their attention away from themselves and towards God and Jesus.

We notice, once again, Paul's emphasis, in this context, on the crucifixion.

And, finally, the circumstances of his first arrival in Corinth are credibly related in Acts 18. Paul's 'fear and trembling' may have been either because of the kind of place that Corinth was, where only the streetwise survived, or because of failure in Athens, when they had laughed at him on the Areopagus because he had spoken of resurrection.

The quotation about 'the one who boasts' is from Jeremiah 9:23.

The difference between the human and the divine approaches

6-16 We speak of 'cleverness' among initiates: but not the cleverness of this world nor of the rulers of this world, who are being abolished. Instead we are speaking of the cleverness of God, which is wrapped up in a mystery, [the cleverness] which God marked out beforehand, before the worlds [existed], for our glory. This 'cleverness' [or: 'wisdom'] none of the rulers of this world recognised. For if they had done, they would never have crucified the Lord of Glory. Instead, as it is written,

'What eye has not seen and ear not heard,
and [what] has not come on the human heart,
what God has made ready for those who love him.'

It is to us that God has revealed [it] through the Spirit. For the Spirit searches everything, even the depths of God. For who among humans knows the affairs of the human person, except the spirit of that person which is in them?

Similarly, no one knows the affairs of God except the Spirit of God. We, however, have not received the spirit of the world, but the Spirit that comes from God, so that we may know the free gifts that God has lavished on us, the things that we speak of, not in the learned rhetoric of human cleverness, but in the 'rhetoric' that is taught by the Spirit, interpreting spiritual things to spiritual people. The person who lives merely on the human level does not accept what belongs to the Spirit of God; for they regard it as stupidity, and they can't grasp it, because it is discerned spiritually. But the spiritual person investigates everything spiritually; but the spiritual person herself or himself is not investigated by anybody. For 'Who has known the Lord's mind, so as to instruct him?'

But as for *us*, we have the mind of Christ!

> You will see that it is very difficult to decide between 'cleverness' and 'wisdom' as alternative translations of the Greek word *sophia*, because, as Paul uses it here, there is a bit of both. The heart of the matter here is the profound distinction, not to say yawning abyss, between God's way of doing things, and the way of the 'flesh' or 'unreformed humanity'. Paul speaks of the 'natural' or 'unspiritual' person; the Greek word *psychikos* is used rather oddly here, but clearly it is intended to contrast with the 'spiritual' person, who operates in God's way. I have tried to express the contrast by way of the idea of the 'person who lives merely on the human level', but nothing quite captures the sense of the original. The point is that the Corinthians were so flaunting their 'wisdom' that they did not grasp that it was merely 'cleverness' when set against what God was about in Christ.
>
> The citation 'What eye has not seen . . .' is from Isaiah 64:3; 'Who has known the Lord's mind . . .' is from Isaiah 40:13.

Two metaphors for unity: a garden, and a building

3 ¹⁻¹⁷ My brothers and sisters, it was impossible for me to address you as spiritual beings; [I could only address you] as belonging to the flesh, as 'infants' in Christ. I gave you milk to drink, not solid food, because you weren't up to it. And even now you are not up to it; for you are still belonging to the flesh. Because whenever there is factionalism and squabbling among you, aren't you still belonging to the flesh? [Aren't you still] behaving as human beings?

For example, whenever someone says, 'Well, *I* belong to Paul', and someone else says, '*I* belong to Apollos' – aren't you merely human? So what is 'Apollos'? Or what is 'Paul'? [Merely] servants, through whom you came to faith, in each case according as the Lord granted them. It was I who planted; it was Apollos who irrigated, but it was God who made it grow. The one who planted and the one who irrigated are just the same; each of them will get their own reward, according to their labour.

For [Apollos and I] are just God's collaborators. You are God's garden.

Or [if you like], you are God's building. In accordance with God's grace given to me, like a clever master builder, I laid a foundation, and someone else built on top. Let each one check how they build on top. In fact, no one can put down any foundation other than the existing one, which is Jesus Christ. And if a person builds on top of the foundation, gold, silver, precious stones, timber, hay, or straw, each one's work will become clear. For the Day will show it up; because it is revealed through fire. And the fire will test each person's work, [and reveal] what the quality is. If the work that a person has built on [to the foundation] turns out to be permanent, they'll get their reward; but if a person's work gets burnt up, they'll be punished (but they will be saved, although with a scorching, as it were). Don't you know that you people are the Temple of God, and that the Spirit of God dwells among you?

If someone destroys the Temple of God, God will destroy that person: for God's Temple is holy – and it is you people who are that Temple!

Paul starts by reminding his Corinthians (and, once again, we may envisage a not entirely comfortable silence as this portion of the letter is read out in the house-church) of how immature they were when he first evangelised them. And things do not appear to have progressed, sadly enough, for they are *still* immature! The evidence is their readiness to divide into factions, principally, it would seem, 'Apollonians' and 'Paulists'. When they do so, they are missing the point, which is that Christ is the foundation, and Christ 'is' the Church.

To get the message across, Paul uses two metaphors. The first is that of a garden, where Paul and Apollos are only gardeners (although the reader will perhaps reflect that as the planter, Paul may have a certain priority over Apollos!); and what matters is what God does.

The second metaphor will run throughout the letter; it is the idea of a 'building', where Paul (once again quietly claiming priority) laid the foundation, while Apollos (and others) has built the superstructure, in materials of varying quality. Once again, the key point concerns Christ: Christ is the foundation. This leads into a further development of the image, that of the congregation as Temple of God, and now we can see, clearly exposed for the first time, the seriousness with which Paul views any division in the Church, and his horror of those who cause such division. We are not far here from the image of the 'body', which in Chapter 12 Paul is going to use, creatively and with humour, to urge the cause of Christian unity. God is the one who matters.

Summarising the argument so far

3 ¹⁸-4 ⁵ Let no one fool himself or herself. If someone thinks they are 'clever' by modern standards, let them become stupid, in order to become [really] clever. For this world's 'cleverness' is stupidity before God. For it is written,

'The one who seizes the clever in their craftiness', and again,

'The Lord knows the reasonings of the "clever" – they lead nowhere.'

So – let no one boast in human beings. For *everything* belongs to you: Paul, Apollos, Kephas, the universe, life, death, things present and things to come – *everything* belongs to you. And you belong to Christ. And Christ belongs to God.

So a person should account us as servants of Christ, and as stewards of God's mysteries. What people look for in stewards is that they should turn out to be reliable.

It is of absolutely no interest to me that I should be judged by you, or by any human Day [of Reckoning]. I don't even judge myself. For I have nothing on my conscience; but that does not mean that God acquits me – it is the Lord who judges me. So – no premature judgement of anything, until the Lord comes; and he will shed light on the secret places in the darkness, and reveal the thoughts of hearts. So each one will get their praise from God.

> Here Paul pulls the argument together; his tone is a bit irritable at this point, which suggests that the criticisms (presumably of the 'Apollonians') have got to him. He is still using the word 'clever' or 'wise' (it is obviously on the table, between him and the Corinthians), still reminding them of the centrality of God, and the relativity of all human factions and all human assessment.
>
> 'The one who seizes the clever . . .' is Job 5:13; the next line is from Psalm 94:11.

'Puffed up' – Paul turns to sarcasm

6-13 All this, my fellow Christians, I have applied to myself and Apollos, on your account. I want you to learn from our situation the [meaning of] 'nothing beyond what is written', so that you should not get 'puffed up' on behalf of one [of us] against the other.

For who is distinguishing you? What do you have that you did not receive? And if you received [everything], why boast, as though you had not received it? You are already sated! You are already wealthy! Without any help from us you are already reigning monarchs!

If only you *were* already reigning – then we could reign along with you!

You see, I think that God has shown us apostles up as last in the queue, as [gladiators] who are going to die; because we have become a public spectacle, for angels and for human beings. We are fools on Christ's account, whereas you are intelligent in Christ. We are weak, whereas you are strong. You are glorious, whereas we are dishonoured. Right down to this present moment we are both hungry and thirsty; we are poorly clothed, and roughly treated, and of no fixed abode, and we struggle away, working with our own hands. When [they] revile us, we bless [them]; when they persecute us, we put up with it. When they slander us, we are conciliatory. We have become the scum of the universe, and everybody's scrapings, right down to this moment.

> For the first time, Paul uses the word that I have translated 'puffed up'. Apart from once in Colossians (2:18), 1 Corinthians is the only New Testament text that employs the word (see 4:6, 18, 19; 5:2; 8:1; 13:4). It is possible that it was a term already 'on the table', between Paul and his Corinthians, and so I have put it into inverted commas. It carries the idea of one of those toads that frightens off

its enemies by blowing itself up into a kind of football, and Paul uses it of his opponents, to indicate that they are not 'the real thing'.

So the issue here is not that between Apollos and Paul, but the problem between different Corinthian factions. Paul is very cross, though, as the sarcasm of this passage indicates. We also notice that he hints at the suffering that he has endured for the gospel's sake; and the Corinthians must have known about it, or there would have been no point in Paul's mentioning it. But the sarcasm, and the insistence on his own suffering, also reveals something of the slightly uncertain relationship he had with the Corinthian Christians.

Corinthian factionalism – the final appeal

14-21 [Don't get me wrong] – I'm not writing this to you in order to make you ashamed, but to admonish my beloved children. You may have had ten thousand tutors in Christ – but not all that many fathers. For in Christ Jesus, through the gospel, it is *I* who fathered you.

So I'm begging you, sisters and brothers, start behaving like me. That's why I send Timothy (he is my beloved and reliable child in the Lord), for him to remind you of my ways of doing things in Christ Jesus, just as I teach them everywhere, in every church.

Some people got 'puffed up' [thinking that] it was not me that was coming. I shall come to you soon enough (if the Lord wills), and then I shall find out, not the rhetoric of those 'puffed-up' people, but what they can do.

For the kingdom of God is not about rhetoric but about what people can actually do. So it's your choice: do you want me to come to you with a cane, or do you want me to come to you in love, and with a gentle spirit?

> Paul is shortly to move on to another issue, so he is bringing this issue of their divisions to an end. The Corinthians may (if Paul was not looking at them when they did so) have raised a quizzical eyebrow at his claim that he was not trying to make them 'ashamed', especially when he concludes with a threat to administer corporal punishment. We should notice, however, the unmistakable affection that Paul feels for those whom he regards as his children.
>
> Nevertheless, they have to get it right, and there is a firm warning (to which he will return later) that they must be respectful to Timothy when he comes; but it is clear that Paul would prefer the relationship to remain affectionate.

Incest in the community!

5 1-8 It is actually reported that there is sexual immorality among you; and it is sexual immorality of a sort that [you will] not even [find] among the Gentiles: one [of you] has his father's woman!

You people really are 'puffed up' – shouldn't you rather be in mourning, and have the one who commits the crime removed from your community?

I am physically absent; but in the spirit I am present, and as one who is virtually present, this is my final verdict on the person who has committed this crime:

In the name of Our Lord Jesus
with you gathered as a community, and my spirit being there with you,
with the power of Our Lord Jesus,
a person of this sort is to be handed over to Satan
for the destruction of his flesh
so that his spirit may be saved on the Day of the Lord.

There is nothing pretty about your boasting. Don't you realise that [it only takes] a little leaven to leaven the whole lump of dough? Purge out the old leaven, so that you may be a new dough, just as you have none of the [old] leaven.

You see, our Passover has been sacrificed – it is Christ! So let us celebrate the Passover festival, not with the old leaven, the leaven of evil and wickedness, but with the unleavened bread of sincerity and truth.

Paul's horror here is unmistakable. As a good Jew, he had been brought up to believe in the ancient wisdom that our sexual drive is too important and too powerful to be deployed outside the bond of marriage. Corinth, however, like many another international city (particularly, for some reason, cities with harbours and docks), was notorious for its sexual behaviour, although it is possible that the reputation was overdone. The crime here is that of incest with a stepmother. Paul would have been hardly less alarmed at the effects of the so-called 'sexual revolution' of the 1960s; and it is an open question whether the change in patterns of sexual behaviour in the years since that time has increased or diminished the sum of human happiness.

The reference to the Passover may plausibly be taken as an indication of the time of year when the letter was written. In 16:8 he announces his intention of remaining in Ephesus until Pentecost, so it is quite possible that he was writing at Easter time.

Relations with the sexually liberated outside the community – a clarification

9-13   In [my] letter, I wrote that [you were] not to consort with the sexually immoral. [I did] *not* [mean] those 'in the world' who are sexually immoral, or [for that matter] the covetous, and those who are swindlers, or idolaters; because in that case you would have to leave the world entirely! I am now writing to you not to have anything to do with a so-called fellow Christian who is sexually immoral or covetous or idolatrous, or a reviler or a drunkard or a swindler: [you should] not even eat with a person of that sort.

I have no interest in judging outsiders! Isn't it you people [in any case] who will judge insiders? Outsiders will be judged by God. 'Take the evil one from your midst.'

Paul's horror of sexual immorality has led the Corinthian Christians to a confusion that is perhaps pardonable. They thought that he meant eschewing contact with anyone at all who was that way inclined; but that is not his problem. As he half jokingly indicates, if you were to adopt that policy, you wouldn't have a great many people to talk to in contemporary Corinth. His problem is with having people of that sort inside the community, because they contaminate the rest. Here it may be helpful to think of his image of the old and new leaven. And we are verging here on the doctrine that we shall encounter later, of the Church as Body of Christ: if it is Body of Christ, then certain activities may not go on within it.

It may be worth noting that 'take the evil one from your midst' is a quotation from Deuteronomy (13:16; 17:7, 12; 21:21; 22:21), where it refers to the capital punishment of false prophets, idolaters, those who disobey the legal decision of parents, disobedient sons, and girls who are not virgins on their wedding night. Clearly that is not what Paul has in mind here.

A further complaint: litigation in the community!

6 ¹⁻¹¹ [Is it true that] one of you has the audacity, when he has a case against another, to seek judgement from the unjust, and not from fellow Christians? Don't you realise that it is Christians who will judge the world? And if it is among you that the world is judged, are you incompetent to judge small claims? Don't you realise that we shall be judging *angels*, never mind mundane matters? So – if you have competence over mundane matters, [why] are you appointing those of no importance in the Church as judges over you?

Now I [really] am speaking to make you ashamed. So is no one among you clever enough to judge a fellow Christian's case? Instead, are Christians going to law against each other? And before unbelievers?

It's already a defeat to you that you have cases against one another. Shouldn't you prefer to suffer injustice? Why don't you voluntarily let yourselves be defrauded? As it is, you people go in for injustice and fraud yourselves – *and* against your fellow Christians!

Don't you realise that the unjust will not inherit God's kingdom? Don't be led astray: those who are sexually immoral, idolaters, adulterers, pederasts and sodomites, thieves and the covetous, drunkards, revilers, and swindlers, will *not* inherit the kingdom of God. And that is what some of you were:

> Instead of this, you were washed clean;
> instead, you were consecrated;
> instead, you were justified by the name of the Lord Jesus Christ,
> and by the Spirit of our God.

Paul is quite clear that Christians have to be different; he is also clear that Christians belong together, so that if I am being unfaithful to God's covenant, then the body of Christ is thereby damaged. This is not the place to consider whether Paul's strictures on homosexuality can answer our modern questions; but we cannot evade the challenge. Being a Christian is a summons to integrity, and if we are to be members of the Body, we have to put God, and Christ, and not our own instinctual drives, in the centre of our lives. No one said it would be easy.

What's wrong with a bit of sexual hanky-panky?

12-20 'Freedom in everything' [is the slogan]. Yes – but not everything is profitable. 'Freedom in everything.' Yes – but that doesn't mean that I'll surrender my freedom to anything.

'Food is for the belly, and the belly is for food. And God will put an end to both of them.' Yes – but the *body* is not for sexual immorality but for the Lord; and the Lord for the body. God raised the Lord; and, thanks to his power, he will raise us also. Don't you get it? Your bodies are Christ's members! So am I going to take Christ's members and put them into a prostitute's members? No way! Or don't you realise that someone who is intimate with a prostitute is one body [with her]? For it says 'the two shall become one flesh'. Whereas the one who is intimate with the Lord is one spirit [with him].

Steer clear of sexual immorality. Every other sin that a person might commit is outside the body; but the one who commits sexual immorality sins against their own body. Or don't you realise that your body is the Temple of the Holy Spirit in your midst? [The Holy Spirit] is what you have received from God, and you are not your own property; for you were bought at a price. So – glorify God in your body.

Paul is arguing with very great passion here, and it is in consequence not always easy to follow his argument. Notice, however, that the theme of the 'body', which has been just below the surface of the text for a while now, here comes to the top. Paul uses it three times. The first time, we think that it certainly must refer to our physical body, until we read that it is 'for the Lord'. The second time seems at first to refer to the physical body, until we reflect that gluttony, drug addiction and drunkenness might also be classed as sins in this category. So it is possible to read these two both as the physical body and as the Body of Christ. The third use sounds ambiguous also, at least in English; in Greek, however, the body which is the 'Temple of the Holy Spirit in your midst' is the body of 'you-plural'. So in our conduct, and apparently especially in our sexual conduct, our task is to put ahead of our own immediate satisfaction not only God and Christ, but also our fellow members of the Body, who are affected by what we do, especially in the all-important area of sexuality.

Paul Answers the Corinthians' Letter at Last (7:1–11:34)

While the tirade has been going on, those in the house-church who had not been stunned into a mental blank may have been wondering if he was ever going to get round to answering their (perhaps rather self-satisfied) letter. Those near enough to whoever was reading it out to them will have noticed that the scroll was now getting on for halfway through, and may have asked themselves if Paul was going to have time to reply. Those further away may have been glancing at the water clock or the declining movement of the sun's rays to know where they were at.

Is sex allowed for Christians?

7 1-7 Now for what you wrote, 'It is good for a man not to have intercourse with a woman'. No – because of cases of sexual immorality, let every man stay with his own wife, and let every woman stay with her own husband. Moreover, the husband should give his wife her due, and similarly the wife her husband. The woman does not have the freedom of her own body – it is the man's; and similarly the man does not have the freedom of his own body – it is the wife's. Don't deprive each other, except by agreement, and for a time, [for example] in order to have leisure for prayer; and then you should come back together again, so that Satan may not tempt you because of your problem with self-control. I'm saying this as a concession rather than as a command. I'd like everyone to be like me – but [of course] everyone has their own gift from God, some like this, some like that.

> Paul seems to be dealing with a group in Corinth who thought that sex was Bad. Paul wants to deny this, and also to acknowledge that it is a powerful (God-given) drive. Notice his emphasis on the equality between husband and wife and on marriage as a partnership. The final sentence seems to imply that Paul is a celibate, or at least widowed (which makes life difficult for those who locate a 'Mrs Paul' in Philippi – see Philippians 4:3; unless he is one of those able to remain celibate within marriage).

On marital status

8-11 My message to the unmarried and widows is this: it is good for them to stay as I am. If, however, they are not [managing to] control themselves, then let them marry – for it is better to marry than to burn.

To those who are married, my advice (not mine but the Lord's) is that a wife should not separate from her husband; but if she does separate, she should remain unmarried or be reconciled to her husband. And I advise a husband not to abandon his wife.

> The context of this passage, we shall see later, is Paul's sense that the end is coming soon, so placing him and his Corinthians in a situation quite different from our own. He remains, too, passionately opposed to any kind of sexual immorality – it does not fit with the Body of Christ.
>
> What does he mean by 'burn'? Scholars are divided between burning passions, and burning in Hell, or in the fire of judgement. You must make your own decision.
>
> Paul does not countenance separation under these circumstances, and certainly not in order to marry someone else!

What if you're married to a non-Christian?

12-16 As for the others (this is me talking, not the Lord): if a Christian man has a wife who is a non-believer, and she is happy to live with him, he should not divorce her. And if a [Christian] woman has a husband who is a non-believer, she should not divorce her husband.

You see, the non-believing husband [can] be sanctified by his [Christian] wife; and the non-believing wife through her Christian [husband]. Otherwise your children [would be] unclean; but as it is they are holy. But if the non-believer [opts for] separation, let them separate; under circumstances like these, the Christian husband or wife is not enslaved: God has called you [to be] in peace. How do you know, wife, but that you'll save your husband? Or, husband, if you'll save your wife?

> This is an admirably balanced judgement. Paul is quite realistic about the strains of 'mixed marriages', but also knows of their possibilities.
>
> A general rule in this part of the letter is that Paul is trying to think his way through a new problem, so it represents something closer to a beginning than an end of the Church's positioning with regard to marriage and divorce. And because Paul thought that the present dispensation might not last much longer (perhaps Jesus' Second Coming would be next Wednesday at the latest) he is, as we have said, in a rather different position from ourselves.

What about circumcision and slavery?

17-24 Anyway, as the Lord has given each one their [allotted] portion, as God has called each of them, let them walk in that way. This is the rule I make in all the churches. If someone was circumcised when they were called, let them not undergo the operation to remove the circumcision. If they are called as uncircumcised, let them not be circumcised. Circumcision and uncircumcision are wholly unimportant; [what matters] is the keeping of the commands of God. Everyone should remain in the calling to which they were originally called. If you were called as a slave, don't worry about it. Even if you are able to get free, rather make use of your situation. For the one who is called in the Lord as a slave is the Lord's freedman. Similarly, the one who was free when called is Christ's slave.

You were purchased at a price – don't get enslaved to human beings. [So], brothers and sisters, as each of you was called, so you should remain before God.

> Obviously the Corinthians have asked whether turning to Christ meant an end to social and ethnic and religious distinctions such as slavery and circumcision. Paul wants them instead to concentrate on what God has done for them in Christ (although he is clear that these conventional distinctions are irrelevant within Christianity). So they are not to bother about changing status, including the status of slavery, interestingly enough, although here Paul's Greek is so skeletal that it could mean either 'make use of your status as slave' or 'make use of your opportunity to be free'.
>
> Once again, notice how the word 'Lord' is used: is it God, or Christ, and what difference does Paul make between them?
>
> 'Circumcision' and 'Slavery' were burning issues in Paul's world, in a sense in which they are not today.

What about virgins?

25-38 About the unmarried, I have no command of the Lord; instead, I am giving my opinion as one whom God's mercy has enabled to be faithful. So – I think the following is appropriate, because of the constraints of the present time; it is good for a person to be as they are. If you are bound to a wife, don't seek for a dissolution; if you are free, don't look for a wife. But you don't sin if you get married; and if the unmarried woman gets married, she does not sin. [The only thing is] people like that have trouble in the flesh, and I'm [trying to] spare you that.

This is what I mean, my fellow Christians: the time is contracted. For what remains, let those who have wives be as though they had none; and those who weep, as though they were not weeping, and those who rejoice as though they were not rejoicing and those who are in commerce as though they had nothing, and those who have dealings with the world [must be] as though they were not dealing completely with it. For the outward form of this world is passing away.

I want you to have no worries. The unmarried person is worried about the Lord's affairs – how are they going to please the Lord? Whereas the person who gets married is worried about the world's affairs – how is he going to please his wife? And he is divided.

Likewise, the unmarried woman who is not in marriage, and the virgin, are concerned about the Lord's affairs – to be holy in body and in soul. Whereas the woman who gets married is concerned about the world's affairs – how can she please her husband? I'm saying this to help you, not to put a halter on you. [It's just that] I want everything to be [done] properly and with constancy to the Lord, without distraction.

If, however, someone thinks they are behaving badly towards their young woman, if it's going too far and it is appropriate that it happens in this way, they're not sinning: let them get married. But anyone who remains steadfast in their heart, and is not under strain, but is exercising mastery over their own will, and has decided on this in their own heart, to keep her as a virgin – he will be doing all right. So: the one who marries his young woman does well, and the one who does not marry will do even better.

> We have to read this passage with some care, mainly because it speaks to us from a world that at first sight seems utterly different from our own. We shall do well, however, to remember that with Corinth's reputation for sexual misbehaviour, Paul may well have seen a 'sign-value' in people deliberately remaining unmarried. In addition, of course, we must pick up his references to the 'time' and the sense that everything was coming to an end: remaining unmarried might be difficult, but it would perhaps not be for very long, is the underlying argument. We shall misread the apostle if we see him as a miserable old Puritan, thundering 'Sex is bad, sex is dirty' from his office in Ephesus.

What about marriage after bereavement?

39-40 A wife is bound for as long as her husband is alive; but if the husband dies, she is free to marry whomever she wants, but only in the Lord. She'll be happier, however, if she remains as she is, in my opinion.

And I also think I have the Spirit of God!

Paul is making a similar point here (and we may care to notice that this argument appears again, in slightly different disguise, in Romans 7); but observe that he is quite balanced about it. The impression one gets is that his opponents were claiming possession of the Spirit and decrying marriage: 'Asceticism: good; sex: bad', might have been their slogan. Paul's view is that both are good, according to the gifts of God.

What about food offered to idols?

8 ¹⁻¹³ Now Paul proceeds to answer another of the Corinthians' questions: are they allowed to eat food that has been sacrificed in pagan ceremonies? The advantage would be that the meat would be sold off cheap in the market; the disadvantage would be the impression given that Christians who ate such food were in fact participating in pagan ceremonies.

As for food offered to pagan deities, we realise that all of us have 'knowledge'. Knowledge 'puffs up' – but love *builds* up. If someone thinks that they've got 'knowledge', they don't yet have this 'knowledge' as they ought to know it. On the other hand, a person who loves God is known by God.

As regards eating what has been sacrificed to idols: we know that 'idols have no existence in the world' (Isaiah 41:24) and 'there is only one God' (Deuteronomy 6:4).

For there are so-called 'gods' in heaven and on earth, just as there are many 'gods' and many 'lords'. BUT:

We have one God (the Father),

from whom everything comes – and we [are made] for him.

And we have one Lord, Jesus Christ,

through whom is everything – and we are through him.

But not *everyone* has this 'knowledge'. Some people, through force of habit, eat meat as an offering to the pagan deity; and their conscience, because it is diseased, is defiled. Food will not bring us before God'[s judgement-seat]. It is neither the case that if we refrain from eating we go hungry nor that if we eat we have a surplus. But just make sure that this freedom of yours doesn't become a cause of stumbling to those who are [still] sick. You see, if someone sees you (you who have 'knowledge') reclining at dinner in a pagan temple, won't their conscience (because they are still sick) get built up so as to eat food offered to idols? So your 'knowledge' is the cause of the destruction of this person who is sick, a fellow Christian for whom Christ died. So those of you who sin against your fellow Christians and batter their sick consciences, are sinning against Christ.

Therefore, if food is [going to] scandalise a fellow Christian of mine, I'll never, ever eat meat – so as not to scandalise a fellow Christian.

Eating food offered to idols, and thereby running the risk of making people think that we have changed religion, or take pagan deities seriously, is not really a problem for us, as it was in Corinth. In that city, a) you could get meat on the cheap if it had previously been offered in sacrifice (that's how the priests made their money); and b) you might walk past a temple and see someone you knew sharing in a banquet, and either be shocked because they have become a worshipper of Asclepius or Aphrodite, or decide, 'well, in that case I can be a Christian *and* worship the Roman or Greek gods.'

What matters to us is the principle Paul uses to solve the problem; the pagan deities are non-existent and therefore unimportant. The focus for us is God and Christ, not the 'knowledge' to which the squabbling Christians were laying enthusiastic claim. It is not knowledge that counts, but love; once again, Paul reverts to the term 'puffed up'; once again, by contrast, he adverts to the image of 'building up'. If you are to be a Christian, it is not theological or technical expertise that counts, but your loving concern for the well-being of the other.

One passage to think about is verse 6, Chapter 8: 'We have one God . . .' Here Paul is deliberately echoing the great Jewish prayer of the Shema ('Hear, O Israel, the Lord your God is One God . . .' – Deuteronomy 6:4; compare Malachi 2:10), asserting monotheism against the polytheism of 'the nations'; and here Paul has cleverly demonstrated how he can assert his native monotheism, and *at the same time* give Christ the very lofty title of Lord. He does this by way of deft contrast with the pagan world and its many 'gods' and many 'lords', this last a clear side-swipe against the increasing tendency of Rome to insist on emperor-worship. There is a good deal going on in this passage.

Paul's freedom

9 ¹⁻²⁷ As we read this section, it is important for us to see that Paul is still dealing with the same question: Christians are free, as he has already told the Corinthians, and as they are now quoting back at him. But Christian freedom does not mean that we can do what we like – we are restrained by the Law of God, and by consideration for others. To illustrate this principle, and still with his mind on the question of food offered to idols, and the deeper issue underlying it, of 'liberty or licence', Paul speaks of an issue in his own life which (it seems) his opponents have used against him, the fact that though he is a preacher and therefore entitled to material support, he has, as it happens, paid his way (as a tent-maker, according to Acts 18:3); and although he would have been entitled to have his wife with him, he has not done so.

What about me? Aren't I free? Aren't I an apostle? Haven't I seen Jesus Christ our Lord? Aren't you my work in the Lord?

If I'm not an apostle to others, I am at least an apostle as far as you are concerned – for you are the certificate of my apostolic mission in the Lord. This is how I defend myself against the people who are putting me on trial.

Clearly we have the right to food and drink. Clearly we have the right to take a Christian wife around with us, like the other apostles, and the Lord's brothers, and

Kephas. Or is it only I and Barnabas who do not have the freedom not to work? Whoever fought in a campaign at their own expense? Who plants a vineyard and doesn't eat of its fruit? Who shepherds a flock and is not fed on the flock's milk?

Am I just arguing from a human point of view – doesn't the Law say this? For in the Torah of Moses it is written, 'You shall not muzzle an ox that is treading the grain.' Do you think God is worried about oxen? Or is he not certainly talking about us? It was on our account that it was written that the ploughman ought to plough in hope, and the thresher in hope of having his share. If we have sowed spiritual seed among you, is it a very big deal if we harvest your material crops? If [certain] other people have a share in your freedom, should we not, even more so?

Instead, [however] we have not made use of our freedom, but are silent about everything, so as not to throw a spanner in the works of Christ's gospel.

Don't you realise that those who perform the sacred rites eat from what the temple affords? Those who serve at the altar share in its profits. So the Lord laid it down for those who proclaim the gospel to live off the gospel.

Now I have made use of none of this; and I am not writing all of this so that this should happen in my case. You see, I'd rather die than – no one will invalidate my reason for boasting. If I preach the gospel, that's no grounds for me to boast. For it's something I *have* to do: I'm in *pain* if I don't preach the gospel. If I do this voluntarily, I get my salary; if I do it reluctantly, I'm entrusted with a commission. So what's my salary? It is [simply] to offer the gospel free of charge, so as not to abuse my freedom in the gospel.

I'm free of anybody's claims; and yet I've enslaved myself to everybody, in order to gain more people. And [so] to the Jews I was like a Jew, in order to win over Jews, under the Torah to those under the Torah, even though I wasn't myself under the Torah, in order to win over those under the Torah. To those outside Torah, I became like one outside the Torah; it wasn't that I was outside God's Torah, for I was within Christ's Torah, in order to win over those not under Torah. To the weak I became weak, in order to win over the weak. To everybody I became everything, in order in every way to save some of them. I do everything for the gospel's sake, in order that I may have some partnership in it.

[Think of the Isthmian Games]: you're surely aware that the people who are running in the stadium, all of them run, but only one gets the gold medal. Run in such a way as to win it. Everyone who is in training is under all kinds of discipline. Now they do it to win a glory that passes; but our training is for a glory that never passes. So my running is done with a clear end in view; and when I box, I make sure that my punches don't miss their target. Instead, I treat my body roughly, and make it my slave, because my fear is that having preached to others, I myself might not pass the test.

This chapter starts with an angry series of rhetorical questions (and when you meet Paul, you will do well to answer all of them with a solid affirmative; his temper is just a shade uncertain), and ends with an athletics metaphor. We speak nowadays of 'inculturation', which (among many other things) can mean preaching the gospel in terms that the host culture can understand. The Corinthians lived only a few miles from the site of the biennial Isthmian Games, and may have appreciated the metaphor Paul uses, while perhaps reflecting that (as a good Jew) he was not perhaps entirely at home in the world of the locker room.

In between the angry questions and the attempt to win their interest by a familiar allusion, Paul pursues his central argument, that in order to make sure that the gospel is properly preached, he has foregone his rights. The Corinthians, if they are listening carefully, should be reflecting on how this applies to their question about eating the meat that has been sacrificed in the temples of their city.

Two other points: first, the word he uses early in the fifth paragraph, which I have translated 'we are silent about . . .' can also mean 'we bear everything'. It is not a particularly common word, and it appears again in 1 Corinthians 13. Perhaps Paul's mind is running ahead of itself already to that beautiful hymn, which is his third answer to all their divisions, the 'hymn to love'.

Second, notice the broken syntax, probably expressing his deep emotion, two paragraphs later: 'You see, I'd rather die than – no one will invalidate my reason for boasting'. We shall not understand Paul unless we realise how much the preaching of the gospel means to him.

Appeal to biblical precedent: how to read the Old Testament

10 **1-13** My fellow Christians, I want you to be absolutely clear that our ancestors were all under the cloud, and all of them went through the sea. They were all baptised into Moses in the cloud and in the sea. They all ate the same spiritual food and all drank the same spiritual drink. For they drank from the spiritual Rock that followed them – and the Rock was Christ. But God was not pleased with most of them – for they were slain all over the desert. These things happened as 'types' for us, to discourage us from desiring evil, just as they did. And don't be idolatrous, as some of them were, as it is written,

'The people sat down to eat and drink and rose up to play.'

And let us avoid sexual immorality, as some of them committed sexual immorality, and three thousand of them fell in a single day.

And let us not put Christ to the test, as some of them tested him, and they were destroyed by snakes.

And don't complain, as some of them complained, and were destroyed by the Destroyer.

These things [as I say] happened to them as a 'type'; but they were written down to admonish us, on whom the ends of the ages have arrived.

So let everyone who thinks that they are secure watch out for a fall. The only temptation that has seized you is of a human kind. God is faithful; and God will not permit you to be tempted beyond what you can manage. Along with the temptation, he will fashion a successful outcome, so that you['ll] be able to bear up under it.

Paul is still trying to deal with the question of eating food that has been sacrificed to idols, while not surrendering his belief in the freedom of Christians. Unless you keep your eye on the ball, however, you may not see quite where he is going.

He appeals to the Exodus story in the Old Testament, especially recalling by his quotation of Exodus 32:6 that terrible memory of the episode of the Golden Calf. This may perhaps indicate that it was Corinthian *Jewish* Christians who were most anxious about this issue; but because for him Christ is God's last word, he feels entitled to reread the Old Testament story from a Christian point of view. So he speaks of the desert ancestors as 'baptised into Moses', and (without having to argue for it) of the 'Rock' (from which they drank) as Christ. The worst thing they did in all that time was to worship the Golden Calf (see Exodus 32); but (like some Corinthians) they also committed sexual immorality, and complained about their leaders. No one can think themselves immune. So even if they think they are strong, it may be better to forgo their right.

Should Christians always be prepared to forgo their rights?

Summarising the debate

10^{14}**-11**^{1} Therefore, my beloved ones, avoid idolatry. I am speaking to prudent people: judge for yourselves what it is that I am saying. The cup of blessing which we bless – is it not an act of communion with the blood of Christ? The bread which we break – is it not an act of communion with the body of Christ?

Because there is one loaf, we who are many are one body; for we all partake of the one loaf.

Look at Israel according to their physical ancestry: those who eat the sacrifices are in communion with the altar of sacrifice.

What is my point? That stuff sacrificed to idols, or an idol itself, is of any importance? No – what I am saying is that their sacrifices are sacrificed to demons, and not to God; and I don't want you to end up in communion with demons. It is just not possible to drink both the Lord's cup, and the cup of demons. It is just not possible for you to share the Lord's table and the table of demons. Or are we provoking the Lord to jealousy? We're not stronger than him, are we?

Yes, 'freedom in everything'; but not everything is profitable.

'Freedom in everything'; but not everything builds up [the body]. No one should be looking for their own interests, but for the interests of the other person.

Eat anything that is bought in the market; and don't ask too many awkward questions, because of [your] conscience. 'The Lord's is the earth, and the fullness thereof' (Psalm 24:1). If a non-Christian invites you to a meal, and if you are minded to go, eat everything that is put before you, asking no awkward questions, because of [your] conscience. If, however, someone tells you 'this was sacrificed in a temple', don't eat it, because of the person who pointed it out to you, and for the sake of conscience. When I say 'conscience', I don't mean yours, but theirs. For why should my freedom come under judgement from someone else's conscience? If I have a share in grace, why am I slandered because of what I give thanks for?

To sum up: whether you eat or drink, or whatever you do, do everything for the glory of God. Don't give offence to [anyone]: Jews, Greeks, the Church of God, just as in every way I please everybody, not seeking my own advantage, but the advantage of the greater number. [I want] them to be saved. Be imitators of me, just as I am [an imitator] of Christ.

Paul brings this complex and difficult argument together with splendid simplicity; but he takes the opportunity to cast the net wider than just the question of food offered to idols. Obviously idolatry is out; but deeper than that is the unity of the Christian group, symbolised and made actual by the bread and wine of communion. Once again the idea of 'Body of Christ' comes to the surface; here it has two meanings, the 'eucharistic body' and the 'body of Christians', and Paul makes intelligent use of the ambiguity.

Once again he touches on the word *koinonia* (union, communion, solidarity, etc.), and emphasises that we have to choose: Christ or demons? So our Christian 'freedom' is not to be asserted without further ado: our obligation is not to ourselves, but to look out for the interests of our fellow members of the body.

Finally, but only after this necessary preliminary has been carefully laid out (remember that it was in all probability the first time that the Church had had to face this particular question), Paul makes a sensible practical suggestion: it's all right to eat this food, but not if someone makes a thing of it. Notice that the last word in the section is 'Christ'. It is in for ever coming back to Christ that Paul solves all his problems.

Styles of headdress in worship

2-16   I applaud you [when you tell me] that you remember me in every way, and that you hold fast to the traditions, just as I passed them on to you.

I want you to be clear that of every man, Christ is the head; and the man is the head of his wife; and Christ's head is God.

Any man who has anything on his head when praying or prophesying brings shame on his head. Whereas any woman who has her head uncovered when she prays or prophesies brings shame on her head – for it's exactly the same as a woman who has been shaved. For if a woman doesn't wear a covering, let her have it [her hair] cut short. But if it is disgraceful for a woman to have it cut short or shaved – let her wear a covering.

You see, a man ought not to have his head covered, because he is the 'image and glory of God' (Genesis 1:26). Whereas the woman is the 'glory of the man': for the man did not come from the woman, but the woman from the man. And then the man was not created on the woman's account, but the woman on the man's account. This is the reason why the woman ought to have control over her head, on account of the angels.

But, of course, in the Lord there is no such thing as woman without a man or man without a woman. For just as the woman is from the man, so the man is through the woman: and it all comes from God.

Judge for yourselves: is it decent for a woman to pray to God with her head un-covered? Doesn't nature teach you that if a man has long hair it is his disgrace, while if a woman has long hair it is her glory? Because long hair is given her as a covering.

And if anyone wants to pick a fight, we have no such custom, and neither do the churches of God.

In our day we approach this passage with some trepidation, because we are shy of anything that would seem to argue that women are inferior to men, and therefore nervous even of stressing (as Paul does here) the difference between women and men. In reading this passage, the following observations may be helpful:

- Paul is displaying much emotion here, so it is obviously a matter of considerable importance to him.

- He may, however, be aware that his arguments will not, perhaps, convince all of his Corinthian audience. So he argues from creation (the chain that goes God-Christ-man-woman), from liturgical propriety ('because of the angels'), from natural law (short hair for men, long hair for women), and, finally, perhaps feeling that he needs a coup de grâce, from authority ('we have no such custom, and neither do the churches of God').

- The words for man and woman also mean husband and wife in Greek, and we need to read this into the passage.

- Paul is definitely not arguing the inferiority of women: they are allowed the same liturgical function as men (praying and prophesy-ing), and he is adamant about their mutual independence in the Lord. So he will not surrender his 'gospel of freedom', whatever is the issue in Corinth (and many scholars suggest that the problem may have been men dressing as women and women dressing as men).

- The force of the arguments (e.g. 'because of the angels') is now lost to us, and we have to assume that they meant more to Paul and his Corinthians. Scholars have spilt much ink on them, but the jury is still out.

- Part at least of the argument depends on two different meanings of 'head': that which you find at the top of the body, and 'authority'.

- Paul starts by applauding the Corinthians for observing his traditions. Now he goes on to criticise their failure to observe an important tradition that he gave them.

Divisions at the Eucharist!

17-34   In giving you this direction, I am not [able to] applaud you on another matter. When you gather as a community, you do more harm than good.

For in the first place, when you gather as a church, I hear that there are splits among you, and I partly believe it. For it's inevitable that there should be dissensions among you, so that the tried and true among you may be revealed.

So: when you gather in the same place as a community, it is not for eating the Lord's Supper. For each of you wolfs down your own supper ahead [of the others]: and this person goes hungry, while that person is drunk! Don't you have homes for eating and drinking in? Do you have contempt for God's Church? Do you embarrass the 'have-nots'? What can I say to you? Shall I applaud you? On this matter I cannot applaud you.

For *I* received from the Lord, what I also passed on to you, that the Lord Jesus, on the night when he was handed over, took bread, and, giving thanks, broke it and said, 'This is my body, which is for you: do this in memory of me.'

Likewise, the cup, after supper: 'This cup is the new covenant in my blood. Do this, as often as you drink it, in memory of me.'

For as often as you eat this bread and drink this cup, you proclaim the Lord's death until he comes.

So – whoever eats the Lord's bread or drinks the Lord's cup unworthily is guilty of the Lord's body and blood. Let a person examine themselves, and in that frame of mind eat of the bread and drink of the cup. For the one who eats and drinks, eats and drinks condemnation for themselves if they do not discern the body.

This is the reason that many people among you are sick and ill – and quite a few have died. If we have an accurate discernment of ourselves, we shouldn't get condemned. But if we are condemned by the Lord we are punished, in order not to share in the world's condemnation.

So, my brothers and sisters, when you come together for the meal, show hospitality to each other. If one of you is ravenous, have a meal at home, so that your community gathering may not be a source of condemnation. The other matters I shall put in order when I come.

The opening of this section tells us that the reports about divisions were not included in their letter; the end of it apparently dismisses 'the other matters' in their letter as of no urgency.

Central, however, to Paul's understanding of what it is to be a Christian community, is the question of unity, especially at the Eucharist. Paul is horrified to hear of the class distinctions operative at the Corinthians' communion service: some are drunk, and others are starving! As always with Paul, the solution goes back to Jesus, and, in this case, to what he did 'on the night when he was handed over'. It goes back to the extraordinarily weighty significance that Paul (and Christians before and since his time) attached to Jesus' mysterious words and gestures at the Last Supper, 'This is my body . . . This cup is the new covenant in my blood'. Whatever the precise meaning of this formula, it is not something to be treated lightly.

Paul here once more makes good use of the idea of 'body', which has resonances of both the 'community of Christians' and the 'eucharistic body of Christ' (and there is probably also a hint of the body of Jesus that suffered on the Cross, in what he says here).

We should notice also Paul's reference to the fact that 'quite a few have died', looking ahead to an issue that he will have to confront in Chapter 15.

What about the charismatic gifts? (12:1–14:40)

One of many sources of division in the Corinthian community was evidently the distribution of 'spiritual gifts', and my easy assumption that I'm a better Christian than you because I speak in tongues, or prophesy, or work miracles, or whatever, and you don't. Paul spends quite a long time now (three chapters in our division of the letter), trying to work out the principles on which to resolve this one.

A simple test

12 ¹⁻³ As regards spiritual gifts, my fellow Christians, I don't want you ignorant. You know that when you were pagans, you would get led astray, taken off to dumb idols. So I'm telling you: no one who is speaking with the Spirit of God can say 'Jesus is cursed.' Likewise, no one can say 'Jesus is Lord,' except by the Holy Spirit.

> As always, Paul brings it back to Jesus, and a simple test: what is the charismatic's attitude to Jesus? If they (charismatics) proclaim Jesus as 'Lord' as Paul does, again and again, then they are led by the Spirit. Could one imagine anyone uttering the opposite statement, that 'Jesus is anathema?' One possibility is in time of persecution, when perhaps Christians were invited to say this, and to proclaim that 'the Emperor is Lord', to avoid torture or a horrid death, although it is not clear that, by the time 1 Corinthians was written, the Church had met with the persecution that would soon afterwards start to be the inevitable concomitant of the proclamation of the gospel. Perhaps also this odd-sounding statement is a rule of thumb whereby to assess the utterances of charismatics in the Church.

Diversity and unity in the Church

⁴⁻¹¹ There are different kinds of spiritual gifts, but the same Spirit.

There are different kinds of service, and the same Lord.

There are different kinds of activities, but the same God who enacts everything in everybody.

To each [of you] the revelation of the Spirit is apportioned – to build up [the Church]. This person, through the Spirit, may have clever rhetoric apportioned to him, and another person rhetoric of 'knowledge', according to the same Spirit. Another person may have faith, in the same Spirit, while someone else has the gift of healing in the same Spirit, and another person the power to work miracles, another person prophecy, another discernment of spirits, another, different kinds of languages, and another the interpretation of languages. It is one and the same Spirit that empowers all these things, privately apportioning to each one as the Spirit wills.

> You can see how all these different (and perhaps clashing) gifts might cause division in the Church. How do you prioritise the gifts, and how do you prevent the Christian liturgy from becoming a zoo, if all these gifts are on offer? Paul's response is to go back to the Spirit, source of all gifts, and principle of unity in the Christian Church. And now Paul proceeds to give a full-blown account of the 'Church as Body', which we have glimpsed in occasional 'straws in the wind'. He does so with humour and originality.

The Church as Body

¹²⁻³¹ᵃ For just as the body is one, and has a number of members, and all the body's members, though many, [constitute] a single body, the same is true of Christ. For

it was by a single Spirit that all of us were baptised into one Body: Jews, Greeks, slaves, free; and all of us were given one Spirit to drink.

You see, the body is not a single member, but several. If the foot [for example] says, 'I'm not a hand, therefore I don't belong to the body' – does that really mean that it *doesn't* belong to the body?

And if the ear says, 'I'm not an eye, therefore I don't belong to the body' – does that really mean that it *doesn't* belong to the body?

If the whole body were eye, how would it hear? If it were all ear, what about the nose? In fact, God has placed the members, each one of them, in the body, according to his disposition. But if they were all just one member, where would the body be? As it is, there are several members, and just one body.

It is no good the eye saying to the hand, 'I can do without you,' or, again, the head saying to the feet, 'I can do without you.' No – those bits of the body that seem less powerful are essential; and we give increased honour to the bits of the body that we think are less honourable, and our unpresentable bits are made presentable in a way that our presentable bits can do without. God made up the body by giving greater honour to the part that most wanted it, to prevent there being a division in the body. [God's intention was that] the members should care for each other; and so if one member is suffering, all the other members are suffering along with it, and if one member gets glorified, all the other members are rejoicing along with it.

You people are the Body of Christ, and individually you are members of that Body. God has appointed in the Church first some who are apostles, in the second place prophets; third are teachers. Then come miracles, then gifts of healing, then the corporal works of mercy, then administrative gifts, and different kinds of languages.

Are all apostles? Are all prophets? Are all teachers? Do all do miracles? Do all have healing powers? Do all speak in tongues? Do all interpret?

Be jealous for the gifts that are most significant.

> This is a lovely piece of writing. Many political thinkers in the ancient world had made use of the idea of the 'body' in this way, but none with Paul's sense of fun and his individuality. The reader will notice that apostles and prophets come first in his list, and speaking in tongues comes last. What matters is that the body should work as one.

Love as the final solution to the problems at Corinth

12 31b–13 13

This loveliest of all Paul's compositions is clearly from his pen, and clearly fits the Corinthian situation, although some have observed that it seems to interrupt the flow of Chapters 12–14. But they may be missing the point. Paul has established, in Chapter 8, that love 'builds up', while knowledge 'puffs up', and that is what Paul is talking about in Chapter 14, responding to the problems outlined in Chapter 12. There is more, however: the problems in Corinth as a whole, of divisions and squabbling, find their final solution in Chapter 13. The answer to all the difficulties of that church is, quite simply, love.

And now I'm going to show you a way that is even more outstanding.

If I speak in the languages of human beings and of angels, but do not have love, then I have turned into a sounding brass or a clashing cymbal.

And if I have the gift of prophecy, and I know all mysteries and all knowledge, and if I have complete faith, so as to move mountains, but have no love, I am nothing.

And if I divide all my possessions into bits, and if I hand over my body in order that I may boast, but do not have love, I am not helped in any way.

Love waits patiently, shows kindness. Love is not jealous, does not brag, is not 'puffed up', does not behave improperly, does not seek self-interest, doesn't get provoked, doesn't reckon up evil, doesn't rejoice at injustice, but rejoices at integrity.

Love copes with everything; is always committed, always hopeful, always endures to the end; love never collapses.

You have your skills at prophecy – they'll be brought to an end. Tongues? They'll cease. Knowledge? It will be brought to an end. For we know only partially, and we prophesy only partially; but when what is complete comes, the partial will be brought to an end.

When I was an infant, I would talk like an infant, I would think like an infant, and I would calculate like an infant. But when I became an adult, I put an end to infants' stuff.

For just now we're looking in a distorting mirror; but then [it will be] face to face. Now I know partially, but then I shall recognise, just as I have been recognised.

So now there remains faith, hope, and love, these three. But the greatest of these is love.

> There is perhaps no need to comment on this passage, except to make the point that this 'solution' to the problems at Corinth could also be read as Paul's portrait of his beloved Jesus Christ. With Paul, it always comes back to Jesus.

The application of love to the problem of spiritual gifts

14 1-25 Make a special thing of love, but be eager for [all] spiritual gifts, especially, however, that you should prophesy. For the person who speaks in a tongue does not speak to human beings but to God. For no one is listening, while the person speaks of mysteries in the Spirit. Whereas the one who prophesies speaks upbuilding, comfort, and consolation to human beings. The one who speaks in a tongue builds him- or herself up, whereas the one who prophesies builds up the [entire] Church.

I'd like all of you to speak in tongues; but I'd prefer you to prophesy. The one who prophesies is more important than the one who speaks in tongues (unless they interpret it), so that the church may receive 'upbuilding'.

See here, my brothers and sisters, if I come to you talking in tongues, how am I going to help you, unless I speak to you, either with a revelation or with knowledge or with prophecy or with teaching?

Similarly, inanimates that can give a sound, like a flute or a guitar, if they don't produce different notes, how will people know what tune is being played on the flute or the guitar?

Another example: if a trumpet gives an unclear signal, who will make ready for war? So with you: if you don't give a clear message, how will people know what is being said? You see, you'll just be talking to empty air. There's any number of kinds of languages in the world, and every one of them makes a sound; but if I don't know the sound's force, I'll be a foreigner to the speaker, and the speaker will be a foreigner to me.

So with you – if you are keen on the spiritual gifts, be keen on having lots of them, that you may build up the church. Therefore let the person who speaks in a tongue pray to interpret [it]. For if I pray in a tongue, my spirit prays, but my mind gets no profit. What then? I shall indeed pray in the Spirit, but I'll also pray in the mind. I shall sing praise in the Spirit, but also in my mind. For if you pronounce a blessing in the Spirit, [what about] the person who fills the rôle of the outsider? How will they [be able to] say their 'Amen' to your thanksgiving? Because they have no idea what you are saying. You do a very nice line in thanksgiving; but the other person is not 'built up'. Thank God, I speak in tongues more than any of you; but in church I'd prefer to speak five intelligible words, in order to instruct others, than a million words in a tongue.

Brothers and sisters, don't be childish in your thinking; you can be infants in regard to doing evil, but in your thinking [I want] you to be mature. In the Torah it is written,

'In strange tongues and on foreign lips shall I speak to this people,
and even so they will not listen to me, says the Lord.'

So tongues function as a sign, not for believers but for unbelievers, while prophecy is a sign, not for unbelievers but for those who believe. Therefore if the entire Church gathers as a community in the same place, and they all speak in tongues, and outsiders or unbelievers come in, won't they say that you're all mad?

If, on the other hand, everyone prophesies, and some unbeliever or outsider comes in, they are convicted by everybody and judged by everybody, and the secrets of their heart are revealed, so that they fall on their face and worship God, proclaiming that 'Indeed God is among you.'

> It is not having the spiritual gifts that makes the difference, but the use to which they are put: do they operate, as love always does, in a way that benefits the community ('upbuilding') and outsiders (bringing them to a knowledge of their need for God)?

How to ensure 'upbuilding' in the Church

26-40 What about it, then, brothers and sisters? When you come together as a community, each one has a song, or a teaching, or a revelation, or a tongue, or an interpretation: let everything work for 'upbuilding'. If someone speaks in a tongue, [let it be] two or at most three, and in order; and let one [of them] interpret. If, however, there is no interpreter, let's have a bit of silence in the church, and let everyone speak to themselves and to God. And let two or three prophets speak, and let the rest discern. And if someone else gets a revelation, when they are sitting down, let the first one be silent. For you can all prophesy one by one, so that all may be instructed, and all be encouraged. And the prophets' spirits are under the control of the prophets; for God is not a God of unruliness but of peace.

As in all the churches of the saints, let wives refrain from speaking in the churches. For it is not permitted for them to speak; rather, let them be subordinated, as the Torah says. If, however, they wish to learn something, let them enquire of their own husbands at home. For it is a disgrace for a woman to speak in the assembly. Or is it from you people alone that the Word of God emerged? Was it to you people alone that it came?

If someone thinks that they are a prophet or spiritual, I want them to recognise that what I am writing to you is the Lord's command. If a person doesn't recognise this, they aren't recognised.

So, my brothers and sisters, be keen to prophesy, and don't put a bar on speaking in tongues. But let everything happen properly, and in good order.

This is all about avoiding liturgical chaos, a particular danger (presumably) for charismatics. The keyword here is 'upbuilding', which Paul has long since identified as the effect of love. And up-building will not take place if the liturgical celebration turns into a free-for-all. Clearly all that Paul says here is meant to subserve that basic end; and it is in that context that we must read the apparently rather forbidding injunction on women (or wives) to be 'silent in church'. We do not know the 'other side' of the conversation, but we must assume that both Paul and the Corinthians know the precise issue that he had in mind. There is some uncertainty about the manuscript tradition here, but on balance it is held that the teaching about women probably came from Paul.

It does not follow from this, of course, that Paul was enacting legislation whereby no woman, even in the third millennium, must open her mouth in the Christian assembly. For one thing, Paul would have been rather surprised to know that we should still be reading his letter, written on a particular occasion, for the problems of a particular church, almost two thousand years later. For another, unless we can be sure what kind of anarchy he was attempting to avoid, we cannot confidently state what he is telling the Corinthian women not to do. As always with Paul, notice how he comes back to 'the Lord' at the end of his instructions.

The gospel as originally preached – a reminder

15 [1-11] Fellow Christians, I am making known to you [again!] the gospel which I gospelled to you, which you received, on which you stand secure, through which you are being saved, the terms in which I gospelled you, if you still hold it fast (unless, of course, you came thoughtlessly to faith).

So, in the first place [you will recall], I passed on to you, what I had also received, that Christ

- died for our sins according to the scriptures;
- that he was buried;
- that he was raised on the third day according to the scriptures;
- and that he appeared to Kephas, then to the Twelve.

Then he appeared to more than five hundred brothers and sisters at once, of whom the majority still remain [alive], although some have fallen asleep. Then he appeared to James, and then to all the apostles. Last of all, as though to an abortion, he appeared also to me. I am, you see, the least of the apostles; I'm not fit to be called an 'apostle', because I persecuted God's Church. By God's grace, I am what I am, and God's grace towards me hasn't turned out unprofitably. Actually, I worked harder than all of them – not really me, though, so much as God's grace [working] with me. So, whoever, they or I, that's how we preach, and that's how you came to faith.

> Paul turns here to a very different subject, that of resurrection, but for many scholars this is the climax of the letter, the point it has been aiming at from the beginning. We have to work out, from what Paul says, precisely what the Corinthians had got wrong; but it seems to have been (at least in Paul's view) a matter of denying the gospel as it had originally been preached to them. Some have called this the 'gospel of four verbs': Christ 'died', 'was buried', 'was raised', and 'appeared'. Paul is quite clear that it is a non-optional part of Christianity.

So what are some of you getting up to?

12-19 Now, if the proclamation is that Christ is raised from the dead, how is it that some among you are saying that there is no such thing as resurrection from the dead? But if there is no such thing as resurrection from the dead, then nor has Christ been raised. And if Christ has not been raised, then our proclamation is void, and your faith is void; and we turn out to be false witnesses for God, because we bore witness against God that he raised Christ, when [in fact] he didn't raise him [at all], if [it is really true that] the dead aren't raised. You see, if the dead aren't raised, then Christ wasn't raised, either. And if Christ wasn't raised, then your faith is futile, and you are still in your sins, and, moreover, those who have slept in Christ are lost. If in this [present] life our hope has been in Christ alone, then we are the most pitiable of all human beings.

> Resurrection is the hardest thing to believe, 'news too good to be true', in some people's view, and quite clearly the Corinthians, or some of them, were finding it hard to believe that Christians they knew who had died, and whose rotting corpses were presumably available (at least in theory) for inspection in some Corinthian cemetery, might in any sense be said to be still alive. Paul takes them through the logic of their position: the heart of Christianity is the resurrection of Christ; but if there is no such thing as resurrection, then Christianity is built on a lie, and (what is worse) a slander against God. If that is the case, then their conversion was a fairy tale. Paul lays it all bare, and invites them to choose; and the invitation is extended to us also.

The structure of resurrection

20-28 As it is, however, Christ *has* been raised from the dead, the 'first-fruits' of those who have fallen asleep. For since [it was] through a human being that death [happened], it was also through a human being that the resurrection from the dead happened. That is to say, in Adam everybody dies, and in just the same way everybody will be brought to life, but each in their own order: Christ (as the first-fruits), then those who belong to Christ, at his coming. Then, finally, when he hands over the kingdom to the [one who is] God and Father, [comes the end] when he cancels out every rule and every authority and power. For it is required that he should reign until 'he place all enemies beneath his feet'. It is death that is the final enemy [to be] cancelled out. For 'he subjected everything under his feet'; however, when he says 'everything has been subjected', clearly that does not include the One who subjected everything to him. When he subjects everything to him, then the Son himself will be subjected to the one who subjected everything to him, in order that God may be all in all.

In this section, Paul traces the pattern of resurrection, and he picks up the parallel between Adam and Christ that we read in Romans 5, and extends it. The pattern is as follows: Adam brought in death; Christ is God's answer to death, which will be progressively eliminated from the universe; Christ, then Christians, then, finally, the whole of creation, as it is restored to the proper order that God designed, and which Adam shattered. All that is opposed to God will be defeated, and the final (and perhaps most intractable) enemy is going to be death, but death, too, will be defeated, and then the universe will once more be as it should be.

There is, however, one important difference: Christ has come into the picture. So far in this letter, we have seen that Paul gives Jesus a very high status indeed, calling him 'Lord', and clearly under-standing by this some kind of equivalence to God. At this point, however, he moderates it somewhat, and as Christ hands over our restored universe to the Most High God, Paul makes it clear that the Son is also subject to God. The Christian community was only at the beginning (and perhaps we have not advanced much further) of the enquiry into how God and Christ are related.

Appeal to a Christian practice

29-34 Because what will those people be doing who get themselves baptised for the sake of the dead? If the dead aren't raised, why are they getting baptised for their sakes?

And what about us? Why do we take risks all day long? Every day I'm on the point of death. Yes – by the pride in you which I have in Christ Jesus our Lord! If (in human terms) I have fought with wild animals here in Ephesus, what's in it for me? If the dead aren't raised,

'Let's eat and drink, for tomorrow we die.'
Don't be fooled – 'Bad company corrupts even excellent morals.'

Sober up properly; stop sinning. Some people have an un-'knowledge' of God. I am speaking to shame you.

Paul now argues from what they know. First, from the practice of 'being baptised for the sake of the dead'. It has been estimated that there are some thirty explanations of what this might mean. All we can say for certain is that it was a practice that the Corinthians recognised, but which is absurd, unless the Christian proclamation of resurrection is true.

Next Paul appeals to his own experiences as an apostle: the risks he endures are clearly pointless unless it is true about resurrection. Then he offers a couple of quotations. The first may be from Isaiah 22:13, or from contemporary criticism of the Epicurean philosophers, and the second is from a Greek poet. Finally, perhaps feeling that he is running out of arguments, he adds a touch of asperity: 'get your act together'.

The obvious next question is: 'All right, then; what will resurrection *look* like?' To that question Paul now turns; and the reader must judge whether or not he succeeds in finding the answer.

What will Resurrection look like? Arguments from nature

35-58 But someone will object, 'How are the dead raised? What body do they come wearing?'

Fool – what you sow doesn't get turned into life unless it dies. In this instance, what you sow in the ground is not the body that will be, but a bare grain, as it might be of wheat, or one of those things. But God gives it 'body', as he intended, and each of the different seeds has its own 'body'. Not all flesh is identical. No – you have one kind for humans, another kind for cattle, another for birds, and another kind of flesh for fish. Then there are heavenly bodies and earthly bodies, and their glory is of two different kinds. The sun's glory is quite different from that of the moon; and that of the stars is different again. For different stars are different in their glory.

[Have you got that?] Well, that's how it is with the resurrection of the dead. A corpse is sown in corruption, and raised in un-corruption. A corpse is sown in dishonour, and raised in glory. A corpse is sown in weakness, and raised in power. A human body is sown; it is a spiritual body that is raised. If there is a human body, there is also such a thing as a spiritual body. So it is also written, 'The first man, Adam, came to be as a living human' (Genesis 2:7), while the final Adam came to be as a life-giving spirit.

However, the order is not spiritual first, but human first, then spiritual. The first human came from the earth, made of dust; the second human came from heaven.

As is the Person of Dust, so are his successors in dust; as is the Heavenly One, so are his successors from heaven. And as we have carried the likeness of the Person of Dust, so we shall carry the likeness of the Heavenly One.

This is what I mean, brothers and sisters: flesh and blood cannot inherit the kingdom of God; corruption does not inherit un-corruption. Look! I am telling you a mystery. We shall not all fall asleep; but we shall all be changed, in a nanosecond, in the blink of an eye – at the final trumpet.

For the trumpet will signal – and then the dead shall be raised undecayed. And for ourselves, we shall be changed. For this decaying part must put on un-decay, and this mortal part put on immortality. But when this decaying part puts on un-decay, and this mortal part puts on immortality, then the word of Scripture will come true: 'Death has been swallowed up into victory' (Isaiah 25:8). 'Where, death, is [your] victory? Where, death, is your sting?' (Hosea 13:14).

The sting of death is sin; and the power of sin is the law. Thanks be to God who gives us the victory through our Lord Jesus Christ!

So, my beloved fellow Christians, be firm of purpose, unbudging, always doing all in your power in the Lord's work, knowing that – in the Lord – your labour is not useless.

> We may not have followed every twist and turn of the argument here, but we should be heartened by Paul's massive certainties. Resurrection may indeed seem like 'news too good to be true'; but that is not a discovery of the twenty-first century – Paul has been there before us and faced the difficulty. What makes the difference for him is his certainty of the unfailing presence of Christ.

Arrangements for the collection

16$^{1-4}$ About the collection for the saints, as I instructed the churches of Galatia, so you must do. On the first day of the week, let each of you put something aside at home, saving up whatever fits in with how they are doing financially; this is to avoid doing the calculations when I come. But when I do come, I'll give a letter of introduction to whoever meets your criteria, to carry your generous gift to Jerusalem. And if it is appropriate for me to go too, they'll come with me.

> The 'collection', for the impoverished Jerusalem Church, was of enormous importance for Paul. It is a statement for him of Christian solidarity. Those who are better off are, in his view, obliged to look after fellow Christians who are struggling materially. That is a part of what being Christian means – looking after the other bits of the Body, as he might have said in Chapter 12 above.
>
> It may not be too fanciful to read here evidence of some lack of trust in the Corinthian Church. For, first, Paul tells them to 'put something aside' each Sunday, rather than (as we should expect) bringing it to church, to put in the collection. So perhaps the Corinthians could not even trust each other with charitable money. And, second, Paul is not at all sure whether they are prepared to allow him to escort the collection to Jerusalem. This Church is not at ease with itself, nor with its founder.

Paul's travel plans

$^{5-9}$ I'll come to you when I pass through Macedonia. For I am passing through Macedonia, and perhaps I'll stay a while with you, and even spend the winter with you, so that you can send me on wherever I am going. For this time I don't want to see you just in passing; I'm hoping to remain quite a while with you, if the Lord permits. I'm staying at Ephesus until Pentecost, because a powerful door has opened wide for me – and several people are opposing me.

> In the opening chapter of 2 Corinthians, we shall see that it looks as though Paul was over-optimistic here, and he never actually made it. All kinds of things could intervene in his missionary work. In winter,

snow on land and storms at sea, as well as the various kinds of opposition he might encounter. In addition, Paul's deepest question was always 'What does Jesus want me to do now?', and that was not always identical to what the Corinthians might want him to do.

Be nice to Timothy. Apollos won't be coming

10-12 If Timothy comes, make sure that he comes to you without cause for fear. For he is doing the Lord's work, just as I am. So don't let anyone disdain him; send him on his way in peace, for him to come to me. For I'm waiting for him, with the Christians here.

With regard to our brother Apollos, I begged and begged him to come to you with the other brothers and sisters, but it was definitely not his [or: God's] wish that he should come to you at this moment. He will come when the time is right.

> There is a hint of unease in these verses also. Paul is quite menacing as he tries to ensure that Timothy is received properly, reminding them that he will soon find out whether or not they did the right thing. He does not tell us why the Corinthians might not receive Timothy properly; it may have been a general sense of 'We want the organ-grinder, not his monkey.' And Apollos's absence also suggests looming mistrust; some may have thought that Paul was preventing him from coming because he was the leader of a faction opposed to Paul. Or it may have been (more piously) that Apollos was so horrified at having his name used by a particular splinter group in Corinth that he thought it better to leave it awhile. It is striking, however, that Paul does not make it clear whose will it wasn't for Apollos to come to Corinth (Apollos? Paul? God?).

Final greetings

13-24 Stay awake; stand firm in the faith; be courageous; grow in strength. Let all your business be done in love.

One thing I'm asking of you, brothers and sisters. You know Stephanas's household – they were the first converts in Asia, and they have set themselves to serve the saints. I want you people to be subject to people like this, and to all collaborators and workers. I'm really happy at the presence of Stephanas and Fortunatus and Achaicus; because these are people who have made up for the lack of you, for they refreshed both my spirits and yours. So – give recognition to people of this sort.

The churches of Asia greet you. Aquila and Prisca greet you in the Lord, along with the church that meets in their house. All the Christians here greet you. Greet each other with a holy kiss.

Here's the greeting in my hand: PAUL

If anyone doesn't love the Lord, let him or her be accursed.

Marana Tha.

The grace of Our Lord Jesus be with you.

My love be with all of you in Christ Jesus.

There is a breathlessness about the last lines of the letter, and no let-up in the tension. The conclusion begins with a reminder of certain virtues that they had been ignoring in Corinth. It continues with what is presumably a reprimand for their lack of respect for the 'household of Stephanas', whose name suggests that he may have been a freedman, and perhaps therefore not taken seriously by the Corinthian Christians, despite his evident good will.

Then come the usual greetings: 'The churches of Asia send you their love' might capture the mood a bit better than my translation does. The reference to Aquila and Prisca reminds us that Acts 18 has Paul working and living in Corinth with this husband and wife team, who were also responsible for capturing the gifted Apollos.

As usual, Paul makes his mark on the papyrus of the letter, with an insistence on 'loving the Lord', and an Aramaic prayer, 'Our Lord, come', and a characteristic conclusion, where Jesus is twice mentioned, and love is given its proper place.

So ends perhaps Paul's most remarkable letter.

The Second Letter to the Corinthians

Opening greeting

1 **1, 2** Paul, apostle of Jesus Christ through the will of God, and Timothy our fellow Christian, to the Church of God which is in Corinth, along with all the saints who are in the whole of Achaia. Grace to you and peace, from God our Father and the Lord Jesus Christ.

> This is an entirely characteristic opening to a Pauline letter; notice his distinctive emphasis that his vocation as an apostle is 'through the will of God'; his mention of Timothy (1 Corinthians 16:10-11 appears to suggest that they had been less than respectful of him); the extension of the greeting beyond the confines of Corinth to 'the whole of Achaia'; Paul's use of the words 'grace' and 'peace', which are very important elements in his understanding of what God has done in Christ; and, finally, the mention, virtually in the same breath, of God the Father and Jesus. All of this sets the scene for what is to follow.
>
> This is perhaps Paul's most passionate and emotional letter. In consequence, it is very often hard to see precisely what he is saying, and the sound of the Greek is jerky and at times impenetrable. The translation has left Paul obscure where he has been obscure (generally noting when this was the case); but the reader needs to be assured that no disrespect is thereby intended to the apostle.

Thanksgiving

3-7 Blessed be the God and Father of our Lord Jesus Christ, the Father of mercies and the God of all comfort, who comforts us in all our affliction, so that we can comfort people in all [kinds of] distress, through the comfort with which we ourselves have been comforted by God. Because just as Christ's sufferings overflow to us, so, through Christ, our comfort also overflows. If we are being afflicted [it is] for your comfort and salvation. If we are being comforted, it is for your comfort, which works itself out in enduring the same sufferings that we are undergoing. And our expectation for you is solidly based; we know that just as you are partners in the suffering, so also [you will be partners] in the comfort.

> Notice the tension here, between 'comfort' and 'affliction'. In one guise or another, this will run through all of the letter; at present the reader does not know, although presumably the Corinthians who

first heard this letter read out did know, what are the 'afflictions' for which comfort is on offer. But clearly there is a continuity between the sufferings of Christ, those of Paul, and whatever the Corinthians were currently having to put up with. Notice also the word 'partners', which translates two words that are familiar from 1 Corinthians, *koinonos* and *koinonia*, which refer to ideas like partnership, union, communion, and solidarity. And, as in the opening of 1 Corinthians, the series of passive verbs may carry a warning to the Corinthians not to pride themselves too much.

Some unidentifiable troubles

8-11   My fellow Christians, we do not want you to be ignorant of the affliction that happened to us in Asia, [when] we were weighed down, far beyond our resources. The result was that we even despaired of living; we actually had the death sentence on us; this was so that we should not trust in ourselves, but in God who raises up the dead. God is the one who rescued us from so great a [danger of] death, and will rescue us again; that is the God in whom we still hope that he will rescue us once more, as long as you join in helping us with your prayers, in order that thanksgiving may be made on our behalf from many people, because of the favour granted to us through many prayers.

The translation of the last sentence is, frankly, anyone's guess; and indeed, for what we know, it is anyone's guess what the life-threatening troubles were to which Paul refers, though evidently he expected the Corinthians to know. They may be hinted at in 1 Corinthians 15:32; 16:9, and in the account in Acts 19 of the riots in Ephesus. What comes out with absolute clarity is Paul's total dependence on God, his insistence on the Resurrection, and his affirmation of the importance of prayer as something that Christians do for each other.

Boasting: only in God, and in Jesus Christ

12-14   For this is our boast, the witness that our conscience bears, that we have conducted ourselves in the world, more especially towards you, with the simplicity and purity of God, not by human cleverness, but by God's grace. For all we write to you is nothing other than what you read, and what you recognise. And my hope is that you will [continue to] recognise to the end, just as you partly recognised us, that we are your boast, just as you are our boast on the day of our Lord Jesus.

Look out for the idea of boasting in this letter; this section, obviously, begins and ends with it; we shall see it again. Probably we may read 'between the lines' here, that the Corinthians have been complaining about Paul. They may well have been complaining that he is different in person to how he presents himself in his letters.

Paul's abandoned travel plans

15-22   It was with this confidence that I was wanting to come to you before, for you to have a second chance of the gift; [the idea was] to come via you to Macedonia, and

then to come back to you again after Macedonia, and have you send me on my
way to Judaea. So when I was planning this, was I 'behaving irresponsibly'? [Are
you saying that] my decision was an unspiritual decision, so that in my case 'yes'
should mean 'yes' and 'no' should mean 'no'?

It is God who is reliable: our word to you is not 'yes-and-no'. For the Son of
God, Jesus Christ, the one who was proclaimed among you through us, that is to
say through me and Silvanus and Timothy, wasn't 'yes-and-no' but 'yes'. For as
many as are the promises of God, in [Jesus they find their] 'yes'. So it is through
him that the 'Amen' is [given] to God for glory, through our [preaching]. It is God
who confirms us – along with you – into Christ; and God who anoints us; God
who gives us the certificate of authenticity, and who provides the 'down-payment'
of the Spirit of God in our hearts.

> Clearly there have been complaints from Corinth (for another
> example, later in the letter, see 2 Corinthians 10:1, 10, 11); and the
> ground for complaint is that in 1 Corinthians 16:5-9 Paul said that
> he would come, and never turned up. They seem to have accused
> him of irresponsibility and selfishness ('unspiritual decision') and
> vacillation. Paul is not pleased, that much is clear; but notice how,
> as always, he brings the question back to God and to Jesus Christ, or
> to God-in-Jesus-Christ. There is an untranslatable pun towards the
> end of this section, when Paul speaks of Christ ('The Anointed
> One' or 'Messiah'), and then, immediately afterwards, of 'God who
> anoints us'. His apostolate, he never tires of saying, is from God, as
> is Christ's mission. If they don't like it, it is Christ they have to
> blame, not Paul.

Paul's attitude to the Corinthian Christians

1 ²³-2 ⁴ I call on God as my witness (I stake my life on it) that it was in order to spare
you that I did not after all come to Corinth. This was not because we lord it over
your faith. No – we are working with you, to bring you joy. For it is by faith that
you stand.

For my decision was not to return to you in grief. For if I cause you grief, who is to
cheer me up, other than the one whom I have grieved? And this is the reason why I
wrote this letter: [I didn't want to] come and have grief from the ones who ought
to bring me joy. I am convinced with regard to all of you that my joy is that of you
all. It was out of great affliction and anguish of heart that I wrote to you, with many
tears; [I didn't want] you to grieve, but to know the love I have especially for you.

> There had obviously been a major breakdown in relations between
> Paul and the Christians in Corinth, and both sides have been upset.
> Paul is here trying to rebuild the relationship, without retreating
> from whatever position it was that he had adopted. Quite clearly he
> is very fond of his Corinthians, even when they irritate him.

Punishing (but with love) a person who has done wrong

5-11 If someone has caused grief, it wasn't to me that they caused it, but to all of you, in
a way (I don't want to exaggerate). For a person like that this punishment is

appropriate, at the hands of the majority, so that – on the contrary – you should rather forgive the person and comfort them; we don't want a person like that to be overwhelmed with greater grief. So I'm encouraging you to reaffirm your love for that person. This was the reason I wrote, to know your quality, to see if you are obedient in every respect. If you forgive someone, so do I: for any forgiveness that I have granted (if I *have* granted any), is for your sakes, in the person of Christ. We don't want to be outwitted by Satan; for we are well aware of Satan's intentions.

> The translation is tricky here; to follow what is going on, and to decide how to take some of the Greek words and phrases that Paul uses, we would need to hear both ends of the 'telephone conversation' at once. Without that, the translation depends on interpretative guess-work. Clearly someone (perhaps the incestuous person of 1 Corinthians 5:1, or perhaps a visitor from elsewhere who has challenged Paul's right to be an apostle) has done something that requires drastic measures in response; Paul regards the offence (whatever it was) as utterly evil, the work of Satan, and, clearly, he was not too pleased with how the Corinthians had coped with it. And, in all probability, someone has been questioning Paul's authority, which is never a good idea.

A slightly mysterious travel detail

12, 13   When I came to Troas, for the gospel of Christ, and because a door opened for me in the Lord, I could not relax spiritually, because I didn't find Titus, my fellow Christian. Instead, I said goodbye to them, and left for Macedonia.

> Troas is a regular port from which to leave Asia Minor for Europe (see Acts 16:11, and consult a map); so clearly Paul was on his way to Corinth after some arrangements had broken down. Once again, we cannot be clear what has happened, but he seems still to be referring to his failure to come to Corinth (which was partly through a desire not to cause more pain).

God's is the victory; and Paul is God's apostle

14-17   Thanks be to God, who always leads us in triumph in Christ, and who always makes known the fragrance of the knowledge of him, through us, everywhere we go. Because we are Christ's 'sweet scent' to God, among those who are being saved, and among those who are being lost. For some it is a scent that leads them from death to death; for others, it is a smell that leads from life to life – and who is equal to this [task]? For we aren't (as many people are) putting God's word up for sale. No – it is with pure motives that we speak in Christ. No – it is from God and before God that we speak.

> Once again we should very much like to know what those Corinthians knew; they must have understood precisely what he was telling them. Paul uses a metaphor ('lead in triumph') from a Roman victory parade, which shows him to be God's willing prisoner; he

then uses (almost battering it into the ground) another (the sweet smell of sacrifices) from Old Testament religion. Both of these images emphasise how God and Christ are at the heart of Paul's life and ministry. He sees his ministry as a daunting task, but one that he thinks he is at least performing with integrity. And it is a matter of 'life and death'.

From the Corinthian complaints to Paul's ministry

3¹⁻³ Are we starting to 'commend ourselves' again? Surely we don't need any letters of recommendation, either to you or from you! *You* are our letter, a letter written on our hearts, known and read by everyone; you are revealed to be Christ's letter, served up by us, written not in ink but in the Spirit of the Living God, not on stone tablets, but on the tablets of hearts of flesh.

Implicit in the complaints that the Corinthians have evidently been making is a protest about how Paul has been approaching his ministry, and possibly also about his reaction to criticism – the idea of 'commending oneself' will appear again and again in this letter, and may have been a quotation from his Corinthian opponents. Paul has heard their protest, and now shifts, almost imperceptibly, into a defence of his apostolate. But it is not just prickly defensiveness; as we shall see in what follows, Paul is now thinking his way through his theory of what it is to be an apostle, and what it is to be a church. What comes next is an account of what God is doing in Christ, and in Paul, and why it matters, for Corinth, and for the world at large. The idea of the letter 'known and read' by everyone, contains another untranslatable pun: see 1:13. The metaphor of a letter may perhaps have been suggested by what Paul was actually doing, and perhaps reflects his discovery of just how powerful a letter can be as a means of communication.

The ministry of the living God

4-11 We have as much confidence as this in God through Christ. It is not that we are sufficient from our own resources, to credit anything as coming from us. No – our resources come from God, who has given us the resources to be ministers of the New Covenant, which is a covenant not of the letter but of the Spirit. For the letter kills, but the Spirit gives life.

If the ministry of death, carved in stone letters, made its appearance in radiance, so that the children of Israel were unable to look on the face of Moses, because of the transient nature of the radiance of his face, will not the ministry of the Spirit all the more appear in radiance?

If the ministry [that led to] condemnation had its own radiance, all the more will the ministry of righteousness be saturated in radiance. You see, that which has been endowed with radiance is not in this case given radiance because of its own surpassing radiance. If that which is transient has radiance, how much more that which is permanent?

If you did not understand a word of this, don't worry; it is not easy, and scholars are divided about what it might mean. What is clear is that Paul is emphasising the superiority of the New Covenant to the old. Once again, we see his insistence that it is life over death; and on the side of life, Paul speaks of spirit and of righteousness.

Why could the children of Israel not look on Moses' face? Because he had been close to God (see Exodus 34:29-35); and, some scholars suggest, the children of Israel had already indicated that they didn't want to get too close to the living God (see Exodus 20:18-21).

What has this got to do with Paul and his Corinthians? They need to accept this opportunity for direct access to the New Covenant of the Living God, and willingly.

Unrestrained access to God

12-18   So since we have a hope as great as this, let us behave with great boldness. Let's not be like Moses, who put a veil on his face, so that the children of Israel should not look upon the end of what was transitory. Instead, their thoughts were hardened. Right up to the present day, there is still the same veil at the reading of the Old Covenant; the veil is not lifted up, because in Christ [the Old Covenant] is transitory.

Instead, right down to today, whenever Moses is read, a veil lies over their hearts. 'But whenever he turned to the Lord, the veil was lifted' (Exodus 34:34). Now the Lord is the Spirit, and where there is the Spirit of the Lord, there is freedom. But all of us, with uncovered faces contemplating [or: 'reflecting'] the Lord's radiance, are transformed from radiance into radiance, as from the Spirit of the Lord.

This is still difficult to follow; but a few things are clear:

- 'boldness' is an important idea. The children of the New Covenant enjoy (and should make use of) unrestrained access to God;
- Moses' veiled face prevents the children of Israel from encountering God's radiance, and from seeing that the Old Covenant is transitory;
- Jesus, on the other hand, is the likeness of God; and Paul has gazed on that likeness – but the radiance is not to be hidden. Instead, there is the opportunity for all to be transformed;
- Spirit, Lord, Jesus, God, are all part-names for the bright reality that is being offered;
- we may also notice how, in this letter, Paul makes use of the metaphor of 'letter'. In 3:1 he contrasts 'letters of recommendation' with the living 'letter' that the Corinthians are, a 'letter of Christ', written not in ink but in the Spirit of the Living God, on the heart, not on stone tablets (and we think of Ezekiel 36:26). Later on he will refer to 'The Letter' (7:8), which caused them pain, and is part of the history of their complicated relationship. Chapter 3:6 contrasts 'writing' and 'Spirit', and verses 7 and 8 contrast stone-death with radiance-life. Verse 9 drifts from the metaphor, but note how the contrast continues: condemnation-righteousness. In verses 14 and 15, the metaphor of 'letter' recurs with the idea of 'reading'. We have unrestrained access, and the access can transform us.

This is difficult material, but the broad landmarks are clear enough.

No veil over our hearts

4 ¹⁻⁶ Because of this, since we have this ministry, just as we have received mercy, we do not lose heart; instead, we have renounced the things that we hide out of shame. We do not behave in a crafty manner; we do not falsify God's word. Instead, we recommend ourselves to the conscience of all people before God, by revealing the Truth. If our gospel is a hidden one, it is [only] hidden for those who are on the way to destruction, those among whom the god of this age has blinded the thoughts of unbelievers, so that they do not see the gospel's illumination, the radiance of Christ, who is the likeness of God.

We do not, you see, preach ourselves, but the Lord Jesus Christ, and ourselves as your slaves because of Jesus. For it is God who said, 'out of darkness light shall shine'; and that is the God who has shone in our hearts, to illuminate the knowledge of the radiance of God, in the person [or face] of Jesus Christ.

> To grasp what is going on here, it is important to see that Paul is still thinking of the experience of the children of Israel in the desert. He seems to be saying that because they did not want to see the living God, Moses wore a veil, which also had the effect of hiding from them the fact that the dispensation was not going to last. Now, however, the vision is available, because Christ is the likeness of God, and God can therefore be known, and the world ('all people') transformed.

The power is God's, not ours

7-18 But we hold this treasure in clay pots, so that the immense power should be [seen to be] from God and not from us.

In every way we are afflicted, but not crushed; we are perplexed, but not despairing. We are persecuted, but not utterly abandoned, struck down but not destroyed, always carrying around Jesus' putting-to-death in our body, so that Jesus' life might be revealed in our body.

For all the time we who are alive are being handed over to death because of Jesus, so that Jesus' life may be revealed in our mortal flesh.

The result is that death is doing its work in us, but life in you. We have the same Spirit of faith, according to the Scripture, 'I believed, and so I spoke.' In just the same way, we believe, and so we speak, knowing that the one who raised the Lord Jesus will raise us also with Jesus and will set us before him, along with you.

For everything is because of you, in order that increasing grace may, through the thanksgiving of the many, overflow to the radiance [or: 'glory'] of God.

So [as I say] we do not lose heart; no – even if our outer being is wasting away, our inner being keeps being renewed, day in and day out.

For the present lightweight of our affliction is bringing about an incomparable, immeasurable, solid weight of glory for us. We keep our eyes, not on the things that are visible, but on the things that are invisible; for visible things are just temporary, while invisible things are eternal.

> Now, you may feel, we are emerging into the sunlight, and that difficult passage in the last chapter starts to make sense. As always, Paul's eyes are on God, not on himself; hence the contrast between the 'treasure' and the 'clay pots' in which the treasure is contained.

The clay pots represent apostles for Paul; but the attention of Paul and of his Corinthians must always be on the glory of God. This 'glory' is invisible, but it exercises an unmistakably transforming power – Paul clearly expected to be able to see it make a difference.

The word that I have translated as 'radiance' is often rendered as 'glory'; the reader needs to have both ideas in mind.

Notice how important resurrection is in Paul's thinking. It seems to him entirely appropriate that he and his fellow ministers should be suffering, because the same God who raised Jesus from the dead is still at work, bringing out the 'glory' that (at the moment) can't quite be seen.

God is working our transformation

5 1-10 For we know that when our earthly home [which is no more than a tent] is destroyed, we have a building from God, a house not made by hand, eternal, in heaven. For in our present [home] we are groaning, longing to put on, over the top, our home from heaven. That is, assuming that once we strip off we shall not turn out to be naked. For while we are in the tent, we groan and are weighed down, because we do not want to strip off, but to put on additional clothing, so that what is deathly in us may be swallowed up by life. It is God who is working on us for this very purpose, God who gives us the down-payment of the Spirit.

So let us always take courage, and know that when we are at home in the body we are away from the Lord. The thing is, it is through faith that we proceed, not through outward appearance. We take courage, and we prefer to be away from the body and at home with the Lord. Therefore it is our ambition, whether at home or away, to be pleasing to him. For all of us must appear before Christ's tribunal, so that each one may receive a reward for the things they have done through the body, whether good or evil.

For Paul, resurrection is central and indispensable to the gospel. This means looking beyond what is present and tangible. It is not something we can take for granted (we might easily miss out on it) – but we can be confident that God is unceasingly at work to bring about resurrection. How do we know? As far as Paul is concerned, it is through the Spirit, a palpable presence. Have we lost something here?

The reference to Christ's tribunal may remind the alert reader about the tribunal in Corinth before which Paul was hauled, according to Acts 18:12. More than that, it may serve as a reminder that Jesus is Judge for Paul; that is to say, he is (yet again) taking over a function hitherto reserved for God.

The 'down-payment of the Spirit'. What does Paul mean by this (which also appears at 1:22)?

What God-in-Christ has done; what the Corinthians should do

11-21 So, since we know the fear of the Lord, we are trying to persuade human beings – to God we are transparent. But I hope that we are transparent also to your consciences. We are not (once more) 'recommending ourselves' to you, but giving you an incentive for boasting about us, so that you may have [something to say] to those who boast about appearances, and not in the heart. For if we are 'out of our minds', it is for God; if we are in a calm state, that is for you. For Christ's love constrains us. Our verdict is this: if one has died on behalf of all, then all have died. And he died for all, in order that those who live might no longer live to themselves, but to the one who died for them and was raised.

So then: from now on, we regard nobody from a worldly point of view. Even if we knew Christ in the flesh, we no longer do so. The result is that if someone is 'in Christ', they are a new creation. What is old has passed away – look, [the] new has come! Everything comes from God, who, through Christ, reconciled us to himself, and who gave us this ministry of reconciliation. That is, that God was in Christ reconciling the world to himself, not reckoning their transgressions to them, and putting his message of reconciliation in us.

So we are Christ's ambassadors: [imagine] that God is pleading through us. On Christ's behalf we *implore* you: be reconciled to God. [Christ] who had no knowledge of sin, God made into 'sin' for our sakes, so that in Christ we should become God's righteousness.

Even in translation, Paul's passion is unmistakable here. What is he trying to get the Corinthians to do? *Not* to admire Paul, but to 'be reconciled to God'. Some of them may have dismissed him, perhaps because he is so passionate about Christ, as 'out of his mind'; but as far as Paul is concerned, he is speaking of the deepest reality of all, God's Resurrection victory over Death; and that deepest reality is not just a gift to Jesus. It is available to transform the lives of absolutely everybody, such is God's generosity. But God will not force us. So 'be reconciled to God', says Paul to the Corinthians (dressing up as 'God's diplomat', although not perhaps in diplomatic language) and be astonished at God's generosity: he made Christ into 'sin', all for us!

Paul's plea

6 1-10 So we are working along with you, and we beg you not to make God's gift useless, once you have accepted it. You know how he says, 'At the acceptable time I listened to you, and on the day of salvation I helped you' (Isaiah 49:8). Look! *Now* is the beautifully acceptable time! Look! *Now* is the day of salvation! We do not give any occasion of offence, so that our ministry should not be censured. Instead, in every respect, we 'commend ourselves' as ministers of God: we put up with much affliction, calamities, difficulties, floggings, imprisonment, political disturbance, hard work, nights without sleep, days without food. We endure in sincerity and knowledge, in patience and decency, in the Holy Spirit, in unfeigned love, in speaking the truth, in the power of God. Our means are the armour of righteousness, to right and to left, through glory and dishonour, through ill repute and good repute. [We are regarded] as deceitful – and yet we are true; as unrecognised – and yet we are known; as dying – and look! we are alive; as punished – and yet not put to death; as distressed – and yet always rejoicing; as beggars – and yet we make many people rich; as having nothing – and yet possessing everything.

There is no main verb in the list of disasters and triumphs that starts with 'We do not give any occasion of offence'; so even saying 'we' here is only an intelligent guess at translating a string of participles. It is clear, though, what Paul is saying: seen in the light of the Resurrection, his ministry (and presumably that of Silvanus and Timothy also) is not the string of catastrophes that his opponents are suggesting. Clearly Paul's life as an apostle has been an eventful one, though it is beyond us to reconstruct exactly what it had involved, or to fit his account with what is reported in Acts.

The plea resumed (after the dramatic autobiographical interlude)

11-13 We have spoken openly to you, Corinthians; you have a place in our affections. It is not in us that you are cramped, but in your own emotions. In return, open yourselves also up to us (I am speaking as [a father speaks] to children).

Avoid anything that is not the living God

6 14–7 1 Don't get mismated with unbelievers; for what do righteousness and lawlessness have in common? How can light and darkness be partners? Can Christ and Beliar sing in harmony? What has a believer in common with an unbeliever? What agreement can there be between the Temple of God and idols? You see, we are the Temple of the living God, as God said,

'I shall dwell and walk among them
and I shall be their God and they shall be my people.'

Therefore 'Come out of the midst of them and be separated,' says the Lord, and

'Do not touch what is unclean
and I shall welcome you
and I shall be as a Father to you
and you shall be as sons and daughters to me,'
says the Lord Almighty.

So, my dear ones, since we have these promises, let us purify ourselves from every defilement of flesh and spirit, bringing about sanctification by the fear of God.

It is not altogether easy here to know what target Paul has in mind, and some scholars, noting that the previous section and that which follows flow easily into each other, have suggested that it is an interpolation, perhaps part of another letter that Paul wrote to his Corinthians. For a variety of reasons it seems better to read it here as Christians have read it for twenty centuries, and to admit that while we cannot be clear precisely what Paul has in view, the Corinthians will have been in no doubt.

When Paul tells the Corinthians not to get 'mismated with unbelievers', it is undeniably strong language – but it is what he wrote.

The three quotations above are from Exodus 29:45; Isaiah 52:11 and 43:6 respectively.

The plea resumed

2-4 Make room for us. There is nobody we have wronged, nobody we have ruined, nobody we have taken advantage of. What I say is not to condemn [anybody]; for I have already said that you are in our hearts, to live and die together. I have great confidence in you; I boast a good deal about you; I am filled with comfort, and overflowing with joy, after all our affliction.

Reviewing their intimate and painful relationship

5-16 For when we came into Macedonia, our flesh had no rest – we were afflicted in every respect, with assaults from outside and fears within. But God, who comforts the lowly, comforted us through Titus's arrival, and not just his arrival, but also the comfort he had received in regard to you. He reported to us your longing for us, your grieving, and your enthusiastic support for me – so that I rejoiced all the more.

Because even if I caused you pain by 'The Letter', I don't feel any regret. Even if I had had some regret (because I observe that 'That Letter' caused you pain, even if it was only for a while), now I'm glad, not because you experienced pain, but because your pain led to your repenting. The pain you felt was in God's way, so that in no respect did you lose anything at our hands, because pain that is in God's way leads to repentance, and to salvation that is [certainly] not to be regretted. Whereas the world's pain brings about death. Look what this very business of being pained 'in God's way' has brought about in you, how much eagerness – but also a desire to defend yourselves, but also some indignation, but also some fear, but also some longing, but also some zeal, but also some vindication. In every respect, you 'commend yourselves' to be innocent in the affair.

So then, even if I did write to you, it wasn't because of the person who had done wrong, nor because of the person who had been wronged, but because of this eagerness of yours that has been shown on our behalf, before God. Because of this we have been comforted.

In addition to the comfort we received, we rejoiced even 'abundantlier' at Titus's joy – because his spirit was refreshed by all of you. Because if I had boasted to him a bit about you, I wasn't embarrassed. Instead, as we told you, just as we had told you the truth in every respect, so also our boasting before Titus came true. And his heart goes out to you all the more abundantly when he remembers the obedience you all showed, how you welcomed him 'with fear and trembling'. I'm delighted that in every respect I can count on you.

This is an extraordinarily warm and intimate passage, from this most emotional of Paul's letters. His affection is plain to see, even as he admits that there have been difficulties. Notice how all the time Paul brings the issue back to God, and what God is doing in the situation.

The syntax in the last-but-one sentence of the second paragraph is very hard to represent in English in any satisfactory way, and is a poor representation, but the best that I can do, of Paul's use of a conjunction that means something like 'but', only rather stronger.

The horrid word 'abundantlier' is an attempt to express Paul's rather ungrammatical enthusiasm.

The collection

8 ¹⁻²⁴ I am letting you know, brothers and sisters, [about] God's collection [literally: 'grace'; see also 1 Corinthians 16:3], which was given by the churches of Macedonia, because it was through trial and much affliction that the overflowing of their joy and their profound poverty overflowed into the wealth of their simplicity; because I am witness that of their own accord, in line with what they could manage, and even beyond what they could manage, they begged us, most earnestly, for the grace and communion of the ministry to the saints, not as we had expected – instead, they gave themselves in the first place to the Lord, and to us through the will of God. The result was that we asked Titus, just as he had already made a beginning, so he would also complete this work of generosity among you.

But, as you overflow in every way, in faith and rhetoric, and knowledge and all eagerness, and in the love among you that comes from us, may you abound also in this work of grace. I am not saying this as a command, but through the eagerness of others, and testing the genuineness of your love; for you know the grace of our Lord Jesus Christ, that because of us he became poor although he was rich, so that you might be rich through his poverty. And let me give you my opinion in this matter; this is for your benefit. A year ago you had already begun, not just to act but also to want to act; now bring the action to completion, so that your enthusiastic wanting may be matched by our bringing it to completion (so far as you are able). For if the enthusiasm is there, it is acceptable in proportion to what a person has, not in proportion to what a person does not have.

The idea is not that other people should get relief, while you get affliction; it is a question of equalisation – your present surplus balanced against their present need. Then their surplus may assist your need, so that there may be equalisation, as it is written,

> 'The one who [gathered] much did not have a surplus;
> the one who [gathered] little did not go in want.'

Thanks be to God, who put into Titus's heart this eagerness for you, because he accepted the request; but because he was so very eager, of his own initiative he went off to [visit] you.

Along with him we sent the Christian, who is [widely] commended in all the churches [for his service to] the gospel. Not only that, but he was appointed by the churches as our travelling-companion, for this collection that was served up by us to the glory of God himself, and our good will. We tried to avoid anyone finding fault with us because of this lavish gift that is being served up by us; for we took careful thought, about not just how the Lord might see it, but also about how humans might see it. With them we sent that fellow Christian of ours, whose quality we have frequently tested, in many different circumstances: he is in earnest, and much more so now, with great confidence in you. If there is any problem about Titus, he is my partner and a fellow worker as far as you are concerned. If [about] our brethren, they are apostles of the churches, the glory of Christ. So give them proof of your love, and of our boasting on your behalf, in the presence of the churches.

> The collection was of enormous importance to Paul, not just for the relief it brought to Christians in Jerusalem, who had no access to the welfare system that Jewish inhabitants operated there. The importance was also theological: this is how we do things in the

Body of Christ. So we notice the number of 'theologically weight-bearing' terms that he uses here, and their flexibility. The word for 'collection' is the word he uses also for God's 'grace', for 'generosity', and even for 'thanks'. In addition he uses the root of the words for 'ministry' (which I have translated also as 'served up' and 'administered'), 'affliction', 'simplicity' (see 2 Corinthians 1:12; 8:2; 9:11, 13; 11:3, and not much used outside this letter, so it is clearly a term of some importance for this situation), 'comfort' (also translated as 'beg' or 'ask'), and 'communion' ('fellowship' or 'solidarity'). See how many other words you can see that are frequent in 2 Corinthians. Paul's theological insight here is: if this is how God has acted towards us in Christ, that is how we should act towards others who are 'in Christ'.

The 'equalisation' quotation, 'the one who [gathered] much did not have a surplus . . .' is from Exodus 16:18, where it refers to God's astonishing (and very precise) generosity with the manna. The point here is that Paul is trying to encourage the Corinthians to live out their generous desires, and not to fear that they will thereby be deprived.

There are occasional signs of haste here, and it is sometimes difficult to translate individual elements with any confidence; but the overall meaning is clear. Notice (as in 1 Corinthians 16) the occasional hints that the Corinthians may not quite trust Paul in financial matters. We have no very clear idea who is the 'Christian' or 'fellow Christian' of whom Paul speaks.

A reminder to be generous in the collection

9 1-15   As regards the ministry to the saints, it is superfluous for me to write to you. For I am well aware of your eagerness (about which I have boasted to the Macedonians!), that Achaia has been all ready since last year; and your ardour spurred most of them on. But I sent the brethren, so that our boasting about you might not prove hollow – I wanted you to be all ready, as I had told them. I didn't want us (never mind you!) to be embarrassed by this confidence, for example if some Macedonians accompanied you and found you unprepared! So it was necessary for me to ask those brethren to go on ahead to you and make the advance arrangements for the generosity that you had previously promised, [so that it would] be ready, like an act of generosity, and not [as something reluctantly conceded] by greedy people.

[Think of] this: the one who sows sparingly will also reap sparingly, and the one who sows generously will also reap generously. Each one as he has decided in advance, not sadly or under compulsion, for God loves a cheerful giver. For God is strong enough to overflow every kind of grace on you, so that always and in every way you may have enough of everything, and you may overflow into every kind of good deed. As it is written,

> 'He scattered, he gave to the poor;
>   his righteousness remains for ever' (Psalm 112:9).

The one who organises 'seed for the sower and bread for food' will also organise and increase your seed, and multiply the produce of your righteousness. [You will be] enriched into total simplicity, which brings about thanksgiving to God through us. Because the ministry of this service doesn't just provide for the needs of the saints, but also overflows through much thanksgiving to God. Through the quality of this ministry, [you are] glorifying God in the obedience of your confession of faith in the gospel of Christ, and by the simplicity of your solidarity with them and with all. And by their prayer for you they long for you because of the exceptional grace of God [that has come] upon you. Thanks be to God for his inexpressible gift.

> Once again, Paul is utterly passionate in what he is saying here, and occasionally he is dictating so fast that we can see what he is saying, but not quite how it fits together. The second and third sentences from the end, for example, are completely without a main verb in Greek.
>
> The collection is of huge importance to Paul, and, as before, there are many words that we have already recognised as important in the letter: ministry, superfluity (also overflow or abundance), eagerness, boasting, ardour, promise, grief, quality, thanks (or grace), glory, simplicity, fellowship (or communion or solidarity), and the whole notion of generosity: Christians should act as God has acted towards them. That is how the transforming power of God-in-Christ works in the world.
>
> We can allow ourselves a little smile at Paul's appeal to inter-provincial rivalry with his mention of 'Macedonians', but we do not know enough of the circumstances to be sure what his point is here.
>
> Lastly, read through the passage again, and see if you detect any hints that Paul is here soothing ruffled feathers. People can get very agitated where money is concerned.

A sudden change of tone

10 ¹⁻¹⁸ I myself, Paul, beg you, through the meekness and gentleness of Christ, I who am 'humble face to face' among you, but 'courageous when absent' with regard to you. I implore you that, when I am present, I won't [have to] be courageous with the confidence which I reckon on [in order] to face down certain people who reckon that we are operating in a merely human way.

For although we may behave in a merely human way, our strategy is not merely human: for the weapons [we use in] our military campaign are not merely human, but powerful, and on God's side, able to destroy fortresses: [they can] demolish sophistries, and every high tower that is raised up against the knowledge of God. And [they can] take prisoner every intellectual concept, to make it obey Christ; and they remain at the ready, to avenge all disobedience, whenever your obedience is fulfilled.

Look at what is staring you in the face. If a person is confident in himself or herself that they belong to Christ, let them consider this fact for themselves, that just as they [may] belong to Christ, so also do we. For if I start boasting a little too extravagantly about this authority of ours which the Lord gave us (for upbuilding, and not for destruction), I shan't be embarrassed. [I don't want] to seem as if I'm [trying to] terrify you through the 'Letters'. Because someone says, '[Paul's] letters are weighty and powerful, but his physical presence is unimpressive and his rhetoric contemptible.' Someone like that should reckon that we are just the same when present, and in action, as we are at long distance, and by letter.

We wouldn't have the nerve to put ourselves in the same class or compare ourselves to those who 'commend themselves'; but those people who measure themselves by their own standards, and compare themselves with one another, don't understand. We, however, won't boast outside the proper measure. No – our boasting will be in accordance with the measure of the rule that God apportioned to us as our measure, to reach as far as you. For we are not over-extending ourselves, as though we had not reached you; for we were actually the first to reach as far as you in [preaching] the gospel of Christ. You see, we don't boast inappropriately about the work that others have done; our expectation is that as your faith grows it has increased [according to our measure], so that it overflows to preach the gospel in the regions that are beyond you, not to boast about someone else's work in places which are already evangelised. 'Let the one who boasts, boast in the Lord.' For it's not the person who 'commends himself' who is trustworthy, but the one whom the Lord commends.

> There is a very sudden change of tone at the beginning of Chapter 10. Paul once again seems very cross, and it is not absolutely clear to the reader what he is cross about. This has led some scholars to argue that Chapters 10 and 11 are part of another letter that Paul sent to Corinth. We shall read it as it stands – but the reader should note that as it stands it is hard to be quite sure precisely what Paul is saying, except that in the final paragraph it looks as though some of his opponents in Corinth have been 'boasting inappropriately', and perhaps claiming Paul's work of evangelising as their own. Paul may well be quoting from what his Corinthian opponents have been saying about him. That is why 'humble face to face' and 'courageous when absent' are printed in inverted commas.
>
> Compare different translations of the last few sentences of this passage, to get a feel of the difficulties in knowing what he was saying. The alert reader will have noticed several words that are important in both 1 and 2 Corinthians: 'upbuilding', 'beg/comfort', 'reckon', 'rhetoric', 'commend'. Some, perhaps all, of these words are clearly 'on the table' between Paul and his Corinthians, but without hearing both sides of the discussion, we cannot say more than that. Notice, too, his reference to 'sophistries'. Paul's readers or listeners in Corinth would have known all about these: the empty cleverness of skilled rhetoricians, intended to bolster weak arguments.

Don't abandon the gospel

11 ¹⁻⁴ If only you would put up with me, with a little bit of my foolishness! No – please put up with me. For I am jealous for you with the jealousy of God; I betrothed you to one husband, to present you to Christ as a chaste virgin. But I'm afraid that perhaps as the snake cheated Eve in its wickedness, it may corrupt your minds away from the simplicity and chastity that lead to Christ. For if anyone comes and proclaims a Jesus different from the one whom we proclaimed, or if you receive a Spirit different from the one you [originally] received, or a gospel different from the one you [originally] accepted, you put up with it quite easily.

It now becomes clearer why Paul is cross; other Christian evangelists have been disparaging his work, never a wise thing to do with Paul, and arguing that he has preached 'the wrong gospel'. But he does not tell us exactly what the disagreement was about; the Corinthians obviously knew, and he did not expect us to be reading the material two millennia later. So we should be careful not to embrace too enthusiastically all the scholarly attempts to construct a picture of Paul's opponents.

Paul is very cross

5-11   You see, I reckon that I am no way inferior to the 'Superapostles'. I may be untrained in rhetoric – but not in knowledge; in every respect we have made it plain to you, in every way. Or did I commit a sin by humbling myself so that you might be raised on high, when as a free gift I preached to you the gospel of God? I robbed other churches when I accepted wages in order to support my ministry to you, and when I came to you and was in need, I didn't burden anyone. For the Christians who came from Macedonia supplied my needs, and [so] in every respect I kept myself from being a burden to you. And I shall continue to do so. It is the truth of Christ in me: this 'boasting' will not be silenced for me in the whole region of Achaia. Why? Because I don't love you? God knows . . .

There is sarcasm here, and we can only dimly reconstruct the charges that had been laid against Paul. Clearly, however, someone else has been at work in Corinth. See the reference to 'Superapostles' and to Paul's lack of training, as well as the earlier references to a 'different gospel', and his insistence on not being supported by the church he was evangelising. Once again, Paul mentions 'Macedonia' to the Corinthians, possibly meaning his generous (and much-loved) Philippians. For Paul everything always comes back to Christ and to God.

Testing for fake apostles

12-15   That is what I do – and what I shall continue to do – in order to remove the opportunity (from those who desire an opportunity) for them to be regarded as just like us. For people like that are fake apostles, dishonest workmen disguised as apostles of Christ. And no wonder – for Satan himself disguises himself as an angel of light. So it is nothing extraordinary if his ministers disguise themselves as ministers of righteousness. Their end will be in accordance with the work they have done.

Now we can see more clearly what has been going on. Some people in Corinth have been alleging that Paul wasn't a proper apostle, possibly because he had persecuted the Church, or because he had never known Jesus; but there was also a problem, apparently: he had not been charging for his services (perhaps making rather a point of this), but then asked them to give him money for Jerusalem. Trust between the Apostle and this most prominent of all his churches was at an all-time low. Notice, however, that he turns the argument back on his opponents: it is *they*, not Paul, who are the 'fake apostles'!

Paul's 'boasting'

11 ¹⁶–12 ¹³   Again, I say, don't let anyone imagine me to be a fool. Otherwise you must accept me as a fool; let me too boast for a little while. What I am saying, I am not saying in the way of the Lord, but as it were as an example of foolishness, in boastful self-assurance. Since many people are boasting in a human way, I'm going to boast, too. For you people, who are so wise, gladly put up with fools. For you put up with it if someone enslaves you, or if someone eats you up, or captures you, or puts on airs, or hits you in the face! To my shame, I must confess that we were indeed weak.

If someone has courage (I am speaking out of foolishness), I have courage also.

Are they Hebrews? I am, too.

Are they Israelites? I too.

Are they descended from Abraham? I too.

Are they ministers of Christ? I am, and more [than that]. (I am speaking as though I were out of my mind!)

My labours have been more [than theirs]; I have spent more time in prison; I have been flogged far more often; often in mortal danger. Five times I got forty-minus-one from the Jews; three times I was beaten with rods; once they stoned me; three times I have been shipwrecked: I have spent twenty-four hours out in the deep. Often I have had road journeys, threatened by rivers, by muggers, by my own people, by Gentiles; threatened in the city and in the desert and at sea, threatened by fake Christians, with hard work and heavy labour, often going without sleep; hungry and thirsty, often going without food; cold and without clothes.

And apart from everything else, there is my daily preoccupation, my care for all the churches. Who is weak, and I am not weak? Who is affronted, and I am not blazing?

If boasting is the name of the game, then I'm going to boast of things to do with my weakness.

The God and Father of the Lord Jesus knows, blessed be he for ever, that I am not lying: [once], at Damascus, the governor of King Aretas was guarding the city of the Damascenes, to arrest me, and I was let down through a window in the wall in a basket, and escaped his hands!

Boasting is the name of the game; it serves no good purpose, but I'll come to 'visions and revelations of the Lord'.

I know a man in Christ fourteen years ago (in the body? I don't know. Outside the body? I don't know, God knows). [Anyway] a person like this was snatched up as far as the third heaven. And I know a person like this (in the body? out of the body? I don't know, God knows); he was snatched up into paradise, and he heard unspeakable words, which it is not permissible for a human to utter.

I'll boast of a person like that; but I'll only boast about myself in regard to my weaknesses. You see, if I should wish to boast, I shan't be a fool, for I shall be telling the truth. But I am being lenient; I don't want anyone to reckon any more of me than what he sees of me, or what he knows from [my lips]. And because the revelations were so exceptional, so that I shouldn't get elated, there was given me a 'thorn in the flesh', an 'angel of Satan' to batter me, so that I shouldn't get elated. With regard to this I three times begged the Lord that it would go away, and he told me, 'My grace is enough for you – for power is made perfect in weakness.' So I shall most gladly boast of my weaknesses, that Christ's power may come to rest on me. So I'm content with weaknesses, insults, torture, persecutions and difficulties, for Christ's sake. For when I am weak, then I am powerful.

What a fool I've been! You forced me! For I should have been recommended by *you*! For I'm no way inferior to the Superapostles, even if I'm nothing! The 'apostolic signs' were worked among you, in all patience: signs, and portents, and miracles. How did you come off second-best to all the other churches? Was it just that I wasn't a 'burden' to you? Forgive me the monstrous injustice!

> We are inevitably rather taken aback by this. What has happened to Paul? He seems to have lost his temper, and to be indulging in some savage sarcasm, and perhaps (as he says in self-accusation) some 'foolish boasting'.
>
> We have to focus on Paul's main purpose in life: he lives, breathes and sleeps Jesus Christ, and anything that takes people away from Christ, especially people who put themselves above the gospel, sends him into a fury.
>
> We can be grateful, however, to the people who were causing so much trouble in Corinth. Without them we should know far less about 'a day in the life of an apostle of Christ'!

Paul's apostolic instincts

14-18 Look! This is now the third time that I'm all ready to come to you, and I shan't be a 'burden': I'm not after what belongs to you – it's *you* I'm after! Children shouldn't have to save up for their parents: no – it's parents who should save up for their children! As for me, I'll cheerfully spend – yes, and be utterly spent – for the sake of your lives. If I love you so intensely, am I to be loved any the less? All right – I didn't weigh you down; but I'm a crafty fellow, and got you by a trick. Was it one of those I sent to you? Was it through him that I defrauded you? I begged Titus, and I sent the Christian along with him. Was it Titus that defrauded you? Didn't we walk in the same Spirit? And along the same path?

> Once again, the Corinthians know more than we do of what was going on here, and they aren't saying; but evidently Paul has been charged with some kind of deceit; possibly someone had accused him of stealing the money intended for Jerusalem. Clearly, though, Paul is certain that as soon as they think about it they won't believe the accusations, whatever they were.

A final warning

19-21 Do you think that we have been a long time making our defence to you? We are speaking before God, and in Christ, and everything, my dear ones, in order to build you up; for I'm afraid that when I come I'll find you not quite what I want you to be, and you'll find me not quite what you want. I don't want strife and fanaticism, and outbursts of anger, and outbreaks of selfishness, acts of defamation and tittle-tattle, instances of being 'puffed up', and examples of unruliness. My fear is that when I come back, God will humble me in your presence, and I shall be mourning for many of those who committed sins earlier, and who did not repent of impurity and sexual immorality and debauchery that they had committed.

> Paul is clearly fearful that things have gone dreadfully wrong here among his Corinthian Christians. It looks as though some of what has gone wrong is sexual misbehaviour, although that might be no more than a metaphor for not living a godly life. Whatever precisely they have got wrong, the situation requires urgent remedy.

Paul's final crack of the whip

13 ¹⁻¹⁰ This is now the third time that I'm coming to you; 'every legal matter shall be substantiated on the evidence of two witnesses or three'. I have said it before, and now I am saying it in advance of my visit, as when I was present on the second occasion, so now in my absence, to those who committed sins earlier, and to all the rest, that if I come I shall not be lenient again, since you are looking for proof that Christ is speaking in me: he is not 'weak' with regard to you, but powerful among you. For he was crucified in weakness, but lives in the power of God. For we are also 'weak' in him – and we shall show ourselves very much alive with him in the power of God with regard to you.

Examine *yourselves*, to see if you are still in the faith; test *yourselves*. Or do you not recognise that Jesus Christ is among you? Unless, that is, you fail the examination. I hope that you will realise that *we* are not failures. But I pray to God to do you no evil, not so that we may be shown to have passed the examination, but so that *you* may do what is right, and *we* may fail the test. For we can do nothing against the truth; we can only act on the side of truth. You see, we rejoice whenever we are 'weak', and whenever you are strong. What we are praying for is your restoration to perfection. That is why I am writing these things while I am away from you, so that when I am present I may not have to deal severely [with you], in accordance with the authority that the Lord gave me (for upbuilding, not for destruction).

> Paul is operating in legal mode here; the quotation at the beginning is from Deuteronomic law about valid evidence: 'two or three witnesses' is here adapted into 'two or three visits', and he wants to make sure that there is no evidence of misbehaviour when he next comes – or else! But he is not just playing authority games, like a schoolmaster who fears that he is losing control; see how, as always, he comes back to God-in-Christ and to the Resurrection. The Corinthians (or some of them) have been making accusations against him; in return he forcefully argues that they should look in the mirror and put the accusations to themselves, not so that he can punish them, but so that he can avoid punishing them.
>
> The contrast between 'present' and 'absent' in this section is a deliberate reference to certain criticisms that his opponents in

Corinth have been making. But it also goes back to the beginning of this section of the letter (if it is indeed a part of the letter as a whole), and forms an 'inclusion' with it.

Final (and unusually curt) greetings

11-13 For the rest, my brothers and sisters, be glad, mend your ways, and think the same [as each other], keep the peace, and the God of love and peace will be with you. Greet one another with a holy kiss. All the saints greet you.

The grace of the Lord Jesus Christ, and the love of God, and the communion of the Holy Spirit be with all of you.

> With a degree of (perhaps relieved) exhaustion we come to the close of a letter which has maintained its tension – and our attention – right to the end. It is an uncharacteristically brief closing salutation, perhaps indicating how cross Paul is with the Corinthians. This 'postlude' pulls together many of the themes of Paul's correspondence with this difficult and divided community. It is a beautiful and providential irony that one of the loveliest and best-known of New Testament prayers, the 'Grace', with its Trinitarian echoes, is the closing sentence of this tempestuous epistle.

The Letter to the Galatians

Introduction

This is, it has to be said, a very ill-tempered letter. Some scholars regard it as Paul's first surviving work (though a majority would give the accolade to 1 Thessalonians). In this letter, Paul covers the same issues (what God has done in Christ) as in Romans, but with considerably less diplomatic skill. One of the great joys of this letter is that Paul is forced to tell us a good deal about his faith-journey.

Opening greeting

1 [1-5] Paul, an apostle (not [appointed] by human beings, or through any human being, but through Jesus Christ, and through God the Father, who raised him from the dead), and all the Christians who are with me, to the churches of Galatia, grace to you and peace from God our Father and the Lord Jesus Christ, who gave himself for our sins, that he might rescue us from the present evil age, according to the will of our God and Father, to whom be glory for ever and ever. Amen.

For Paul, the opening greeting is never a mere formality; words are always made to work. Notice his insistence that he is an apostle, whose appointment has no human source, but is authenticated by God and Jesus Christ; note, too, Paul's insistence on the link between his mission and the Resurrection. Paul does not here mention anyone else as joint author of the letter, but characteristically stresses that it comes from 'all the Christians who are with me'; the letter, dealing with mighty matters, is not just his own. Nor is it addressed to particular awkward individuals, but to 'the churches of Galatia'. As always, Paul wishes his readers 'grace' and 'peace', words which carry a great weight of meaning; they are not just idle religious platitudes. In connection with this, we should note that Paul believed that you could detect a clearly visible transformation when people became Christian. So when he speaks of 'rescue' from 'the present evil age' he has solid content in mind. Notice, finally, how God the Father has been mentioned several times in this short greeting.

What, no thanksgiving?

[6-9] I am astonished that you are so quick to turn away from the one who called you in Christ's grace, to another gospel. *There is no other gospel*: but there are people who are unsettling you, and who are aiming to pervert Christ's gospel. No – even if we ourselves, or an angel from heaven were to preach you a gospel different from the gospel that we preached to you, let them be accursed! We have said it before, and now we are saying it again: if anyone preaches the gospel to you contrary to the gospel that you received, *let him or her be accursed.*

In all Paul's other letters, the opening greeting is followed by a thanksgiving, which acts as a kind of foretaste of the themes of the letter. In Galatians, however, he is so cross with what has been going on in Galatia that he substitutes 'I am astonished' for the expected 'I thank God'.

What is it that has gone wrong? They have abandoned 'the gospel (he) preached', the gospel of 'grace', for a different gospel. Paul expresses his fury at this by solemnly cursing anyone who preaches the 'perverted' gospel, even if it should be himself or 'a messenger of God', as he suggests, with more than a touch of exaggeration.

We can be grateful, however, to those who got the gospel wrong, because they forced him to remind the Galatians of elements of his faith-journey, which we should otherwise not have known. He tells the story in three sections.

Paul's faith-journey: first section

10-17 Am I now trying to win over human beings or God? Or am I seeking to please human beings? If it were still human beings that I were trying to please, I should not be a slave of Jesus Christ. I want you to know, brothers and sisters, the gospel that was preached by me: it was not of human origin. I didn't receive it from human beings, nor was I taught it by them. No – it came through a revelation of Jesus Christ.

You've heard of my manner of life once upon a time within Judaism, how violently I used to persecute God's Church, and how I tried to destroy it, and how I made progress within Judaism beyond many of my contemporaries who were of the family; I was far more fanatical about the ancestral tradition. But when it was God's good pleasure (God who had marked me out from my mother's womb and had called me through his grace) to reveal his Son to me, that I might preach the gospel [about] him to the Gentiles, I didn't immediately consult with human beings; and I didn't go up to Jerusalem to [see] those who were apostles before me. Instead, I went off to Arabia, and came back again to Damascus.

> We may guess from this that someone had been accusing Paul of concentrating too much on human beings, and not enough on God. Certainly he is emphatic that what happened to him came from God. Hence the word 'receive', which Paul uses elsewhere to describe the tradition that he wishes to defend, and the emphasis that it 'came through a revelation of Jesus Christ'. As in the opening of Romans, he calls himself a 'slave of Jesus Christ', as a title that he and the Galatians can agree about. For Paul, the reality that matters is Jesus, and nothing else; and for Paul 'Jesus' includes, in one direction, God (source of his vocation) and, in the other direction, the Church, which Paul had been persecuting. This must guide our interpretation of the two references to Judaism in this passage. It was not that Paul thought of himself as an 'ex-Jew' or a convert from Judaism; Romans 9-11 makes it clear that he still thought of himself as very much a Jew. What had made all the difference was a personal encounter with Jesus Christ, and his consequent belief that God had raised Jesus from the dead, and then his sense of being called to preach God-in-Jesus to all the world, beyond the bounds of Judaism. Note that Paul regards himself as an apostle on just the same level as the Twelve ('those who were apostles before me').

Paul's faith-journey: second section

18-24 Thereafter, after three years, I went up to Jerusalem, to visit Kephas; and I remained a fortnight with him. I saw none of the other apostles, except for James the brother of the Lord.

(Look – what I am writing to you, before God, I am not telling lies.)

After that I came back to the regions of Syria and Cilicia. The churches of Judaea that are in Christ did not know me by sight; they had only heard that 'our one-time persecutor is now preaching the gospel of the faith, which once he tried to destroy' – and they glorified God in me.

The autobiography continues. The point here is how little contact he had with the Twelve, just a fortnight with Peter after three years in Arabia or Damascus, and a session (perhaps no more) with James the brother of the Lord. Where had Paul learnt the gospel? Basically, he is claiming, from the risen Jesus.

Paul's faith-journey: third section

2 ¹⁻¹⁰ Then, fourteen years later, I went back to Jerusalem, taking Barnabas and Titus with me. I went up in accordance with a revelation. And I put before them the gospel which I proclaim among the Gentiles (but privately, to the 'influential ones': I didn't want my present and past efforts to be useless). But they didn't even make my companion Titus (he was a Greek) get circumcised. However, because of some fake Christians who had been smuggled in – they had sneaked in to spy on our freedom that we have in Christ Jesus. Their aim was to reduce us to slavery; but we didn't give in to them even for a moment. We wanted the gospel's truth to remain continually with you.

Now from the so-called 'influential ones' (it makes no difference to me what kind of people they once were; God is not a snob) . . . for the 'influential ones' made no addition. No, on the contrary, seeing that I was entrusted with the gospel of uncircumcision, just as Peter was [entrusted with the gospel] of circumcision (for the One who had worked in Peter, for his mission to the circumcised, had worked also in me for the Gentiles); and when they realised that [God's] grace had been bestowed on me, James and Kephas and John, the so-called 'pillars', gave me and Barnabas the right hand of fellowship: we were to go to the Gentiles, and they to the circumcised. The only thing was, we were to remember the poor – and I was eager to do that very thing.

Some of the sentences in this passage are incomplete, or lose their way, which may be an indicator of how passionately Paul feels the issue as he dictates.

This third stage covers a huge period of time; very likely the visit to Jerusalem that he mentions here is the same as that referred to in Acts 15, but scholars are divided about it, and it need not worry us. What Paul is emphasising is, first, his independence from the 'influential ones' and his dependence on God. Second, Paul insists on his vocation to preach to non-Jews, just as Peter (does he only call him Kephas when he wants to keep him in his place?) had the vocation to preach to Jews. The instruction at the end to 'remember the poor' is something that Paul refers to also in Romans, as well as in the two Corinthian letters that we have. It was very important to him.

Confronting Kephas's hypocrisy: first statement of the gospel

¹¹⁻²¹ But when Kephas came to Antioch, I opposed him in person, because he stood condemned. For before the arrival of some people from James, he used to eat with Gentiles. But after their arrival, he drew back and held himself aloof – he was terrified of the circumcision people! And all the rest of the Jews joined him in playing the hypocrite, so that even Barnabas was led to join in their hypocrisy. But

when I saw that they were not advancing in the direction of the truth of the gospel, I said to Kephas, in front of all of them, 'If you, who are Jewish by race, no longer live according to Jewish custom, how come you are forcing Gentiles to become Jews? You and I are Jews by nature, not sinners of Gentile stock. We know that a person is not made righteous by works of the law, but by faith in Jesus Christ. And we have come to faith in Jesus Christ, that we might be made righteous by Christ's faith, and not by works of law: because no human being is made righteous by works of law. Now – if we, who seek to be made righteous in Christ, ourselves turn out to be sinners, does that mean that Christ is a servant of sin? No way. For if I start building up all these things that I pulled down, then I show that I am a transgressor. For through law I died to law, in order that I might live to God; I have been crucified along with Christ. But now I live [and it is] no longer I, but Christ lives in me. The life I now live in the flesh, I live in faith in the Son of God, who loved me, and who gave himself up for my sake. I do not make God's grace null and void; for if righteousness comes through law, then Christ's death is in vain.'

It is reassuring, somehow, to find these distinguished apostles locked in controversy. The Greek does not tell us where Paul's speech to Peter ends, and where the theological comment begins. My translation opts to take the theological argument as part of what Paul said to Kephas, inviting the Galatians to listen in on the argument, and so to grasp it for themselves, before he turns on them.

The word 'hypocrite' originally means an actor, someone who plays a part that is not really his or hers.

You stupid Galatians!

3 1-5   You *stupid* Galatians – who has bewitched you? It was before your eyes that Jesus Christ was exhibited as crucified. Tell me just this one thing: the Spirit – did you get it from works of law or from obedience to the faith? Are you so stupid? You made your beginning in the Spirit – are you now coming to an end in the flesh? Have you experienced so much for nothing? (That's assuming that it *was* for nothing.) Look – the one who laid the Spirit on for you and worked miracles among you, was that the result of works of law or of faith in what you heard?

Paul is very cross: most Christian pastors avoid addressing their flock in language quite as strong as this, but Paul thinks that the Galatians are in life-threatening danger of missing the point. And notice that it is Paul's assumption that he could appeal to their experience of having 'seen' Christ crucified, and of having the 'Spirit'. For Paul, the Christian experience is tangible, palpable; Paul takes it for granted that they had actually seen things happening when he first was among them.

The argument from Abraham

6-29   Just as Abraham 'believed God, and it was reckoned to him as righteousness' (Genesis 15:6), you know that those who are 'of faith' are the ones who are children of Abraham. However, Scripture foresaw that God [would] reckon the Gentiles as righteous as a result of faith, and gave Abraham a foretaste of the gospel: 'in you all the Gentiles will be blessed' (Genesis 12:3). So that those who are 'of faith' are blessed along with faithful Abraham.

You see, all those who are of law-works are under a curse. For it is written 'accursed is everyone who does not abide by all the things that are written in the book of the law, so as to perform them' (Deuteronomy 27:26). Now it is clear that no one can be made righteous before God by the law, because 'the righteous one by faith shall live' (Habakkuk 2:4). Now the law is not 'by faith'; but 'those who do them shall live by them' (Leviticus 18:5). Christ has bought us back from the law's curse; he became a curse for our sake, because it is written, 'cursed is the one who is hanged on a tree' (Deuteronomy 21:23), in order that Abraham's blessing might extend to the Gentiles in Christ Jesus, in order that we might receive the promised Spirit through faith.

Brothers and sisters, I am speaking in a human way. Likewise [or: 'nevertheless'] no one sets aside a will that has been ratified, or adds a codicil to it. Now the promises were uttered 'to Abraham and to his seed' (Genesis 12:7). It doesn't say 'to his seeds', in the plural; no, it's in the singular, 'and to your seed', and that is Christ! This is my argument: the will [or: 'covenant' or 'Testament'] that had already been validated by God *can't* be set aside by the law (which came 430 years later), so as to annul God's promise. You see, if the inheritance is a matter of law, it's no longer a matter of promise: it is to Abraham that God has shown himself gracious through the promise.

So what is the law? It was an added extra, because of transgressions, until the 'seed' should come to whom the promise had been made; it was ordered through angels, by the agency of a mediator. Now you can't have a mediator where there is only one party – and God is one.

'So the law is in contradiction to the promises of God?' No way! Because if the law that was given had the power to bring life, then indeed righteousness would be 'from the law'. Instead, law locked up everything under sin, so that the promise which is the fruit of Jesus Christ's faith is given to those who have faith.

However, before faith came, we were held in custody under law, locked up [to wait] for the faith that was destined to be revealed. So the law became our instructor, leading us to Christ, so that we might be made righteous by faith. But when faith came, we are no longer under the instructor. For you are all children of God, through the faith that was in Christ Jesus; you see, as many of you as were baptised into Christ, you have put on Christ. There is no such thing as Jew or Greek, no such thing as slave or free, no such thing as male and female. For you are all one in Christ; and if you belong to Christ, then you are the 'seed of Abraham', heirs according to [God's] promise.

> The argument is difficult, but perhaps would have been more easily grasped by the Galatians, who had heard Paul talk, than by us. We have always to remember that Paul did not expect us to be reading this letter, so he has not given us the key to crack its code.
>
> Clearly, though, the person of Abraham is important. He was an iconic figure, as the ancestor of all Jews, but he was not yet circumcised when he was 'justified by faith' (so faith is prior to circumcision or works of law); and second, Abraham's blessing was for 'all Gentiles' (or nations). Third, and the argument is stretched thin here, 'seed' is

in the singular, not the plural, and therefore (according to Paul) was referring to one of Abraham's descendants in particular, namely Christ.

Paul has to hold together two not wholly compatible positions, that law is the gift of God, and that law is limited; so he hints at the idea that law (or Torah) is a 'teacher' (with all the negative emotions that idea can arouse). Much more important, though, is that the law is not Christ, around whom everything revolves for Paul; and if baptism (see how Paul keeps coming back to the Galatians' own experience) is a matter of 'putting on Christ', like an actor's costume, then all human divisions, ethnic (Jew or Greek), cultural (slave or free) and sexual (male and female) are irrelevant. What counts is, quite simply, the promise of God.

Notice that three of the Old Testament citations (those from Genesis 15:6; Habakkuk 2:4 and Leviticus 18:5) are used again at important moments in the argument of Romans (4:3, 22, 23; 1:17; 10:5). Romans is Paul's second, and more diplomatic, attempt at defending the case he makes in Galatians. It is interesting to note that Paul clearly expected his Galatian converts (Gentiles as well as Jews) to know the Jewish scriptures, and to accept arguments based on them.

Argument from the law, about an heir who is still a minor

4 1-11 This is my meaning: while the heir is a minor, he is no better than a slave, even though he is master of everything; he is under guardians and house managers until the time set by his father. So with us: when we were 'minors', we were enslaved under the elemental spirits of the universe. When, however, the fullness of time came, God sent out his Son, born of a woman, born under law, in order to buy back those under law, that we might receive adoption-as-sons. But because you are sons, God sent the Spirit of his Son into our hearts, crying 'Abba, Father'. So you are no longer a slave; you are a *son*. Now, if you are a son, then you are an heir, through [what] God [has] done.

But at that time, you did not know God, and you were enslaved to what were not really gods at all. Now, however, you know God – or rather you are known by God – how is it that you are reverting to the weak and destitute elemental spirits? Why do you want to be enslaved to them all over again? You are religiously observing days and months and special feasts and holy years. I fear for you – perhaps my labour for you was in vain!

The analogy of a son (and I fear that there is no way here of maintaining inclusive language and still preserving the force of Paul's argument; but it is only an analogy) who has not yet entered into his inheritance is presumably meant to illustrate what was wrong with the law: it was not the real thing, but only a teacher. The real thing is what God (Father) has done for us, by sending the Son and Spirit, who enable us to cry 'Abba, Father'. The Galatians are being asked to remember what it was like before they met Christ, and not to revert to their old captivity.

Reviewing the relationship between Paul and the Galatians

12-20 Be like me, my fellow Christians, I implore you, because I was like you. You did me no wrong; but you are well aware that it was because of a weakness of the flesh that I preached the gospel to you the first time; and you didn't despise the [trial that I experienced] in my flesh. Nor did you vomit [spit] me out: no – you received me as God's messenger, as Christ Jesus! So where is your happiness now? For I swear to you that, if possible, you would have dug out your eyes and given them to me. So have I become your enemy, by telling you the truth?

Their cultivation of you is not honourable; they want to lock you up, so that you can cultivate them! But it is honourable to be cultivated in an honourable way all the time, and not just when I'm with you. My children: I am suffering birth-pangs with you until Christ is formed among you. But I wanted to be present with you now, and adapt my tone to you – I'm puzzled about you.

> Paul is annoyed with his Galatians; but also there is no mistaking the affection he has for them; and he can appeal to the happy memories that they share: 'if possible, you would have dug out your eyes and given them to me,' he says of their first meeting.
>
> Some readers have deduced from this that Paul was suffering from a disease of the eyes; they point to the 'big letters' of his handwriting (see 6:11), and suggest that an eye disease may have been the 'thorn in the flesh' of 2 Corinthians 12:7, and even link it to Paul's allegedly unimpressive presence, referred to in 1 Corinthians 2:3 and 2 Corinthians 10:10.
>
> The reference to 'spitting out' might suggest either disdain or a gesture to ward off evil spirits.

Slave and free: Hagar and the mother of Isaac

21-31 Tell me, you who are so keen on being under the law – don't you listen to the law? For it is written that Abraham had two sons, one from the slave girl and one from the free woman. But the one born of the slave girl was born according to the flesh, while the one born of the free woman [was born] through the promise. This is an allegory – for the women are the two covenants, one from Mount Sinai, born into slavery, and that's Hagar. Now Hagar is Sinai – a mountain in Arabia; it corresponds to present-day Jerusalem, because, along with its children, it is in slavery. Whereas the Jerusalem [which is] above is free – that is our mother. For it is written,

> 'Rejoice, O barren woman, who does not give birth.
> Break out and shout, you who have no birth-pangs.
> For many are the children of the deserted one,
> more than the one who has a husband' (Isaiah 54:1).

Now you, brothers and sisters, are children of the promise after the manner of Isaac. But just as the one born according to the flesh used to persecute the one born according to the Spirit, so it is now. But what does Scripture say? 'Expel the slave girl and her son; for no way will the son of the slave girl inherit on equal terms with the son of the free woman' (Genesis 21:10-12). So, brothers and sisters, we are not children of a slave girl, but of the free woman.

It is striking that in this comparison, deeply offensive to many Jews, Paul does not mention the name of Sarah, but only that of Hagar. The point that he is trying to make is that the Galatians are actually looking to go back into the slavery from which the gospel of Jesus has rescued them. It is an ingenious and bold stroke of Paul to use Abraham's wife and concubine to illustrate his argument.

Freedom and circumcision

5 1-12 By [this] freedom, Christ set us free; so hold your ground, and don't go back to being burdened by the yoke of slavery.

Look, I, Paul, am telling you that if you are circumcised, Christ is of no use to you. My testimony for every man who is circumcised is that he is under an obligation to perform the whole law. You have been estranged from Christ, you who find your righteousness in the law; you have fallen away from [God's] gift. For *we*, by the Spirit and as a result of faith, are waiting eagerly for the righteousness that we hope for. For in Christ Jesus, neither circumcision nor uncircumcision is of any use – no, [what matters is] faith, achieving its effects through love.

You were running nicely: who impeded you, so as not to obey the truth? That persuasion does not come from the One who called you. A little leaven leavens all the dough. I am confident in you in the Lord, that you will not think any differently: whoever he is, the one who is unsettling you will carry the blame. As for me, brothers and sisters, if I proclaim that circumcision still matters, why am I being persecuted? So the scandal of the Cross is eradicated.

I wish that those who are disturbing you would castrate themselves.

> The last line (which will have offended many to whom it was reported) shows how passionately Paul views the issue. For him what was wrong with the law was that it was not Christ, and therefore insisting on obeying the law's precepts simply meant undoing all that Christ had done for them.
>
> Paul has clearly been accused of still giving importance to circumcision (hard though that may be to credit); but his 'bottom line' is the 'scandal of the Cross'.

Spirit and flesh

13-26 For, my brothers and sisters, you were called to be free; but don't let your freedom become an opportunity for your unreformed humanity. Instead, be each other's slaves through love. For the whole law is fulfilled in a single saying, in 'You shall love your neighbour as yourself' (Leviticus 19:18). But if you are biting and devouring each other, watch out that you aren't consumed by each other.

I'm telling you: walk in the Spirit, and absolutely do not yield to the desire of the flesh. For the desire of the flesh is against the Spirit; that of the Spirit against that of the flesh: for they are opposed to each other. I don't want you to be doing the things that you don't want to be doing.

If you are led by the Spirit, you are not under the law. The works of the flesh are evident: sexual immorality, impurity, debauchery, idolatry, drugs, outbursts of hatred, quarrelling, fanaticism, fits of rage, outbreaks of selfishness and dissension, factions and envy, drunkenness and revelry, and all that sort of thing.

I am giving you advance warning, as I have already done, that people who do that sort of thing will not inherit God's kingdom.

The fruit of the Spirit, on the other hand, is love, joy, peace, patience, kindness, goodness, faith, gentleness and self-control. There is no law against that sort of thing. Those who belong to Christ Jesus have crucified the flesh along with [its] passions and desires. If we live by the Spirit, let us also follow the Spirit. Let us not turn into empty-heads, provoking each other and envying each other.

> It is important here to keep our eye on what really matters for Paul: belonging to Christ Jesus, being willingly crucified with him, accepting the Spirit. And, of course, we have to make a choice: are we to go with the flesh or with the Spirit? That was what the Galatians were failing to do when they flirted with law observance, as far as Paul is concerned.

General instructions

6 ¹⁻¹⁰ Brothers and sisters, if a person is caught out in some transgression, you are of the Spirit, so set him right in a spirit of gentleness; and keep an eye on yourself, in case you get tempted. Carry one another's burdens, and in this way you will fulfil the law of Christ. For if a person thinks they are something, when they are nothing, they are fooling themselves. Let everyone test their own work, and then they will have reason for boasting over themselves, not over the other person. For everyone will carry his or her own load.

Let the teacher of the word teach his or her pupil in everything that is good. Don't be misled – God is not to be outwitted. You see, what a person sows is what they will reap; because the person who sows in the field of flesh will bring in a harvest of destruction from that source, while the person who sows in the Spirit's field will bring in a harvest of eternal life. Let us not grow weary of doing what is good, for when our own time comes we shall bring in a harvest, provided that we don't slacken. So then, since we have our opportunity, let us do good to all, but especially to those in the family of the faith.

> We only hear one side of the 'telephone conversation' between Paul and his Galatians, and we need to remember that fact whenever we are inclined to dismiss these closing instructions as weary religious clichés ('hate evil and do good'). Paul does not waste words, and we have to assume that these instructions will have had a very precise meaning to those who were more aware of the problems that the Galatian churches were experiencing.

In his own write

¹¹⁻¹⁸ Look what big letters I'm drawing for you in my handwriting! All those who want to make a good showing in external matters are the ones who are trying to force you to get circumcised, just so as to avoid being persecuted for the Cross of Christ. You see, not even the circumcised keep the law – but still they want you circumcised, so that they can boast of your flesh! As for me, may I never boast on any grounds but those of the Cross of Our Lord Jesus Christ, through whom the

world is crucified to me and I to the world. For circumcision is irrelevant, and uncircumcision is irrelevant: what matters is 'new creation'; and all those who follow this rule, peace upon them, and mercy, and on the Israel of God.

For the rest, let no one cause me problems. For I carry the scars of Jesus on my body.

The grace of Our Lord Jesus Christ be with the spirit of you all, my brothers and sisters. Amen.

> The phrase 'new creation' is an important idea for Paul. He uses the phrase, for example, at 2 Corinthians 5:17. The idea of the 'new human' appears in Ephesians 2:15; 4:24 and Colossians 3:10 (but not everyone agrees that both of these letters are by Paul). The idea is also lurking, probably, beneath the text of Romans 6:4; 7:6; 8:2, 21. 'In Christ', there is no longer the polarisation of the world in which Paul had grown up, between 'Jews' and 'non-Jews'. What matters now is simply a new symbolic universe, without the old identity markers, which the Galatians and Paul have experienced and can refer to as a 'new creation'. Galatians and Romans cannot really be understood apart from this idea.
>
> It looks as though Paul wrote all these last verses out with his (rather unskilled) hand. As he brings this angry letter to a close, notice his emphasis on the Cross of Christ, and his sense of sharing in Christ's sufferings, all in order to encourage the Galatians not to abandon the gospel that he had preached. Notice also Paul's sense of mission ('the world is crucified to me, and I to the world'); and ponder his remarkable phrase 'the Israel of God'.

The Letter to the Ephesians

Introduction

This is a very different letter from its predecessors, and there is uncertainty about whether it was written by Paul, and whether it was in fact written to Ephesus; this need not worry us too much. Certainly, though, its style is fuller than what we are accustomed to in Paul. There are elaborate groups of nouns strung together, and the sentences are rather long. I have tried, not entirely successfully, to make these long sentences more manageable by the use of bullet points. Someone who was quite at home in Paul's thought wrote this document. It is a letter of great richness, and steeped in the liturgy of the early Church. It is many people's favourite Pauline epistle.

Opening greeting

1[1,2] Paul, an apostle of Christ Jesus, through the will of God to the saints who are [at Ephesus], and to those who are faithful in Christ Jesus, grace to you and peace from God our Father and the Lord Jesus Christ.

> As is frequently the custom today, I have left the addressee town in brackets, as a reminder of the uncertainties in the manuscripts and among the early witnesses. Otherwise this is a standard opening to a Pauline epistle.

Blessing

3-14 Blessed be the God and Father of our Lord Jesus Christ,

- the one who blessed us with every spiritual blessing in the heavenly regions in Christ, just as he chose us in him before the foundation of the world, for us to be holy and unblemished before him in love,
- the one who predestined us for adoption-as-sons through Jesus Christ to him, according to the good pleasure of his will, to the praise of the glory of his grace with which he graced us in the Beloved,
- the one in whom we have redemption through his blood, the forgiveness of transgressions according to the wealth of his grace, which overflowed to us, in all wisdom and understanding,
- the one who revealed to us the mystery of his will, according to his good pleasure which he proposed in him, for the plan for the fullness of times, recapitulating everything in Christ, the things in the heavens and the things on earth,
- in him in whom we have our lot cast, in accordance with the design of the one who carries out everything, according to the plan of his will, so that we should be for the praise of his glory, we who have been the first to hope in Christ,
- in whom you also have heard the word of truth, the gospel of your salvation,
- in whom you believe, and have been sealed with the Holy Spirit of promise, which is the down payment of our inheritance, for the redemption of the [God's] property, to the praise of his glory.

> This section is an immense single sentence and the longest in the entire New Testament (but by no means the last long sentence we shall encounter in Ephesians); and you have to admire the way in which the author has held it together, with a series of no less than seven relative clauses, four referring to God the Father, and three referring to Christ, which we have signalled with a series of bullet points, to show how it all works. It is a lovely hymn of praise, and even when we cannot follow in detail what the author is saying, we can nevertheless sit back and relish his profoundly spiritual theology. You will notice the series of nouns, often turned into adjectives by translators, which marks the style of the author of this epistle, such as, for example, 'to the praise of the glory of his grace'. This piling up of nouns gives density to the language and depth to the spiritual theology of the epistle.

This 'blessing' comes where we should normally expect to find the thanksgiving in a Pauline letter. That thanksgiving perhaps now follows.

The fourth 'bullet point' speaks of the 'mystery of his will' and of 'recapitulating everything in Christ'. Many people have been inspired by the mystical vision of God gathering everything into Christ. Does it help you to open up to God's work in our world? (You might like to look at Paul's remarks about the 'groaning' of creation in Romans 8:19-23.)

Thanksgiving (or is it?)

15-23 Because of this, I too, having heard of the faith that is among you in the Lord Jesus, and the love for all the saints, do not cease from giving thanks, making remembrance of you in my prayers,

- that the God of our Lord Jesus Christ, the Father of glory, may give you a spirit of wisdom and revelation in the knowledge of him, the eyes of your heart enlightened so that you may know
- what is the hope of his calling,
- what is the wealth of the glory of his inheritance among the saints,
- and what is the overarching greatness of his power for us who believe according to the exercise of the might of his strength,
- which he exercised in Christ [by] raising him from the dead, and making him sit on his right hand in the heavenly regions, above all rule and authority and power and lordship, and every name that is named, not only in this age, but also in the coming age,
- and 'he subordinated everything beneath his feet', and gave him as head over the entire Church, which is his body, the fullness of that which fills everything in every respect.

This is another immense sentence, and we may feel, as we admire the rich theology of it, that the author has overdosed on nouns once more. It is easier to stand back and admire the broad picture he paints than to stand close and work out the detail; and it must be admitted here that our attempt to pick out the structure of the sentence by the use of bullet points is less successful than in its predecessor. The word translated as 'Church' is a very important one in Ephesians, and there is something to be said for taking it, slightly more literally, as 'Assembly', except that it does not work quite so well in every instance in this letter; but whenever you see it, the reader should bear in mind the slightly different nuance that the word 'assembly' offers.

The citation in the final bullet point, 'he subordinated everything beneath his feet', comes from Psalm 8:6, where it refers to the authority of human beings over all creation (see Genesis 1:26, 28). Interestingly, both here and at Hebrews 2:8, 9, it is made to refer to Christ. Jesus of course often referred to himself as Son of Man, which might account for this rather free use of the psalm.

What God has done for the readers

2[1-10] And you, who were dead because of your transgressions and sins,

- in which once you walked in keeping with the age of this world, in keeping with the ruler of the power of the air, the spirit that is now at work among the children of disobedience
- among whom we all once lived because of the desires of our flesh, doing the wills of the flesh and of the intellects, and we were by nature children of anger, just like the rest,
- but since God is rich in mercy, because of the great love with which he loved us,
- and us who were dead because of transgressions

he made alive together with Christ
(It is by God's gift that you have been saved)

and raised you with him
and made you sit in the heavenly regions in Christ Jesus

in order that in the coming ages he might demonstrate the surpassing value of his free gift in kindness to you in Christ Jesus.

For it is by [God's] free gift that you have been saved through faith – and it has nothing to do with you; it is God's gift. It is not dependent on what you have done (so that no one should boast). For we are his 'poem', created in Christ Jesus for good works, which God prepared in advance, so that we might walk in them.

> The reader is here invited to be astonished at the generosity of God, to feel its impact on his or her life, and to concentrate on the central building blocks of Pauline belief, that a) God raised Jesus from the dead, b) the Resurrection has a clearly visible impact on the lives of Christians, and c) that this is not because Christians have been particularly deserving, but because of God's loving generosity. I have put the key phrases in bold italics, to simplify the reader's task.
>
> The reader may like to know that the word 'poem' is simply a transcription of what Paul wrote. It might equally be translated as 'work of art'.

Remember what you once were, and where you are now

[11-22] Therefore recall that once you were Gentiles, in unredeemed human nature, those who are called 'uncircumcision' by the so-called 'circumcision' (which is in the flesh, made by human hands),

- that you were at that time separated from Christ, alienated from the commonwealth of Israel, strangers to the covenants of the promise, hopeless and godless in the world,
- but now in Christ Jesus you who were once far off have come near in the blood of Christ.

For he is our peace, who in his flesh made the two into one, and has dissolved the dividing wall that acts as a fence, the hatred,

- who has cancelled out the law of commandments that consisted of regulations

- so that he might thereby fashion the two into a single human person, making peace and reconciling the two to God in a single body through the Cross, putting the hatred to death in [Christ].

And he came and preached the gospel of peace to you who were far off, and peace to those who were nearby, because through him both of us have, through a single Spirit, access to the Father.

So therefore you are no longer foreigners and strangers. No – you are fellow citizens of the saints, and members of the family of God, built upon the foundation of the apostles and prophets, with Christ Jesus himself as the cornerstone,

- in whom the whole building is crafted together and grows into a holy temple in the Lord
- in whom you are built up into God's dwelling place in the Spirit.

> The long sentences of Ephesians are not really what we are used to in the letters that are certainly written by Paul, and it is important to take them slowly, to make sure that you see how they work; use the bullet points to find your way into the structure. Notice, though, that the ideas owe a good deal to the thinking that Paul has already done: the uniting of Gentiles and Jews, the tension between the two, the tangible difference that Christ makes, the centrality of Jesus, his death-resurrection and his peace, the cancellation of the law, the metaphor of a building, the emphasis on the Spirit, and the extraordinarily rich and powerful idea of the Church as the Body of Christ. All these are ideas that are already in 1 Corinthians and Romans.

The difference that the gospel makes, to those who preach and to those who hear

3 **1-7** For his sake, I, Paul, a prisoner of Christ Jesus, on behalf of you Gentiles (assuming that you have heard of the stewardship of God's grace that was given me for you),

- because by a revelation the mystery was made known to me, as I have written briefly above, in accordance with which you are able to read and comprehend my understanding in the mystery of Christ
- which in earlier generations was not made known to the 'sons of men'
- as now it is revealed to his holy apostles and prophets by the Spirit,
- for the Gentiles to have a share in the inheritance, and in the body, and in the partnership of the promise in Christ Jesus through the gospel
- of which I became a minister, according to the free gift of the grace of God, which was given to me according to the activity of his power.

> This is not difficult to understand, but quite hard to translate. At times one feels that the author has only a tenuous grasp on his clauses, which seem about to fly off in all directions. The sentence starts 'I, Paul', but we are never introduced to the main verb that this leads us to expect.
>
> Many readers will anxiously ask if there is not some dishonesty in the author pretending to be Paul, if indeed this document is not

written by the apostle. It may be helpful to think of a successor of Paul, one who knows his thought well, telling the reader or hearer, 'this is what Paul would be telling us today', rather than to worry about a forger trying to deceive us.

The apostle's ministry summed up

8-13   To me, the least significant of all the saints, this grace was given, to preach to the Gentiles the unfathomable wealth of Christ, and to shed light

- on what is the stewardship of the mystery which had been hidden from the ages by the God who fashioned everything
- that the many-sided wisdom of God might be made known now to the powers and authorities in the heavenly regions, through the Church according to the purpose of the ages which he fashioned in Christ Jesus our Lord,
- in whom we have full assurance and free access in confidence through his faith.

Therefore, I beg you not to despair at my afflictions on your behalf, which is your glory.

> This is the verdict on Paul's apostolic task, and we can hardly follow (but must try to follow) the author as he scales mystical heights, the obsession with God, and the astonishment at what God has done, and his sense of where the Church fits into the picture.

The apostle's prayer

14-21   For his sake I bend my knees to the Father,

- from whom all fathering in heaven and on earth is named,
- that he might grant you, in accordance with the wealth of his glory, to be mightily strengthened through his Spirit with regard to the 'inner person',
- that Christ should dwell through faith in your hearts,
- [that you may be] rooted and founded in love that you may have the strength
- to comprehend with all the saints
- what is the breadth and length and height and depth, to know
- the overarching love of Christ which transcends knowledge,
- that you may be filled with regard to all the fullness of God.

To the one who is able above all, quite beyond all measure of what we ask or understand according to the power that is at work in us, to him be the glory in the Church and in Christ Jesus to all generations for ever and ever. Amen.

> This beautiful prayer clearly comes from the same hand as has constructed the rest of the letter, with its complex sentences and piles of nouns; but more important than that for the reader is the certainty about the accessibility (to all!) of the mystery of God in Christ. As with Paul's undisputed letters, God and Christ and love are right in the centre of the author's intention.

Unity in the Spirit of the Body of Christ

4 **1-16** Therefore I beg you, I who am the prisoner in the Lord, to walk worthily of the calling to which you have been called, with all humility and gentleness, with patience, putting up with one another in love, being eager to keep the unity of the Spirit, in the bond of peace: One body and one Spirit (just as you were called in one hope of your calling), one Lord, one faith, one baptism, one God and Father of all, who is over all and through all and in all.

To each one of us the grace is given according to the measure of Christ's free gift. Therefore it says,

'Going up to the height, he took captivity captive;
he gave gifts to human beings.'

Now what is 'he went up', other than that 'he went down' to the lower regions of the earth? The one who 'went down' is the same as the one who 'went up', far above all the heavens, that he might fill everything.

And he himself gave some as apostles, others as prophets, others as evangelists, others as shepherds and teachers, for the equipping of the saints for a work of service, for the upbuilding of the Body of Christ, until all of us arrive

- at the unity of faith and the knowledge of the 'sons of God',
- at the perfect human being,
- at the measure of the stature of the fullness of Christ,
- so that we may no longer be infants, tossed here and there by waves, and carried here and there by every breeze of teaching, by the craftiness of human beings, by readiness to do anything bad as regards deceitful scheming,
- but that we may be truthful in love and make everything grow into him, who is the Head,
- Christ, from whom the whole body is joined together and knit together, through every supporting ligament according to the activity that is proper to each individual part;
- it may bring about the increase of the body for its own upbuilding in love.

Once again, it is reasonably clear what the author means here, though it is less obvious how the individual parts hang together. Three principles are affirmed here:

1. the unity of the Church in the Spirit

2. the identity of Christ, now in glory, with the One who 'came down' to earth

3. the intimate connection of Christ and the Church (seen as Body of Christ).

The quotation in the second paragraph, 'Going up to the height . . .' is from Psalm 68:18, where it celebrates God's ascent to Mount Zion (or perhaps Mount Sinai); God's reign is symbolised by the fact that he received slaves and other gifts. Here it is applied to Jesus, triumphantly entering heaven; and the wording has been changed, rather daringly, so that he now gives gifts.

How to behave in the Body of Christ

4 ¹⁷-5 ²⁰   This is my statement, and my testimony in the Lord: no longer [ought] you to walk as the Gentiles walk, in the futility of their intellects, being darkened in [their] understanding, alienated from God's life because of the ignorance that is in them because of the hardness of their hearts, who have become devoid of feeling and given themselves over to debauchery, to the practice of every kind of impurity to excess.

You, however, did not learn Christ that way (assuming, that is, that you *did* hear him and *were* taught in him) as the truth is in Jesus, for you to set aside the person you once were, according to your previous way of life, a person on the way to destruction according to deceptive desires. Instead, get yourselves renewed in the spirit of your mind and put on the new person, the one who is fashioned according to God, in the righteousness and holiness of truth.

Therefore put away falsehood, 'let each one speak truth with their neighbour' [Zechariah 8:16, freely cited], because we are parts of each other, 'be angry, but do not sin' [Psalm 4:5, freely cited]. Let the sun not go down on your anger, and do not give space to the devil. Let the thief stop stealing, rather let him labour, producing good with his own hands, that he may have something to share with the one who has need.

Let no evil speech come from your mouth; but nothing other than good [speech], to build [people] up in case of need, in order that it may give grace to those who hear.

And do not grieve the Holy Spirit of God, by whom you are sealed for the Day of Redemption. Let all bitterness and passion and anger and clamour and blasphemy be taken away from you, along with all that is evil. Be kind to one another, compassionate, forgiving each other, just as God in Christ forgave you.

So become imitators of God, like beloved children, and walk in love, just as Christ loved us and handed himself over for our sakes as an offering and a sacrifice to God, to make a fragrant smell.

Sexual immorality and all kind of impurity or excess should not even be named among you, as is fitting for holy people – and the same goes for wickedness and foolish talk or dirty jokes, which ought not to happen, but rather thanksgiving. For be quite certain that no one who is sexually immoral or impure or covetous (that's idolatry) has an inheritance in the kingdom of Christ and of God.

Let no one fool you with insubstantial talk; for this brings the wrath of God on the children of disobedience. Don't go into partnership with them: for once upon a time you were darkness. Now, however, you are light in the Lord – walk as children of the light, for light's fruit is all about goodness and righteousness and truth; test what is pleasing to the Lord, and don't go shares in the unfruitful works of darkness – instead [you should] expose them. For the things that are secretly done by them are too disgusting to mention, while everything that is exposed by the light is revealed, because everything that is revealed is light. Therefore it says,

> 'Awake, you who sleep
> and arise from the dead,
> and Christ shall shine upon you.'

So look carefully at how you are behaving: not as [the] unwise but as [the] wise, making the most of the time, because the days are evil. Therefore do not become foolish, but [try to] understand what is the Lord's will. And don't get drunk on wine, in which there is dissipation, but be filled with the Spirit, talking to yourselves in psalms and hymns and spirit-filled canticles, singing and playing musical instruments in your heart to the Lord, always giving thanks for everything in the name of our Lord Jesus to [our/his] God and Father.

> This is a very long section on the kind of behaviour that is appropriate in the Body of Christ. Once again, the sentences are long, but never quite fly out of control. The moral teaching is far more diffuse, far less precise, than in Paul, and yet the author shares the apostle's sense of what does and does not fit if you are Christians.
>
> The lines 'Awake, you who sleep . . .' may be a fragment of an early Christian hymn, or, just possibly, a loose translation of Isaiah 60:1, 'Arise, shine, for your light has come and the glory of the Lord has risen upon you.' Our author is quite free in his handling of the Old Testament.

How Christian families are to operate

5 21-6 9   Be submissive to one another in the fear of Christ:

- *wives* to their own husbands as to the Lord, because the husband is the head of the wife, as also Christ is the head of the Church – he is the Saviour of the body. But as the Church is submissive to Christ, so also wives to their husbands in every respect.

- *husbands*, love your wives, just as Christ loved the Church, and gave himself for her, so that he might make her holy by the washing in water, accompanied by a form of words, that he himself might present the Church to himself as resplendent, with no stain or wrinkle or anything like that, but that she might be holy and blameless. That is how husbands ought to love their own wives, as their own bodies. The one who loves his own wife loves himself. For no one ever hates his own flesh, but nourishes and cherishes it, as Christ [does with] the Church, because we are limbs of his body. 'For this reason, a man will leave his father and his mother and will cling to his wife, and the two will become one flesh.'

This is an enormous mystery – and I am speaking of it with reference to Christ and to the Church. But you too, individually, let each of you love his own wife as you love yourself – but the wife should revere her husband.

- *children* – obey your parents in the Lord; for this is right: 'honour your father and your mother', which is the first commandment in the promise, 'that it may be well with you, and you may have a long life on the earth'.

- And *parents* – don't make your children angry, but look after them with the Lord's discipline and admonition.

- *slaves* – obey those who are your 'lords' according to the flesh, with fear and trembling, in simplicity of your hearts, as though [they were] Christ, not as doing your service to attract attention, as though you were 'pleasing people' – but as Christ's slaves, doing God's will from the heart, doing your slavery with enthusiasm, as for the Lord, and not for human beings, confident that whenever each one does anything good, they will get this from the Lord, whether they are slave or free.

- And '*lords*', do the same to them; give up menacing [them], confident that your Lord and their Lord is in heaven; and there is no snobbery in him.

The 'household code' is always a tricky passage to handle. It is our belief, of course, that all are equal before God, and many readers, properly anxious about the rights of women, children and slaves, are dismayed by what they read as a sanctification of a 'hierarchy of relationships' in the Body of Christ.

But look again. What the author of this epistle does in the 'household code' is to relativise all that his contemporary society would have taken for granted. It starts with a command of universal submission (not just women, slaves, children) 'in the fear of Christ', and all that follows serves only to relativise human hierarchies. So just as husbands, parents, and slave owners are turning to their 'inferiors' and saying 'Did you hear what the man said?', they find themselves under review: 'husbands, love your wives . . . as your own bodies'; 'parents – don't annoy your children'; 'slave-lords . . . know that their Lord and yours is in heaven'. We are not to read this simply as reinforcing the social stratification of contemporary society: the mention of 'love' rules that out.

Notice the instruction to children and parents; it looks at first like a simple quotation from Exodus 20:12 and Deuteronomy 5:16; but our author is quite daring in expecting it to include the responsibility of parents to their children, not to make them angry!

Concluding prayer: the 'suit of armour'

10-20 For the rest, be strong in the Lord, and in the might of his power. Put on God's suit of armour, so as to be able to stand against the devil's craftiness, because our struggle is not against blood and flesh; no – it is against the rulers, the powers, the world rulers of the present darkness, against the spirit forces of evil in the heavenly regions.

For that reason, take up God's suit of armour, that you may be able to resist on the Evil Day, and having won through against everything, to stand firm. So stand firm, with your loins girded with truth, and putting on the breastplate of righteousness, and putting sandals on your feet in readiness for the gospel of peace; in everything taking up the shield of faith, by which you will be able to extinguish all the Evil One's incendiary devices. And accept the helmet of salvation, and the sword of the Spirit, which is God's word.

Praying in all prayer and supplication, on every occasion in the Spirit, and for that reason staying awake in all patience and in supplication for all the saints – *and* for me, that I may be given speech when I open my mouth, to make known with complete confidence the mystery of the gospel, for which I am an ambassador-in-chains, so that in him I may utter freely, as I ought to speak.

Much of this is the slightly fanciful analogy of the 'suit of armour', which has so seized the Christian imagination. Notice the powerful sense that the author has, that Christians are engaged in a real battle, the importance of prayer, and (once again) the absolute centrality of God, and the mission to preach the gospel.

Do you feel embarrassed by all the military language that the author applies here to Christian life? Many people would say that this is because we have forgotten that Christian life is a battle against the evil powers.

Final salutations

21-23 But that you may know about me (what I'm up to), Tychicus, the beloved fellow Christian, and faithful minister in the Lord, will tell you everything. I have sent him to you for this very purpose, that you may know about us, and that he may comfort your hearts.

Peace to the brothers and sisters, and love with faith, from God the Father and the Lord Jesus Christ. Grace be with all those who love our Lord Jesus Christ in immortality.

So ends the Letter to the Ephesians; these last few lines show why many scholars do not regard the letter as coming from the apostle himself, despite the personal references: 'love with faith' and 'grace' used in this way, as well as the odd reference to 'Jesus Christ in immortality' all sound different from Paul. Nevertheless, the author of the epistle certainly both knew and understood Paul's thinking; and I have to say that of all the Pauline corpus, it was this document that most seized me and moved me while I was doing the translation.

The Letter to the Philippians

Introduction

This is Paul's most joyful letter, even though it was written in a prison from which he might not emerge alive. The Philippians were perhaps his favourite community (though the Corinthians might be characteristically disposed to argue the point); they were almost the first of his foundations in Europe – see Acts 16 for the details.

Opening greetings

1 [1, 2] Paul and Timothy, slaves of Christ Jesus, to all the saints in Christ Jesus who are in Philippi, with the overseers and assistants, grace to you and peace from God our Father, and from the Lord Jesus Christ.

> A characteristic opening from Paul and his co-worker. Not for the first time, he describes himself as 'Jesus' slave'. The words translated as 'overseers' and 'assistants' later turned into 'bishops' and 'deacons', but it is unlikely that they had that meaning at this early stage.

Thanksgiving

[3-11] I give thanks to my God every time I think of you, all the time in each one of my prayers on behalf of all of you, making the prayer with joy, because of your solidarity in the gospel, from the first day until now, confident of this, that the one who started a good work in you will bring it to completion by the day of Christ Jesus, as it is [only] right for me to be thinking about all of you, because I keep you in my heart, both in my imprisonment and in the defence and establishment of the gospel, since all of you are in solidarity with me in grace.

For God is my witness that I long for all of you in the heart of Christ Jesus. And this is my prayer, that your love may overflow more and more in knowledge and in all insight, that you may test out the things that are superior, that you may be pure and blameless for Christ's Day, filled with the fruit of that righteousness that comes through Jesus Christ to the glory and praise of God.

> In the thanksgiving of Pauline letters, it is always wise to look out for themes that will reappear in the rest of the letter. Three times here he uses the phrase 'all of you', which may be a sly reference to their disunity, something of which he will speak later on. Notice also the first reference to 'joy', which we shall often meet again in this letter. Though Paul is writing from prison (we cannot be sure where or when) this is nevertheless the most joy-filled of all his letters. And, finally, there are various words derived from the root *koinonia*, which I have translated as 'solidarity', but carries hints of partnership, union, communion, fellowship. The reader should keep all these ideas in mind when thinking about this word.

Some of Paul's difficulties

[12-17] My brothers and sisters, I want you to know that my circumstances have actually led more to the progress of the gospel, so that my imprisonment has (in Christ) become well known among the entire praetorium, and to everyone else, and the majority of the brothers and sisters in the Lord have, because of my imprisonment, had the confidence and, increasingly, the courage to speak the word fearlessly. Some preach Christ out of envy and rivalry, while others proclaim him out of good will. Some do it for love; they know that I am put here in order to mount a defence of the gospel. While others proclaim Christ with mixed motives; they think that they will stir up trouble for me in prison.

It is quite hard to reconstruct what is going on while Paul is in prison, though presumably his Philippians knew what he was talking about; but notice his calm contemplation of the odd fact that people are actually using the gospel to upset him (and Paul is not always the calmest of souls!), and his eye for the main point, that, one way or another, the gospel gets preached.

The 'praetorium' to which Paul refers is anywhere where the local Roman governor might live, and includes also the troops that form his bodyguard.

Only Christ matters

18-26 So what? But in every way, whether for false motives or true, Christ is proclaimed; and I rejoice at that.

No – but I *shall* rejoice. For I am sure that through your prayers and through the support of the Spirit of Jesus Christ, all this will turn out for my deliverance, according to my eager expectation and hope, that I shall in no way be ashamed; no – Christ will be glorified in my body, with all boldness, both now and always, whether by [my] life or by [my] death.

You see, for me, to live is Christ, and to die is a gain; but if continuing to live in the body means that my work will bear fruit, then I do not know which I shall choose. I am torn between the two: I have a desire to depart and be with Christ (for that is far better). On the other hand, to remain in the body is more necessary because of you; and since I am convinced of this, I know that I shall remain and stay by you all, for your own advancement and the joy of your faith, so that your boasting may overflow in Christ Jesus by means of my being present to you once more.

This is a charming passage, and reveals Paul's profound sense of the things that really matter: a) Jesus Christ; b) the proclamation of the gospel of Christ; c) the welfare of Christ's Church.

He is profoundly convinced that death would mean being once more with his beloved (and is therefore a welcome gift), but is prepared to stay with the Church despite his own preference. Notice how once again he speaks of 'you all'.

Faith is not easy: sporting metaphors

27-30 Just conduct your life in a way that is worthy of the gospel of Christ, so that whether I come and see you, or whether I am absent and hear all about you, [I may know] that you stand fast in one Spirit and in one mind, fighting side by side for the gospel faith, and not being intimidated in any way by your opponents; for [the faith] is a sign of destruction for them, but [a sign] of salvation for you – and [it comes] from God. Because being on Christ's side has been given as a free gift to you, not just for you to believe in him, but also to suffer for him, sharing the same struggle as you saw, and now hear about, in my case.

Paul acknowledges here that the Philippians are not having an easy time of it; but then, as he points out, neither is he. He uses various sporting metaphors ('fighting side by side', 'opponents', 'struggle'), possibly drawn from Stoic philosophy, or possibly because that was language that the Philippians easily understood.

The word 'gospel' is another important idea in Philippians: it is used twice in this section, making six times in all in Chapter 1 of the letter.

Please be united

2 [1-18] Therefore if there is any comfort in Christ, if there is any consolation of love, if there is any solidarity of the Spirit, if there is any compassion or pity, fill up my joy: [I want] you to think the same, have the same love, and be of one mind, with just a single thought, with no thoughts that are in line with selfish ambition or empty conceit. No – in humility, think of each other as your superiors; don't be each of you looking to your own [interests]; instead, look to each other's interests. Let your thinking be what was in Christ Jesus,

> who, being in the form of God,
> did not think it plunder to hang on to
> (the being equal to God).
> Instead, he emptied himself,
> taking a slave's form,
> coming to be in the likeness of human beings.
> And being found in appearance like a human being,
> he humbled himself!
> He became obedient even to the point of death
> (death on a cross!).
> Therefore God superexalted him
> and gave him the free gift of the name
> which is above every name,
> that at the name of Jesus
> every knee should bow
> in heaven and on earth and under the earth
> and every tongue confess
> that Jesus Christ is Lord
> to the glory of God the Father.

So, my dear ones, just as you have always been obedient, not just when I have been present, but now all the more when I am absent, with fear and trembling work out your own salvation. For it is God who is bringing about in you the willing and the working for [God's] good will. Do everything without any muttering or argument, so that you may become blameless and innocent, unblemished children of God in the middle of a crooked and perverse generation, among whom [I want you to] appear like stars in the world. Hold on to the word of life, so as to give me something to boast about on the Day of Christ, to prove that I did not train in vain, or labour in vain. No – even if I am poured out as a sacrificial offering for your faith, I rejoice – and share my joy with all of you. In just the same way, you must rejoice – and share your joy with me.

Now we can see what we have been suspecting for a while, that Paul is addressing a problem of disunity at Philippi; his tactic is to urge them to 'think the same' as each other, but also to have the same attitude as his beloved Jesus, an attitude of not seeking to 'hang on to what you have', but of 'self-emptying', and regarding others as superior. That is how you build the 'solidarity' that for Paul was the mark of a Christian Church, as he stresses in his correspondence with the Christians of Rome, and, especially, Corinth. This tactic leads him into the 'hymn to Christ'. Whether or not it really was a hymn, and whether Paul composed it, or used existing material that was already a part of the Christian liturgy, cannot now be determined for certain, though in the translation I have followed one of the ways of setting it out as a hymn. It is a lovely passage, and has remained a favourite with Christians ever since; its theology of 'who Jesus was' is a very exalted one (at least on the most obvious way of reading it). But notice how Paul's theology is intimately linked to his pastoral concerns.

Once again, we see the words 'joy' and 'solidarity'. Reflect on why they are important to Paul in his dealings with the Philippians.

Timothy and Epaphroditus

2 ¹⁹-3 ¹ I hope in the Lord Jesus to send Timothy to you soon, so that I too may be heartened by hearing about you. For I have no one who is on the same wavelength, who genuinely cares about your interests. For they are all pursuing their own interests, not those of Jesus Christ. But you know his quality; [you know] how he slaved at my side for the gospel, like a child with his father. So that's the one whom I'm hoping to send, immediately, as soon as I see what is going to happen to me. And I trust in the Lord that I also shall come soon.

I thought it necessary to send you Epaphroditus, my fellow Christian and co-worker and comrade-in-arms, and your apostle, and the one who has served my need; because he was longing for all of you, and was much distressed, because you had heard that he had been ill. He had indeed been ill, close to death; but God had mercy on him, and not just on him, but on me also, so that I should not have sorrow upon sorrow. So I despatched him all the more enthusiastically, so that when you saw him, you would rejoice once more, and I might have my sorrow relieved. So welcome him in the Lord with all joy; and hold people like that in honour, because it was on account of the work for Christ that he came near to death, risking his life, so that he might fill up your lack by giving service to me.

For the rest, my brothers and sisters, rejoice in the Lord. (It is no problem to me to repeat what I have written, and it is a safeguard for you.)

Paul regarded those whom he sent as equivalent to him; and in Timothy and Epaphroditus the churches may have felt they were getting 'second-best' (see 1 Corinthians 16:10, 11); and the language Paul uses to commend Epaphroditus will remind the reader of how he dealt with the Corinthians in their disdain for Stephanas (1 Corinthians 16:15-18), whose Greek name may suggest that he and Epaphroditus were of a similarly lowly social status.

Once again, the word 'joy' appears (once as a noun, and twice in the verbal form, 'rejoice'). Once again, the phrase 'all of you', possibly another reference to Philippian disunity, appears.

A sudden change of tone

2-11   Watch out for the dogs; watch out for evil workers; watch out for the 'chopping-cision' party. For *we* are the 'circumcision party', we who worship by the Spirit of God, and who boast in Christ Jesus, and who do not place our reliance in the flesh. Although I have reliance in the flesh also: if someone else thinks they [can] rely on the flesh, I am more capable of doing so: [I am] of the eighth-day circumcision, of the race of Israel, of the tribe of Benjamin, a Hebrew born of Hebrews, a Pharisee as regards the law, a persecutor of the Church as regards fanatical enthusiasm, I became irreproachable as regards law-righteousness.

No – whatever was on my credit-side, I regarded it as loss, because of Christ. In fact I regard everything as loss, because of the supreme good of the knowledge of Christ Jesus my Lord, for whose sake I lost everything, and I regard it as dung, in order that I may gain Christ, and take my place in him, without any righteousness of my own that comes from the law, but only the righteousness that comes through Christ's faith, the righteousness that comes from God on those who believe: so as to know him and the power of his resurrection, and solidarity with his sufferings, being conformed to his death, if somehow I may reach up to the resurrection from the dead.

Some scholars, observing that the beginning of Chapter 3 ('for the rest . . . ') looks like the start of the conclusion of the letter, and that suddenly the tone changes in the very next verse, have suggested that this is part of another letter. In fact, however, Paul often changes his tone rather suddenly; and in any case, the angry note does not continue throughout the section, as Paul turns to speak of God's righteousness and Paul's share in his Christ's resurrection and sufferings.

Once again, we must be grateful to whoever it was that annoyed Paul sufficiently for him to indulge in reminiscences of his past life, which otherwise we should never have had. He indulges in a slightly cumbersome metaphor, difficult to put smoothly into English, about the 'profit' and 'loss' side of ancient accounting practice, to describe the importance of Christ to him, in comparison with what he once had.

The reference to 'chopping-cision' in the first line of this section is a heavy attempt to reproduce Paul's somewhat offensive pun on 'circumcision'.

A sporting metaphor

12-14   Not that I've already received the gold medal, or reached perfection, but I'm in pursuit of it, in the hope of winning it, seeing that I've been won by Christ Jesus. My fellow Christians, I do not reckon that I have won: but one thing [I do]. Forgetting the previous laps, I am pushing towards those which lie ahead, in pursuit of the finishing line, towards the medal, which consists in the summons [that comes] from God in Jesus Christ, [to go] higher.

We may find that the awkwardness of this metaphor conveys at one and the same time Paul's determination to catch his readers' attention by using an image from the athletics field, and his own lack of familiarity with the sport. Or, more prosaically, the image may have come to him by way of Stoic philosophy, which seems to have been a part of his cultural baggage. It would be pushing a harmless metaphor too far if we started asking whether the analogy with training for a sport does not signal a return to 'righteousness by works'!

Christ should make a difference to the way we behave

3¹⁵-4¹ So those who are 'perfect', let us keep thinking this way; and if your thoughts are different in some way, God will reveal this also to you – only [we should] hold to whatever we have attained.

Join [with the others] in following my example, brothers and sisters; keep an eye on those who are behaving like us, whom you have as your model. For many people are behaving – whom I have mentioned to you, and now I am in tears as I mention them – [as] enemies of the cross of Christ, whose end is destruction, whose god is their belly, and whose glory is their shame, those whose thoughts are earthbound. For our country is in heaven, from which we are waiting for a saviour, the Lord Jesus Christ, who will transform our humble body, conforming it to his glorious body, according to his power which enables him to subordinate everything to him.

So, my beloved and longed-for brothers and sisters, my joy and my crown, stand firm like this in the Lord, beloved.

> Paul is never shy about offering himself as an example. The encounter with Christ had transformed his life, made a visible difference. He is quite clear about the kind of behaviour that is appropriate for Christians, and that which is not.
>
> Occasionally, in his enthusiasm, the syntax falls apart; or perhaps his secretary could not keep up with his dictation! One example would be the sentence beginning 'For many people are behaving . . .'

Stop quarrelling

2, 3 I beg Evodia, and I beg Syntyche to think the same in the Lord. Yes, and I ask you too, my true partner, give them help; for these women have fought side by side with me in the arena of the gospel, and also with Clemens, and the rest of my fellow workers, whose names are in the book of life.

> We have on several occasions in the letter so far seen possible hints of disunity at Philippi, often in connection with the word 'thinking' (see Philippians 1:7; 2:2; 2:5; 3:15; 3:19; 4:10); here we see a clear instance, where named people are causing scandal in the body. The word translated as 'partner' (for which the Greek is *Syzygos*) is thought by at least one eminent scholar to refer to Paul's wife. It is certainly a thought-provoking possibility, although it is also just possible that *Syzygos* is a personal name.

Peace and joy

4-9 Rejoice at all times in the Lord; again I shall say [it]: rejoice! Let your decency be known to all people. The Lord is near: don't be anxious about anything, but in all your prayer and intercession, with thanksgiving let your requests be known to God; and the peace of God which is beyond all imagining will guard your hearts and your minds in Christ Jesus.

For the rest, brothers and sisters, whatever is true, whatever is honourable, whatever is righteous, whatever is holy, whatever is agreeable, whatever is attractive, anything that is virtue or praise – think of these things.

And whatever you have learnt and received and heard and seen in me – do these things.

And the God of peace will be with you.

> Again the letter seems to be coming to a close; it's a lovely passage, which starts with our familiar 'rejoice', and focuses the Philippians on God, on prayer, and, in a few charming lines, on all that it is proper for us to think of and all that we should do. Then there is what sounds like the beginning of a Pauline farewell: 'the God of peace will be with you'. But there is more to come.

The gift Epaphroditus brought to Paul

10-20 I rejoiced greatly in the Lord that already, some time ago, you had revived your [habit of] thinking about me (insofar as you were thinking about me, but you lacked the opportunity). Not that I am talking because of any need: for I have learnt how to be content, where I am. I know how to be humbled, and I know how to have enough and to spare. In everything and in every respect I am an expert: being satisfied and being hungry; being in surplus and being in want. In every respect I am strong in the one who empowers me.

Nevertheless, it was a lovely thing that you did, when you showed me solidarity in my trouble. You too know, Philippians, that in the beginning of the gospel, when I came out of Macedonia, no church showed me any solidarity of debit and credit, except for you people alone; because even in Thessalonica, on two or three occasions, you sent me something towards my needs. Not that I am fishing for the gift; what I am fishing for is the profit that increases to the settlement of your account. I have received payment in full, and I have enough and to spare. I am fully supplied, having received your contribution from Epaphroditus, an odour of fragrance, an acceptable sacrifice, pleasing to God.

My God will fill up all your need, according to his wealth in glory in Christ Jesus: to our God and Father be the glory, for ever and ever. Amen.

> Notice the familiar words 'rejoice' and 'think'. Clearly the Philippians have, in the past and more recently, been generous in their contributions to Paul, but perhaps he is in need again. As always with Paul, everything begins and ends with Christ.
>
> Once again he uses the fiscal metaphor of 'debit and credit', and it bumps along, a little uncomfortably. He is more at ease when he turns to an image from the Old Testament cult: 'an odour of fragrance, an acceptable sacrifice'.

Closing greetings

21-23 Greet every single saint in Christ Jesus. The brothers and sisters who are with me send greetings; all the saints send you greetings, especially those from Caesar's household.

The grace of our Lord Jesus Christ be with the spirit of you [all].

The closing greetings have fewer names than in other Pauline epistles; the reference to 'Caesar's household' may be a reminder to his hearers or readers that Paul is not a complete failure as an evangelist!

The Letter to the Colossians

Introduction

This is a lovely letter, perhaps written by Paul towards the end of his life, or by someone else (Timothy?) under Paul's instruction, or shortly after his death, to let third- and fourth-generation Christians know 'this is what Paul is saying to us today'. Colossae is about a hundred miles east of Ephesus, and quite near Laodicea (whose church is mentioned in Chapter 4). There are connections with the letter to Philemon; see the references in Chapter 4 to Epaphras, Luke, Aristarchus, Onesimus and Demas.

Opening greetings

1 [1,2] Paul, an apostle of Christ Jesus through the will of God, and Timothy [our] fellow Christian, to the saints at Colossae, faithful brothers and sisters in Christ, grace to you and peace, from God our Father.

> This is a standard opening to a Pauline letter, whether or not Paul wrote it.

Thanksgiving

[3-8] We give thanks to God, [the] Father of our Lord Jesus Christ, all the time, when we pray for you, having heard of your faith in Christ Jesus, and the love which you have for all the saints, on account of the hope which is laid up for you in heaven, which you heard about before, in the word of truth of the gospel which has come to you, just as it is bearing fruit and growing in the whole world, so also in you, from the day when you heard and recognised the grace of God in truth, as you learnt from Epaphras, our beloved fellow slave, who is a faithful minister of Christ for you, who told us about your love in the Spirit.

> This thanksgiving is a single sentence in Greek, and we have left it so in English, at some cost, perhaps, to the reader's patience; you are advised to take it gently, and count the number of different things for which the author is thanking God. Like Ephesians, but to nowhere near the same extent, we have in this letter a frequent piling-up of nouns, such as 'the word of truth of the gospel', for example.

The author's prayer

[9-14] Because of this, we also, from the day when we [first] heard, do not cease praying for you, and asking that you may be filled with the knowledge of his will in all wisdom and spiritual understanding, to walk worthily of the Lord, to please him in all things, bearing fruit and growing in every good work, through the knowledge of God, being empowered with all power, according to the might of his glory, with a view to all patience and fortitude.

Joyfully giving thanks to the Father who made us fit for the portion of the lot of the saints in light, who delivered us from the authority of darkness and changed us into the kingdom of the Son of his love, in whom we have redemption, the forgiveness of sins.

> Some scholars think of these verses as part of the thanksgiving, but it seems easier to read it as the author's prayer for his hearers or readers. The attentive reader will notice that the phrase 'bearing fruit and growing' makes its second appearance in the letter. The first time, it refers to the spread of the gospel; on the second occasion, it is something that is desired for the Christians of Colossae. Possibly it is something that, in the author's view, they lack.

The hymn to Christ

15-20

> [He] is the icon of the invisible God,
> the first-born of all creation.
> Because in him all was created,
> in heaven and on earth,
> what is visible or invisible:
> whether thrones or lordships,
> whether rules or authorities,
> through him and for him was all created.
> And he is before all,
> and all has come to exist in him.
> And he is the head of the body, the Church;
> [he] is the beginning, first-born from the dead,
> that he himself might become Number One in all.
> Because in him all the Fullness was pleased to dwell
> and through him to reconcile all to him,
> having made peace through the blood of his cross
> through him, whether the things on earth or the things in heaven.

This is an extraordinary piece of writing, and scholars have not fully agreed on what it is. Often, though, it is described as a hymn to Christ, perhaps one already in use in the liturgy at Colossae, to which the author has added some elements in order to make a theological point. As it stands, it sings about Christ as 'Number One', in creation, and in redemption. Some scholars see it as a meditation on the opening words of the Bible, 'In the beginning, God created the heavens and the earth'.

What Christ has done for the readers

21-23

And you, who were once alienated, and enemies in your mind, because of wicked works, now he has reconciled [you] by the body of his flesh, through death, to offer you as holy and blameless and irreproachable before him – as long as you remain established and steadfast in the faith, not shifting from the hope of the gospel you heard, which was proclaimed in all creation under heaven, of which I, Paul, became a minister.

Many scholars regard this as the summary of the message of Colossians, a statement of what Christ has done for Paul's addressees, and an indication of what their response might be.

What Paul is doing for his people

1 24-2 5   Now I rejoice in my sufferings on your behalf; and I fill up what is lacking in the affliction of Christ-in-my-flesh, on behalf of his Body, which is the Church,

- of which I became a servant according to God's arrangement,
- which was given me for you, to bring God's word to completion,

- the mystery that was hidden from the ages and from the generations
- but now has been revealed to his saints,
- to whom God wished to make known what is the wealth of the glory of this mystery among the Gentiles,
- which is Christ among you, the hope of glory,
- whom we proclaim, admonishing everybody, and teaching everybody in all wisdom,
- that we may present everybody as perfect in Christ – that is the goal towards which I am labouring,
- struggling in accordance with his action that is active in me in power.

For I want you to know what a huge struggle I have, for you and for those in Laodicea, and those who have not physically seen my face, so that their hearts may be comforted, united by love, and for them to have all wealth of the assurance of understanding, and [for them to have] the knowledge of the mystery of God, Christ, in whom all the treasures of wisdom and knowledge are hidden.

This is what I am saying: let no one fool you by plausible arguments. For even if I am physically absent, nevertheless I am with you in spirit, rejoicing as I look at your orderliness, and the firmness of your faith in Christ.

> As so often in Ephesians, here we have a long and slightly unwieldy sentence, whose structure I have tried to show by means of bullet points. As so often in Paul's genuine letters, theology and pastoral practice walk closely together, hand in hand.

Be confident in the gospel of the Resurrection

6-15 So, as you have received Christ Jesus as Lord, walk in him, rooted in him and built on him and established in the faith, as you have been taught, overflowing in gratitude.

Watch out that someone does not take you prisoner through philosophy and empty falsehood,

- according to the tradition of human beings, according to the elementals of the universe, and not according to Christ,
- because in Christ dwells all the fullness of divinity, in bodily form, and you are fulfilled in him,
- who is the head of all rule and authority
- in whom also you have been circumcised, with a circumcision not made by hands, by the stripping off of the body of flesh, by Christ's circumcision, being buried with him in baptism
- in which you have also been raised through faith in the activity of God, who raised him from the dead.

And you, who were dead because of [your] transgressions, he made you alive along with him, freely forgiving us all our transgressions, wiping out the written evidence against us, the bond, and its requirements, which was opposed to us – and he took it out of the field of play, nailing it to the Cross, stripping off the rules and authorities, he made a public example of them, confidently holding a triumph over them in it.

Another long sentence holds together the warning against alternative doctrines and the reaffirmation of the gospel tradition. The author here reminds his hearers or readers of the tradition that they have received, and of their absolute grounds for confidence in Jesus, in his divinity, his resurrection, and his conquest of everything that threatened them.

The phrase that I have translated 'rule and authority' appears frequently in Colossians and in the Pastoral Letters. The author here uses metaphors from moneylending ('the bond'), sport ('the field of play') and Roman military parades ('triumph') to underline the completeness of God's victory over the 'authorities'.

Warning against following false teachings

16-23   So let no one pass judgement on you with regard to food and drink, or in respect to a festival, or new moon or Sabbath. These things are [merely] shadows of what is to come – the reality belongs to Christ. Don't let anyone cheat you of your prize, through insisting on self-abasement and angel-worship, entering upon [a description of] what they have seen, foolishly puffed up by their fleshly mind, and not holding on to the head, from whom the whole body is supported and held together by sinews and ligaments, and will grow the growth of God.

If you have died with Christ and [are liberated] from the elements of the world, why let yourselves be dictated to, as though you were still living in the world? 'Don't handle; don't taste; don't touch.' These things are all heading for destruction by wear and tear, in keeping human commandments and teachings; they have a rhetoric of cleverness with their self-chosen worship and humiliation, and their severity on the body, with no value against the indulgence of the flesh.

Scholars have made valiant, and mutually contradictory, attempts to establish what the false teaching might have been, though certainly the Colossians will have known what Paul was talking about. Rather than pry any deeper into these murky thickets, the reader should make for what really interests the author; for him, the prime concern is to not let go of death-with-Christ and rising-with-Christ. Nothing else matters.

The phrases 'destruction by wear and tear' and 'with no value against the indulgence of the flesh' more or less accurately translate the Greek, but it is not absolutely clear what the author is getting at. This is because we really do not know what the 'false philosophy' was; but the basic point seems to be that the practices into which the Colossians are being seduced are merely human, and therefore transitory, and, although aimed at restricting self-indulgence, will turn out to be ineffective.

How to live in Christ

3 1-17   So, if you have been raised with Christ, seek the things that are above, where Christ is seated at God's right hand;

- think of the things that are above, not of things on earth.
- For you have died, and your life is hidden with Christ in God.
- When Christ appears, [who is] your life, then also you will appear with him in glory.
- So put to death your earthly parts: fornication, impurity, passion, evil desire, and greed (which is idolatry);
- through these things the anger of God is coming on the children of disobedience;
- among them you once walked, because you lived among them;
- now, however, you have also put everything aside: anger, rage, evil, blasphemy, filthy talk from your mouth;
- don't tell lies to others,
- having put off the old person, with all its practices, and
- having put on the new person who is made new in knowledge, in accordance with the likeness of the one who created him,
- where there is no 'Greek and Jew', 'circumcision and uncircumcision', 'barbarian', 'Scythian', 'slave', 'free',
- but Christ is all in all.

So, as God's chosen ones, holy and beloved ones, put on new clothes: merciful compassion, goodness, humility, gentleness, patience, putting up with each other, and forgiving each other, if anyone has a complaint against another: as the Lord forgave you, so you must also do.

On top of all these, [put on] love, which is the bond that unites perfectly. And may Christ's love referee in your hearts, to which you were called in one body – and become grateful!

Let Christ's word live richly in you, teaching and admonishing yourselves in all wisdom, with psalms, hymns, spiritual canticles, singing with thanks in your hearts to God. And everything that you do, in deed or word, do everything in the Lord Jesus' name, giving thanks to God the Father through him.

It is a consistent theme in the Pauline letters, both those that are clearly from the apostle's hand, and those that may have come from later disciples, that being a follower of Christ makes a visible difference. The basic attitude is 'upwards', a heart set on God; and that means that some kinds of behaviour are ruled out, while others are expected. Another consistent theme is that what God has done in Christ means that there is no room for artificial distinctions, racial, religious, or social. All that matters is Christ, who is mentioned no less than six times in these verses.

The Scythians were a group from modern Russia, of notorious crudeness and cruelty. The point is that no one is excluded from the mystery of God-in-Christ, no matter who they are or what they have done.

The reference to Christ as 'referee' translates a word that means to 'umpire' in the Games, such as the Olympics, where the function of the umpire was a great deal more unchallenged than in their modern equivalent. The point is the absolute completeness of Christ's (peace-giving) command over the Christian.

The 'household code'

3 [18]–**4** [1]   *Wives* – be subject to your husbands, as is proper in the Lord.

Husbands – love your wives, and don't get embittered against them.

Children – obey your parents in every respect; for this is pleasing in the Lord.

Fathers – don't irritate your children, so that they don't get dispirited.

Slaves – in every respect, obey those who are your 'lords' according to the flesh, not in 'serving to attract attention', like those who try to please human beings, but in simplicity of heart, fearing the *Lord*. Whatever you do, work from the heart, as for the *Lord*, and not for human beings, knowing that [it is] from the *Lord* [that] you will receive the reward of the inheritance. Be slaves to *the Lord Christ*. For the one who does what is unrighteous gets the reward of the unrighteousness he has done – and there is no snobbery.

'*Lords*' – give what is righteous and fair to your 'slaves', knowing that you also have a '*Lord*' in heaven.

> At first reading, this passage gives us a bit of a shock, for it seems to undo the sense of equality of all Christians before the Lord; but notice how the author relativises what looks like rampant hierarchy. It is true that wives and children and slaves are told to keep their places, but so are husbands, fathers, and slave-lords. And look at the last pairing – see how much longer is the section given to slaves, and how the wordplay between 'slave-lord' and 'Lord' puts all human rankings into perspective. Though it is sadly true that some Christians have read this text in such a way as to justify exploitation and subordination, it simply means that they have not looked attentively enough at it.

Final instructions

2-6   Be persistent in prayer; be wide awake about it, in gratitude; at the same time, pray for us, that God may open for us a door for the word, to speak of the mystery of Christ, for which I am in prison, so that I may make it plain, as I must speak. Behave 'cleverly' towards outsiders; make the most of the time. Let your speech always be agreeable, seasoned with salt, to know how you must answer each one.

> The obligation to pray for one another is frequently stressed in Paul, as is the eagerness for mission, and the emphasis on Christ (as well as the connection between being an apostle and being in prison). Paul nearly always stresses the importance of correct relations with outsiders.

Final greetings

7-18   Tychicus, beloved fellow Christian, faithful servant, and fellow slave in the Lord, will tell you all about me; I am sending him to you for that precise purpose, that you may know about us, and he may comfort your hearts, along with Onesimus, a faithful and much-loved fellow Christian, who is one of you. They'll inform you of everything at this end.

Aristarchus, my fellow prisoner, greets you, as does Mark, Barnabas's cousin (about whom you have received instructions; if he comes to you, give him hospitality), and Jesus (the one called 'Justus'), who are [all] of the Circumcision; these alone are my fellow workers to [build up] the kingdom of God, and have been a comfort to me.

Epaphras greets you, who is one of you and a slave of Jesus Christ, who is all the time fighting on your behalf in his prayers, that you may stand perfect and fully assured in all that God wills. I can testify to him, that he has much hard labour on your behalf, and also on behalf of those in Laodicea and Hierapolis. Luke the beloved doctor greets you all, as does Demas.

Greet the brothers and sisters in Laodicea, and Nympha and the church that meets at her house; and when this letter has been read among you, make arrangements for it to be read in the church of the Laodiceans; and I want you also to read the one from Laodicea. And tell Archippus, 'Watch out for the ministry that you have received in the Lord; make sure that you fulfil it.'

The greeting in my hand: PAUL. REMEMBER MY CHAINS.

Grace be with you.

The list of names, including that of Onesimus, makes a clear link between the letters to the Colossians and to Philemon. Indeed some scholars suspect that the rather sharp-sounding reminder to Archippus to 'watch out for the ministry' may be addressed to the actual addressee of Philemon, and may refer to Paul's demand that he set Onesimus free. Notice how the author commends his various fellow workers, to give them standing in both Colossae and Laodicea (the letter is to be read in both places). Titles like 'fellow slave', 'fellow captive', 'slave of Christ Jesus', 'beloved doctor', and adjectives like 'faithful' and 'beloved', all tend in that direction. Certainly something like the message to Archippus, whether or not it is about freeing Onesimus, makes it harder to imagine that the letter is entirely pseudonymous. Recently a strong case has been made for Timothy having written Colossians, under Paul's supervision; and that is entirely possible.

The First Letter to the Thessalonians

Introduction

In the view of many scholars, this is the first of Paul's letters, in which case the opening verse contains the first words of the New Testament to have been written. (If you find yourself puzzling about why, in that case, this letter is positioned so late in the collection of Paul's letters, the answer is quite simple: they are collected in order of their length!) We should read them in awed tones.

We share with Paul and his readers the problem of living our Christianity in a hostile and pagan culture.

Opening greeting

1[1]   Paul and Silvanus and Timothy to the Church of the Thessalonians in God the Father and the Lord Jesus Christ, grace to you and peace.

> It may be worth looking at a map to see where Thessalonica is, and at Acts 16, to see how Paul came to found the Church there. This first document of the New Testament apparently has three authors (but outside of this opening verse you would hardly know that Silvanus and Timothy are involved). Notice that Paul thinks of 'God the Father' and 'the Lord Jesus Christ' as practically the same.

The thanksgiving

2-10   We give thanks to God for all of you, always making mention of you in our prayers, remembering your work of faith and the labour of love, and the perseverance of hope of our Lord Jesus Christ in the presence of our God and Father, knowing as we do, beloved brothers and sisters, the fact that you have been chosen, because our gospel did not come to you just in rhetoric, but also in power and in the Holy Spirit, and with full conviction, as you know the kind of people we were among you for your sake.

And you became imitators of us and of the Lord, welcoming the message in considerable affliction, and with joy in the Holy Spirit, so that you became a model to all the believers in Macedonia, and in Achaia as well. For from you the Lord's word has sounded forth, not just in Macedonia and Achaia, but in every place your faith in God has gone out, so that we have no need to say anything. For it is they who report about us what kind of a welcome we had from you, and how you turned to God from idols, to become slaves of the living and true God, and to wait for his Son [coming] from heaven, whom he raised from the dead, Jesus, who delivers us from the wrath that is coming.

> Letters in the ancient world tended to have a thanksgiving, after the introduction, and Paul follows that pattern. In the thanksgiving of his letters, which are rather longer than other letters of his time, we find that he plays out the themes that will appear again in the letter. Such themes might include, in this case, the fact of waiting for Jesus to return, and the belief that Jesus 'delivers us from the wrath that is coming'. In addition, notice the teaching, so central to Paul's theology, that God raised Jesus from the dead. Note, too, the word 'Lord', which appears three times in Chapter 1. To whom does it refer? The Holy Spirit appears twice; we also have the mention of the three virtues of faith, love and hope, which will reappear in a different form in 1 Corinthians 13.
>
> Three other points will be useful to notice at this stage: First, the Thessalonian Christians had obviously come from paganism (the reference to idols would have been impossible if they had been Jews). Second, Jesus is 'Son of God'. This is very familiar to us now; but what does Paul mean by it? Who is Jesus for Paul? Third, notice that the opening section of this sentence is very long, and has a

string of nouns ('labour of love', 'perseverance of hope of our Lord'), so the appearance of a string of nouns does not mean that Paul did not write a particular passage.

Paul's arrival at Thessalonica

2 ¹⁻⁴ For you yourselves know, brothers and sisters, about our arrival with you, and that it was not useless. No – although we had, as you know, previously experienced suffering and insults at Philippi, we had full confidence in our God to speak the gospel of God to you amid strong opposition. You see, our comfort is not from deception or impure motives or by trickery. No – as we have been found worthy by God to be entrusted with the gospel, so we speak, not pleasing human beings, but pleasing God who tests our hearts.

> Paul starts with what is common ground between him and his Thessalonians. The word 'useless' (literally 'empty') is a frequent concern in his later letters, as is his emphasis on suffering and opposition for the sake of the 'gospel'. The word 'gospel' is worth watching, to see how Paul uses it. Absolutely at the heart of Paul's self-consciousness is his certainty that he is called by God to proclaim the gospel, and his insistence that he does it with integrity.
>
> The reader must decide whether 'our comfort', of which Paul speaks, is the comfort he gives or the comfort he receives.

How Paul preached in Thessalonica

5-12 For, as you know, it was not with any verbal flattery, nor, as God is my witness, through concealed greed, nor with an eye on honour from human beings, whether from you or from any other people; we can wield authority as apostles of Christ. We, however, became like infants in the midst of you, just as a nursing mother cherishes her children, so in our longing for you we were determined to share with you, not merely the gospel of God, but also our own selves, because you had become dear to us.

For remember, brothers and sisters, our labour and our toil; night and day we worked so as not to be a burden for any of you, and we proclaimed the gospel of God. You and God are our witnesses that we behaved to you who believe in a holy and righteous and blameless manner; as you know, we comforted each of you as a father comforts his own children, and consoled you, and testified before you, so that you should behave worthily of the God who calls you into his own kingdom and glory.

> Twice in this passage Paul calls God to witness; twice he speaks of the 'gospel of God'; twice he likens himself to a parent in his dealings with the Church he has evangelised. These are aspects of Paul's attitude to his mission that surface again and again in his letters. Also present is just a touch of boastfulness, something that can be found elsewhere in Paul.

How the Thessalonians responded

13-16   And because of this we give thanks to God unceasingly, because when you received the 'word of hearing' from us, you accepted it from God, not just a 'word of human beings'; no – as it really is [you accepted it] as a 'word of God', who is active among you who believe. For, my brothers and sisters, you became just like the churches of God which are in Judaea and in Christ Jesus, because you also suffered from your own fellow countrymen, precisely as they did from the Jews, who had killed both the Lord Jesus and the prophets, who chased us out, who do not please God, and are hostile to all humanity, who prevent us from talking to the Gentiles in order that they might be saved, so that they all the time fill up the measure of their sins; but the wrath has come upon them to the full.

> Paul is cross here (not for the last time in his letters), but not with his correspondents, who had clearly accepted his teaching unexpectedly well. Then, in a long and slightly lost sentence, he compares them to Christians in Judaea, who have likewise endured persecution; then the sentence turns into an assault on his fellow Jews, which reads uncomfortably to us. Paul's anger, however, is the kind that can surface 'within the family'. This passage is not often read in church!

Paul wants to see the Thessalonians

17-20   We, however, brothers and sisters, separated from you for a brief while (in person, but *not* in our hearts), were more eager than ever, with a passionate longing to see your faces, because we intended to come to you, *I, Paul*, on two or three occasions; and Satan thwarted us. For what is our hope, or our joy, or the crown of which we boast before our Lord at his coming – is it not you? For you are our glory and our joy.

> Overcoming absence by a token of presence is what a letter is all about; and Paul is showing a new way for Christians to be Christian (something that you cannot do without others) in this first surviving Christian letter. Paul's love for the Thessalonians is neither forced nor exclusive; that same love can be seen in all his letters, even to the vacillating Galatians and the intractable Corinthians.

Why Timothy was sent

3 1-5   Therefore, since we could not bear it any longer, we decided it was best to be left alone in Athens; and we sent Timothy, our fellow Christian and co-worker of God in the gospel of Christ, to make you resolute and to counsel you about your faith, [so as] not to be agitated in any way in all these troubles. For you yourselves know that we are destined for this. For when we were with you, we predicted to you that we were about to be persecuted, and it turned out that way, as you know. For that reason, I sent to find out about your faith (I couldn't bear it any longer), we didn't want the Tempter to tempt you, for then perhaps our labour would be made useless.

Paul's evident affection for the Thessalonians continues; but it is possible that they thought he was giving them 'second-best' by sending Timothy, not coming himself. Certainly that was how the Corinthians were to feel later on. Notice that Paul takes it for granted that where the gospel is preached there will be persecution, and that it will put some Christians off.

Timothy's report

6-10   But Timothy came to us recently from you, and he gave us the good news about your faith and love, and that you make continuous mention of us, longing to see us, just as we long to see you; on this account we were comforted, brothers and sisters, about you, in all our distress and trouble, through your faith, because now we continue to live, if you stand firm in the Lord. For what thanksgiving can we return to the Lord for you, in all the joy with which we rejoice before our God, day and night begging most earnestly to see your face, and to make good what is lacking in your faith?

Once more, Paul's affection for the Thessalonians is unmistakable, and his desire to praise them. It seems that he was anxious about whether their faith would survive the pressure of his absence; Timothy has reassured him. Just as Christians cannot be Christians on their own, so wandering apostles need a combination of letters, agents and personal contact.

A prayer for the Thessalonians

11-13   May Our God and Father himself, and our Lord Jesus, straighten our road to you. May the Lord make you rich and overflowing in love to each other and to all, just as we do to you, to confirm your hearts as blameless in holiness before our God and Father at the coming of our Lord Jesus with all his saints. Amen.

This is a charming and affectionate prayer, and perhaps a subtle reminder to the Thessalonians that they still have a way to go. The reader might ask what it means for a good monotheist Jew like Paul to call Jesus 'Lord', and to place him as closely as he does here with 'God and Father'. Jesus is not quite identical with 'God and Father', of course, but there is a certain 'unity of action'. Notice, too, the reference to Jesus' 'coming' (Greek *parousia*), an idea which is more prominent in 1 Thessalonians than in other Pauline letters.

Keeping the traditions and observing sexual purity

4 1-8   For the rest, brothers and sisters, we ask and beg you in the Lord Jesus, that as you received from us how you should behave and, please God, as in fact you are behaving, that you do so even better. For you know what promises we gave you through the Lord Jesus.
    For this is the will of God, your sanctification, that you should abstain from fornication, that each of you should know how to keep his own vessel in holiness

and honour, not in undergoing passion, like the Gentiles who do not know God, [so as] not to transgress and take advantage of one's fellow Christian in the matter, because the Lord is the one who exacts punishment for all these things, as we told you before and solemnly testified [to you]. For God did not call us to impurity but in holiness. Consequently anyone who disregards this is not disregarding human beings but God, who also gives his Holy Spirit for you.

Paul frequently uses language about 'receiving' and 'passing down', that refers to the traditions that he has given to his churches. For Paul, they could not pick and choose what to believe. And one problem he always had with converts who had not been brought up in the strict morality of Judaism was that they tended to ignore rules about sexual behaviour. For Paul, sexuality was too important to mess about with, and misuse of sexuality incompatible with the holiness to which they were called.

'Keeping one's own vessel in holiness' might refer to one's body or one's wife; scholars are not agreed.

Lastly, notice the use of the Holy Spirit, slightly less frequent in 1 Thessalonians than in other letters (see 1:5; 1:6; 5:19), but still clearly something that they could experience and feel.

Relations within the community and without

9-12 About your love of fellow Christians, you have no need for me to write to you, for you are taught by God to love each other; for this is what you do to all the Christians in the whole of Macedonia. We beg you, fellow Christians, to be even more generous and to have it as your ambition to live in peace, to do your own thing, and to work with your own hands, just as we directed you, that you may behave decently towards outsiders, and have no need of anybody.

Sometimes, when a group is under external pressure, as the Thessalonians were, it is tempting for them to retreat behind a barrier, and to exclude the outside world from their considerations. Paul is not prepared to allow his Christians to operate in this way, in two respects. First, they must be generous to fellow Christians; very possibly he is talking here about the 'collection', so very much a concern of his and in regard to which he was later to boast to the (relatively wealthy) Corinthians of the generosity of Macedonia (1 Corinthians 8:1-7). Second, this group is to 'behave decently towards outsiders', and to work with their own hands.

What about Christians who have died?

13-18 About those who have fallen asleep, we want you to know, brothers and sisters; we do not want you to grieve, like those others who have no hope. For if we believe that Jesus died and rose again, so also God will bring with him those who have fallen asleep through Jesus. For this is our statement, on the basis of a word of the Lord, that we who are alive, who survive till the Lord's coming, will not have any advantage at all over those who have fallen asleep. For the Lord himself, at a word of command, at the sound of an archangel and at the trumpet of God, will come down from heaven; and the dead-in-Christ shall be raised first, then we who are alive, who survive, will be snatched up together with them in the clouds to meet the Lord in the air; and so we shall be all the time with the Lord. So comfort each other with these words.

> At the heart of Paul's gospel is his faith in the Resurrection; it looks also as though he believed in a fairly imminent coming of Jesus. This, of course, raises the question as to whether or not those who are still alive when Christ comes have somehow won the race against those who have died (and some Christians must have died between the bringing of the gospel to Thessalonica and the writing of this letter). To answer this, Paul uses some symbols from Jewish speculation about the end-time. The main thing is not to worry; and that is not because of any pious fiction, but because of what Paul and his Thessalonians know God has done in Christ.

Waiting for the unknown Day

5 1-11 About dates and times, brothers and sisters, you have no need of anything in writing to you. For you know precisely that the Day of the Lord is coming, just like a burglar at night. When they say 'peace and security', then a sudden destruction looms over them, as the labour pains come on a pregnant woman; and no way are they going to escape. But you, brothers and sisters, are not in darkness, that the day should come upon you like a burglar. For you are all children of light and children of day. We do not belong to night or to darkness. So let us not sleep, then, like the rest; no – let's stay awake and be sober. For people who sleep, sleep at night, and those who get drunk, get drunk at night. We, however, who belong to the Day, are sober; we put on the breastplate of faith and love, and the helmet of faith in salvation. Because God did not put us [here] for wrath, but for obtaining salvation through our Lord Jesus Christ, who died for us, so that whether we are awake or asleep we may be alive with him. Therefore comfort each other and build each other up, just as you are doing.

> Paul clearly believes that Jesus will return; but life has to continue, and he will not allow them to speculate about when this might happen. What matters is their attitude, not their watching of the cosmic clock. God's visitation is always at an unexpected time; the essential thing is to remain 'on-side', on the team of light and day, to be awake and clear-headed, and confident in what God has done in Christ.

Respect for church leaders

12, 13 We ask you, brothers and sisters, to acknowledge those who labour among you, and are appointed over you in the Lord, and who admonish you, and to have immense regard for them, because of their function. Live at peace with each other.

> In Christianity, all are equal before God; but in the history of Christianity it has always been found necessary to have leaders, whatever they were called, for the stability of the group. It has also

always been the case that Christians are sinful and squabbling, including, of course, sniping at church leaders. Hence the admonition to 'live at peace'. It is not that church structures are there to be worshipped, simply that they are necessary, human nature being what it is.

How to behave in the Body of Christ

14-22 We beg you, brothers and sisters, admonish the undisciplined, console the faint-hearted, pay attention to those who are sick, be patient with everybody. See that no one returns evil for evil to anybody. Instead, always keep going for what is good for each other and for all.

Rejoice always.
Pray without ceasing.
In everything give thanks
(for this is the will of God in Christ Jesus for you).
Do not extinguish the Spirit.
Do not despise prophecy,
but test everything (hold fast to what is good).
From every form of evil – keep away!

It is interesting for us at this distance to see what are the fundamental moral requirements, as far as Paul is concerned. There must be good order and compassion, respect for all and joy (a word frequently on Paul's lips), prayer and gratitude, and, above all, the Spirit. That means, at least sometimes, the gift of prophecy; but, as Christians have always known, it is necessary to test the spirits.

Concluding prayer and greetings

23-28 May the God of peace himself sanctify you through and through; and may your spirit be preserved undamaged and your body irreproachable at the coming of our Lord Jesus Christ.

The One who calls you is faithful – he will also perform!
Brothers and sisters, pray for us.
Greet all the brothers and sisters with a holy kiss.
I adjure you by the Lord to have the letter read to all the Christians.
The grace of our Lord Jesus be with you all.

So ends our earliest surviving New Testament document. Perhaps Paul, as he does elsewhere, has seized the pen, two lines from the end, and speaks of 'I' instead of 'we'. The farewell conveys his sense of absolute dependence on God, on the love that Christians should have for one another, of their mutual support in prayer, and of the physical means of building community, the 'holy kiss' and the exchange of letters. All, however, goes back to God, 'the One who . . . is faithful', and to 'the grace of our Lord Jesus Christ'.

The Second Letter to the Thessalonians

Opening greetings

1 ^{1, 2} Paul and Silvanus and Timothy, to the Church of the Thessalonians in God our Father and the Lord Jesus Christ, grace to you and peace from God our Father and the Lord Jesus Christ.

> For a variety of reasons, scholars today are increasingly of the view that 2 Thessalonians was written much later than 1 Thessalonians, and by a different author, whose concern was to oppose the view that 'Jesus has already come'. If 2 Thessalonians is by Paul, then it must have been written quite soon after 1 Thessalonians, when Paul and Silvanus were still together. It is difficult, however, to find a really plausible setting for the letter on the assumption of Pauline authorship.

Thanksgiving

3-12 We ought to thank God always for you, brothers and sisters, as is proper, because your faith is increasing remarkably, and the love of each one of you for the other is on the increase, so that we ourselves rest our boast on you, among the churches of God, because of your courage and faith in the midst of all your persecutions and oppressions that you put up with, [which is] evidence of God's righteous judgement, to count you worthy of the kingdom of God, for whose sake you are suffering, since in God's eyes it is appropriate to repay those who oppress you with oppression of their own, and [to repay] you who are oppressed with relief [from oppression] along with us, at the revelation of the Lord Jesus from heaven with the angels of his power in a flaming fire, who gives out punishment to those who have not come to know God, and to those who refuse to obey the gospel of our Lord Jesus, who will pay the penalty of eternal destruction, removed from the presence of the Lord and from the glory of his might, when he comes to be glorified in the midst of his saints, and to be a source of wonder for all who believe, because our witness has been shown to be reliable in you, on that day; to which end, we pray all the time about you, that our God may make you worthy of [your] call, and fulfil all [your] desire or goodness, and the work of faith in power, so that the name of our Lord Jesus may be glorified among you, and you in him, according to the grace of our God and the Lord Jesus Christ.

This difficult passage, where several words could be translated in a number of ways, is a single sentence in Greek, though the author manages it with some assurance. We can use the thanksgiving of Pauline letters as an indicator of the themes uppermost in the author's mind. Here the interest is principally on Jesus' fearsome Second Coming, and the Thessalonians' present difficulties, and the importance of them not getting despondent.

The instruction to the brethren

2[1,2] We ask you, brothers and sisters, with regard to the coming of our Lord Jesus Christ, and our being gathered to him, not to be quickly shaken from your way of thinking, neither through the Spirit, nor through the word, not through any letter supposedly from us, saying that the Day of the Lord has come.

Clearly the issue is that some people have been saying that the Day of the Lord has come (we shall see later with what undesirable consequences), and they have been claiming that Paul has lent his backing to this view.

What must come before the Day of the Lord

[3,4] Don't let anyone deceive you in any way. Because [that day will not come] unless the Rebellion comes first, and [unless] the Man of Iniquity [is revealed], the Son of Destruction, the Adversary and the One who exalts himself above everything that is called a god or an object of worship, to the point of taking his seat in the Temple of God and making himself out to be a god.

Before the end, there has to be (according to the author) a rebellion, and the revealing of the Rebellious One. Scholars have not been able to identify this character with any historical person, nor even with any celestial or infernal figure.

The reader will notice that in the second sentence above, the word 'unless' makes us look for a main verb, which never appears.

Rebellion and the Lawless One

[5-12] Don't you remember that when I was still with you I used to tell you these things? Now you know what is restraining him, so that he may be revealed at his own proper time. For the mystery of iniquity is already at work, only until the one who is restraining [it] is removed from the scene. And then the Lawless One will be revealed, whom the Lord Jesus will destroy with the breath of his mouth, and will annihilate him at the manifestation of his Presence. The coming of the Lawless One, by the activity of Satan with all false power, signs and portents, and all deceptive iniquity for those who are being destroyed, because they did not accept the love of truth so as to be saved. And because of this God is sending them a deceiving power, so that they should believe what is false, that all those who did not believe the truth, but consented to unrighteousness, should be condemned.

This passage is far from easy to understand, still less to translate, and scholars are not agreed on how to read it, though the basic meaning is clear: there is to be an apostasy before the end-time, and there will be a 'Lawless One' who is somehow restrained, by a 'thing' or a 'person'; and the opponents of God are going to be condemned.

Keep going; God is at work

13-17 We ought to thank God always for you, fellow Christians beloved by the Lord, because God has chosen you as first-fruits for salvation through sanctification by the Spirit and by faith in the truth, to which he has called you through our gospel, to possess the glory of our Lord Jesus Christ. So then, brothers and sisters, stand firm and hold fast to the traditions which you have been taught, whether by what we said or by what we wrote. The Lord Jesus Christ himself and God our Father who loved us and who give unfailing comfort and good hope in grace, comfort your hearts, and strengthen them in every good work and deed.

> This exhortation is a little bit vague, but the readers or hearers of this letter are to keep going, confident that the Lord Jesus Christ and God our Father (note the unusual order here) are guiding the enterprise.

Prayer and reassurance

3 1-5 For the rest, keep on praying for us, brothers and sisters, that the word of the Lord may run freely and be glorified, as it has done also with you, that we may be delivered from evil and wicked people. For not everybody has faith. The Lord is faithful, and he will strengthen you and guard you from the evil one. We rely on the Lord with regard to you, because you are doing, and will continue to do, what we command. May the Lord direct your hearts to the love of God and to the constancy of Christ.

> This exhortation is not very specific but both the hearers and the author are to pray for each other, and they can rely on God.

Final exhortation: keep everyone hard at work

6-15 We command you, brothers and sisters, in the name of our Lord Jesus Christ, that you should try to avoid any fellow Christian who behaves in an undisciplined manner, and not in accordance with the tradition that they have received from us. For you yourselves know how you are to imitate us, because we were not undisciplined [when we were] among you, nor did we eat bread at anyone's house without payment; no – we worked, toiling and labouring night and day so as not to be a burden to any of you. This was not because we had not the right [to be fed], but so that we should offer ourselves as a model to you, for you to imitate us. For indeed when we were with you, we commanded you this, that 'if anyone is unwilling to work, let them not eat, either'.

For we hear that some of you are behaving in an undisciplined manner, not being busy at work, but on the contrary behaving like 'busybodies'. We beg and command people like this in the Lord Jesus Christ that they should work peacefully and so eat their own food. As for you, brothers and sisters, don't give up on doing what is good.

And if anyone fails to obey our teaching in this letter, take note of that person; have nothing to do with him or her, that they may be ashamed. Don't think of them as an enemy – but just admonish them as a brother or sister.

> Obviously one of the purposes of the letter has been to deal with Christians who thought that the coming of the Day meant that they no longer had to work. The author is very opposed to anything that looks like 'indiscipline', and uses Paul's 'receive' and 'tradition' vocabulary to make the point. It is quite characteristic of Paul to use himself as an example for young Christians, and, under certain circumstances, to contemplate expulsion from the community of believers. 2 Thessalonians is a good document to read when we get the gloomy feeling that all was sweetness and light in the early Church, and that it has been getting worse ever since.

Closing greeting

16-18   May the Lord of peace himself grant you peace, through all and in every way. The Lord be with all of you.

The greeting in my handwriting: PAUL, which is the identifying mark in every letter – this is how I write.

The grace of our Lord Jesus Christ be with all of you.

> The closing greeting is familiar enough, down to the reference to Paul's handwriting. It is curious, however, that the 'identifying mark' seems to refer to a whole collection of letters by Paul, when, if 2 Thessalonians were really his composition, it would be only the second of his surviving letters. It still makes interesting reading, however.

The First Letter to Timothy

Opening greetings

1 [1,2] Paul, an apostle of Christ Jesus, by the command of God our Saviour, and Christ Jesus our Hope, to Timothy, true child in the faith, grace, mercy and peace from God our Father and Christ Jesus our Lord.

> With these words we start the 'Pastoral Epistles', two addressed to Timothy and one to Titus, which come as a set, and which almost no modern scholar would ascribe to Paul's hand (though Luke Timothy Johnson's recent commentary in the Anchor Bible series makes a worthy attempt at such ascription). The first argument against Paul's authorship is that despite the occasional personal asides, the vocabulary seems different from that of Paul's undisputed letters. The second is that the Church organisation presupposed in these letters seems to reflect that of the end of the first century and the beginning of the second, rather than what you find in Paul's lifetime. In the foregoing passage, God as 'Saviour' and Christ as 'Hope' are unusual titles. And the attentive reader will note the insertion of 'mercy', a common theme in the Pastorals, between the more familiar Pauline terms 'grace and peace'.

Beware of false teaching

[3-11] As I asked you to stay on at Ephesus while I journeyed into Macedonia, for you to command certain people not to teach a different doctrine and not to pay attention to stories and endless genealogies, which provide useless speculation rather than the dispensation of God in faith. But the aim of [my] command is love, whose source is a pure heart and a good conscience, and a faith that involves no pretence. Some people have gone wide of the mark of all these things, and have turned to futile talk, because they wanted to be 'teachers of the law', with no idea what they were saying, nor what they were making such confident assertions about. We know that the law is good, if someone makes use of it in a lawful way, knowing that the law is not instituted for the righteous person, but for the people who are lawless, rebellious, impious, sinners, unholy and godless, who kill their mother and father, murderers, fornicators, sodomites, kidnappers, liars and perjurers, and anything else that contradicts healthy teaching, according to the glorious gospel of blessed God, with which I myself have been entrusted.

> It is virtually impossible to reconstruct the enemies that the author has in mind; and indeed it is hard to imagine this entire list of vices

contained within a single person or even school of thought; but the author is warning of the kind of thing that is likely to go on once you start to 'teach a different doctrine'.

The leaving of Timothy in Ephesus while Paul went to Macedonia does not fit anything that we know of from Paul's correspondence or from Acts; but that need not matter; if Paul did not write this letter, then these details would be the author's attempt to give the letter a Pauline 'feel', when its function is to answer the question, 'What would Paul be saying to us today?' One of the tendencies that we shall see in the Pastorals is a desire to keep doctrine under control, because of the undesirable consequences of getting it wrong.

Paul's own experience of God's mercy

12-17 I give thanks to Christ Jesus our Lord, who empowered me, because he thought me trustworthy enough to appoint me for ministry; I had earlier been a blasphemer and a persecutor and braggart; but I was treated with mercy, because what I did as an unbeliever [was done through] ignorance; but the grace of our Lord was present in great abundance, with faith and love in Jesus Christ. The saying is reliable, and worthy of approval, that 'Christ Jesus came into the world to save sinners', of which I am number one. But for this reason I was treated with mercy, that in me first of all Christ Jesus might show all his forbearance, as a prototype of those who would believe in him to [receive] eternal life. To the king of the ages, the immortal, invisible, only God, [be] honour and glory for ever and ever. Amen.

The contrast here between human sinfulness and God's mercy is there in the undisputed letters of Paul; but it is worth noticing the tendency here to rationalise Paul's previous persecution of the Church, that he 'didn't know what he was doing'.

The expression 'the saying is reliable' appears five times in the Pastorals (1 Timothy 1:15; 3:1; 4:9; 2 Timothy 2:11; Titus 3:8), and not at all in the certainly genuine letters of Paul.

A command to Timothy

18-20 This command I entrust to you, Timothy, my child, in accordance with the former prophecies about you, that in them you may fight the good fight, with faith and a good conscience, which some people have rejected with regard to the faith, and been shipwrecked. Examples of this are Hymenaeus and Alexander, whom I have handed over to Satan, that they may learn not to blaspheme.

It is quite hard to know precisely what is the command that the author is enjoining on Timothy, unless it refers to all that follows. When, on the other hand, it seems that we are coming to a concrete case, that of Hymenaeus and Alexander, we have no evidence whatever as to what the problem was.

Prayers for everybody

2 **1-7** First of all, I ask that petitions and prayers and intercessions and acts of thanksgiving be made on behalf of all people, on behalf of kings and all those who are in authority, so that we may live a tranquil and quiet life, in all piety and holiness. This is good and acceptable before our Saviour God, who wants everybody to be saved and come to the recognition of the truth. For,

> 'there is one God
> and one mediator between God and humanity,
> the human being Jesus Christ
> who gave himself as a ransom for all,
> a testimony at the proper time.'

For this I was appointed a herald and an apostle (I am speaking the truth; I am not lying), a teacher of the Gentiles in faith and truth.

> Some of this sounds very much like the real Paul, such as the reference to his mission, and the remark that 'I am speaking the truth; I am not lying' – see Romans 9:1; 2 Corinthians 11:31; Galatians 1:20). But the attentive reader will notice the reference once again to the 'Saviour God' and the understanding of salvation as coming 'to the recognition of the truth', which is not how the Paul who wrote Galatians, Romans and 1 Corinthians would have expressed it.

The conduct of women

2 **8-3** **1a** So I want the men to pray in every place, lifting up holy hands without any anger or argument. In just the same way, [I want] women to adorn themselves with tasteful deportment, in modesty and restraint, not with braided hair or gold or pearls or expensive clothing, but in a manner that is fitting for women who lay claim to reverence for God, through good works. Let a wife do her learning in tranquillity, in all submission. However I do not permit a wife to do any teaching, nor to have authority over a husband – she must be in tranquillity. For Adam was formed first, then Eve. And it was not Adam who was deceived; it was his wife who was deceived and fell into transgression. But she will be saved by childbearing, provided that they remain in faith and love and holiness, along with self-control. The saying is reliable.

> Nowadays we read this passage with some embarrassment, and want to reassert the basic Christian (and Pauline) insight that all people, including both men and women, are equal before God; but here women are told how they may dress, and what their role is in the Christian Church, namely to be quiet, and not to have authority. This claim, which will not be congenial to many readers today, is then supported by an argument from Scripture, slightly reminiscent of Paul's argument in 1 Corinthians 11, but not really attentive to the actual text of Genesis. It is important to see this passage in context. Our author is of a conservative cast of mind, writing at a time when, all over the Mediterranean world, women were adopting a higher

profile, and at this stage of the Church's development he does not wish to give the enemies of Christianity grounds for criticism. It does not mean that today Christian women must be 'silent and submissive'.

The qualities of an 'overseer': don't rock the boat

1b-7   If anyone aspires to the office of 'overseer', it is a good job that he desires. So the 'overseer' must be irreproachable, the husband of [only] one woman, temperate, self-controlled, respectable, hospitable, a good teacher, not addicted to wine nor a bully. No – he should be gentle, peaceable, not obsessed with money, well able to take care of his own household, keeping his children in good order, with complete dignity (if he has no idea how to conduct his own household, how is he going to take care of the Church of God?). He should not be a recent convert, so that he doesn't get conceited, and fall under the devil's condemnation. He must also have a good reputation among non-Christians, so that he doesn't fall into disgrace, which is a devil's snare.

The Greek word for 'overseer' turned eventually into the English word 'bishop', but at this stage it is not at all clear what the function was, so it is better in translation to use a word that reflects the basic meaning. We notice that the overseer is to be a family man, and to have no publicly obvious moral flaws. Those who argue against Paul's authorship of this letter point out that the two conditions at the end, about the overseer not being a recent convert, and having a good reputation among non-Christians, would, so the argument goes, be unimaginable in Paul's day; almost everyone would have been a 'neophyte' (new convert), so this could not have been a disqualification for Church leadership in Corinth. Similarly, Paul expected the Church to be persecuted by outsiders, so he would never have made public esteem from non-Christians a qualification for holding office within the Church. The author is writing in an age where Christianity needed acceptance from outsiders.

The qualities of a 'servant'

8-13   'Servants' likewise should be honourable, not insincere, nor addicted to lots of wine, nor greedy for dishonest gain; they should hold the mystery of faith with a clean conscience. And these people should be tested first; then let them serve, if they are irreproachable.
Their wives should likewise be honourable, not slanderers, but temperate, faithful in every respect. 'Servants' should be husbands of only one wife, well able to take care of their children, and of their own households. For those who perform their service becomingly win a good standing for themselves, and much assurance in the [life of] faith in Christ Jesus.

The word translated as 'servants' is that which eventually turned into the English word 'deacon'. It is noticeable that 'servants' or 'deacons' require very much the same qualities as 'overseers' or 'bishops' in the preceding verses; presumably the author and his readers know the difference.

A sentence in the middle might either refer to women 'deacons' or to the wives of such 'servants' – it is impossible to be sure.

Christ in the Church

14-16 I am writing this, hopeful of coming to you soon. But if I delay, I want you to know how one must behave in the house of God, which is the Church of the Living God, the pillar and foundation of the truth. And, undeniably, the mystery of godliness is a great one, who

'appeared in the flesh,
was justified in the Spirit,
appeared to angels,
was proclaimed among the Gentiles,
was believed in the world,
was taken up in glory.'

This rather odd passage starts with a colourable account of how the letter might fit into the life of Paul, but continues the emphasis on behaviour in the Church (which at this stage, of course, is a community not a building), and relates it to the presence of Christ, the 'mystery of godliness'. What the author says here lacks the warmth with which Paul ordinarily speaks of his beloved Jesus.

Warning against opponents

4 1-5 The Spirit explicitly says that at the last times some people will fall away from the faith, paying attention to deceptive spirits and the teachings of demons, with the hypocrisy of liars, branded in their own consciences, discouraging marriage, [telling people] to abstain from foods which God had created for the faithful and those who know the truth to accept gratefully. Because everything created by God is good; it is not to be rejected but to be accepted gratefully. For it is made holy by God's word and by prayer.

If we can filter out the propaganda here, the author is warning against those who are over-keen on asceticism, especially those who advocate celibacy and selective approaches to food (such as vegetarianism, for example). 'We are not fanatics' would appear to be his slogan for dealing with the outside world.

Timothy's task

6-10 If you make this known to the brothers and sisters, you will be a good servant of Christ Jesus, nourished by the words of the faith and of the correct teaching which you have followed; but reject the profane stories of old women. Train yourself for godliness; for physical training is of little use, whereas godliness is useful for everything, since it holds the promise of life now *and* life to come. The saying is reliable and worthy to be accepted by all. For that is the point of our labour and struggle, that our hope is in the Living God, who is Saviour of all people, especially of those who do believe.

> This tells Timothy, in the most general terms, what he is to do. Timothy is described here as a 'servant' or 'deacon', which may suggest that the word has not yet taken on a precise hierarchical sense. The reader will notice that the final sentence is grist to the mill of those who cannot believe in a God who condemns all unbelievers, simply because of being unbelievers; for this author, God is the Saviour of all people.
>
> We notice a third example of the expression, the 'saying is reliable'.

Timothy the teacher

11-16 Insist on these things, and teach them. Let no one show contempt for your youthfulness; instead, become a model for believers, in word, in behaviour, in love, in faith, in all propriety. While I am coming, pay attention to reading, and exhortation, and teaching. Never neglect the gift of grace which was given you through prophecy, along with the laying-on of hands of the council of elders. Put these things into practice; be [immersed] in them, that your progress may be evident to all. Be attentive to yourself and to your teaching; remain steadfast in them. For if you do this, you will save both yourself and those who hear you.

> This is how the Christian teacher is to operate; if the letter is not by Paul, the instruction has been given a veil of personal detail to cover the fiction. Regardless of whether or not Paul wrote it, however, it could still be an instruction to teachers today.

Domestic relations in the Church

5 1-22 Don't strike an older man; instead, encourage him as your father. Treat younger men like your brothers, older women like your mother, younger women as your sisters – in all purity.

Widows: honour those who are genuinely widows; but if a widow has children or grandchildren, let them first learn to act piously towards their own household, and to make a return to their forebears. For this is pleasing to God. The genuine widow, however, who has been left on her own, has placed her hope in God, and sticks at her intercessions and prayers night and day – but the one who lives a life of self-indulgence is already dead. Give them this command, that they should be irreproachable; but if someone does not take care of their own people, and particularly of their own family, they have denied the faith and are worse than an unbeliever.

A person should not be registered as a widow under the age of sixty, and [only] married once; she should have a reputation for good works; it is conditional upon her having brought up children, having given hospitality to strangers, having washed the feet of the saints, having come to the aid of those in trouble, and devoted herself to every good work. Don't accept younger widows; for whenever sensuality turns them against Christ, they want to get married, and they come under condemnation because of abandoning their first commitment. At the same time they are lazy, and they go round [people's] houses; and it's not just that they are lazy – but they are also gossips and busybodies, and they talk about things that they should not.

So I want *younger women* to get married, to have children, to manage their household, to give the adversary no pretext for abuse. For already some have turned aside to follow Satan. If some woman believer has widows [in her family] she should look after them, and not let the Church be burdened, so that the Church may look after the real widows.

Elders who show themselves good leaders are to be accounted worthy of double salary, especially those who work at preaching and teaching. For Scripture says, 'You shall not muzzle the threshing ox' and 'The worker is worthy of his hire'. Don't accept an accusation against an elder, unless it is 'on the word of two or three witnesses'. Reprimand those who sin publicly, so that the others may show wariness. I solemnly charge you, by God and Christ Jesus and the chosen angels, that you observe these things without prejudice, doing nothing in a spirit of partiality. Don't be in a hurry to lay hands on [or: 'ordain'] anyone, and don't take part in other people's sins. Keep yourself pure.

> The regulations dealing with how various sectors in the Church should treat each other, and the criteria for being enrolled as a widow, are now almost beyond our reach. For example, Timothy has to be warned not to hit an older man (but presumably *could* strike a younger man!), and 'not to be in a hurry to lay hands on anyone' (but presumably might if he does it after a pause for reflection), whereas we live in an age that is less at ease with corporal punishment. The author's animadversions on 'merry widows', and his sense that they should 'marry, have children, and run the household' do not today find a ready reception, even though they could be read as stressing the importance of the woman's role in Church and society.
>
> The word for 'elder' has turned into the English word 'priest'; and the instruction about not accepting accusations against them, except where there are two or three witnesses, has posed problems in our day.
>
> All that having been said, a society where everyone knows their part and plays it, not out of compulsion, but enthusiastically, because that is what they want to do, can be a happier place than many that we see today.

Some instructions, with no particular theme

5 ²³-6 ²ᵃ Stop drinking water, but make use of a little wine, for your stomach's sake, and your frequent attacks of weakness.

Some people's sins are known to all, going ahead of them to judgement; while others they follow. In just the same way, good deeds are known to all, and those that are otherwise cannot be indefinitely suppressed.

Those who are slaves under the yoke, let them regard their own masters as worthy of all honour, so that God's name and teaching should not be blasphemed. But those who have masters who are believers should not despise them because they are fellow Christians; but they should be all the more enslaved to them because they are believers and beloved, those who devote themselves to good service.

The material seems less well organised at this point, a pseudo-medical injunction, which probably does not contradict the criterion for 'overseers' that we saw in 3:3 – that had to do with **addiction** to wine! Then comes a general comment about people's deeds becoming known (whether it refers to elders or to the congregation as a whole is not clear). Finally, there are instructions to slaves who are, frankly, told not to get above themselves if they belong to a Christian master. Again, we no longer belong in a world where the institution of slavery can go unquestioned, and we struggle to think our way into such a world. Our author is undoubtedly somewhat conservative in his social attitudes – but he is also well aware of the need to make Christianity acceptable to his contemporaries.

A collection of teachings

2b-19 Teach and exhort these things. If someone teaches a different doctrine, and if they do not agree with the health-giving words of our Lord Jesus Christ, and the teaching that goes along with godliness, they are conceited, knowing nothing. They have a sick craving for controversies and verbal squabbles, from which come envy, strife, blasphemies, wicked suspicions, and the mutual friction of people whose morals are corrupted and deprived of the truth, because they suppose that godliness is a way to make money.

Now [it is true] that godliness, with self-sufficiency, is enormously profitable, for

'we brought nothing into the world,
because neither can we take anything out of it.
If we have food and covering,
we shall be satisfied with these.'

But those who wish to be wealthy fall into the tempting trap of many senseless and harmful desires, which plunge people into death and destruction. For the root of all evils is the love of money. Some people have lusted for money and wandered away from the truth, and have been shot through with many pains.

But you, O man of God, flee from these things.
Look for righteousness, godliness, faith,
love, fortitude, gentleness.
Play the great game of faith;
take hold of the everlasting life to which you have been called,
and make the great acknowledgement before many witnesses.

I charge you, before the God who gives life to all things, and before Christ Jesus, who bore testimony under Pontius Pilate to the great acknowledgement, to keep

the commandment spotless and without reproach until the appearance of our Lord
Jesus Christ, which

> he will show at his own proper time [– he who is]
> the blessed and sole Sovereign
> the King of all who reign as kings
> the Lord of all who rule as lords,
> the One who alone has immortality,
> dwelling in unapproachable light,
> which no human has seen or is able to see,
> to whom be honour and eternal power. Amen.

Impress upon the wealthy in the present age not to think haughty thoughts, nor to
set their hopes on the uncertainty of riches. Instead, [they should have their hopes
set on] God, who provides us with everything richly for our enjoyment; they
should be doing good, rich in good deeds, generous, ready to share, laying up for
themselves a good foundation for the future, that they may take hold of what is
really life.

> One major problem that the author sees is that of wealth, and in
> this respect, 1 Timothy may have much to say to a consumerist and
> materialist society that appears to have lost its way.
>
> The 'great acknowledgement' mentioned above is something that
> Timothy has to do, both as Church leader and as Christian; it is also
> something that Jesus has already done. What precisely the author
> has in mind is not absolutely clear, but it is at least 'standing up to
> be counted' and telling the truth, no matter how risky.
>
> Are we called to make this 'acknowledgement' or 'confession'?

Concluding greetings

20, 21 O Timothy, keep what has been entrusted; turn aside from profane and empty talk
and the contradictions of what is falsely called knowledge, which some people have
professed, and have gone wide of the mark of faith.

Grace be with you.

> This is not quite the conclusion that we should expect from what
> we know of other Pauline letters; there are, for example, no
> greetings to or from anyone but Timothy. On the other hand, this
> letter is only written to Timothy. If we knew more about the situation
> that the author has in mind, we should be able to comment more
> exactly on what he is really saying.

The Second Letter to Timothy

Introduction

This differs in many ways from 1 Timothy, though some of the issues remain the same. It is much more personal, and far more names are mentioned. It can also be described as Paul's 'last will and testament', and for some scholars this is the most likely of the three 'Pastoral Letters' actually to have come from Paul's hand. It has far more echoes of other Pauline letters than we find in 1 Timothy or Titus.

Opening greetings

1 [1, 2] Paul, an apostle of Christ Jesus through the will of God, with a view to the promise of life which is in Christ Jesus, to [my] beloved child Timothy, grace, mercy and peace from God the Father and Christ Jesus our Lord.

> As in the opening of 1 Timothy, the author has inserted 'mercy' between the standard Pauline pair of 'grace' and 'peace'. Otherwise this is a characteristic Pauline introduction.

Thanksgiving and overture

[3-14] I give thanks to God, whom I worship, following my ancestors, with a clear conscience, when I make unceasing remembrance of you in my prayers, night and day, [because] I long to see you, in order to be filled with joy when I receive a reminder of your unfeigned faith, which dwelt first in your grandmother Lois and your mother Eunice, and (I am persuaded) also in you. For this reason I am reminding you to rekindle God's gift of grace, which is in you through the laying-on of my hands. For God did not give us a spirit of cowardice, but a spirit of power and love and of self-discipline. Don't, therefore, be ashamed of witnessing to our Lord, nor of me, his prisoner. Instead, join [with me/us] in suffering for the gospel, under the power of God,

> who saved us
> and called us with a holy calling
> not because of our works
> but because of his own purpose and grace
> which was given us in Christ Jesus
> before the eternal ages and has now appeared
> through the appearance of our Saviour Christ Jesus,
> who has destroyed death
> and brought life and immortality to light through the gospel

for which I was appointed herald, apostle and teacher. That is also the reason that I am suffering these things. But I'm not embarrassed, because I know in whom I have put my trust; and I am persuaded that he has the power to preserve my deposit for that day. You have a model of healthy words which you heard from me in the faith and the love [that is] in Christ Jesus. Keep the noble trust through the Holy Spirit who dwells in us.

> The thanksgiving is always a part of a Pauline letter, but (in keeping with the rest of this letter) this one is very personal, with its reference to Lois and Eunice. If Paul is writing shortly before his execution in the mid-60s AD, then that is just about enough time for Timothy to be a third-generation Christian. As in 1 Timothy, there is a relative clause introducing a reference to the 'Saviour', and to Paul's 'appointment' (as 'herald, apostle and teacher'; see 1 Timothy 1:1; 2:7).

Personal details: traitors and helpers

[15-18] You know that all those in Asia turned their backs on me, among whom were Phygelos and Hermogenes; may the Lord grant mercy to the house of Onesiphorus, because

he frequently refreshed me, and was not embarrassed by my imprisonment; but when he got to Rome he promptly sought me out and found me. May the Lord grant him to find mercy from the Lord on that day; and you know better [than I do] what great services he rendered in Ephesus.

> We know nothing about any of these names; but they have a ring about them, and it is hard to see why a forger would have included them.

Advice to a young minister

2 1-7   But you, my child, be empowered by the grace that is in Christ Jesus, and the things that you have heard from me before many witnesses, entrust them to reliable people, who will be competent to teach others. Take your share of suffering hardship, like a good soldier of Christ Jesus. No one who is on active service gets entangled in civilian pursuits, in order to satisfy the one who recruited him. But if someone competes in a race, they don't get the gold medal unless they have competed in accordance with the rules. The labouring farmer should be the first to have a share in the crop. Think what I am saying; for the Lord will give you insight in every respect.

> Timothy might, after all, be very young indeed, perhaps a teenager, who is finding his vocation difficult, and not easily able to grasp Paul's teaching. Here Paul offers three metaphors, from soldiering, sports and farming, each with a slightly different point: Timothy should focus on what he is doing, operate according to the rules, and then expect to get his reward.

The message: Christ is all

8-13   Remember Jesus Christ who was raised from the dead, of the seed of David, according to my gospel because of which I am suffering evil, even imprisonment like a criminal – but God's word can't be locked up. Therefore I endure everything on account of the elect, that they too may gain salvation that is in Christ Jesus, along with eternal glory. The saying is sure:

> For if we have died with him, we shall also live with him.
> If we endure, we shall also reign with him.
> If we disown [him], he will also disown us.
> If we are faithless, he remains faithful.
> For he cannot disown himself.

> This is a kind of summary of the author's message. Timothy must concentrate on Christ and, as always with Paul, above all on Christ's death and Resurrection, and the need for Christians to belong to that mystery and not to try to evade its uncomfortable consequences.

Coping with false teachers

14-26 Remember these things as you adjure [people] before God not to go in for verbal quibbles, which serve no useful purpose, [but only] to destroy those who hear them. Be eager to present yourself to God as tried and tested, a worker with nothing to be ashamed of, who cuts a straight path for the word of truth. But avoid godless and empty chatterings, for they will make ever-greater advances in impiety, and their word will devour like cancer [or: eat its way like gangrene]. Among these are Hymenaeus and Philetus, who have gone astray with regard to the truth, claiming that the Resurrection has already taken place; and they are overturning some people's faith. But God's solid foundation stands firm, and it has this seal, 'The Lord knows those who are his' and 'Let them keep away from wickedness, all those who name the Lord's name'. In a great house, there are not only gold and silver vessels; there are also vessels of wood and of earthenware; and some are for honourable use, others for dishonourable use. So if people cleanse themselves from these things, they will be a vessel for honourable use, sanctified, useful to the master, prepared for every [kind of] good work.

Avoid youthful desires; make a thing of righteousness, faith, love, peace, along with those who call upon the Lord out of a pure heart. Discourage stupid and uneducated speculations; be aware that they breed quarrels. But the Lord's slaves must not quarrel; they should be gentle to all, good at teaching, forbearing, gently correcting opponents. It might perhaps be the case that God will give them a change of heart, leading to knowledge of the truth, and they may come to their senses and escape the devil's trap, those who have been held captive by him to perform his will.

> More than anything else, the author is concerned to discourage false teaching; he is painfully aware of the damage it can do, and uses an alarming medical metaphor for it: cancer (or perhaps 'gangrene'). He uses three other metaphors here, that of a forester, who 'cuts a straight path', that of earthenware vessels, also used in 2 Corinthians 4:7 (and see also Romans 9:21), and (an old Pauline favourite), that of a building or 'great house' for the Church (see especially 1 Corinthians 3:9-17). All three images point to the function of a Church leader to ensure that orthodoxy is preserved.
>
> The challenge for our day may be to accept this challenge, while avoiding the dead hand and repellent tedium that the word 'orthodoxy' can sometimes project.
>
> For a positive understanding of orthodoxy, however, the reader is recommended to read G. K. Chesterton's book of that title, which has still much to say to us today.

Problems at the end-time

3 1-9 Know this, that in the last days difficult times will be threatening. For people will appear who are lovers of self and lovers of money, braggarts and arrogant blasphemers who disobey their parents, ungrateful and unholy, unloving and implacable, slanderers and dissolute, untamed, unloving-of-the-good, traitors and reckless, conceited and loving pleasure rather than God, people who have the appearance of piety, but

have refused its reality. These too you should avoid. For from them come those who worm their way into households and captivate silly women who are overwhelmed by their sins, who are led by desires of various kinds, who are always attending lessons, but never able to come to a knowledge of the truth. Just as Jannes and Jambres defied Moses, so these men defy the truth; they are people depraved in mind and unqualified with regard to the faith. But they will not advance any further; for their mindlessness will be evident to all, just like that of [Jannes and Jambres].

It is hard to be sure of the precise problems that the author has in mind here, but they have three aspects: moral failings, resistance to orthodoxy, and an attraction to the women members of the Church, perhaps especially those who want to study their faith in greater depth. Our author would not be the first man, nor the last, to deprecate the study of theology by women; but his problems and ours are not necessarily identical, and for us today what is of interest is the general principle rather than its particular applications.

On surviving the difficulties as Paul did

10-17 You, however, have carefully followed my teaching, my way of life, the tendency of my thought, my faith, patience, love, endurance, and the persecutions and sufferings that came my way in Antioch, Iconium and Lystra. I endured these persecutions, and from them the Lord delivered me. All those who want to live a godly life in Christ Jesus will be persecuted. Wicked people and charlatans will go from bad to worse, deluding and deluded. You must stick with what you have learnt and been convinced of, knowing the people from whom you learnt it. Because since you were a child you have known the sacred scriptures, which have the ability to make you wise on the way to salvation through faith in Christ Jesus. All Scripture is breathed-by-God, and useful for teaching, for refutation, for improvement, for training, that the man of God may be proficient, prepared for every good work.

If it were Paul who is writing, facing the fact of his imminent death, then it would hardly be surprising if he gave Timothy a tip or two about coping with the difficulties that lie ahead. Nor would it astonish us if he were to point to his own example as something to follow (compare 1 Corinthians 4:16; 11:1; Philippians 3:17; 1 Thessalonians 1:6).

The author's emphasis on the importance of Scripture is also quite characteristic of Paul, of course; and it would be quite normal for him to offer the Old Testament to Timothy as a way out of any difficulties.

The phrase 'every good work' can sound a bit jarring to those who think that Paul has no place for 'works' in his map of salvation, but see 2 Corinthians 9:8, and, in the Pastorals, see 1 Timothy 6:18; 2 Timothy 2:21; Titus 1:16; 3:1. Though everything is God's gift, Paul is well aware that we have to respond, by 'presenting our bodies to God as instruments of righteousness' or (in a frequent metaphor), 'running the race' (see Philippians 3:12-14; 1 Corinthians 9:24-27).

Urgent instructions to Timothy from the dying Paul

4 [1-8] I adjure you, before God and before Christ Jesus, who is going to come to judge the living and the dead, and by his manifestation and by his kingdom: proclaim the word; be ready, whether it is convenient or inconvenient; admonish, rebuke, console, in all patience and teaching. For a time will come when they will not put up with healthy teaching; instead, they will pile up teachers for themselves, titillating their ears, and turning their ears away from the truth, while directing them towards fables. But you must stay sober in every respect, bear hardship patiently, do the job of an evangelist, fulfil your service.

As for me, I am being offered up, and the time for my death has come. I have played the great game; I have completed the race; I have kept the faith. For the future, the gold medal of righteousness is reserved for me, which the Lord, the Righteous Judge, will award me on that day; and not just me, but all those who have loved his appearing.

> This is a stirring passage; it has an urgency about it, and an eye for what really matters. The author knows that death is almost upon him, and the tone of these lines makes a literary fiction hard to imagine; he wants his addressee to be clear about the task that lies before him, as Timothy picks up the baton that Paul is passing to him.
>
> Not for the first time, he uses a metaphor from athletics, to indicate that he is almost there, and to affirm his confidence in God and in Christ (who is clearly the 'Lord' who is mentioned in the final lines). The word for 'death' derives from a nautical metaphor, and it refers to the activity of untying the ropes and casting off.
>
> The notion of 'healthy' teaching is a frequent one in the Pastorals: see 1 Timothy 1:10; 6:3; 2 Timothy 1:13; Titus 1:9; 2:1, 2.

The author's personal situation

[9-15] Make an effort to come quickly to me. For Demas has abandoned me; he loved the present world and went off to Thessalonica, Crescens to Galatia, Titus to Dalmatia. Luke is the only one with me. Pick up Mark and bring him with you, for he is useful to me for the ministry. Tychicus I have sent to Ephesus. When you come, bring the cloak which I left in Troas, at Carpus's house, and the scrolls, especially the parchments. Alexander the coppersmith did me great harm. The Lord will repay him according to his deeds. Watch out for him – for he is utterly opposed to our teaching.

> There are several names here; none of them can be identified with any certainty. Though some of the names appear in other Pauline letters and in Acts, we do not know if they refer to the same people. So we cannot say whether the 'Luke' and 'Mark' mentioned here have anything to do with the Gospels that bear those names. The reader gains a sense of a Church on the move, which certainly squares with both Acts and the indisputably genuine Paulines.

The apostle is never utterly abandoned

[16-18] In my first defence, no one was at my side; they *all* abandoned me. May it not be put down to their account. But the Lord stood by me and empowered me, that the

preaching might be fulfilled through me, and that all the Gentiles might hear; and I was delivered from the lion's mouth. The Lord will deliver me from every evil deed, and will save me for his heavenly kingdom. To him be the glory for ever and ever. Amen.

> We cannot say what this 'first defence' might have been; but the author's faith comes powerfully through the text. There is nothing that can finally dismay him – or us.

Final salutations

19-22 Greet Prisca and Aquila, and the house of Onesiphorus. Erastus stayed in Corinth, and I left Trophimus at Miletus – he was sick. Make an effort to come before winter. Greetings to you from Euboulos and Pudens and Linus and Claudia, and all the brothers and sisters.

The Lord be with your spirit. Grace be with you.

> We know some of these names, notably Prisca and Aquila, and Erastus, but not others (except that Onesiphorus appears at 1:16). There is a profound longing for Timothy to come soon; on the whole, winter was not propitious for travelling around the Mediterranean basin: storms at sea and snow on the mountains made marine and land journeys equally problematic.

The Letter to Titus

Introduction

Like 1 and 2 Timothy, Titus is regarded by most scholars as not being by Paul (although see Luke Timothy Johnson's commentary in the Anchor Bible series for a vigorous presentation of the case for Pauline authorship).

Opening greetings

1 ¹⁻⁴ Paul, a slave of God, and an apostle of Jesus Christ, according to the faith of God's elect, and according to the knowledge of the truth in accordance with godliness, in the hope of eternal life, which God, who is free of all deceit, promised before the eternal ages, and has revealed his word in his own proper time by the preaching with which I was entrusted by the command of our Saviour God, to Titus, true child according to the common faith, grace and peace from God the Father and Christ Jesus our Saviour.

> This is a single sentence, longer and more complex than the opening greetings in the other Pastoral Letters. The word 'Saviour' is used twice in this passage, once of God and the second time of Christ Jesus. 'Faith' is a matter of content rather than commitment. It also emphasises Paul's own commission, introduced, as elsewhere in the two letters to Timothy, by a relative clause.

The job of an 'overseer', in Crete and elsewhere

5-9 This was the reason that I left you in Crete, for you to put right what remains, and set up elders in individual cities, as I myself commanded you, provided someone is irreproachable, the husband of only one wife, who has children who are of the faith, are not accused of debauchery, or rebellious. For the 'overseer' must be irreproachable as God's steward, not self-willed, not quick-tempered, nor addicted to wine, not a bully, nor fond of dishonest gain, but hospitable, loving all that is good, temperate, righteous, holy, self-controlled, holding fast to the teaching of the trustworthy message, that he may be able also to comfort with sound teaching and refute opponents.

> We notice here that 'overseer' and 'elder' are used as equivalent; and the office described here demands more or less the same qualities as the officials mentioned in 1 Timothy 3. Modern Church leaders may be alarmed at the requirement that their children should be believers, and not profligate or rebellious.

The opponents in Crete

10-16 For there are many who are rebellious, who go in for meaningless discussions, and create illusions – especially those of the Circumcision Party. These people must be silenced – they turn entire households upside down by teaching what they should not, in order to make a base profit. One of them, one of their very own prophets, said,

> 'Cretans are always liars, vicious brutes, idle gluttons.'

The testimony is true. For that reason, reprimand them severely, that they may be healthy in the faith, not paying any attention to Jewish fables and the commands of human beings who repudiate the truth. Everything is clean for those who are clean; but for those who are tainted and unbelievers, nothing is clean – their understanding and their consciences are tainted. They claim to know God, but deny it by what they do; they are detestable and intractable, and incapable of any good work.

Here it looks as though the opponents that the author has in mind are Jewish Christians, wanting to observe the dietary laws of the Old Testament. Apart from the references to Cretans, these animadversions could apply to anyone who Paul thought was going back on the freedom of the gospel. It is worth noticing, perhaps, that there is not a single church built in the name of St Paul in the whole island of Crete.

Household code

2 ¹⁻¹⁰ As for you, say the things that are appropriate for healthy teaching.

- Tell the *older men* to be sober, dignified, healthy in faith, love and perseverance.

- Tell the *older women*, likewise, to be sober in their behaviour, not slanderers, nor addicted to lots of wine; they are to teach what is noble and good,

- so that they may encourage the *young women* to love their husbands; they should love their children, be temperate, pure, good household managers, and submissive to their own husbands – so that people don't blaspheme God's word.

- Encourage the *young men* likewise to be temperate in every respect; offer yourself as a model of good works, and integrity in doctrine, reverence, and a sound preaching that is beyond reproach, so that the opponent may be put to shame, having nothing dreadful to say of us.

- Tell *slaves* to be submissive to their own masters in every respect, to be obliging rather than argumentative, not misappropriating [property], but showing all good faith, so that they make the teaching of our Saviour God attractive in every way.

As in other New Testament documents, we have here a household code, perhaps rather starker than the one in Ephesians, which was subversively suffused with love. This one, perhaps reflecting a situation wherein it seemed important to underplay the radical challenge of Christianity, seems much more inclined to go along with the status quo; slaves, for example, are told to submit to their 'masters'; the word 'Lord', which tends in other household codes to undermine the master-slave relationship, is, perhaps significantly, not used here. The passage about the 'young women' (if that is to whom it refers; grammatically, it could be a reversion to the older women) may give the clue, 'so that people don't blaspheme God's word'. Throughout its history, Christianity has had to walk uneasily between fidelity to its entirely radical message and making itself attractive to a majority that is at ease with something a little more comfortable.

Like Paul, Titus is to be fairly up-front about offering himself as an example. (The syntax of the relevant sentence is puzzling, but the meaning is clear.)

A people for Christ

11-15 For the saving grace of God has appeared to all people, correcting us, so that with moderation we may renounce ungodliness and worldly desires, and live soberly, justly and reverently in the present age, waiting for the blessed hope [which is] the appearance of the glory of our great God and Saviour Jesus Christ, who gave himself for us, in order to ransom us from [the slavery of] all iniquity, and purify for himself a chosen people, fanatical about good works. Say these things, urge them, and make the reprimands with all authority.

Let no one despise you.

> There is a coherence between doctrine and ethics; if the Church is to be a place where Christ can appear, then Church leaders need to have a hand on the rudder, to make sure that the appropriate patterns of behaviour are operative, and that there are no signs of 'ungodliness' and 'worldly behaviour', and every indication of being a 'chosen people, keen on good works'. But notice that this is not a reversion to 'justification by works'; it is simply a response to the fact that 'Jesus gave himself for us in order to ransom us'.
>
> The phrase 'the glory of our great God and Saviour Jesus Christ' is a slightly more natural reading than the alternative, which would translate 'the glory of the great God and of our Saviour Jesus Christ'. But to call Jesus 'God' is not an impossibly enormous step forward from Paul's own Christology.

Relations with authority

3 ¹,² Remind them to be submissive to rulers and authorities, to be obedient, ready for every good work, to slander nobody, to be peaceable, considerate, showing gentleness to all human beings.

> Once again, we see the author's concern for the infant Church (in Crete) not to wear so radical a hat that it alienates the authorities or public opinion. There are some situations in which it is a Christian's duty to challenge fearlessly. In other circumstances it may be more appropriate to keep one's head down.

Why treat outsiders decently?

3-11 For we also were once foolish, disobedient, deluded, enslaved to different kinds of desires and passions, spending our lives in malice and spite, hateful and loathing one another,

'but when the kindness and love of humankind of our Saviour God made its appearance,
not in consequence of works of righteousness which we have done,
but in accordance with his mercy,
he saved us through the washing of rebirth
and the renewal of the Holy Spirit
which he poured richly upon us,
through Jesus Christ our Saviour,
so that having been made righteous by his grace,
we might become heirs in accordance with [our] hope of eternal life.

The saying is reliable; and with regard to this, I want to insist with you, that those who have come to faith in God should take care to be outstanding in good works; for these are good and beneficial to human beings. But avoid foolish speculations and genealogies and controversies and wrangles about the law. For they are useless and lead nowhere. Drive out a person who is causing divisions, after a first and a second warning; know that such a person is perverted, and sins because he is self-condemned.

> This passage, couched in entirely Pauline terms, explains the previous one, on having good relations with the authorities and other non-Christians. The argument is that Christians have no cause to look down on their non-Christian neighbours, because they were in the same boat until God intervened in Christ, through no merit of theirs. This puts the onus on Christians to seek to benefit humanity, and to avoid the foolish factionalism to which we sometimes give ourselves.
>
> The word translated as 'kindness' would, it may be useful to recall, have sounded in Greek something like 'Christ-ness'.

Final instructions

12-15 When I send Artemas or Tychicus to you, make an effort to come to me at Nicopolis; for it is there that I have decided to spend the winter. Send Zenas the lawyer and Apollos on their way with alacrity, so that nothing may be lacking to them. And let our people also learn to be outstanding in good works, to relieve essential needs, that they may not be unproductive.

All those who are with me greet you. Greet those who love us in faith. Grace be with you all.

> The letter ends, as Pauline letters so often do, with various personal greetings and instructions; two of the four names here are unknown to us, nor do we know which Nicopolis this might be (it is the only time when the place is mentioned in the entire New Testament). Once again the Christians are exhorted to good works, apparently in favour of non-Christians.

The Letter to Philemon

Introduction

This is a 'charming postcard' of a letter; there is no doubt about it having been written by Paul, though the reader will need to decide what is Onesimus's situation: Is he (as most people have assumed) a runaway slave? Or is he in some ways at odds with his master? Or did Philemon send Onesimus to look after Paul in prison, as some scholars have suggested recently? Or, as some argue, is the letter really addressed to Archippus? (See Colossians 4:9, 17 in support of this theory.)

Depending on your decision about that, you may want to consider the claim of some scholars that Paul here writes in a bullying, manipulative way, leaving Philemon no choice about his response.

Why do you think Paul does not here launch an attack on the institution of slavery?

Opening greetings (to a community, not an individual)

1-3 Paul, a prisoner of Christ Jesus, and Timothy our fellow Christian, to our beloved Philemon, our co-worker, and to Apphia our sister and Archippus our fellow campaigner, and to the church in your house, grace to you all and peace, from God our Father and the Lord Jesus Christ.

> Clearly we should be mistaken in supposing that this is just a private letter; it has two authors, and is addressed to Philemon, Apphia (Mrs Philemon?), Archippus, and an entire church; and the 'you' to whom the greetings are addressed is unmistakably plural, but the 'your' in the phrase 'the church in your house' is singular, and it follows the name of Archippus. Archippus is mentioned in Colossians 4:17 and Onesimus in Colossians 4:9. There are clear connections between the two letters.

Thanksgiving

4-7 I give thanks to my God, all the time making mention of you in my prayers, when I hear of your love and your faith which you have in the Lord Jesus and towards all the saints, so that the solidarity of your faith may become operative, in the knowledge of all that is good in us, [turning us] to Christ. For I have had much joy and comfort through your love; because the hearts of the saints have been refreshed through you, my brother.

> The thanksgiving is conventionally the second part of a letter in the ancient world, and, except in Galatians, Paul always followed the convention. That having been said, Paul is particularly grateful for some loving attention that Philemon (or Archippus) has shown, which is variously characterised as 'joy', 'comfort', and (a phrase that we shall meet again) 'refreshing the hearts of the saints'.

Paul's request – Part I (but what is he asking for?)

8-14 Therefore, although I have full authority to command you to do what is your duty, because of [my] love, I [would] rather ask you, being who I am, Paul, an old man, and now a prisoner of Christ Jesus. I am asking you about my child, whom I have fathered in prison, Onesimus, the one who was once Useless to you, but is now Useful to both you and me, whom I am sending you, that is my heart, whom I should have liked to keep for myself, so that in your place he might serve me in my gospel-prison; but without your consent I didn't want to do anything, so that your good deed should not be done under compulsion, but willingly.

> The standard interpretation of the request in Philemon has been that Paul is asking the slave-owner to be nice to the returned runaway slave, and not punish him as he deserves. An alternative reading is to understand it as the rather more radical demand, that Onesimus be set free and returned to Paul.
>
> It is clear that Paul wants something, and that he is applying some pressure to get it. He stresses that he is 'an old man and a prisoner',

in a bid for sympathy. Another tactic is some witty wordplay. The slave's name is Onesimus, given emphasis by the position it has in the sentence. Now the name means 'profitable', and right next to it, Paul places two adjectives to refer to 'profitable', namely 'useless' and 'useful', whose significance we have tried to emphasise by the use of capitals. It does not stop there, however; for the sound of the two words in Greek would have suggested something like 'Christ-less', and 'Christ-well'. Paul is using a number of stratagems, including puns and a scarcely veiled reference to his authority. Another wordplay is involved in calling Onesimus 'my heart'; Paul has already said that Philemon (or Archippus) 'refreshes the hearts of the saints'; now Paul wants a piece of the action.

The request – Part II

15-20 For perhaps this was the reason that he was separated from you for a while, in order that you might have him back for all eternity, no longer as a slave, but as [something] more than a slave, a much-loved fellow Christian, beloved especially by me, and how much more by you, both in the flesh and in the Lord, So, if you regard me as a partner, accept him as though it were me. But *if* he has done you some wrong, owes you anything, put it down to my account. I, PAUL, AM WRITING IN MY OWN HAND, I SHALL REPAY. (I don't want to be telling you that you owe yourself to me!)

Yes, my brother, let me have this profit in the Lord. Refresh my heart in Christ.

What precisely does Paul want? It is impossible to be sure from what he writes whether he wants Onesimus's freedom so that he can return to be Paul's collaborator, or whether it is simply a matter of the slave-owner not exacting the draconian penalty to which he was entitled. One might in any case suppose that after this has been read out to the Church it would be extremely difficult for Philemon/Archippus not to give Onesimus his freedom. The word that we have translated as 'partner' is from the *koinonia* root, meaning union, communion, fellowship, solidarity, and so on. When Paul says 'if he has done you some wrong' he might mean not 'if (as you suggest)', but 'given that he has done you some wrong (as you and I are both well aware)'; so Onesimus has not necessarily robbed his boss.

There are two more wordplays here: 'let me have this profit' is a play on Onesimus's name, and 'refresh my heart in Christ' is the third use in the letter of this idea of 'refreshing', which was first employed for what Philemon/Archippus does for the saints. It is clearly part of Paul's tactics here.

Concluding remarks

21-25 I am writing to you, confident in your obedience, knowing that you will do even more than what I say. But at the same time, prepare a guest room for me; for I am hoping that through your prayers I shall be given to you as a free gift.

Epaphras my fellow prisoner sends greetings in Christ Jesus, [as do] Mark, Aristarchus, Demas and Luke, my fellow workers.

The grace of the Lord Jesus Christ be with the spirit of you all.

Paul ends the letter with some hidden menace, perhaps. He is asking for obedience (and then some), but he has not precisely formulated a command. He is also hinting that he may be with them soon ('prepare a guest room for me'), so despite the imprisonment they may need to get something done.

'Given . . . as a free gift'. This is how God always gives and what is expected of the slave-owners.

Some readers think that Paul is not 'playing fair' here.

The Letter to the Hebrews

Introduction

Hebrews is a letter that many readers tend to skip, perhaps fearful of what seems like rather difficult argumentation, and hoping to find 'real Christianity' and 'less of that dogmatic stuff' elsewhere in the New Testament; but hold your horses, and take a good look at Hebrews. Try to think of it as telling its readers (and we can no longer confidently say who they originally were) that 'Jesus is the real thing'. It is not, we must admit, always easy to see precisely where the argument is going, and at times the Greek is a little awkward; at those places we have tried to preserve the awkwardness in the English. Stay with it, however, and persistence will be rewarded.

Introduction

1 [1, 2]   God, who spoke bit by bit, and in many guises, of old to [our] ancestors through the prophets, in these last days has spoken to us in [his] Son, whom he made heir of everything, through whom he also created the worlds.

> This is an astonishing beginning, elegantly written, and carefully blending:
>
> - the continuity of the news about Jesus with what God has always been doing, as recounted in Scripture;
> - an assertion of the discontinuity: there is something new and different about Jesus (who has yet to be mentioned by name – but the hearers or readers instantly know who the author is talking about);
> - three points about Jesus – that he is Son, that he is heir, and that the 'ages' or 'worlds' were created through him. These are lofty claims.
>
> Throughout this epistle, the author argues on the basis of Old Testament texts; since they are more frequent, and more central to his argument even than Paul's quotations of Scripture, I have foot-noted the references. The reader is advised to look them up.

The Son's difference and superiority proved from Scripture

[3-14]   [The Son is] the radiance of the glory, and an exact representation of [God's] nature.

[The Son] bears everything by his all-powerful word, bringing about a purification from sins. [The Son] sat down on the right of the Majesty on high. [The Son] became as much superior to the angels as the name which he had inherited was more excellent [than theirs]. For to which of the angels did he ever say,

> 'You are my Son, I have begotten you today'?[56]

And again:

> 'I shall be a father to him; and he will be a son to me.'[57]

And again (when he introduces the first-born into the world), he says:

> 'And let all the angels of God worship him.'[58]

And with regard to the angels he says,

> 'The one who makes his angels spirits
> and his servants a flame of fire.'[59]

---

56. Psalm 2:7
57. 2 Samuel 7:14
58. Psalm 97:7
59. Psalm 104:4

Whereas with regard to the Son [he says]:

'Your throne, O God, for ever and ever
and the staff of righteousness is the staff of your kingdom.
You loved righteousness and hated lawlessness.
Because of that, God (your God) has anointed you
with an oil of exultation over and above your fellows.'[60]

And:

'You in the beginning, Lord, founded the earth,
and the work of your hands are the heavens.
They will be destroyed, but you will remain
and they shall all grow old like a garment
and like a cloak you will roll them up,
and like a garment they shall also be changed,
while you are the same, and your years shall not fail.'[61]

To which of the angels did he ever say,

'Sit on my right, until I make your enemies a footstool for your feet'?[62]

Are they not all ministering spirits, missioned for service, on account of those who are about to inherit salvation?

> A major challenge for the Christians of that first century (indeed a major challenge for those of the present century) is that of getting right the language they (and we) use about Jesus. Clearly Jesus is human; equally clearly, the language appropriate to humans falls short of the full reality of Jesus. So in this passage the author of our letter starts by insisting on the closeness of his relationship to God (without having yet mentioned the name of Jesus): he is close to God ('the radiance of the Glory' and even 'Your throne, O God, for ever and ever' is addressed to the Son) but not quite identical, because the phrase translated as 'an exact representation' translates the word that the Greeks used for the mark made by a signet-ring in sealing wax. As one of my teachers used to say, 'If you want to know what God is like, look at Jesus.'
>
> Now if Jesus is close to God, but different from God, what about 'angel' as a category to describe him? Our author, hot in pursuit of Jesus as the 'real thing', will have none of that, and collects a series of sayings that are applied to the Messiah, and insists that they cannot be applied to angels.

A warning

2 [1-4]   For this reason, we must pay more and more attention to what [we] have heard: otherwise we might drift away. For if the message that was spoken through angels was valid, and every transgression and act of disobedience receives a just punishment, how shall we escape, if we ignore such a great salvation, which was first

---

60. Psalm 45:6, 7
61. Psalm 102:25-27
62. Psalm 110:1

spoken through the Lord, and was confirmed to us by those who heard, and [to which] God bore witness by signs and portents and distributions of the Holy Spirit according to his will?

> Warnings like this are strung out throughout the Letter to the Hebrews, underlining the urgency of getting Jesus right. Reading this passage we have the impression of a community that is in danger of losing its first fervour. Clearly they are not the first generation of Christians; but they had received confirmation of the message by 'signs and portents and gifts of the Holy Spirit'.
>
> It always seems that the New Testament clearly expects us to receive these gifts in a palpable, tangible way.

The Son superior to the angels (*continued*)

5-9 You see, it was not to angels that he subjected the world to come, about which we are speaking. Someone, somewhere, solemnly affirmed,

> 'What is the human person that you should remember him?
> Or the Son of Man that you should visit him?
> You have made him for a short time lower than the angels,
> with glory and honour you crowned him,
> you subjected everything under his feet.'[63]

You see, when it talks of 'subjecting everything', he left nothing unsubjected to him. For the moment, we do not yet see 'everything subjected to him'; what we do see is Jesus 'for a short time made lower than the angels', because of his experience of death 'crowned with glory and honour', so that by the grace of God he might taste death on behalf of all.

> Once again, by careful Scripture exegesis, and armed with the assumption that Psalm 8 applies to Jesus (who did, after all, commonly refer to himself as the Son of Man), the author shows how any subjection of Jesus 'below the angels' is purely temporary; and we can already see him 'crowned with glory and honour' in the Resurrection.
>
> This is the first time that the letter has explicitly referred to the mystery of the death and resurrection of Jesus; and, indeed, it is the first time that Jesus has been mentioned by name.

Jesus' solidarity with those for whom he came (Jesus is the 'real thing')

10-18 You see, it was appropriate for [God] (for whom and through whom everything [came into existence]) to lead many sons and daughters into glory, and to make perfect through suffering the prince of their salvation. For the one who consecrates and those who are consecrated are all from the one source. Therefore he was not embarrassed to call them brothers and sisters, saying,

---

63. Psalm 8:4-6

> 'I proclaim your name to my brothers and sisters,
> in the middle of the assembly I shall sing a hymn to you.'[64]

And again,

> 'I shall be reliant on him.'[65]

And again,

> 'Look! I and the children whom God gave me.'[66]

So since the children shared blood and flesh, he also in just the same way partook of the same, in order that through death he might nullify the one who has the power of death, namely the devil, and release those who, through fear of death, all their lives were subject to slavery. For of course he does not take on [responsibility for] angels; no – it is the offspring of Abraham [for] whom he takes on [responsibility]. Hence he had to be like his brothers and sisters in every respect, in order to make atonement for the sins of the people. For insofar as he has suffered himself, by being put to the test, he can help those who are being tested.

Does the author of the Letter to the Hebrews think that Jesus is God? To put the question in this way is to address the matter altogether too brutally. Clearly God takes the initiative, according to our author; and in some sense God is above (the source of) both Jesus and the 'brothers and sisters'. The Scripture quotations here are put on the Messiah's lips, and we are to imagine him looking up and praying or singing to God. At the same time, however, his humanity is seen as something different from ours, something that Jesus has 'taken on', because it was fitting, not because he was naturally the same as the brothers and sisters. We may put it like this: if he was not like them, he was no use to them; if he was not also different from them, he was no use to them.

Jesus is superior to Moses (Jesus is the 'real thing')

3 **1-6** So, holy brothers and sisters, sharers in the heavenly calling, reflect on Jesus, the Apostle and High Priest of our profession, because he was faithful to the one who appointed him, just like Moses, in his house. For this one was regarded as worthy of more glory than Moses, insofar as the builder of the house is more valuable than the house itself. For every house is built by somebody, but it is God who builds everything. And, while Moses was 'faithful in all his house', like a servant, to testify to the things that had been uttered, Christ was [faithful] like a son, in charge of his house. We are his house, if we hang on to our confidence, and the pride of our hope.

The author has argued that Jesus is in some ways like an angel, but superior to any angel. Now he turns to comparing Jesus with another important symbol of God's dealing with the people of God,

---

64. Psalm 22:22
65. Isaiah 8:17
66. Isaiah 8:18

namely Moses, to whom Jesus' opponents (unfavourably) and his supporters (favourably) frequently compare him.

Two rather odd titles are given to Jesus here: 'Apostle' and 'High Priest'. They are not used of Jesus in other New Testament documents, but Hebrews makes a good deal of the idea of Jesus the High Priest. The author does not make much of 'Jesus the Apostle', but, obviously, it carries the notion of 'one who is sent'. The heart of the matter here is that Jesus is even more significant than Moses.

Notice that in this passage the author turns directly to the reader ('holy . . . sharers of the heavenly calling'), and that leads into an exhortation to them, one of many in this Letter, that they should remain faithful. This is continued in the Scripture-based warning that now follows.

Another warning, based on Scripture

7-19 Therefore, as the Holy Spirit says,

'Today if [only] you would listen to his voice;
    do not harden your hearts as at the rebellion,
        in the day of testing in the desert
when your ancestors tested [me] in the examination,
        and they saw my works for forty years.
Therefore I was offended at this generation, and I said,
    "Always they are astray in heart – they do not know my ways."
So I swore in my anger: "Never shall they enter my place of rest." '[67]

Watch out, brothers and sisters: we don't want there to be in any of you an evil and unbelieving heart, to make you fall away from the living God. No – comfort one another each day until the 'Today' is called; none of you is to be hardened by sin's deceitfulness. For we have become sharers in Christ, provided that we hold fast to our first assurance, firm to the end. When it is said, 'Today if [only] you would listen to his voice; do not harden your hearts as at the rebellion' – who were the ones who heard and rebelled? Wasn't it all those who had come out of Egypt through Moses? And who were the ones he was offended at for forty years? Wasn't it those who sinned, whose corpses fell in the desert? And of whom did he 'swear that they wouldn't enter his place of rest' if not those who disobeyed? And we see that because of their unbelief they were unable to enter.

Hebrews is full of warnings, and clearly the people it is written to had, in the view of its author, rather lost their first fervour. The careful explanation of scriptural texts, making them applicable for today, is a mark of this letter, and perhaps has a good deal to teach us.

The explanation of Psalm 95 continues for some lines further, examining what it means to 'enter his place of rest'.

---

67. Psalm 95:7b-11

'Entering the place of rest'

4 [1-10]   So let's be afraid: we don't want any of you to think that you have missed out on it, while the promise to 'enter his place of rest' still remains [open]. For we were given the good news just as they were; but the word they heard did not help them, because they were not linked in faith with those who heard. For we who have faith are entering the place of rest, as he said, 'As I swore in my anger: "Never shall they enter my place of rest,"' even though the works were done from the creation of the world. For he spoke somewhere about the seventh day in this way, 'And God rested on the seventh day from all his works.'[68] And again in this one: 'Never shall they enter my place of rest.' So since the fact remains that some enter it, and because those who had previously heard the good news did not enter, because of disobedience, again he appoints a certain day, 'today', speaking through David such a long time afterwards, as has already been said, 'Today if only you would listen to his voice; do not harden your hearts.' For if Joshua had brought them into their rest, [God] would not have spoken of any subsequent 'day'. Therefore the Sabbath rest is still waiting for the People of God. For the one who has entered his place of rest has also rested from his works, just as God did from his own works [after completing the Creation].

> The argument here depends on linking a) the Sabbath rest at the end of the seven days of creation to the rest promised to the people in the desert at the end of the Exodus and b) Jesus to Joshua; these are the same name in Greek and in Hebrew, but not, alas, in English. The argument is that Joshua did not lead them into the promised rest, but Jesus has done: Jesus is the real thing, as opposed to angels, Moses, Joshua, or anyone else.

Third warning – don't miss out on the rest

[11-13]   Therefore let's be eager to enter into that place of rest – we don't want anyone to perish through disobedience, as in that example. For God's word is alive and powerful, and sharper than any two-edged sword; and it reaches as far as the point of division of soul and spirit, of joints and marrow, and it examines critically the reflections and thoughts of a heart. And nothing created is concealed before him: everything is naked and exposed to the scrutiny of the one to whom we have to give an account.

> Notice how the warning is not separate from the careful explanation of who Jesus is, but builds on all that has hitherto been established about 'rest' and its enemy, 'disobedience'. There is nothing comfortable about this, and we shiver as we recollect that a two-edged sword cuts first on the way in, with one blade, and then with the other on the way out. The word 'exposed' is an attempt to translate the image of an animal prepared for sacrifice which has had its neck broken, or possibly its throat bared for sacrifice, or perhaps its entrails opened up for inspection. We shift uncomfortably.

---

68. Genesis 2:2

Jesus the High Priest: access for all, weak like us, called by God, heard by God

4 ¹⁴**-5** ¹⁰   So since we have a great High Priest who has gone through the heavens, Jesus, the Son of God, let us hold fast to the confession. For we don't have a High Priest who is unable to sympathise with our weaknesses; [this one] has been tested just like us in every respect – apart from sin. So let us confidently approach the throne of grace, that we may receive mercy and find grace, and so be helped at the right time.

For every other high priest, taken from among human beings, is appointed to act on behalf of human beings in relation to God, to offer gifts and sacrifices for sin, able to moderate his feelings towards those who are ignorant and off the track, because he himself is subjected to weakness, and because of the weakness has to make sin-offering not only for the people but also for himself. And a man does not take the honour for himself, but [only when he is] invited by God, just as Aaron was.

So Christ did not glorify himself so as to become High Priest – it was the one who said to him, 'You are my Son – I have begotten you today,'[69] just as in another [place] it says, 'You are a priest for ever according to the order of Melchisedek.'[70] In the days of his flesh he offered prayers and entreaties to the one who could save him from death, with a loud cry and tears; and he was heard because of his piety. Although he was Son, he learnt obedience from what he suffered, and having been made perfect, he became, for all those who obey him, the source of eternal salvation, having been designated by God as High Priest according to the order of Melchisedek.

> Hebrews now starts its consideration of Jesus as High Priest. Here the letter makes several points: Jesus shares our condition (apart from sin); Jesus provides access to God; Jesus is invited by God to the high priestly task; Jesus painfully gave obedience to God. The passage ends with the double reference to 'Melchisedek', which will be taken up in Chapter 7.

Another warning

5 ¹¹**-6** ³   We have much to say about this, and it will be hard to explain, because you have become lazy listeners. You see, after all this time you ought to be teachers; instead you yourselves need someone to teach you the ABC of the most elementary level of God's message; and you have become needy for milk, and not solid food. For everyone who partakes [only] of milk has no experience of teaching about righteousness, for they are just infants. Solid food belongs to the perfect, people who through practice have their senses trained to distinguish good and evil.

So let us leave behind the first stages of Christ's word; let us fly onwards towards perfection; don't let us lay the foundation all over again, of repentance from dead works, and faith in God, and teaching about baptisms, and laying-on of hands, and resurrection from the dead, and eternal judgement. And this is what we shall do, if God permits.

---

69. Psalm 2:7
70. Psalm 110:4

This is quite stern stuff; the people the writer is addressing have not moved on as they should, and he is fearful that they are forever having to 'reinvent the wheel' as far as their spiritual growth is concerned. The contrast between 'infants' and 'initiates' or (as we have here translated it) the 'perfect' is found elsewhere in the New Testament (see, for example, Ephesians 4:13-15; Philippians 3:14, 15; 1 Corinthians 2:6; 3:1; 13:10, 11; 14:20) and may owe something to the Greek mystery religions. The Greek and Roman mystery cults were rather exclusive sects, which played an important part in feeding the religious hunger of the centuries when Christianity was developing. In that sense, they resemble the eclectic mix of rites and philosophies that today is lumped under the New Age umbrella, except that they generally operated in secret, and we cannot easily reconstruct what they did.

Yet another warning, but also some reassurance

4-12 You see, it is impossible to restore to repentance those who have once received the light, who have tasted the heavenly gift, and become sharers in the Holy Spirit, and have tasted God's lovely word, and the miracles of the age to come, and then fall back, crucifying the Son of God themselves, and making a fool of him. For land that drinks up the rain which often comes upon it, and produces a plant that is usable for those on whose account it is being farmed, receives its share of blessings from God. But when it produces thorns and thistles, it is worthless, and close to a curse; its destiny is the bonfire. But I am certain of you, my beloved ones, with regard to the higher things, and those which relate to salvation, even though we are not talking in this way. For God is not unjust enough to overlook your work, and the love that you showed for his name, with your past and present service to the saints. We want each of you to show the same enthusiasm for the realisation of your hope, right to the end. We do not want you to become lazy; [we want you] to imitate those who through their patient faith inherited the promises.

This warning is regarded by some scholars as something of a rest from the main argument; but there is no doubt about the author's seriousness. He is anxious that they don't get things wrong, and fears that they may be about to do so. On the other hand, he does not want to discourage them, so he acknowledges what they have already done, in order to stimulate them to keep going to the very end. Now he offers them the example of Jesus, their predecessor, to whom the promise was made. This is supposed to encourage them.

From Abraham (recipient of the promise) to Jesus, via Melchisedek

13-20 For God made the promise to Abraham, and since he had nothing greater to swear by, he swore by himself, saying, 'Indeed I shall bless you with a blessing, and increase you with increase.'[71] And so it was that he had the patience to obtain what he had been promised. For human beings swear by something greater than

---

71. Genesis 22:16, 17

themselves, and for them the oath [means] an end of all argument, and provides a guarantee. And so, since God wanted to demonstrate even more tellingly to the heirs of the promise that his intention was unshakable, he guaranteed it with an oath, so that through two 'unshakables' (in which it is impossible that God should tell a lie) we who have taken refuge [in him] might have a powerful reassurance that we shall lay hold of the hope that lies before us. We have this hope as a reliable and firm anchor for our soul, one that enters the inner [sanctuary], behind the curtain, where Jesus has gone in as a forerunner for us, having become a priest according to the order of Melchisedek for ever.

> This is very neatly done. The author has moved smoothly back to Jesus-as-Melchisedek (a topic that he is now about to resume) from the warning, which led into a reassurance for the readers. The reassurance was of course based on the promise to Abraham, where God swears by himself; and Abraham, of course, had a mysterious encounter with the enigmatic figure of Melchisedek. The first hearers of this letter, more in tune than we are with the story of Abraham, would not have needed to have this pointed out to them. On the other hand we are perhaps in a better position to admire his adroitness.

Priesthood I – Melchisedek

7 [1-10] For it was this 'Melchisedek, King of Salem, priest of God Most High, who met Abraham as he returned from the defeat of the kings and blessed him, to whom [Abraham] apportioned a tenth of everything';[72] first of all [his name] is translated 'King of Righteousness'. Second, he is also 'King of Salem', which is King of Peace.

He has no father, no mother, and no family tree, no beginning of his days, and no end to his life; [so] he resembles the Son of God, and remains a priest for all time.

Consider how great this man must have been, 'to whom Abraham gave a tenth', the patriarch [giving] the first-fruits! And those of the descendants of Levi who receive the priesthood have a command to take a tenth from the people in accordance with the law, to tithe their brothers and sisters, that is to say, even though they came from Abraham's loins. [Melchisedek], the one with no family tree, tithed Abraham, and blessed the one who had the promises! Beyond all dispute, it is the lesser that is blessed by the greater. In the one case, human beings who die take their 'tenths'; but in the other case, the evidence is that he is alive. And, so to say, through Abraham, Levi, who exacts tithes, is himself tithed – for he was still in his father's loins when Melchisedek met him.

> This is a gloriously simple argument, even though we may scratch our heads wondering if we can really say that Levi was in his great-grandfather's loins. Remember that we are talking about Jesus ('the real thing') and arguing that he is a High Priest 'like Melchisedek', and here the point is that Melchisedek's high priesthood is superior to that of Levi, because of the incident where Abraham is revealed as inferior to Melchisedek.

---

72. See Genesis 14:18-20

Priesthood II – Jesus and the Levitical Priesthood

11-19   So if perfection came through the Levitical priesthood (for the people had been given a law about it), why would there still be a need for another priest to arise 'according to the order of Melchisedek' and for him not to be named 'according to the order of Aaron'? You see, given that there is a change in the priesthood, then necessarily there is a change in the Law. For the one about whom these things are said belongs to another tribe; and no one from that tribe has ever served at the altar. For it is known to all that our Lord arose from Judah; and Moses made no mention of that with regard to priesthood. And it is still more abundantly clear when a different priest arises 'according to the likeness of Melchisedek', one who did not appear in accordance with the law of a fleshly command, but according to the power of indestructible life. For it is testified that 'you are a priest for ever according to the order of Melchisedek'.[73] For an annulment of an existing commandment takes place because that commandment is ineffective and useless (for the Law brought nothing to perfection), and a better hope is being introduced, through which we draw near to God.

> The argument here is not so easy, but the broad line is clear, and we find it in many other places in the New Testament. Jesus is superior to what has gone before, and his 'priesthood' (we are talking in metaphors here) takes the place of the Mosaic Law that precedes it. The point is not the inferiority of the previous covenant, but the radical novelty of what God has done in Jesus.

Priesthood III – the radical superiority of Jesus' priesthood, proved from Scripture

7 20–8 13   Next stage: to the extent that it was not done without an oath (for *they* became priests without an oath being sworn, but this one [became a priest] through the swearing of an oath, by the one who said to him, 'the Lord swore an oath and will not change this mind, you are a priest for ever'),[74] to that extent Jesus is the guarantee of a better covenant. And those who became priests are numerous, because death stops them remaining [in office], whereas he has a priesthood that is permanent, because he remains for ever. Therefore he is totally able to save those who approach God through him, living all the time to intercede for them. That's the kind of High Priest that was appropriate to us: holy, innocent, undefiled, separated from sinners, and set higher than the heavens. He has no need (as do the [other] High Priests) to offer sacrifice every day for his own sins [first] and then for the people's sins. For this is what he did, once and for all, when he offered himself. You see, the Law appoints people as High Priests, people with weaknesses, but the word, sworn on an oath that was uttered subsequent to the Law, appoints a Son, who has been made perfect for all time.

The main point in what has been said is this: we have just such a High Priest, who has sat down on the right of the Throne of Majesty in Heaven, a minister in the Sanctuary and in the True Tent, which the Lord (not human beings) has erected.

---

73. Psalm 110:4
74. Psalm 110:4

You see, all other High Priests are appointed in order to offer gifts and sacrifices; it follows necessarily that this one must have something to offer. And so if he were [still] on earth, he wouldn't be a priest, since there are those who offer the gifts according to the Law. These people worship a shadowy version of the heavenly things, just as Moses was admonished by God, when he was about to complete the Tent. For he says 'See to it that you do these things in accordance with the model that was shown you on the mountain.'[75] As it is, [Jesus] has gained a ministry that is all the more superior because he is the mediator of a superior covenant, whose law-giving was done with superior promises.

For if that first [covenant] had been flawless, no place would have been sought for a second one, for he says (pointing to their flaws), 'Look! The days are coming, says the Lord, and I shall complete a new covenant with the house of Israel and with the house of Judah, not according to the covenant which I made with their ancestors, on the day when I took their hand to lead them out of the land of Egypt, because they did not remain in my covenant, and I lost interest in them, says the Lord. Because this is the covenant, which I shall make with the house of Israel after those days, says the Lord, putting my laws into their mind, and I shall write [them] on their hearts. And I shall be God for them, and they shall be my people. And no longer shall each one teach their fellow citizen, and each one their brother or sister, saying "Know the Lord" – because they will all know me, from the littlest to the greatest of them, because I shall be merciful towards their iniquities, and I shall remember their sins no more.'[76] When he speaks of a 'new covenant', he has made the first one 'old', and what is old and obsolete is close to destruction.

> Here our author underlines the superiority of what God has done in Christ. He continues the metaphor of Jesus as High Priest, building on the quotation from Psalm 110, but with the added feature that Jesus' High Priesthood a) is permanent and b) provides access for believers. This is then connected with the point (already made earlier) of Jesus' sinlessness. And, just as Jesus is the 'Real Thing', so the liturgy at which he presides is real, in a way that the liturgy of the old dispensation simply could not be, since it was only a 'shadow' and a 'copy'. This is then all backed up by a chain of four Old Testament quotations, put together anyhow, and with no explanation; presumably our author knew that his readers didn't need much in the way of explanation.

Priesthood IV – the superiority of the new covenant, proved from Scripture

9 [1]–**10** [18]   So the first covenant had regulations for ministry, and the earthly sanctuary. For a tent, the first one, was constructed; in it was the menorah, and the table, and the shewbread, which is called Holy. And after the second curtain the tent is called Holy of Holies; it has a golden altar, and the Ark of the Covenant, covered on all sides with gold, in which [was] the golden jar with the manna, and Aaron's staff that burst into bud, and the tablets of the covenant; and above it the cherubim of

---

75. Exodus 25:40
76. Jeremiah 31:31-34

glory overshadowing the mercy seat. Now is not the time to speak of these things in detail.

When these things were laid out in this way, the priests who were performing the rituals always entered the first tent. But the second tent only the High Priest entered, once a year, not without blood, which he offers on his own behalf and for the sins the people had committed in ignorance. The Holy Spirit showed that the way of the saints had not yet been revealed while the first tent still had existence. This is an image for the present time; according to this image, gifts and sacrifices are offered which are unable to bring the worshipper's conscience to perfection, [since they are] only on the level of food and drink, and various ceremonial washings, regulations about material things which are imposed until the time is put right.

Whereas Christ has appeared as the High Priest of the good things that have come to be, through the greater and more perfect tent, the one not made by hands, that is to say, not of this creation; and it was not through the blood of goats, but through his own blood, that he entered, once and for all, the Holy of Holies having got hold of eternal redemption. For if the blood of goats and bulls, and the ashes of the [red] heifer [can] sanctify by a sprinkling those who have been defiled, so as to purify their flesh, how much more will the blood of Christ, who through the eternal Spirit offered himself, a flawless offering to God, purify our consciences, so as to worship the living God!

And he is in consequence the mediator of a new covenant, so that when a death takes place for the redemption of the transgressions in the days of the first covenant, those who have been invited may receive the promise of the eternal inheritance. You see, where there is a covenant [or: will, or: testament], it is necessary that the death of the one who made the covenant be established. For the covenant is valid on the basis of dead people, since it is not yet operative while the covenanter [or: testator] is alive. Hence the first covenant is not inaugurated without blood. For after every commandment according to the Torah has been enunciated by Moses to the whole people, taking the blood of calves and of goats, with water and red wool, and hyssop, he sprinkled both the book itself and the whole people, saying,

'This is the blood of the covenant which God has commanded you.'[77]

And likewise he sprinkled with blood the Tent and all the vessels of the sacred ministry. And almost everything is sprinkled with blood according to the Torah; and: no shedding of blood, no forgiveness.

Therefore it is a requirement that the imitations of the heavenly things be purified by these means; but the heavenly things themselves must necessarily be purified by sacrifices that are superior to these. For Christ did not enter a Holy of Holies made by human hands, some copy of the true Holy of Holies. No, Christ entered heaven itself, to appear now in the Presence of God on our behalf, not in order to offer himself a number of times, as the High Priest enters the Holy of Holies year after year, with blood that is not his own, since it would have been necessary [in that case] to have suffered many times from the creation of the world. As it is, it is revealed once, at the climax of history, for the abolition of sin, through his sacrifice. And just as it is the destiny of human beings to die once, and after that [there is] judgement, so Christ, having offered himself, in order to take the sins of many upon himself, will appear a second time, regardless of sin, for the salvation of those who wait for him.

---

77. Exodus 24:8

For the Torah has [merely] a shadow of the good things that lie ahead, not the image of the realities themselves; it is unable to bring to perfection those who draw near, with the same sacrifices, year after year, which they offer continually. For would they not have ceased to be offered, because of the worshippers no longer having any consciousness of sins, having been purified once and for all? Instead, in these sacrifices remembrance of sin is made year after year. You see, it is impossible for the blood of bulls and goats to take away sin. Therefore when he comes into the world, he says,

> 'You did not want sacrifice and offering; you prepared a body for me.
> You are not pleased with whole burnt offerings.
> Then I said, "Look, I have come
> (in the scroll of the book it stands written about me)
> to do your will, O God." '[78]

And earlier [he] says,

> 'Sacrifices and offerings and whole burnt-offerings and sin-offerings you do not want, nor are you pleased with them.'[79]

[The sacrifices he refers to here are those] which are offered in accordance with the law.

Then he said, 'Look! I have come to do your will.'[80] He takes away the first, so that the second might stand. By that will we have been made holy through the offering of the body of Jesus Christ, once and for all.

And while every other priest stands doing his ministry every day, and frequently offering the same sacrifices, which have no power to remove sins, this priest, having offered a single sacrifice for sins, sits for ever at the right hand of God, waiting from now on until his enemies are placed 'as a footstool for his feet.'[81] For by means of a single offering he has made perfect, and for ever, those who are being sanctified. And the Holy Spirit adds his evidence, for after saying, 'This is the covenant which I shall covenant with them, after those days, says the Lord, putting my laws on their hearts, and on their minds I shall write them', [he goes on to say] 'and their sins and their lawlessness I shall remember no more.'[82] Where there is forgiveness of these there is no more sin-offering.

This is a long passage, but the Scripture-based argument flows so easily that it seems a shame to break it up. The argument is intended to demonstrate (as part of the general thesis that Jesus is the 'Real Thing') how much better is Jesus' new covenant than that which preceded it. It may be helpful for us to recall that the word for 'covenant' can also here mean 'will' or 'testament'. This accounts for the talk about 'death'.

The argument makes four points:

1. What Jesus has done provides access for all believers, access to where it matters (the 'Real Thing') as opposed to the lesser access

---

78. Psalm 40:6-8
79. Psalm 40:6-8
80. Psalm 40:7
81. Psalm 110:1
82. Jeremiah 31:33, 34

that the old covenant provided, which in any case had to be repeated year after year, and only the High Priest was allowed to enter.

2. What Jesus has done really succeeds in coping with human sinfulness.

3. Blood is shed in both covenants; but in the case of what Jesus has done, the blood is 'once and for all', not year after year.

4. What Jesus has done is connected to his radical obedience to the Father's will ('I have come to do your will').

Encouragement based on the foregoing

19-25   Therefore, brothers and sisters, since by the blood of Jesus we have confidence in our access to the Holy of Holies, [and since] he has made a new route through the curtain for us, one that is recent and living, that is his flesh; and since we have a great priest over God's house, let us advance with a true heart in the fullness of faith, our hearts sprinkled, so that our conscience is no longer bad, and our bodies washed in pure water; let us hold fast to our unwavering profession of hope – for one can rely on the one who gave the promise; and let us pay careful attention to each other, and incite each other to love and to good works, not abandoning our own meetings, as is some people's custom, but encouraging one another, and all the more so in proportion as you see the Day drawing near.

> One thing always to notice in Hebrews is how close is the link between theology and exhortation. This 'pep-talk', aimed at keeping the group going, even when they don't feel like it, is based firmly on all the argument that has gone before.

A warning: judgement is coming

26-31   For if we voluntarily sin after we have received knowledge of the truth, there no longer remains any sacrifice for sins, but a fearsome expectation of judgement and a raging fire which is going to eat up those in its way. Someone who flouts the Torah of Moses 'dies on the evidence of two or three witnesses',[83] with no mercy. How much worse a punishment do you think a person will be thought to deserve who tramples on the Son of God, and regards the blood of the covenant (by which they have been sanctified!) as profane, and who insults the Spirit of Grace? For we know the one who said, 'Vengeance is mine – I shall repay',[84] and again, 'The Lord will judge his people'.[85] It is a terrible thing to fall into the hands of the Living God.

> As the Letter goes on, the warnings become sterner, more urgent. For our author, this is life and death. For our purposes, it is important to notice how the warning is all of a piece with his theological argument.

---

83. Deuteronomy 17:6
84. Deuteronomy 32:35
85. Psalm 135:14

Encouragement: look to your previous experience

32-39 Remember those earlier days when you received the light, and you endured a great battle with suffering; sometimes you were publicly exposed to abuse and persecution; sometimes you showed solidarity with those who were being treated in this way. For you shared the sufferings of prisoners, and you joyfully accepted the plundering of your possessions, knowing that you had better possessions – possessions that will last. So don't throw away your confidence, which is a huge reward. For you need endurance, so as to do God's will and obtain the promise. For 'just a little while, the Coming One comes and will not delay. My just one shall live by faith, and if he draws back, my soul is not pleased with him.'[86]

But you and I do not belong to those who draw back [and fall into] destruction. No, we belong to those who have faith, so as to make our life secure.

> The author shows here a calm and unshakable confidence, which he tries to impart to his wobbly community. His confidence is based simply on his quiet certainty about Jesus, the Real Thing.
> 'Received the light'; in Hebrews, this refers to baptism.

What faith can do – some examples

11 1-40 Faith is the confident assurance of the things that we hope for, the inner conviction about things that are invisible. People in the past were noted for this [quality of] faith. It is by faith that we know that the worlds were created by God's word, in such a way that what is seen came to be from that which does not appear. By faith Abel offered God a greater sacrifice than Cain, through which he was attested as righteous, because God himself gave testimony over the gifts; through faith, Abel still speaks, even though he died. By faith Enoch was taken up, so that he did not see death, and he was not found, because God had taken him up. For before his taking-up, he was accredited as having pleased God. Without faith, it is impossible to please. For the one who approaches God must have faith that God exists and that God rewards those who seek him. It was by faith that Noah, after he had been warned of the things that had not yet been seen, took heed, and built an ark for the welfare of his household, through which he condemned the world, and became an heir of the righteousness that comes with faith.

It was by faith that when Abraham was summoned he obeyed and went out to a place that he was going to receive as an inheritance, and he went out, not knowing where he was going. It was by faith that he migrated to the land of promise, a land that was not his own, living in tents with Isaac and Jacob, fellow heirs of the same promise; for he was waiting for the city that has foundations, the city whose designer and craftsman is God.

It was by faith that Sarah herself (who was barren) received the power to conceive, even though she was past the age, since she regarded the one who made the promise as worthy of faith. Therefore there were born from one person (and that one, moreover, as good as dead), [offspring] like the stars of heaven in number, and like uncountable grains of sand by the seashore.

In faith all these people died; they did not receive the promises, but glimpsed them from a long way off, and they hailed them, and acknowledged that they were

---

86. Isaiah 26:20, 21 (Septuagint)

foreigners and exiles on earth. People who say that sort of thing make it clear that they are looking for a homeland. And if they had been thinking of the one they had come out from, they would have had time to return. As it is, they are longing for a better one, their heavenly homeland. Therefore God is not ashamed to be called their God, for he has prepared a city for them.

It was by faith that Abraham offered up Isaac when he was tested, and he was ready to sacrifice his only son. [This was the] Abraham who had received the promises, to whom it had been said, 'In Isaac seed shall be called [up] for you.'[87] He calculated that God was able even to raise from the dead; and therefore he symbolically got him back. It was also by faith in what was to come that Isaac blessed Jacob and Esau. By faith Jacob on his deathbed blessed each of the sons of Joseph, and 'worshipped, leaning over the tip of his staff'.[88] It was by faith that when Joseph was dying he mentioned the exodus of the children of Israel, and gave instructions about his bones.

It was by faith that when Moses was born he was hidden for three months by his parents, because they saw that the child was beautiful, and they were not afraid of the king's decree. It was by faith that when he grew up, Moses refused to be called the son of Pharaoh's daughter – instead he chose to be maltreated with the people of God, rather than to have a shortlived enjoyment of sin; he thought Christ's disgrace was of more significance than the treasures of Egypt, for he was looking ahead to the reward.

It was by faith that he abandoned Egypt, unafraid of the king's anger; he persevered as though he [could] see the Invisible One. By faith he kept the Passover, and the sprinkling of the blood, so that the Destroying Angel should not touch their first-born children. It was by faith that they crossed the Red Sea, as though it were dry land (and when the Egyptians tried it out, they were devoured!).

It was by faith that the walls of Jericho fell, after they had been encircled for seven days. It was by faith that the prostitute Rahab did not perish with the unbelievers, when she gave hospitality and peace to the spies.

And what more can I say? For time would run out on me if I were to tell the story of Gideon, Barach, Samson, Jephthah, David and Samuel, and the prophets, the people who through faith overcame kingdoms, practised righteousness, attained the promises, blocked the mouths of lions, quenched the power of fire, escaped the sword's edges, were made strong when they had been weak, became mighty in war, broke the formations of alien [invaders]. Women received their dead as a result of the Resurrection; others were tortured when they had refused release, in order to gain a greater Resurrection. Others experienced jeering and flogging, others got chains and imprisonment; they were punished by stoning or by being sawn in two; or they died, killed by the sword; they went around in sheepskin and goatskin, destitute, oppressed and ill-treated: the world was not worthy of them – they wandered in deserts and on mountains, and caves and holes in the ground.

And all those people, whose faith is attested, failed to gain the promise. God had foreseen something better for us, so that they should not be made perfect without us.

> This is a magnificent chapter, a long list of people who have been distinguished by faith. One of them is Moses. Readers may be brought

---

87. Genesis 21:12
88. Genesis 47:31 (Septuagint)

up short by the phrase 'he thought Christ's disgrace was of more significance than the treasures of Egypt . . .' The point here, as so often in the New Testament, is that for our author Christ was already there in the Old Testament. At the end, though, there is a twist. The reader has supposed all the way through that we are being invited to admire these splendid examples of faith for their own sakes. Only in the final verses do we realise that the author is saying something slightly different; these characters are entirely admirable, but we are in an even better situation than they are, because the promise is ours for the taking. All the more, then, should we be ready to exercise faith.

Warning: examples from the discipline of the training-ground, and of home

12 [1-17] For that very reason, since we have such a great cloud of witnesses around us, we should lay aside every burden, including sin, which easily impedes our running, and run with endurance the race that lies ahead of us. We should fix our eyes on Jesus, our pacemaker and trainer in faith. Instead of the short-term joy that was within his grasp, he endured the Cross, disdaining the shame, and took his seat on the right hand of the throne of God. Just think of the one who endured such hostility towards himself at the hands of sinners. This will prevent you from getting exhausted, worn out in your souls.

You have not yet resisted to the point of bloodshed in your struggle against sin; and you have completely forgotten the encouragement which speaks to you as to sons, 'My son, do not despise the Lord's discipline; and don't lose heart when you are reprimanded by him. For the Lord disciplines the one he loves, and he whips every son whom he accepts.'[89] Keep on enduring, to gain discipline; God is treating you as sons – for what son is there whom his father does not discipline? But if you have none of the discipline in which all have shared, then you are illegitimate, and not proper sons. Then again, we had our human fathers, who imposed discipline on us, and we respected them. Should we not be much readier to be submissive to the Father of Spirits and live? For [our human fathers] disciplined us just for a short time, as they felt like it, whereas God disciplines us for our benefit, so that we might have our share in his holiness. All discipline, at the time we get it, seems to be a matter for sadness rather than joy – but later on it produces fruit that yields peace and righteousness in those who have been trained by it.

Therefore brace up your drooping hands and your weakened knees, and make straight tracks with your feet, in order that what is lame may not be dislocated, but rather cured. Pursue peace with everybody; pursue holiness, without which no one will see the Lord. See to it that no one falls short of God's grace, 'that no root of bitterness grow upwards and cause trouble', and through it many people might be defiled. [See to it] that no one is a fornicator or irreligious like Esau, who for the sake of a single meal sold his right as the first-born. For know that when later on he wanted to inherit the blessing he was rejected; for he was given no chance to change his mind, even though he sought for it with tears.

---

89. Proverbs 3:11, 12

The examples continue to be urgent in their appeal, and the author treats his readers as though he were one of the legendary coaches of athletics or football; you can almost hear him bellowing, 'It's only pain!', as they wearily contemplate how much of the Marathon they still have to run. He also invites them to consider the discouragement of children whose parent is over-inclined to corporal punishment, an example that is perhaps less typical of our own day than of his. The point is clear: they (and we) must keep going, right to the end.

The approach to Mount Sion

18-29 For it is not the tangible [mountain] that you have approached, burning fire and darkness and gloom and whirlwind, and the noise of a trumpet and the sound of words which when they heard it they begged [the speaker] not to add any more, for they could not cope with the command 'even if an animal touches the mountain, it shall be stoned';[90] and so fearful was the spectacle that Moses said, 'I am fearful and trembling'.[91]

No – you have approached Mount Sion and the city of the Living God, heavenly Jerusalem, and thousands upon thousands of angels, and the festal assembly of the firstborn who are recorded in heaven, and God the Judge of all, and the spirits of the just who have been made perfect, and Jesus, the mediator of the new covenant, and the blood of sprinkling which speaks more fully than Abel's.

Watch out that you do not disregard [Jesus] when he speaks. For if those people did not escape when they disregarded the one who admonished them on earth, how much more will [that be true of us] who turn away from the one who speaks from heaven, the one whose voice then shook the earth, but now has promised, 'Yet once more I shall shake not only earth but also heaven'?[92] That 'yet once more' reveals the removal of the things that are shaken, as created things, that the things unshaken may remain. Therefore since we are receiving an unshakable kingdom, let us be grateful; that will enable us to give worship in a way pleasing to God, with reverence and awe – for our God is a consuming fire.

This is a powerful passage, and we are half understanding, half baffled, but certain that the warning is urgent, and that Mount Sion is worth risking everything for, and that we want to hear the voice of Jesus when he speaks.

Final exhortations

13 1-17 Let the love of the brothers and sisters remain [in you]. Don't forget about hospitality; because that has enabled some people to entertain angels without noticing it. Remember those in prison – [think of yourselves] as their fellow prisoners. [Remember] those who are being maltreated, as though you were yourselves also in their bodies.

---

90. Exodus 19:12, 13
91. Deuteronomy 9:19
92. Haggai 2:6

Let marriage be valued by everybody, and let the marriage-bed be undefiled – for God will condemn fornicators and adulterers. Let your manner of life not be money-oriented, but [be] content with what you have. For he himself has said, 'I shall not fail you nor forsake you,'[93] so that undaunted we may say, 'The Lord is my help – I shall not be afraid; what can a human being do against me?'[94]

Remember your leaders, who spoke the Word of God to you. Consider the outcome of their way of life, and imitate their faith. Jesus Christ, the same yesterday and today and for ever.

Don't get carried away by various outlandish doctrines. For it is good for the heart to be strengthened by grace, not by foods – people who follow that way of life are not helped by it. We have an altar from which those who worship in the tent do not have authority to eat. For the animals whose blood is brought to the sanctuary as sin-offering by the High Priest are burnt outside the camp. Therefore Jesus also, in order to sanctify the people through his own blood, suffered outside the gate. Therefore let us go out to join him, outside the camp, bearing his reproaches. For we do not have a permanent city here; instead we look for the city that is to come. Through him, therefore, let us continually lift up a sacrifice of praise to God, that is to say the produce of lips that praise his name. Don't forget good deeds and fellowship – for God is pleased by sacrifices of this sort. Obey your leaders and submit to them, for they are keeping watch over your souls, as people who will have to submit an account; they should [be able to] do this joyfully, and not groaning as they do so. For that would do you no good.

> These last instructions do not tell us much about what the community was like, nor, really, what were the problems that affected it. Not for the first time, the author stresses the superiority of the new dispensation to the old. And, above all, he emphasises the central importance of Jesus and of looking ahead to the city that will last. The 'leaders' are clearly of some importance in his view of this group – but we can say very little about them.

Final greetings

18-25   Pray for us, for we are persuaded that we have a good conscience; in every respect we want to live properly. Above all, I beg you to pray that I may be restored to you quite soon.

May the God of peace, the one who by the blood of the eternal covenant leads up from the dead the Great Shepherd of the sheep, our Lord Jesus, make you complete in every good thing, so as to do his wish, bringing about in you that which pleases him through Jesus Christ, to whom be glory for ever and ever.

I beg you, brothers and sisters, put up with this message of encouragement; for I have written to you briefly.

Know that our brother Timothy has been released; I shall see you in his company, if he arrives soon.

Greet all your leaders and all the saints. Those from Italy greet you.

Grace be with all of you.

---

93. Joshua 1:5
94. Psalm 118:6

At the end here, the author turns personal, and speaks in the first person, although he does not tell us who he is. The mention of 'our brother Timothy' does not, alas, identify Paul as the author. We notice his mention (not for the first time in this letter) of the 'leaders', whom he clearly regards as having an important function in the Church, but we do not know who they are or what they do.

We notice that the author describes this document as 'a message of encouragement', which many understand to mean 'a sermon'; so presumably the theology is meant to support the passages of exhortation, rather than the other way round. We also observe that the author feels that he has written 'briefly', and ask ourselves what he might have done had he felt that time and space allowed.

The Letter of James

Opening greetings

1 ¹ James, a slave of God and of the Lord Jesus Christ, to the Twelve Tribes in the
Diaspora, greetings.

> This follows the regular pattern for beginning a letter in the Mediter-
> ranean world at this era, with the author and addressees identified,
> and with the characteristic Christian addition of a reference to God
> and to Jesus. As in the Pauline letters, these two are strikingly mentioned
> in the same breath. We also notice the very Jewish theme of the
> greeting to the 'Twelve Tribes in the Diaspora'. This is the standard
> term for Jews who live outside the Holy Land, but here clearly refers
> to Jewish Christians.

Overture: on temptations

2-18 My brothers and sisters, consider it all joy when you fall into different kinds of
temptations; be aware that the testing of your faith results in endurance. And let
endurance have a perfect outcome, so that you may be perfect and complete,
lacking in nothing.

If however one of you is lacking in wisdom, let them ask from God, who gives
indiscriminately to all, without reproach – and it will be given to them. Let them
ask in faith, not doubting at all. For the person who doubts is like a wave in the
sea, moved and tossed by the wind. You see, that person should not think that they
will receive anything from the Lord, being in two minds, unstable in all their ways.

Let the brother or sister who is of low status boast of their high status, and the
rich brother or sister boast of their low standing: because they will pass away like
the wild flower. For the sun rises, with its burning heat, and dries up the grass, and
its flower fades, and its beautiful appearance is lost. So the rich person will fade
away, along with all his enterprises.

Congratulations to the person who endures temptation: that person will pass the
test and receive the crown of life which [God] promised to those who love him. No
one who is being tempted should say, 'I am being tempted by God': God cannot
be tempted to do evil, and God himself does not tempt anybody. Each of us is
tempted by our own passions, dragged off and enticed [by them]. Then desire
conceives and gives birth to sin, and sin comes to term and brings death into the
world.

Don't get led astray, my beloved brothers and sisters. Every good gift, and every
perfect present, comes down from above, from the Father of Lights, with whom

there is no variation, no shadow of change. [God] deliberately brought us to birth through the word of truth, so that we should be a kind of first-fruits of God's creation.

It is impossible to recreate with any confidence the original purpose of this letter, but many scholars think that its author may have been that 'James, the brother of the Lord' who became such an important figure in the early Church, and who was martyred in AD 61. If this was so, it may be that somebody else subsequently revised the letter. It is a very Jewish document, but the reader will notice the references to Matthew 7:7 ('Ask and you shall receive'), Matthew 13:6 (the sun's burning heat), and to the link of sin and death in Romans 7.

We may also notice a certain Christian audacity in the claim that we should rejoice when afflicted by temptations, and the downgrading of the status of the rich, which is so much a feature of Christian teaching.

Listen, and act

19-27 Be sure of this, brothers and sisters; let everyone be quick to listen, slow to speak, slow to get angry. For a person's anger does not bring about the righteousness of God. So: gently put aside all moral filth, and excess of evil, and accept the implanted word that has the power to save your souls.

Be doers of the word, not just listeners who deceive themselves. Because if someone is just a listener and not a doer of the word, they're like a man contemplating in the mirror the face that nature gave him: he contemplates himself and goes off and immediately forgets what he was like. But the one who peers closely at the perfect law of freedom, and stays with it, turns into a doer of deeds, not a hearer-and-forgetter. Such a person will be happy in what they do.

If anyone thinks they are religious, but does not restrain their tongue, and instead deceives themselves, then their 'religion' is useless. This is [the meaning of] religion that is pure and unstained before [our] God and Father: visiting orphans and widows when they are in difficulty, and keeping ourselves unstained by the world.

For our author, religion is more than just sitting in church; it needs to be tested by what happens in real life, the link between what we claim and what we do. That includes restraint in what we say, a distance from 'the world' and difficult things like showing love for the marginalised and the poor.

Some sharp social comment

2 1-13 My brothers and sisters, don't make belief in our glorious Lord Jesus Christ a matter of snobbery. For example, if a man with gold jewellery and smart clothes comes into your assembly [or: 'synagogue'], and at the same time a poor man in dirty clothes comes in, you look at the one in the smart clothes and say, 'Have a nice seat here'; and if you say to the poor man, 'You! Stand there,' or 'Sit under my footstool,' aren't you making distinctions among yourselves, and assessing people on evil criteria?

My beloved brothers and sisters, listen: isn't it the case that God chooses those who are poor as far as the world is concerned, to be rich in faith and to inherit the kingdom that he has promised to those who love him? But you people insult the poor man. Isn't it the rich who oppress you? Isn't it they who drag you off to the law courts? Aren't they the ones who slander the noble name that God has added to the name you were given?

If you are really accomplishing the royal law ('you shall love your neighbour as yourself')[95] in accordance with Scripture, you're doing a noble deed. But if you go in for snobbery, you're committing sin, and you're convicted by the Torah as transgressors. For anyone who keeps the whole Torah, but stumbles over one point [of it], is answerable for the whole [Torah]. The One who said, 'Thou shalt not commit adultery'[96] also said, 'Thou shalt not kill'[97]; [so] if you avoid adultery, but commit murder, you have become a transgressor of Torah.

Speak and act in a way appropriate to those who are judged by the law of freedom. For those who do not act mercifully there will be condemnation without mercy – mercy overrides our condemnation.

> James (like Jesus) is not afraid to be remarkably direct about what he sees as the hypocrisy of believers. We shiver uncomfortably at the comedy acted out when the affluent are treated with so much more warmth than the poor when they come to church, and we notice how this goes against Jesus' teaching that 'love your neighbour as yourself' is the second commandment. This appears at Matthew 22:39, and we notice also in our passage the echo of Matthew's fifth beatitude (Matthew 5:7), on being merciful, and the dramatisation of it in the story of the unforgiving servant in Matthew 18.

Faith leads to action

14-26 Brothers and sisters, what's the use, if someone claims to have faith, but [there's] no action? Can faith save that person? If a fellow Christian is without clothes and doesn't even have enough food for the day, and one of you says to them, 'Go in peace – be warm and well fed,' but doesn't supply their physical needs, what's the use? In just the same way, faith on its own is lifeless, if it doesn't lead to action.

'Aha,' someone will object, 'you've got faith, and I've got actions.' [All right –] show me your faith, that doesn't lead to actions, and I'll show you my faith in the actions that I perform. You have faith, quite rightly, that God is one: even the demons have that faith – and they shudder.

You want convincing, do you, that faith that doesn't lead to action is useless? You really are inane! Wasn't it actions that justified our ancestor Abraham when he offered up his son Isaac on the altar? Do you see that faith collaborates with Abraham's actions, and that it is the actions that bring faith to perfection? And the Scripture is fulfilled, 'Abraham had faith in God, and it was reckoned to him as righteousness';[98] and he was called a friend of God.

---

95. Leviticus 19:18
96. Exodus 20:14
97. Exodus 20:13
98. Genesis 15:6

Similarly the prostitute Rahab – wasn't she justified by her actions? She gave hospitality to the messengers, and sent them out by another route. You see, just as the body is lifeless without the spirit, so faith is lifeless if it doesn't lead to actions.

> Sometimes when one reads this passage, it seems uncomfortably as though James might be attacking Paul: he uses the words 'faith' and 'works' (or 'actions'), and the example of Abraham, even the quotation of Genesis 15:6, of which Paul makes so much in Romans and Galatians. It was this that led Luther to dismiss James as 'a rather strawy epistle'; and it may well be that James has in view some more extreme interpretations of Paul. Nevertheless, James and Paul are not too far apart. The 'actions' that James has in mind are what are clearly demanded of all Christians: treating the brethren as human beings, whatever their social status, feeding the hungry, and clothing the naked. Paul has to tell his Corinthians about the central importance of the command to love. What Paul objected to was Christians attacking his gospel of freedom by arguing the need for Christians to be circumcised and observe the dietary laws and so on, not the obvious fact that faith may be expected to lead to visible results in the real world.
>
> The reference to demons shuddering reminds the reader of Jesus' control over these shadowy enemies of the human race. See, for example, Matthew 8:28-34.

Dangers of teachers, and other spin doctors

3 ¹⁻¹² Not many of you should become teachers, brothers and sisters, because you should know that we [who are teachers] will receive a harsher judgement. For all of us stumble in many respects; if someone does not stumble in what he says, then he is a perfect man, who is also able to rein in his whole body. Now if we put reins in horses' mouths, to make them obey us, we also steer the horse's whole body. And look at ships, how big they are, and how they get driven by stiff winds: they are steered by a tiny rudder, wherever the pilot's impulse determines. In just the same way, the tongue is a tiny part of us, and boasts of great things. Look at how a tiny fire can set alight a huge wood. And the tongue is a fire; the tongue shows itself to be a world of wickedness in our limbs; it pollutes the whole body and sets fire to the cycle of existence, and it is set on fire by Gehenna. For all nature, beasts and birds, serpents and sea creatures, are being tamed and have been tamed by human nature. But the tongue no human being can tame: it is a restless evil, full of lethal venom. With the tongue we bless our Lord and Father; with the tongue we curse human beings, made in God's likeness. Blessing and cursing come out of the same mouth. Brothers and sisters, it ought not to be like this: does a fountain pour out sweet and bitter from the same hole? Brothers and sisters, can a fig tree produce olives, or a vine figs? Nor can a salty spring produce sweet water.

> This is common sense, but it is solidly within the Jewish and Christian traditions, and it represents a wisdom of which our world stands in grave need. The tongue is a tiny thing, but can do immense

damage. James makes his point by way of illustration from horse-riding, navigation and fire to show how difficult it is to control the tongue, and how much damage it can do.

True wisdom

13-18 Who is wise and knowledgeable among you? Let that person show that his achievements come from a noble way of life, with the lack of pretension [that is appropriate to] wisdom. If, however, you have bitter partisanship and selfishness in your heart, don't go boasting and telling lies against the truth. This is not the wisdom that comes from above: no – it is earth-bound, unspiritual, demonic. For where there is partisanship and selfishness, there [you get] disorder, and evil of every kind. The wisdom [that comes] from above, however, is, in the first place, pure. After that it is peaceful, gentle, obedient, full of mercy and good fruits, impartial and unfeigned. The fruit of righteousness is sown in peace, for those who make peace.

> James here contrasts 'wisdom from below' with 'wisdom from above', rather as one finds in Qumran's 'Manual of Discipline' (many scholars find a link between James and Qumran). But we might also think of the virtues listed by Paul at Galatians 5:22, 23, and their opposed vices (5:19-21). 'Those who make peace' may allude to the seventh beatitude of the Sermon on the Mount (Matthew 5:9).

Avoiding trouble in the community

4 1-12 What is the source of wars, what is the source of battles in your community? Don't they come from the pleasures that are on active service in your limbs? You have desires, and you don't get what you desire; you murder and covet, and you can't obtain [what you want]. You go to war and battle, and you don't get, because you don't ask. You ask and you don't receive, because you ask in an evil way, to spend money on your pleasures. You are [like] adulterous women – don't you realise that the world's friendship is enmity with God? So anyone who wants to be the world's friend is a self-appointed enemy of God. Or do you think that Scripture speaks pointlessly? Does the Spirit which [God] has caused to live in us go in for envious desire? God gives greater grace. Therefore he says, 'God opposes the arrogant: but gives grace to the humble.' Therefore oppose the devil, and he will flee from you. Draw near to God and he will draw near to you. Clean your hand, sinners, and purify your hearts, you waverers. Be wretched, mourn and weep; let your laughter be turned to mourning, and your joy to dejection. Humble yourselves in the presence of the Lord, and he will raise you up. Brothers and sisters, don't slander each other. The one who slanders a fellow Christian slanders the Law, and condemns the Law; but if you condemn the Law, you're not a doer of the Law but a judge over it! There is one Lawgiver and Judge, one who is able to save and to destroy; but who are you to condemn your neighbour?

> You may feel that there is not much here that you could call specifically Christian; you may protest that it's all good common sense. But it is common sense that we shall do well to observe, and

it would have been no bad thing if Christian communities down the ages had observed it, or if they would do so today. We know nothing for certain about the community that James was addressing, but we may get the feeling that it was in some respects very much like our own.

There seems to be an echo of the 'Sermon on the Plain' (see Luke 6:25) in the instructions about laughter turning into mourning; and Luke 14:11 may lie behind the injunction to 'humble yourselves in the presence of the Lord', and possibly an allusion to Matthew 10:28 in the reference to 'one who is able to save and to destroy'. And, of course, when James says, 'you ask and you don't receive', the Christian reader instinctively thinks of Jesus' teachings at Matthew 7:7-11 and Luke 11:9-13.

Watch out, wealthy wheeler-dealers!

4 ^{13}-5 ^{6} Come now, you who say, 'Today or tomorrow we shall journey to such-and-such a city, and we'll spend a year there, and make a profit', when you don't know anything about tomorrow. What is your life like? You are mist, which appears for a little while, then disappears. Instead of saying, 'If the Lord wills, we shall both live and accomplish this or that', you go boasting arrogantly. All boasting of that sort is evil. So, then, anyone who knows what is the right thing to do and fails to do it, that's a sin for them.

Come now, you who are affluent, weep and cry aloud over the miseries that are coming upon you. Your affluence has gone rotten, and your clothes have become food for moths; your gold and silver has gone rusty, and their rust will [serve] as evidence against you, and will eat up your flesh like fire. You have stored up treasures in the last days. Look! The wages of the workers who harvested your lands, wages that you have deprived them of, cry out against you. The cries of [your] harvesters have reached the ears of the Lord of hosts. On earth you have lived a life of self-indulgence and luxury; you have fattened your hearts on the day of [your] slaughter. You have condemned and murdered the Just One – he does not resist you.

The reader cannot avoid the conclusion that many of the community to which James is writing were wealthy people who saw no connection between their faith and the way they lived, making grandiose plans for new commercial enterprises, for example, and failing to pay workers the wages they are owed. Not only is this foolish investment, since the wealth does not last; it is also exploitation of the poor, and will therefore be punished. Worst of all, they are doing it to Christ himself, identified here as 'the Just One' (and we are reminded of the parable of the sheep and the goats, Matthew 25:31-46).

Waiting for the Coming

7-20   So, brothers and sisters, be patient until the coming of the Lord. Look! The farmer waits for the valuable fruit of the earth; he is patient with it, until it gets the early rain and the late rain. You [must] also be patient; make your hearts resolute, because the coming of the Lord has drawn near. Brothers and sisters, don't complain against each other, so as not to be judged. Look! The Judge is standing at the gates. Brothers and sisters, take the prophets who spoke in the Lord's name as examples of how to endure evil and how to be patient. See — we congratulate those who showed endurance. You've heard of Job's endurance, and you have seen the outcome [that] the Lord [brought about], because the Lord is merciful and compassionate.

Above all, brothers and sisters, don't swear by heaven or earth, or any other oath. Let your 'yes' mean 'yes', and your 'no' mean 'no', that you may not fall under condemnation.

If someone among you is in trouble, let them pray; if someone is cheerful, let them sing a song of praise. If someone is sick, let them summon the elders of the Church, and let them pray over the person, anointing him or her with oil in the Lord's name, and the prayer offered in faith will save the one who is ill, and the Lord will raise them up. And if they have committed sins, it will be forgiven them: confess your sins to each other, and pray for each other that you may be healed. The prayer of a just person is effective and achieves much. Elijah was a human being like us, and in prayer he prayed that it would not rain; and it didn't rain on the land for three and a half years! And he prayed again, and heaven gave rain, and the earth produced its fruit.

My brothers and sisters, if someone among you has wandered from the truth, and someone turns him back, let the person know that one who turns a sinner from wandering on the road will save his soul from death, and 'will cover a multitude of sins'.[99]

> Whoever the group is that James was writing to, they are clearly Christians: see, for example, the reference to Jesus' teaching in the Sermon on the Mount about swearing oaths (Matthew 5:33-37). They are also clearly a community who practise their faith together and have effects on each other (not always desirable effects, it would seem). They and James would have little patience with the idea that 'Christianity is something you do on your own'. James is, moreover, quite realistic about their difficulties, and knows that Christian living is in a variety of ways (anxiety about the end-time, or its non-appearance, questions about oaths, what to do about sickness and sinfulness in the community) quite problematic for them. This is a letter to return to again and again.

---

99. Proverbs 10:12

The First Letter of Peter

Introduction and greetings

1 [1,2] Peter, apostle of Jesus Christ, to the chosen exiles in the Diaspora of Pontus, Galatia, Cappadocia, Asia and Bithynia, according to the foreknowledge of God the Father, by the Holy Spirit, which leads to obedience and to sprinkling with the blood of Jesus Christ, may grace and peace be yours in ever greater measure.

> Clearly the letter claims to be written by Peter, leader of that first group of Jesus' companions, but the high standard of the Greek of this letter suggests to many scholars that it is written in his name, perhaps some years after his death (which was traditionally said to have taken place in AD 64). The letter is a circular, addressed to five Churches in modern Turkey. The provinces mentioned (look at a map) might represent the order in which the letter was to be delivered.

Prologue – the focus on Christ

[3-12] Blessed be the God and Father of our Lord Jesus Christ, who in accordance with his great mercy has caused us to be born again into a living hope, through the Resurrection of Jesus Christ from the dead, to an incorruptible, undefiled and unfading inheritance, which has been preserved in heaven for you who have been kept safe by the power of God, through faith, for a salvation that is ready to be revealed at the end-time. You rejoice in him, even if you have for a little while now to be distressed by various trials, so that the genuineness of your faith, more valuable than gold (which is perishable, yet tested in fire), may be discovered to lead to your praise and glory and honour at the revelation of Jesus Christ. You did not see Christ, but you love him; and now you believe in him without seeing him, and you rejoice with an inexpressible, glorious joy, as you obtain the end [to which] your faith [is directed], the salvation of your souls. The prophets who uttered their prophecies about the grace [that has been destined] for you searched for this salvation and inquired carefully about it; they investigated the 'who' and the 'when' that the Spirit of Christ was indicating, the Spirit who predicted Christ's sufferings and the glory that would follow them. It was revealed to them that they were not doing this service for themselves, but for you, ministering to you the things that have been declared to you through those who preached the gospel to you, by the Holy Spirit sent from heaven, at which the angels long to steal a glance.

> What can we say about this? First and foremost, the focus is on Jesus Christ, as long since predicted by the prophets (and peered at by angels), and as subsequently risen. The Resurrection is the proclamation with which Peter starts. Now this is true of every document in the

New Testament, but it gets particular emphasis here because the Christians Peter is addressing either have experience of, or are likely to experience, 'various trials', and Peter is assuring them of the glory (watch out for the number of times this word, or its related adjective, appears in this letter) that lies beyond, but which they can already glimpse. In the same breath he reminds them that God has kept them safe.

We also learn that these Christians are of the second generation; they did not know Jesus personally, but had the gospel of Jesus' resurrection preached to them. And still they love him.

Exhortation, based on their experience of Christ

1 [13]-**2** [3]   Therefore gird up the loins of your mind; be sober; have perfect hope in the grace that is being conferred on you at the revelation of Jesus Christ. Be like obedient children; don't be conformed to the old desires [that you had when] you were ignorant. Instead, like the Holy One who called you, you also must be holy in your entire way of life, because it is written, 'You shall be holy, because I am holy.'[100] And if you call on him as Father, the one who judges impartially, in accordance with what each one has done, then live in fear for the period of your exile; be aware that it was not by perishable things [like] silver or gold that you were redeemed from the useless way of life handed down from your ancestors. No – it was by the precious blood [of Christ], as of a lamb, spotless and without blemish, Christ, who was foreknown before the creation of the world, and then appeared at the end of the ages, for the sake of you who through him are faithful to God who raised him from the dead and gave him glory, so that your faith and hope is in God.

After purifying your souls in obedience to the truth, to the point of sincere love of your fellow Christians, love one another eagerly, having been reborn not from perishable procreation, but through the imperishable word of the Living and Abiding God. Because

'All flesh is as grass, and all its glory is as the wild flower.
The grass withers and the flower fades,
but the word of the Lord remains for ever.'[101]

This 'word' is the good news that has been proclaimed to you.

So set aside all evil and all guile, and insincerity and envy, and all kinds of slander and, like newborn babies, drink spiritual, unadulterated milk, so that it may help you grow into salvation, seeing that 'you have experienced that the Lord is kind'.[102]

Clearly Peter thinks that the various groups he is addressing need a bit of a boost (what Christian does not, at times?); and notice how he can appeal a) to their experience of the way their life changed after they met Christ, and b) to Scripture. The final Scripture quotation referred originally to God, but in Greek it would sound like ' . . . that Christ is the Lord'.

---

100. Leviticus 1:44, 45; 19:2
101. Isaiah 40:6-8
102. Psalm 34:8

Christ the foundation stone; and other kinds of stone

4-10 Approach [Christ] as the Living Stone, rejected by humans, but in God's eyes select and precious; and you yourselves are being built up as a spiritual house, into a priesthood holy [enough] to offer spiritual sacrifices to God through Jesus Christ. Because it says in Scripture, 'Look – I am placing in Sion a cornerstone, select and precious; and the one who believes in him will not be disappointed.'[103] So to you who believe it is precious, but to those who do not believe 'a stone which the builders rejected; this has become the cornerstone',[104] and 'a stone of stumbling and a rock of offence'.[105] The unbelievers stumble against the word, disbelieving as they were destined to do. You on the other hand are 'a select race',[106] 'a royal priesthood, a holy nation',[107] 'a people [that has become God's] possession',[108] so that you may announce the glories of the One who summoned you out of darkness into his marvellous light; those who once were 'No People',[109] but are now the People of God, those who did not receive mercy, but now have received mercy.

> Here Peter puts together some Scripture texts on the ideas of 'stone' and 'rock' (it may have occurred to his first readers that his nickname meant 'Rock', of course). He is making several points: a) Christ is the foundation of Christians; b) Christ was rejected, but ultimately accepted; c) non-believers simply do not see the point and will come a cropper; d) believers on the other hand are already in a good place.

On living in the real world

2 11-3 7 Beloved, I encourage you, as strangers and exiles, to keep away from sensual desires, which war against the soul. Maintain a noble rule of conduct among the Gentiles, so that when they denounce you as evildoers, they may observe [your conduct], because of the noble deeds that you do, and glorify God on the Day of Visitation.

Be subject to every social institution on the Lord's account, to the Emperor as supreme, to governors who are sent by him to punish evildoers and to praise those who do good. Because this is God's will, that people who do good should silence the ignorance of silly human beings, like people who are free, and not making freedom a pretext for evil, but [acting] as God's slaves. Give honour to everybody, love the Christian community, fear God, honour the Emperor.

Slaves [should] be subordinated to their masters with all reverence, and not only masters who are good and considerate, but also those who are harsh. For this is also a grace, if someone puts up with suffering sorrows unjustly, because that person is aware of God. What merit is there if you endure it when you do wrong and are beaten? No – if you suffer after doing good and endure it, *that's* a grace in God's eyes. For this is what you were called to, that Christ suffered on your behalf,

---

103. Isaiah 28:16
104. Psalm 118:22
105. Isaiah 8:14
106. Isaiah 43:20
107. Exodus 19:6
108. Exodus 19:15
109. Hosea 1:10; 2:23

leaving behind an example, for you to follow in his footsteps. He did not commit sin, 'nor was any guile found in his mouth'.[110] He was insulted, and did not return insults; when he suffered, he did not threaten, but handed himself over to the One who judges justly. He himself offered up our sins in his body on the tree, in order that we might die to sin and live to righteousness: by his wound you have been healed. For you were 'wandering like sheep',[111] but now you have turned back to the Shepherd and Overseer of your souls.

Wives likewise should be subordinated to their own husbands, in order that even if some of them disobey the gospel, because of the behaviour of their wives they may be won over without a word, when they see the reverence and purity of your lives. Yours must not be exterior adornment: the braiding of your hair and wearing gold rings or putting on cloaks. [Your adornment should be] the person hidden in the heart, in the incorruptibility of a gentle and quiet disposition, which is of great value before God. For that was how, once upon a time, the holy women who hoped in God adorned themselves, by submitting to their own husbands, as Sarah obeyed Abraham, calling him 'Lord'; you were born from her, children who do good and do not fear any intimidation.

Husbands likewise, who are living prudently with their wife as with a weaker vessel, show honour to them as fellow heirs of the free gift of life, so that your prayers may not be blocked.

> In every generation, Christians have had to face the question of how to live in and with the prevailing culture. Are we to go quietly about our business, or set up Christian communes of the like-minded, or bravely stand out against contemporary morals, or try to convert the world, or excommunicate it as hopelessly evil? The Book of Revelation takes the last of these options; 1 Peter on the whole takes the first. The Book of Revelation saw the Emperor and his representatives as utterly evil; Peter sees them as doing God's will. In different times and places Christians have to take a decision about their stance towards secular authority. In my own South Africa, Christians responded in very different ways to the government that introduced and maintained the evil of apartheid.
>
> The fact that Peter's longest set of remarks here is to the slaves may simply reflect the actual composition of the communities to which he was writing. If they were largely slaves who had no realistic prospect of obtaining their freedom, but who found hope and inspiration in the weekly meetings of Christians, then this may be the best advice: put up with unjust punishment (that happens) and keep your eyes on Christ. Peter then underlines this with what may be a hymn, filled with scriptural allusions about the example of Jesus.
>
> The instruction to wives to be 'subordinated' rings less comfortably in our ears; but equality of the sexes was something unheard of in that world, although we should notice that Peter clearly believes in such equality. For all this talk of 'weaker vessels' (which may be

---

110. Isaiah 53:9
111. Isaiah 53:5, 6

alluding to the physical facts of the relative strength of men and women), he is quite clear that women are co-heirs with their husbands.

How to cope with persecution and other difficulties

8-22 Finally, all [of you should be] of one mind, sympathetic, loving the brothers and sisters, compassionate, humble-minded, not returning evil for evil, or abuse for abuse; on the contrary, [you should] bless [others] – because that is what you were called for, to inherit a blessing,

> 'For the one who wants to love life and see good times,
>> should restrain his tongue from evil
>> and his lips from speaking treachery.
> They should turn away from evil and do good.
> They should seek peace and pursue it.
>> For the Lord's eyes are on the just,
>> and his ears on their petition.
> The Lord's face is against those who do evil.'[112]

And who will harm you if you become ardent for what is good? And even if you were to suffer because of righteousness – congratulations!

Do not be disturbed by fear of them. Treat the Lord Christ as holy in your hearts, always ready to give an explanation to everyone who asks you for an account of the hope that is in you; but do it gently, and with respect, with a clear conscience, in order that those who slander your good way of life in Christ may be embarrassed on the very point on which you are being slandered. For it is better to suffer (if that is what God wants) as people who do good than as evildoers.

Because Christ also suffered once, for sins, a just person on behalf of the unjust, in order to bring you to God; he was put to death in the flesh but brought to life in the Spirit; and in the Spirit he also went and proclaimed to the spirits in prison, to those who had once been disobedient, when God patiently waited, in the days of Noah, when the Ark was being prepared, into which a few (that is, eight people) were brought safely through, by means of water. And water now saves you too, who are the anti-type [of Noah and his company], that is the water of baptism, [which is] not putting off physical dirt, but is an appeal to God, proceeding from a clear conscience, through the resurrection of Jesus Christ, who is at the right hand of God, having made the journey into heaven, once the angels and authorities and powers were made subject to him.

Here Peter offers some practical help, which would be useful for those who face religious persecution (and it seems that some at least of those to whom he is writing may be suffering in this way); but it would also be helpful for the slaves and wives, mentioned not long ago, if they were experiencing the kind of oppression to which patriarchal society tends to expose them. Notice that the instructions here have three elements: they have a basis in the Old Testament; they are linked to the gospel (the congratulations to those who suffer for righteousness echoes Matthew 5:10); and they relate, as all

---

112. Psalm 34:12-16a

Christian living must, to Christ's death and resurrection. There is also the slightly mysterious reference to Christ preaching to the 'spirits in prison'; scholars are divided as to whether these are the pre-Christian dead or imprisoned angels. Either way, Peter's readers are invited to share in Christ's victory, as he goes on to demonstrate.

Some scholars read this paragraph as evidence that 1 Peter is a homily addressed to those who are about to be baptised. Notice the author's understanding of baptism: it is not just a matter of water, and being clean, but of direct access to God, and profoundly connected with the Resurrection.

Christians must expect to be different

4 1-11 Therefore, since Christ has suffered in the flesh, you also [should] arm yourselves with the same frame of mind, because the one who has suffered in the flesh is free from sin, so that for the time that remains in the flesh he lives no longer by human longings, but by the will of God. Let the time that has elapsed be sufficient for people who live their lives in debauchery, passions, drunkenness, carousing, drinking parties, and unlawful idolatry to accomplish what the Gentiles like to do. They are surprised when you do not rush with them into the same flood of dissipation; they slander you, but they will [have to] give an account to the one who is ready to judge the living and the dead. This was why the gospel was preached to the dead, so that although they may have been condemned as human beings in the flesh, they may live the life of God in the Spirit.

The end of everything has drawn near. So keep your heads and be sober for your prayers. Before everything else, have an eager love for one another, because 'love covers a multitude of sins'.[113] Be hospitable to each other, without grumbling, each one giving the same service to others as they have received the gift, like good stewards of God's multi-coloured grace. If someone speaks, let them speak as though it were God's words; if someone serves, then [do it] from the resources that God endows, so that in every respect God may be glorified through Jesus Christ, to whom is the glory and the power for ever and ever. Amen.

Christians march to the beat of a different drum. What marks us out is the relationship with Christ, and we should both expect and desire to share his experiences. This will not necessarily win us friends from among those for whom Christ is not equally important. Also Christians live according to a different time-frame: 'The end of everything has drawn near.' Human relations, especially within the Christian community, and everything that they do, should be seen from this perspective.

Suffering with Christ is a privilege

12-19 My beloved, don't get surprised (as though something strange were happening to you) at the ordeal by fire with which you are being tested. Instead, rejoice as you share Christ's sufferings, so that you may rejoice and exult at the revelation of his

---

113. Proverbs 10:12

glory. Congratulations if you are reviled in Christ's name, because the Spirit of Glory and of God rests upon you. For let none of you suffer as a murderer or a thief or an evildoer or as a busybody. But if it is as a Christian that a person suffers, let them not be embarrassed, but glorify God on the grounds of this name. Because it is time for the judgement to begin with God's household; and if it begins with you, what will be the end, for those who disobey God's gospel? And if 'the just person is scarcely saved, where shall the impious and the sinner appear'?[114] So those who suffer according to the will of God should entrust their lives to their trustworthy Creator, by doing good.

> We may feel a little uncomfortable at the idea that suffering is what God wants for us; but Peter is writing to Christians who (like Christians ever since) are enduring suffering, and they need to find some landmarks in the storm. The idea that Christ has been there before us is undeniably helpful, as is the careful distinction between suffering as a Christian and suffering because of crimes that we have committed.

All encouraged to live as a community in the face of persecution

5 [1-11] So I encourage those who are *elders* among you; I am a colleague of theirs in this office, and I have my share in the glory that is going to be revealed. Shepherd the flock of God that is among you, overseeing them not under compulsion but voluntarily, in God's way, wholeheartedly rather than out of desire for dishonest gain, and not like people who lord it over their allotted portions [of the flock], but acting as models for the flock. And with the appearance of the Chief Shepherd you will receive the unfailing crown of glory. *Younger people*, likewise, submit to the elders; all of you [should] clothe yourselves with humility, because God 'is opposed to the arrogant, but to the humble he gives grace'.[115]

Therefore be humbled under God's powerful hand, that he may raise you up at the right time, throwing all your cares on to God, because God is concerned for you. Be sober, stay awake, for your opponent, the devil, like a roaring lion goes about seeking someone to gobble up. Resist him, firm in the faith, knowing that the same kinds of suffering are laid upon [all] the Christian community. And the God of all grace, who invites you to his eternal glory in Christ Jesus, after you have suffered for a little while, will himself restore you, and give you support, strength, and a secure foundation. To him be the power for ever, Amen.

> Clearly these groups are facing persecution of some kind; and Peter invites them to draw together as a community in the face of the threat. The office-bearers ('elders') must unselfishly look after them all, and the younger ones also have their part to play. Notice how Peter brings them back, again and again, to God (while darkly reminding them of the activity of the Opponent, the devil) – but overall the tone is one of quiet confidence.

---

114. Compare with Proverbs 11:31
115. Proverbs 3:34

Final greetings and encouragement

12-14 I write to you briefly, I think, through Silvanus, that faithful brother, encouraging [you] and testifying that it is the grace of God in which you stand. The Elect [Church] here in 'Babylon' greets you, as does my son Mark. Greet each other with the kiss of love.

Peace to all of you who are in Christ.

In these final words, we learn (it seems) that 'Peter' wrote through a secretary, Silvanus, which in the view of some scholars would explain the high standard of Greek in the letter (and perhaps his apparent uncertainty as to whether or not he has been brief). The reference to 'my son Mark' has often been interpreted as a reference to the author of the second Gospel – but we know far too little about what lies behind the reference to either of these names to make any very confident claims. Presumably Peter's addressees knew a good deal more. 'Babylon' is almost certainly Rome, as in the Book of Revelation. The letter comes to a calm and firm end.

The Second Letter of Peter

Introduction

1 [1,2] Symeon Peter, a servant and apostle of Jesus Christ, to those who have been allotted a faith equal to ours, through the righteousness of our God and Saviour Jesus Christ, may grace and peace be multiplied for you through the knowledge of God and of Jesus our Lord.

> The Greek of this letter is so different from that of First Peter (and we shall try to make this clear in the translation) that very few scholars regard the two letters as having been written by the same author. It is possible that a scribe who was given a good deal of latitude wrote it under Peter's direction. Or perhaps it was written to 'say what Peter would be telling us today', some time after his death. In many ways (the self-identification of the author, the prayer for 'grace and peace', and the echo of Titus 1:3 in the phrase 'our God and Saviour Jesus Christ') this resembles the opening of a Pauline letter. It is clearly, though, intended to claim Peter, leader of the Twelve, as its author; and the way the word 'righteousness' is used here is quite different from the way Paul uses it in Romans and Galatians.

The overture

[3-15] Since divine power has bestowed everything on us that [we need] for life and for godliness, through the knowledge of the One who called us by his own glory and power, through which the precious and sublime promises have been freely given to us, so that through these you may become sharers in the divine nature and escape the destruction that is in the world because of lust.

And for this very reason make every effort to add virtue to your faith, and knowledge to your virtue, and self-control to your knowledge, and endurance to your self-control, and godliness to your endurance, and affection for the community to your godliness, and love to your affection for the community. For if these things are yours, and if they are on the increase, they make you productive and fruitful, and [lead you] to the knowledge of our Lord Jesus Christ. You see, if anyone lacks these things, they are short-sighted to the point of blindness, oblivious of the purification of their sins [which they received] long ago. Therefore, brothers and sisters, be all the more eager to make your calling and your election secure. For if you do this, you will never, ever stumble. That is how your entry into the eternal kingdom of our Lord and Saviour Jesus Christ will be amply provided for.

Therefore I am always going to remind you about these things, even though you know [them] and are confirmed in them by the truth that has come to you. I think it proper, for as long as I am in this tent, to give you a wake-up call by way of reminder, knowing that the time for me to put off this tent is soon, as our Lord Jesus Christ revealed to me; and I shall make every effort that on every occasion you may be able to remember these things, after my death.

> Peter (for so we shall call him) is quite clearly anxious that those he is writing to should not go wrong in any way, although we only form the vaguest possible impression of what he fears might happen to them. Jesus Christ is absolutely essential to his and their experience, and he does not want them to lose any of their enthusiasm. We also notice a possible reference to 2 Corinthians 5:1 in the reference to 'putting off the tent', and quite likely also to John 21:18, 19 in the phrase 'as Our Lord Jesus Christ revealed to me'.

Peter the eyewitness

16-21 You see, we were not following cunningly concocted myths when we revealed to you the powerful presence of Our Lord Jesus Christ. No – we had seen his majesty for ourselves. For he received honour and glory from God the Father, when such a powerful voice came from the Sublime Glory: 'This is my beloved Son in whom I am well pleased'.[116] And we heard this voice ourselves coming from heaven when we were with him on the holy mountain. And we have the prophetic word, which is all the more reliable; you do well when you pay attention to it, as to a lamp shining in a dark place, until the day dawns, and the morning star rises in your hearts. Know this first, that no prophecy in Scripture is a matter of one's own interpretation. For prophecy was never brought about by the will of human beings; no – human beings gave utterance when they were borne along by the Holy Spirit from God.

> Here there is an explicit claim to be writing as or in the name of Peter the Apostle, eyewitness to the Transfiguration. Many readers feel discomfort at so palpable an attempt to deceive (if Peter was not in some sense the author of this letter) and argue for a secretary writing in his name.
>
> Notice the appeal to the 'prophetic word': this could either be the Old Testament prophecies, or 'what Jesus is saying to us today', enabling Christians to keep faithful as they await Jesus' return. Notice, too, the lovely image of the lamp that keeps going through the night until the light comes. There is also an unease, perhaps a sign of the growing institutionalisation of the Church, at the notion of interpreting Scripture just as people please: the important thing is to listen for the voice of God.

Beware of fakes

2 1-3 There arose false prophets among the people, just as there will be false teachers among you, who will smuggle in destructive heresies, and deny the Master who bought them, bringing rapid destruction upon themselves. Many people will follow

116. Matthew 17:5

their debaucheries, and because of them the way of truth will be reviled. In their rapacity, they will exploit you with fabricated words; their condemnation (long since uttered) is not idle, their destruction is not asleep.

Here we have a profound awareness that not just any expression of Christianity will do. There are frauds, whom you can detect by their immoral way of life – and they will get their come-uppance. Christianity has always had to look very carefully at new expressions of the faith, and test whether or not they ring true. In this case, the frauds are evidently peddling ('spinning') a false view of Jesus. This is the beginning of a passage (going down to 3:3) that 'Peter' has evidently borrowed from the Letter of Judas, or from a document to which both authors had access.

God will look after you, even if you live in a wicked society (proved from Scripture)

4-11   For if God did not spare angels who sinned, but consigned them to hell, handing them over to the chains of the netherworld, [where] they are kept under guard to await condemnation; and if God did not spare the ancient world, but preserved Noah and his eight-man crew as a herald of righteousness, when he brought the Flood on the world of the impious; and if he reduced the cities of Sodom and Gomorrah to ashes, then condemned them to destruction, setting up their condemnation as an example to those who were going to commit impieties, and delivered righteous Lot, who was oppressed by the lifestyle of the immoral and the debauched (you see, the righteous man tormented his righteous soul by what he saw and heard, living among them day after day) then the Lord knows how to rescue the ungodly from their trial, and to keep the unrighteous under punishment until the Day of Judgement, especially those who go after the flesh, desiring pollution and despising the Lordship. They are arrogant and audacious, not afraid to revile the glorious ones, whereas angels who are greater in might and power do not bring a defamatory judgement against them from the Lord.

Peter evidently had particular targets in mind, and presumably those he was writing to knew what he was talking about. We can only guess, on the basis of what he tells us; but it looks as though he has in mind people whose way of life is immoral (in not very specific ways, but perhaps there is a hint of sexual aberrations) and has an uncomfortable effect on Peter's addressees; and perhaps they have unsatisfactory views about the 'glorious ones' (but since we cannot be quite sure who they are, that does not advance us by very much). If in any case this material is borrowed from elsewhere, we are in an even less satisfactory position.

All-out assault on the enemy

12-22   These people [are] like irrational animals, creatures of instinct born to be captured and killed. They blaspheme in matters that they know nothing about; they will be destroyed just like the animals, suffering damage in recompense for the damage they have done, regarding their daytime carousing as a pleasure; they are disfigurements and blemishes as they revel in their love feasts [or, according to some manuscripts: 'deceptions'], and as they share their feasting with you. Their eyes are full of adultery, never abstaining from sin; they seduce unstable souls; their hearts are trained in avarice; they are offspring of the curse. They have abandoned the direct road and have lost their way; they followed the way of Balaam, son of Beor, who loved the reward of unrighteousness, but received the rebuke of his own lawlessness: a dumb beast of burden, speaking in a human voice, prevented the prophet's folly. These people are waterless wells; they are mists driven by a storm; deep darkness is reserved for them. They utter arrogant folly, and with debauched desires of the flesh they entice those who barely escape from the people who live in error. They promise them freedom, but are themselves slaves of destruction (for if someone is defeated by anything, they are its slaves). You see, if they have escaped the world's defilement by knowing our Lord and Saviour Jesus Christ, but then get defeated by getting entangled in them again, their 'last state' would have become 'worse than the first'! For it would have been better for them not to have known the way of righteousness than to have known it and then to turn back from the holy commandment handed down to them. What happened to them was the truth of the proverb: 'A dog returning to its own vomit and a washed pig rolling in mud.'[117]

> Who are the enemy that Peter has in mind? Clearly he views them with extreme misgivings. They are apparently close to the people to whom he is writing, and were evidently Christians at some stage, but are so no longer (at least in Peter's view); and it is not so much their beliefs that he objects to as their dissipated behaviour. We have not, of course, heard 'the enemy's' version of events.
>
> The contrast of 'the last state' with 'the first' is, clearly, an allusion to Matthew 12:45.

Don't be fooled – the end is coming

3 ¹⁻¹⁰ Beloved, I am writing this second letter to you. In both letters I [have been trying to] arouse your sincere understanding by way of a reminder, to remind you of the words spoken in advance by the holy prophets and the command (from your apostles) of the Lord and Saviour. Know this first and foremost, that in the last days mockers will come mocking, living in accordance with their own desires, and saying, 'Where is his promised coming? For from the day when your ancestors died, everything remains just as it was from the beginning of creation.' They deliberately let the fact pass them by that the heavens and the earth long ago came into existence, out of water and through water by the word of God, through which the world as it then existed was flooded by water and destroyed.

Beloved, don't let this fact pass you by, that for the Lord a single day is like a thousand years, and a thousand years like a single day. The Lord is not being slow in his promise (as some people think of slowness). No – he is being patient with you; he doesn't want any of you to be lost. He wants all of you to reach repentance. The Day of the Lord will come like a thief. On that day, the heavens will pass away

---

117. See Proverbs 26:11

with a thunderous roar, and the elements will burn and be dissolved, and the earth, and the works that take place in it, shall be discovered.

> An issue that seems to have dominated the early Church was that of the expectation, apparently going back to Jesus himself, that the end was coming quite soon. But it didn't happen, and that inevitably meant that people raised questions about it. Peter is determined to hang on to his view that it is still on its way; what matters is a) the reliability of God, and b) (closely connected) the reliability of the prophets. Peter's answer to the delay is a double one: first, God does not see time as we see it; second, God is giving us all time to repent. But, he says, don't be fooled: the Day of Judgement is coming.

So keep living properly, to the very end

11-13   So when all these things fall apart, what sort of people must you be? [People who live] holy and godly lives, eagerly waiting for the coming of the day of God, because of which the heavens will be dissolved in flames, and the elements melt and burn. Let us wait for 'new heavens and a new earth',[118] in accordance with his promise, where righteousness dwells.

> Given the imminence of the Day of Judgement, Peter is anxious to make sure that they are not tempted by the world around them. Whether he thought them particularly prone to backsliding we cannot really say; but he wants them to stay on the right path, and he does not mind if a certain healthy fear is part of their stimulus in the direction of correct behaviour.

Final exhortation

14-18   So, beloved, as you wait for these things, make every effort to be found spotless and stainless, in peace; and think of Our Lord's patience as salvation. That was how our beloved brother Paul wrote to you, in accordance with the wisdom that was given him, speaking of these things, as he does in all his letters. In these letters there are some things that are obscure, which uneducated and unstable people distort (as they do with other scriptures), to their own destruction.

So, beloved, you know it in advance; be on your guard. Don't be led away by the error of the ungodly, and drift away from [the source of] your own stability, but grow in the grace and knowledge of Our Lord and Saviour Jesus Christ. To him be the glory now and to the day of eternity. Amen.

> Peter retains his sense of urgency to the very end, but he is maddeningly vague about precisely what he expects of his addressees.
> We notice that Peter already knows Paul's letters, apparently as a collection, and perhaps also as something to be regarded as 'Scripture', although the word can also mean 'writings'. Possibly one of Paul's letters was written to whomsoever Peter is addressing, though it is

---

118. Isaiah 65:17

hard to be sure which letter Peter has in mind here. Quite correctly he points to the difficulty of understanding some of what Paul writes, very likely with regard to the end-time.

As so often in the New Testament, the author ends by giving glory to Jesus, in terms that put him on the same level as God.

The First Letter of John

The prologue

1 ¹⁻⁴ What was from the beginning, what we have heard, what we have seen with our eyes, what we beheld, and our hands touched, with regard to the Word of Life: and the Life appeared, and we saw, and we bear witness, and we are announcing to you the Eternal Life that was with the Father and appeared to us. What we have heard and seen, we are announcing also to you, in order that you also may have communion with us; and our communion is with the Father and with his son, Jesus Christ. And we are writing these things in order that our joy may be fulfilled.

What kind of a document is 1 John? It does not at all look like a letter, and some scholars regard it as a kind of theological commentary on the Gospel of John, perhaps intended to affirm the full humanity of Christ, which readers of the Fourth Gospel may have been inclined to underplay. You can hear the echoes of John's Gospel here: 'from the beginning', 'Word', 'Life', 'Eternal Life', and the references to Father and Son. But the Word and the Life are not here explicitly presented as 'incarnate' to quite the same extent as they were in the Prologue to the Gospel. The reader should keep open the question of what 1 John is trying to do.

Notice the word that I have translated as 'communion'. The Greek word is *koinonia*, and it is a very important idea in the New Testament. It can also be translated as 'fellowship', 'union', 'partnership', 'community', and 'solidarity'. I have translated it here as 'communion' in order to stress the importance of the chain that runs: Father-Son-the author-the readers.

The message

⁵⁻¹⁰ And this is the message that we have heard from him, and which we pass on to you, that God is light, and that in God there is no darkness at all. If we claim to have communion with God and we are walking in darkness, [then] we are lying, and not performing the truth. But if we are walking in the light, as God is in the light, we have communion with each other, and the blood of Jesus his Son purifies us from all sin.

If we say that we have no sin, we are deceiving ourselves, and the truth is not in us. If we admit our sins, God is faithful and just in forgiving us [our] sins, and purifying us from all unrighteousness. If we claim that we have not sinned, we turn God into a liar, and his Word is not in us.

There are two points here at which the epistle is different from the Fourth Gospel. First, here it is God who is light, whereas in the Gospel of John it was the Incarnate Word. Second, there is the emphasis on Jesus' blood. Each of these represents a subtle shift in the direction of stressing the humanity of Jesus, and a corresponding down-playing of his divinity. The stress on the fact of our sinfulness may suggest that the opponents whom this epistle has in mind not only over-emphasised Jesus' divinity at the expense of his humanity, but also claimed not to be sinners (and therefore not to stand in need of the death of Jesus). We may also notice that it is hard to decide whether or not to capitalise the word 'Word': does the author have in mind the 'message' or Jesus, the 'Word Incarnate'?

What Jesus does

2 [1,2] My children, I am writing these things in order that you should not sin. And [yet] if anyone does sin, we have a Paraclete before the Father, Jesus Christ the Just One. And he is an expiation-sacrifice for our sins, and not just for our sins, but for [those of] the whole world.

John combines here a desire that people should not sin, with an awareness that in fact they do. He describes Jesus here as the 'Paraclete' (Advocate, Prisoner's Friend), a role which in the Fourth Gospel was filled by the Holy Spirit. And, once again, the author insists on Jesus' humanity ('the Just One') and on his death (the 'expiation-sacrifice'). He also looks outwards to 'the whole world', whereas in certain moods (see, for example, the Last Supper Discourse in John 13–17) the Fourth Gospel tends to concentrate more on the beleaguered little group from which the Gospel emerged.

The test of knowing Jesus

[3-6] And this is how we know that we have come to know him, if we keep his commandments. The one who says 'I have come to know him' and does not keep his commandments is a liar, and the truth is not in that person. But whoever keeps Jesus' word, God's love is made perfect in that person. This is how we know that we are in [Jesus]. Anyone who says that they remain in him should themselves walk as he walked.

Here, in language profoundly reminiscent of John's great Last Supper Discourse (Gospel of John, Chapters 13–17), we are given the test whereby we can find out if someone really knows Jesus: Do they 'keep his command' (14:21 etc.)? Do they have truth in them (8:44)? Do they 'remain in Jesus' (15:1-10)?

Walking in the light and in the darkness

[7-11] Beloved, it is not a new commandment that I am writing to you – it is [the] old one, which you had from the beginning. The old commandment is the word that

you heard. Again I am writing a new commandment for you, which is true both in him and in you, because the darkness is passing and the true light is already shining. Anyone who says they are in the light and who hates their brother or sister is in darkness until the present moment. The one who loves their brother or sister remains in the light, and there is no occasion of stumbling in that person. But the one who hates their brother or sister is in the darkness, and walks in the darkness, and they do not know where they are going, because the darkness has blinded their eyes.

> The charming tradition that 1 John was written by the evangelist as an old man presumably takes its origin from passages such as this, where there may seem to be confusion (is it a new or an old commandment?) and repetition. For the same reason, it is desperately difficult to be confident about the structure of the letter. But we can at least say that there are unmistakable echoes of the Gospel.

To various sectors of the community

12-14   I am writing to you, *children*, because your sins have been forgiven for his name's sake.

I am writing to you, *fathers*, because you have come to know the One who was from the beginning.

I am writing to you, *young men*, because you have conquered the evil one.

I write to you, *children*, because you have come to know the Father.

I write to you, *fathers*, because you have come to know the One who was from the beginning.

I write to you, *young men*, because you are strong, and God's word remains in you, and you have conquered the evil one.

> It is probably better not to press the text too hard here, and find differences between the various exhortations, appropriate to the different addressees. Note that the word that I have translated 'because' could also mean 'that' (with, oddly enough, not very much difference in meaning). Notice also that the 'One who was from the beginning' could be God or Jesus; probably the latter makes the best sense.

The World's desire

15-17   Do not love the world, nor the things that are in the world. If someone loves the world, the love of the Father is not in that person; because everything that is in the world, the desire of the flesh and the desire of the eyes, and the ostentatious way of life, are not from the Father – they are from the world. And the world is passing away, and so does its desire; but the one who does God's will remains for eternity.

> In the gospel, the world is very often (as here) a symbol of what is opposed to God. Sometimes, though, as in 'God so loved the world', it has a more positive sense. Here, it is uniformly negative in meaning.

Traitors in the community

18, 19   Children, it is the final hour, and as you have heard that Anti-Christ is coming, so now many Anti-Christs have appeared; that is how we know that it is the final hour. They went out from us, but they were not of our number. For if they had been of our number, they would have remained with us. But [this happened] that they might be shown up as not of our number.

> In this passage, it seemed a good idea to hyphenate 'Anti-Christ', because the idea is not so much that of an opposing, alternative Messiah; it is rather, as the following passage indicates, that some people, once of the Johannine community but now its opponents, are denying (among other things) that Jesus is the Christ or Messiah.

Truth and falsehood in the community

20-25   And you have anointing from the Holy one; and you all know. I do not write to you because you do not know the Truth, but because you do know it, and no lie belongs to the Truth. Who is the Liar, if not the one who denies that Jesus is the Christ? That is the Anti-Christ, the one who denies the [relationship of] the Father and the Son. Anyone who denies the Son lacks the Father also; the one who acknowledges the Son has the Father also.

As for you – what you heard from the beginning, let it remain in you. If what you heard from the beginning remains in you, you also remain in the Son and in the Father. And this is the promise that he promised you: Eternal Life.

> John's claim is that those who have left the community have gone against what they 'heard from the beginning'. In particular, they have denied that Jesus is the Messiah, and tried to drive a wedge between Father and Son. Interestingly, the word that I have translated as 'anointing', here and in the following section, is closely related to the word 'Christ'.
>
> The goal of this letter is the same as that of the Gospel: Eternal Life (see John 20:31; 5:24 etc.).

Remain in him

26-29   I write this with regard to those who are misleading you. And as for you, the anointing which you received from him remains among you, and you have no need for anyone to teach you; but as his anointing teaches you about everything, and is true and not a lie, and as he taught you, remain in him.

And now, children, remain in him, in order that when he appears we may have confidence and not be embarrassed and shrink from him when he comes. If you know that he is righteous, you know that everyone who performs righteousness is born of him.

> The language is familiar from the Gospel (look at 15:1-10, for example), and from what we have seen hitherto in the epistle; but it is very hard to be precise about what the author has in mind. The

invitation is evidently to stay within the community, and to live appropriately, but we cannot confidently say much more than that.

The mystery of love and sin in the community

3 ¹⁻¹⁰ See what great love the Father has given us, that we might be called children of God; and we are! This is the reason that the world does not know us, that it did not know him. Beloved, as it is we are children of God; and it has not yet appeared what we shall be. We know that when he appears we shall be like him, because we shall see him as he is. And everyone who has this hope in him purifies himself or herself, just as he is pure.

Everyone who does sin also does lawlessness; and sin is lawlessness. And you know that he has appeared in order to take away sin; and there is no sin in him. Everyone who remains in him does not sin. Everyone who sins has failed to see him or to know him.

Children – don't let anyone lead you astray. The one who does righteousness is righteous, precisely as he is righteous. The one who does sin comes from the devil, because the devil has been sinning since the beginning. This was why the Son of God appeared, to undo the devil's works. No one who is born of God does sin, because his seed remains in that person, and that person cannot sin, because they are born of God. This is how to distinguish the Children of God and the Children of the devil. Everyone who fails to do righteousness does not belong to God, and [likewise] everyone who fails to love their brother or sister.

> Once again, we can see the kind of thing that John is saying, without knowing quite how it all hangs together. At times it is very hard to be sure whether the 'he' of whom the author speaks is God or Jesus. The reader can decide which the author has in mind.

The Message is: love not hate

¹¹⁻¹⁸ Because this is the message which you heard from the beginning, that we should love each other, not like Cain, who was of the evil one, and slaughtered his brother. And why did he slaughter him? Because his works were evil, while his brother's works were just.

Brothers and sisters, don't be surprised if the world hates you. We know that we have transferred from death to life, because we love the brothers and sisters. The one who fails to love remains in [the realm of] death. Everyone who hates their brother or sister is a murderer – and you know that no murderer has eternal life remaining in them. This is how we have come to know [what] love [is], that he laid down his life for our sakes – and we in our turn should lay down our lives for our brothers and sisters. If someone who has worldly goods sees their brother or sister in need, and closes their heart to them, how does the love of God remain in them? Children – let's not love [just] with a word or [just] with [our] tongue; let's love in deed and in truth.

> It is a perfectly reasonable assumption that our faith should make a visible difference. We should expect opposition, from those opposed to God; but likewise people should expect to see in us a life, and a policy about actions, that fit the gospel that we proclaim.

How do we know?

19-24 And this is how we shall know that we are of the truth, and in his presence we shall reassure our heart, whatever our heart may accuse us of, that God is greater than our heart, and knows everything. Beloved, if the heart does not condemn us, we have confidence before God, and whatever we ask we receive from him, because we keep his commandments and do what is pleasing before him. And this is his commandment, that we believe in the name of his son Jesus Christ, and love each other, just as he gave us [the] command. And the one who keeps his commandments remains in him and he in that person. This is how we know that he remains among us, from the Spirit that he gave us.

> John is endeavouring here to give his readers confidence, in language that makes us think of the Fourth Gospel: 'we shall know that we are of the truth' (John 18:37); 'whatever we ask we receive from him' (14:13); 'we do what is pleasing before him' (8:29); 'love each other' (15:17); 'remains in him, and he in that person' (6:56). It is clear that the letter and the Gospel come from the same circles, if not necessarily from the same author.
>
> What does the 'Spirit' do, according to this passage? (Read it *carefully*).

The critical importance of Jesus' humanity; telling the spirits apart

4 1-6 Beloved, don't believe every spirit. Instead, test the spirits [to see] if they come from God, because many fake prophets have come out into the world. This is how you know the Spirit of God: every spirit that acknowledges Jesus Christ as having come in the flesh is from God. And every spirit that does not acknowledge Jesus is not from God; and this is the spirit of the Anti-Christ; you have heard that he is coming – well, now he is already in the world. You are from God, children, and you have conquered them, because the One who is among you is greater than the one who is in the world. They are from the world, [and] because of this they speak from the world, and the world hears them. We are from God, and the One who is from God listens to us; the one who is not from God does not listen to us. This is how we know the Spirit of truth and the spirit of deception.

> One of the standing anxieties of John's audience seems to be the question: how can we be *sure*? His answer is to distinguish God (truth) and the world (deception), convincing perhaps more by the atmosphere he creates than by the compelling logic of his answer. Notice also the characteristic insistence on the key issue of Jesus' humanity.

The absolute centrality of love

7-11 Beloved, let us love each other, because love is from God. And everyone who loves is born of God and knows God. The one who does not love does not know God, because God is love. This is the way that the love of God appeared among us, that God sent his only Son into the world, that we might live through him. Love consists in this: not that we have loved God, but that God loved us and sent his Son as an offering for our sins. Beloved, if God loved us in this way, we in our turn should love each other.

> The root word 'love' appears (in different forms) no less than thirteen times in these five verses; and the basic model is the prior love of God, to which we subsequently respond.

Loving God means loving the community

12-21 No one has ever seen God. If we love each other, God remains in us, and his love is made perfect in us. This is how we know that he remains in us and we remain in him, that he has given us of his Spirit. And we have seen and have borne witness that the Father has sent his Son as the Saviour of the world. Whoever acknowledges that Jesus is the Son of God, God remains in that person, and that person in God. And we have come to know and to believe the love which God has among us. God is love; and the one who remains in love remains in God – and God remains in them. This is how love is made perfect with us, that we might have confidence on the Day of Judgement, that just as he is, so also we are in this world. Fear is not a part of love – instead perfect love expels fear, because fear involves punishment, and the one who fears is not made perfect in love. We love because he loved us first. If someone says 'I love God' and hates their brother or sister, they are a liar. Because the one who fails to love their brother or sister (whom they have seen!) can't possibly love God (whom they haven't seen!). And we have this commandment from him, that the one who loves God should also love their brother or sister.

> Once again the language echoes that of the Fourth Gospel, as the author builds the links between God's Spirit, mutual indwelling, accepting Jesus as Son and Saviour, and love. At the same time, he refers to the familiar contrast between God and the world, love and fear, eternal life and punishment.
>
> How should Christians demonstrate the existence of the invisible God?

The importance of the humanity of Jesus

5 1-12 Everyone who believes that Jesus is the Christ is born of God, and everyone who loves the Father also loves the one who is born of the Father. This is how we know that we love God's children, when we love God, and perform his commandments. For this is the love of God, that we should keep his commandments; and his commandments are not heavy, because everyone that is born of God conquers the world. And this is the conquest that conquers the world: our faith!

But who is the one who conquers the world, if not the one who believes that Jesus is the Son of God? He is the one who came through water and blood: not just in water alone. No – in water and in blood. And the Spirit is the one that bears witness, because the Spirit is truth. Because there are three who bear witness: the Spirit, the water, and the blood. And the three are one. If we accept the witness of human beings, God's witness is greater: because this is God's witness, that he has borne witness about his Son. The one who believes in the Son of God has the witness in himself; the one who does not trust God makes God a liar, because that person has not trusted the witness that God has given about his Son. And this is the witness, that God gave us eternal life; and this life is in his Son. The one who has the Son has life. The one who does not have the Son does not have life.

> As so often in this epistle, it is better to absorb the atmosphere rather than examine the logic. Notice, though, the absolute insistence on Jesus' humanity ('the blood') over against a spiritualising emphasis on Jesus' divinity, which for John does not do sufficient justice to the reality of what God has done for us in Christ, which our author sums up as 'eternal life'.

Grounds for confidence

13-15   I am writing this to you, so that you may know that you have eternal life, you who believe in the name of the Son of God. And this is the confidence that we have in our access to him, that if we ask for anything in accordance with his will, he hears us. And if we know that he hears us in whatever we ask for, we know that we have the requests that we asked for from him.

> Some scholars see these verses, and those which follow, as a kind of commentary on John 20:30, 31, the Fourth Gospel's original ending: 'that you may believe that Jesus is the Christ, the Son of God, and that believing you may have life in his name'. Certainly this passage, exhorting his readers to have confidence in Christ, is imbued with the language and the thought of the Gospel.

If one of the community sins

16, 17   If someone sees their brother or sister sinning, a sin that is not fatal, they will ask, and [God] will give them life, those whose sin is not fatal. There is a sin that is fatal: I am not saying that they should ask about that sin. All unrighteousness is sin, and there is a sin that is not fatal.

> This passage has caused some anxiety in the centuries since it was written. Perhaps what we should say is that the author and his first readers had a much better idea than we do what he was talking about; and when we interpret it, we shall do well to remember John's insistence on the absolute centrality of love.

Conclusion

18-21   We know that everyone who is born of God does not sin: no, the one born of God holds fast to [God], and the evil one does not touch him or her. We know that we are of God and that the whole world lies in the power of the evil one. We know that the Son of God has come and has given us understanding, that we might know the True One; and we are in the True One, in his Son Jesus Christ. This is the True God and Eternal Life.

Children – guard yourselves against idols.

> Once again we need here to breathe the air of the letter, rather than unpick the logical steps of the argument. John's readers are reminded, in conclusion, of the choice that lies before them: God or sin? God or the evil one? The Son of God or the world? Anything that is not God is an idol (the epistle's last word, significantly enough), and will let us down. The choice is ours.

The Second Letter of John

Opening greetings

1-3 The elder [or: 'presbyter'] to the chosen lady and to her children. I love you [all] in truth, and not just I, but all those who have come to know the truth, on account of the truth that remains among us and will be with us for ever. Grace, mercy and peace will be with you from God the Father, and from Jesus Christ, the Son of the Father, in truth and love.

> Unlike 1 John, this is clearly a real letter, its size possibly tailored to the space available on a sheet of papyrus. This opening is standard for a letter of the time, except that the 'chosen lady' is almost certainly a Church rather than an individual; and instead of a prayer for 'grace and peace' to his addressees, the 'presbyter' offers a quiet confidence that they will receive these gifts, and the unusual addition of 'mercy' (which we also saw in the Pastoral Letters). We can see links to the Johannine tradition represented by the Gospel of John and by 1 John: the emphasis on 'truth' and 'love', the word 'remains', and the insistence on Jesus as Son of the Father.
>
> The 'presbyter' does not tell us who he is, but few scholars see a problem in identifying him as the author of 1 John.

Grounds for rejoicing

4-6 I rejoiced enormously that I found some of your children walking in truth, just as we received [the] commandment from the Father. And now I ask you, lady, not like someone writing a new commandment to you – no, this is the commandment we had from the beginning, that we should love each other. And this is what love is, that we should live in accordance with his commandments. This is the commandment, as you heard from the beginning, that you should walk in it.

> Once again, the language is that of the Johannine community: 'truth', '(new) commandment', 'the Father', 'beginning', are all ideas from that stable. There may be a hint of trouble in that only 'some' of the chosen lady's children are walking in love. The 'it' which is the final word of the passage may refer to either 'commandment' or 'love'.

Warnings against fraternising with the enemy

7-11 For many deceivers have come out into the world: people who do not acknowledge that Jesus Christ comes in the flesh. These are the real deceivers and Anti-Christs.

Look out for yourselves, so as not to lose what we have achieved, so as to receive instead the full reward. Anyone who leads and who does not remain in Christ's teaching [or: 'teaching about Christ'], does not have God. The one who remains in the teaching has both the Father and the Son. If someone comes to you and does not bring this teaching [with them], don't accept them into your home, and don't [even] say 'Hallo' to them. For anyone who says 'Hallo' to them is in solidarity with their evil actions.

> Once again, the language is familiar from the Fourth Gospel and from 1 John. Clearly, as in 1 John, the most objectionable feature of the opponents is that they deny Jesus' humanity. We may feel uncomfortable about the exclusivism that the presbyter commends; but we do not know enough about their situation to judge.

Closing greetings

12, 13 Though I have much to write to you, I didn't want to do it in papyrus and ink; instead, I am hoping to come to you and speak face to face, so that your joy may be filled. The children of your chosen sister send you greetings.

> A fairly standard conclusion to a letter, which (as the presbyter indicates) is only a substitute for direct contact. Notice the presbyter's sense that when a Christian communicates with another Christian, it is their two Churches that greet each other.

The Third Letter of John

Opening greetings

1, 2   The elder [or: 'presbyter'] to beloved Gaius, whom I love in the truth. My beloved, I pray that in every way you are doing well, and in good health, as your soul is doing well.

> This is the shortest epistolary greeting in the New Testament (3 John is the shortest document), and the one that most resembles the examples we have of non-Christian Greek letters. The references to 'love' and 'truth' and to Gaius's 'soul' mark it out as belonging to the Johannine world.

Thanksgiving

3, 4   For I rejoiced enormously, when some of the brothers and sisters came and bore witness to your [life in] the truth, just as you are living in the truth. I have no greater joy than this, to hear that my children are living in the truth.

> This is a fairly standard thanksgiving, except that God is not brought into the matter. Once again we have the familiar Johannine emphasis on living in the truth. As before, we see the early Christian concern for one another, represented by the intelligence brought by the 'brothers and sisters'.

Christian hospitality – the contrast between Gaius and Diotrephes

5-12   Beloved, you are doing a work of faith, when you do it for fellow Christians (and actually people whom you don't know, at that!). They have given evidence of your love before the Churches, those people to whom you have given a good send-off, in a manner worthy of God himself. Because they came out for the sake of the Name, accepting nothing from the Gentiles. So we should give hospitality to people of this sort, so as to become fellow workers with the truth.

I wrote something to the Church; but Diotrephes, who likes to be their Number One, doesn't accept us. Because of this, if I come, I shall remember the things he does, talking evil nonsense about us. And not content with that, he does not give hospitality to Christians, and expels from the Church anyone who does want [to give hospitality]!

Beloved, don't imitate what is evil; imitate what is good. The person who does good is from God. The person who does evil has not seen God.

Everyone has given evidence about Demetrius; Truth Herself has given evidence about him; we ourselves give evidence – and you know that our evidence is true.

> It is impossible to reconstruct what has caused this breach in the Johannine community; but it is a story that has (sadly) repeated itself throughout the course of Christian history. We know nothing of Diotrephes beyond what is said here.
>
> Once again we notice the abundance of Johannine terminology in this passage.
>
> Hospitality is obviously an important Christian value for the author of this letter.

Conclusion – hoping to visit

13-15　I had many things to write to you; but I don't want to write to you with papyrus and ink. I hope to see you immediately, and we shall speak face to face.

Peace be with you. The friends send you greetings. Greet the friends by name.

> This is a fairly standard epistolary conclusion, but Gaius may have reflected 'you say that to everybody' if he knew that the presbyter had in 2 John also told the chosen lady (likewise as an excuse for not writing more) that he hoped to visit and 'speak face to face'. Rather as moderns say, 'See you soon.'

The Letter of Judas

Introduction

This is another short letter. It is undeniably difficult to be confident about its structure. There are a good many points of interest: firstly, the fact that Judas, or something very like it, has been in large part (though in a different order) taken over by 2 Peter. Second, Judas uses a good deal of material outside the Old Testament canon, not just the quotation from the Book of Enoch, and perhaps the Assumption of Moses, but also allusion to exegetical traditions that have gone beyond what is found in the Old Testament, with regard to Cain and Balaam. Third, the manuscript traditions are rather complex, and it is not always easy to be certain of the correct text. Finally, it is extremely difficult to be sure precisely what is the group that Judas is attacking, although it is absolutely clear that he is attacking someone.

Some readers find themselves wondering why the book is in the canon of the New Testament at all. Read it through slowly, and then ask if you agree.

Introduction

1, 2   Judas, a slave of Jesus Christ, and brother of James, to those who are called, beloved by God the Father, and kept safe for Jesus Christ, may mercy, peace and love abound for you.

> This is a characteristic introduction for a New Testament letter (and for a letter in the ancient world, for that matter). Judas (who is not the Iscariot!) is presumably, or is intended to be, the same 'brother of James', and therefore also brother of Jesus, who is mentioned at Mark 6:3 and Matthew 13:55.

The reason for writing

3, 4   Beloved, I was [already] anxious to be writing to you about our shared salvation; but [I felt] I [really] had to write to you, encouraging you to strive for the faith that was once and for all given to the saints. For some people, impious ones long ago predestined for this condemnation, have stolen in, and have perverted our God's grace into debauchery, and they deny our only Master and Lord, Jesus Christ.

> Clearly there is a crisis in the Church to which Judas is writing. There are two evidently connected possibilities. Firstly, 'grace' has been turned into debauchery, and, second, there has been a denial of Jesus.

The crisis outlined

5-13   I want to remind you, although you know all about [it] how, having once saved the people from Egypt, the second time the Lord destroyed those who did not believe, and he kept the angels who did not keep to their own domain, but abandoned their own habitation, in eternal chains, under darkness, for the judgement of the Great Day, as Sodom and Gomorrah, and the cities round about them, committed fornication, and went off in pursuit of unnatural lust, are set before us as an example, undergoing the punishment of eternal fire. Likewise, however, these people in their sleep defile the flesh, reject [Christ's?] Lordship, and defame the glorious ones. But Michael the archangel, when he disputed with the devil, argued about the body of Moses, and did not dare to bring charges of blasphemy, but said, 'May the Lord rebuke you.' But these people revile whatever they do not know, and they are destroyed by whatever they know by instinct, like irrational animals. Woe to them, because they have gone down Cain's road, and they have abandoned themselves to Balaam's error for a reward, and have been destroyed by Korah's rebellion. These are the ones who, unscrupulously feasting at your love-feasts [or: 'feasting on their deception of you'], looking after their own interests, are submerged rocks, clouds that bring no rain, trees that bring no fruit in autumn, dead twice over, plucked up by the roots, wild waves of the sea that foam with their deeds of shame, stars out of orbit, for whom the deepest darkness has been permanently reserved.

> We cannot pretend to be clear about the nature of the crisis. There is an appeal to events narrated in Scripture, and also (apparently) to the Book of Enoch, not a text that is nowadays regarded as scriptural by either Jews or Christians.

What have they been up to? It looks like some kind of sexual immorality; except that in the Old Testament 'fornication' is often a metaphor for going after other gods, or 'idolatry'. And the reference (found also in the related passage in 2 Peter) to 'rejecting the Lordship', defaming 'the glorious ones', and to Michael not daring 'to bring charges of blasphemy', all suggest that the opponents are wrong about God, or perhaps Jesus, rather than in their private life.

They won't get away with it!

14-16 It was of them that Enoch, seventh in line from Adam, said, 'Look! The Lord has come with his tens of thousands of angels, to execute judgement on everybody, and to examine every soul for all their deeds of impiety, which they impiously committed, and for all the harsh things which sinners spoke against him.' These people are grumblers and disgruntled; they go along in accordance with their own desires, and their mouths speak arrogance, showing partiality to people for the sake of profit.

> Our author clearly approves of Enoch, and of the literature that gathered in his name; but the point here is to encourage Judas's readers by telling them that the crisis will pass, that their opponents will not be victorious.

How to survive the crisis

17-23 But you, beloved, remember the words that were spoken earlier by the apostles of Our Lord Jesus Christ; they told you that at the end of time there will be mockers, who behave according to their own desires (the impious ones). These are the ones who create division, worldly people, who lack the Spirit. But you, beloved, build yourselves up on your most holy faith; pray with the Holy Spirit; keep yourselves in the love of God; welcome the mercy of Our Lord Jesus Christ, which leads to eternal life. Have mercy on some people who doubt; save other people, plucking them from the fire; have mercy on others (but with reverence); hate the garment that has been stained by the flesh.

> It is, many people find, obscurely reassuring that those early Christians also had their problems: we often find ourselves thinking 'it was easy for them'. But it wasn't: like us, they needed to remember what Jesus' apostles had said; they needed to cope with mockery and divisions; they needed to be 'built up . . . in the faith'; they needed the Holy Spirit. Like us, too, they needed to know how to cope with different kinds of tension in the Church.

Final doxology

24, 25 To the one who can keep you free from stumbling, and set you flawless before his glory in joy, to the only God our Saviour, through Jesus Christ our Lord, glory, majesty, power and authority, before all time, now and for ever. Amen.

> This final doxology is about the only part of this letter which many churchgoers will recognise.

The Revelation of John

Introduction

1 ¹⁻³ The Un-Veiling of Jesus Christ, which God gave him to show his servants what must happen soon, and what he signalled, sending by means of his angel to his servant John, who bore witness to God's message, and the witness of Jesus Christ which he saw.

Happy is the one who reads out; and those who listen to the words of the prophecy; and those who keep what is written in it. For the time is near.

Here we are told the name of the author of this extraordinary work: 'John', though there is no indication as to which John it might be (for example John the Baptist, John the son of Zebedee, or the 'John' to whom the Fourth Gospel and three letters are attributed). We are also told what kind of a document John thinks it is: an 'Un-Veiling' or 'Apocalypse' ('Revelation' is simply the Latin, and Apocalypse the Greek, equivalent of 'Un-Veiling'). We learn, further, that it is an 'unveiling of Jesus Christ', without any clue as to whether that means 'a revelation about Jesus' or 'a message transmitted by Jesus'. Perhaps it is both, as there is a clear chain which goes: God-Jesus-angel-John-slaves-of-God. However, we are also told that the book is a 'prophecy', the speech of God to human beings (and not necessarily, it is important to emphasise, a prediction of the future).

The author also distinguishes three separate stages of communicating this document, while congratulating those who are involved in it. First it must be read out loud (most of the intended recipients will have been illiterate). Reading it will have been therefore a skilled activity, from a difficult manuscript, to what may have been, on any given occasion, quite a sizeable group. Second, it must be listened to; the hearers have to be both open-minded and attentive. Third, it must be 'kept'. This is a very important idea in the Book of Revelation (as also in the Gospel and first Letter of John), and it is always used of those who 'hang on to' what God wants or commands them to do (see in addition 2:26; 3:3, 8, 10; 12:17; 14:12; 16:15; 22:7, 9). This 'Un-Veiling' is supposed to change people's lives.

Finally, we learn that there is a degree of urgency about it all: 'the time is near'. We should continue our reading with immense attentiveness.

The addressees

⁴⁻⁸ John, to the seven churches who are in Asia. Grace to you, and peace, from 'The Is and the Was and the Coming One', and from the seven Spirits who are before his

throne, and from Jesus Christ, the witness, the reliable, the first-born from the dead, and the ruler of the kings of the earth.

To the One who loved us and freed us from our sins by his blood; and he made us a kingdom, priests for his God and Father, to him be the glory and the power for ever and ever. Amen.

Behold, he is coming with the clouds; and every eye shall see him, and those who pierced him, and all the tribes of the earth shall mourn over him. Yes! Amen! 'I am the A and the Z ['the Alpha and the Omega']', says the Lord God, 'the Is and the Was and the Coming One, the Almighty.'

This is a compelling passage, and we must be sensitive to the profound emotions that are at work in it, for it is these that give the Book of Revelation its power.

What do these verses tell us about the book? First, that it is addressed to 'the seven churches that are in Asia' (modern-day Turkey; we are not to be thinking of India or points east). We shall soon be reading seven letters to these seven churches, each tailored, so far as we can see, to the needs of the particular addressees; and the order in which they appear is (look at a map) the order in which a messenger might travel, starting from the seaport of Ephesus, and following the best available roads. However, we need also to recall, all the way through the Revelation, that seven is a significant number, the symbol of perfection, so that the document is addressed not only to particular churches, but also to the whole Church (or at least all the Christians of Asia).

Second, this address, and the familiar Pauline greeting of 'grace and peace' makes it sound like a letter, as well as an Un-Veiling and a prophecy. So we shall need to watch and listen attentively if we are to do justice to this document.

Third, we are also told who the 'letter' is from; it is from John, to start with, but it also appears to be from God: 'The Is, and the Was and the Coming One'. This phrase is my rather clumsy attempt to render the title. When you see it in Greek, it looks at first sight horridly ungrammatical, and has made some people think that the author is writing in a language that is not his own. But the author manages to make the language do what he wants of it, and so we should probably not think of John as incompetent in Greek. It is more likely that he is writing in a dialect of Greek that is heavily influenced by Hebrew and Aramaic.

Fourth, the greetings come from the 'seven Spirits before the throne'. We recall that seven is the number of perfection; we shall see these 'seven spirits' again, at 3:1; 4:5, and perhaps 5:6, and readers may wonder if we should think here of the 'Holy Spirit'. Certainly the 'seven spirits' are closely related to God.

Fifth (and again ungrammatically, as far as the Greek is concerned), Jesus Christ is the sender of greetings. He is described, in terms that we shall hear again, as 'the witness, the reliable, the first-born from the dead, and the ruler of the kings of the earth'. These last two titles refer, of course, respectively to the central Christian doctrine of the Resurrection, and to the subversive creed that Jesus is the real ruler of the world, despite all appearances to the contrary. Jesus is also described as 'the One who loved us' and 'who freed us from our sins by his blood' and 'he made us a kingdom, priests for his God and Father'. And then, just as we thought that Jesus is being presented as distinct from God, we realise that he is getting a salutation that one would expect to be reserved for God: 'glory and power for ever. Amen.'

Then the Lordship of God is reasserted: 'the A and the Z', and the ungrammatical title is repeated, indicating God's control of present, past and future, all summed up as 'the Almighty'. The author is asking us to be very attentive indeed at this point.

John's vision of Jesus: the instruction to write seven letters

9-20 I, John, your brother, and your co-partner in the trouble and in the kingdom, and in endurance in Jesus, I was on the island known as Patmos because of God's word and because of witness [to] Jesus. On the Lord's Day, I fell into a trance, and I heard behind me a loud voice (it was like a trumpet) saying, 'Write what you see into a book; and send it to the seven churches: to Ephesus and Smyrna and Pergamon, and Thyatira and Sardis and Philadelphia and Laodicea.'

And I turned round to see the voice that was speaking with me; and when I turned round I saw seven golden lamp-stands, and in the middle of the lamp-stands a 'person like a Son of Man',[119] clothed in a garment that reached to his feet, and with a golden girdle round his chest. His head and his hair were white as wool, white as snow, and his eyes were like flaming fire, and his feet were like bronze, refined in a furnace; and his voice was like the voice of many waters.

And in his right hand he held seven stars; and from his mouth there came out a sharp two-edged sword. And his appearance [or: 'face'] was as the sun shines in its power. And when I saw him, I fell at his feet like a corpse; and he placed his right hand upon me and said, 'Do not be afraid; I am the First and the Last, and the Living One. And I was dead, and look! I am alive for ever and ever. And I possess the keys of death and [the keys] of hell.

'Therefore write down what you saw: both the things that are and the things that are about to happen after this, the mystery of the seven stars which you saw at my right, and the seven golden lamp-stands. The seven stars are the angels of the seven churches, and the seven lamp-stands are the seven churches.'

Again, this is an extraordinarily powerful piece of writing. Some people think of Revelation as just a literary composition, without any necessary basis in fact; but it doesn't feel like that. It is hard to avoid the impression that John is recounting an actual vision, even though he uses many biblical quotations and allusions.

The grammar, once again, is such as to make a teacher of Greek shiver, at several points; but significantly it never comes between the reader and the author's meaning.

There are some other points to notice:

---

119. Compare Ezekiel 1:26; Daniel 7:13

- The word that I have here translated 'endurance' is a common idea in the Book of Revelation (see 1:9; 2:2, 3, 19; 3:10; 13:10; 14:12). Elsewhere it has seemed better to translate it as 'stamina' and 'constancy'. But it is a clue about the kind of world that our author and his readers lived in: they had to keep going in their faith, against all the odds.

- 'John' is no more than a Christian, along with other Christians, their co-partner; and if they have been suffering, he has shared in their sufferings. He also asserts Jesus' 'kingship', which excludes the kingship of anybody else (such as the Roman emperor currently reigning).

- He also appears to have been exiled to Patmos ('because of God's word and Jesus' witness').

- He is there on 'the Lord's Day' (most likely Sunday), and has this quite extraordinary experience, 'a voice like a trumpet', which is so powerful that he baffles us by turning round 'to *see* the voice'!

- Before that, however, he is given instructions to 'write to the seven churches'. This may introduce the seven letters that will shortly follow; or it may refer to the whole book.

- Then the 'sound' turns into a 'vision': seven lamp-stands (later interpreted as 'seven churches') and in the middle of them 'one like a Son of Man'. Obviously there is a glance here at the vision in Daniel 7 (have a look at it, if you can't recall how it went); but equally it clearly refers to Jesus, who in the Gospels often referred to himself as 'Son of Man'. It is a magnificent and impressive vision, and it sounds and feels like a vision of God, as the author indicates by falling down like a corpse. The impression is continued when the vision says 'Do not be afraid, for I am the First and the Last', which a few verses earlier, under the guise of 'A and Z', had clearly referred to God; and the reference to the 'Living One' confirms this interpretation. However, when we read that it is the one who 'was dead and behold I am alive for ever and ever' it can only be Jesus, who is giving the instruction to start writing. Beneath the surface of the text, our author is making for Jesus some very grand claims indeed.

Letters to the Seven Churches (2:1–3:22)

John has been told to write his vision and send it to the seven churches, 'the things that are and the things that are going to happen after this'. It is not clear whether it is the seven letters or the book as a whole that represents his response to this command. The letters all have very much the same shape: each starts with the address, and with some defining quality of Jesus; each then has something about what the particular church has been up to (both good and bad); and then come a promise to 'the one who conquers' and an encouragement to 'listen to the Spirit', not always in that order. Each of them is directed by Jesus, through John, to the 'angel' of the particular church. 'Angels' are of great importance in Revelation; some scholars think that in the letters it may be the title of a leader in the local church.

The letter to Ephesus

2 1-7 'To the angel of the church at Ephesus write:

This is what the one who holds the seven stars in his right hand says, the one who walks in the middle of the seven golden lamp-stands:

I know your deeds, and your labour, and your endurance. [I know] that you cannot endure evil people, and that you tested those who said that they were apostles – and aren't! – and you found that they were fakes. [I know] that you have stamina, and that you endured because of my name, and [that] you didn't get weary.

But I have something against you: you abandoned your first love. So recall where you have fallen from, and change your ways, and do the deeds you did in the beginning. Otherwise, I'm coming to you; and I shall move your lamp-stand from its place, unless you change your ways.

But you have this point in your favour, that you hate the deeds of the Nicolaitans – which I hate, too.

Let the one who has an ear listen to what the Spirit is saying to the churches.

The one who conquers, I shall give them to eat of the tree of life, which is in the garden of God.'

In this letter, Jesus is described as 'holding the seven stars in his right hand', as in the initial vision, but also, as in the initial vision, as living 'in the middle of the golden lamp-stands'. He has, in other words, some of the qualities of God, but is also involved in the world of the seven churches; in the language of John's Gospel, we should speak of 'incarnation'. The Ephesian Christians are praised for having stuck at it (we don't know what), and for their dislike of the activity of the 'Nicolaitans'. (We have no notion of who these might have been, though plenty of scholars have made their guesses.) The Ephesians are, however, criticised for some kind of loss of fervour, and given an unmistakable, if obscure, warning.

They are also invited to 'listen to what the Spirit is saying'. This expression, which appears in each of the seven letters, suggests that when Jesus speaks it is identically the Spirit speaking. This would fit what the Gospel of John and the First Letter of John say about the relationship of Jesus and the 'Paraclete'.

The promise to Ephesus is a charming one, of eating from the tree of life. Some scholars think that there may also be a reference here to a tree in the Temple of Artemis at Ephesus, where there was a right of refuge for asylum-seekers. The word translated as 'garden' is actually a Persian word that has come into English as 'Paradise'.

The letter to Smyrna

8-11 'And to the angel of the church in Smyrna write:

This is what the First and the Last says, who became dead and lived: I know your trouble and your poverty (but in fact you are rich!). And [I know about] the blasphemy from those who claim to be Jews and are not (in fact they are the synagogue of Satan!). Don't be afraid of any of the things that you are going to suffer. Look! The devil is going to throw some of you into prison, so that you may be tested; and you'll have trouble for ten days. Be faithful until death, and I shall give you the crown of life.

The one who has an ear, let them listen to what the Spirit is saying to the churches. The one who conquers is certainly not to be injured by the second death.'

This letter has, obviously, the same shape as its predecessor. Notice how, once again, it uses language about Jesus that is elsewhere used of God.

We cannot (on the evidence of this text) say much about the trouble that the Christians of Smyrna are enduring, nor whether it could be described as persecution. The threat of imprisonment might count as persecution, of course, and the exhortation to 'be faithful until death' might hint at a possible martyrdom. The 'crown of life' is in contrast to the athlete's gold medal or 'crown': the faithful Christian will be receiving the real thing. The 'second death' will appear later in the text, in chapters 20 and 21.

The letter to Pergamon

12-17 'And to the angel of the church in Pergamon, write:

This is what the one who holds the sharp and two-edged sword says:
I know where you live, where Satan's throne is: and you hold on to my name, and you did not deny my faith, even in the days of Antipas, my faithful witness, who was killed in your town, where Satan dwells.

But I have a few things against you: you have some people there who hold on to the teachings of Balaam, who taught Balak to put a stumbling block before the children of Israel, to eat food offered to idols, and to fornicate. Similarly, you also have some people who likewise hold on to the teaching of the Nicolaitans. So change your ways. Otherwise, I'm coming soon, and I shall wage war on them with the sword of my mouth.

Let the one who has an ear listen to what the Spirit is saying to the churches. To the one who conquers, I shall give some of the hidden manna, and I shall give a white pebble, and a new name written on the pebble, which no one knows except the one who gets it.'

Pergamon became the seat of government of the Roman proconsular province of Asia, with a Temple in honour of Rome and Augustus, as early as 29 BC, and that might account for its being called the place of 'Satan's throne'; but the author may also have in mind the existence there of a temple of Asclepius. Healings often took place in the temples of Asclepius, who may therefore have been regarded as a rival to Jesus; and in addition, the 'serpent' was Asclepius's emblem, and that was an ancient Jewish symbol for Satan. There was also a temple of Zeus at Pergamon, and that may have been yet another reason why it would have been classed as the place of 'Satan's throne'.

We do not know who Antipas was; it is a Jewish name, and clearly he died a martyr's death. Nor can we be sure whether the teaching of 'Balaam' is the same as or different from that of the Nicolaitans.

'Fornication' is a standard Old Testament image for idolatry, so we cannot say if the Balaamites had one charge against them or two. The 'white pebble' is an entry ticket; the colour is that of Jesus' victory.

The letter to Thyatira

18-29   'And to the angel of the church in Thyatira, write:

This is what the Son of God says, the one who has eyes like fiery flame, and his feet are like bronze:

I know your deeds, and your love and your faithfulness and your service, and your ability to endure, and your latest deeds, that are greater than your first deeds. Nevertheless, I hold it against you that you put up with the woman Jezebel, who calls herself a prophetess, and teaches my slaves, leading them astray [so that] they fornicate, and eat food offered to idols. And I gave her time to change her ways, and she does not want to change her ways, away from her fornication. Look! I am throwing her on a bed, and those who commit adultery with her into great trouble, unless they change their ways from her [evil] deeds; and I shall kill her children with death. And all the churches shall know that I am the one who searches minds and hearts, and I shall give you each according to [what] your deeds [deserve].

And to the rest of you in Thyatira, you who do not accept this teaching, who did not know what they call "Satan's Depths", I throw no further burden upon you: but just this – hold on to what you have until I come.

And the one who conquers, and who keeps my deeds to the end, I shall give them authority over the nations (and they will rule them with an iron rod, as clay vessels are smashed), just as I have received [authority] from my Father; and I shall give them the Morning Star.

Let those who have an ear listen to what the Spirit says to the churches.'

In this letter, Jesus is called 'Son of God', the only time the title is used in the Book of Revelation. As always, the writer knows a good deal about the church that he is addressing. We can say nothing for certain about Jezebel, except that the author does not particularly care for her, and that her offences are similar to those of the 'Balaamites', who may be the same sort of person as the 'Nicolaitans'. The note of urgency is, once again, unmistakable.

The letter to Sardis

3 1-6   'And to the angel of the church in Sardis, write:

This is what the one who has the seven Spirits of God and the seven Stars is saying: I know your deeds. You have the reputation of being alive – and you are dead! Get alert; strengthen the remaining parts that were about to die; for I have not found your deeds to be perfect in the presence of my God.

So remember how you have received, and how you heard; and keep it, and change your ways. Unless you wake up, I shall come like a thief; and no way will you know at what hour I shall come upon you. You have, however, a few people in Sardis who have not defiled their garments; and they shall walk with me in white clothes, because they are worthy.

The one who conquers will be clothed in white robes, and I shall not blot their name out of the Book of Life; and I shall acknowledge their name before my Father and before his angels.

Let the one who has an ear hear what the Spirit is saying to the churches.'

> Sardis was a very well-defended fortress, and had only been captured twice in its history, both times by a trick; and there may be a reference to this in the mention of 'like a thief'. There may also, though, be an echo of Matthew 24:43 and perhaps 1 Thessalonians 5:2. We can almost certainly detect another reference to the Gospel tradition in the line 'I shall acknowledge their name . . .' (see Matthew 10:32).

The letter to Philadelphia

7-13   'And to the angel of the church in Philadelphia write:

This is what the Holy One says, the True One, the One who has the Key of David, the one who opens, and no one shall close, the one who closes and no one opens: I know your deeds. Look! I have put an opening door in front of you, which no one can shut, because you have little power, and yet you have kept my word and did not deny my name. Look! I am granting that some of the Synagogue of Satan, who call themselves Jews (and are not, but are liars) – look! I shall bring it about that they will come and fall at your feet, and know that I love you. Because you have kept my message of constancy, I in my turn shall keep you from the hour of testing that is going to come on the whole world, to test those who dwell on the earth. I am coming soon. Hold on to what you have, so that no one take your crown.

The one who conquers, I shall make them a pillar in the Temple of my God and they will never come out again, and I shall write on that person the name of my God, and the name of the city of my God, the new Jerusalem that comes down from heaven, from my God, and my new name.

Let the one who has an ear listen to what the Spirit says to the churches.'

> Christ is here seen as carrying the Key of David; the reference here is to the passage in Isaiah 22:15-23, the dismissal from office of the steward Shebna, and his replacement by Eliakim; but the key is not so much the power of hiring and firing, as the opportunity to bring the Jews of Philadelphia into the family of Christ.

As we read Revelation, one of the questions that should be surfacing is: Who does the author think that Jesus is? This passage may help us towards an answer: if Jesus can speak of 'my God', then we cannot simply identify Jesus with God.

The 'new Jerusalem' is a phrase that we shall meet again, in Chapter 21. It is perhaps appropriate that it is mentioned in a letter addressed to Philadelphia, a city that took a 'new name' (a phrase that also appears here) of 'Neo-Caesarea', in a sycophantic endeavour to please the Emperor Tiberius (Roman emperor from AD 14–37, under whom Jesus died).

The word here translated as 'constancy' is, as I have said, a prime virtue in these letters, which elsewhere it has seemed better to translate as 'stamina' or 'endurance' or 'ability-to-endure'. But it is the same word. It serves to remind us that the author envisages some trouble for this church (and others of the seven); but scholars are not agreed on whether the trouble is a general persecution, smaller local difficulties, or tribulations ahead of Jesus' Second Coming. Whatever it is, the Christians will require an ability to 'endure'.

The letter to Laodicea

14-22 'And to the angel of the church in Laodicea, write:

This is what the Amen says, the Faithful and True Witness, the Beginning of God's Creation: I know your deeds: You are neither cold nor hot. If only you *were* cold or hot! But as it is, because you are lukewarm, I am about to vomit you out of my mouth. Because you say, "I am rich, and I've been enriched, and I have no needs," and you have no idea that you are wretched and pitiable and poor and blind and naked, I advise you to buy from me gold refined in the fire, that you may [really] be rich, and white garments to put on, so that the shame of your nakedness may not appear, and eye-salve to put in your eyes, that you may see. As for me, those whom I love, I reprove and discipline. So be keen; and change your ways.

Look! I am standing at the door, and I am knocking. If anyone hears my voice and opens the door, I shall come in to them, and dine with them, and they with me.

The one who conquers, I shall give them the privilege of sitting with me on my throne, just as I conquered and sat down with my Father on his throne.

Let the one who has an ear listen to what the Spirit is saying to the churches.'

Poor old Laodicea has nothing good to be said about them at all; but John seems to have more local knowledge of it than of the other churches to which he writes. Laodicea was well known for a glossy black wool produced by the local sheep, to which the 'white garments' may be an ironic reference (though we shall read later on about the white garments of the martyrs); the city was also famous for a particular ointment applied to ears, as well as an ingredient in the making of 'eye-salve', to which John also refers. It was a wealthy city, too, so they may have been startled to be told of their poverty. 'Hot' and 'cold' perhaps refer also to nearby hot and cold springs, at Hierapolis and Colossae. The point (for us as well as for them) might be that 'hotness' and 'coldness' are good things, in water and in the spiritual life, but they are not to be mixed. 'Lukewarmness' is no good to anybody.

In this letter, the 'one who conquers' is identified for the first time as the Jesus who has conquered; and the link is definitively established between Jesus, the throne, and Jesus' Father.

The Liturgy in Heaven (4:1–5:14)

At this point, having alerted the churches of Asia to some features of their situation to which they should be paying attention, John allows us to see the heavenly liturgy in progress. All good liturgy serves to make it easier to live out our life in this world; the reader is invited to see how it works here.

The imagination is enticed: God is in charge

4 **1-11** After this I saw, and look! A door which was open in heaven; and the first voice that I had heard, like [the sound] of a trumpet speaking to me and saying, 'Come up here, and I shall show you the things that must happen after this.'

Immediately I fell into a trance; and look! A throne was placed in heaven, and there was someone sitting on the throne. And the appearance of the One Sitting was like precious stone, jasper and cornelian; and a rainbow around the throne like emerald. And around the throne [were] twenty-four thrones, and on the thrones twenty-four elders sitting, clothed in white robes, and on their heads golden crowns. And from the throne came flashes of lightning and peals of thunder, and seven fiery lamps [were] burning before the throne. These are the seven Spirits of God; and in front of the throne a sea of glass, like crystal. And in the middle of the throne, and around the throne, four animals, full of eyes in front and behind. And the first animal [was] like a lion; and the second animal [was] like a bull; and the third animal had the face like that of a human being; and the fourth animal [was] like an eagle in flight. And the four animals, each one of them had as many as six wings, around and inside full of eyes, and they have no rest, night and day, as they say,

> 'Holy, holy, holy, the Lord God, the Almighty,
> the Is and the Was and the Coming One.'

And each time the animals give glory and honour and thanksgiving to the One Sitting on the Throne, the One who Lives for Ever and Ever, the twenty-four elders fall down before the One Sitting on the Throne, and they shall worship the One who Lives for Ever and Ever, and they shall throw their crowns before the throne, saying,

> 'Worthy are you, our Lord and God
> to receive glory and honour and power
> because you created all things,
> and at your will they came into existence and were created.'

We have learnt from the letters that their addressees, the seven churches of Asia, are facing a difficult period. Now, in this 'Un-Veiling' of the heavenly liturgy, we are given an inkling of how they are to cope. They are allowed a glimpse, enticing the imagination, of the reign of God over the troubled world, to encourage them in the face of trouble. Despite all appearances to the contrary, God is really in control. And so, at the heart of the matter, at the centre of the liturgy, we see God, the One Sitting on the Throne, addressed as the 'Thrice-Holy' from Isaiah, and the ungrammatical but telling title that we have already heard: 'The Is and the Was and the Coming One'. The reality is that it is God and not the Beast, whom we shall see later, who is omnipotent, powerful though the Beast appears to be.

The precious stones and the rainbow, and the twenty-four elders in white garments and golden crowns, the four animals and seven Spirits, and the lightning and thunder, are all about creating an atmosphere of awe: at the centre of our lives is the Creator God, the only proper object of worship; and that means that all shall be well.

The throne is important: God has a throne, and it is more power-ful than that of any Roman Emperor. God himself, though, is not described, only hinted at.

The reader reassured: the Lamb can do it

5 1-14 And I saw, on the right hand of the One Sitting upon the Throne, a scroll, written inside and on the back, sealed with seven seals. And I saw a mighty angel, proclaiming in a loud voice, 'Who is worthy to open the scroll and to undo its seals?' And no one could do it: [no one] in heaven, nor on earth, nor under the earth [was able] to open the scroll, nor to look at it. And I wept greatly, because no one was found worthy to open the scroll, nor to look at it. And one of the elders said to me, 'Don't weep. Look! The Lion from the tribe of Judah, the Root of David, has conquered, to open the scroll and its seven seals.'

And I saw, standing between the throne with its four animals and the elders, a Lamb, slaughtered, so to say, with seven horns and seven eyes, which are the seven Spirits of God sent out to all the earth. And he came and took [the scroll] from the right hand of the One Sitting on the Throne.

And when [the Lamb] received the scroll, the four animals and the twenty-four elders fell before the Lamb. Each of them had a harp, and golden bowls full of incense, which are the prayers of the saints. And they are singing a new song:

'Worthy are you to take the scroll and to open its seals,
because you were slaughtered and you bought for God with your blood
people from every tribe and language and people and nation,
and you made them a kingdom and priests for our God,
and they shall reign upon the earth.'

And I saw, and I heard the voice of many angels around the throne and the animals and the elders (and their number was myriads of myriads, and thousands of thousands), saying in a loud voice,

'Worthy is the slaughtered Lamb
to receive power and wealth and wisdom and strength and honour and glory
and blessing.'

And [I heard] every creature in heaven and on earth and under the earth and in the sea, and I heard everything in them saying,

'To the One Sitting on the Throne and to the Lamb
blessing and honour and glory and power for ever and ever.'

And the four animals were saying 'Amen.'
And the elders fell down and worshipped.

Again, this is a passage of immense power. The scroll, presumably, represents God's plan: it is written 'inside and on the back', and it has seven seals (we notice how many times the number appears in this scene). The scroll is beyond the capacity of any creature to open. John grieves at this – so he knows that it is important for it to be opened. Reassurance, however, is the name of the game, and our attention is directed to the conqueror, draped in biblical titles: 'Lion of Judah, Root of David'. Then the conqueror appears; the setting is encouraging, with the elders and the four animals, but a Lamb doesn't sound much use, particularly when it turns out to have been slaughtered (the term is decidedly brutal). Now, however, things look up: we remember the 'Lamb of God, who takes away the sin of the world', of John 1:29 (though the Greek word there is slightly different). We notice, next, that this Lamb has seven horns and seven eyes, defined as the 'seven Spirits of God'. And (here's the rub) the seven Spirits are sent out into the world. Then the elders and animals sing to the Lamb in terms that would be appropriate for addressing God, except that the Lamb is clearly Jesus: 'you were slaughtered, and you bought [people] for God with your blood'. Then we learn that these people are going to be 'kings', and to 'rule over the earth'. They are, that is to say, a challenge to the Roman imperial authorities. And the whole scene ends with massed choirs of angels praising the Lamb, and then (in the same breath) both God and the Lamb, as the animals respond 'Amen', and the elders adopt the position of silent worship. This is a scene to stay with.

The Opening of the Seven Seals (6:1–8:6)

Introduction

This is an intense and powerful passage: the slow undoing of the seven seals, as the Lamb opens the scroll, with, towards the end, a pause to allow us to take in what is happening. It is important, however, not to become so obsessed with the cosmic horrors that are to come (partially represented by the four horsemen) that we miss the absolutely central (literally crucial) message that the vision seeks to convey, above all in its liturgical allusions, that *God is in charge*.

The first to the fourth seals: the four horsemen

6 1-8 And I saw that the Lamb opened one of the seven seals; and I heard one of the four animals saying (like the sound of thunder): 'Come.' And I saw, and look! A white horse, and the one sitting on it had a bow, and a crown was given him; and he came out, conquering and in order to conquer.

And when he had opened the second seal, I heard the second animal say 'Come,' and another horse came out, a red one. And to the one who sat on the horse it was given to take peace from the earth, and that they should slaughter each other; and to him a great sword was given.

And when he opened the third seal, I heard the third animal say 'Come,' And I saw, and look! A black horse, and the one sitting on it had a set of scales in his hand. And I heard something like a voice in the middle of the four animals saying, 'A quart of wheat for a denarius, and three quarts of barley for a denarius – and don't harm the olive crop and the wine crop.'

And when he opened the fourth seal, I heard the voice of the fourth animal saying 'Come.' And I saw, and look! A bay horse, and the one sitting on it, his name was Death, and Hades followed along with him, and to him was given power over a quarter of the earth, to kill with the sword, and with hunger, and with death, and by the beasts of the earth.

> Obviously we read all this, the opening of the first four seals, and the arrival of the four horsemen, with a chill in our hearts. Nevertheless we are supposed to take courage from it all. There are trials yet to come: war, and slaughter, and economic crisis (the wheat and barley is expensive, but not impossibly so), and Death; but these are allowed (rather than decreed) by God, and, as the vision of the slaughtered Lamb has already shown us, God is in charge, and God's purposes are not to be neglected.
>
> Not for the first time, John's revelation comes through both seeing and hearing.

The fifth and sixth seals: the alarmed response

9-17 And when he opened the fifth seal, I saw underneath the altar the souls of those slaughtered because of God's word, and because of the witness they had given. And they cried out in a loud voice, 'How long, Holy and True Master [before] you come to judgement and avenge our blood on those who dwell on the earth?' And to each of them was given a white garment, and God told them to rest for a little while, until [the number of] their fellow servants, and their brothers and sisters, should be completed, those who are going to be killed as they have been.

And I saw when he opened the sixth seal, and there was a great earthquake; and the sun turned as black as sackcloth, and the whole moon was like blood; and the stars of heaven fell on the earth, as a fig tree drops its late figs when it is shaken by a great wind. And the sky was split, like a rolled-up scroll, and every mountain and all the islands were shifted from their places. And the kings of the earth, and the magnates, and the mighty ones, and every slave and every free person hid in caves and in the mountain rocks. And they say to the mountains and the rocks, 'Fall on us and hide us from the face of the One Sitting on the Throne, and from the anger of the Lamb, because the great day of their anger has come – and who can stand?'

> Both these seals are accompanied by phenomena to make us quail, but both serve to emphasise that God is in charge. The fifth seal reveals that there are people who have been slaughtered 'because of

the word of God and because of their witness'. John has already used these two phrases to explain why he is on Patmos (1:9), and will use them again at 20:4 for those who have been beheaded. The slaughtered ones cry out and are given reassurance: wait a little – there are others who will be joining you. The reader may be alarmed by these tidings, but it does at least signify that God is in charge.

The sixth seal reveals trouble of a different kind: cosmic disorder, and this time it is not the believers who clamour for assistance, but the powerful, mainly those who run the Roman Empire. They, however, get no answer, as they try to escape the wrath of God and the 'anger of the Lamb'. This is, we may feel, a particularly striking notion: we do not normally think of lambs as 'angry' creatures. Once again, the message is that God is in charge, and that the world is therefore to be viewed upside down.

A vision: four angels, the number of those anointed, and a liturgical commentary

7 1-17 After this, I saw four angels standing on the four corners of the earth, holding back the four winds of the earth, so that the wind should not blow on the land, nor on the sea, nor on any tree. And I saw another angel going up from the rising of the sun; [the angel] had the seal of the Living God, and cried out in a loud voice to the four angels to whom it was granted to harm the land and the sea, saying, 'Do not harm the land or the sea, or the tree, until we seal the slaves of our God on their foreheads.'

And I heard the number of those sealed: a hundred and forty-four thousand, sealed from every tribe of the children of Israel:

Of the tribe of Judah, twelve thousand [were] sealed
Of the tribe of Reuben, twelve thousand [were] sealed
Of the tribe of Gad, twelve thousand [were] sealed
Of the tribe of Asher, twelve thousand [were] sealed
Of the tribe of Naphthali, twelve thousand [were] sealed
Of the tribe of Manasseh, twelve thousand [were] sealed
Of the tribe of Simeon, twelve thousand [were] sealed
Of the tribe of Levi, twelve thousand [were] sealed
Of the tribe of Issachar, twelve thousand [were] sealed
Of the tribe of Zebulun, twelve thousand [were] sealed
Of the tribe of Joseph, twelve thousand [were] sealed
Of the tribe of Benjamin, twelve thousand [were] sealed.

First comes the vision of those who belong to Israel (perhaps the *new* Israel); and only then (see below) comes that of those who belong to the rest of humanity: still the point is that no matter how alarming things are, for those who remain faithful to God, all will be well. We must never forget that there is a good deal of liturgy in Revelation; and the function of all good liturgy is to remind us that all things shall be well, no matter how disastrous they may appear.

After this I saw, and look! A huge crowd, whom no one could number, from every nation and tribe and people and language standing before the throne and before the Lamb, wearing white robes, and with palms in their hands, and they cry out in a loud voice, saying,

'Victory to our God who sits on the throne, and to the Lamb.'

And all the angels stood in a circle [round] the throne and the elders and the four animals, and they fell down on their faces before the throne, and they worshipped God, saying,

'Amen! Blessing and glory and wisdom and thanksgiving
and honour and power and strength
to our God for ever and ever. Amen.'

And one of the elders responded and said to me, 'Those who are wearing white garments – who are they, and where are they from?' And I said to him, 'Lord – you know.'

And he said to me, 'These are those who come from the great trouble. And they washed their clothes and whitened them in the Lamb's blood. Because of this they are before God's throne, and they worship him day and night in his Temple. And the One Sitting on the Throne shall pitch his tent with them. They shall not hunger and thirst any more; the sun shall not fall upon them, nor any burning heat, because the Lamb that is in the middle of the throne shall shepherd them, and shall guide them to streams of living waters,[120] and God shall wipe away every tear from their eyes.[121]

> When the sixth seal was opened, we were left with the panic-stricken question, 'Who can stand?' Our anxiety is sharpened as we see the four angels 'holding back' the destructive winds, and then relieved as we hear the fifth angel ordering a pause in the destruction until God's slaves are sealed. Then we are back to liturgy, and to two visions (or is it really only one? The reader must decide) that calm us. Notice what the visions do *not* say. They do not pretend that things will be easy; they only claim that all will be well in the end.
>
> You could read the 144,000 as Israel, or see it as the Christian community ('the new Israel'). And the un-numberable crowd could be the same group (144,000 is not an exact number, but 'lots and lots and lots'). Clearly, though, they come from all over the world. They are singing liturgical hymns, and liturgical gestures are being performed. But they are martyrs: they are carrying palm branches, and they have 'washed their robes white in the Lamb's blood'. There is a real shock here: blood, as anyone will tell you, is not recommended as a bleach. But the Lamb's death has turned all worldly wisdom upside down.
>
> Alert readers may notice here a couple of echoes of John's Gospel: God's tent-pitching reminds us of John 1:14, and the 'streams of living waters' recalls not only Psalm 23, but also the conversation with the Samaritan woman (see John 4:10, 11, 14).

---

120. Psalm 42:1
121. For this touching maternal image, see Isaiah 25:8; Revelation 21:4

The seventh seal

8¹   And when [the Lamb] opened the seventh seal, there was silence in heaven, about half an hour.

> We saw that there was a pause after the opening of the sixth seal, during which we were given a glimpse of the chasm yawning ahead of us, and then in the liturgy we were shown that all would be well. Now, at this climactic point, comes another of those moments that all good liturgy should have: 'there was silence in heaven for about half an hour'. We should savour this moment.

Seven angels and seven trumpets, and a liturgical pause

2-6   And I saw the seven angels who stand before God, and there were given to them seven trumpets.

And another angel came and stood at the altar, with a golden censer; and much incense was given him, for him to offer with the prayers of all the saints on the golden altar before the throne. And the smoke of the incense went up with the prayers of the saints, from the hand of the angel [who stood] before God. And the angel took the censer, and filled it with the fire from the altar, and threw it on the earth; and there were peals of thunder and sounds and flashes of lightning, and an earthquake.

And the seven angels who had the seven trumpets prepared them, to blow the trumpet-blast.

> And now we have another dramatic pause; we already know that these seven trumpets, like the seven seals before them, mean that there is going to be trouble. John is the master of the artistic delay, and before he charts what happens as the trumpets blow, he reminds us that we are watching a liturgy unfold, whose function is to assert that, whatever happens, God is running the universe: so between the handing-out of the trumpets, and their being put to the angelic lips, we have a glimpse of the scene in heaven – the angel before the altar, offering 'the prayers of the saints', which is itself a reassurance that those prayers are going to be heard by God. But there is no longer silence in heaven; instead, there is thunder and lightning, and a sense that everything is about to explode.

The first four trumpets

7-13   And the first angel blew a trumpet-blast. And there came hail, and fire mixed with blood, and it was thrown on the earth. And one third of the earth was burnt up, and one third of the trees were burnt up, and all the green grass was burnt up.

And the second angel blew a trumpet-blast, and [something] like a great mountain, burning with fire, was flung into the sea, and one third of the sea turned to blood, and one third of the living creatures in the sea died, and one third of the boats were destroyed.

And the third angel blew a trumpet-blast; and a great star fell from the sky, burning like a torch. And it fell upon one third of the rivers, and upon the sources of [their] waters. And the name of the star is called Wormwood. And one third of the waters turned into wormwood, and many human beings died from the waters, because they had been made bitter.

And the fourth angel blew a trumpet-blast; and one third of the sun was struck, and one third of the moon, and one third of the stars, so that one third of them might be darkened, and the day might withhold one third of its brightness, and the night likewise.

And I saw, and I heard a single eagle in flight in mid-heaven, crying in a loud voice, 'Woe, woe, woe to those who live on the earth from the remaining blasts of the trumpets of the three angels who are about to blow their trumpets!'

> The trumpets bring unmixed disaster; but it is very important for us, as we read this text, not to read it as prediction, so much as a highly symbolic account of the mess into which the world falls when it abandons God. The picture is one of the most appalling destruction; the second trumpet, especially, threatens well-to-do merchants who travelled with such apparent ease through the Roman Empire. The third trumpet is a frightening prospect for those who know the scarcity of clean water and the dangers that go with it. The darkening of the sky tells the horrified reader that nothing in the natural world is to be relied on. We should not, however, press too far to find out what it might mean that the 'night' withholds one third of its brightness.
>
> Then, with consummate artistry, John uses the device of the eagle, to make us look forward in fascinated horror to what will come next.

The fifth trumpet

9 ¹⁻¹² And the fifth angel blew a trumpet-blast. And I saw a star that had fallen out of heaven on to the earth; and the star was given the key to the depths of the Abyss. And it opened the depths of the Abyss, and smoke rose up from the depths, like the smoke of a great furnace. And the sun and the air were darkened by the smoke from the depths. And out of the smoke there came locusts on the land, and they were given power like the power that the scorpions of the earth have. And they were told not to harm the grass of the earth, nor any plant, nor any tree, but only those human beings who do not have God's seal on their foreheads. And they were not allowed to kill them, but [only] that they should be tortured for five months. And their torture was like the torture of a serpent when it afflicts a human being. And in these days, human beings will seek for death, and shall not find it; and they shall long to die, and death shall run away from them.

And what were the locusts like? They were like horses armed for war; and on their heads crowns like gold, and their faces like the faces of human beings. And they had hair like women's hair, and their teeth were like lions' teeth, and they had breastplates like breastplates of iron, and the sound of their wings was like the sound of many horse chariots racing to war; and they have tails and stings like scorpions, and with their tails their power is to harm human beings for five months. They have over them the angel who is King of the Abyss. His name in Hebrew is 'Abaddon', and in Greek he has the name 'Destroyer'.

The first woe has gone. Look! Two [further] woes are coming after this.

> We quail as we read. The description of the destruction is so power-
> fully told (and the intensity is perhaps increased by the fact that this
> fifth trumpet explicitly goes beyond, does not even bother with, the
> destruction of grass, plants and trees signalled by the first trumpet),
> and the events seem so unnatural that there appears to be no hope.
> John's contemporaries, however, may have pricked up their ears at
> the reference to the 'sound of many horse chariots racing to war',
> and the 'King of the Abyss': are we talking here, they might ask, of
> the power of Rome? The word Apollyon (here translated as Destroyer)
> may echo the sound of the name of the God Apollo, worshipped in
> the eastern half of the Roman Empire under that name, and as
> Mercury in the west.

The sixth trumpet

13-21 And the sixth angel blew a trumpet-blast. And I heard a voice from the four
corners of the altar of gold before God, saying to the sixth angel, the one that held
the trumpet, 'Release the four angels who are held prisoner at the river, the Great
Euphrates.' And the four angels were released, those who had been prepared for the
hour and the day and the month and the year, to kill a third of human beings. And
the number of the troops of cavalry was twenty thousand times ten thousand – I
heard the number of them. And this is how I saw the horses in the vision, and
those riding upon them, with breastplates the colour of fire and violet and
sulphurous yellow. And the heads of the horses were like lions' heads; and out of
their mouths came fire and smoke and sulphur. As a result of these three plagues
(the fire and the smoke and the sulphur that came forth from their mouths) one
third of humanity was killed. For the power of the horses is in their mouths and in
their tails. For their tails are like snakes; they have heads, and with them they do
damage.

And the remainder of humanity, who had not been killed by these plagues, failed
to repent of the deeds of their hands, so as not to fall down before the demons, the
idols of gold and silver and bronze and stone and wood [idols] that cannot see or
hear or walk. And they did not repent of their murders, or of their witchcraft, or of
their fornication or of their thieving.

> This is a passage of unrelieved grimness; but you should start, as
> John does, from the point of view that God is in charge. He foresees
> destruction coming, but it is coming on those who refuse God's law;
> and even those have room for repentance. But people do not trouble
> to 'change their ways', and it is for the failure to observe the command-
> ments of God, despite a warning, that the destruction will come,
> not so much as a punishment, more as an inevitable consequence.

The pause before the seventh trumpet

10 ¹⁻11 ¹⁴ And I saw another mighty angel coming down from heaven, clothed in a
cloud, and a rainbow on his head, and his face like the sun, and his legs were like

pillars of fire, and in his hand he had a little scroll, opened. And he placed his right leg on the sea, and his left [leg] on the land. And he cried out in a loud voice, as a lion roars. And when he cried out, the seven thunders uttered their own sounds. And when the seven thunders uttered, I was about to write [it] down, and I heard a voice from heaven saying, 'Seal up what the seven thunders have uttered, and do not write them down.'

And the angel whom I had seen standing on the sea and on the land lifted his right hand up to heaven, and swore by the one who lives for ever and ever, the one who created the heaven and the things that are in it, and the earth, and the things that are on it, and the sea, and the things that are in it, that 'There shall be no more time, but in the days of the sound of the seventh angel, when he is about to blow a trumpet-blast, the mystery of God will have been accomplished, in accordance with the good news that he had proclaimed to his servants the prophets.'

And the voice which I had heard from heaven I heard speaking a second time, and saying, 'Go – take the scroll which is open in the hand of the angel that stands on the sea and on the land.' And I went to the angel, and told him to give me the little scroll. And he says to me, 'Take it and eat it up, and it will make your stomach bitter; but in your mouth it shall be as sweet as honey.'

And I took the little scroll from the angel's hand, and I ate it up, and in my mouth it was like sweet honey, and when I had eaten it, my stomach was made bitter; and they tell me, 'You must prophesy again to the peoples and nations and languages and to many kings.'

And there was given me a measuring rod, like a staff, saying, 'Up you get – and measure the Temple of God, and the Altar, and those who worship in it. And cast out the court which is outside the Temple; [leave it] outside, and do not measure it, for it is given over to the Gentiles, and they shall trample over the Holy City for forty-two months.

'And I shall give power to my two witnesses, and they shall prophesy for 1260 days, wearing sackcloth. These are the two olive trees, and the two lamp-stands which stand before the Lord of the Earth and if anyone desires to harm them, fire comes out of their mouths and devours their enemies, and if anyone desires to harm them, this is how that person must be killed. These have the authority to close up heaven, so that no rain may fall in the days of their prophecy; and they have authority over the waters, to turn them into blood and to strike the earth with every kind of plague, as often as they want.

'And when they complete their witnessing, the Beast which comes up from the Abyss will make war against them, and will conquer them and kill them, and their corpses shall lie in the main square of the great city, which is called, spiritually, Sodom and Egypt, where their Lord was crucified. And from the peoples and tribes and languages and nations, there will be those who look upon their corpses for three-and-a-half days; and they do not permit their corpses to be placed in a tomb. And those who dwell on the earth are glad and rejoice over them, and they'll send each other presents, because these two prophets tormented those who dwell on the earth.

'And after three-and-a-half days, the Spirit of Life from God entered into them, and they stood on their feet, and great fear fell on those who saw them. And they heard a great voice from heaven, saying to them, "Come up here." And they went up to heaven in a cloud, and their enemies saw them. And at that hour there was a great earthquake, and one tenth of the city fell; and in the earthquake, seven thousand human beings were killed. And the remainder became fearful, and gave glory to the God of heaven.

'The second woe has gone. Look! The third woe is coming soon.'

Once again, as we read this passage, it is with an increasing sense that the world as we know it is falling apart (as indeed is the case); but the fact that it is foretold means that we are being invited to see it in the light of God's purpose. So the angel who swears by the Living One gives us great reassurance, as he dominates land and sea.

And John follows Ezekiel in eating the scroll,[122] and receiving a prophetic mission, in this case to 'peoples and nations and languages and many kings'. He also follows Ezekiel in measuring around the Temple.[123] He foresees, however, a long (but not unending) domination of the Holy City by the Gentiles. In this context, we encounter the mysterious 'two olive trees and two lamp-stands',[124] and the reader will have to decide (on the basis of all that you read in Revelation) who these are. Clearly they are on the side of God; clearly they are to suffer a humiliating death; clearly that death is not the end of the story.

The alert reader will notice that the tense changes rather abruptly from future to present to past, partly because the past tense is that of the quotation from Ezekiel's vision (37:1-10) of the Valley of the Dry Bones. It also reflects the fact that tenses in Hebrew and Aramaic are not as clear-cut as they are in English (and Greek); but for the reader it offers a sense that the vision (or is it a 'hearing'?) is somehow timeless.

The reference to the mystery of God being 'accomplished' may be yet another link to John's Gospel (19:30). The 'two witnesses' may remind us of Moses and Aaron before Pharaoh, as they called down plagues, in Exodus 5-12.

The mention of the Beast, clearly an enemy of God, is the first of more than 30 in the Book of Revelation.

The seventh trumpet-blast: another liturgical moment

15-18 And the seventh angel blew a trumpet-blast. And there were loud voices in heaven, saying, 'The kingdom of the world has become the kingdom of our Lord and of his Messiah. And he will reign for ever and ever.'

And the twenty-four elders who sat on their thrones before God fell on their faces and worshipped God, saying, 'We give you thanks, Lord God Almighty, The Is and the Was, because you have accepted your great power and started to reign. And the nations have become angry, and your anger has come, and the time for the dead to be judged, and to give [their] reward to your slaves the prophets, and to the saints, and to those who fear your name, the small and the great, and to destroy those who destroy the earth.'

---

122. See Ezekiel 2:9–3:4
123. Ezekiel 40–42
124. Which we find already in Zechariah 4:1–14

This seventh trumpet-blast does not, rather to our surprise, immediately unleash another 'woe'. Instead we are returned to the heavenly liturgy, and to the reminder that, whatever the power of 'those who destroy the earth', God is in charge, and that our proper posture is flat on our faces before God's throne, joining in the worship that never ends.

A glimpse into heaven

11¹⁹-**12**¹⁸ And the Temple of God was opened in heaven, and the Ark of his Covenant was seen in his Temple, and there were flashes of lightning and voices and thunderclaps and an earthquake, and great hail.

And a great sign was seen in heaven, a woman clothed in the sun; and the moon was beneath her feet; and on her head was a crown of twelve stars. And she was pregnant; and she cries out in her labour-pains and in the anguish of giving birth. And another sign was seen in heaven, and look! A great red dragon with seven heads and ten horns, and on the seven heads seven diadems, and its tail sweeps away one third of the stars of heaven, and threw them down on to the earth.

And the dragon stood before the woman who was about to give birth, in order to eat her child up when she bore it.

And she bore a son, a male, who is going to shepherd all the nations with an iron rod, and her child was snatched up to God and to God's throne. And the woman fled to the desert, where she has a place made ready from God, in order for them to look after her for 1260 days.

And war broke out in heaven, Michael and his angels to make war on the dragon. And the dragon and his angels made war, and he was not victorious, nor did they have any place in heaven. And the Great Dragon, the Ancient Snake, the one known as Devil and Satan, the one who leads the whole world astray, was thrown down on the earth; and his angels were thrown down with him. And I heard a great voice in heaven saying,

> Now the salvation and the power and the kingdom of our God has come, and the authority of his Messiah, because the accuser of our brothers and sisters was cast down, the one who accuses them before our God day and night. And they conquered him because of the blood of the Lamb, and because of the word of their witness; they did not love their lives to the point of death.
>
> Therefore rejoice, O heavens, and those who dwell in [the heavens]. Woe to earth and sea, because the devil came down to you with a great rage, knowing that he has not much time.

And when the dragon saw that he had been thrown on to the earth he went after the woman who had borne the male child. And the woman was given the two wings of the great eagle, to fly into the desert, to her place, where she is being looked after, for a time and two times and half a time [protected] from the presence of the dragon. And from its mouth, the dragon hurled water, like a river, after the woman, in order to have her swept away like a river. And the earth came to the woman's help; and the earth opened its mouth and swallowed up the river that the dragon hurled from its mouth. And the dragon was enraged against the woman, and went off to make war on the rest of her seed who kept the commandments of God and who had the witness of Jesus.

And he stood on the sand of the sea.

> Once again we are given a glimpse of the heavenly liturgy, to show us what is going on, and to reassure us that God is really in charge. Who is the woman? The most obvious reading is that she is Mary, mother of Jesus (for the child is evidently Jesus); but she has also been read as Eve, Hagar, Israel, the city of Jerusalem and the Christian Church. Perhaps she has elements of all of these.
>
> Who is the dragon? The enemy of God, evidently, and also a kind of parody of God, as is suggested by the seven heads and seven diadems, and the sweeping away of 'one third of the stars'. This is something that we shall see again in this second half of the Un-Veiling. War is inevitable against this 'fake God', but the forces of righteousness will be victorious. The liturgy gives us hope, the glimpse of the dragon compels us to recognise that there is trouble ahead.

The emergence of the Beast

13 ¹⁻¹⁸ And I saw a Beast coming up out of the sea, with ten horns and seven heads, and ten diadems on its horns, and on its heads blasphemous names. And the Beast that I saw was like a leopard; and its feet were like [the feet] of a bear; and its mouth was like a lion's mouth. And the dragon gave [the Beast] its own power, and its throne, and great authority. And one of its heads was as though it had been slaughtered to death; and its lethal wound was healed.

And the whole earth was astounded in the wake of the Beast; and they worshipped the dragon, because it had given [its] authority to the Beast, and they worshipped the Beast, saying, 'Who is like the Beast? And who can make war on it?'

And it was given a mouth to utter boasts and blasphemies; and it was given authority to act for forty-two months. And it opened its mouth for blasphemy against God to blaspheme [God's] name and God's tent, those who dwell in heaven. And it was granted it to make war on the saints and to conquer them; and it was granted authority over every tribe and people and language and nation. And all those who dwell on earth will worship it: its name is not written in the scroll of life of the Lamb slaughtered from the creation of the world.

If anyone has an ear, let them hear!

If anyone [is destined] for imprisonment, [they go] to imprisonment. And if anyone [is destined] to be killed by the sword, [they go] to be killed by the sword. Here is the endurance and faith of the saints.

And I saw another beast coming up from the land, and it had two horns like a lamb – but it spoke like a dragon. And it exercises all the authority of the first Beast in its presence, and it causes the earth and those who dwell in it to worship the first Beast, whose lethal wound was healed. And it performs great miracles, to make fire come down from heaven onto the earth, in the presence of human beings. And it leads astray those who dwell on earth, through the miracles that it was granted to perform in the presence of the Beast, telling those who dwell on the earth to make a statue for the Beast, who has the wound from the sword, and yet lived.

And it was granted to it to endow the statue of the Beast with life, so that the Beast's statue might speak, and bring it about that whoever did not worship the Beast's statue might be killed. And it makes them all, small and great, rich and poor, free and slaves, to give them a mark on their right hand or on their forehead; and it brings it about that no one can buy or sell except a person who has the mark, the name of the Beast, or the number of the Beast's name. This is the secret: let the one who has intelligence calculate the Beast's number – for it is the number of a human being, and his number is six hundred and sixty-six.

Now we meet the Beast; he has been mentioned before, but here we see him in uncomfortable detail. Clearly the Beast stands for the forces opposed to God; it is a horrible sight, made up of different kinds of animal, and in some of its features (power, authority, throne, for example), clearly sets itself up as a rival to God, and a parody of the Lamb. Like the Lamb, it is 'slaughtered'. (This is probably a reference to the rumour that the dead emperor Nero was still alive somewhere. The rumour therefore becomes an evil parody of Jesus' resurrection.) Like the Lamb, it has authority over every tribe and tongue and people and language and nation. Like the Lamb it has horns; like the Jesus of the Gospels, it does miracles. However, it is different from the Lamb in that its authority is not real and in that it speaks like a dragon. Nevertheless, there are two beasts, and this display of power makes us feel nervous.

So we feel uneasy and discomfited, as we watch, and ask who can possibly make war on the Beast. We know already that 'Michael' has won the battle in heaven, which means that all shall be well, and the Lamb will be victorious on earth; but we shiver as we read. Then there is the number of the Beast, the one fact that everybody knows about the Book of Revelation. There are many possibilities for an interpretation, but the most likely is the name of the Emperor Nero, written in Hebrew letters (in both Hebrew and Greek, numbers are expressed by letters, and form the basis of all kinds of interesting calculations). It is quite possibly the case that the Un-Veiling was written not very long after Nero's death, and in the context of 'Elvis lives' rumours of his return.

A liturgy for the Lamb

14 1-5 And I saw, and look! The Lamb standing on Mount Sion, and with him a hundred and forty-four thousand who have his name, and the name of his Father written on their foreheads. And I heard a voice from heaven, like [the] voice of many waters, and like [the] voice of great thunder. And the voice which I heard [was] like harpists playing harp melodies on their harps. And they sing something like 'a new song' in the presence of the Lamb, and in the presence of the four animals and the elders, and no one could learn the song except for the one hundred and forty-four thousand, who are redeemed from the earth. These are the ones who have not been defiled [by going] with women; for they are virgins, those who follow the Lamb wherever he goes. These have been redeemed from [among] human beings, as first-fruits for God and for the Lamb. And in their mouth there is found no falsehood – they are unblemished.

Once again we are in liturgical mode; and, once again, the function of liturgy is to help us to plod on, despite all adversity. The voice is a part of this, and God is clearly present in the voice of waters and thunders and harps that sing a new song; and we should observe the 144,000 now safely with God. John is signalling to his readers that they too will one day be there, if only they will keep their nerve and continue to follow the Lamb, and to avoid the temptations of the world.

More liturgical glimpses: six angels

6-20 And I saw another angel, flying in mid-heaven; he had an eternal gospel to preach upon those who dwell on earth, and upon every nation and tribe and language and people, saying in a loud voice, 'Fear God, and give him glory, because the hour of his judgement has come; and worship him who created heaven and earth and the sea and the springs of water.'

And another angel (the second) followed, saying, 'Fallen, fallen is Babylon the Great, she who caused all the nations to drink of the wine of the rage of her fornication.'

And another angel (the third) followed them, saying in a loud voice, 'If someone worships the Beast and its statue, and accepts [the] mark on their forehead or on their hand, they also shall drink of the wine of God's rage, poured out undiluted in the cup of his anger; and they shall be tormented with fire and brimstone in the presence of the holy angels and in the presence of the Lamb. And the smoke of their torment shall rise up for ever and ever; and they have no respite, day or night, those who worship the Beast and its statue, and anyone who accepts the mark of its name. Here is the endurance of the saints, those who keep the commandments of God and their faith in Jesus.'

And I heard a voice from heaven saying, 'Write: Happy are the dead who from now on die in the Lord. Yes, says the Spirit, that they may have respite from their labours, for their deeds follow along with them.'

And I saw, and look! A white cloud, and on the cloud one sitting like a Son of Man; on his head he had a golden crown, and in his hand a sharp sickle. And another angel came out of the Temple crying out in a loud voice to the one sitting on the cloud, 'Put in your sickle and harvest, because the hour has come to harvest, because the earth's harvest has withered up.' And the one sitting on the cloud put in his sickle, onto the earth; and the earth was harvested.

And another angel came out of the Temple which is in heaven, and he also had a sharp sickle.

And another angel came out of the altar of incense; [the angel] had authority over the fire, and cried out in a loud voice to the one who had the sharp sickle, 'Put in your sharp sickle and pluck the bunches of grapes from the earth's vine, because its grapes are ripe.' And the angel put his sickle on to the earth, and harvested the earth's vine, and put [it] into the great winepress of the anger of God. And the winepress was trodden outside the city, and blood came out of the winepress, as high as horses' bridles, for a distance of one thousand six hundred furlongs ['two hundred miles'].

This view into heaven, with six angels (the alert reader of the Un-Veiling inevitably asks, 'Where is Number 7?') preparing to administer punishment to the enemies of God, is meant to reassure us; we are present at a crisis, but God's forces are mobilised, and cannot fail in their objective.

For the first time in the book we hear mention of 'Babylon', who is clearly the enemy of God. We shall hear more of this name, which is very likely early Christian code for Rome, whose destruction is therefore being prophesied. We mop our brow as we read.

Visions of victory

15 1-8 And I saw another sign in heaven, great and astonishing: seven angels with seven plagues, the final plagues, because in them the wrath of God is consummated.

And I saw something like a sea of glass mixed with fire; and those who conquered and survived the Beast and its statue and the number of its name, they were standing on the glass sea with God's harps; and they sing the song of Moses, God's slave, and the song of the Lamb:

'Great and wonderful are your deeds, Lord God Almighty.
Just and true are your ways, King of the Nations.
Who shall not fear, Lord, and glorify your name?
Because [you] alone are holy,
because all nations shall come and worship before you,
because your judgements have been revealed.'

And after this I saw, and the temple of the tent of witness was opened in heaven, and the seven angels who had the seven plagues came out of the temple wearing clean bright linen, and with golden breastplates around their chests. And one of the four animals gave the seven angels seven golden bowls, full of the wrath of God who lives for ever and ever. And the temple was full of smoke from the glory of God, and from God's power. And no one could enter the temple until the seven plagues of the seven angels were completed.

We shiver with discomfort as we read, but we are struck with the holiness of God, the certainty of his victory, and the roughness of it. Once again a liturgical hymn encourages us to hope, not in our own resources, but in the power of God.

Does this make you feel hopeful?

Seven angels, pouring out seven plagues

16 1-21 And I heard a loud voice from the temple saying to the seven angels, 'Go – and pour out the seven bowls of the wrath of God on the earth.'

And the first went off and poured out his bowl on the earth; and there arose a foul and angry sore on the people who had the mark of the Beast, and those who worshipped its statue.

And the second one went off and poured out his bowl on the sea, and it turned into blood, like that of a corpse, and every living creature that was in the sea died.

And the third one poured out his bowl on the rivers and the springs of water; and [the water] turned to blood. And I heard the angel of the waters saying,

'You are righteous, the Is and the Was, the Holy One,
because you have pronounced these judgements,
because they poured out the blood of the saints and prophets
and you gave them blood to drink – they deserve it.'

And I heard the altar of incense saying,

'Yes, Lord Almighty, your judgements are true and just.'

And the fourth one poured out his bowl on the sun, and it was granted him to burn people up with fire. And the people were burnt up, a massive burning, and they blasphemed the name of God who had authority over these plagues; and they did not repent and give him glory.

And the fifth one poured out his bowl over the throne of the Beast; and his kingdom was darkened, and they bit their tongues from pain. And they blasphemed the God of heaven because of their pains and because of their sores; and they did not repent of their deeds.

And the sixth one poured out his bowl on the great river, the Euphrates; and its water was dried up, in order to prepare the way of the kings from the east. And, out of the mouth of the dragon, and out of the mouth of the Beast, and out of the mouth of the false prophet I saw three unclean spirits, like frogs; for they are the spirits of demons, and they perform miracles, which come out upon the kings of the entire world, to gather them for the war of God Almighty's Great Day. 'Look – I am coming like a thief; happy the one who stays awake, and who keeps his clothes on, so that they do not go about naked, and people see their private parts.' And he gathered them to the place that in Hebrew is called 'Har Magedon'.

And the seventh one poured out his bowl on the air; and there went out a loud voice from the Temple, from the throne, saying 'It is over.' Then there came lightning, and voices, and thunderclaps, and a great earthquake, such as has not happened since humanity came on earth, an earthquake of such magnitude, such a violent one. And the great city was split into three parts; and the cities of the Gentiles fell. And great Babylon was remembered before God, to give her the cup of the wine of the wrath of his rage. And every island fled, and the mountains could not be found. And a great hailstone, weighing a talent, comes down from heaven upon human beings; and the human beings blasphemed God because of the plague of hail; because its plague is very violent.

> Reading this, we are uneasy at being asked to share John's evident enthusiasm for the punishment that is being dished out to the unrighteous. But we must not miss the point, that they deserve it, in John's view; they are given the chance to repent and instead of mending their ways, they carry on blaspheming God's name. In other words, they have opted to stay on the side of the Beast – and that way lies inevitable destruction. The point is not so much the punishment of the unrighteous, as the certainty that Jesus' followers will (despite all appearances) be vindicated.
>
> Does this passage make you gloat or breathe a sigh of relief?

The Great Whore

17 ¹⁻¹⁸ And one of the seven angels who held the seven bowls came and said to me, 'Come here; I shall show you the condemnation of the Great Whore, who sits upon many

waters, with whom the kings of the earth have committed fornication, and those who inhabit the earth have got drunk on the wine of her fornication.' And he carried me away to the desert in the Spirit. And I saw a woman sitting on a scarlet beast, full of blasphemous names, with seven heads and ten horns. And the woman was clothed in purple and scarlet; and she was gilded with gold and precious stone[s] and pearls, with a golden cup in her hand, full of abominations, and the impurities of her fornication. And on her forehead a name [was] written, a secret: 'Babylon the Great, the Mother of the Whores and Abominations of the earth.' And I saw [that] the woman was drunk from the blood of the saints, and from the blood of Jesus' witnesses. And I was astonished as I looked at her – a great astonishment.

And the angel said to me, 'Why are you astonished? I shall tell you the secret of the woman and of the Beast who carries her, who has the seven heads and the ten horns.

'The Beast that you saw was and is not, and is about to come up out of the Abyss, and is going to destruction. And those who inhabit the earth shall be astonished [those] whose name is not written in the scroll of life, from the creation of the world, when they see the Beast, because it was and is not, and shall be at hand. Here is the mind that has wisdom.

'The seven heads are seven hills, on which the woman sits; and they are seven kings: five have fallen, one is, the other has not yet come, and when he comes he must remain a little while. And the Beast which was and is not is both number eight and one of the seven; and he is going to destruction. And the ten horns which you saw are ten kings, who have not yet received the kingship, but they receive authority as kings, for a single hour, along with the Beast. These ones are of one mind; and they give their power and authority to the Beast. These will make war on the Lamb, and the Lamb will conquer them, because he is Lord of lords and King of kings and those with him are called, and chosen, and faithful.'

And he says to me, 'The waters that you saw, where the whore sits, are peoples and crowds and nations and languages. And the ten horns that you saw, and the Beast, these will hate the whore, and they will cause her to be laid waste and naked, and they will devour her flesh, and they shall burn her up with fire. For God put it into their hearts to carry out his purpose, and to carry out a single purpose, and to give their kingly authority to the Beast, until God's words shall be accomplished. And the woman whom you saw is the great city, which has kingship over the kings of the earth.'

Like the Beast that she rides on, the woman represents the forces of evil who are implacably opposed to God, and who are unmistakably the world power that is Rome, and its client kingdoms. The Beast's seven heads and ten horns resemble those of the dragon (12:3). The Beast who 'was and is not', to whom the ten kings give 'authority and power' parodies God, just as the Beast's hatred of the whore, and devouring her flesh, is a parody of Christian love and of the Eucharist. Moreover, we are now quite clear that we are talking about Rome: the woman sits on seven hills like Rome; it is the current Emperor (rather than the Lamb) who is Lord of lords and King of kings; and there can be only one great city which has kingship of the kings of the earth.

What about the seven kings, one of whom is also number eight? They seem to represent Roman emperors, and scholars have suggested various different ways of counting them, in order to find out the date when the Book of Revelation was written. Perhaps we should not worry too much about the mathematics of it all: until recently it was widely supposed by scholars that the Revelation was written at the end of the first century, in the reign of Domitian. Not long ago, however, attention has shifted back to the difficult days after the death of the Emperor Nero in AD 68, and the rumour that Nero was about to return from death as a possible time for the writing of the Book of Revelation. Perhaps it does not matter; John wants us to savour the victory over evil rather than unravel the code.

The fall of Babylon

18 ¹⁻²⁴ After this I saw another angel coming down out of heaven; he had great authority, and the earth was lit up by his radiance. And he shouted in a mighty voice,

'Fallen, fallen is Babylon the Great;
and she has become a dwelling place of demons,
and a prison for every unclean spirit,
and a prison for every unclean bird,
and a prison for every unclean and loathsome beast,
because all the nations have drunk of the wine of the rage of her fornication;
And all the kings of the earth have committed fornication with her;
and the merchants of the earth have become wealthy as a result of the power
of her luxury.'

And I heard another voice from heaven, saying,

'Come out from her, my people, so as not to take part in her sins, and so as not to receive a share of her plagues, because her sins have reached up to heaven, and God has remembered her crimes. Pay her back as she has paid back; and give her double, twice as much as her deeds: the cup that she has mixed, mix her a double dose. For all her glory and her luxury, give her an equal amount of torment and mourning, because in her heart she is saying, "I am enthroned as Queen; and I am not a widow; and I shall not see any mourning." Because of this, her plagues will come in a single day, death and mourning and famine; and she will be burnt up with fire, because the Lord God who has judged her is mighty.'

And the kings of the earth, who committed fornication and lived in luxury with her, shall weep and mourn when they see the smoke of her burning, as they stand afar off, because of [their] fear of her torment, saying,

'Woe, woe, the great city, Babylon the mighty city!
Because in a single hour your judgement has come.'

And the merchants of the earth weep and grieve over her, because no one any longer buys their cargo, cargo of gold and silver and precious stone[s] and pearls and linen and purple robes and silk and scarlet clothes, and every kind of citron wood, and every kind of ivory vessel and every kind of vessel that is made of very precious wood, and bronze and iron and marble, and cinnamon and spices and incense, and myrrh and frankincense and wine and olive oil and fine flour and wheat and cattle and sheep and horses and carriages and slaves – and the souls of human beings.

And the fruit your soul craved has departed from you; and all your glamour and splendour are lost to you, and no way will they ever be found again.

The merchants of these things, who got rich by her, will stand afar off, in fear at her torment, weeping and mourning and saying,

> 'Woe, woe, the great city, that wore linen and purple and scarlet
> and was gilded with gold and precious stones and pearls,
> because in a single hour so much wealth was devastated.'

And every ship's captain, and every seafarer, and sailors, and all who make their living from the sea stood afar off, and they cried out as they saw the smoke of her burning, and said, 'Who is like the great city?' And they threw dust on their heads, and they cried out, weeping and grieving, saying,

> 'Woe, woe, the great city,
> through whom all those who had ships on the sea
> grew rich from her high prices,
> because in a single hour she has been laid waste.
> Rejoice over her, heaven, and saints, and apostles, and prophets,
> because God has executed your judgement on her.'

And one mighty angel lifted up a stone, like a great millstone, and hurled it into the sea, saying,

> 'So shall Babylon, the "great city", be hurled down with violence and not be
> found again. And the sound of harpists and musicians and flute players
> and trumpeters
> shall not be found in you again.
> And no craftsman of any craft shall be found in you again.
> And the sound of the millstone shall not be heard in you again,
> and the light of the lamp shall not be seen in you again,
> and the voice of the bridegroom and of the bride shall not be heard in you again,
> because your merchants were the great ones of the earth,
> because by your magic spell all the Gentiles were led astray.
> And in the city the blood of the prophets and saints,
> and of all those slaughtered on earth, was found.'

> There is for many readers an unattractive note of gloating triumph at the fall of Babylon; but try to read this passage with the eyes of those who felt gloomily that Rome was there for ever, and would never be overthrown, so that the followers of Jesus would always be persecuted. On the lips of the kings and merchants and shipowners, in their lamentation at the fall of Babylon, we hear a parody of the hymns we have overheard in the heavenly liturgy. The message is the same: God is in charge.

The heavenly liturgy: victory songs

19 ¹⁻¹⁰ After this, I heard [something] like [the] mighty sound of a large crowd in heaven, saying,

> 'Alleluia! Salvation and glory and power belong to our God,
>> because his judgements are true and just,
>> because he has condemned the great whore,
>> who was destroying the earth with her whoring,
> and he has avenged the blood of his slaves [and freed them] from her power.'

And a second time they said,

> 'Alleluia! And her smoke goes up for ever and ever.'

And the twenty-four elders and the four animals fell down and worshipped God who sits on the throne, saying,

> 'Amen! Alleluia!,'

and a voice came out of the throne, saying,

> 'Praise to our God, all you his slaves, and those who fear him, small and great.'

And I heard something like the sound of a large crowd, and like the sound of many waters and like the sound of mighty thunder saying,

> 'Alleluia! Because the Lord God Almighty has started his reign,
>> let us rejoice and exult and give him glory,
>> because the Lamb's wedding feast has come,
>>> and his Bride has prepared herself,
>> and it has been granted her to put on a clean and radiant linen [garment].
>> (For the linen is the righteous deeds of the saints.)'

And he says to me, 'Write: "Happy are those who are invited to the Lamb's wedding feast."'

And he says to me, 'These are God's true words.'
And I fell down before his feet, to worship him.
And he says to me, 'Don't even think of it: I am the fellow slave of you, and of your brothers and sisters who have Jesus' testimony. Worship God. For Jesus' testimony is the spirit of prophecy.'

> Once again we are permitted to eavesdrop on the heavenly liturgy, and this enables us to see the destruction of 'Babylon' as God's improbable victory. And at the end we are reminded that the only proper objects of worship are God and the Lamb; hence not angels, and certainly not Roman emperors or their statues.
> Is worship of the wrong objects a problem for us, too?

Glimpses of God's victory

¹¹⁻²¹ And I saw heaven opened, and look! A white horse, and the one sitting on it, called Faithful and True, and he judges with justice, and with justice he makes war. His eyes are like a fiery flame, and on his head are many diadems, with a name written

that no one knows except himself, and he is clothed in a garment that has been dipped in blood, and his name is called 'The Word of God'. And the heavenly armies followed him, on white horses; and they were clothed in clean white linen. And from his mouth there came out a sharp sword, so that he might strike the nations with it, and he shall shepherd them with an iron rod; and he will trample the winepress of the wine of the rage of God Almighty's wrath; and on his garment and on his thigh a name is written, 'King of kings and Lord of lords'.

And I saw an angel standing on the sun; and the angel shouted in a loud voice, saying to all the birds that fly in the mid-heavens, 'Come – gather to the banquet, to eat the bodies of kings, and the bodies of commanders, and the bodies of the mighty, and the bodies of horses, and the bodies of their riders, and the bodies of all free people, and all slaves, and of small and great!'

And I saw the Beast, and the kings of the earth, and their armies gathered to make war on the one who sits on the horse, and on his army. And the Beast was made prisoner, and his false prophet along with him, the one who performed miracles before him, with which he fooled those who accepted the mark of the Beast, and those who worshipped its statue. The two of them were thrown alive into the lake of fire which burns with sulphur. And the remainder were killed with the sword of the one sitting on the horse, the sword that came out of his mouth, and all the birds gorged themselves on their bodies.

> A vision here to take away the unpleasant taste of the whore. The victorious one rides on a white horse instead of a beast, and it is the victory of truth and fidelity, against all the odds, that we are invited to celebrate. This is the one who, unlike the Roman Emperor, is properly called 'King of kings and Lord of lords', and who is given the title, familiar to us from the Prologue of John's Gospel, of 'The Word of God'. We are not invited to feel sorry for the powerful enemies of God as they receive the punishment that they have deserved.

The thousand-year captivity of the enemy

20 1-10 And I saw an angel coming down from heaven, with the key of the Abyss, and a great chain in his hand. And he seized the dragon, the snake, the Ancient One, who is the Devil and Satan. And he tied him up for a thousand years, and threw him into the Abyss, and locked it and put a seal on it, so that he would no longer lead the nations astray, until the thousand years should be completed. After that he must be released for a brief time. And I saw thrones, and people sat on them, and judgement was given to them; and [I saw] the souls of those who had been beheaded because of their witness for Jesus and because of the Word of God; and [I saw] those who had not worshipped the Beast, nor its statue, and who had not accepted [its] mark on their foreheads and on their hands. And they came to life, and they reigned with Christ for a thousand years. The remainder of the dead did not come to life until the thousand years were completed.

This is the first Resurrection. Happy and holy is the one who has a part in the first Resurrection; over these people, the second death has no power, but they shall be priests of God and of Christ; and they shall reign with him for the thousand years.

And when the thousand years are completed, Satan shall be set free from his prison, and he will come out to lead astray the nations who are in the four corners of the earth, Gog and Magog, to gather them for war: their number is like the sand of the sea. And they went up to the broad plain of the earth, and encircled the camp of the saints, and the beloved city, and fire came down out of heaven and devoured them. And the Devil who leads them astray was hurled into the lake of fire and sulphur, where the Beast and the fake prophet [are]; and they shall be tortured day and night for ever and ever.

> The 'thousand-year captivity' is said to have caused a good deal of anxiety at the end of the tenth century AD, and the end of the twentieth century was not without its anxieties. But all that comes from a misunderstanding of the text. The Book of Revelation is not a prediction, but a dramatic statement; and its message is that because God is in charge, all will be well, no matter how unpleasant things may appear to be. So we should rejoice at John's confidence in the Resurrection, rather than tremble at the alarming but transient phenomena.

The final judgement

11-15 And I saw a great white throne, and the One sitting on it. And earth and heaven fled from his presence; and there was no place for them. And I saw the dead, the great and small, standing before the throne. And scrolls were opened, and another scroll was opened, which is [the Scroll] of Life; and the dead were judged on the basis of what was written in the scrolls, according to their deeds. And the sea gave up the dead that were within her, and Death and Hades gave up the dead that were in them, and each one was judged on the basis of their works [or: what they had done]. And Death and Hades were thrown into the lake of fire. This is the second death, the lake of fire. And if anyone is not found written in the Scroll of Life, they are thrown into the lake of fire.

> At this point comes the judgement; and, once again, the point is not to tremble in fear that one's name might have been missed out of the 'Scroll of Life', so much as to assume that we each have our place in the new creation (earth and heaven, the old creation, having fled), and to rejoice at the destruction of 'Death and Hades'.

The vision of the new creation

21 1-8 And I saw a new heaven and a new earth; for the first heaven and the first earth had gone away – and the sea no longer exists. And I saw the Holy City, New Jerusalem, coming down out of heaven from God, prepared like a bride adorned for her husband. And I heard a mighty voice from the throne, saying, 'Look! God's tent with human beings; and God will pitch his tent with them; and they shall be his peoples, and God himself will be with them as their God. And he will wipe away every tear from their eyes. And Death shall be no more; and sadness, and crying, and pain shall be no more – for the former things have gone.'
And the One Sitting on the Throne said, 'Look! I am making all things new.' And he says, 'Write, because these words are reliable and true.' And he said to me, 'It is done. I am the Alpha and the Omega ['the A and the Z'], the Beginning and the End. I shall give to the one who is thirsty, from the fountain of the water of life – at no cost. The one who conquers shall inherit these things, and "I shall be God

584

to him and he shall be my son".[125] But as for the cowards and the faithless, and those who have gone in for abominations; as for murderers and fornicators and sorcerers and idolaters, and all liars – their portion is in the lake that burns with fire and sulphur, which is the second death.'

> This is a beautiful vision of the new creation, God intimately present to his people, and an end to all that threatens humanity; and it is full of charming scriptural echoes: the water at no cost, from Isaiah 55, and the water of life that reminds us of Chapter 4 of John's Gospel. But there is another note, too, of judgement and death, which we must take seriously if we are to understand the Book of Revelation, including, perhaps, an echo of the death of Jesus in the Gospel of John: the cry 'It is done' (though the Greek word used is different), and the reference to 'thirst' (see John 19: 28, 30). 'He shall be my son': this refers, of course, to anyone who conquers, not just Jesus – but I have left the 'exclusive' language of the original, because of the apparent reference to 2 Samuel 7:14.

The vision of the Holy City – like no city you ever saw

21 ⁹-22 ⁵ And one of the seven angels who have the seven bowls filled with the seven plagues, the final ones, came and spoke with me, 'Come – I shall show you the Bride, the wife of the Lamb.' And he took me away in the spirit, to a great and high mountain, and he showed me the Holy City, Jerusalem, coming down out of heaven from God; it had the glory of God. Its splendour was like very precious stone, like jasper, crystal clear. It has a great high wall, with twelve gateways, and on the twelve gateways it has twelve angels, and names inscribed, which are the names of the twelve tribes of the sons of Israel. On the east, three gateways, and on the north three gateways, and on the south three gateways, and on the west three gateways. And the wall of the city has twelve foundation stones, and on them twelve names, of the Twelve Apostles of the Lamb.

And the one who was speaking to me had a golden measuring rod, to measure the city, and its gateways, and its wall. And the city lies four-square; and its length is the same as its breadth. And he measured the city with the rod: all of twelve thousand stades; its length and breadth and height are all identical. And he measured its wall: one hundred and forty-four cubits in the human (that is, angelic) measuring. And the enclosure of the wall is of jasper, and the city is pure gold, like clear glass. The foundation stones of the wall of the city are adorned with every [kind of] precious stone. The first foundation stone is jasper, the second is sapphire, the third is chalcedony, the fourth is emerald, the fifth is sardonyx, the sixth is carnelian, the seventh is chrysolite, the eighth is beryl, the ninth is topaz, the tenth is chrysoprase, the eleventh is hyacinth, the twelfth is amethyst; and the twelve gateways are twelve pearls – each one of the gateways was from a single pearl. And the street of the city was pure gold, transparent as glass.

And I saw no temple in her, for the Lord God Almighty is her temple – and the Lamb. And the city has no need of the sun or of the moon to give her light, for the glory of God illuminated her; and the Lamb is her lamp. And the nations shall

---

125. Roughly, 2 Samuel 7:14

walk by means of her light, and the kings of the earth bring their glory into her; and her gateways shall not be shut by day (for there will be no night there); and they shall carry the glory and the wealth of the nations into her. And nothing profane shall enter her, nor anyone who does abomination and falsehood – only those who are written in the Lamb's Scroll of Life.

And he showed me the river of the water of life, bright as crystal, coming from the throne of God and of the Lamb. In the middle of the city's street, and its river, on both sides is the Tree of Life, yielding twelve fruits, every month each one yielding its fruit; and the leaves of the tree [serve] for the healing of the nations. And no longer will there be any cursed thing there. And the throne of God and of the Lamb shall be in her; and his slaves shall worship him, and they shall see his face, and his name shall be on their foreheads. And night shall be no more, and they have no need of the light of a lamp or the light of the sun, because the Lord God shall shine upon them; and they shall reign for ever and ever.

> This concluding vision is majestic; and we must simply let it work on our imagination, not trying to worry too much about precise details, simply basking in the light of this radiant vision of God's victory over the Beast (whose existence is dimly recalled in the reference to the 'name . . . on their foreheads'). It is not just God's victory, of course, for God's slaves will also be victorious, and 'shall reign' (or 'be kings and queens') – so the end is coming for the Roman Empire and those who live by it. Notice the line about the Temple, and the quiet assumption of an equivalent between 'God' and 'the Lamb'.

Concluding observations

6-21 And he said to me, 'The words are reliable and true; and the Lord God of the spirits of the prophets sent his angels to show his slaves what must happen soon. And look! I am coming quickly. Happy the one who keeps the words of the prophecy of this scroll.'

And [it is] I, John, who hear and see all these things. And when I had heard and seen, I fell down to worship before the feet of the angel that showed me these things. And he says to me, 'Don't even think of it – I am your fellow slave, and the fellow slave of your brothers and sisters the prophets, and those who keep the words of this scroll. Worship God.'

And he says to me, 'Do not seal up the words of the prophecy of this scroll, for the time is near. Let the wrongdoer continue to do wrong, and the one who is defiled continue to be defiled; and let the just person continue to do justice, and the holy one continue to be holy. Look! I am coming soon, and my reward with me, to repay each one according to their work. I am the Alpha and the Omega [the 'A and the Z'], the First and the Last, the Beginning and the End.

'Happy are those who wash their robes, so that they may have the right to the Tree of Life, and enter the city through its gateways. Out with the dogs and the sorcerers and the fornicators and the murderers and the idolatrous, and everyone who loves falsehood and does it.

'I, Jesus, sent my angel to bear witness of these things to you, for the churches. I am the root and the lineage of David, the bright Morning Star.'

And the Spirit and the Bride say, 'Come.' And the one who hears, let them say, 'Come.' And let the one who is thirsty come; but let the one who wishes receive the water of life for free. I testify to everyone who hears the words of the prophecy of this scroll. If anyone should add to them, God will add to that person the plagues written in this scroll; and if anyone takes away from the words of the scroll of the prophecy, God will take away that person's portion from the Tree of Life, and from the holy city, which are written in this scroll.

The one who bears witness to these things says, 'Yes, I am coming soon.' Amen, come, Lord Jesus.

The grace of the Lord Jesus be with the saints.

> The Revelation (or Un-Veiling) and, as things stand, the New Testament, comes to its end now, with some words of reassurance. It is a vision of a prophecy from God, and for God's 'slaves'; it is to reassure them that, despite everything, God is in charge. It is witnessed to by John (hearing and seeing) who encourages us to worship God alone and to keep the prophecy open and unsealed – but to change nothing in it. It affirms our faith in Jesus and encourages those who must suffer; finally, it implores Jesus to 'come'. This is the attitude of all attentive Christians.
>
> The final words are a neat epilogue to the New Testament: 'The grace of the Lord Jesus be with all the saints.'

Maps

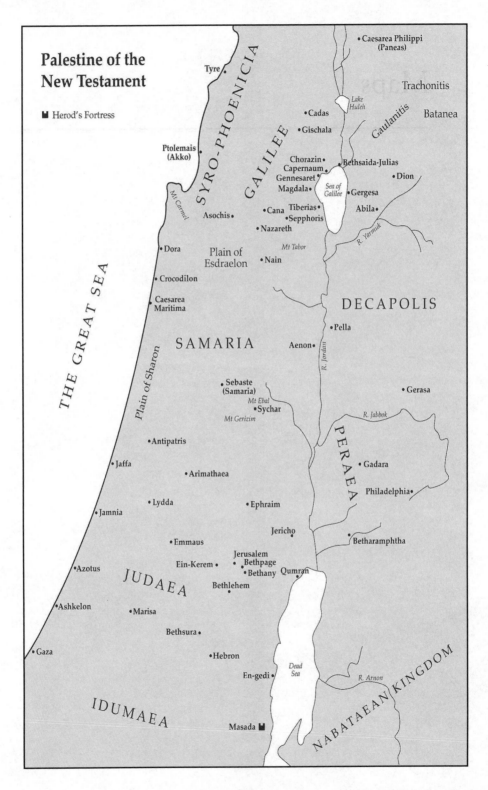

Palestine of the New Testament

◼ Herod's Fortress

SYRO-PHOENICIA

Tyre

Ptolemais
(Akko)

Mt Carmel

Asochis•

•Dora

Plain of
Esdraelon

•Crocodilon

Caesarea
Maritima

THE GREAT SEA

SAMARIA

Plain of Sharon

•Sebaste
(Samaria)
Mt Ebal
•Sychar
Mt Gerizim

•Antipatris

•Jaffa

•Arimathaea

•Lydda

•Jamnia

•Emmaus

•Azotus

JUDAEA

•Ashkelon

•Marisa

Bethsura•

•Gaza

•Hebron

En-gedi•

IDUMAEA

Masada ◼

GALILEE

•Cadas

•Gischala

Chorazin•
Capernaum•
Gennesaret•
Magdala•

•Cana   Tiberias•
•Sepphoris
•Nazareth

Mt Tabor
•Nain

Lake
Huleh

Sea of
Galilee

Caesarea Philippi
(Paneas)

Trachonitis

Gaulanitis   Batanea

Bethsaida-Julias

•Dion

•Gergesa

Abila•

R. Yarmuk

DECAPOLIS

•Pella

Aenon•

R. Jordan

•Gerasa

R. Jabbok

PERAEA

•Gadara

Philadelphia•

Ephraim•

Jericho•

•Betharamphtha

Jerusalem
Ein-Kerem • •Bethpage
•Bethany   Qumran•
Bethlehem

Dead
Sea

R. Arnon

NABATAEAN KINGDOM

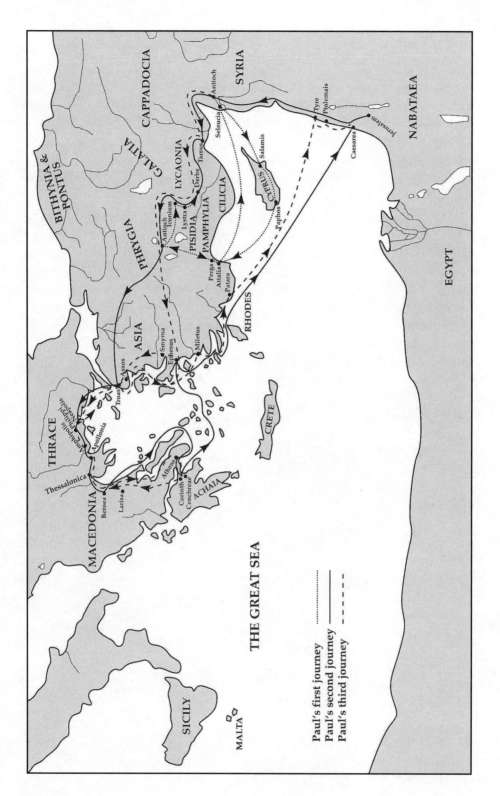